E. G Kern

Warren County History and Directory

The Farmers Manual and Business Mens Guide

E. G Kern

Warren County History and Directory
The Farmers Manual and Business Mens Guide

ISBN/EAN: 9783337215859

Printed in Europe, USA, Canada, Australia, Japan

Cover: Foto ©Lupo / pixelio.de

More available books at **www.hansebooks.com**

WARREN COUNTY
HISTORY AND DIRECTORY

—:OR:—

THE FARMERS' MANUAL

—:AND:—

BUSINESS MENS' GUIDE.

CONSISTING OF

PART I—CONTAINING A BRIEF HISTORY OF THE STATE AND OF WARREN COUNTY.

PART II—MISCELLANEOUS DEPARTMENT CONTAINING BRIEF, PRACTICAL INFORMATION FOR THE FARMER, BUSINESS MAN AND HOUSEKEEPER.

PART III—CONSISTING OF HISTORY, DESCRIPTION OF PHILLIPSBURG, WASHINGTON, HACKETTSTOWN AND BELVIDERE AND EACH OF THE TOWNSHIPS OF WARREN COUNTY, TOGETHER WITH NAMES OF RESIDENTS, OCCUPATION AND POST OFFICE.

COMPILED BY
WEAVER & KERN
WASHINGTON, N. J.

1886.
PRESS OF THE REVIEW
WASHINGTON, N. J.

PREFACE.

In presenting this, the first general directory of Warren county, to our patrons, we ask only that reasonable consideration which the beginning of every new business enterprise demands and which all charitably inclined persons are willing to accord. We feel assured that all fair minded business men will grant this. We do not claim for our work absolute freedom from mistakes, but we do claim that we have constantly aimed at accuracy, and that our purpose has been so far reached as to render the Directory adequate for all the practical purposes for which it is intended.

In the preparation of our work we have encountered a vast deal of prejudice, the cause of which is obvious, but we have persevered honestly, and now hope to satisfy the most incredulous of the utter absence of all thought on our part, to impose upon or in any measure whatever, deal unfairly with the people. It has been our aim to make this work valuable not only to the business man, but to every resident of the county. If we have succeeded we shall only be rewarded for honest labor and money expended, and if, in the judgment of our patrons, we have failed to do so, we shall still have the satisfaction of an honest purpose faithfully pursued.

As to the mistakes that may be found in the Directory a word will suffice. Some names may be misspelled, some addresses and occupations wrongly stated, but it is impossible that these things should not occur. These facts are due not to any lack of effort on our part, but to the mistakes of men employed by us and to typographical errors.

Moreover, we claim that our Directory of Phillipsburg, (although there has been a number of Directories published of the town,) is the most accurate and complete of any ever issued. An examination of its contents we think will prove it.

This work cannot fail to be of benefit to the county, and in return we solicit a liberal patronage.

WEAVER & KERN, Compilers.

TABLE OF CONTENTS.

	PAGE.
History of New Jersey	5
History of Indians in New Jersey	40
Some early Laws	61
New Jersey—Descriptive	65
History of Warren County	69
French and Indian War	83
Warren and Sussex in the Revolution	93
The war of the Rebellion	99
Organization of Warren County	104
Miscellaneous Department	107
Directory of Washington Borough	183
" Hackettstown "	213
" Belvidere "	237
" Phillipsburg "	255
" Allamuchy Township	327
" Blairstown "	332
" Frelinghuysen "	343
" Franklin "	349
" Greenwich "	359
" Hope "	366
" Hardwick "	375
" Harmony "	380
" Independence "	389
" Knowlton "	395
" Lopatcong "	407
" Mansfield "	417
" Oxford "	431
" Pahaquarry "	451
" Pohatcong "	455
" Washington "	466

LIST OF ADVERTISEMENTS.

	PAGE.
Cornish & Co	182
S. S. Teel	190
E. B. Webb	192
E. P. McCann	204
Misses Berscherer's	205
F. G. McKinstry, M. D	207
Kinnaman & Co	208
William M. Baird, M. D	212
Centenary Collegiate Institute	216
A. B. Buell	217
William F. Shields, Ph. G	218
T. G. Plate	221
R. Q. Bowers & Son	223
John Toepfer	225
L. H. Salmon	227
Charles Hairhouse	230
F. H. Bryan & Co	233
Aug. Dickerson	236
Faust Brothers	239
H. K. Ramsey	239
J. Diesel & Sons	240
King's Pharmacy	241
S. J. Raub	254
Robert H. Lerch	261
C. C. Cocklin	271
Thomas Carrol	274
John Eilenberg	277
John H. Haggerty & Sons	286
Clemens Kupka	290
John Lee	293
O. D. McConnell	295
A. Moenig	299
Samuel A. Metz	298
O. Kidney	307

J. M. R. Shimer	321
William H. Walters	322
Riegel & Luch	325
Washington Star	326
A. C. Howell	328
Blairstown Press	334
John Bunnell	336
Joseph M. Mann	339
Blair Presbyterial Academy	340
J. T. Bowers	350
Washingtown Review	350
Prof. J. L. Rosenbery	351
Thatcher & Wandling	352
Creveling & Co	353
Daniel Pittenger	354
William A. Stryker	355
F. A. Bowlby & Bro	356
Dr. J. P. Hoff	357
J. M. Butler	358
G. C. Young, M. D	360
C. W. Garis	365
Washington Review	365
William Dean	369
Israal R. Gibbs	370
James F. Hildebrant	372
Depue. Son & Co	381
Cornish & Co	382
J. C. Butler	386
Charles L. Free	388
Washington Review	390
Dr. H. M. Cox	403
George C. Rice	406
E. W. Alleger & Son	408
William H. Keller	412
St. Cloud Hotel	416
Thompson & Co	421
Mark Cyphers	424
John W. Forker	426
Charles A. Miller	428
H. M. Cregar	429
Charles Force	430
Thomas Craig	437
Marvin A. Pierson	439
S. J. Odsted	440
Dr. G. Orlando Tunison	441
John Zulauf	442
James A. Allen	444
Rockafellow & Weller	446
J. Fitts & Son	448
Philadelphia Shoe Manufacturing Company	449
Oscar Jeffery	450

Washington House	454
Michael Meagher	456
Victor Castner	465
William Jennings	469
Jacob Hill, Jr	470
Williamson's Restaurant	471
A. B. Groff & Co	472
Myers' Meat Market	473
C. C. Bowers	474
J. H. Mattison	475
Brass Castle Store	476
H. W. Alleger	Inside front cover.
Dr. H. M. Cox	Inside back cover.
Simon W. Nunn	Fly leaf.
T. Shields, Jr	" "

History of New Jersey.

IT is deemed necessary by the compilers of this volume to precede the history of Warren County by a brief history of the State of which it forms a part.

It was not long after the voyages of Columbus that John and Sebastian Cabot, two Venetians in the service of the King of England, Henry VII. were commissioned ' to discover the isles, regions, and provinces of the heathen and infidels, which had been unknown to all the nations of Christendom, in whatever part of the globe they might be placed." It was under that commission that the Cabots discovered the island of Newfoundland, on the 24th of June, 1497. They sailed from there southward along the coast as far as Cape Florida. We have no proof that they endeavored to form settlements, but they landed in a number of places and took possession in the name of the King of England. But from various reasons the English did not take advantage of these discoveries till almost a century afterward. A patent was granted to Sir Walter Raleigh by Queen Elizabeth of England, in 1584, to discover, occupy and govern "remote, heathen and barbarous countries" not previously possessed by any Christian prince or people. Under that authority Raleigh, in conjunction with his associates, sent two ships to America under the command of Amidas and Barlow. They landed at Roanoke, took possession of the country in the name of the Sovereign whose subjects they were, and called it Virginia. Attempts were made in 1585 and in 1590 to establish settlements, but both were unsuccessful. In 1606, King James, ignoring Raleigh's right, granted a new patent of the country of Virginia, embracing all the territory between the southern boundary of North Carolina and the northern boundary of Maine. It consisted of two districts called respectively *North* and *South Virginia*. The southern district was granted to Sir Thomas Gates and his associates, chiefly residents of London, and therefore styled the London Company. North Virginia was granted to Thomas Hanham and his associates, who were styled the Plymouth Company.

It was in 1609 that Henry Hudson, sailing under the auspices of the Dutch East India Company, in attempting to find a passage through the American Continent, and thus make a short cut from Europe to China, entered the Delaware Bay on the 25th of August. "Proceeding along the eastern coast of New Jersey he finally anchored inside of Sandy Hook on Sept. 3, 1609. On Sept. 5th he sent a boat's crew ashore southward in the vicinity of the Horseshoe, to take the soundings of the depth of the water. Here the boat's crew landed and penetrated into the woods in the present limits of Monmouth county, New Jersey. These were probably the first Europeans who set foot upon the soil of the State. Henry Hudson failed to find the Northwest Passage, but what is of far more importance, he discovered the North River, and sailed up to the head of navigation. What a contrast between the palatial steamers of to-day which ply these waters and the Half Moon on its pioneer voyage.

The Dutch were quick to avail themselves of the advantages which the discovery of Columbus opened up to their view. "In 1610 it appears that at least one ship was sent hither by the East India Company, for the purpose of trading in furs, which it is well known continued for a number of years to be the principal object of commercial attraction to the new world. Five years after Hudson's voyage a company of merchants, who had procured from the States-General of Holland a patent for an exclusive trade on Hudson's River, had built forts and established trading posts at New Amsterdam (New York), Albany, and the mouth of the Rondout Kill. The latter was a small redoubt on the site of what is now the city of Kingston, N. Y. It was known as the 'Ronduit,' from whence comes the name of Rondout. The fort near Albany was upon Castle Island, immediately below the present city, and the one at New York was erected on what is now the Battery."

The exact date of the first European settlement within the present limits of New Jersey does not distinctly appear. It is thought that the first settlement commenced at Bergen—so called from a city of that name in Norway—in 1618 by a number of Danes or Norwegians who accompanied the Dutch colonists to the New Netherlands.

In 1621, the privileged West India Company was formed in Holland. In 1623 this company dispatched a ship loaded with settlers, subsistence and articles of trade, under the command of Cornelius

Mey. He gave his own name to the cape at the northern part of Delaware bay which it still retains—Cape May. He built a fort upon a stream called by the natives *Sassackon*. It is a tributary of the Delaware a few miles below Camden, and it is now called Timber Creek. He named the fortification *Fort Nassau*.

It is highly probable that this was the first attempt ever made to form a settlement on the eastern shore of the Delaware.

David Pieterson De Vries who arrived in the Delaware in the winter of 1630–31 found that *Fort Nassau* had fallen into the hands of the Indians. He built a fort; colonized his immigrants and went back to Holland, and for some years not a single European was left upon the banks of the Delaware.

In 1637 two ships arrived in the Delaware bringing a number of Swedish settlers. Other companies followed, and in 1642 John Printz, a military officer, was sent over as Governor of the colony. He established himself upon the island now known as Tinicum, and built a fort, planted an orchard and erected a church. In 1655 the Dutch, under the command of Peter Stuyvesant, and coming from Manhattan, fell unawares upon the Swedish settlements. They captured fort after fort, made prisoners the principal men and carried them to New Amsterdam. The Dutch, however, retained possession of the country but a short time, for in 1644 Charles II. King of England, sent over Col. Nichols with a fleet and army. He made a complete conquest of New Amsterdam and the surrounding country, and all the Dutch possessions fell into the hands of the English.

Immediately after the subjection of New Amsterdam by Peter Stuyvesant, and even before this had been accomplished, Charles II made an extensive grant of territory to his brother, the Duke of York. This was done by a royal charter dated 20th of March, 1664.

The Duke of York in turn conveyed that portion of it now known as New Jersey to two other persons, Lord Berkely and Sir George Cartaret. The form of the conveyance was as follows:

"This indenture made the three and twentieth day of June, in the sixteenth year of the Raigne of our Sovereign Lord Charles the Second, by the Grace of God of England, Scotland, France and Ireland, King, Defender of the Faith—Anno Dominie 1664. Between his Royal Highness James Duke of York and Albany, Earl of Ulster, Lord High Admiral of England and Ireland, Constable of Dover Castle, Lord Warden of the Cinque Ports, and Governor of Portsmouth, of the one part, John Lord Berkely, Baron of Stratton, and one of his majestie's most honorable privy council, and Sir George Carteret of Strattum in the county of Devon, Knight, and one of his majestie's most honorable privy council, of the other part, Witnesseth, that said James Duke of York, for and in consideration of the sum of ten shillings of lawful money of England, to him in hand paid, by these presents doth bargain and sell unto the said John Lord Berkely and Sir George Carteret all that tract of land adjacent to New England, and lying and being to the westward of Long Island, Bounded on the east part by the main sea, and part by Hudson's River, and hath upon the west Delaware Bay or river, and extendeth southward to the main ocean as far as Cape May at the mouth of Delaware Bay, and to the northward as far as the northermost branch of said bay or river of Delaware, which is forty-one degrees and forty minutes of latitude, and worketh over thence in a straight line to Hudson's River—which said tract of land is hereafter to be called by the name or names of Nova Cesarea or New Jersey."

It is thought that the name of New Jersey was given to honor Cartaret, who had so ably defended the island of Jersey against the Long Parliament, in the civil wars. And the instrument of conveyance above given is thought to be the first one in which the bonds of New Jersey are regularly defined. "The two proprietors formed a constitution for the colony, securing equal privileges and liberty of conscience to all, and appointed Philip Carteret Governor. He came over in 1665, fixed the seat of government at Elizabethtown, purchased land of the Indians, and sent agents into New England to invite settlers from that country. The terms offered were so favorable that many accepted the invitation."

The constitution that was granted by Carteret and Berkely continued entire until 1676, when the province became divided, and was the first constitution of New Jersey.

The colony began to be disturbed by domestic disputes a few years after Governor Carteret began his administration. Some of the proprietors having purchased their lands of the Indians before the conveyance of the Duke of York, refused to pay rent to the proprietors. Because of this and other complaints the people arose in insurrection in 1672, and Sir Philip was obliged to leave for England. His officers were imprisoned and their estates confiscated. The government was then assumed by James Carteret, a weak and dissolute son of Philip.

War occurred with Holland in 1673 and the Dutch sent over a small squadron which arrived at Staten Island July 30th. Captain Manning, who had charge of the town during the absence of Gov. Lovelace, rejected the aid of those who offered to defend the place, sent a messenger to the enemy and struck his flag before the vessels of the enemy had appeared in sight. He surrendered the place unconditionally to the enemy without striking a blow. He was afterward tried by a court martial and pleaded guilty to all the charges made. His sentence, remarkable as his conduct, was as follows: "Though he deserved death, yet, because he had, since the surrender, been in England, *and seen the King and the Duke*, it was adjudged that his sword should be broke over his head, in public, before the city hall, and himself rendered incapable of wearing a sword, and of serving his majesty for the future, in any public trust in the government."

The Dutch dominion lasted but a short time, as the following Spring a treaty of peace was concluded and New Netherlands (comprising the territory of New York and New Jersey) was again restored to the English, who continued in undisturbed possession until the war which secured the independence of the United States of America.

Doubts having arisen as to the validity of the title of the Duke of York, a new patent was issued in 1674 and Edmund Andros was sent over as Governor. Philip Cartaret who had returned to England in 1672 came back in 1675, and was welcomed by the people, who had been uneasy and dissatisfied with Andros' tyrannical rule. Phllip Carteret "postponed the payment of their quit-rents to a future day, and published a new set of "*concessions*" by Sir George Carteret. Peace was again almost restored. These new "concessions" however, restricted the broad grant of political freedom originally framed. Because of Anaros' efforts to enforce the Duke's unjust pretensions much uneasiness still continued. Gov. Cartaret attempted to establish a direct trade between New England and New Jersey, but was opposed by Andros, who even went so far as to confiscate the vessels engaged in such trade, and sent a force to Elizabethtown to arrest Gov. Carteret and convey him a prisoner to New York.

Lord Berkely, dissatisfied with the pecuniary outcome of his colonization scheme, disposed of his interest to John Fenwick, in trust for Edward Byllinge, both members of the Society of Friends. The conveyance to these individuals was executed to the former in trust for the latter, for the sum of one thousand pounds. The tract thus purchased was afterward known as *West New Jersey*, embracing about one-half of the State as now constituted. The division between East and West Jersey was made by Carteret and the trustees of Byllinge, July 1, 1676. The line of partition was agreed on "from the east side of Little Egg Harbor, straight north, through the country to the utmost branch of the Delaware river." "This line was extended from Little Egg Harbor as far as the south branch of the Raritan, at a point just east of the Old York Road. It was run by Keith, the surveyor-general of East Jersey, but was deemed by the West Jersey proprietors to be too far west, thereby encroaching on their lands, and they objected to its continuance. On the 5th of September, 1668, Governors Coxe and Barclay, representing the respective interests entered into an agreement to terminate the dispute. It was that this line, so far as run should be bound, and that in its extension, it should take the following course: "From the point where it touched the South Branch, along the back of the adjoining plantations, until it touches the North Branch of the Raritan at the falls of the Allamitung, thence running up that stream northward to its rise near Succasunny." From that point a short straight line was to be run to touch the nearest part of the Passaic River. Such a line would pass about five miles North of Morristown. The line was to be continued by the course of the Passaic River as far as the Paquanick, and up that branch to forty-one degrees north latitude, and from that point in "a straight line due east to the partition point on Hudson River between East Jersey and New York." This line gave to the northern part of West Jersey the present counties of Warren and Sussex, and portions of Morris, Passaic and Bergen. The Coxe-Barclay agreement was not carried into effect, although the division line constituted the eastern boundary of Hunterdon County until Morris County was erected, in 1738."

Edward Byllinge in consequence of losses in trade was financially embarrassed and compelled to convey in trust his interest to William Penn, Gawen Lawrie and Nicholas Lucas (all Friends or Quakers) "to be used for the benefit of his creditors." Before this, however, he had sold a number of shares, and the trustees sold many of them to different purchasers, who thereby became proprietors in common with them. Fenwick soon after made a like assignment. "As these trustees were Quakers, the purchasers were mostly of that body. Two companies were formed; one in Yorkshire, the other in London, both intent on colonization in America, and in the same year some four hundred persons came over, most of them of considerable means. Daniel Coxe was connected with the London company, and one of the largest shareholders; subsequently he became the owner of extensive tracts of land in old Hunterdon County."

In 1677 commissioners were sent by the proprietors, with power to buy the lands of the natives; to inspect the rights of such as claimed property, and to order the lands laid out; and in general to administer the government pursuant to concessions. These commissioners were Thomas Olive, Daniel Wills, John Kinsey, John Penford, Joseph Helmsley, Robert Stacy, Benjamin Scott, Richard Guy and Thomas Foulke. They came in the *Kent*, commanded by Gregory Marlow. This was the second ship from the East to the Western parts. After a tedious passage they arrived at Newcastle the 16th day of June. King Charles, the Second, pleasuring on the Thames, came alongside in his barge and knowing where they were bound asked if they were all Quakers and gave them his blessing. They landed their passengers, consisting of two hundred and thirty persons, above Raccoon creek, where the Swedes had some scattering habitations. There were too many of them to be all provided for in houses and consequently some were obliged to lay their beds and furniture in cow-stalls and places of that sort. One of the most inconvenient things to which they were exposed was the snakes, which took up their abode frequently upon the hovels under which they slept. Some of the passengers in this ship were of good estates in England, but most of them were Quakers. The commissioners who had left them before this and arrived at Chygoe's Island (afterward Burlington) went to treat with the Indians about the land there and to regulate the settlements. They not only had the proprietors', but Gov. Andros' commission for that purpose; for in their passage they had first dropped anchor at Sandy Hook, while the commissioners went to New York to acquaint him with their design. They believed that the powers they had from the proprietors were sufficient, but due respect for the Duke of York's commission required them to call upon his governor. They were treated courteously by him, but he asked them what they had to show from the Duke, his master. They told him nothing, particularly, but that he had conveyed that part of the country to Lord Berkely, and that he had in turn conveyed it to Byllinge, etc., in which the government was as much conveyed as the soil.

The Governor replied that all that would not clear him and that if he should surrender without the Duke's orders it would be as much as his head was worth. If they had but a line or two from the Duke he would be as ready to surrender to them, as they to ask it. The Commissioners did not ask for any excuse for their neglect to bring such an order, but insisted upon their right and asserted their independence. Andros, however, clapping his hand upon his sword told them that he should defend the Government from them till he received orders from the Duke to surrender it. Afterward, however, he backed down from that position somewhat and told them that he would do all that was in his power to make them easy, till they could send home to get redress; in order, thereto, he would commission the same persons mentioned in the commission they produced. They accepted that and commenced to act as magistrates under him, till further orders came from England, and proceed in relation to their land affairs according to the methods prescribed by the proprietors.

"When arrived at their Government, they applied to the Swedes for interpreters between them and the Indians. Lacy Cock, Peter Rambo and Israel

Helmes were employed. Through their help a purchase was made from Timber Creek to Rankokas Creek, and another from Oldman's Creek to Timber Creek. After this they purchased land through another interpreter that they employed—Henric Jacobus Falconbre—from Rankokas Creek to Assunpink. They had not enough Indian goods to pay for the last purchase, but gave them what they had to get the deed signed. They, however, stipulated not to settle on the land till the remainder was paid.

"The deed for the lands between Rankokas Creek and Timber Creek bears date the 10th of September, 1677; that for the lands from Oldman's Creek to Timber Creek, the 27th of September, 1677; and that from Rankokas Creek to Assunpink, the 10th of October, 1677. By the consideration paid for the lands between Oldman's and Timber Creek, a judgment may be formed of the rest. It consisted of 30 match-coats, 20 guns, 30 kettles and one great one, 30 pair of hose, 20 fathoms of duffelds, 30 petticoats, 30 narrow hose, 30 bars of lead, 15 small barrels of powder, 70 knives, 30 Indian axes, 70 combs, 60 pair of tobacco-tongs, 60 scissors, 60 tinshaw looking glasses, 120 awl blades, 120 fish hooks, 2 grasps of red paint, 120 needles, 60 tobacco boxes, 120 pipes, 200 bells, 100 jewsharps and 6 anchors of rum."

"Having travelled through the country and viewed the land, the Yorkshire Commissioners, Joseph Helmsley, William Emley and Robert Stacy on behalf of the first purchasers, chose from the falls of the Delaware down, which was hence called the first tenth. The London Commissioners, John Penford, Thomas Olive, Daniel Wills and Benjamin Scott, on behalf of the ten London proprietors chose at Arwaumas—in and about where the town of Gloucester now is. This was called the second tenth. To begin a settlement there Olive sent up servants to cut hay for cattle he had bought. When the Yorkshire Commissioners found that the others were likely to settle at such a distance they told them that if they would agree to stay by them they would join in settling a town, and that they should have the largest share in consideration that they—the Yorkshire Commissioners—had the best land in the woods. Being few, and the Indians numerous, they agreed to it. The Commissioners employed Noble, a surveyor, who came in the first ship, to divide the spot. After the main street was ascertained he divided the land on each side into lots: the one on the East among the Yorkshire proprietors, the other among the Londoners. To begin a settlement ten lots of nine acres each were laid out. The London commissioners also employed Noble to divide the part of the island yet unsurveyed, between the ten London proprietors in the manner before mentioned. The town thus by mutual consent laid out, the commissioners gave it the name of New-Beverley, then Bridlington, but soon changed it to Burlington. Among the heads of families which came in the ship last mentioned were John Wilkinson and William Perkins. They died on the passage and their families were exposed to additional hardships, which were greatly alleviated by the care of their fellow-passengers. Perkins was, during his youthful days, impressed with the principles of the Quakers, and lived well in Leicestershire; but coming across an account of the country written by Richard Hartshorne he was impressed with the advantage that it might be be to himself and family and though fifty-two years old embarked in this ship with his wife, four children and servants. It being late in the Fall when they arrived. Winter was almost gone before they began to build their habitations. In the meantime they lived in temporary shelters built after the manner of the Indian's wigwam. The supplies of Indian corn and venison brought by the Indians was their chief food. These poor red men were at that time comparatively free from the curse of strong liquors, and generally very friendly to the English, although it was thought that endeavor had been made to make them otherwise by telling them that the English sold them the small-pox in their matchcoats.

The next ship that came over was the *Willing Mind*, commanded by John Newcomb and having on board some sixty or seventy passengers. She dropped anchor at Elsingburg. Some settled at Salem; others at Burlington. In this year, 1677, the "Flie-boat Martha" also sailed from Hull the latter end of the Summer with one hundred and fourteen passengers designed to settle the Yorkshire tenth. Several settlements were started and West Jersey became as early as 1680 quite populous. Some heads of families who came over in the "Flie-boat Martha" were Thomas Wright, William Goforth, John Lynam, Edward Season, William Black, Richard Dungworth, George Miles, William Wood, Thomas Schooley, Richard Harrison, Thomas Hooten, Samuel Taylor, Marmaduke Horsman, William Oxley, William Ley and Nathaniel Luke; the families of Robert Stacy and Samuel Odas; and Thomas Ellis and John Botts, servants, sent by George Hutchinson, also came in the ship. Twenty of the passengers, perhaps more, were living forty-five years afterward."—*Smith's Hist. N. J.*

"The following, extracted from a letter from Mahlon Stacy, one of the first settlers of New Jersey, to his brother Revell and some others, is descriptive of West Jersey at this period. It is dated 26th of April, 1680 :

"But now a word or two of those strange reports you have heard of us and our country; I affirm they are not true, and fear they were spoke from a spirit of envy. It is a country that produceth all things for the support and sustenance of man, in a plentiful manner ; if it were not so I should be ashamed of what I have before written. But I can stand, having truth on my side, against and before the face of all gain-sayers and evil spies. I have travelled through most of the places that are settled, and some that are not; and in every place I find the country very apt to answer the expectation of the diligent. I have seen orchards laden with fruit to admiration, their limbs torn to pieces with the weight, and most delicious to the taste, and lovely to behold. I have seen an apple tree from a pippin-kernel yield a barrel of curious cyder; and peaches in such plenty that some people took their carts a-peach-gathering; I could not but smile at the conceit of it. They are a very delicate fruit and hang almost like our onions that are tied on ropes. I have seen and known this summer forty bushels of bold wheat of one bushel sown ; and many more such instances I could bring which would be too tedious here to mention. We have, from the time called May until Michaelmas, great store of very good wild fruits, as straw-berries, cranberries and hurtleberries, which are like our bilberries in England, but far sweeter ; they are very whole-some fruits. The cranberries are very much like cherries for color and bigness, which may be kept till fruit comes in again. An excellent sauce is made of them for venison, turkeys and other great fowl ; and they are better to make tarts than either gooseberries or cherries, We have them brought to our houses by the Indians in great plenty. My brother, Robert, had as many cherries this year as. would have loaded several carts. It is my judgment, by what I have observed, that fruit trees in this country destroy themselves by the very weight of their fruit. As for venison and fowls, we have great plenty; we have brought home to our houses by the Indians, seven or eight fat bucks of a day, and sometimes put by as many having no occasion for them. And fish, in their season, are very plenteous. My cousin, Revell and I, with some of my men, went last third month into the river to catch herrings; for at that time they came in great shoals into the shallows. We had neither rod nor net, but after the Indian fashion, made a round pinfold, about two yards over and a foot high, but left a gap for the fish to go in at; and made a bush to lay in the gap to keep the fish in; and when that was done we took two long birches and tied their tops together, and went about a stone's cast above our said pinfold; then hauling these birch boughs down the stream, where we drove thousands before us, but as many got into our trap as it would hold. And then we began to haul them on shore, as fast as fast as three or four of us could, by two or three at a time; and after this manner, in half an hour, we could have filled a three-bushel sack of as good and large herring as ever I saw. And as to beef and pork, there is plenty of it, and cheap; and also good sheep. The common grass of this country feeds beef very fat; I have killed two this year and therefore I have reason to know it. Besides, I have seen killed this fall in Burlington, eight or nine fat oxen or cows on a market day, and all very fat. And though I speak of herrings only, lest any should think we have little other sorts, we have great plenty of most sorts of fish that I ever saw in England, besides several other sorts that are not known there—as rocks, catfish, shads, sheep's heads, sturgeons; and fowls plenty—as ducks, geese, turkeys, pheasants, partridges and many other sorts that I cannot remember and would be too tedious to mention. Indeed, the country, take it as a wilderness, is a brave country; though no place will please all. But some will be ready to say, he writes of conveniences and not of inconveniences. In answer to those I honestly declare, there is some barren land, as (I suppose) there is in most places of the world, and more wood than some would have upon their lands; neither will the country produce corn without labor, nor cattle be got without something to buy them, nor bread with idleness — else it would be a brave country indeed. And I question not but all then would give it a good word. For my part I like it so well I never had the least thought of returning to England, except on the account of trade.   Mahlon Stacy.

In a letter to William Cook, of Sheffield, and others, Stacy wrote thus :

"This is a most brave place; whatever envy or evil spies may speak of it, I could wish you all here. Burlington will be a place of trade quickly; for here is way for trade; I, with eight others, last winter, bought a good ketch of fifty tons, freighted her out at our own charge, and sent her to Barbadoes, and so to sail to Saltertugas, to take in part of her lading in salt and the rest in Barbadoes goods as she came back ; which said voyage she hath accomplished very well and now rides before Burlington, discharging her lading, and so to go to the West Indies again. And we intend to freight her out with our own corn. We have wanted nothing since we came hither but the company of our good friends and acquaintances. All our people are very well, and in a hopeful way to live much better than ever they did ; and not only so, but to provide well for their posterity. They improve their lands, and have good crops ; and if our friends and countrymen come, they will find better reception than we had by far at first, before the country was settled as now it is. I know not one among the people that desires to be in England again —I mean since settled. I wonder at our Yorkshire people that they had rather live in servitude and work hard all the year, and not be three pence better at the year's end, than stir out of the chimney-corner, and transport themselves to a place where, with the like pains; in two or three years, they might know better things. I never repented my coming hither, nor yet remembered thy arguments and outcry against New Jersey with regret. I live as well to my content and in as great plenty as ever I did ; and in a far more likely way to get an estate. Though I hear some have thought I was too large in my former, I affirm it to be true ; having seen more with mine eyes, in this time since, than ever yet I wrote of.

MAHLON STACY.

"*From the Falls of Delaware, in West New Jersey, the 26th day of the 9th month, 1680.*"

The death of Sir George Carteret, sole proprietor of East Jersey, occurred in 1679, and by will he ordered that province to be sold to pay his debts. This was done by his "widow and executors, by indenture of lease and release, bearing date the 1st and 2d of February, 1681-82, to William Penn, Robert West, Thomas Rudyard, Samuel Groome, Thomas Hart, Richard Mew, Thomas Wilcox of London (goldsmith), Ambrose Rigg, John Haywood, Hugh Hartshorn, Clement Plumsted, and Thomas Cooper, their heirs and assigns; who were thence called *the twelve proprietors*. They, being together so seized, in this year published an account of their country, a fresh project for a town, and method of disposing of their lands."

The following are extracts from the above:

SECOND. The conveniency of situation, temperature of air and fertility of soil is such that there are no less than seven considerable towns, viz: Shrewsbury, Middletown, Bergen, Newark, Elizabethtown, Woodbridge and Piscataway; which are well inhabited by a sober and industrious people, who have necessary provisions for themselves and families, and for the comfortable entertainment of strangers and travellers. And this colony is experimentally found generally to agree with English constitutions. * * *

FOURTH. For fishery, the sea banks there are very well stored with variety of fish — for not only such as are profitable for transportation, but such also as are fit for food there; as whales, codfish, cole and hake-fish, large mackerel, and also many other sorts of flat and small fish. The bay also, and Hudson's river, are plentifully stored with sturgeon, great bass, and other scale-fish, eels, and shell-fish, as oysters, etc., in great plenty, and easy to take. *   *   *

SEVENTH. The land or soil (as in other places) varies in goodness and richness; but generally fertile, and with much smaller labor than in England. It produceth plentiful crops of all sorts of English grain, besides Indian corn, which the English planters find not only to be of vast increase, but very who'esome and good in its use; it also produceth good flax and hemp, which they now spin and manufacture into linen cloth. There is sufficient meadow and marsh to their uplands; and the very barrens there, as they are called, are not like some in England, but produce grass fit for grazing cattle in summer season.

EIGHTH. The country is well stored with wild deer, conies and wild fowl of several sorts — as turkeys, pigeons, partridges, plover, quails, wild swans, geese, ducks, etc., in great plenty. It produceth variety of good and delicious fruits — as grapes, plums, mulberries; and also apricots, peaches, pears, apples, quinces, watermelons, etc., which are here in England planted in orchards and gardens. These as also many other fruits, which come not to perfection in England, are the more natural product of this country.

NINTH. There is also already great store of horses, cows, hogs, and some sheep, which may be bought at reasonable prices, with English moneys or English commodities or man's labor, where money and goods are wanting.

"TENTH. What sort of mines or minerals there are in the earth, aftertime must produce, the inhabitants not having yet employed themselves in search thereof; but there is already a smelting furnace and forge set up in this colony, where is made good iron, which is of great benefit to the country."

"ELEVENTH. It is exceedingly well furnished with safe and convenient harbors for shipping, which are of great advantage to that country; and affords already, for exportation, great plenty of horses, and also beef, pork, pipe-staves, boards, bread, flour, wheat, barley, rye, Indian corn, butter and cheese. which they export for Barbadoes, Jamaica, Nevis, and other adjacent islands; as also to Portugal, Spain, the Canaries, etc. Their whale-oil and whale fins, beaver, mink, raccoon and martin skins (which this country produceth), they transport to England."

"THIRTEENTH. The Indian natives in this country are but few comparative to the neighboring colonies; and those that are there are so far from being formidable or injurious to the planters or inhabitants, that they are really serviceable and advantageous to the English — not only in hunting and taking the deer and other wild creatures, and catching of fish and fowl fit for food, in their seasons, but in the killing and destroying of bears, wolves, foxes, and other vermin and peltry, whose skins and furs they bring the English, and sell at less price than the value of time an Englishman must spend to take them. * *
As for passages to this province ships are going hence the whole year about, as well in winter as in summer, Sandy Hook bay being never frozen. The usual price is five pounds per head, as well masters or servants, who are above ten years of age; all under ten years and not children at the breast, pay fifty shillings; sucking children pay nothing. Carriage of goods is usually forty shillings per ton, and sometimes less, as we can agree. The cheapest and chiefest time of the year for passage is from midsummer till

the latter end of September, when many Virginia and Maryland ships are going out of England into those parts; and such who take them their voyage, arrive usually in good time to plant corn sufficient for next summer. The goods to be carried there, are, first, for people's own use; all sorts of apparel and household stuff; and also utensils for husbandry and building; secondly, linen and wool cloths and stuffs, fitting for apparel etc., which are fit for merchandise and truck there in the country, and that to good advantage for the importer — of which farther account will be given to the inquirer.

LASTLY. Although this country, by reason of its being already considerably inhabited, may afford many conveniences to strangers, of which unpeopled countries are destitute, as lodging, victualling. etc., yet all persons inclining unto these parts must know that, in their settlement there, they will find their exercises. They must have their winter as well as summer. They must labor before they reap; and, till their plantations be cleared (in summer time), they must expect (as in all those countries) the mosquitoes, flies, gnats, and such like, may, in hot and fair weather give them some disturbance where people provide not against them — which, as land is cleared, become less troublesome.

The twelve proprietors' plans and purposes were well received especially by the people of Scotland, many of whom came across the ocean and took up their abode in East Jersey.

Each of the twelve proprietors soon took another partner and made over the particular deeds and they were afterwards designated as the twenty-four proprietors. On the 14th of March, 1682, the Duke of York made a new grant of East New Jersey to these twenty-four proprietors.

At this time there were supposed to be about seven hundred families settled in the towns of East Jersey, which, reckoning five to a family, were three thousand and five hundred inhabitants; besides the out plantations which were thought to contain half as many more."

Philip Carteret continued to be the governor of East New Jersey after the "quinty-partite" division till about the year 1681. "His salary was generally £50 a year paid in country produce, at prices fixed by law; and sometimes four shillings a day besides, to defray his charges while a sessions was held. The wages of the council and assembly, during their sitting in legislation, was to each member three shillings a day. The rates for public charges were levied at two shillings per head for every male above fourteen years old."

For the most part the assembly sat at Elizabethtown and held its sessions there, occasionally, however, at Woodbridge, and once or more at Middletown and Piscataway.

"Some of the first laws as published by the legislature at Elizabethtown, were, in substance: That persons resisting authority should be punished at the discretion of the court; that men from sixteen to sixty years of age should provide themselves with arms, on penalty of one shilling for the first week's neglect, and two for every week after; that for burglary, or highway robbery, the first offence, burning the hand; the second, in the forehead — in both to make restitution; and for the third offence, *death*. For stealing, the first offence, treble restitution, and the like for second and third offence, with such increase of punishment as the court saw cause, even to death, if the party appeared incorrigible; but if not, and unable to make restitution, they were to be sold for satisfaction or to receive corporal punishment. That conspiracies or attacks upon towns or forts should be death; that undutiful children, smiting or cursing their father or mother, except provoked thereunto for self-preservation, upon complaint of, and proof from their parents, or either of them, should be punished with *death*; that in case of adultery, the party to be divorced, corporally punished or banished, or either or all of them, as the court should judge proper; that for night-walking and revelling after the hour of nine, the parties to be secured by the constable, or other officer, till morning, and then, not giving a satisfactory account to the magistrate, to be bound over to the next court, and there receive such punishment as should be inflicted. That the meeting of the assembly should be always on the first Tuesday in November, yearly, and oftener if the Governor and Council thought necessary; and that they should fix the Governor's salary — the deputies of each town to be chosen on the first of January, according to the concessions. Any deputy absenting himself at such times was to be fined forty shillings for every day's absence. That thirty pounds should be levied for provincial charges — i. e., £5 to be paid by each town in winter wheat, at five shillings a bushel, summer wheat at four and six pence, peas at three shillings and six pence, Indian corn at three shillings, rye at four shillings, barley at four shillings, beef at twopence half-penny per pound, and pork at three-pence half-penny. That no son, daughter, maid or servant should marry without the consent of his or their parents, masters, or overseers, without being three times published in some public meeting or kirk, near the party's abode, or notice being set up in writing at some public house near where they lived, for fourteen days before; then to be solemnized by some approved minister, justice, or chief officer, who, on penalty of twenty pounds, and to be put out of office, were to marry none who had not followed those directions."

Robert Barclay, a Scotchman, was one of the new proprietors of East Jersey. He was the author of the noted "Apology" in defence of the Friends and Quakers. He was appointed governor of East Jersey for life by the unanimous voice of his colleagues, with dispensation from personal residence and authority to nominate his deputy. He appointed Thomas Rudyard, who arrived about the beginning of 1683. He was superseded, however, as deputy-governor, at the close of the year, by Gawen Lawrie, likewise of London, the same who had been one of Byllinge's trustees for West Jersey. Lawrie was succeeded by Lord Niel Campbell, and he by Alexander Hamilton, Esq.

West Jersey added a great many settlers to its population in 1680 and was tolerably populous. In 1681, Samuel Jennings having received a commission from Byllinge as deputy governor, came to West Jersey, called an assembly, and with them agreed upon a constitution and form of government. From this time on assemblies were held each year; courts were established in several places and "justice was administered in due course of law." Jenning's successors in the executive department were, Thomas Olive, John Skeine, William Welsh, Daniel Coxe and Andrew Hamilton. The last named continued to hold the governorship until the charter of the proprietors was surrendered to the Crown.

The Duke of York was in 1685, by the death of Charles II, raised to the throne as James II, and, notwithstanding he had thrice conveyed and confirmed to others all the rights, powers and privileges he had in New Jersey, he resolved to extend his royal prerogative over it in order to increase his revenues. The proprietors were not silent under this arbitrary action of the King. In a petition to the King in council they recited some of the encroachments of Dongan in relation to the seizure of vessels trading to New Jersey as calculated to "overthrow one of the most hopeful colonies in America." In a remonstrance subsequently presented to the King they reminded him that they had not received the province as a gratuity, but had expended for it twelve thousand pounds; that under his own confirmation of their title and assurance of protection they had sent thither several hundred people from Scotland, but as yet had received no returns; and that notwithstanding these guarantees their rights had been violated by the governor of New York. They indicated their willingness to submit to an imposition of the same customs that were levied in New York, and among other prayers requested that a customs officer might be appointed at Perth Amboy. The last request was the only one granted, as it promised additional revenue and did not conflict with the designs he then had in view.

"On the 6th of April, 1686, the assembly met for the first time at the new seat of government, Perth Amboy. Lawrie was succeeded by Lord Neil Campbell in the same year. His council was composed of Gawen Lawrie, Major John Barry of Bergen, Isaac Kingsland of New Barbadoes, Capt. Andrew Hamilton of Amboy, Richard Townly of Elizabethtown, Samuel Winder of Cheesequake, David Mudie and John Johnson of Amboy, and Thomas Codrington of Raritan.

"This year, 1686, seems to have been a dangerous one if the law against wearing swords was properly founded. According to that several persons had received abuses and were put in great fear from quarrels and challenges; to prevent it for the future, none, by word or message, were to make a challenge, upon pain of six months' imprisonment, without bail or mainprize and a ten pound fine. Whoever accepted or concealed the challenge was also to forfeit ten pounds. No person was to wear any pocket pistols, skeins, stillaters, daggers, or dirks, or other unusual weapons, upon pain of five pounds forfeiture for the first offence, and for the second to be committed, and on conviction imprisoned for six months; and moreover, to pay a fine of ten pounds. No planter was to go armed with sword, pistol or dagger, upon penalty of five pounds. Officers, civil and military, soldiers in service, and strangers travelling upon lawful occasions were excepted."

In 1687 there was a partial failure of crops in West Jersey, and many of the settlers were put to great difficulties. Many families were forced to accept the charities of the few who were luckily better provided for. Those who lived near the rivers were forced to live upon fish for weeks, and some who did not, lived upon herbs. A vessel laden with corn going from New England to Philadelphia proved an agreeable surprise, and readily sold its cargo. Other vessels speedily followed and the settlers were not at any time afterward put to such straits for want of food.

"The year 1701 was a memorable era in the history of New Jersey on account of the disturbances and confusions that agitated the minds of the people. Each province had many and different proprietors, who promoted separate and intervening schemes and interests. To promote particular purposes, one party would have the choice and management of the governor, while another refused any but of their own nomination; and a third objected to proposals from either. Discord prevailed, and every expedient to restore order, union and regularity proved unsuccessful. The disorders in East Jersey made such an impression on the minds of many of the people, that they readily hearkened to overtures made for a surrender of the proprietary government. A considerable part of West Jersey was also, for similar reasons, disposed to a resignation. The proprietors, weary of contending with each other, and with the people, drew up an instrument, whereby they surrendered their right of government to the crown, which was accepted by Queen Anne on the 17th of April, 1702."

As soon as the transfer of the right of government from the proprietors to the Queen had been made, Queen Anne again united East and West Jersey and gave its government into the hands of her kinsman, Edward Hyde, Lord Cornbury, grandson of the Chancellor, Earl of Clarendon. "The commission and instructions which Cornbury received formed the constitution and government of the province, until its declaration of independence. The new government was composed of the Governor and twelve councilors, nominated by the Crown, and an assembly of twenty-four members, to be elected by the people, for an indefinate term, whose sessions were to be held, alternately at Perth Amboy and Burlington. Among the numerous instructions given to the Governor was one directing 'to permit liberty of conscience to all persons (except Papists,) so they may be contented with a quiet and peaceful enjoyment of the same, not giving offence or scandal to the government;' also stating that, 'Forasmuch as great inconveniences may arise by the *liberty of printing* in our said province, you to provide by all necessary orders, that no person keep any press for printing, nor that any book, pamphlet or other matters whatsoever, be printed without your special leave and license first obtained.'"

At this time it is said that there were about 20,000 inhabitants belonging to the province — 1,200 of whom belonged to East and 8,000 to West Jersey. There were about 1,400 militia. The trade of the province was considerable. To the West Indies it sent agricultural produce; to the English market, furs, skins and tobacco; to Spain, Portugal and the Canary Islands, oil, fish and other provisions.

Lord Cornbury came over from England in 1703 and held the office of Governor for five years, when the loud complaints of the people forced the Queen to revoke his commission. He was heavily in debt and as soon as he lost his office his creditors pounced upon him and put him in prison in the same province that he had governed. There he remained till his father died. He was by his father's death elevated to the peerage and entitled to his liberty. Lord Cornbury was almost universally detested by his people. His behavior was trifling, mean and extravagant. He would dress himself *in women's clothing* and patrol the fort in which he lived. Such low freaks exposed him to ridicule and contempt. He kindled the indignation of the people by his despotic rule, savage bigotry, insatiable avarice, and injustice, not only to his private creditors, but to the public as well.

The successor of Cornbury was John, Lord Lovelace, Baron of Hurley, who summoned the council to meet him at Bergen, December 20th, 1708. The hopes entertained, from his exalted character, of a peaceful and happy time during his administration, were not realized. He died on the succeeding 5th of May. The governorship now devolved upon Lieutenant-governor Ingoldsby, who laid before the assembly the design of the Crown respecting an expedition against Canada. "The assembly prepared three bills, one for raising £3,000 and another for enforcing its currency, and a third for the encouragement of volunteers going on the Canada expedition. These bills having received the Governor's assent, the house was adjourned to the first of November, to meet at Burlington. They met accordingly, but deferred business till December, when they sat ten weeks, passed eighteen bills, were then adjourned, and afterward prorogued, from time to time till dissolved by Governor Hunter in 1710.

According to *Smith's Hist. of N. J.* this action of the Assembly in raising £3,000 "began the paper currency in New Jersey. The care of the legislature respecting it, in this and all the succeeding emissions, being to render the funds for sinking, according to the acts that created it, secure, and to prevent the currency failing in value; by changing the bills as they became ragged and torn, and allowing no reemissions on any other account whatever. It has thence, from the beginning, preserved its credit and proved of great service to the proprietors in the sale of their lands, and to the settlers in enabling them to purchase and contract, and pay English debts and go on with their improvements. The securities, when issued on loans, were double the value in lands, or treble in houses, and five per cent interest; but now (1765) there is none current on this footing. The funds for sinking, by tax, the money created for the expedition and other purposes are mortgages (secured in the acts that make the respective emissions) on the estates, real and personal, in the province; hence they are secured as firmly as the province itself. They are legal tender to all the inhabitants in the province, and elsewhere, but not to others, except while in the province. The remittances of this province to England, being chiefly from New York and Philadelphia, and the bills no legal tender there, they can never operate to the prejudice of English debts, let exchange be as it may; because none there are obliged to take them. This is a particularity only belonging to the state of trade of New Jersey and renders a paper currency there free from the objection usually made against it in England."

Governor Hunter administered the affairs of the province for ten years, from 1710 to 1720, and then returned to England, having resigned in favor of William Burnet, the son of the celebrated Bishop. He loved money and had a ready art of procuring it. He drifted into gambling schemes and lost considerable money. He made a tolerably acceptable officer. During Governor Burnet's administration the assembly passed some remarkable bills, one of which was to fix the salary of the Governor for five years at £500 per annum, and that authorizing the issue of £40,000 in bills of credit, with the view, principally, of increasing the circulating medium of the colony. "The country had been drained of its metallic currency, and as the paper currency of the neighboring colonies was not a legal tender in the payment of debts, much embarrassment was produced. They sometimes paid their taxes in broken plates, ear-rings and wheat. Forty thousand pounds in bills the value of from one shilling to three pounds, were issued by the government to borrowers, on the pledge of plate or real estate, at five per cent per annum. The whole sum was apportioned to the counties in which loan offices were established; the bills were made current for twelve years, and were made a legal tender for debts. In 1730 another act added £20,000 to this medium and were made current for sixteen years. All these issues (although at one period they were at a discount of sixteen per cent) were fully and duly redeemed."*

Governor Burnet after this continued to preside over New York and New Jersey, till 1727; when he was removed to Boston and succeeded by John Montgomery, Esq. He continued till his death, which happened in the summer of 1731. To him succeeded William Crosby, Esq. He continued till his death in 1736.

The government here then devolved upon the president of the council, John Anderson, Esq. He died about two weeks afterward and was succeeded by John Hamilton, Esq. (son of Andrew, governor in the proprietors' time.) He governed nearly two years. In the summer of 1738 a commission arrived to Lewis Morris, Esq., as governor of New Jersey, separate from New York. He continued till his death in the spring of 1746. He was succeeded by President Hamilton. He dying, it devolved upon John Reading, Esq., as the next eldest councilor. He exercised the office till the summer of 1747, when Jonathan Belcher, Esq., arrived. He died in the summer of 1757, and was succeeded by John Reading, Esq., president. Francis Bernard, Esq., arrived as governor in 1758; he was removed to Boston and succeeded by Thomas Boone, Esq., in 1760. He was removed to South Carolina and succeeded here by Josiah Hardy, Esq.,

---

* See Gordon's Hist. of New Jersey, pp. 94-96.

in 1761. He was removed and afterward appointed consul at Cadiz."

The next and last of the royal governors was William Franklin, Esq., son of Dr. Benjamin Franklin. During the year 1763 a treaty of peace was signed by Great Britain and France. By its terms Canada was ceded to the British king, "and the colonies secured from the ravages of French and Indian wars, which had continued for more than half a century."

When the English government through their prime minister, the celebrated Mr. Pitt, called upon the colonies to do something to subdue the French in America, "the Assembly of New Jersey, instead of raising, reluctantly, five hundred men, doubled that number, and, to fill the ranks in season, offered a bounty of twelve pounds per man, increased the pay of the officers, and voted $200,000 for their maintenance. They at the same session directed barracks to be built at Burlington, Trenton, New Brunswick, Amboy and Elizabethtown, competent reach for the accommodation of three hundred men. This complement of one thousand men New Jersey kept up during the years 1758, 1759 and 1760; and in the years 1761 and 1762 furnished six hundred men, besides in the latter year a company of sixty-four men and officers, especially for garrison duty; for which she incurred an average expense of $200,000 per annum."

New Jersey was from the first among the foremost in resisting the arrogant demands of British tyranny.

The people, early in July, 1774, met in the different counties and passed resolutions stoutly condemning the acts of parliament. "They nominated deputies to meet in convention for the purpose of electing delegates to the general congress about to meet in Philadelphia."

The delegates that were sent from New Jersey reported the proceedings of this congress to the assembly January 11, 1775, by whom they were unanimously approved.

"The joint action of the colonies was opposed by their royal governors, who threw every obstacle in their power to prevent its accomplishment. Gov. Franklin refused to summon the assembly, notwithstanding the petitions of the people; therefore the first delegates to congress were elected by a convention. The second provincial convention met at Trenton, May 23, 1775, and directed that one or more companies of eighty should be formed in each township or corporation; and in order to raise necessary funds, imposed a tax of ten thousand pounds. The provincial congress of New Jersey reassembled August 5th, 1775, and directed that fifty-four companies, each of sixty-four minute men, be organized. These troops were formed into ten battalions; in Bergen, Essex, Middlesex, Monmouth, Somerset, Morris, Sussex, Hunterdon and Burlington, one each; in Gloucester and Salem, one; while in the counties of Cumberland and Cape May were independent light infantry and rangers. But the chief measure of this congress was the perpetuation of the authority which they had assumed; they therefore resolved and directed, that, during the continuance of the controversy between Great Britain and America, the inhabitants qualified to vote should yearly choose deputies to the provincial congress, who now took upon themselves the management of the affairs of the colony, relating to their rights and liberties."

The legislature was convened by Gov. Franklin the 16th of November, 1775. He made a speech to the assembly seemingly for the purpose of getting an assurance of personal safety from them, and a denial of all intentions to proclaim independence. He prorogued the house on the 6th of December till January 3d, 1776, but it never came together again; and thus terminated the provincial legislature of New Jersey.

At the time the provincial congress of New Jersey, (June 10, 1776) convened at Burlington the *General Congress* of the United Colonies was in session in Philadelphia, and on the memorable Fourth of July declared themselves free and independent States. On the 18th of July the provincial congress assumed the title of the "State Convention of New Jersey." Governor Franklin was powerless during the progress of these events as the tide of public opinion was too strong for him to attempt to interfere. He made a proclamation, however, on the 30th of May summoning the house in the name of the King to meet on the 20th of June. The provincial congress took notice of this proclamation and by a vote of thirty-five to eleven decided that it ought not to be obeyed and further that Governor Franklin had by this proclamation shown himself an enemy of the people and their liberties and that for their safety his person ought to be secured. "This was done; and by an order of the Continental Congress, on the 25th of June, the deposed Governor was sent, under guard, to Governor Trumbull of Connecticut, who was desired to take his parole, and in case he refused, to treat him agreeably to the resolution of Congress respecting prisoners. This request was immediately complied with. On his release he sailed for England where he received a pension for his losses."

"The first legislature of independent New Jersey convened at Princeton, August 27th, 1776, and on the 31th of the same month *William Livingstone*, Esq., was, in joint ballot, chosen governor of the State; and, being annually re-elected, continued in office for fourteen years. During his administration, the State was the theatre of war for several years. In the revolutionary struggle, her losses, both of men and property, in proportion to the population and wealth of the the State, was greater than any other of the thirteen States. As General Washington was retreating through the Jerseys almost forsaken, her militia were at all times obedient to his orders, and for a considerable time composed the strength of his army. There is hardly a town in the State that lay in the progress of the British army that was not signalized by some enterprise or exploit. At Trenton the enemy received a check which turned the tide of war. "In the summer of 1778 Sir Henry Clinton retreated with the British army from Philadelphia through New Jersey to New York. The battle of Monmouth signalizes this retreat. The military services performed by the soldiers of New Jersey, and the suffering of the people during the Revolutionary War, entitle her to the gratitude of her sister States. Because of her patriotic spirit, her sacrifices of blood and treasure, her good and true men who marched gallantly to battle and death at their country's call, she is entitled to stand in the foremost rank among those who fought and struggled for American freedom.

HISTORY OF THE INDIANS IN NEW JERSEY.

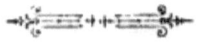

"IT would be in vain to pretend to give a particular account of all the different tribes or nations of Indians that inhabited these provinces before the Europeans came among them, there being a tribe, probably, in some parts, for every ten or twenty miles, which were commonly distinguished by the names of creeks or other noted places where they resided; thus, there were the Assunpink, the Shackamaxon, the Rankokas, the Mingo, the Andastaka and the Neshamine Indians; and those around Burlington were called the Mantas; but these and others were all of them distinguished from the Indians farther back, who were a more warlike people, by the general name of the Delawares. The nations most noted from home that sometimes inhabited New Jersey, and the first settled parts of Pennsylvania, were the Naraticongs, on the north side of Raritan River, the Capitinasses, Gacheos, the Manseys, the Pomptons, the Senecas, and the Maugnaas; this last was the most numerous and powerful. Different nations were frequently at war with each other, of which husbandmen sometimes find remaining marks in their fields. A little below the Falls of Delaware on the Jersey side, at Point-no-point in Pennsylvania and several other places, were banks that had been thrown up for intrenchments against incursions of the neighboring Indians, who, in their canoes, used sometimes to go in warlike bodies from one province to another.'

"It was customary with the Indians of West Jersey, when they buried their dead, to put family utensils, bows, and arrows, and sometimes money (wampum) into the grave with them as tokens of their affection. When a person of note died far from the place of his own residence, they would carry his bones to be buried there; they washed and perfumed the dead, painted the face and followed singly. They left the dead in a sitting posture and covered the grave like a pyramid. They were very careful in preserving and repairing the graves of their dead and pensively visited them. They disliked to be asked their judgment twice about the same thing. They generally delighted in mirth; were very studious in observing the virtues of roots and herbs, by which they usually cured themselves of many bodily distempers, both by outward and inward applications. They frequently used sweating and the cold bath." "The manner for a bath was first to inclose the patient in a narrow cabin, in the midst of which was a red-hot stone; this frequently wet with water, occasioned a warm vapor; the patient sufficiently wet with this and his own sweat, was hurried to the next creek or river, and plunged into it; this was repeated as often as necessary, and sometimes great cures performed. But this rude method at other times killed the patient, notwithstanding their hardy natures; especially in the small-pox and other European disorders." They had an aversion to beards and would not suffer them to grow, but plucked the hairs out by the roots. The hair of their heads was black, and generally shone with bear's fat, particularly that of the women who tied it behind in a large knot, sometimes in a bag. They called persons and things by the name of things remarkable, or birds, beasts and fish; as, *pea-hala*, a duck; *coo-hawnk*, a goose; *quink-quink*, a tit; *pul luppa*, a buck; *shingas*, a wild-cat; and they observed it as a rule, when the rattlesnake gave notice by his rattle before they approached, not to hurt him; but if he rattled after they had passed they immediately returned and killed him. They were very loving to one another; if several of them came to a Christian's house, and the master of it gave one of them victuals and none to the rest, he would divide it into equal shares among his companions; if the Christians visited them they would give them the first cut of their victuals; they would not eat the hollow of the thigh of anything they killed. Their chief employment was hunting, fishing, fowling, making canoes, bowls and other wooden and earthen ware; in all which they were, considering the means, ingenious. They boiled their water in their earthen bowls. Their women's business chiefly consisted in planting Indian corn, parching or roasting it, pounding it to meal in mortars, or breaking it between stones, making bread and dressing victuals; in which they were sometimes observed to be very neat and cleanly and sometimes otherwise. They also made mats, ropes, hats and baskets (some very curious) of wild hemp and roots, or splits of trees. Their young women were originally very modest and shame-faced, and at marriageable ages distinguished themselves with a kind of worked mats, or red or blue baga, interspersed with small rows of white and black wampum, or half rows of each in one, fastened to it, and then put round the head, down to near the middle of the forehead. Both young and old women would be highly offended at indecent expressions unless corrupted with drink. They would not allow the name of a friend after his death, to be mentioned. They sometimes streaked their faces with black, when in mourning; but when their affairs went well they painted red. They were great observers of the weather by the moon; delighted in fine clothes; were punctual in their bargains, and observed this so much in others that it was very difficult for a person who had once failed therein to get any dealings with them afterward. In their councils they seldom or never interrupted or contradicted one another till two of them had made an end of their discourse; for if ever so many were in company only two must speak to each other; and the rest be silent till their turn came. Their language was high, lofty and sententious. Their way of counting was by tens, that is to say, two tens, three tens, four tens, etc.; when the number got out of their reach they pointed to the stars or the hair of their heads. They lived chiefly on maize, or Indian corn, roasted in the ashes, sometimes beaten and boiled with water; they also made an agreeable cake of their pounded corn, and raised beans and peas. But the woods and rivers chiefly supplied them with food. They pointed their arrows with a sharpened, flinty stone. They had a larger sort with withes for handles with which they cut their wood. Both of these sharpened stones are frequently found in the fields. They ate on the ground morning and evening. They were naturally reserved, apt to resent and conceal their resentments and retain them long, but were liberal and generous to the English. They were observed to be uneasy and impatient in sickness for a present remedy, to which they commonly drank a decoction of roots in spring water, forbearing flesh, which if they ate at all, must be of the feminine gender. They took remarkable care of their sick while hope of life remained; but when that was gone some of them were apt to neglect the patient.

Their government was monarchial and successive and mostly of the mother's side to prevent a spurious issue. They commonly washed their children in cold water as soon as born; and to make their limbs straight tied the child to a board and hung it to their backs when they travelled. The children usually walked at nine months old. Their young men married at sixteen or seventeen years of age, if by that time they had given sufficient proof of their manhood by a large return of skins. The girls married at thirteen or fourteen, but stayed with their mothers to hoe the ground, bear burdens, etc., for some years after marriage. The women in travelling usually carried the luggage. The marriage ceremony was sometimes thus: the relations and friends being present, the bridegroom delivered a bone to the bride, she an ear of Indian corn to him: meaning that he was to provide meat, she bread. It was not unusual to change their mates upon disagreement; the children going to the one that loved them best. The expense was of no moment to either. In case of disagreement about the children the man was allowed the first choice if the children were divided, or if there was but one. Very little can be said as to their religion. Much pains were taken by the early Christian settlers to inform them respecting the use and benefits of the Christian revelation and to fix restraints, but generally with unpromising success, though instances have now and then happened to the contrary. They are thought to have believed in a God and immortality and seemed to aim at public worship. When they did this, they sometimes sat in several circles, one within another. Their worship consisted of singing, dancing, jumping and shouting, but performed as something handed down from their ancestors, without

any knowledge or inquiry as to its seriousness or
origin. They said that the great king who made
them dwelt in a glorious country to the southward,
and that the spirits of the best should go there and
live again. Their most solemn worship was the sacrifice of the first-fruits, in which they burnt the first
and fattest buck, and feasted together upon what else
they had collected; but in this sacrifice broke no
bones of any creature they ate. When done they
gathered them up and buried them very carefully.
These have since been frequently plowed up. They
distinguished between a good and evil manetta, or
spirit; worshipped the first for the good they hoped;
and some of them are said to have been slavishly dark
in praying to the last for deprecation of evils they
feared; but if this be true in a general sense some of
the tribes much concealed it from our settlers. They
did justice upon one another for crimes among themselves, in a way of their own. Even murder might be
atoned for by feasts or presents of wampum. The
price of a woman killed was double that of a man,
because *she bred children, which man could not do.*
If sober they rarely quarreled among themselves.
They lived to sixty, seventy, eighty or even ninety before rum was introduced, but rarely have they attained
to that age since. Some tribes were commendably careful of their aged and decrepit, endeavoring to make
the last of life as comfortable as they could. It was
pretty generally so except in cases of desperate decays;
then indeed they were apt as in other cases of the like
kind to neglect them. They were keen and strict
observers of property, yet to the last degree thoughtless and inactive in acquiring and keeping it. None
could excel them in liberality of the little they had,
for nothing was thought too good for a friend; a

knife, gun or any such thing given to one, frequently passed through many hands. Their houses or wigwams were sometimes together in towns, but mostly movable, and occasionally fixed near a spring or other water, according to the conveniences for hunting, fishing, basket-making or other business of that sort, and built with poles laid on forked sticks in the ground, with bark, flags or bushes on the top and sides with an opening to the south, their fire in the middle; at night they slept on the ground with their feet towards it; their clothing was a coarse blanket or skin thrown over the shoulder, which covered to the knee, and a piece of the same tied round the legs, with part of a deerskin sewed round their feet for shoes. As they had learned to live upon little, they seldom expected or wanted to lay up much. They were also moderate in asking a price for anything they had for sale. When a company travelled together they generally followed each other in silence. Scarcely ever were two seen by the side of one another. In the road the man went first with his bow and arrow, the woman after, not unfrequently with a child on her back and other burdens besides; but when these were too heavy the man assisted. To know their walks again, in unfrequented woods they heaped stones or marked trees.

In person they were upright, and straight in their limbs, beyond the usual proportion in most nations. Their bodies were strong, but of a strength rather fitted to endure hardships than to sustain much bodily labor; very seldom crooked or deformed. Their features were regular; their countenances sometimes fierce and more resembling a Jew than Christian; the color of their skin a tawny reddish-brown and the whole fashion of their lives of a piece, hardy, poor and squalid. When they began to drink they generally continued it as long as they could find anything with which to purchase more. When drunk they often lay exposed to the inclemencies of the weather, which introduced a train of new disorders among them. They were grave, even to sadness upon any common, and more so upon any serious occasions; observant of those in company and respectful to the old; of a temper cool and deliberate; never in haste to speak but waited for a certainty that those who spoke before them had finished all he had to say. They seemed to hold European vivacity in contempt, because they found such as came among them apt to interrupt each other and frequently speak all together. Their behavior in public councils was strictly decent and instructive; every one in his turn was heard, according to rank of years or wisdom, or services to his country. Not a word or whisper or murmur while any one was speaking; no interruption to commend or condemn; the younger sort were totally silent. They obtained fire by rubbing wood of particular sorts (as the ancients did out of the ivy and bays), by turning the end of a hard piece upon the side of one that was soft and dry; to forward the heat they put dry, rotten wood and leaves; and with the help of fire and their stone axes, they would fell large trees and afterward scoop them into bowls, canoes, etc. From their infancy they were educated to endure hardships, to bear derision and even blows patiently; at least with a composed countenance. Though they were not easily provoked, it was hard to appease them when it did happen. Liberty in its fullest extent was their ruling passion; to this every other consideration was subservient. Their children were trained up to cherish this disposition to the utmost; they were indulged to a great degree, seldom chastised with blows, and rarely chided; their faults were left for their reason and the habits of the family to correct. They said these could not be great before their reason commenced. They seemed to abhor a slavish motive to action as inconsistent with their notions of freedom and independency. Even strong persuasion was industriously avoided as bordering too much on dependence, and a kind of violence offered to the will. They dreaded slavery more than death. They laid no fines for crime, for they had no way of exacting them; the atonement was voluntary. Every tribe had particulars in whom they reposed confidence, and unless they did something unworthy of it, they were held in respect. What were denominated kings, were sachems distinguished among the above. The respect paid them was voluntary and not exacted or looked for, or the omission regarded. The sachems directed in their councils and had the chief disposition of lands. To help their memories in treaties they had belts of white and black wampum; with these closed their periods in speeches, delivering more or less according to the importance of the matter treated of. This ceremony omitted all that they said passed for nothing. They treasured these belts when delivered to them in treaties, kept them as the records of the nation, to have recourse to upon future contests. Governed by customs and not by laws they greatly revered their ancestors, and followed them so implicitly that a new thought or action seldom intruded. They long remembered kindnesses; families that endeavored to deal with them fairly and treat them hospitably even if no great kindness were received were sure of their trade. It must be allowed that the uncorrupted heart seldom fails to be grateful for real favors received. And notwithstanding the strains of perfidy and cruelty which in 1754 and since have disgraced the Indians on the frontier of these provinces, even these, by an uninterrupted intercourse of seventy years, had, on many occasions, given unimpeachable proofs of liberality of sentiment, hospitality of action, and impressions that seemed to promise a continuance of better things. But of them enough at present."

"Among a people so immediately necessary to each other, where property was little thought of, and the anxiety of increasing it less, the intercourse naturally became free and unfettered with ceremony. Hence every one had his eye on his neighbor and misunderstandings and mistakes were easily rectified. No ideas of state or grandeur; no homage of birth, rank or learning; no pride of house, habit or furniture; very little emulations of any kind to interrupt; and so much together they must be friends, as far at least as that term could be properly applied to them; this was general in some of the tribes. Attachments of particular ones to each other were constant and steady in some instances far exceeding what might be expected. Companies of them frequently got together to feast, dance and make merry. This sweetened the toil of hunting. They scarcely knew, however, what it was to toil, for hunting and dancing comprised it all. A life of dissipation and ease, of uncertainty and want, of appetite, satiety indolence and sleep, seemed to be the sum of their character and the chief thing that they aimed at.

"Notwithstanding the government was successive, it was, for extraordinary reasons, sometimes ordered otherwise. Of this there is an instance in the old king Ockanickon, who dying about this time at Burlington, declared himself to this effect:

"'It was my desire that my brother's son, Iahkursoe, should come to me, and hear my last words; for him have I appointed king after me.

"'My BROTHER'S SON, this day I deliver my heart into your bosom; and mind me, I would have you love what is good, and keep good company; refuse what is evil, and by all means avoid bad company.

"'Now, having delivered my heart into your bosom, I also deliver my bosom to keep my heart in; be sure always to walk in a good path, and if any Indians should speak evil of Indians or Christians, do not join in it, but look at the sun from the rising of it to the setting of the same. In speeches that shall be made between the Indians and Christians, if any wrong or evil thing be spoken, do not join with that; but join with the good. When speeches are made, do not you speak first; be silent and let all speak before you, and take good notice what each man speaks, and when you have heard all, join to that which is good.

"'BROTHER'S SON, I would have you cleanse your ears, and take all foulness out that you may hear both good and evil, and then join with the good and refuse the evil; and also cleanse your eyes that you may see good and evil, and where you see evil, do not join with it, but join to that which is good.

"'BROTHER'S SON, you have heard what has passed; stand up in time of speeches; this do, and what you desire in reason will be granted. Why should you not follow my example? I have had a mind to be good, and do good, and therefore do you the same. Sheoppy and Swampis were to be kings in my stead, but understanding, by my doctor, that Sheoppy secretly advised him not to cure me, and they both being with me at John Hollingshead's house, I myself saw by them, that they were given more to drink than to take notice of my last words; for I had a mind to make a speech to them, and to my brethren, the English commissioners; therefore I refuse them to be kings after me, and have now chosen my brother's son, Iahkursoe, in their stead to succeed me."

"'BROTHER'S SON, I advise you to be plain and fair with

all, both Indians and Christians, as I have been; I am very weak, otherwise I would have spoken more."

"After the Indian had delivered this council to his nephew, T. Budd, one of the proprietors, being present, took the opportunity to remark that 'there was a great God who created all things; and that he gave man an understanding of what was good and bad; and after this like rewarded the good with blessings, and the bad according to their doings.'

"He answered:

"'It is very true, it is so; there are two ways, a broad and a straight way; there are two paths, a broad and a straight path; the worst and the greatest number go in the broad, the best and fewest in the straight path.'"

This king dying soon afterward, was attended to his grave in the Quaker's burial-place in Burlington, with solemnity, by the Indians in their manner, and with great respect by many of the English settlers, to whom he had been a sure friend. The foregoing history of the Indians is as given in *Smith's History of New Jersey*.

The following interesting matter in regard to the Indians is taken from *New Jersey Historical Collections* and was published in the *Newark Sentinel*, entitled "Glimpses of the Past in New Jersey":

"During the dominion of the Dutch, hostile relations existed on two or three occasions. De Vries tells us (New York Historical Collections) that, in 1630, thirty-two men were killed by the Indians on the Delaware; and he gives a detailed account of difficulties with those of East Jersey in 1640 and 1643. In the former year an expedition fitted out against those on the Raritan, accused, although wrongfully, of having committed thefts and other trespasses, caused some of the leading chiefs to be maltreated, and led to retaliatory measures upon the settlers of Staten Island, who were killed and their plantations broken up.

"This matter, in connection with the refusal of the Indians to give up the author of a murder subsequently committed, brought on hostilities. The Dutch authorities were guilty of great duplicity, in beguiling the natives into the belief that 'no evil was brewing against them; for they directed that 'the kind intercourse and the trade in corn should be continued with them as before, till God's will and proper opportunity is offered.' This opportunity came early in 1643. The Indians in the vicinity of Fort Orange (Albany) having commenced a war with their more southern brethren, Gov. Kieft joined with them and, on the night of the 25-26th of January a detachment of troops was sent over to Pavonia, and eighty Indians were murdered in their sleep, or in attempting to escape. 'This was the feat,' says De Vries, alluding to a remark of the Governor in relation to it, 'worthy of the heroes of old Rome, to massacre a parcel of Indians, and to butcher them in the presence of their parents, and throw their mangled limbs into the fire or water. Other sucklings had been fastened to little boards, and in this position they were cut to pieces. Some were thrown into the river, and when the parents rushed in to save them, the soldiers prevented their landing, and let the parents and children drown.' As the orders given to the officer commanding the expedition, as they appear on the record, were 'to spare as much as it is possible their wives and children, and to take the savages prisoners,' we might attribute this cruelty entirely to the excited passions of the men; but the same author tells us they were rewarded, and that 'the same night forty

Indians more were murdered at Corlaer's plantation."

Such a warfare could not fail to exasperate the natives; and we are told that, as soon as they became aware that these massacres were by the whites (for from the secrecy observed and the darkness of the night, they thought they had been attacked by their enemies, the Maquas), they murdered in the country all the men they could find; but more human than the whites, spared the females and children. Houses and barns, grain and hay, were destroyed, and war waged for a month or more. In March, a peace was concluded which lasted only till October; when three or four soldiers, stationed at Pavonia for the protection of a family, having been attacked, war was renewed; and so serious was its character, that in March, 1644, the authorities of New Amsterdam, proclaimed a solemn fast, to deprecate the anger of Jehovah.

Peace was permanently restored the following year; and as, in their distress, they had fasted, so now the good burghers rejoiced, and kept a day of public thanksgiving and praise. We hear of no further disturbances from this time; and in 1664 the English came into possession of the country. Of course, the unsettled state of the intercourse with the Indians had interfered most materially with the settlement of this portion of New Netherlands.

There are no data by which a true estimate can be formed of the number of Indians within what are now the limits of New Jersey, when first population began to change the character and aspect of the country; but probably there were more than two thousand when the province was taken under the dominion of the English. An old pamphlet in the Philadelphia Library, printed in 1648, to induce emigration under the grant to Sir Edward Ployden, states that the natives in this section of the country were under the dominion of about twenty kings; that there were "twelve hundred under the two Raritan kings on the north side, next to Hudson's river, and those come down to the ocean about Little Egg Bay and Sandy Barnegat; and about the South Cape two small kings, of forty men apiece, called Tirans and Tiascans; and a third reduced to fourteen men at Reymont. The seat of the Raritan king is stated to have been called (by the English) *Mount Ployden*, 'twenty miles from Sandhaysea, and ninety from the ocean; next to *Amara hill, the retired paradise of the children of the Ethiopian emperor*—a wonder, for it is a square rock, two miles compass, one hundred and fifty feet high, a wall-like precipice, a straight entrance easily made invincible, where he keeps two hundred for his guards, and under is a flat valley, all plain, to p'ant and sow.'

"The writer is at a loss to locate this 'Mount' and 'retired paradise', if such actually existed, save in the imagination of 'Beauchamp Plantagenet, Esq'; as he knows of no place answering the description. On early maps of New Jersey, an Indian path is designated, running from the mouth of Shrewsbury river in a northwesterly direction, crossing the Raritan a little to the westward of Amboy; and thence in a northernly direction to Minisink island, in the Delaware River, near the northern boundary of the State. This was probably their great thoroughfare. The *Sanhicans*, the deadly enemies of the *Manhatas*, but whom DeLaet characterizes as a better and more decent people, inhabited that part of the province lying west of Staten Island; and further south were the *Naraticongs, Mararancongs*, and other branches of the great Delaware tribe.

"When the province came into the possession of

Lords Berkely and Carteret, they consulted the peace and happiness of the settlers, by the establishment of the best regulations for intercourse with the natives. They say to their governor and councilors should they 'happen to find any natives in our said province, and tract of land aforesaid, that then you treat them with all humanity and kindness, and not in any way grieve or oppress them, but endeavor by a Christian carriage to manifest piety, justice and charity; and in your conversation with them; the manifestation whereof will prove beneficial to the planters, and likewise advantageous to the propagation of the gospel (East Jersey Records).' And in order that they might be protected from the arts of designing men, their lands were not allowed to be purchased excepting through the Governor and council, in the name of the lords proprietors.

"It was to be presumed, however, that intercourse with such varied characters as ever constitute the first population of a new country, would present many causes for outbreaks and disputes. The assembly, therefore, early took measures to guard against such difficulties by prohibiting all trade with them; and in 1675, when some apprehensions were entertained the sale to them of ammunition was prevented, as well as the repairing of their firearms; and the continuance of peace was, in subsequent years, still further secured, by prohibiting the sale, gift, or loan to them of any intoxicating drink. These wholesome restrictions, modified as, occasion required, continued in force under the government of the twenty-four proprietors, and that of the crown which succeeded. Mrs. Mary Smith in a manuscript account of the first settlement of Burlington, quoted in Watson's Annals, says, 'the Indians were very civil, brought them corn, venison, and bargained also for their land.' It was said that an old Indian king spoke prophetically, before his death, of the increase of the whites, and the diminution of his race. Such predictions were current among them as early as 1680. At the time Perth Amboy was settled (1684), there appears to have been only a few natives in that vicinity; and those who visited the place are represented as very serviceable to the settlers, from the game they caught, and the skins and furs they procured and sold to them."

The first serious outbreak occurred in 1755, but, so soon as a hostile feeling became apparent, the legislature appointed commissioners to examine into the causes of dissatisfaction. A convention was held at Crosswicks, for the purpose, in January, 1756; and in March, 1757, a bill was passed calculated to remove the difficulties which had grown out of impositions upon the Indians when intoxicated, the destruction of deer by traps, and the occupation of lands by the whites which they had not sold.—(Neville's Laws, Vol. II, p. 125.) During this year, however, and the first part of 1758, the western borders of the province were in much alarm from the hostile feeling prevalent among the Minisink and neighboring tribes—from May, 1757, to June, 1758, twenty-seven murders having been committed by them on the West Jersey side of the Delaware. A constant guard was kept under arms, to protect the inhabitants; but it was not always able to check the predatory excursions of the savages.

In June, 1758, Gov. Bernard of New Jersey consulted General Forbes and Gov. Denny of Pennsylvania, as to the measures best calculated to put a stop to this unpleasant warfare; and through *Teedyescung*, king of the Delawares, he obtained a conference with the Minisink and the Pompton Indians, protection being assured them. It shows no little regard for truth, and the prevalence of a humane and forgiving spirit, on the part of the whites, as well as confidence on the part of the Indians, that the one party should venture, after what had passed, to place themselves so completely in the hands of their enemies, and the other to profit not thereby.

"The conference took place at Burlington, August 7th, 1758. On the part of the province, there were present the Governor, three commissioners of Indian affairs of the house of assembly, and six members of the council. Two Minisink or Mansey Indians, one Cayugan, one Delaware messenger from the Mingoians, and one Delaware who came with the Minisinks, were the delegates from the natives. The conference opened with a speech from the governor. He sat holding four strings of wampum and thus addressed them: 'Brethren, as you are come from a long journey, through a wood full of briars, with this string I annoint your feet, and take away their soreness; with this string I wipe the sweat from your bodies; with this string I cleanse your eyes, ears and mouth that you may see, hear and speak clearly; and I particularly annoint your throat, that every word you say may have a free passage from the heart. And with this string I bid you heartily welcome.' The four strings were then delivered to them. The result of the conference was, that a time was fixed for holding another at Easton, at the request of the Indians; that being, as they termed it, the place of the 'old council fire.'

"The act passed in 1757 appropriated £1,600 for the purchase of Indian claims; but, as the Indians living south of the Raritan preferred receiving their proportion in land specially allotted for their occupancy, 3044 acres, in the township of Evesham, Burlington county, were purchased for them. A house of worship and several dwellings were subsequently erected, forming the town of Brotherton; and as the selling and leasing of any portion of the tract was prohibited, as was also the settlement upon it of any persons other than Indians, the greatest harmony appears to have prevailed between its inhabitants and their white neighbors (Allison's Laws, p 221).

"On the 8th of October, 1758, the conference commenced at Easton. It was attended by the Lieutenant-governor of Pennsylvania, six of his council, and an equal number of the house of representatives; Gov. Bernard of New Jersey, five Indian commissioners, George Croghan, Esq. (deputy Indian agent under Sir William Johnson), a number of magistrates and freeholders of the two provinces, and five hundred and seven *Indians*, comprising delegations from fourteen different tribes. Governor Denny, being obliged to return to Philadelphia, the business of the conference was mainly conducted by Gov. Bernard, who in its management evinced no small degree of talent and tact. It was closed on the 25th of October; and the result was the release, by the Minisink and Wopping Indians, of all lands claimed by them within the limits of New Jersey for the sum of £1000. Deeds were also obtained from the Delawares and other Indians, and they were all desired to remember 'that by these two agreements the province of New Jersey is entirely freed and discharged from all Indian claims.' At least such was the opinion of Gov. Bernard and the Indians; but the assembly, the ensuing March, in answer to the Governor's speech, mention a small claim of the Totamies, and some private claims, still outstanding. The minutes of this interesting conference are printed at length in *Smith's History*. The Governor recommended to the succeeding assembly the continuance of a guard, and the establishment of a regular trading house; but neither measure was adopted. The amicable relations thus happily begun, remained undisturbed for several years. In 1764, a frontier guard of two hundred men was again kept up for some time, in consequence of disturbances in Pennsylvania; but the alarm soon subsided.

"In 1769, Gov. Franklin attended a convention held with the six nations, by several of the colonial governors, and informed the assembly, on his return, that they had publicly acknowledged repeated instances of the justice of the New Jersey authorities in bringing the murderers of Indians to condign punishment; declared that they had no claim or demand whatsoever on the province; and in the most solemn manner conferred on its government the distinguished title of *Sagorighwiyogstha* or the *great arbiter*, or doer of justice—a name which, the governor truly remarked, reflected high honor upon the province.

"In 1802, the small remnant of these original possessors of the soil, remaining in Burlington county, obtained permission to sell their lands and remove to a settlement on the Oneida Lake, in the state of New York, where they continued till 1824; when, with other Indians, they purchased from the Menominees a tract bordering on Lake Michigan, and removed thither. In 1832, the New Jersey tribe, reduced to less than forty souls, applied to the legislature of the State for remuneration on account of their rights of hunting and fishing on enclosed lands, which they had reserved in their various agreements and conventions with the whites. Although no legal claim could be substantiated, yet the legislature in kindness and through compassion for the wanderers, directed the treasurer to pay their agent two thousand dollars, upon filing in the office of the secretary a full relinquishment of all the rights of his tribe (Gordon's New Jersey). Thus was extinguished every legal and equitable claim of the Indians to the soil of New Jersey — a fact which must gratify every citizen of the State."

SOME EARLY LAWS.

"For the beastly vice of drunkenness the first laws inflicted fines of one shilling, two shillings and two shillings and sixpence, for the first three offences, with corporal punishment, should the offender be unable to pay; and if unruly he was, to be put in the stocks until sober. In 1682 it was treated more rigorously; each offence incurred a fine of five shillings, and if not paid the stocks received a tenant for six hours; and constables not doing their duty under the law, were fined ten shillings for each neglect. This increase of punishment indicates that there was a growth in the vice, which may have been attributable in part to the removal of restrictions on the sale of liquors, in small quantities, which had previously been imposed."

"In 1668 each town was obliged to keep an 'ordinary' for the relief and entertainment of strangers, under a penalty of forty shillings for each month's neglect; and ordinary-keepers alone were permitted to retail liquors in less quantities than two gallons. In 1677 the quantity was reduced to one gallon, and in 1683 liquor dealers were debarred the privilege of recovering debts for liquor sold; but whatever good this might have done was destroyed by the assembly authorizing others than keepers of inns to retail strong liquors by the quart. In 1692, 'forasmuch as there were great exorbitances and drunkenness observable in several towns, occasioned by tolerating many persons in selling drink in private houses' an attempt was made to establish an excise; but the following year it was repealed, and the licensing of retailers confided to the Governor."

"The observance of the Lord's day was required by abstaining from all servile work, unlawful recreations, and unnecessary travelling. Any disorderly conduct could be punished by confinement in the stocks, fines, imprisonment or whipping. In 1704, under the administration of Lord Cornbury, many of the early prohibitions were re-enacted; but by that time, it would seem that the use of ardent spirits began to be considered necessary and essential for man's happiness, as keepers of public houses were not to 'allow tippling on the Lord's day, *except for necessary refreshment.*'"

"'All prizes, stage plays, games, masques, revels, bull-baitings, and cock fightings, which excite the people to rudeness, cruelty, looseness and irreligion' were to be discouraged and punished by courts of justice, according to the nature of the offence. Night-walkers or revellers, after nine o'clock were to be secured by the constable till morning; and, unless excused on examination, to be bound over to court.

"Swearing or 'taking God's name in vain,' was made punishable by a shilling fine for each offence, as early as 1668, and such continued to be the law until 1682, when a special act provided that the fine should be two shillings and sixpence; and if not paid the offender was to be placed in the stocks or whipped according to his age, whether under or over twelve."

"The resistance of lawful authority, by word or action, or the *expression of disrespectful language referring to those in office*, was made punishable either by fine, corporal punishment, or by banishment. Subsequently all liars were included — for the second offence incurring a fine of twenty shillings; and if the fines were not paid, the culprits received corporal punishment, or were put in the stocks."

The following proclamation is interesting. It was made by Mr. Basse, who was sent over by the ten proprietors in 1697 as governor of the Eastern province. He seems to have adopted the motto which the common seal of the twenty-four had upon it, viz.: "Righteousness exalteth a nation."

By the Governor — A Proclamation.

"It being necessary, for the good and propriety of this province, that our principal care be, in obedience to the laws of God, and the wholesome laws of this province, to endeavor as much as in us lyeth the extirpation of all sorts of looseness and prophanity, and to unite and join in the fear and love of God and of one another, that by the religious and virtuous carriage and behavior of every one in his respective station and calling, all heats and animosities and dissensions may vanish, and the blessings of Almighty God accompany our honest and lawful endeavors, and that we may join our affections in the true support of his majesty's government over us, who has so often and so generously exposed his royal person to imminent danger to redeem us from the growing power of popery and arbitrary government, and hath, by a singular blessing attending his endeavors, procured our deliverance and a happy and honorable peace, and is a great example and encourager of religion and virtuous living. — I have therefore thought fit, by and with the advice of the Council of this province of East Jersey, strictly to prohibit all inhabitants and sojourners within this province from cursing, swearing, immoderate drinking, Sabbath breaking and all sorts of lewdness and prophane behavior in word or action; and for the true and effectual performance hereof, I do, by and with the advice aforesaid, strictly charge and command all Justices of the Peace, Sheriffs, Constables, and all other officers within the province, that they take due care that all the laws made and provided for the suppressing of vice and encouraging of religion and virtue, particularly the observation of the Lord's day, be duly put in execution, as they will answer the contrary at their peril. Given under the seal of said province this eighth day of April, Anno Dom., 1698, in the tenth year of the reign of our Sovereign Lord William the Third over England, etc., King.   J. BASSE.

"*By the Governor's command,*
"*John Barclay,*
"*Dep' Sec'y and Reg'r.*"

NEW JERSEY DESCRIPTIVE.

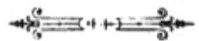

NEW Jersey, one of the original thirteen States, is situated between the Delaware River and Bay and the Hudson River and Atlantic Ocean. Its extreme length is 167 miles, greatest breadth 59 miles, least 32 miles, giving an area of 7815 square miles. It lies between latitude 38 degrees, 56 minutes, and 41 degrees, 21 minutes, north, and longitude 73 degrees, 54 minutes, and 75 degrees, 33 minutes, west. It has a coast front of 120 miles, not counting the coasts of Raritan and Delaware Bays. Its harborage embraces New York Bay, besides Newark and Raritan Bays. There are several estuaries which pierce the State from Little Egg Harbor, Barnegat, Manasquan, affording means of transportation by vessels. Besides these the whole surface of the State is drained by numerous rivers and small streams, emptying into the Atlantic from its eastern watershed or from its western slope into the Delaware, which forms the western boundary. Immense saline marshes stretch along the banks of Delaware Bay and adjoin many of the interior streams; nearly all of them, however, are utilized as meadows. Some of the low lands along the coast have been redeemed from the sea by levies thrown up to keep back the tides, with trap sluices for drainage in low tide.

The north-western portions of the State are diversified by precipitous mountain ranges rising to the height of from

1,000 to 1,800 feet above tide water. On one of these peaks, near Ramapo, is a projecting rock called the Torn, where tradition says General Washington (whose encampment laid in the valley close by) often stood with his telescope to get a glimpse of the movements of the British when they held New York.

Iron ore is found in Sussex, Passaic, Morris and Warren counties. Rich beds of zinc ore are found in Sussex county. Various kinds of sandstone, among which is the famous red variety, magnesian limestone, blue-tinted and other kinds of stone are quarried in large quantities for building purposes. Slate, for roofing and school purposes are extensively quarried on the eastern slope of the Blue range. Fire clay and Potsdam clay are extensively dug in the vicinity of Woodbridge, Amboy and Trenton. Sand, for glass manufacture, is procured in large quantities, near Millville, Winslow and Jackson.

The soil has been greatly improved by the best system of agriculture known, the incentive to which is found in the large demand for fruits, berries and vegetables from the adjacent cities of New York and Philadelphia. To supply this demand the central portions of the State, especially those nearest to these cities have been converted into immense gardens, from which these products are speedily sent to market during their season.

New Jersey is among the foremost in manufacturers, especially those of iron and glass. The largest of these are at Jersey City, where steam is the power used, but these factories are distributed throughout the State where water power is found.

The Morris Canal extends from Jersey City to Phillipsburg, a distance of 101 miles, and has a large carrying trade in coal and heavy merchandise. The Delaware and Raritan Canal connects Trenton on the Delaware, with Brunswick on the Raritan, and has a feeder 22 miles long from Bull's Island. It has about 2,000 miles of railroad, the most important of which are those which connect New York and

Philadelphia, and the New York and Erie and its feeders.

The proximity of the State to two cities of such magnitude as New York and Philadelphia, prevents the centralization of trade to any portion of her own territory sufficiently to produce metropolitan cities, but it is only a fair hypothesis that the State receives from the cities of her adjacent States a larger tribute in supplying their wants, than she pays to them in purchasing their wares.

In summer resorts the State is especially favored. Long Branch and Ocean Grove are crowded with visitors from the great cities. Cape May, Atlantic City, Seabright, etc., also present great attractions to the seekers of pleasure and comfort, and throughout the whole State at farms and villages are scattered, during the hot months, thousands who flee from the cities.

The public schools of New Jersey are excellent, about 210,000 pupils being enrolled and 3,300 teachers.

The State Normal School at Trenton is of great excellence, and has connected with it a model training school. The higher schools of the State are justly celebrated, and number 4 colleges, 4 collegiate schools for women, 3 scientific schools (one being the State Agricultural and Scientific College connected with Rutgers), and 4 schools of theology. The New Jersey State Lunatic Asylum is at Trenton, which has also a State Industrial School for Girls; and there is a State Reform School for juvenile delinquents, near Jamesburg, and a well-managed home for soldiers' children at Trenton, with a branch for colored soldiers' orphans at Bridgewater. At Hoboken is Stevens' Institute of Technology, one of the leading schools of its kind in the United States.

The churches of all denominations report 1,504 church organizations, 1,455 church edifices, 573,303 sittings, 1,421 ministers, 185,160 members, and $19,043,510 value of church property. The Methodists number 71,43 members, almost double that of any other denomination. The Presbyterians come next with 40,093 members. New Jersey has 192 newspapers, with an aggregate circulation of 243,600.

GOVERNORS OF NEW JERSEY.

William Livingston,	1789-90	Daniel Haines,	1843-44
William Patterson,	1790-94	Charles C. Stratton,	1844-48
Richard Howell,	1794-1801	Daniel Haines,	1848-51
Joseph Bloomfield,	1801-12	George F. Fort,	1851-54
Aaron Ogden,	1812-13	Rodman M. Price,	1854-57
Wm. S. Pennington,	1813-15	William A. Newell,	1857-60
Mahlon Dickerson,	1815-17	Charles S. Olden,	1860-63
Isaac H. Williamson,	1817-29	Joel Parker,	1863-66
Peter D. Vroom,	1829-32	Marcus L. Ward,	1866-69
Samuel L. Southard,	1832-33	Theo. F. Randolph,	1869-72
Elias P. Seely,	1833	Joel Parker,	1872-75
Peter D. Vroom,	1833-36	Jos. D. Bedle,	1875-78
Philemon Dickerson,	1836-37	Geo. B. McClellan,	1878-81
William Pennington,	1837-43	Geo. C. Ludlow,	1881-84
	Leon Abbett,	1884-87.	

POPULATION.

Atlantic County,	18,704	Middlesex County		52,286
Bergen "	36,786	Monmouth	"	55,538
Burlington "	55,402	Morris	"	50,861
Camden "	62,942	Ocean	"	14,455
Cape May "	9,765	Passaic	"	68,860
Cumberland "	37,687	Salem	"	24,579
Essex "	189,929	Somerset	"	27,162
Gloucester "	25,886	Sussex	"	23,539
Hudson "	187,944	Union	"	55,571
Hunterdon "	38,570	Warren	"	36,589
Mercer "	58,061	Total,		1,131,116

HISTORY OF WARREN COUNTY.

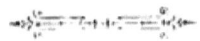

AN act was passed by the General Assembly in 1709 erecting and bounding the old counties of New Jersey. Previous to this, however, eight had been formed. In 1675, Salem, Monmouth and Essex were formed; in 1677, Gloucester; in 1682, Middlesex; in 1688, Somerset; in 1692, Cape May, and in 1694, Burlington. In 1702 upon the proprietors surrendering their charter to Queen Anne, East and West Jersey were united under one government and the royal authority extended over them. The first four assemblies, held at Bergen and Burlington, did nothing toward defining the civil divisions of the province.

The fifth assembly held at Burlington in 1709, passed an act dividing the boundaries of all the counties in the province as follows: " In the Eastern division, the county of Bergen should begin at Constable's Hook, and so run up along the bay and Hudson River to the partition point between New York, and so to run along the partition-line between the provinces and the division-line of the Eastern and Western divisions of this province to Pequanock River; and so to run down the said Pequanock River and Passaic River to the Sound, and so to follow the Sound to Constable's Hook where it began.

"Essex began at the mouth of the Rahway river where it falls into the Sound, and ran up said river to Robinson's Branch; thence west to the division-line between the Eastern and Western divisions, and so to follow the said division-line to the Pequanock River, where it meets the Passaic River; thence down the Passaic River to the bay Sound; thence down the Sound to where it began.

"The county of Somerset began where Bound Brook empties itself into the Raritan River; thence down the stream of Raritan to the mouth of a brook known by the name of Lawrence's brook; thence running up the said Lawrence's brook to Canbury brook; from thence south forty-four degrees, westerly to Saupinck brook, to the said division-line to the limits of the aforesaid county of Essex; thence east along the line of Essex county to Green brook and Bound Brook to where it began.

"Middlesex county began at the mouth of the creek that parts the lands of George Willocks and what were formerly Capt. Andrew Brown's; thence along the said Capt. Andrew's line to the rear of said land; thence upon a direct course to Warne's bridge, on the brook where Thomas Smith did formerly live'; thence upon a direct course to the southeast corner of Barclay tract of land that lies near Matchaponix; thence to the most southeastermost part of said tract of land in Middlesex county; thence upon a direct line to Saupinck bridge on the high road, including William Jones, William Story, Thomas Buchanan and John Guberson, in Monmouth county; thence along the said road to Aaron Robin's land; thence westerly along the said Robin's land and James Lawrence's line to the line of the eastern and western divisions aforesaid, including Robin's and Lawrence's in Monmouth county; thence northerly along the said line to Saupinck brook, being part of the bounds of said Somerset county; thence following the lines of the said Somerset and Essex counties, and so to the Sound; and thence down the sound to Amboy Point; and from thence down the creek to where it first began. The partition-line between Burlington and Gloucester counties began at the mouth of Pensauquin, otherwise Cropwell, creek; thence up the same to the fork; thence along the southernmost branch thereof—sometimes called Cole's branch—until it comes to the head thereof, which is the bounds between Samuel Lipincote's and Isaac Sharp's lands; thence upon a straight line to the southernmost bank of Little Egg Harbor's most southerly inlet; thence along the line of the seacoast to the partition-line between East and West Jersey; thence along the said line of partition, by maidenhead and Hopewell, to the northernmost and uttermost bounds of the township of Amwell; thence by the same to the river Delaware; thence by the river Delaware to the first-mentioned station.

"The beginning point of Gloucester county was at the mouth of Pensauquin creek; thence up the same to the forks thereof; thence along the said bounds of Burlington county to the sea; thence along the seacoast to Great Egg Harbor River; thence up said river to the forks thereof; thence up the southernmost and greatest branch of the same to the head thereof; thence upon a straight line to the head of Oldman's creek; thence down the same to the Delaware River; thence up the Delaware River to the place of beginning.

"Cape May county began at the mouth of a small creek on the west side of Stipson's Island, called Tecak's creek; thence up the said creek as far as tide floweth; thence along the bounds of Salem county to the southernmost main branch of Great Egg Harbor River; thence down the said river to the sea; thence along the seacoast to the Delaware bay, and so up the said bay to the place of beginning.

"This last section subjected Somerset county to the jurisdiction of the courts and officers of Middlesex, for want of a competent number of inhabitants to hold courts and supply jurors, and enacted that jurors might be taken promiscuously from both to either of the said counties, but was altered on March 11, 1713.

"The people of western New Jersey previous to March 11th, 1713, attended court in Burlington. This was, however, very inconvenient and an act was passed by the General Assembly March 11th, 1714, erecting the county of Hunterdon, to wit:

"That all and singular of the lands and upper parts of the said western division of the province of New Jersey, lying northward or situate above the brook or rivulet commonly called Assanpink, be erected into a county named, and from henceforth to be called, the county of Hunterdon; and the said brook or rivulet commonly known and called Assanpink shall be the boundary-line between the county of Burlington and the said county of Hunterdon."

The General Assembly passed an act in 1738 by which Morris county was taken from Hunterdon.

"Sussex County was erected from the upper part of Morris county by an act of the General Assembly passed June 8, 1753, with boundaries as follows:

"That all and singular the lands and upper part

of Morris county, northwest of Musconetcong river, beginning at the mouth of said river where it empties itself into the Delaware River, and running up said Musconetcong river to the head of the Great Pond; from thence northeast to the lines that divide the province of New Jersey; thence along the said line to the Delaware River aforesaid; thence down the same to the mouth of the Musconetcong, the place of beginning, and the said Musconetcong river, so far as the county of Hunterdon bounds it, shall be the boundary-line between that county and the county of Sussex."

Sussex remained in that way till it was reduced to its present dimensions by the detachment of Warren County in 1824.

EARLY SETTLEMENTS.

The first settlement in Sussex County, which then included Warren, was part of a general movement towards the west made from the Dutch settlements on the Hudson, and was located in the upper valley of the Delaware. "The settlers were of the same Huguenot and Holland stock—the former born in France, from which they had been driven by persecution but a few years before, while the latter, if not themselves natives of Holland, were the immediate descendents of those born in that country, which then offered an asylum for the persecuted and oppressed of all nations, and whose struggles in behalf of civil and religious liberty were so memorable."

"The first settlers came here directly from Ulster County, N. Y., the tide of immigration setting up the Mamakating Valley and thence to the Delaware, down which it flowed until it was met by another current ascending from Philadelphia. The two currents of population which thus met and mingled in the ancient valley of the Minisink and spread along the border of these counties from the Neversink to the Musconetcong were of divers nationalities, yet all uniting in one common characteristic,—a native love of liberty and a desire to find freedom from the civil and ecclesiastical restraints which had burdened and hampered them in the Old World. Those coming in from the north were Huguenots and Hollanders; those from the south were Welsh, Quakers, Germans and Scotch-Irish, with a considerable intermixture of the Puritan of New England, all noted for their struggles for civil and religious liberty in the several European countries from whence they came. These formed the basis of the early population not merely of Sussex and Warren counties, but of the upper Delaware valley generally, including the river settlements in the three States of New Jersey, New York and Pennsylvania."

The precise time when the Minisink valley was settled by the Dutch and Huguenots is not clearly established. The "Old Mine Road" which it is thought was made and used as early as 1650 by a company of miners from Holland, was abandoned as a mining-road upon the accession of the English rule in 1664.

"The main body of these men are believed to have returned to their native land, yet a few undoubtedly remained and settled in the vicinity of their abandoned mines. Here then we have the point at which the first settlement in the County was made. Here log cabins were built and orchards planted, when the site of Philadelphia was a wilderness. The Swedes in West Jersey, and the Dutch and Norwegian settlers in Bergen, antedate the pioneers of Pahaquarry but a few years."

Settlements in Other Parts of Sussex and Warren Counties.*

"Our purpose is to give under this head a brief summary of the first settlements in Sussex and Warren counties outside of the Minisink valley.

While the latter portion of our territory was being peopled as we have described, immigrants were coming in to the southward from quite a different direction. Lands were patented and settled near Phillipsburg by Messrs. Lane and Morrill, from Ireland, about the beginning of the eighteenth century. In 1735 three brothers named Green settled in that part of old Greenwich now known as Oxford township. They were soon followed by the McKees, McMurtrys, McCrackens, Axfords, Robesons, Shippins, Andersons, Kennedys, Stewarts, Loders, Hulls, Scotts, Brands, Bowlbys, Swayzes, Shackletons, and Armstrongs, all of whom were Scotch-Irish Presbyterians, with the exception of Robeson, the Greens, and possibly one or two others. Here as a consequence of this unanimity of religious faith and nationality, the first Presbyterian church in the two counties was erected in 1744, following the old Dutch Reformed churches of the Minisink within a very few years of their date. It may be mentioned that the first pastor of the Presbyterian church of Greenwich was Rev. James Campbell, and that he was followed by David Brainerd, the celebrated missionary to the Indians, whose labors called him frequently into the vicinity. He lived for some time at the "Irish Settlement" in Pennsylvania, now known as Lower Mount Bethel, about five miles from Belvidere, where the site of his ancient cabin is still pointed out to the curious trav-

---

*History of Sussex and Warren, 1880, p. 30.

eller. In speaking of Rev. Brainerd it may be well to notice a singular mistake made by Rev. Peter Kanouse in his "Historical Sermon." He speaks of the Neversink emptying into the Delaware and constituting what in Dr. Brainerd's time was called "The Forks of the Delaware" and where was the field of his labors in an Indian settlement named Shakhawotung, now known as "Carpenter's Point." It is well known that "The Forks of the Delaware" where Brainerd had his chief mission, was at Easton, the forks being formed by the Delaware and Lehigh, which form a confluence at that point. "Shakhawotung," the name of the Indian town, signifies "where a smaller stream empties into a larger one, or the outlet," *shakunk* being the general Delaware word for "the mouth of a river."

"The first furnace for the manufacture of iron in Sussex county was erected by Jonathan Robeson, in the then township of Greenwich. It was commenced in 1741, but iron was not run till March 9, 1743. He called this Oxford Furnace in compliment to Andrew Robeson, his father, who had been sent to England and educated at Oxford University. From this furnace the town of Oxford — which was formed twenty years afterward — took its name. Jonathan Robeson was one of the first judges of Sussex county. His father and grandfather both wore the ermine before him in Pennsylvania, while his son, grandson and great-grandson, each in his turn occupied seats on the judicial bench. Wm. P. Robeson of Warren county was the sixth judge in regular descent from his ancestor, Andrew Robeson, who came to America with William Penn and was a member of Governor Markham's Privy Council. In this country, where the accident of birth confers no special right to stations of honor, and where ability and honesty are — or ought to be — the only passports to public distinction. This remarkable succession of officers in one family affords a rare example of hereditary merit, and is, so far as we know, without a parallel in our judicial annals."

Another of the first settlements in Sussex and Warren was made by members of the Society of Friends in that part of ancient Hardwick called "the Quaker Settlement." The pioneers in this locality came from Maiden Creek (now Attleborough, Pa.) and from Crosswicks, N. J., from 1735 to 1740. They were the Wilsons, Lundy's and others and must be set down as among the very first settlers of ancient Harkwick. The settlers here were so few in number that when the first farm-house in the settlement was erected they were obliged to secure help from Hunterdon county. The heavy timbers then put into frames required a greater force to lift them to their place than is needed in raising modern frame structures, and this may account for the fact that this first frame building erected in the settlement stood the blasts of more than a century and a half without having been seriously impaired.

The deed for the ground on which the Friend's meeting-house in this place was built was given by Richard Penn, a grandson of William Penn, in 1752. Previous to the erection of a mill in this neighborhood the people took their grain to Kingwood, in Hunterdon county, to be ground.

Mr. Edsall from reliable date furnished him has summed up the settlements in other portions of Sussex and Warren as follows: "In that part of ancient Newton known as Vernon township there were some early settlements principally consisting of those who had first tried their fortunes in Orange county. One Joseph Perry, who had prepared for the erection of a house there about the year 1740, could not raise the timbers without procuring help from New Windsor. Col. De Kay settled in New York upon the edge of this township in 1711; some of his lands which he held under a New York patent now lie this side the boundary line. The McComleys, Campbells, Edsalls, Winans, Hynards, Simonsons, etc., did not come in until just before the Revolution at which period a considerable amount of population had spread not only over Vernon, but throughout Hardystown. Joseph Sharp—the father, I believe, of the late venerable Joseph Sharp of Vernon—who had obtained a proprietary right to a large body of land stretching from Deckertown to the sources of the Wallkill, came from Salem county a few years before the Revoluton and erected a furnace and forge about one mile south of Hamburg, which were known for some years as the 'Sharpsborough Iron Works.' This was the second furnace erected in Sussex county Sharp lost a great deal from this enterprise; and particularly from the annoyance which he met with from the sheriff of the county,—who, under certain circumstances, is well-known to be a most unwelcome visitor—he abandoned the works." Robert Ogden removed from Elizabethtown and settled in Vernon in 1765 or 1766. He was long one of the judges of the courts of the county, and one of its most prominent and patriotic citizens. Three of his sons fought in the war for independence, and one of them—Col. Aaron Ogden—commanded the honored regiment known as General Washington's Life-Guard.

"From the year 1740 to the close of the Revolution there was a considerable immigration of Germans. Among the first of this class were John Bernhart and Casper Shafer, his son-in-law. They had purchased lands where Stillwater village now is, of persons in Philadelphia, and in the year 1742 by the Delaware and the valley of the Paulinskill, they journeyed to their destination and took possession of the tract indicated by their title-deeds. They were followed in a few years by the Wintermutes, the Snovers, Swartswelders, Staleys, Merkels, Schmucks, Snooks, Mains, Couses, and a large number of other Germans, who settled principally in the valley of the Paulinskill, although a portion branched off in other directions. Mr. Bernhardt lived only a few years after his arrival. He died in 1748, and was the first person buried in the cemetery of the old German church,—the cemetery having been used before the church was built, which was not erected till 1771. In the beginning of his life in the backwoods, Mr. Shafer found it necessary to cross the Pahaqualin Mountain to get his grist ground; the mode adopted was that of leading a horse along an Indian trail, upon whose back the bag of grain was borne. This inconvenience suggested to him the expedient of constructing a mill upon his own property, which he did in the following primitive manner: First, he built a low dam of cobblestones, filled in with gravel, across the kill, to create a water-power; he then drove the piles into the ground, forming a foundation for his building to rest upon; then upon these he built a small frame or log mill-house, furnishing it with one small run of stones, and other equally simple and primitive machinery. His mill being thus furnished and put in operation, was capable of grinding about five bushels a day; yet it was a great convenience and was resorted to from far and near. 'In a few years he built a better mill and commenced shipping flour to Philadelphia' loading it on a flat-boat and running it down the Paulinskill and the Delaware to its place of destination. 'Mr. Shafer was the first man in this region to open a business intercourse with Elizabethtown; he heard from the Indians in his vicinity that there was a large place far away to the southeast which they called "Tespatone", and he determined to ascertain the truth of this assertion. He travelled over mountains and through bogs and forests, and after a rough journey of some fifty miles he arrived at the veritable "Old Borough". He opened a traffic in a moderate way at this time, and thus laid the foundation of that profitable intercourse between the southeastern towns and cities and Northern New Jersey which has increased from that time to the present, and almost entirely excluded Philadelphia from participation in the trade from this part of the State.'

"Robert Paterson was the first settler at Belvidere according to the 'Historical Collections,' about the year 1755. 'Shortly after, a block house was erected on the north side of the Pequest, some thirty or forty yards east of the toll-house of the Belvidere Delaware bridge. Some time previous to the Revolutionary war a battle was fought on the Pennsylvania side of the river between a band of Indians who came from the north and the Delawares residing on the Jersey side.' The name 'Belvidere' was given to the village by Maj. Robert Hoops because of the beauty of its situation. It was made the county-seat of Warren county, when the latter was set off from Sussex, in 1824.

"The Greens, Armstrongs, Pettits, VanHorns, Simes, Hazens, Dyers, Cooks, Shaws and others settled in and around the present village of Johnsonburg, formerly called the 'Log Jail,' where the county-seat of Sussex was first located and the first jail built.

"In 1769 the Moravian Brethren, from Bethlehem, Pa., purchased fifteen hundred acres of land of Samuel Green for the sum of five hundred and sixty-three pounds, or about two thousand five hundred dollars, and founded the village of Hope. This Samuel Green was a deputy surveyor for the West Jersey proprietors, and owned several tracts of land in ancient Hardwick and Greenwich.' The Moravians remained at Hope some thirty-five years, when they commenced selling their property and returned to Bethlehem. Sampson Howell, who settled at the foot of Jenny Jump Mountain, near Hope, a year or two before the Moravians arrived, erected a saw-mill and supplied the lumber for the construction of the very substantial buildings erected by the United Brethren."

We have thus glanced briefly at the first settlements in the principal parts of Sussex and Warren. They were made for the most part within a period of about fifty years, embracing the first half of the eighteenth century,—that is by the year 1750 permanent settlements had been made in most of the important parts of the two counties. When Morris county was set off in 1738, northern New Jersey began to attract attention. It was then ascertained that, although this section had at a remote period evidently been a favorite residence of the Indians, most of them had departed and occupied hunting grounds farther to the north and west. Little danger was therefore to be apprehended from the red men by those who settled in the central portions of the territory; for, even if they should become hostile, the line of settlements on the Delaware from the Musconetcong to the Neversink would be more apt to bear the brunt. Hence immigrants flowed in, and by 1750 they had become so numerous and had experienced so much inconvenience from being compelled to go to Morristown to attend to public business, that they very generally petitioned the Provincial Assembly to "divide the county" and allow them "the liberty of building a court-house and gaol." This request was granted, resulting in the erection and organization of Sussex county in 1753. As to the nationalities constituting the base of population, Mr. Edsall made as complete a list as practicable from the public records for the first six years of the existence of the county. "This list contains four hundred and two names, of which those indicating an English and Scotch origin are the most numerous; those pertaining to Holland and Germany follow next, and the residue are derived from France, Ireland, Wales and Norway."

One thing which stood very much in the way of the prosperity of the early settlers was the appropriation by the proprietors of many portions of the best land in the county. As early as 1715, when as yet but two or three points in the whole territory had been settled, the sagacious proprietors of West Jersey, foreseeing that these lands would ultimately become very valuable, sent their surveyors, who penetrated the heart of the country establishing "butts and bounds" of many of the most desirable tracts. Among others William Penn located three tracts of land, containing ten or twelve thousand acres, in around the vicinity of Newton. "In this way the best locations were generally entered before any immigrants had arrived in the central portions of the county, and they had to cultivate the soil, when they did come, as tenants or trespassers."

FRENCH AND INDIAN WAR, 1755.

THE people of New Jersey treated the Indians with exceptional fairness and the troubles begun in 1755 by the Indians were not reincited by any act of injustice. The people of the province of New Jersey had never shed any of their blood or cheated them out of their lands. Nevertheless the frontiers of Sussex and Warren counties were the sites of much carnage and bloodshed from 1755 to 1758. The causes of this savage attack and massacre, were, however, entirely beyond their control. It was at a time when France and England were at war and the colonies belonging respectively to the above-named nations "had secured the alliance of the various Indian tribes, on one side or the other in the great contest then pending." The Iroquois, or Six Nations, of New York, were for the English and were great factors in the struggle that resulted in the defeat of the French. The Iroquois were the hereditary enemies of the Delaware and Susquehanna Indians. The French had at this time extensive possessions in the vicinity of the St. Lawrence and had forts extending from Quebec to Mobile Bay, and their agents, traders and missionaries were widely scattered among the Indians of all that region of country. Although "Lake Champlain, Niagara and Pittsburg were at that time the nearest points to New Jersey fortified by the French, yet her frontier was accessible by a few days' march along the great trails leading to the Susquehanna and Delaware rivers." These parts were then much exposed, as the Iroquois were away fighting for the English at other places. It is very probable that the Indians who murdered on the borders of Sussex and Warren were incited to their deeds of blood by the French.

There was another cause more local in its character, which embittered and prolonged the strife. William Penn had obtained his lands of the Minsies, through his agents, by the famous "walking purchase" of 1737. This the Indians deemed unfair, and distrust and jealousy took the place of the confidence which they had before had in the whites. They smothered their resentment till 1755 and then resolved to seek revenge and again obtain possession of the country that had been procured from them by treachery and fraud. It is, however, to be deplored that the innocent as well as the guilty suffered in the storm of blood and carnage which swept over the valley during those terrible years of war. The savage, in the height of his fury, seldom pauses to consider whether the scalp belongs to friend or foe. The conflicts were mostly confined to the Pennsylvania side of the Delaware, but New Jersey also felt the shock of the conflict.

In December of the same year the Legislature passed an act authorizing the erection of four blockhouses on the Delaware in Sussex county. John Stevens and John Johnson were designated to superintend their erection. They had "voluntarily offered themselves for that service *gratis*." Two hundred and fifty men were enlisted to garrison the block-houses and ten thousand pounds were granted to pay the expenses of protecting the frontiers.

The troops that were enlisted were to serve one month, or until their places could be filled by others.

The block-houses that were erected were numbered from 1 to 4. They were garrisoned as soon as possible yet the Indians continued to make incursions into the neighborhood and to form ambuscades so near to the forts that parties going out hunting or fishing were on one or two occasions surprised and killed. It became necessary to issue an order to the effect that all officers and soldiers should remain within their garrisons. During times of general alarm whole neighborhoods flocked to the block-houses.

With all the vigilence of the garrisons the Indians would sometimes elude them and get inside and do their bloody work. They did so when they came over into Hardwick and captured the Hunts and Swartwouts. "A party of five Indians, who had formerly resided in the neighborhood but had removed to Pennsylvania, determined to capture three men — Richard Hunt, Harker and Swartwout — having become disaffected towards them because of the part they had taken in the colonial service. They accordingly crossed the Delaware near where Dingman's ferry now is, and in the evening reached the log house of Richard Hunt, having travelled about fifteen miles on the Jersey side of the river. Richard Hunt was absent from home and the only occupants of the house at the time were Thomas Hunt, a younger brother, and a negro servant. The latter was engaged in amusing himself and companion by playing on a violin, when their sport was suddenly interrupted by the Indians. Quick as thought the boys sprang to the door, closed and bolted it. Their fun was at an end, and the negro, in his terror, 'threw his fiddle into the fire and awaited in trembling suspense the result of the unwelcome visit.' The Indians disappeared and were gone about an hour. It was discovered, by their footprints in a newly plowed piece of ground, that during their absence they had reconnoitred the house of Mr. Dildine, where Richard Hunt happened to be at the time ; but they evidently dared not make an attack at that place. Returning to Mr. Hunt's house, they made a movement to set it on fire, threatening to burn the inmates alive if they did not surrender. The boys yielded and were forced to accompany the savages, who proceeded toward the Delaware by the way of the southerly end of Great Pond, and soon came to the house of Swartwuot, who lived on the tract now occupied by the village of New Paterson. Mrs. Swartwout, soon after their approach to the house, went out to the milk-house without a thought of danger, and was instantly shot down. They then attempted to enter the house, but Swartwout seized his rifle and held them in check. Finally he agreed to surrender if they would spare his life and the lives of his son and daughter. They consented to this proposition, but they either themselves violated their pledge or, what was worse, procured a white man to do it, for Swartwout was murdered, and a man named Springer was arrested, convicted and hung for the murder. Swartwout's two children were taken to an Indian town on the Susquehanna, while Hunt and the negro were taken to Canada. Hunt was sold by his captors to a French military officer and accompanied him as his servant. His mother, anxious for his deliverance if alive, attended the general conference at Easton, in October, 1758, where a treaty was made with the Six Nations, and, finding a savage there who knew her son, she gave him sixty pounds to procure his freedom and return him to his friends. This proved money wasted. Hunt was soon after liberated under that provision of the treaty of Easton which made a restoration of prisoners obligatory upon the Indians, and reached home in 1759. after a servitude of three years and nine months. Swartwout's children must have been freed about a year after their capture, for we find his son in New Jersey in 1757, active in causing the arrest of a white man named Benjamin Springer. whom he charged with being the murderer of his father."

Springer was tried in Morris county according to an act passed by the Assembly Oct. 27, 1757. The trial was transferred to Morris county "because the Indian disturbances in Sussex rendered it difficult, if not dangerous to hold a Court of Oyer and Terminer there." Springer had a fair trial and was convicted, but many afterwards believed him to have been wrongly accused.

When the troubles began with the Indians in 1755, most of the settlers along the slopes of the Blue Mountains took the precaution to fortify their houses by building stockades around them. A number of Indians lived in the neighborhood at that time and though openly friendly it was not known how soon they might rush forth with the tomahawk and scalping knife. Mr. Casper Shafer lived in this neighborhood and his house was quite a resort during any unusual alarm. One night, however, when he was alone, the Indians came, surrounded his house, and by their yells, etc., showed unmistakable signs of hostility. He barred up his house, and started across the fields to get assistance. "Soon he found himself hotly pursued by one of the enemy, and likely to be overtaken; whereupon he turned upon his pursuer, and, being an athletic man, seized the Indian, threw him and bound him hand and foot with his garters, while he went on his way and procured the desired assistance. Mr. Depue, in Walpack, also had a narrow escape from the tomahawk and scalping knife. A party of Indians broke into his house at midnight, with murderous intent, and he, being aroused from slumber, seized his loaded gun and aimed it at the foremost aggressor, who, realizing his danger, uttered the peculiar Indian Ugh! dodged away and fled. So acted the next, and another, and another ; and thus without firing his gun, he succeeded in driving the whole gang from his dwelling."

Yielding to petitions that were sent, the General Assembly on June 3d, 1757, "enacted that one hundred and twenty men be immediately raised with the proper number of officers: that Jonathan Hampton be appointed paymaster and victualer for the company and that he provide and allow each officer and soldier the following provisions every week, viz : seven pounds of bread, seven pounds of beef, or in lieu thereof, four pounds of pork, six ounces of butter, three pints of peas, and half a pound of rice."

A year after this, 1758, when everything was supposed to be quiet, Nicholas Cole and family of Walpack were attacked and the most of them murdered. Those who were not murdered were carried away into captivity. Other murders followed. The people again petitioned for protection and the General Assembly ordered another levy of one hundred and fifty men. It was ordered, however, that none, except officers, be taken from the militia of Sussex as they might be needed at any time in case of a formidable attack. Twenty guides, who were well acquainted with the country were to be hired by the commanding officer to conduct the troops through the woods of

Sussex. It was further provided "that inasmuch as the Indians are a very private and secret enemy, and as it has been thought dogs would be of great service in discovering them in their secret retreats among the swamps, rocks and mountains, frequent in those parts; therefore be it enacted, etc., that it shall and may be lawful for the paymaster aforesaid to procure upon the best terms he can fifty good, large, strong and fierce dogs; and the same so procured to be supplied with food necessary to their subsistence, equal to ten men's allowance in quantity; which said dogs shall be disciplined for and employed in the service, in such manner as the said Major, in conjunction with the Commission officers, or the major part of them shall think proper."

EXTRACTS FROM "NEW AMERICAN MAGAZINE". *

"PERTH AMBOY, June 30.—On the 12th instant one Walter Vantile, a sergeant of the forces stationed upon the frontier of this province in the county of Sussex, having received information that a party of Indians had crossed the river Delaware into Pennsylvania, took nine soldiers with him and went over the river in pursuit of them. They made diligent search after the Indians in different ways, but could make no discovery of them. However, for that night they encamped upon the river about six miles from Cole's Fort, and in the morning they scouted back from the river about four miles; at last they discovered an Indian walking towards the place where they had lain the night before, whom they pursued, but he got into a swamp and made his escape. The sergeant and his party then took the same course towards the river which the Indian

---

* This magazine was edited by Samuel Neville, who presided as principal judge, during the first courts held in Sussex county. It was the first publication of the kind in New Jersey.—*History of Sussex and Warren*, 1881.

was steering, and when they came to the bank of the Delaware, they heard some Indians chopping on a small island in the river, and saw ten of them making a raft in order to cross the river. Vantile and his men watched them very strictly the whole night. In the morning, early, the Indians packed up their clothes and other things and waded the river, drawing their raft after them. Vantile, perceiving by their course that they would land higher up than where he and his men were posted, crept privately up the river until they came within one hundred yards of them, when they saw a smoke upon the shore and an Indian rise up, who came towards the soldiers, but he soon returned to the fire and took up his gun; upon which about fifteen Indians rose up and took hold of their guns. The sergeant then ordered his men to fire upon them, and the Indians returned their fire and advanced ; the aforesaid ten Indians who were coming from the island also fired very briskly. The sergeant and his men sustained the attack with great courage, and after fighting six rounds and boldly advancing towards the enemy the Indians fled in great confusion, leaving behind them four guns, four tomahawks, three pikes, fifteen pairs of maccasins, fifteen pairs of stockings, and other sundry things. These are supposed to be the same Indians who had attacked Uriah Westfall's and Abraham Cortwright's houses."

"His Excellency, Governor Bernard, hath sent up orders to the officers upon the frontiers to restrain the soldiers from leaving their quarters and straggling into the woods to shoot and hunt as the same is certainly a dangerous and pernicious practice ; for on Friday last Wm. Ward was shot and scalped, as he was hunting within a half-mile of No. 3, in the county of Sussex ; and the same day about noon a house was burned on the opposite side of the river. The Indians shouted and fired several guns while it was burning.

"Some days since a man and a boy, traveling along the public highway in the said county of Sussex, were attacked by the Indians. The man was shot dead; the boy was surprised, but, finding one of the Indians in pursuit of him, he had presence of mind, as the last refuge, to turn and fire upon him and saw him drop. The other Indian still pursued, and the boy perceiving his gun so retarded his flight that he must be taken, broke it to pieces against a rock, that it might not fall into the enemy's hands, and made his escape from them. He then alarmed the people, who immediately went out upon the scout with guns and dogs, and, coming to the place where the boy shot the Indian, found a great deal of blood, but not the body. They searched very diligently about the woods, when at last one of the dogs began barking; and, going to see what was the matter, they found him barking at a bunch of brush, and turning it aside they found the Indian buried with his clothes and tomahawk, upon which they scalped him and brought away the things they found buried with him. On Tuesday, the 16th of June, Justice Decker, of the county of Sussex, brought the said Indian scalp and tomahawk to Perth Amboy. This savage proved to be the notorious bloody villain well-known by the name of Capt. Armstrong, a noted ring-leader of the Delawares, who, with other Indians, was concerned with Benjamin Springer (lately executed in Morris county) in the murder of Anthony Swartwout, his wife and children."

There were a number of attempts made to treat with the Indians and establish peace. In 1756 a committee was appointed by the Legislature to treat with them. They met the Indians at Crosswicks during the winter, heard their grievances and reported to the Legislature which passed acts to relieve them.

Another conference was held at Burlington Aug. 7, 1758. This was brought about through the diplomacy of the noted chief Teedyuscung, king of the Delawares. Nothing came of it, however, except the understanding to meet again at Easton, the place of the "Old Council" as the Indians termed it. This council was held Oct. 8, 1758. The result of it was that the Indians released all the lands claimed by them within the limits of New Jersey for the sum of one thousand pounds.

Deeds were also obtained, and it was declared "that by these two agreements the province of New Jersey is entirely freed and discharged from all Indian claims."

WARREN AND SUSSEX IN THE REVOLUTION.

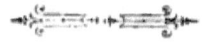

WARREN county was a part of Sussex during the Revolution, hence our history of those times will cover the territory of both. These counties were much exposed to the savage allies of the British during the struggle for independence, owing to their frontier situation along the Delaware.

Many were the battles with the Indians that these people had been compelled to fight during colonial times, and consequently here were a people whose experience had made them familiar with military discipline and the use of arms. Moreover they were a people who had inherited a love of liberty and were somewhat trained in the principles of self government. They were intelligent and patriotic and had among them men capable of filling almost any position in life and taking the lead in any emergency. The two counties then numbered about thirteen thousand. A series of resolutions adopted at a meeting of a number of Freeholders and inhabitants of the county of Sussex, A. D. 1774 declared "That it is our duty to render true and faithful allegiance to George the Third, King of Great Britain, but, that it is undoubtedly our right to be taxed only by our own consent given by ourselves or our Representatives etc." At a meeting held in New Brunswick, July 23, 1774, a commission of fourteen persons was chosen to represent New Jersey in the General Congress that convened at Philadelphia, Sept. 5, 1774. At this time a separation from the mother country was not contemplated, although the people were determined to secure their just rights as British subjects. They had no desire to provoke a war but tried to settle the controversies amicably. It was not till blood was spilt at Concord and Lexington that the people were convinced that all attempts at reconciliation were useless. This was "the straw that broke the camel's back" and cemented the people in one grand and united purpose to declare and maintain their freedom. The people were aroused. "The fathers of Sussex county showed 'an eye to the main chance' in petitions to restrain shopmen from raising the price of their goods. In fact the whole province was in a ferment; Tories were called to repentance, strollers, vagabonds, horse-thieves, and other nuisances were summarily abated; the freemen of the State gathered around the altar of Liberty, and 'pledged their lives, their fortunes and their sacred honor' to the defense and triumph of popular rights. They hardly knew what was to come of it; but, having put their hand to the plow they did not look back."

Committees of safety were organized in all the townships of Sussex county, and representatives from the township committees, formed the county committee of safety, which met at the Court House at Newton once a month. "This committee exercised a general supervision over the township organizations, provided means for promoting the popular cause, and procured the oath of abjuration to be administered to every citizen of the county, carefully noting down the names of those who refused, with the grounds upon which they based such refusal, and causing the recusants to be presented by the grand inquest of the county, to the end that they might appear in court and openly recant, or give bonds for their peaceable behavior. The minutes of the sittings of this important committee were carefully written out for the information of subordinate committees, and, with a little care might have been preserved." At one of these meetings " returns were called for from the several townships of the names of those who refused to sign the articles of association for the respective townships. In Greenwich seven persons were returned as having refused to sign, four of whom were Quakers, who declared it to be against their conscience to take up arms ; one gave no reason and the remaining two would 'take time to consider.'. From Mansfield two names were returned, but no reason for refusal assigned. In Sandystown all signed except two 'who are willing to do so when opportunity offers.' In Montague every citizen signed and in Wantage all agreed except Joseph Havens and one or two more Quakers, 'who are Whigs and are willing to contribute.' The other towns, says the record not having had the association particularly carried to the inhabitants, ordered that the committee of said towns wait upon the people and make return at the next meeting of the committee."

"What report was made from 'the other towns' is not known, but may be inferred from the returns just given. These items afford us an insight into the state of feeling which pervaded the county at that early stage of the conflict, and conclusively refute the gross imputations which have been recklessly and maliciously cast upon the patriotism of our Revolutionary citizens.

"At this meeting means were taken to raise by tax the county's quota of ten thousand pounds ordered by the Provincial Congress of New Jersey for the purpose of raising money to purchase arms and ammunition, and for other exigencies of the province. Casper Shafer was appointed collector of the county, to take charge of the funds to be raised under the authority of the Committee of Safety. It was also ordered that the captains of the respective companies of militia send an account to the next meeting of the committee of all persons upwards of sixteen and under fifty years old in their several districts who refuse to sign the muster roll, that their names may be forwarded to the Provincial Congress.'

"Captain John McMurtry and Lieut. William White, of Oxford township, being desirous to go to Boston, where the Americans were rallying under the standard of Washington, then just appointed Commander-in-Chief of the Continental forces, requested the committee to certify as to their 'place of abode, character and reputation,' which was at once complied with.

"On motion, it was 'Resolved, *mem. con.*, That any person thinking himself aggrieved by any merchant or trader in this county taking an exorbitant price for any article of goods make application to the chairman of the town committee where such merchant or trader resides, who is to call a meeting of said committee as soon as convenient thereafter, which said meeting is to consist of five members at least. And the said committee, when convened, shall notify the said merchant or trader to appear and show why he has taken so great a price; and if it shall appear that he has taken an unreasonable profit, or shall refuse to attend or give any satisfaction in the premises, that he be cited by the said committee to appear at the next meeting of the county committee, there to be dealt with according to the rules of the Continental Congress."

"A memorial on this subject was also drawn up and ordered to be presented to the Continental Congress, praying that the latter body would make inquiry and ascertain if the Philadelphia and New York merchants of whom the traders in this county purchased their goods were not at the bottom of the system of corruption, speculating upon the public necessity by affixing exorbitant prices upon their merchandise."

According to reports the above restrictions were loudly called for as fifty bushels of wheat were required to get one bushel of salt; calico cost fifteen shillings a yard, while rye sold for one shilling eight pence per bushel. "Only one pair of shoes a year could be purchased, which were generally bought about Christmas time, and which the fair owners carefully preserved from dilapidation through the summer by going barefoot, like the enchanting goddesses that figure in ancient mythology."

The Provincial Congress changed the government of New Jersey from the colonial to a constitutional government, or State, on June 21st, 1776. Ten men were appointed to draw up a draft of a constitution for the State of which committee, Rev. Jacob Green of Morris county was chairman. That eminent lawyer, Jonathan Dickinson, and Dr. John Witherspoon, president of Princeton College, were members of this committee. The draft was submitted and adopted as the first constitution of New Jersey.

The country of the Minisinks which had suffered severely through the French and Indian war did not have any better fortune during the Revolution. All the horrors of an Indian warfare were experienced by the settlers in this region. The Indians were incited by the British to acts of horrible brutality. Brant, the noted Mohawk chief, was the bravest and most ferocious leader among these savage allies of the British.

Sussex county enjoys the distinction of furnishing Congress with cannon-balls and steel during their struggle for independence.

The old iron-works at Andover had been erected by an English company. The company were protected by the army at Philadelphia down to the beginning of 1778, when it changed hands and was run by Americans.

"Passing from the control of those who had no interest in the American cause, and who had probably used them in aid of enemies of the country, they came into the hands of men whose fervid patriotism was fitly symbolized in the glow of their rekindled fires." The Andover works continued until the end of the war to furnish supplies to the Continental army. The remainder of the history of Sussex during the Revolution we are compelled for want of space to pass over. Suffice it to say that she fully sustained her reputation; and in the display when necessary of truly heroic qualities her sons were not exceeded by any in the land.

THE WAR OF THE REBELLION.

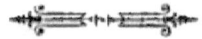

IT is not possible for us to recall the events of 1861 with the same vividness and reality with which the stirring scenes of the first year of the war then struck the public mind. Only those who participated in them can fully appreciate those times. The present generation can only know of them by the light of tradition and history. The "great uprising" of popular feeling and patriotism that was occasioned by the firing on Fort Sumpter penetrated into every State, county, village and hamlet, awakening the people to a realization of the crisis that was upon them. The country had been pausing in anxious suspense to see what result would follow the secession of South Carolina and what she would do with the garrison of Fort Sumpter and the flag that so proudly waved above her walls.

The moment that flag was struck the pause was at an end and the shock of the bitter struggle that followed thrilled the whole land. The President called for troops and immediately flags were hoisted and recruiting stations established in every town and school district in the North. Business was suspended for the time and men marched along with patriotic feeling to the sound of the fife and drum. The North awoke to the necessity of the occasion and responded with alacrity to the call of the President for the men and means with which to decide the question of union or secession.

"New Jersey was not behind the other States of the North in responding to the call. Governor Olden, her executive, was patriotic and energetic. He was greatly assisted in the selection of officers by a board of examiners composed of Adjt.-Gen. Stockton, Lieut. T. A. Torbert, and Gen. William Cook. Lieut. Torbert was at an early day assigned for duty at Trenton and rendered most important service in organizing the first New Jersey regiments for the field."

Sussex and Warren began in season to send forward their quota of troops. Four regiments were called for from the State and twenty-four of the principal banks pledged Governor Olden four hundred and fifty-one thousand dollars. Sussex Bank, at Newton, subscribed twenty thousand and the Farmers' Bank of Wantage ten thousand. Not a week had passed after President Lincoln's first call for troops before Judson Kilpatrick—then unknown to fame and a cadet lieutenant in the United States Military Academy at West Point—had offered his services to Governor Olden and begged to be allowed the privilege of sharing with the soldiers of the State the dangers and honors of the field. All through the war the counties of Sussex and Warren patriotically bore their share of the burden in the great struggle for the supremacy of our laws and the Union. Her sons voluntarily came forward and enrolled their names in a large number of regiments from this and other States. Recruiting began at Newton and Belvidere as soon as the President had made his first call for three months' men, on April 15th, 1861. It was only three days after the call that Capt. Edward L. Campbell had raised a company in Belvidere, consisting of seven officers and fifty privates, but when the company was taken to Belvidere the next day the State authorities were not ready to muster them into service. About a month after this, May 18th, a portion of this company with other recruits went into the Third Regiment, then mustered into the United States service for three years. Capt. DeWitt Clinton Blair, son of John I. Blair, raised a company in Warren county and Capt. James G. Fitts one in Sussex. Capt. Blair presented his company at Trenton, but no further call being made for more troops, they returned home; afterwards, however, nearly every man enlisted. Captain Blair went out in the Twenty-second New York Infantry as a private and served the time of his command. Capt. Fitts' company was not mustered but became Co. D. of the Third Regiment. There were some militia organizations which were a little in advance of these companies in tendering their services, but with this exception these were the earliest companies raised in the State expressly for this emergency.

The following is extracted from an address delivered by Col. Chas. Scranton at Belvidere, July 4th, 1876.

"In 1861, when the plot of treason was laid which threatened the life of our beloved country, and the seat of government itself seemed in danger, a young man, whom many of you know, the private secretary of my deceased brother, was in Washington City where he volunteered as a private in Col. Lane's company, and served until troops arrived from Massachusetts, Pennsylvania and New Jersey, when he was honorably discharged, receiving the thanks of the President and Secretary of War, Cameron. Capt. Jos. J. Henry was the first volunteer from Oxford,

Warren Co., of this State, in the great Civil war, as John McMurray and Thomas White were in the Revolutionary war, and although afterwards entering the Ninth New Jersey Volunteers, he was the first officer from New Jersey to fall in battle. The late war is so fresh in your memories that I shall only briefly refer to it. Sumpter was fired on; its garrison taken prisoners. The call for men to arms was made by President Lincoln. You all know what the response was. Most of you remember the first meeting in yonder court-house where I had the honor to preside; how Campbell, Kennedy and others rallied round the old flag and quickly formed a company and moved for Trenton. Of the meeting at Phillipsburg, and how Mutchler, Sitgreaves, Schoonover, and others flocked to the standard; and again at Oxford, how the gallant McAllister, Henry, Warner, Brewster, and other good men and true joined the phalanx; and again at Clinton, under the brave and gallant Taylor. As aide to the late lamented good Governor, Charles S. Olden, I attended four meetings in as many days, and we had our quota more than full before we had a place for the men to quarter. We were without uniforms, arms, or equipments. What memories cluster around those days of April and May, 1861, and all through the terrible war! And later, as further calls for troops came, how nobly did our county of Warren respond! You knew those noble, brave young men. I knew them by the thousand in the State. I loved them and cherish their memories. Thousands and thousands fell with their face to the foe! Henry, Brewster, Lawrence, Hilton, Hicks, Armstrong, and scores of other noble heroes from old Warren fell. I shrink from calling the roll of those honored dead. Our county furnished one thousand four hundred and thirty-seven men, besides those from other counties and States, of whom one hundred and seventy-six fell in battle, or died of disease contracted in the army, or from inhuman treatment in prisons. Of these brave men who thus died some lie in our own cemeteries, some on the field where they fell, in graves unknown, and though no 'storied urn or animated bust' or marble shaft or granite pile mark their last resting place here on earth, yet their memories will live in story and history, and annually as their loved ones gather flowers to strew on their tombs, or bedew themselves with their tears, will there grow an increasing love for their memories. Fellow-citizens, soldiers, survivors of the war for the Union, very many of whom it became my duty to give an outfit for the war, as I see you before me my heart warms in admiration of your gallantry, of your honored actions towards myself while you were in New Jersey camps. Before this audience I pronounce the fact that, in all the work performed by me in feeding, clothing and paying New Jerseymen who enlisted for the war, no one, so far as I can recollect, ever gave me one single cause for reproof. I place this also on record as a fact: no volunteer (save one crazy man) ever deserted the camps where I acted. Your subordination and gallantry, with the thousands from other counties and states, under the guidance of a wise providence directing the great mind of the immortal Lincoln and his coadjutors, has made this nation in truth free."

It would please us had we the space to go on and chronicle the history of each company and regiment, which contained Warren's brave sons, in the war against secession. Our history, however, has already gone over its allotted space and we are compelled to let it pass.

ORGANIZATION OF WARREN COUNTY.

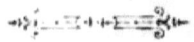

THE Legislature of New Jersey passed an act Nov. 20, 1824, by which Warren County was erected from Sussex with boundaries as follows:

"All the lower part of the county os Sussex beginning on the river Delaware at the mouth of Flatbrook, in the township of Walpack, and running from thence a straight course to the northeast corner of Hardwick church, situated on the south side of the main road leading from Johnsonburg to Newton, and from thence in the same course to the middle of Musconetcong creek, &c, and the same is hereby erected into a separate county, to be called 'the County of Warren'; and a line running from thence down the middle of the said Musconetcong creek to where it empties into the Delaware, shall hereafter be the division-line between the counties of Morris and Hunterdon and the said county of Warren."

Warren County is bounded on the west and northwest by the Delaware River and on the southeast by the Musconetcong. The upper part of the county is about sixteen miles in width and holds that measurement with a slight increase, for nearly half the length of the county, when it is suddenly reduced to about half that width by the bend of the Delaware coming in from Pahaquarry to Manunka

Chunk, where it runs almost at right angles with its former course. If the river continued on in this direction, it would strike across the country from Manunka Chunk to Changewater in the line of the Delaware, Lackawanna & Western Railroad; but the river makes a bend westward again and then eastward, forming the point above Belvidere, whence it proceeds in a southwesterly course past the western point of Harmony township, and then runs in a southerly zig-zag course to the great bend at Holland, in Hunterdon county. The Musconetcong valley on the opposite side of the county is much more uniform, that stream flowing in a curve which varies not more than two miles from a direct line, from one extremity of the county to the other. The extreme length of the county from the Sussex line near Waterloo to Musconetcong Station is about thirty miles, and as near as can be measured on the map its superficial area is three hundred and seventy square miles."

The principal ranges of mountains in Warren County are the Kittatinny, or Blue Mountains in the northwestern part, the Jenny Jump in the central part, Scott's Mountains between Harmony and Oxford townships and the Pohatcong mountains in the southwest. The principal streams are the Paulinskill and its tributaries, Beaver Brook, Pequest, Pohatcong and Musconetcong.

Warren county was originally part of West Jersey. It was included in Hunterdon when that county was erected in 1713-14 and remained a part of it till Morris was set off in 1738-39. It was a part of the territory of Sussex county when that county was erected in 1753 and so remained till the Legislative enactment of November 20, 1824, made a separate county of it.

The first settlements were made along the Delaware river at what is now Phillipsburg and Pahaquarry before the territory of West Jersey was organized into the county of Hunterdon. The townships of Warren county at time of its organization were Greenwich, Hardwick, Pahaquarry, Mansfield, Oxford, Knowlton and Independence.

The first board of chosen freeholders met at Belvidere May 11th, 1825, and these townships were represented in it. Belvidere was selected by a vote of the citizens of the county—taken April 19 and 20 1825—as the County seat. The grounds on which the public buildings are located were donated to the county by Gen. Garrett D. Wall of Trenton by will dated June 7, 1825. The buildings were erected on the grounds thus donated in 1826 at a cost of about ten thousand dollars.

The Poor-house and farm were purchased by the county of Nathan Sutton in 1829 for the sum of $8950. It then contained about 590 acres. William McDaniel was the first steward and Dr. J. T. Sharp the first physician.

PART II.

MISCELLANEOUS DEPARTMENT.

Containing brief, practical information for the Farmer, Business Man and Housekeeper.

AGRICULTURE.

THE BIRTH OF AGRICULTURE.

When God said, "In the sweat of thy face shalt thou eat bread," the birth of Agriculture was foretold. Almost contemporaneous with man's birth was that of the oldest and most important of the arts, Agriculture. This is the only art contemporaneous with man, and was the first if not the only one foretold by the Creator. Agriculture is spoken of as the "Mother of Civilization," and truly such she is: but not such alone. She may quite as appropriately be called the "Mother of all the Arts and Sciences," and hence, the "mother of all that engages and enriches the entire human family to-day." As such the farmer may well be proud of his occupation, though many a thoughtless opinion would hint to the contrary. It is difficult to tell just when Agriculture as an art began to assume the mien of importance. The earliest successful farming of which we have any record was carried on in the valleys of the rivers supposed to water the Garden of Eden. The primitive farmers dwelt along the banks of the Euphrates, the Tigris and the Nile. The old Bible patriarchs were farmers. Among these were Noah, the owner of vineyards; Abraham, and Lot who had in their possession large herds of cattle and sheep. Jacob was the first to comprehend the importance of selecting stock for the purpose of improving it, as is evident from his dealings with Laban. He gave to Esau 580 head of cattle. Moses, the great Jewish law-giver, and the type of the Messiah, was himself a shepherd. Gideon was engaged on the threshing floor. Saul was a cattle herder. David delighted in his flocks. Elisha, the prophet, ploughed with many yokes of oxen. As far as reliable information can be gathered from the inscriptions and hieroglyphics found upon the ancient tombs of the Egyptians, Chaldeans, and Chinese, they were the first to encourage practical agriculture and its literature, and were among the earliest farmers who applied animal power to the cultivation of the soil. Agriculture flourished also in Greece at an early day, perhaps as early as 1000 B. C. They used as a plough, a forked stick with handles attached, and had fine breeds of horses, sheep, and hogs. They imported stock from older countries for the purpose of improving their own. The Greeks were the first to comprehend in any important degree the practical value of manures. Much of their land was poor, and had to be reclaimed from sand-banks, morasses, and swamps. This led them to the practice of a careful cultivation. They ploughed the ground over three times with their oxen and mules, and frequently subsoiled before planting. They raised fruit in abundance. Their knowledge of agriculture and agricultural literature was of a very practical nature and comparatively extensive for their day. Among the Romans agriculture was highly appreciated and held as a most fundamental idea. The Roman State provided each citizen with a farm (or garden spot as we would term it) of seven acres (equal to about six of ours), to which he was rigidly restricted. Any Roman, dissatisfied with his tract was considered a bad citizen and a dangerous man. After Rome, by means of conquest, had extended her dominion, as much as fifty acres were sometimes allotted, and the highest expression of commendation that could be given a man was to say of him, "He has well cultivated his spot of ground." A citizen's worth to the Roman State, either in time of war or in peace, was largely estimated by this principle. Rome's most illustrious citizens, her Senators, and Dictators, and other nobility, during intervals of public business, applied themselves in person to agricultural labors. To cultivate his estate was the Roman's duty; to ornament it, his luxury and delight. Cincinnatus, the illustrious old farmer of Rome, left his estate to serve his country as Dictator in time of danger, and when peace again reigned he returned to his farm, the pride of his heart. Regulus left the Senator's seat to follow the farmer's plough. Distinguished men wrote useful and practical works upon this important science. A compilation of these works was made by the Emperor Constantine, who after conquering the Saracens and Arabians, turned his attention to agriculture as the surest basis of his country's safety and prosperity. The love of the Roman for the pursuit of agriculture made him both careful and scientific. His crops, as a natural consequence, were large. Pliny declared that the soil loved to be tilled by the hands of men. He states that 400 stalks of wheat, the fruit of a single grain, were sent to the Emperor Augustus, and 340 from one seed to Nero. The plough invented in Rome, and still used in the south of Italy and in France, consists of a beam attached to a yoke, with a clumsy, ponderous mould-board and sticks for handles. With this they ploughed about a quarter of an acre a day. That agriculture is the foundation of all prosperous nations is abundantly attested by history. During the golden age of agriculture, when the first men of Rome themselves held the plough, the empire flourished and became the mightiest on the globe; but when her agricultural interests passed out of the hands of her nobility into the hands of menials, and the nation came to rely on the productions of conquered provinces, the zenith of her glory was passed and her decline was begun. Vast hordes swept down upon her from the North, and the once mighty empire fell to rise no more. So has it been in the history of every nation. When a nation prides itself in its agricultural interests, then that nation grows and prospers. When agriculture is neglected the nation becomes weak and helpless. The science of drainage was first introduced by Sparta; an extensive system of irrigation and practical farming was the basis of the glory of Spain, China, India and Babylonia, derived sustenance from systems of minute divisions and thorough cultivation of lands. The first important steps in modern scientific agriculture were taken in the eighteenth century. New methods of culture, new practices, new modes of fertilizing, new forms and great improvements in machinery became universal; chemistry, geology and botany began to illuminate the field of the farmer. Chemistry, especially, began to enlighten the farmers' intelligence and scatter his prejudice, leading him to see that scientific knowledge is a valuable acquisition at least, if not an indispensable requisite for the successful agriculturist. Scientific agriculture has made marvelous strides of development in this country, and hence it will be a matter of interest and profit to trace briefly

THE HISTORY OF FARMING IN AMERICA.

The early settlers on our shores had to begin life anew in the midst of untold hardships, privations, and dangers. Whether in Virginia, New England, New York State, or Maryland, they found themselves under a climate and surrounded by conditions altogether strange to them. Everywhere they were environed by a wilderness infested by wild beasts and savage men, ready to prey on their cattle, destroy their crops, and constantly threatening their own lives and those of their families. When we add to this that a majority of the first colonists were not only unskilled in agriculture, but unused to labor of any kind, it need not surprise us that the progress they made was slow, but rather we wonder that they maintained themselves at all in the midst of such difficulties and dangers.

The very first need of pioneers in a wild country is cattle. These supply him and his family not only with subsistence, and partly with clothing, but also with the means of draught and tillage as well as manure to enrich his crops. Whether the earliest colonists in America, the settlers on the James River, Virginia, brought cattle with them on their arrival in 1607 is matter of doubt. We find, however, that some had been imported into Jamestown by 1609, and that some cows were landed in 1610, and one hundred more in 1611. These were probably from the West Indies, and descendants of the cattle brought by Columbus. So important was it held that domestic cattle should multiply that an order was issued forbidding their slaughter on pain of death. Thus protected, their number had increased by 1639 to 30,000.

The first cattle brought to New England arrived at Plymouth in 1624 and consisted of a bull and three heifers, imported by Governor Winslow. These were followed by others in 1626 and 1629, while in 1633 we find 100 head landed for the Governor and Company of Massachusetts Bay. In the mean time, the Dutch West India Company had imported into New York State 103 cattle and horses from the island of Texel, Holland. In 1627 the settlements along the Delaware were supplied by the Swedish West India Company; while in 1631 and following years many large yellow cattle were brought over by Captain John Mason from Denmark to New Hampshire. By means of other unrecorded importations, but more by natural increase, these Northern cattle multiplied also rapidly till they numbered many thousand head.

Such, then, were the sources of our "native" or common breed of cattle. It must be observed that in those old days the stock of the mother country was not improved to its present high condition. Even so late as in the beginning of last century the average dressed weight of neat cattle sent to Smithfield Market, London, was not over 370 pounds, and of sheep, 28 pounds, whereas now these weights are over 800 pounds and 80 pounds respectively. Then the colonists had not the means of keeping stock so as to obviate deterioration. They had no notion of raising grass and hay by artificial means, but relied on natural meadows, and the grasses in the salt-marshes along the shores. Even so late as 1750 grain and forage for stock had to be imported from England to keep man and beast from starving. Glover, a contemporary, gives us the following glimpse of the mode of keeping cattle in Virginia: "All the inhabitants give their cattle in winter is only the husks of their Indian corn, unless it be some of them that have a little wheat straw; neither do they give them any more of these than will keep them alive." Clayton, another contemporary, says: "They neither housed nor milked their cows in winter, having a notion it would kill them." Of their cropping, Kalm, a Swedish traveller, writing in 1749, tells us: "They (the James River colonists) make scarce any manure for their cornfields, but when one piece of ground has been exhausted by continued cropping they clean and cultivate another piece of fresh land, and when that is exhausted proceed to a third. Their cattle are allowed to wander through the woods and uncultivated grounds, where they are half starved, having long ago extirpated all the annual grasses by cropping them too early in the spring before they had time to form their flowers or shed seeds." That the ox of those days was small and ill-shaped no one who knows anything of stock-rearing needs to be told, and the effects of such treatment are full of suggestion to any one who wishes to rear a thrifty and profitable herd of cattle. But bad management reacts in various ways. Not only did the cattle, originally poor, degenerate under it, not only were the pastures ruined, but the proper cultivation of the farm was impossible. Every farmer knows that if the manure is allowed to go to waste, if what has been taken from the soil is not carefully and systematically restored to it the farm is being run down and exhausted. The fatal results of this old style of farming is being felt in Virginia to this day, where, such is the force of custom, some occupiers of land—we can scarce call them farmers—to this day leave their cows out in the pines during winter, sacrificing thus both the animal and the means of enriching their fields. "Previous to our Revolutionary War," says the Hon. James M. Garrett, speaking in 1842, "no attempts were made to collect manure for general purposes; all that was deemed needful being saved for the gardens and tobacco lots by summer cow-pens. These were filled with cattle such as our modern breeders would hardly recognize as belonging to the bovine species. In those days they were so utterly neglected that it was quite common for the multitudes starved to death every winter to supply hides enough for shoeing the negroes on every farm. My own grandfather was once very near turning off a good overseer because cattle enough had not died on the farm to furnish leather for the above purpose. When cattle were fattened for beef, almost the only process was to turn them into the cornfield to feed themselves. Sheep and hogs were equally neglected."

Improvement of cattle did not set in till after the systematic culture of natural grasses. Even in England there is no evidence of such culture till 1677, when perennial rye-grass was introduced, and no other variety was sown till toward the close of the last century on the introduction of timothy and orchard-grass. Red clover had been introduced in 1633, saintfoin in 1651, yellow clover in 1659, but white or Dutch clover not till 1700. Even in Scotland the practice of sowing grass-seed was not known previous to 1792. No one can think it strange that the colonists, who had vastly greater hardships to encounter, allowed their cattle (poor as first) to degenerate persistently. One fact only in some measure compensated for this: from the unlimited extent of their browsing-grounds the stock continued ever increasing in numbers, so that by the middle of last century the keeping of stock assumed considerable importances in the older settlements, that by this time were comparatively free from molestation, and shortly after the Revolution systematic efforts began to be made for improvement in quality.

One of the chief obstacles experienced by the colonists was the want of implements. Most of their tools were made at home of wood, and were heavy and rude in construction. For the few pieces in which iron was employed either the metal was shaped on an anvil fixed up at home or the aid of the neighboring blacksmith was called in. In 1617 some ploughs were set to work in Virginia. In that year the governor complained that " the colony did suffer for the want of means to set their ploughs in work, having * * almost forty bulls and oxen, but they wanted *, * iron for the ploughs and harness for the cattle." In Massachusetts Colony it was the custom for some one owning a plough to go about and do the ploughing over a considerable district, and a township sometimes paid a bounty to some one who would keep a plough in repair and go about in this way. The massive old plough required three men to use it—one stout man to bear on, one to hold, and a third to drive. The other tools were a heavy spade or clumsy wooden fork, and, later, a harrow. The ploughs used by the French settlers upon the "American Bottom," in Illinois so late as 1812 were made of wood, with a small point of iron fastened upon the wood by strips of rawhide and the yokes were fastened to the horns of the oxen by raw-leather straps. No small plough was used by them to plough corn till 1815. Their carts had not a particle of iron about them. All the ploughs were not so primitive, and some, as the Carey plough, the barshore or bull plough, the shovel plough, and the hog plough, had more than a local reputation, and were in use down into the present century. Of these the Carey was the most extensively used, but the " shovel " was the favorite in the Middle and Southern colonies. In both cases the particular form varied much according to the skill or taste of the blacksmith or wheelwright who made it. In the Carey the landside and the standard were made of wood, and it had a wooden mould-board, often roughly plated over with pieces of old saw-plate, tin or sheet-iron. It had a clumsy wrought-iron share, while the handles were upright, held in place by two wooden pins. It took almost double the strength of team to pull that a modern plough does. The other implements were few and rude. Slow and laborious hand-labor was the rule, machine-work the exception. Thrashing was done with the flail, winnowing by the wind. Indeed, it has been said that a strong man could have carried on his shoulder all the implements used on a farm previous to the present century.

Of the principal crops raised by the early settlers, corn, pumpkins, squashes, tobacco, and potatoes were new to them, and their cultivation they had to learn from the Indians. Their method of planting corn, which was followed with little change to the present century, was to dig holes four feet apart, put in a fish or two, and drop the seed. The Indians' implement was a large clam-shell; for this the colonists soon substituted the grub-hoe. Corn was thus raised in the James River settlement in 1608. The Pilgrims similarly began its cultivation in 1621, the fish used by them for manure being alewives or shad. An early chronicler says: "According to the manner of the Indians, we manured our ground with herrings, or rather shads, which we ... take with great ease at our doors. You may see in one township one hundred acres together set with these fish, every acre taking a thousand of them, and an acre thus dressed will produce as much corn as three without fish."

In Virginia wheat was sown so early as 1611, but its culture soon began to give way to that of tobacco, and for more than one hundred years it was almost neglected, and Indian corn—and, later, potatoes—came to be relied on much more as means of sustenance. As a matter of fact, wheat has never been a reliable or profitable crop on our eastern shores, especially in the Middle and Southern States. Even at the present day, with all our improved modes of tillage, it would be grown to a very limited extent were it not for the sake of the grass crop which is seeded along with it. Rye and barley were introduced early, and it became a common practice to mix rye meal with Indian meal in making bread. Oats also were introduced on the Massachusetts coast as early as 1602, but they were used chiefly as food for animals. The practice of sowing grass-seed did not become general till the Revolution. Here, as in the mother-country, this culture is the result of modern improvement. The culture of the potato, though introduced early, was not recognized as of importance till the middle of last century, when the root became esteemed as an article of food. In 1747 seven hundred bushels were exported from South Carolina.

Tobacco began to be cultivated in Virginia from the very origin of the colony. It is recorded that in 1615 the gardens, fields, and the very streets of Jamestown were all planted with tobacco, which became not only the staple crop, but the currency of the colony. By 1622 the product amounted to 60,000 pounds, and it more than doubled in twenty years. Its culture was introduced into the Dutch colony of New York in 1646, but there with only moderate success; but Maryland, the Carolinas, Georgia, Louisiana, and, later, Kentucky, made it a leading object almost from their settlement. It long constituted the most valuable export from the colonies, but even before the Revolution, owing to its exhausting effects on the soil, the product per acre had been diminishing for many years. From 1744 to 1756 this crop averaged 40,000,000 pounds a year.

MISCELLANEOUS DEPARTMENT.

From what has been said, it will be seen that before the Revolution the American farmer had clumsy and insufficient tools, poor and miserable cattle, meagre crops, and wretched ideas of farming. During the Revolution-years agriculture was brought to a standstill, and for long after it was in a state of extreme depression. Gradually the necessity of making some effort toward its development began to dawn on the more intelligent and public-spirited, and as a result we had the inauguration of local agricultural societies. The earliest of these seems to have been the South Carolina Society, founded in 1784; the Philadelphian in 1785; New York in 1791; Massachusetts, in 1792. The first agricultural exhibition took place under the auspices of the Columbia Society at Georgetown, D. C., May 10, 1810, and others followed. In 1816 the Massachusetts Society offered premiums and instituted a ploughing match. The plough-makers were there with their eyes wide open; and this meeting, if it did not absolutely inaugurate the new era of agricultural mechanics, certainly gave no mean impulse to this important agent in the development of American husbandry. The old wooden plough gave place to the cast-iron plough of New Jersey, which is in turn being supplanted by the polished steel plough of to-day. A better knowledge has enabled our inventors to reduce the weight of the parts of the implements and at the same time secure more effective work while the application of steam is multiplying our resources indefinately, and it has become the main agent in the development of the great West. Forty acres a day are now ploughed by steam, instead of little over a quarter of an acre in ancient times. The steam thrasher now does the work of a thousand flails, the classic sickle has been supplanted by the great reaping and binding machine, and the scythe by the mower. Hay is raked and stacked by horse-power, and the boy, bag, and hoe are being superseded by the automatic corn-planter. Space would fail us were we to try to enumerate a tithe of the successful labor-saving implements introduced within the last half century—cultivators, horse-hoes, grubbers, drills, seed-sowers, etc. etc.; and invention is still maintaining its stately march. Not a year passes that does not offer to the almost bewildered farmer new discoveries to economize labor and accelerate work.

PRACTICAL INFORMATION FOR THE FARMER.

Knowing that the circulation of this book is but local and not universal, we compile such material as we deem useful to the already practical farmer, and omit all such as might be of value simply to the pioneer or inexperienced one. One of the best codes a farmer can form for himself is that given by an old Scottish farmer, who on almost every occasion carried off the prize for the best managed farm in his district and the best crops. His simple code was: "I have a good subject (farm); I pulverize deeply and well, clean well, and manure well." This lies at the bottom of successful farming. We now pass to the consideration of practical farm topics. First let us look at the subject of

DRAINING.

It has been well termed "the most valuable improvement connected with agriculture." Drainage does the same service for the soil that the hole in the bottom does for the flower-pot.

But drainage produces several other effects that are important: (1) The stagnant water being removed and the earth rendered less moist at the surface, far less evaporation takes place there; wherefore, as evaporation cools the surface very considerably, a drained field keeps the heat better, and as a consequence, the crop ripens earlier. (2) Lands well-drained and deeply tilled bear the drought better than others, by enabling the roots to penetrate deeper down to the moist earth, and by the increased porosity enabling the soil to retain moisture longer. (3) By carrying the redundant moisture readily away at all seasons it enables you to cultivate sooner after wet weather, thus lengthening your season for tillage and thoroughly mellowing the soil, which cannot be done if it be too wet. (4) It avoids the danger of plants being frozen out in a hard winter, which they often are if the surface is full of water on the approach of severe frost. (5) The drains (especially if laid with pipes) open the soil to the free access of air, and the soil is thus rendered fit to absorb and retain the fertilizing gases of the atmosphere—carbonic acid and ammonia—as well as the nutritious substances brought into it by the rain-water, and keep them laid up for the nourishment of plants. (6) General drainage lessens or removes malarious influences, there being no curse so baneful to a farmer's family as fever and ague. To these it may be added that cold and stagnant water checks the decomposition of manures and prevents them feeding the crop.

Drainage is effected either by open ditches or by covered drains. Open ditches are objectionable for the following reasons: they occupy land which might otherwise be productive; they interfere with the proper cultivation of the land; they are liable to cave in and become dammed up; they carry off much of the best of the manure washed into them by heavy rains; weeds are liable to grow along their sides.

Under-drains are constructed in various ways. Where wood is plenty, surface stones scarce, and tiles not to be had, logs or large poles are sometimes used. One pole is laid lengthways along either side of the bottom of the ditch, which must be broad enough to allow a free run for the water between the poles. This opening is covered by a larger log resting on the two bottom ones, and the whole is covered with brush laid with its cut ends towards the outlet, or straw, which, again, should be covered with sods with the grassy side downward, the object being to keep the run clear from being stopped up by earth. The whole is then filled in with earth packed close. Stone drains are made much in the same way, except that in place of logs largish stones are used to form the run, or the ditch is filled to the depth of nine to twelve inches with small or pounded stones. Stone drains can only be made where there is abundance of stones on the surface of the land.

Tile drains are undoubtedly the best. They are less liable to get stopped; the tiles are out of reach of the plough; air passes upward through the bore, thus ventilating and enriching the soil; they last longer (a properly-laid drain will be good for half a century), and are, in the end, more economical. For a tile drain a trench of a foot wide at top and four inches at bottom is sufficient. For the pipe a simple round tube is found to be the best shape, and for the interior drains which enter into the larger main drains a bore of two inches in diameter is the right size. The distance commonly allowed between tile drains is 25 feet for three feet deep; 40 feet for 4 feet deep; 80 feet for 5 feet deep. If the drains are 20 feet apart, about 2000 tiles to the acre are required; if 40, about 1000; if 80, 500. Tiles can be purchased for from $10 to $12 a thousand. Deep digging saves money for tiles, and is generally believed to be more effective. A tile drain must be deep enough to be out of the reach of frosts and to be beyond the reach of roots; 30 inches is a common depth; but a drain of this depth is not so effective as one from 6 to 30 inches deeper. The deep drain acts farther and with more effect than the shallow, catching springs the other passes over.

Tiles with a two-inch bore are the most common capacity, and they are usually made about fifteen inches long, the continuity of the drain being maintained by collars. It is of course impossible in our space to give minute details as to the distance, grade, and digging of your drains, or as to the arrangement of main and lateral drains, for these vary in accordance with circumstances. One point, however, the farmer must attend to—viz. to secure a competent outlet, for without this all his toil and labor is thrown away. Make it as low as circumstances will permit, in order to secure as great a fall as possible, which should never be less than one inch to the rod. The outlet should be protected by either brick or stone-work, and have a grate over the same, to prevent obstructions getting into the pipe.

PLOUGHING.

All cultivation, whether with the plough, harrow, or hoe, has for its object the reducing of the soil to such a fine and loose condition that it will permit the air to circulate freely through it. This hastens the decay of vegetable matter, and retain the gases escaping from such decomposition to be used as plant-food. It is only in finely pulverized soil that seeds can with ease send down their tender roots and receive the nourishment essential to their vigorous development. Hence the necessity for thorough ploughing as the first and most important process in pulverization. Ploughing done in the fall and winter has this great advantage, that it exposes the upturned soil to the action of frost, which is the most powerful agent in crumbling down and pulverizing the soil at the same time destroying the roots of many weeds. The objects of ploughing may be summed up as follows: To destroy existing vegetation ; lossen the soil and aid in preparing the seed-bed ; prepare the lower portions of the soil for the better use of plants by exposure to frost and atmospheric influences ; gradually deepen the productive surface-soil ; cover fertilizing materials ; admit air and water among the roots of the plants.

The common plough is the instrument commonly used in breaking up the land, and is the most economical that can be employed. In passing through the soil the plough separates and cuts off a slice of its surface, cutting it both vertically and horizontally, turning it over in such a way as to leave it exposed to the action of the harrow, which follows the plough and pulverizes the soil more completely. The furrow should be deep, straight, and of such a width that the slice cut off may be turned over or left on its edge as the ploughman may wish. It is best to deepen the arable soil gradually by ploughing about an inch or half an inch deeper each time, till it is worked deep enough, say from seven to twelve inches, according to the crops it is designed to cultivate. If much of a poor subsoil should be brought up to the surface at once, the farmer will have to wait two, three, or four years before he obtains the good effects of deep tillage. Deep ploughing has much the same effect as thorough draining, though in a less degree, and is especially needed in the cultivation of deep or tap-rooted plants, like carrots, parsnips and ruta-bagas.

One important principle must always be kept in view, that clay or tenacious soil should never be ploughed when either too wet or too dry. If ploughed wet, clay soils will bake and their fertility is injured for years. On wet, stiff soils there is no rule more essential than to open them as early as possible, that they may have the full benefit of the frost. If left till spring the soils may be too wet for ploughing, or if the season be dry the earth when turned up will be in clods very unfit for vegetation. On farms having a proportion of clay and light soils it is necessary that the strong, wet land be ploughed first if the weather will allow.

In working keep your team as close to the plough as possible, the plough perpendicular, and the furrow straight. A furrow seven inches deep should be ten inches wide. Let the furrow or "land" be as long as possible, to avoid loss of time in turning. Wherever practicable, plough from the centre of the field. Keep your team moving at a regular pace.

SUBSOILING.

The subsoil plough is designed to follow in the furrow of the common plough, loosening and breaking up the lower layers of the soil without bringing them to the surface. With this instrument it is easy to loosen the subsoil six or eight inches below the furrow left by the ordinary plough, stirring the land to a depth of twelve or eighteen inches. The benefits of subsoil ploughing are very similar to those of deep ploughing, enabling the roots of the plants to reach the nitrogen and other fertilizing substances that exist deep below the surface, as also to get beneath the reach of drought, while it permits air and rain to penetrate deeper. On land well underdrained subsoiling has a beneficial effect; on land that needs draining no permanent effect is derived.

HARROWING.

The harrow is an ancient implement, its most common use being to follow the plough, to break down and mellow or pulverize the furrow-slice, and so to prepare a fine seed-bed. It is also of material use in clearing the ground of such weeds as the plough has brought near the surface, as well as in covering seeds sown broadcast. In fact, the harrow is to the farmer much what the rake is to the gardner. In preparing a fine surface it is necessary to go over the ground several times in different directions—that is, to cross-harrow repeatedly. No specific number of times can be indicated; the farmer must judge for himself when the ground is brought to a sufficient fineness and cleanliness.

The cultivator may be regarded as a modification of the harrow, but in some respects more efficient, because with its plough-shaped teeth it lightens up and mellows the soil, instead of pressing it down hard, as the harrow is apt to do everywhere except on new, rough land. In cultivating hoed crops care is needed to avoid cutting the roots. In the early stages of growth cultivate as deeply, and late in the season as shallow, as possible—just deep enough to kill the weeds. When plants have obtained one-half their growth you may take it for granted their roots occupy all the space between the rows.

The horse-hoe is a modification of the cultivator with special reference to the destruction of weeds. The profit derived from the use of cultivators and horse-hoes depends almost entirely on the frequency with which they are used and the depth to which cultivation reaches.

It is a general thing in the district in which we write to cultivate corn at least three times, and then "to lay it by." Cabbages, beans, potatoes, turnips (when drilled,) carrots, beets, and root-crops generally can scarcely be cultivated too frequently. Keep the earth about them always loose and fine, and destroy every weed.

ROLLING AND CLOD-CRUSHING.

Among the principal uses of the roller are the following: By passing it over the land after ploughing it settles the furrows, so that they will not be disturbed by the harrow; it grinds to dust most of the clods on the surface; it presses down such stones as the harrow has exposed, thus preparing a smooth surface for the mower or reaper; if used in the spring on winter grain, meadow, or pasture, it settles the frost-heaved plant back in its place and compresses the soil about its roots. It is often useful on newly-sown grain, hastening the germination by preserving the moisture. The roller may be used to advantage in the driest weather, but when the soil is so wet as to pack instead of crumble it does more harm than good.

On compact clay soils, where the clods are often nearly as hard as bricks, a homemade clod-crusher is often more efficient than the ordinary roller.

MANURES.

The term "manure" is applied to all substances added to the soil with the view of increasing its ability to produce vegetable growth. Chemistry teaches us that the food of all plants is very much alike, though some classes must be supplied with certain substances in greater abundance than others. The great mass of all vegetables is resolved into carbonic acid, water, and ammonia. But besides, these plants on being burned leave lime, potash soda, magnesia, silica, sulphates, and phosphates as ash. If any one of these elements is absolutely wanting in the soil, the plants to which that element is essential could not sprout there, and if planted would pine and die of starvation. Plaster, for example, is essential to clover, and clover-seed sown in a soil destitute of plaster would not come up, or if it were present in insufficient quantity the plant would be proportionally feeble and small. The same holds of every plant, and the obvious remedy is to add artificially to the soil the nutritive elements in which it is deficient. It would plainly transcend the scope of this paper to enumerate the various elements necessary for the food of different plants and to describe their mode of action; that is the province of agricultural chemistry. We must limit ourselves to the directly practical.

Manures may be classified in accordance with the way they act into nutritive, or those whose ingredients are taken up by the roots of the plants and go to form part of their structure; solvents, or those which give to water greater power to dissolve the plant-food contained in the soil; absorbents, or those which add to the power of the soil to absorb the fertilizing parts of other manures, of rain- and snow-water, and of the air in the soil; mechanical, or those which improve the texture of the soil, as clay on sandy or peaty soil, peat or sand on clayey soil; sometimes the last class of manures are termed amendments.

Another division of fertilizers is into inorganic or mineral, and organic or vegetable and animal.

INORGANIC FERTILIZERS.

In their general character inorganic fertilizers are both manures and amendments. They nourish the plants and exert mechanical action upon the texture of the soil—its lightness, stiffness, compactness. The leading mineral fertilizers are lime, marl, plaster, wood-ashes, sulphates and other salts of ammonia, phosphates and superphosphates of lime, salts of potash, etc., etc.

Lime amends a soil by decomposing some of its ingredients, especially all kinds of vegetable matter. It corrects acidity in organic matter, and destroys weeds favored by such a condition of soil. It aids in the decomposition of certain salts whose bases form the food of plants. On certain lands the finer grasses do not grow till the ground has been limed. It is especially an important element in the clovers, tobacco, peas, and turnips. As has already been said, it is unequalled for quickening a rich but dormant virgin soil into active energy. It may either be spread on the ground before ploughing and ploughed in, or it may be spread after ploughing and harrowed in, or simply spread over pasture and left on the surface. A hundred or two hundred bushels is a fair allowance, good land bearing a larger dose than poor, thin land. A convenient way of spreading lime regularly is to divide your land by furrows into checks resembling those of a checker-board, but from twenty to thirty feet square. You calculate how many of these checks are in an acre, and, having determined how many bushels you are going to allow to an acre, you easily fix how much is to be placed in each of the checks. This may be placed there in the lump and allowed to slake by the action of the atmosphere, but it is better to cover it with earth, as the slaking is more gradual and thorough. After being slaked it is easily spread over its check with a shovel.

Marl is a mixture of lime and clay or lime and sand. When exposed to the atmosphere, it should crumble easily, as its action is in proportion to its readiness to mix perfectly with the soil. Though less energetic, it has all the permanent effects of lime, and is very valuable as an amendment. Clayey marl should be applied to sandy soils, and sandy marl to clayey.

Plaster or gypsum (often called plaster of Paris) is a sulphate of lime, and the valuable effects it produces on soils are owing to its supplying them not only with lime, but with the important and sometimes essential element sulphur. A good way of using plaster is to scatter it in the shape of the finest impalpable powder in the spring, just as vegetation is beginning, while the dew of the morning or evening is on the plants, so that it may stick. It ought not to be applied in rainy weather. Plas-

...er thus applied is especially good for clover. It is used also for leguminous plants, and for corn, potatoes, and turnips, being put in with the seeds or sprinkled on them after the first hoeing. It is also useful by fixing the ammonia of the atmosphere and laying it up for the future use of plants. As an absorbent of ammonia it is of high value in the stable and poultry-yards, acting as a deodorizes, while its value as a fertilizer is greatly enhanced. From one hundred to two hundred pounds an acre is a dose.

Sulphate of soda is said to be good for clover and other green crops, sulphate of magnesia for these crops and potatoes.

Ashes.—It has been often observed that on strewing wood-ashes on a meadow that has long been mown thousands of clover-plants make their appearance where none were visible before. Ashes are made up of salts, as silicates, phosphates, sulphates, and carbonates. The carbonates and sulphates of potash and soda are dissolved out by leaching. The silicates, phosphates, and carbonates of lime and magnesia are insoluble. Far the largest part of leached ashes is carbonate of lime, the next being phosphate of lime or bone-dust.

Unleached ashes are of great value for Indian corn, turnips, beets, and potatoes, because of the amount of salts of potash they contain; for so important is potash to these plants that they are called "potash plants." The leached ashes have important effects when mixed in the compost-heap. Ashes of sea-coal and anthracite are an excellent top-dressing for grass.

Potash.—Potash is of high value for any land in which it is deficient. It is specially valuable for the plants already enumerated as "potash plants," as well as for oats and cabbage. The cheapest way to get potash is to buy the German mineral kainit, of which potash constitutes 22 per cent. It costs at the port of import about $10 a ton.

Phosphates.—No salts are of greater value to the farmer than these. Mineral phosphates are most readily got by dissolving, by means of sulphuric acid, the coprolites constituting the well-known South Carolina or Charleston rock. These dissolved coprolites contain from 8 to 14 per cent. available phosphoric acid and 2 to 3 per cent. potash. This manure is useful for every crop, phosphates giving bones their great value as a manure. Acid phosphate can be had at Charleston for $15.5 a ton.

Salt.—Common salt is of great value as a fertilizer, especially for certain plants, as asparagus. It is also good for wheat, making the straw brighter, stiffer, and stronger, and less liable to lodge. It not only enriches the soil but kills nearly all weeds, and must therefore be used with discretion. In small proportions it is of value to all cultivated plants, besides rendering grass and clover more palatable to animals. Salt that has been used for curing meat or fish is cheaper and better than pure salt.

ORGANIC MANURES.

The use of organic manures is to furnish the soil with humus or mould, which shall serve as a reservoir to hold in readiness for plants all sorts of food necessary to their growth, especially a supply of carbonic acid, ammonia, and water, which three are the result of the decomposition of vegetable substances. Organic manures should therefore be employed in a condition favorable to decomposition, either in a fermented state or ready to enter into fermentation.

Organic manures are either vegetable, animal, or mixed. The main purely vegetable manures are green crops ploughed under, the best plants for this being clover, lucerne, and sainfoin, vetches, buckwheat, wild mustard, rye, Indian corn, turnip- and potato-tops, etc. For sandy and light soil the best are the clovers, cabbages, rye, and Indian corn turnip- and potato-tops; for clayey, stiff soils, beans and pease, vetches, clovers; but green crops are least suited for clay soils. For calcareous soils that need no lime they are very useful, as also for dry, sandy soils. Green manuring is specially useful in places remote from the homestead, where the expense of carriage of other manure would be considerable.

The land for a green crop meant to be used as manure for winter wheat and rye (for both of which it is suitable) should be ploughed deep in spring, and the seed sown so as to have the crop in full bloom and ready to be ploughed under two or three weeks before the grain is to be sown. The manure, with lime or plaster, should be ploughed in to the depth of four to six inches, and the wheat or rye sown just as decomposition begins.

When land is much infested with weeds two green crops may be grown the same season and ploughed down before the weeds are ripe. This both cleans the land and enriches the soil. The mechanical texture of the soil is improved by ploughing in a green crop, a tenacious soil being loosened and made more friable, and coherence being given to a sandy soil.

Kelp and rock weed are good manures for cabbages, also for flax and hemp, and rye, oats, turnips, and clover are benefited. Their action is immediate, but does not last long.

The straw and leaves of particular vegetables are the best manures for these vegetables—wheat straw for wheat, potato-tops for potatoes, grape-vine prunings for vines, etc. Straw ploughed into stiff soils renders them more porous. For land laid down in grass, damaged hay not fit for animals is a valuable manure. Leaves, grasses, young twigs, and all other green vegetable matter—the very element of humus—are valuable as manures, and may be ploughed in fresh or added to the compost-heap.

ANIMAL MANURES.

These are the most powerful of all, on account of the great quantity of nitrogen they contain. The nitrogen unites with hydrogen and forms ammonia, and this by further combination forms ammoniacal salts, which are dissolved by water and carried to the roots of plants. The flesh of quadrupeds, fishes, etc. contains 50 per cent. carbon, 15 to 17 nitrogen, besides salts of potash, soda, lime, and magnesia, and is therefore one of the very best of manures. The best way to utilize dead carcasses for manure is to put them in a hole two feet deep, cover with quicklime, a layer of earth, then of plaster, and again of earth. In a few weeks the pit may be opened, the bones separated and used for manure, and the remaining mass turned over and mixed with earth. "The body of a dead horse," says Dana, "can convert twenty tons of peat into a manure richer and more lasting than stable manure."

Hoofs, hair, feathers, skins, wool, and blood contain over 50 per cent. carbon and from 13 to 18 nitrogen, besides salts of lime, etc. Made into a compost they are excellent for potatoes, turnips, hops, or for meadow-land. Being slow of decomposition, their action may last seven or eight years. Blood especially, containing 52 per cent. carbon, 17 nitrogen, besides phosphates, sulphates, and carbonates of potash, soda, lime, etc., is, when made into compost, a valuable manure for light soils, acting quickly, but soon carried away. It is good for spring crops and garden vegetables.

Bones.—The employment of bones as a manure is one of the greatest improvements in modern agriculture. The chemical constituents of bones are gelatin 33.30 per cent., phosphate of lime 50 to 60 per cent., besides carbonate of lime, phosphate of magnesia, soda, and chloride of sodium (common salt). Bones are applied either simply reduced to small fragments or a coarse powder called "bone-dust," or dissolved by sulphuric acid. The effect of the acid on bones is to reduce them to a pulpy mass. The value of bones lies in their phosphates, as these salts are largely removed from land by the feeding of cattle and crops. If grass-lands are sterile, it is easy to discover whether a deficiency of phosphorus is the cause by adding crushed or dissolved bone and watching the effect. It is as an application for turnips that bones produce their most marked results. The seed is small, with only a limited supply of phosphates stored up. Unless the roots meet a concentrated supply, the other elements of plant-food—carbonic acid, ammonia, water—cannot be assimilated. Bone-dust may be applied at the rate of ten to twelve hundred-weight to the acre, and its effects will be observed for several years.

The action of bones is accelerated by converting their phosphates into super-phosphates by treating with sulphuric acid diluted with water. The pasty mass may then be mixed with water in the proportion of one barrel to a hundred of water and applied in a liquid state, or it may be mixed with a large quantity of earth, sawdust, soot, or powdered charcoal, and thus applied. No artificial manure is to be so thoroughly relied on as pure bone.

Mixed Manures.—Of all the fertilizers at the disposal of the farmer, none is to be compared in value to farmyard manure. "Without manure," says the French proverb, "there are no good fields; with plenty of manure there are no poor ones." Other manures have great value for particular purposes; this is useful for all. This is just what we should expect. The concentrated essence of the nutritious elements of plant-forms the food of man and animals. All these valuable elements, except the comparatively small portion which is converted into flesh or milk, are returned to the manure-heap, or ought to be. Manure consists not only of that part of the animal's food not assimilated and discarded in the form of dung and urine, but also of the straw, cornstalks, leaves, etc., used as bedding, as well as the waste food and litter from the manger, feed-box and rack. The richer the food upon which stock is fed, so much richer the manure produced. Thus stock fed upon straw have a very poor manure, while turnips, and especially oil-cake, add largely to its value. Although farmyard manure is useful for all plants, there are some to which it is more valuable than others. Potatos and beans are raised with best success with this manure. It also tends to render lands more adapted for carrying clovers, and many farmers apply it to lands to be sown out with grasses. As a top dressing for winter wheat (see Wheat) it is of the highest value, protecting the tender grain from the effects of severe frost and enriching the land far more permanently than any fertilizer sown along with the crop, save, it may be, bones. Speaking generally, we may say cow and ox-manures are more suitable for dry, light soils; that from the horse-stable for stiff, clayey soils; those from the penfold and the pig-stpe are better fitted for meadow-lands, as they often impart a disagreeable flavor to culinary vegetables. Poultry manure is by far the strongest of all, and must therefore be used with great caution, otherwise you run the risk of burning your crop. It ought always to be largely mixed with earth or other proper basis for a compost.

The best materials for bedding horses and cattle are straw, leaves, sedge, reeds, sawdust and damaged hay. Where these cannot be had, then resource may be had to turf, loam, or even sand. When cattle are fed in sheds the whole surface should be covered with such substances. The stables may be kept clean and sweet by sprinkling a little plaster on their floors once a day.

The main object in regard to manure should be that none of it, liquid or solid, be lost or become less efficient than it ought to be. If it be left exposed to the open air and suffered to be drenched with rain or parched up by the sun, a great proportion of the products will be washed away or be volatilized. The best and most convenient arrangement is to have the manure fall into a cellar under the stable. There is danger of it heating here from the process of decomposition which immediately sets in, and of its most valuable constituent, ammonia, escaping. In a cellar where the liquid manure is saved as carefully as the solid, and into which a stream of water may be directed by a spout from the eaves, this will scarcely occur; but if the smell of ammonia is perceived, then a good plan is to cover the heap with a layer of plaster or fresh garden-soil or loam. In no case should the temperature be permitted to rise above 100 degrees Fahr. If there is not a cellar below your stables, it is wise economy to cover the heap with a roof and convey off the water from the eaves.

Guano is largely vegetable in its substance, modified by the processes it undergoes in the animal body. We class it, therefore, as a mixed manure. It is the droppings of sea-fowls collected for innumerable years on certain uninhabited islands on the coasts of Africa and Peru, in a climate not subject to rain, mingled largely with remains of feathers, eggs, food and carcasses. In some places it accumulates to the depth of sixty to eighty feet. Different specimens vary much in quality. The following may be regarded as a sort of average analysis of pure, good guano: Organic matter, containing nitrogen, 50 per cent; water, 14; phosphate of lime, 25; ammonia, phosphate of magnesia, phosphate and oxalate of ammonia, 13; siliceous matter &c. (sand &c.), 1. The above analysis exhibits a strongly concentrated manure. As we have indicated, it is above the medium, as much as 15 to 20 per cent of sand alone being found in some specimens. Guano used to be largely used for roots, grains, and other cultivated crops, and as a top-dressing for grass. Before using it for the latter purpose it should be mixed with twice its weight of fine earth, plaster, charcoal-dust, or ashes. The proper dose is two hundred to four hundred pounds an acre, sown broadcast and harrowed in or supplied in two dressings, the first immediately upon the plants appearing, but so as not to come in contact with them; the other, from ten to fourteen days later, immediately before rain or moist weather. It can be used as liquid manure by dissolving four pounds in twelve gallons of water and letting it stand for twenty-four hours before using. The best guano—viz. that from the Peruvian islands—is now becoming exhausted, and what is in the market is much inferior; therefore its use is not nearly so general as formerly. Another reason for its comparative disuse is the general impression that guano does not enrich the soil, but by its stimulating effects on the plants leaves it rather poorer than before its application.

Useful Farm Recipes and Hints.

An excellent and economical paint for rough woodwork can be made of melted pitch, six pounds; linseed oil, one pint; and brickdust or yellow ochre, one pound.

Lime Whitewash.—Place some freshly-burned quicklime in a pail and pour on sufficient water to cover it (if the lime is fresh great heat is given out); then add one pint of boiled linseed oil to each gallon of wash. For cheapness any refuse fat, such as dripping, may be used instead of the boiled oil. The whole should be thinned with water. Should colored wash be required, one pound of green vitriol added to every two gallons of wash gives a very pleasing drab. The brush should not be left in the lime-wash or the bristles will be destroyed.

Quicklime slaked with skimmed milk and afterward thinned with water makes an excellent wash for outdoor walls, as it is not acted upon by the weather.

Calcimine.—This is a substitute for whitewash and is used for nice work. It is made of Paris white and glue sizing in this proportion: twenty pounds of Paris white to one pound of glue, dissolved in boiling water. Dilute the mixture with water until it is of a creamy thickness.

Whitewash.—Take half a bushel of unslaked lime and slake it with boiling water. Cover it during the process. Strain it, and add a peck of salt dissolved in warm water, three pounds of ground rice boiled to a thin paste put in boiling hot, half a pound of Spanish whiting, and a pound of clean glue dissolved in warm water. Mix it and let it stand several days. Keep it in a kettle, and put it on hot as possible with a brush. It is said to look as well and last nearly as long as oil paint on wood, brick, or stone.

A very simple wash may be made in the following manner: Slake as above, and add to each pailful half a pint of salt and the same quantity of wood-ashes sifted fine; this makes it thick like cream, and covers smoke much better. Use hot. Coloring may be used if desired.

Cheap Wash for Buildings.—Take a clean water-tight cask and put into half a bushel of lime. Slake it by pouring water over it boiling hot and in sufficient quantity to cover it five inches deep, and stir briskly until it is thoroughly slaked. When the lime has been slaked, dissolve it in water, and add two pounds of sulphate of zinc and one of common salt. These will cause the wash to harden and prevent its cracking, which gives an unseemly appearance to the work. A beautiful cream-color may be given to the wash by adding three pounds of yellow ochre, or a good pearl-or-lead-color by the addition of a lump of iron-black. For fawn color add four pounds of umber, one pound of Indian red, and one pound of common lampblack. For stone-color add two pounds of raw umber and two pounds of lampblack. When applied to the outside of houses and to fences, it is rendered more durable by adding about a pint of sweet milk to a gallon of wash.

Damaged Hay may be rendered available by cutting into chaff and dressing with molasses and water.

To Preserve Wooden Buildings.—Mix two parts of tar, one of pitch, half of resin; boil, and paint the wood when quite hot. Give two coats, well sanding with the last.

Flooring for Pig-styes.—Take six parts of gravel, three of sand, and one of cement; mix dry, and then make into mortar. Spread three inches thick over the ordinary floor.

Sulphuring Seed.—A safe plan in sowing any kind of seed is to mix it with sulphur—about one pound to twelve pounds of seed. It serves to impart vigor, and keeps away parasites. The sulphur may be fearlessly mixed with the seed and sown with it.

To Destroy Caterpillars.—These are great pests in the garden, devouring gooseberry and currant bushes, cabbages etc. The best plan is to mix up a quantity of turpentine and water to sprinkle the bushes with. In order to make the turpentine mix well, some fine mould must be mixed with it, and the water added to the required consistency. It need not be very strong, but a fair sprinkling from a watering-pot with a good rose on the spout will kill them or prevent them from doing further damage. Tar-water is also said to be effective, and is excellent for destroying green fly, wood lice, and ants.

To Destroy Potatoe-bugs.—Mix one pound of Paris green with ten pounds of flour or whiting. The mixture should be sifted on the potato-hills while the vines are wet with dew or rain.

To Destroy the Striped Bug on Cucumbers or Melons.—Sift charcoal dust over the plants three or four times in succession, or take a solution of one peck of hen-house manure to one and a half gallons of water, and sprinkle the vines freely after sunset.

For Killing Lice on cows, horses, and hogs the following application is successful: Take the water in which potatoes have been boiled and rub it over the skin of the animal to be treated. The lice will be dead in two hours, and no further progeny appear.

Shelters for Sheep—Sheep should have shelter to run under at all seasons. They need it during the long cold rains of autumn fully as much as any other animal on the farm does. They get soaked to the skin during these long rains, and in that condition suffer great discomfort, which always tells on the flesh and general condition. Sheds for this purpose are easily and cheaply constructed in the pasture or field if it is not convenient to let them up to the stables.

The Best Hay.—To make the best and most nutritious hay the mowed grass should not be allowed to become too dry before being put up. When it "rattles" a great deal of its nutriment is lost, and it will not make as good feed as it otherwise would. The greener it can be put up the better. Hay-harvesting requires considerable intelligent consideration, and the farmer that gives it the most attention is the one that will win.

Cider should be made only from perfectly clean and sound apples if it is expected to be good. Insist on cleanliness being practised at every stage of the making. For perserving it there should first be slow fermentation in a cool place, and after fermentation bung tightly. It will soon become clear, when it should be racked off in bottles.

A pint of mustard-seed put in a barrel of cider will keep it sweet for several months, and make it more wholesome.

The Sunflower.—This plant is truly useful as well as ornamental. The flowers contain a large quantity of honey and are most attractive to bees, and the seeds are much relished by poultry. The seeds yield a large percentage of fine oil, while the leaves and cut stalks are relished by cattle. The first flowers, just before full bloom, furnish a palatable dish for the table, resembling artichokes in flavor. The seeds ground into flour make very good cakes, and if roasted furnish a drink not much inferior to cocoa. Boiled in alum, they make a good blue coloring-matter. The leaf is used as tobacco, the seed-pods made into blotting-paper, and the plants, if grown in damp places — for they will grow anywhere — are a protection against intermittent fever.

Harness Polish.—To make a good harness polish, take of mutton suet two ounces; beeswax, .. ounces; powdered sugar, .. ounces; lampblack, one ounce; green or yellow soap, two ounces; and water, half a pint. Dissolve the soap in the water, add the other solid ingredients, mix well, and add turpentine. Lay on with a sponge and polish off with a brush.

To Oil Harness.—Wet the harness over-night and cover it with a blanket, and in the morning it will be damp and supple. Rub on neats'-foot oil in small quantities. Never use vegetable oils on leather.

To Make Boots and Shoes Waterproof.—Take one pound of fresh tallow or mutton suet and melt it in an earthenware dish with half a pound of beeswax and about half an ounce of resin, and apply the mixture while warm to the soles and uppers, which should be well soaked with it. Soaking the soles in boiled linseed oil in a flat-bottomed vessel renders them waterproof. The oil should not be deeper than the thickness of the soles, as it should not get upon the upper leather, for it would render it hard. To take the stiffness out of boots and shoes when they have been wet, it is well to rub them thoroughly with castor oil, or the following mixture is excellent: Burgundy pitch, half an ounce; spirits of turpentine, one ounce; linseed oil, one gill; these should be melted together, and rubbed into the leather when quite dry before the fire or in the hot sun.

To Destroy Rats.—The following is an effectual mixture: Melt hog's lard in a bottle immersed in water heated to about 150 deg. Fahr.; then put in half an ounce of phosphorus for every pound of lard, and add a pint of whiskey. Cork the bottle tight when the mixture has been heated as hot as the water, and, taking it out of the water, shake it well until a milky-looking liquid is formed. When the liquid cools it will afford a solid compound of phosphorus and lard, from which the spirits may be poured off and used again if needed. Warm the compound a little and pour it into a mixture of wheat flour and sugar. This dough, rolled into pellets, is to be laid in rat-holes. It will be found as efficacious as any rat-poison sold.

New Kegs, etc.—To remove the disagreeable taste from new kegs, churns, or other wooden vessels, first scald them with boiling water, then dissolve some pearlash or soda in lukewarm water adding a little lime to it, and wash the inside of the vessel well with the solution; afterward scald it well with plain hot water before using.

A Good Disinfectant.—Permanganate of potassa in solution, twenty-five grains to two quarts of water, is an excellent disinfectant; it can be used for removing odors in utensils or in rooms. It is excellent for disinfecting mouldy barrels. Two or three tablespoonfuls of the solution, added to a pint of water, will cleanse a cask or barrel, which should be washed and rinsed out well.

Corn-cribs.—A corn-crib should be mounted on posts several feet high, and these capped with inverted metal pans, in order to prevent depredations from rats and mice.

Protecting Horses.—Sponging horses with a solution of a dram of Persian insect-powder to a quart of water is said to be an effectual remedy against the annoyance of flies and insects.

Advice on Sheep-raising.—In winter it is of prime importance that sheep should have plenty of rough feed in connection with their green rations. Corn-fodder nicely cured stands at the head, being relished by the sheep and excellent in assisting the fattening process. The corn used in fattening sheep does not need the preparation necessary for cattle. One of the best rations for fattening is composed of three parts of shelled corn, one part of wheat bran, with a little oil meal added. This, fed in connection with fodder or clover hay, with a plentiful supply of pure water, gives excellent results.

Sheep can best be fattened at from one and a half to two years old. Previous to this time the wool should pay a reasonable profit upon the keeping. At this age sheep will take on more fat from the same amount of feed, and the mutton be of better quality, than if held longer.

The mutton market is most active from about the 1st of February until the 1st of May, after this period the supply generally being full and prices lower. Sheep fattened for the early market require more feed, better shelter and care, but the price received generally pays for this extra cost. Those turned into market during the summer or fall have the advantage of green feed supplied at less cost than the dry.

Weaning Pigs.—In weaning pigs, says an authority, there is something more to be considered than simply taking them away from their mother. They should be weaned gradually, so as not to get any stunt or set-back. To take pigs away from their mother and little home before they have been taught to eat gives them a check for at least two weeks, and this is quite a little part of their lives if they are designed for slaughter when they are six to eight months old. Feeding them in a separate place to which they have access will accustom them to eating, and when deprived of their mother's milk they will refuse to eat until driven to it by hunger.

How to Sharpen a Scythe.—Keep the blade firmly upon the grindstone, with the point drawn toward the body of the holder, at an angle of about forty-five degrees with the edge of the stone. Commence to grind at the heel, and move it steadily along as the work progresses until the point is reached; then grind the other side in the same manner. Never rub the scythe back and forth upon the stone, as though endeavoring to whet it. The revolution of the stone will wear away the steel much better than rubbing it in this manner, by which the edge is likely to be made round and to be set irregularly. It is preferable to hold the scythe so that the stone will revolve toward the edge. In this way the holder can see when the edge is reached, and the particles ground off are carried away clean. In the opposite method of grinding there is risk of making a "feather edge" which will readily crumble off and leave the scythe almost or quite as dull as before. The blade should be ground equally on both sides. In whetting the scythe lay the rifle or whetstone flat against the side of the blade, and give a light, quick stroke downward and forward in the direction of the edge, so that the scratches it makes shall keep the points set in the same direction as was given them by grinding. By following these simple suggestions a scythe may be made to hold its edge twice as long as when the rifle or whetstone is drawn along the edge almost at random. A few strokes carefully taken will enable the workman to keep the proper direction and whet rapidly.

A Simple Mode of Sharpening Edge Tools.—Place the cutting part of the tool in water containing one-twentieth of its weight of sulphuric or muriatic acid; after allowing it to remain there for half an wipe it gently with a piece of soft rag, and in a few hours set it on an ordinary strop. The effect of the acid is to supply the place of the oil-stone, but uniformly corroding the entire surface, so that nothing but a good polish is afterward needed.

Care of the Grindstone.—A grindstone should not be exposed to the weather, as it is not only injurious to the woodwork, but the sun's rays harden the stone so much as in time to render it useless. Neither should the stone be allowed to stand in the water in which it runs, as the part remaining in the water softens so much that it wears unequally, and this is a common cause of grindstones becoming "out of tune."

Farm Bookkeeping.—Nothing conduces more powerfully to the profitable and satisfactory results of any business or undertaking than a regular and systematic registration of every proceeding, from the examination of which a clear and accurate knowledge can at any time be derived of the state and progress of the whole business. Farming is composed of three very chief ingredients—labor, money and stock, live and dead. Each of these elements requires a distinct attention, and also the branches into which the connections are divided; each separate detail implies a statement of its business and a review rendered of the success or defalcation. Expenses of every kind must be exhibited in the weekly and yearly arrangements; outlays in money must be singly exposed, and labor by itself, so that the several items, being individually set to view, are joined into a yearly aggregate. Grain crops must be seen in the quantity and value, the disposal by sale and by domestic use. The animals that are kept for work demand a view of the number and transactions among the sales and casualties, so that any profit or loss in that department is seen by a single reference. The fattened animals are singly kept in view, in order to show the income derived from each kind of beasts that are reared. Sales must be registered, and an account will show the debts outstanding at any period of time. All minor occurrences are noted in a memorandum page and transferred to the standing place when the nature of the affair requires the position.

The books needed by a farmer are a diary, a day-book, and a ledger. Another book will be convenient if an account is kept with each crop, and with separate fields, but this method can hardly be recommended for ordinary use. In the diary a record of each day's work and the weather should be kept. Business transactions of all kind should be noted immediately. In regard to debiting and crediting Mr. Waring gives the following rule: "When you let your neighbor or he with whom you deal have anything from you, it is a charge against him, and you must charge him with it on the debit side of the account; but whenever you receive anything from him it is a credit, and you must credit him with it on the credit side of the account." There are several books prepared expressly for farm bookkeeping, and it is well that every farmer should have one, for they will save much work by their convenient manner of arrangement. But, at any rate, every farmer should keep a set of books. The cost of the books is but a trifle, and but little time is needed to keep them.

The Common Ailments of the Horse.

This treatise has been compiled chiefly from Mayhew's excellent and stand work, though other authorities have been consulted.

The causes of the various ailments are given as well as their treatment, for knowledge of the causes should lead to their avoidance. The ounce of prevention is always better than the pound of cure. The ordinary owner should only attempt to deal with the less serious ailments that afflict horseflesh; when any threatening complications arise a veterinary surgeon should be summoned. No surgical operations are described in the pages that follow, because all such should be attempted only by persons skilled in horse-surgery, and never by persons whose qualifications are that they have read how an operation should be performed. At the end of the treatise on the 'Common Ailments of the Horse" will be found the manner of preparing some excellent articles of diet for sick horses.

Administering Medicine.—Medicine is generally administered to a horse either by making it up in the form of a ball or by giving a drench; that is, giving the medicine in a liquid form, in which case a drenching-horn is used.

To Administer a Ball.—Turn the animal round in the stall so as to bring his head to the light, making the least possible fuss or noise. Stand on a stool on the off side; gently put your hand in the horses mouth and draw the tongue a little out; place the fingers of the left hand over the tongue, and keep it firmly in this position by pressure against the jaw—not holding the tongue by itself, as a restless horse, by suddenly drawing back or sideways while his tongue is tightly held, may seriously injure himself. The ball should be oiled, that it may slip down the throat easily. Take it between the tips of the fingers of the right hand, and, making the hand as small as possible, pass the ball up the mouth by the roof to avoid injury of the teeth. When the ball is landed well upon the root of the tongue, withdraw the right hand, and as soon as it is out of the mouth release the tongue, which will help the ball down. Have a warm drink ready to give just after the ball is taken.

To Give a Drench.—Turn the animal as in giving a ball. The drenching-horn is best made of a cow's horn, the larger end of which is stopped up. A glass bottle should never be used. Pour in the liquid at the narrow end of the horn, the circular mouth of which should be an inch in diameter. The operator should have an assistant; both should be tall or else should stand on firm stools. The assistant should raise the horse's head till his mouth is above the level of his forehead, and keep it steadily in that position while the drench is being given. The operator, standing on the off side and taking the wide end of the horn in his right hand, can steady and assist himself by holding the upper jaw with his left, and leaving the tongue at liberty, he discharges the drench below the root of the tongue if possible. The drenching-horn should always be cleaned after use.

The horse's pulse is easily found by placing the two fore fingers under the middle of the horse's jowl or cheek-bone. A horse's pulse when in good condition beats from about thirty-two to thirty-eight pulsations per minute. The smaller the horse the faster is his pulse.

Bog Spavin.—This caused by brutality of some kind—by abuse of the whip, spur, or bit, which causes repeated shocks to the limb. It resembles wind-galls, though situated in a different locality, and is also liable to the same changes. It is evidenced by a puffy swelling at the front and at the upper part of the hock. Rest and a little sweating blister or pressure maintained by means of an India-rubber bandage are perhaps the best treatment.

Bots.—A horse is liable to be troubled with these parasites after having been turned out to graze in summer. These pests are the progeny of the gadfly, which hovers around horses while out at grass in summer and alights, and deposits its eggs on the hair of the horse, especially about the shoulders and fore legs. The horse licks off the eggs and swallows them, when the larvæ stick to the coats of the stomach, and are known as bots. These ultimately release their grasp and are ejected naturally, but during the months that they remain in the stomach they often impair digestion and appetite and occasion much weakness.

Whenever a horse is running at grass his skin should be scanned carefully once a day, and the eggs of these gadflies, if found, should be washed off with hot water and washing soda. Occasional diarrhœa, capricious appetite, and loss of flesh are indications of bots, or they are often passed in the dung. There is no remedy for bots. In the course of a year the parasites will be ejected naturally.

Broken Wind.—Broken wind is a disorder of slow growth, and may be caused by any abuse ; it is often the result of carelessness in feeding and exercise. The horse is allowed to eat too much hay or straw, or food of great bulk containing little nutriment, and the lungs are squeezed into less than the natural compass. If the horse be suddenly exercised more blood must be purified, and as a consequence some of the cells give way and broken wind is established ; old age, prolonged work, and bad food are its usual generators. Its symptoms are a short, dry, hacking cough, greedy appetite, insatiable thirst, and abundant flatus. The food is but half digested, the belly is pendulous, the coat ragged, and the aspect dejected. Respiration is performed by a triple effort; inspiration is spasmodic and single; expiration is labored and double.

Prevention is easy for broken wind, but cure is impossible. The utmost that can be done is to relieve the distress. Water should never be given except at stated times, and never immediately before work. Four half-pails may be allowed per diem—one the first thing in the morning, another the last thing at night, and the other two at convenient times during the day. In every drink of water it is likewise well to mingle half an ounce of dilute phosporic acid or half a drachm of dilute sulphuric acid.

Allow oats and beans, five feeds each day, with only five pounds of hay—two pounds in the morning when eing dressed, and the remainder in the rack at night. Crush the oats and beans; thoroughly damp all the food before it is presented to the horse, and also scald the corn.

Remove all bed by day, and muzzle when littered down for the night. Place a lump of rock-salt at one end of the manger. and at the other put a block of chalk.

A horse afflicted with broken wind should never be pushed hard or called upon for any extraordinary exertion, otherwise death may speedily ensue.

So much for the alleviation of the disease after it has been contracted; may be well to give a few directions for the ounce of prevention or how to avoid this scourge; (1) Never drive the horse from the shelter of the stable to the exposure of the field. (2) Never turn the steed which has thriven upon prepared food to the starvation of a "run at grass" or the rankness of the "straw-yard" (3) Never for the sake of cheapness buy damaged provender. (4) Never load a famishing stomach. (5) Be attentive that the times of watering are rigidly observed. (6) Never suffer the animal to quit the stable soon after it has drank or eaten. (7) Be very attentive to all coughs; accustom yourself to the sound of the healthy horse's windpipe, that when the slightest change of noise indicates the smallest change of structure you may be prepared to recognize and to meet the enemy before disease has had time to fix upon the membrane.

Cold.—A mild cold, with care, is readily alleviated. A few mashes, a little green food, an extra rug, and a day or two of rest will generally cure a mild cold. When the attack is more severe the horse is dull; the coat is rough; the body is of unequal temperature, hot in parts, in places icy cold. The membrane of the nose at first is dry and pale or lead-colored; the facial sinuses are clogged; the appetite has fled; often tears trickle from the eyes, and a discharge from the nose appears.

Treatment.—The horse should be comfortably and warmly housed, should have an ample bed, and the body should be plentifully clothed.

A hair-bag, half as long and half as wide again as the ordinary nose-bag, should be buckled by a broad strap upon the horse's head ; into this bag should be previously inserted one gallon of yellow deal sawdust ; upon the sawdust, through an opening guarded with a flap on the side of the bag, should be emptied a kettle of boiling water, the superfluity of which may run or drain through the hair composing the bag.

The boiling water should be renewed every twenty minutes, and the bag should be retained upon the head for an hour each time. Should yellow deal sawdust be not obtainable, some of common deal will do, upon which pour an ounce of spirits of turpentine. Mix well and thoroughly before applying the bag to the head. If the horse is weak and the weight of the bag taxes his strength place the bag upon a chair or stool.

While the membrane is dry use the steaming bag six times daily. When a copious stream of pus flows from the nose, its application three times daily will be sufficient. The food should consist of grass with mashes, to regulate the bowels and subdue the attendant fever. No medicine should be given, but, the discharge being established, three daily feeds of crushed and scalded oats, with a few broken beans added to them, will do no harm. Should the weakness be great a couple of pots of stout—one pot at night and the other at morning—will be beneficial. Good nursing, a loose box, fresh air, warmth, and not even exercise till the disorder abates, are also to be commended. Afterward take to full work with caution as much debility is apt to ensue upon severe cold. A cold often ushers in other and more dangerous diseases. The original ailment should then be disregarded, and those measures should be taken requisite to relieve the more important affection.

Colic.—Spasmodic colic, fret, gripes are names for the same illness. Spasmodic colic is caused by fast driving, change of water, change of food, getting wet, fatigueing journeys, aloes, or often no cause can be traced.

Symptoms.—First stage : While the horse is feeding he becomes uneasy and ceases to eat ; his hind foot is raised to strike the belly ; fore foot paws the pavement ; the nose is turned toward the flank, and an attack of fret is recognized. Second stage : While the horse is being watched every indication of disturbance may disappear. His countenance grows tranquil, and the nose is again inserted in the manger ; but in a few minutes the pangs are renewed. The animal has thus alternate fits of pain and then ease, but the intervals of freedom from pain grow shorter, while the attacks grow longer ; the horse crouches, turns round, then becomes erect ; pawing and striking at the abdomen quickly follow ; a morbid fire lights up his eyes. Third stage: If no relief is afforded, the pains go on lengthening, while the intervals of tranquility become shorter ; action becomes more wild ; often one foot stamps on the ground; the animal does not feed, but stares at the abdomen; at length without warning, he leaps up and falls violently on the floor; seems relieved; rolls about till one leg rests against the wall; should no assistance be now afforded the worst consequences may ensue.

Treatment.—Place, if possible, in a loose box, guarded by trusses of straw ranged against the walls. Give one ounce each of sulphuric ether and of laudanum in a pint of cold water, and repeat the dose every ten minutes if the symptoms do not abate. If no improvement be observed double the active agents, and at the periods stated persevere with the medicine. A pint of turpentine, dissolved in a quart of solution of soap as an enema, has done good. If after this the horse's condition does not improve, dilute some strong liquor ammonia with six times its bulk of water, and, saturating a cloth with the fluid, hold it by means of a horse-rug close to the abdomen. It is a blister, but its action must be watched or it may dissolve the skin. If, after all, the symptoms continue there must be more than simple colic to contend with, and a veterinary surgeon had better be summoned.

Flatulent or Windy Colic sometimes arises from gorging on green food, but the more common cause is impaired digestion consequent upon severe labor and old age. It is evidenced by uneasiness after feeding, hanging of the head, laborious breathing; the belly begins to swell and the animal paws, but more slowly and inertly than in spasmodic colic; the eye is sleepy, and wind passes frequently from the body. When such a case occurs a veterinary surgeon should be sent for at once; meanwhile a ball composed of two drachms of sulphuret of ammonia, with a sufficiency of extract of gentian and powdered quassia, may be administered, and be repeated for two consecutive half hours should the surgeon not yet have appeared.

Corns.— Corns generally result from imperfect shoeing. The shoe is either too tight or it is nailed too near the heel. The sole should be kept well pared and dressed with tar. Should the corns suppurate, hot linseed poultice should be applied, and the horse be allowed to rest. Corns must often be treated with the knife.

Cracked Heels.—This affection is generally caused by cutting the hair from the heels or by wet, mud, neglect of cleanliness, or sometimes by too little work and over-feed; it is generally peculiar to the cold and wet months of the year. The animal should rest, at all events until the parts are improved. The heels should be washed with tepid water and mild soap, and thoroughly dried; then the following wash should be applied:

    Animal glycerine   ½ pint
    Chloride of zinc   2 drachms.
    Strong solution of oak bark   1 pint.

Dissolve the zinc in water, then mix, and use thrice daily.

If sloughing and ulceration have set in, the animal should be allowed complete rest, and not be taken out even for exercise until the ulceration is arrested. A few bran mashes or a little cut grass should be given to open the bowels, and the following should be applied to the heels;

Ammalglycerin or phosphoric acid	2 ounces.
Permanganate of potash or creasote	½ ounce.
Water	2 ounces.

Mix, and apply six times daily.

When the ulceration is arrested the first recipe should be again resorted to, and the latter one discarded. A drink each night of the following mixture should be given:

Liquor arsenicalis	½ ounce.
Tincture of the muriate of iron	1 ounce.
Water	½ pint.

This acts directly upon the skin, and is an excellent tonic for the general system.

In all affections whatever of the legs, where the skin is broken, the ground on which the horse stands must be kept free from his evacuations and as dry and warm as possible.

Crib-Biting.—This habit, which one horse seems often to acquire from another, is often occasioned by bad ventilation, by indigestion, and sometimes by sameness of food. To cure it, the ventilation of the stable should be the first thing attended to. Place a lump of rock-salt in the manger; if that is not successful, add a lump of chalk. If these means are unavailing, always dampen the food, and at time of feeding sprinkle magnesia upon it, and mingle a handful of ground oak-bark with each feed of corn. Sometimes the habit may be broken by placing a piece of sheep-skin over the manger and sprinkling it with pepper.

Curb.—Curb consists of an enlargement, or gradual bulging out, of the posterior of the hock; it is accompanied by heat and pain, and often by lameness. It is caused by galloping on uneven ground, wrenching the limb, prancing, etc. It is a great mistake to blister the horse as soon as a curb appears, which is often done, but results always in harm. The horse should have a high-heeled shoe put upon him at once. The part should then be kept constantly wet with cold water to lower the inflammation. A cloth doubled two or three times is easily kept upon the hock by means of an Indian-rubber bandage. This cloth is to be kept cool and wet. The animal should be kept quiet under this treatment until the heat and swelling are diminished and the leg is almost sound; then a blister should be rubbed all over the joint.

Cough.—Cough is a symptom of many and very diverse forms of disease. It may arise from a trivial cause, or it may be the attendant of some of the worst forms of disease that horseflesh is heir to. Broken wind roaring, chronic diseases of the stomach, bowels, and lungs, etc., are all attended by cough, which is more frequently present as a symptom than a disease. Cough as a distinct affection is frequently caused by unhealthy lodging; hot stables, coarse and dusty provender, rank bedding, and irregular work are its general provocatives.

To cure a chronic cough care must be taken, in the first place, that the stable air is pure. The human nose is a good test of atmosphere; the stable should not smell of horses nor of any taint whatever. If the ventilation is good, the drainage clear, and the bedding clean, the interior of the stable will be odorless. Indeed the stable should always be in this condition be the horse sick or well. The oats given to a horse with chronic cough should be scalded and crushed, the hay should be dampened, and thin gruel or linseed tea should be given for drink. The horse should be clothed warmly, and given half a pint of the following mixture in a tumbler of cold water three times daily:

Extract of belladonna, rubbed down in a pint of water	1 drahm.
Tincture of squills	10 ounces.
Tincture of ipecacuanha	8 ounces.

Mix the above.

If no beneficial change be witnessed, try the subjoined:

Barbadoes tar or common tar if none other be at hand	½ ounce.
Calomel	5 grains.
Linseed meal	A sufficiency.

Mix, and give as one ball night and morning.

Should no improvement result, the next may be substituted:

Powdered aloes	1 drachm.
Balsam of copaiba	3 drachms.

Distemper (Strangles).—This form of sore throat is characterized by swelling between the bones of the lower jaw, which terminates in an abscess.

Cause.—A specific poison in the blood, which but few horses escape.

Treatment.—The opinions of different veterinarians vary in regard to the treatment, some recommending poultices, while others forbid it, etc., but the following plan is undoubtedly as good one as any:

Give grass or soft feed, and procure a good powder. If thought best to do anything to hasten the suppuration, apply warm poultices, or some like blistering. The appetite will return when the abscess breaks or is opened.

Epizootic.—This disease attacks many animals at the same time, and originates in one common cause; but just what this cause may be, it is very difficult to ascertain; yet it is evident that it is from a miasmatic influence, which has a tendency to spread rapidly over the country.

Symptoms.—The attack is abrupt. There is debility, stupor, eyes half-closed, disinclination to move, cracking joints, deficient appetite, mouth hot, constipation, urine high-colored and scanty, pulse weak and a little faster than normal, deep, painful cough, trembling at times, hair rough, limbs and ears are alternately hot and cold.

Soon there is a discharge from the nose of white, yellowish, or greenish matter, and the horse may recover, or complications may arise which are liable to cause death.

Treatment.—Give the horse a good comfortable place, with good care, and a good warm blanket. Give bran mashes and other proper nourishment, and then give some good powders, and continue their use freely until the horse is fully convalescent.

Caution.—Do not leave horses sick with this disease without any extra care, or without proper medical treatment, for two reasons: first, it is cruel and inhuman; and second, it is not profitable; for the cases which are left to themselves are very liable to have some complications arise which will either cause death or leave the horse in bad condition, from which he may not recover for a long time, and perhaps never.

Diarrhœa—Diarrhœa is evidenced by the frequent passage of watery stools. It is caused by acrid matter in the intestines, over-succulent food, too much water, change of dry to succulent food, working in the hot sun, mental excitement as seen at the covert-side, an overdraught of cold water whilst heated.

Treatment.—As the bowel movements are very active during waking hours, and still more so during exertion, whilst during rest, and especially during sleep, their movements are least, care should be taken to keep the horse quiet and in as drowsy a state as possible. All coarse succulent food, such as the green food of summer should be avoided, and small quantities of good sound hay, well made gruel, small malt mashes mixed with a handful of oats only, should be fed to the horse. The following is an excellent remedy for diarrhœa:

Raw linseed oil	16 ounces.
Oil of turpentine	2 ounces.
Tincture of opium (laudanum)	1 ounce

Shake well together and give as a draught.

Some horses are subject to repeated attacks of diarrhœa. In them the bowels are over-sensitive, and they are extremely difficult to keep in condition. Dieting is the only thing for them.

Founder (Laminitis):—This disease is inflammation of the sensitive laminæ of the foot, of which there are two kinds, acute and chronic, the latter being a continuation of the former. The acute form is invariably cured, if properly treated, but the chronic form is generally considered incurable; it can be relieved very much, but the feet are always afterwards sore and tender in front.

Cause.—Allowing to drink cold water, when overheated and tired from overwork, standing in the cold air (or where the wind will strike the horse) while warm, driving through a stream of water while warm, long and hard drives over dry roads, etc.

Symptoms.—The horse will stand upon his heels, with fore feet and legs stretched out as far as he can get them, so as to throw the weight off as much as possible; and he can scarcely be made to move. The horse has fever and considerable constitutional disturbance, in the acute form of the disease.

Treatment (of acute founder).—Give the horse a good bedding of straw, in a large, well-ventilated stall, so as to encourge him to lie down, which, by removing the weight from the inflamed parts, will relieve his sufferings very much, and assist in hastening the cure. As soon as his bed is fixed, give him twenty drops of the tincture of aconite root in a half-pint of cold water, poured into his mouth with a bottle, having a strong neck and repeat this dose every four hours until six or eight doses have been given. Also apply a cloth wet in ice water to the feet, and keep wet with the same for several hours, until the severe pain has been relieved. Wet the cloths often, and continue for two or three days, or longer if necessary. Give plenty of cold water to drink. The above treatment should be adopted as soon as possible after the horse has been attacked with founder. Let the horse have rest until he has fully recovered. Give grass or mashes for two or three days, and then give a good and fair amount of feed.

Glanders.—This disease is usually occasioned by vitiated air—that is, by bad stabling—stimulating food, and excessive work operating upon the young horse. Youth and high feeding, together with excessive labor and damp lodging, will certainly produce glanders. Age, starvation, and ceaseless toil generally induce farcy. The glanders and the farcy are however, one and the same disease, modified by the cause which originates them. Glanders is the more vigorous form of the disorder; farcy is the slow type, fastening upon general debility. Glanders is highly infectious and may be communicated hereditarily.

When glanders exist a staring coat generally shows the skin to be affected; the appetite is bad and the pulse is quickened. A mash or two, however, seems to set things all right, and the matter is forgotten. Soon afterward a slight discharge may issue from one nostril, but it is so very slight that it excites no alarm. One of the lymphatic glands on the same side as the moist nostril alters in character. It may remain loose and become morbidly sensitive. Usually, however, it grows adherent to the jaw, turns hard, and from being wholly imperceptible in the healthy animal enlarges to about the size of half a chestnut. At a later period the discharge, retaining its clear appearance, becomes more consistent, and to a slight degree the hairs and parts over which it flows are encrusted. It subsequently adheres to the margin of the nostril, and then in the transparent albuminous fluid may be seen opaque threads of white mucus. This marks the second stage. The next change takes place more rapidly. The transparent fluid entirely disappears, and in its place is seen a full stream of unwholesome pus. At this time there is some danger of glanders being mistaken for nasal gleet. A little attention will enable a person, however, to distinguish these diseases. The smell of glanders is peculiar. It is less pungent, but more unwholesome, suggesting a more deep seated source, than characterizes the disease with which it has been confounded. The ejection of glanders mucus is obviously impure, whereas that of nasal gleet generally flows forth in a fetid stream of thick and creamy matter.

When the third stage is witnessed the disease is rapidly hurrying to its termination. The membrane of the nose changes to a dull leaden color. The margins of the nostrils become dropsical, and every breath is drawn with difficulty. The defluxion exhibits discoloration. Scabs, masses of bone or pieces of membrane mingled with patches of blood next make their appearance, and the internal parts are evidently broken up by the violence of the disorder.

When a horse is suspected of being affected with glanders he should be examined in the following manner: The animal's head should be turned toward the strongest light obtainable; if toward the blaze of the noonday sun, so much the better. The examiner should then place himself by the side of the creature's head not in front, but in a situation where, though the animal should snort, he is in no danger of the ejected matter falling upon him. With one hand the upper and outer rim of the nostril should be raised; when grasping this part between the finger and thumb no fear need be entertained. The case would be something more than suspicious were any risk of contamination incurred. The wing of the nostril being raised, the examiner must note the appearances exposed; this he will best do by knowing where to look and what to expect. His eye has nothing to do with the skin nor with the marks that appear upon it. The opening of the lachrymal duct often challenges observation by being well defined and particularly conspicuous; but that natural development does not concern him; to that no attention must be given. The attention must be concentrated upon the membrane more internally situated than the skin seen at the commencement of the nostrils. The skin, moreover, suddenly ceases, and is obviously defined by a well-marked margin; there is, therefore, no difficulty in distinguishing the membrane by its fleshy and moistened aspect, as well as by its situation. If on this membrane any irregular or ragged patches are conspicuous, if these patches are darker toward their edges than in their centres, and if they nevertheless seem shallow, pallid, moist, and sore, the animal may be rejected as glandered. Should any part of the membrane, after being wiped with a piece of tow or anything soft wrapped round a small stick, seem rough or have evidently beneath its surface certain round or oval-shaped bodies, the horse is assuredly glandered. The membrane may present a worm-eaten appearance or be simply of a discolored and heavy hue. In the first case the animal ought to be condemned; in the second it is open to more than suspicion.

No animal should be permitted to perish slowly of glanders. The disease as it proceeds affects the fauces, pharynx, and larnyx; all become ulcerated; the obstruction offered to breathing grows more and more painful. Farcy breaks forth, and as a consequence superficial dropsy is added to the other torments. The edges of the nostrils enlarge, the membrane lining the cavities bags out, while the fauces and larnyx contract; the discharge becomes more copious, and the breathing is impeded. Ultimately laborious breathing induces congestion of the brain, and the animal dies of suffocation.

There is no cure for glanders. The disease has been described at some length only that it may be known and distinguished; so that a person about to purchase a horse may avoid buying one which shows evidence of this terrible disease; and also that when an owner once fully recognizes the disease in his horse, he may kill it at once. Glanders may be communicated to human beings, so that besides the cruelty of allowing an animal to slowly die in fearful torture, it is absolutely unsafe to have a glandered horse about.

Hide-Bound.—Neglect, hard living, exposure to cold and wet are the usual causes of this distress. Liberal food, clean lodging, soft bed, healthy exercise, and good grooming are necessary for the cure of hide-bound. Twice a day the following mixture may be given:

Liquor arsenicalis	1 ounce.
Tincture of the muriate of iron	1 ounce.
Water	1 pint.

Mix and give as a dose.

Lameness.—Lameness shows itself in unevenness of gait and in unusual attitudes while standing. It arises from structural change, often accompanied by inflammation, in the hard and soft tissues. In examining horses as to lameness, it is well to bear in mind that generally horses lame in front are lame in the feet, and that hind lameness has its seat in the hock.

Concerning the cure of lameness little can be said. The causes are various, as are the different remedies. In any serious case of lameness a veterinary surgeon should be consulted. One thing may be advised and that is to have the shoe taken off and the foot searched. Do not mind the horn being pared away, as a horse may go sound upon a very small portion of horn. If the seat of the injury is ascertained, always soak the foot in warm water before permitting the final use of the knife. The water should be at 70 deg. Fahr. when the foot is immersed, and then gradually raised to 90 deg., at which temperature it should be maintained. The water cleanses the part, favors the discharge of pus, lessens the inflammatory action, softens the anguish, and destroys the harsh character of the dry horn, which cuts much more easily when newly released from the bath.

Larvæ in the Skin.—Larvæ in the skin, like the bots, are caught while out at grass. The flies lay their eggs in the horse's hair; these are hatched, and the larva enters the skin. The next summer an abscess appears, in the centre of which is the insect. The best treatment is to open the abscess with a lancet, and then with finger and thumb applied on either side of the swelling squeeze out the larva. The abscess rapidly disappears, and to close the wound it only requires a few dabbings with a lotion made of chloride of zinc, one grain; water, ne ou ce.

Lice, fleas, and ticks may be got rid of by sponging the animal night and morning with a lotion composed of one part of carbolic acid to twenty of w ter. Care should be taken to wash all clothing worn during the affection, and then bake it in an oven heated to at least 150 deg. Fahr. Harness, brushes, etc., and everything that has come in contact with the skin, should be washed with a vermicide. Henroosts, pigeon-houses, etc., should not be allowed in the immediate vicinity of the stable, as frequently the lice which infest the stable come from the chicken-house. After treating a horse affected with lice look for other diseases, as hide bound, mange, etc.

Mange.—Insufficient food, bad lodging, no grooming, and often turning out to grass are the causes of mange. This disease is highly contagious, and is due to small insects burrowing beneath the scurf ski . It is evidenced by scurf about the hairs of the mane; the hair falls off in patches; sores and crusts appear; and the horse rubs his body against posts, etc. The principles of treatment consist in removing the scurf skin, or as much of it as possible, and then applying a dressing which will kill the insects. The horse, if the weather permits, should be placed in the sun for an hour, or in some warm unoccupied place if the weather is cold, and its coat should then be thoroughly whisked to remove scurf and incrustations; after this the following ointment should be rubbed all over the skin from the tip of the nose to the point of the tail.

Animal glycerin	4 parts.
Creasote	½ part.

Oil of juniper .... ¼ part.

Mix all together, and shake well before using.

About one and a half pints of this mixture is the general quantity employed for one application. Leave the mixture on for two full days, and then wash with soft soap and warm water. Afterward employ the whisk as directed before, and repeat the anointing and washing as directed.

Anything which has come in contact with a mangy horse must be cleansed before it is applied to any other horse or to the same horse after he is cured. Heat of an oven raised to 150 deg. is the best means for killing the parasites. Such things as cannot be placed in this heat should be well washed with carbolic soap or with carbolic acid and water (one part in one hundred), and exposed to the air for a week.

Poll Evil.—Poll evil is a disease most common among agricultural horses. It consists of a deep abscess situated upon the upper part of the neck, at its junction with the head; this abscess ends in an ulcerous sore which has numerous sinuses. The cause of poll evil is external injury of some sort, as blows upon the poll while going under a low doorway, and also blows from heavy whip-shafts often administered by brutal and careless drivers, or chafing of collars, especially during an irritable condition of the skin.

The animal gives evidence of this disease by carrying his head very steadily and poking his nose out. The enlargement, heat, and tenderness on pressure are obvious when the abscess is ripening. The anguish attendant upon the earlier stages of this disease is evidenced by the length of time the horse takes to empty his manger. When forced to bend his head toward the manger, he generally hangs back to the length of the halter. At this stage nothing is apparent, and the collar is often forced over the head regardless of the struggles of the diseased animal; the most careful inspection often fails to detect an indication of probable enlargement. Pressure or enforced motion of the head excites resistance. In some cases the enlargement becomes prominent in a few weeks; in others it is never well developed; the latter cases are most difficult to treat, for in them the disorder is most deeply seated.

In examining for suspected poll evil place the fingers lightly on the part, and let them remain there until the fear excited by a touch upon a tender place has subsided. Then, and not till then, gradually introduce pressure. The more superficial the injury the more speedy will be the response. In any case, little good can be accomplished by mild applications of fomentations or poultices. The seat of the supposed hurt should be lightly painted with spirituous or acetous tincture of cantharides; this should be done daily until copious irritation is produced, and before that dies away repeat the dressing. The soreness should be kept up, but no more. The tincture should not be applied upon active vesication, otherwise a foul sore may result. The poll should be made painful merely. The head should be kept perfectly quiet

As soon as the swelling appears watch it attentively, and when some particular spot points or is softer or more prominent than the surrounding substance, call in the aid of a surgeon, for the knife must be used, and used skilfully. After the operation rub the sides of the wound with lunar caustic. The sore should be thoroughly moistened with solution of chloride of zinc, one grain to an ounce of water, and a rag dipped in a solution of tar should be placed over the wound. After recovery a collar should not be used; a breast strap is far preferable.

Prick of the Foot.—When shoeing horses a blacksmith will often drive a nail either too near the quick or actually into it, or a nail of some sharp-pointed body may pierce the foot while the horse is traveling. When this is suspected from the horse showing lameness, the foot should be squeezed between pincers, then the nails from the shoe should be drawn one by one, and examined carefully as each is removed. If one appears moist or wet, the hole of that nail should be freely opened. Let the shoe be replaced, leaving that nail out. Put a little tow covered with tar over the wound, and shoe with leather. If lameness is still present, a veterinary surgeon had better be consulted.

Ringbone.—Ringbone somewhat resembles splint and spavin; these latter, however, generally occur in horses of speed, while the former is almost confined to the cart-horse. It is caused by the violent efforts the animal makes in dragging a heavy load up a steep hill. It is evidenced by roughness of hair on the pastern and a bulging forth of the hoof; a want of power to flex the pastern; an inability to bring the sole to the ground upon any but an even surface; and general loss of power.

When a horse shows ringbone seek to allay the pain. Apply poultices upon which one drachm of powdered opium and one of camphor has been sprinkled. Rub the diseased part with equal parts of oil of camphor and of chloroform. When the pain has ceased, apply with friction to the seat of the enlargement and around it some of the following ointment night and morning:

Iodide of lead   1 ounce.
Lard   8 ounces. Mix.

Continue treatment for a fortnight after all active symptoms have disappeared, and allow liberal food and rest. When work is resumed let it be gentle at first, and be very careful how the horse goes to his full labor.

Rheumatism.—Exposure to cold and damp are causes of the acute form of rheumatism, though frequently it follows in the train of more serious disorders. The chronic form is often a sequel of the acute, but

MISCELLANEOUS DEPARTMENT.

more often it is a separate constitutional affection very common in old age.

When attacked by the acute form the animal moves very reluctantly; the joints swell and cause painful lameness; fever is present, and the animal's skin becomes bathed in perspiration. Often the disease flies about, the inflammation attacking now some joints and then others.

Treatment.—Give two ounces of tincture of opium (laudanum) in water; then give a drachm of salicylate of soda every two hours, carefully watching the temperature, which it brings down in a marvellous manner. Should the temperature fall decidedly, the remedy must be omitted, but the moment the temperature attempts to rise the remedy must be resumed as before. Warm woolen rags and bandages must be kept on, loosely applied, all cold air scrupulously avoided, so as to encourage the perspiration. Without removing the rags sponge over with a little hot water every six hours. The swollen, painful joints can be greatly relieved by applying the following without pressure:

Powdered mustard	4 to 8 ounces.
Warm water	A sufficiency.

Mix into a thin paste and rub the whole quickly into the skin over the part affected.

Or the following liniment may be applied:

Compound soap liniment,	16 ounces.
Liquor of ammonia,	2 "
Tincture of cantharides,	2 "
Tincture of opium	2 "

The diet should be of a fluid, laxative kind, such as bran mashes, gruel, and hay tea, with a little juice of fresh lemon squeezed into each. When the thermometer shows the fever to have departed, the diet should be improved in the most careful manner possible.

Complications, such as pneumonia, etc., may arise, in which case a veterinary surgeon should be called in.

Chronic rheumatis affects the joints, and is not attended by fever; the joint affected is thicker and stiffer as consequence. Such forms of chronic rheumatism of short duration, such as lumbago, stiff neck, etc., require a few days rest, a laxative, and warm clothing for treatment.

Scald Mouth.—It sometimes happens that the horse's mouth is scalded by carelessness in giving some powerful medicine which has not been properly diluted. Scald mouth is evinced by dribbling of saliva and constant motion and repeated smacking of the horse's lips. In such cases soft food should be given, and the following wash should be used:

Borax,	5 ounces.
Honey or treacle,	2 pints.
Boiling water,	1 gallon. Mix.

When this mixture has cooled, hold up the horse's head and pour half a pint into the mouth. Half a minute afterward allow the head to fall and the fluid to run out of the lips. This mixture should be used several times during the day.

Sitfast.—Sitfasts resemble somewhat a corn upon the human foot, but the hard bare patch is surrounded by a circle of ulceration. They appear upon saddle-horses, and are caused by a badly fitting saddle, by careless and too energetic riding, loose girths, or often by the saddle-cloth when carelessly put on so as to become thrown into folds when the horse is mounted. These, although they may appear trifling, always require treatment; for which time must be taken, during which the horse should not be ridden.

Liquor arsenicalis,	¼ ounce.
Tincture of muriate of iron,	½ ounce.
Water,	1 pint. Mix.

Sore Throat.—Sore throat is frequently a sign of some graver disorder, and so should be very cautiously treated as a local malady. Its symptoms are a perpetual flow of saliva, want of appetite, inability to swallow liquids, the fluid returning partly by the nostrils, and each gulp being accompanied with an audible effort.

A horse so suffering should be given complete rest and, if there is such a thing in the stable, be placed in a loose box. He should be clothed warmly, fed upon green food for a couple of days, and always have present a pail of thick, well-made gruel, which should be regularly changed three times daily. Three feeds of bruised and scalded oats, with a handful of beans, should be given every day. If the bowels prove obstinate, and after the second day remain constipated, the following drink should be given:

Solution of aloes	4 ounces.
Essence of anise-seed,	½ ounce.
Water,	1 pint.

Should the throat not amend, dissolve half an ounce of extract of belladonna in a gallon of water; hold up the animal's head and pour half a pint of the liquid into the mouth, and in thirty seconds let the head down. Repeat this from six to eight times during the day.

If, instead of appearing to heal, the sore throat seems inclined to spread, use at once the following preparation: half a pint of permanganate of potash in a gallon of distilled water, and in the manner directed for the belladonna liquid; or use the following in the same manner:

Chloride of zinc,	3 drachms.
Extract of belladonna,	½ ounce.
Tincture of capsicum,	2 drachms.
Water,	1½ gallon. Mix.

Should the disease not yield, but remain stationary, give a quart of brewers' stout morning and evening. If no change takes place in two days, a veterinary surgeon had better be called in.

Spavin.—Spavin is evidenced by any bony enlargement upon the lower and inner side of the hock. The leg cannot be flexed and the hoof is hindered from being turned outward. The horse leaves the stable limping, but returns seemingly improved by exercise. The foot is dragged along the ground instead of lifted, which causes the front of the shoe to be worn to a state of positive sharpness and the toe of the hoof to be rendered blunt. When the bony enlargement is located high upon the joint it is generally incurable.

Good food and rest are the best treatment for spavin; there are various cruel treatments, such as firing, punching, etc., but their efficacy is questioned. While inflammation exists, apply poultices and rub the part with a mixture of belladonna and opium, one ounce of each rubbed down with an ounce of water; or place opium and camphor on the poultices; or rub the enlargement with equal parts of chloroform and camphorated oil. The pain and heat having subsided, apply with friction some of the following ointment :

   Iodide of lead,   1 ounce.
   Simple ointment,   8 ounces. Mix.

Splint.—Splints are very commonly met with, especially in roadsters and draught horses. Some splints, when they have reached their maturity, cause little or no inconvenience. All are painful when growing, and in that state generally cause lameness. Any swelling upon the inner and lower part of the knee of the fore leg, or any enlargement upon the shin-bone of either limb, may be taken as an evidence of this disease. On the shin they are to be dreaded, as they interfere with the movements of the tendons. In feeling down the leg, any heat, tenderness or enlargement is proof of a splint. If, on the trot, one leg is not fully flexed or the horse "dishes" or turns the leg outward, the proof is confirmed.

Rest and liberal food are the best treatment for splints. When they are acutely painful, a poultice on which one drachm of opium and one drachm of camphor is sprinkled will frequently afford relief. They may also at such times be rubbed with a drachm of chloroform combined with two drachms of camphorated oil. These measures aim merely at mitigating the symptoms. Operations for splints are dangerous remedies, though sometimes resorted to.

When a splint interferes with a tendon, however, the only chance of cure is in an operation. This requires a skilled hand. After the operation the skin should be left open and the wound dressed with the lotion made of chloride of zinc one grain to water one ounce. Nothing irritating to the bone should be employed. Splints sometimes occur on the outer side of the hind leg; these, however, do not occasion severe lameness, and are not worthy of much notice. The following ointment is excellent for preventing the further enlargement of a splint :

   Iodide of lead,   1 ounce.
   Simple ointment,   8 ounces.

Mix and apply with friction three times daily.

Sprain of the Back Sinews.—Sprain of the back sinews often occurs in driving or riding horses over uneven ground or hilly roads. Shaft-horses descending a steep declivity with loads behind them are very liable to sprain the back sinews. Slight sprains may be treated by bandaging the leg with linen rather tightly, and keeping the bandage constantly wet with cold water. The horse should be allowed to rest, and no attempt should be made to work off the complaint. The horse should not be put to work until more than recovered. Bad sprains are very serious affairs, and operations are often necessary. These, however, never fully restore the horse.

Staggers.—Mad staggers and sleepy staggers represent different symptoms or stages of the same disease. Over-feeding is the sole cause giving the horse considerably more at any meal than his usual allowance, especially after much fatigue or a prolonged fast. Eating certain foods such as ripe or fast-ripening rye-grass, is liable to bring on the staggers.

The first symptoms are the sleepy staggers. The horse becomes dull or sleepy; the head hangs downward or is pressed against some prominence; the animal snores when sleeping; the skin is cold and the coat staring. Some animals die in this state. The advent of mad staggers is announced by a raising of the lid and sudden brightening of the eye; the breath becomes rapid and drawn, with a panting action. The whole appearance is altered; the evidences of approaching frenzy can hardly be mistaken.

Treatment.—Allow no water. Give a quart of any oil. Six hours afterward give another quart of oil, with twenty drops of croton oil in it, should no improvement be noticed. If there is still no improvement within another six hours, repeat the oil with thirty drops of croton oil. After a further six hours repeat the dose, and administer the succeeding doses at the intervals before stated until the altered aspect of the horse indicates that the distension has been relieved. Upon the slightest mitigation of the symptoms stop all medicine at once.

If the mad stage becomes fully developed no remedies can avail.

Surfeit.—This is a sudden rash or a quantity of heat-spots bursting out upon the skin, which are round, blunt, and slightly elevated. If the pulse is not affected, the lumps may disappear in a few hours. The diet should be looked to. Eight pounds of hay should be abstracted, and a couple of bundles of cut grass allowed per day. A handful of sound old crushed beans should be given with each feed. The following drink is of service:

Liquor arsenicalis,	1 ounce.
Tincture of the muriate of iron.	1½ ounces.
Water,	1 quart.

Mix, and give once daily, one pint for a dose.

Should the horse be young and have been neglected throughout the winter, a surfeit sometimes appears which is of a different character. The lumps do not disappear, but an exudation escapes from the centre of each. In this case the constitution is involved, and if not attended to the malady is apt to settle upon the lungs. Should the attack assume this appearance, the horse should not be taken from the stable even for exercise; the bed should be kept clean and the stable well ventilated. Feed as previously directed, and give bran mashes if the bowels are constipated, but cease to give them when the constipation is removed. Administer the drink before recommended night and morning, but should the appetite suffer reduce the quantity or withhold all medicine. Clothe warmly. Should the pulse suddenly sink, allow two pots of stout daily. If the appetite is poor, good gruel instead of water should be kept constantly in the manger. The shortest cases of this affection generally last a fortnight, during which time the treatment consists in good nursing and in liberally supporting the body.

Swollen Legs.—Swollen legs mostly occur in heavy animals, and have a tendency to partial dropsy. In mild cases bandages of cloth or flannel wet with cold water afford relief. In more serious cases the horse should be placed in a large, roomy loose box, if possible, for nothing more quickly removes this affection than easy and natural motion. Hay should not be fed to the animal for some weeks. The corn should be damped and a handful of ground oak bark should be sprinkled on each feed. Attend particularly to exercising the horse. Should the legs continue to enlarge, do not apply the bandages, but hand-rub the limb well and long.

Thrush.—This disease is evidenced by a thin foul-swelling discharge, appearing in the cleft of the frog. Thrush may be due to a local origin, as standing in filth in the stable, or it may be caused by a constitutional affection. Local thrush shows itself in the hind foot, and constitutional in the fore foot. To prevent local trush keep the stable clean. Clay, cow dung, and other filth employed for stopping the horse's feet will produce thrush if long continued.

If the affection has a local origin, place the foot in a poultice for twenty-four hours. Afterward cleanse the cleft of the frog by see-sawing a little tow or soft band through it; then ram a little calomel and tow down to the bottom of the cleft with a sharpened piece of wood. Should this treatment not cure the thrush, take the horse to the blacksmith after washing the feet well with water in which is dissolved chloride of zinc in the proportion of two scruples to the pint. When he has pared away the frog till only sound horn remain or the flesh is exposed, the shoe should be tacked on and the horse returned to a clean stall. Apply chloride-of-zinc lotion, three grains to an ounce of water, to the cleft of the frog by means of some tow wrapped round a small piece of stick. When the stench has ceased a little liquor of lead will perfect the cure.

When thrush is constitutional it is best to have the ragged thrush and unsound horn removed. Afterward dress every morning with the chloride-of-zinc lotion. Do not attempt to stop the thrush.

Tread.—Fatigue and overweight are the usual causes of tread. In light horses it occurs toward the end of a long journey. The hind foot is not removed when the fore foot is put to the ground. The end of the fore shoe consequently tears off a portion of the coronet from the hind foot. In cart-horses, after the horse is fatigued, the load has to be taken down a steep hill; the animal, being in the shafts, rocks to and fro the legs cross, and the calk of one shoe, wounds the coronet of the opposite hoof.

The sore should be bathed with chloride-of-zinc lotion, one grain to an ounce of water. Continue to do this three times daily. Feed liberally. A slough will take place and the animal will be well in about a month, the only danger being the after-result of a false quarter.

Overreach, which is akin to tread, occurs only to fast horses. It calls for the same treatment as tread.

Wind-Galls.—These are small enlargements, generally upon the hind legs and below the hocks. They are caused by hard labor. The best form of treatment is the application of pressure. Fold a piece of soft rag several times; saturate the rag with water and lay upon it one drachm each of opium and camphor. Wrap this about the enlargement. Upon the moistened rag place a piece of cork big enough to cover the wind-gall, and above it lace on an India-rubber bandage. This bandage should be constantly worn in the stable.

Worms.—Worms infesting the horse are of four kinds: the tænia or tapeworm, the lumbrici, the strongylus and the ascarides.

The tape-worm mostly affects colts, and is caused by denying the mare proper nourishment when with foal or by breeding from old animals. A foal afflicted with tape-worm grows up with a large head, low crest and long limbs. The abdomen is swollen, the appetite is ravenous, the coat unhealthy and the breath fetid. The animal may rub its nose against the wall or remain straining it upward for a considerable time; it picks and bites its body, often pulling out mouthfuls of hair.

Tape-worm is best destroyed by spirits of turpentine given in the following quantities:

A foal,	2 drachms.
Three months old,	½ ounce.
Six months,	1 ounce.
One year,	1½ ounces.
Two years,	2 "
Three years,	3 "
Four years and upward,	4 "

Procure one pound of quassia-chips; pour on them three quarts of boiling water. Strain the liquor. Cause the turpentine to blend, by means of yolks of eggs, with so much of the quassia infusion as may be necessary. Add one scruple of powdered camphor to the full drink, and give every morning before allowing any food. This may kill the worms, but as every link of the tape-worm is a distinct animal of both sexes and capable of producing itself, the eggs must be numerous. For the destruction of these, nourishing prepared food is essential such as gruel, scalded oats, etc.; little or no hay should be given. The following tonic will be of service:

Liquor arsenicalis,	1 to 8 drachms.
Muriated tincture of iron,	1½ to 12 drachms.
Extract of belladonna,	10 grains to 2 drachms.
Ale or good stout,	½ pint to 1 quart.

Mix; and give every morning, strength being proportioned to age, till the coat of the animal becomes glossy.

The lumbrici worms prey upon weakly horses and those enfeebled by age. Two drachms of tartarized antimony, with a sufficiency of common mass, should be given as a ball every morning until the worms are expelled.

The ascarides and strongyli inhabit the large intestines. The last are difficult to eradicate, because of the extent of bowel which they infest. The ascarides are always located within the rectum. It is best to begin treatment with injections of train oil. Should these be followed by no result by the end of a week, give for seven mornings a solution of catechu, one ounce to a quart of water. Upon the eighth morning give the animal a bran mash, and at night administer a mild physic-ball, composed of about four drachms of aloes and one drachm of calomel. Tobacco smoke enemas are sometimes useful. The itching is sometimes so provoking that the horse will rub the tail and quarter violently against any rough surface within its reach. The itching may be allayed by inserting up the anus a portion of the following ointment night and morning: Glycerine, half an ounce; spermaceti, one ounce; melt the spermaceti and blend; when nearly cold add strong mercurial ointment three drachms, powdered camphor three drachms.

ARTICLES OF DIET FOR SICK HORSES.

Barley and Lentil Gruel.—Take of barley meal six parts, lentil flour two parts, celery-seed half a part; mix. A few handfuls boiled in a gallon of water down to six pints make a capital nutritious drink, used as a change in place of oatmeal gruel.

Bean Meal and Bread Mash.—Soak a loaf of bread, cut in large slices, for two hours in new milk, then make a mash with two handfuls of bean meal and a pinch or two of salt.

Bean Meal and Potato Mash.—Boil some potatoes in their skins, then peel them, and pound them into a small mash, and mix with one or two handfuls of bean meal. Such a mash must not exceed two pounds in weight, and will be better to be smaller, and repeated night and morning or oftener.

Beef Tea.—Take good lean beef, cut it into pieces the size of a walnut, pick off all skin and fat, place it in a stone jar and just cover it with water; place on a cover and let it stand in a slow oven for five hours. Give a large breakfastcupful every four hours in urgent weakness, if necessary, out of a drench-horn.

Beer and Loaf Bread.—Place a quart of beer, ale, porter or stout in the bottom of a pail; then place a whole loaf, with a crust pared off, in the beer, leaving the upper side dry. The horse eats the bread down to the beer, and eventually takes the whole, the beer also, and will afterward take kindly to beer given alone. Beer and loaf bread are capital in long, tedious cases of extreme weakness, such as continued fevers, etc.

Bran Mash.—Place good, recently-made bran in a pail; pour boiling water over it; let this stand near a fire covered with several thicknesses of clean rug; mix thoroughly with a stick. It should be given only in quantities capable of being eaten at once, as it has a tendency to turn sour with standing. It should never be placed in a wooden manger. It is highly useful on account of its laxative properties. A couple of handfuls of bean meal added to a bran mash will make it more valuable as a relish.

Bran Tea.—Place a few handfuls of good fresh bran in the bottom of a pail; fill up the pail with boiling water; let the whole stand covered near a fire, then strain through muslin. Place, when cold, in a fresh clean pail, and squeeze a lemon into it, and give. It is a pleasant demulcent drink after inflamed bowels, diseases of the urinary organs, in fevers, etc.

MISCELLANEOUS DEPARTMENT.

Brandy and Egg Mixture.—Beat up well four fresh eggs; then add a quart of good new milk and two wineglassfuls of brandy. Give such a dose in a clean pail or out of a drench bottle three or four times or oftener in the twenty-four hours. Very useful in a weak state when no food or very little can be taken.

Bread Mash.—Soak two loaves of bread in milk for two hours; reduce to a pulp; add a pinch of salt, and, if thought desirable, a little celery seed also.

Compound Bread Mash.—Take four tablespoonfuls, upheaped, of bread mash, and the same quantity of malt; mix well together; then pierce it all over, after placing it before the horse, with pieces of sliced carrot.

Pulled Bread.—Remove the crust from one or two fresh loaves of bread and pull the crumb or white portion with the fingers into pieces the size of walnuts or larger; place these in a hot oven to brown the surface of each piece, turning the pieces over for this purpose, and afterward put into a cooler oven three or four hours to drive away all moisture. This is highly relished by a sick horse, and may be given at intervals from the hand in any low, weak case.

Carrots.—These are highly relished by horses in sickness and in health. They should be washed and scraped very clean and sliced crosswise or lengthwise. They are better given raw, from the hand or placed temptingly in and around mashes or in corn, etc.

Celery Seed Tea.—Pour a quart of boiling water upon two tablespoonfuls of seed; let it stand half an hour; then place it in heart a pail of water and give cold.

Corn Flour Mash.—Take four tablespoonfuls of corn flour, and mix them with a quart of milk. Boil slowly for eight or ten minutes; then pour into a clean pail and stir in two handfuls of malt. Let it get cold and give it in the pail.

Green Food.—Freshly-cut grass, clover, etc., are of high value in many forms of sickness. But they must not be given indiscriminately in every form of ailment, or harm may result. It is best to give them in small quantities, in order that their easy ingestion may not lead to overeating. In low states of illness, with utter absence of appetite, a little green food may be offered by hand from time to time.

Cut Hay Mash.—Take seven or eight handfuls of bran mash and two handfuls of bean meal; then add the same quantity or more of the chaff of good hay. Mix all together and sprinkle over all a handful of malt.

Hay Tea.—Place some good hay in a pail, so as to half fill the pail when pressed down; then pour over boiling water till the pail is three-quarters full. Let it stand near a fire, cover over with a few thicknesses

MISCELLANEOUS DEPARTMENT.

of a clean rug, for an hour; then pour off the water into a clean pail and give. In fevers a little ice may be added.

Lentils.—These like beans, contain a large amount of nutriment and flesh-giving properties. Lentil flour, mixed with barley meal half and half, may be advantageously sprinkled over bran mashes and other forms of food and mashes to give extra piquancy. A handful or two may be stirred occasionally into the drinking water.

Linseed.—Whole linseed should be always on hand, as it forms a bland mucilaginous, laxative diet.

Linseed Mash.—Boil a pound of good whole linseed in a gallon of water down to six pints; then pour this over good bran instead of the boiling water used in making a bran mash. A handful of malt may be thrown over the surface after the mash is placed for the horse to eat. It is a highly useful, bland, laxative diet during "physic."

Linseed Tea.—A pound of whole linseed, boiled in two gallons of water down to ten or twelve pints, must be strained through muslin; let it get cold, then add fresh lemon juice or ice, or both. It is a highly useful fever drink, and also of great use during and after inflammation of the bowels, kidneys, or any of the urinary organs; especially useful in catarrh and sore throat.

Malt.—The ease with which malt can be digested, together with its power of aiding in digestion, renders it an invaluable agent in the treatment of horses and cattle. A handful or two may be sprinkled over different varieties of diet after placing these before the sick animal.

New Milk.—After or during illnesses where the horse is rapidly losing flesh, good sweet milk given in quart doses from a clean pail is highly valuable.

Oats.—Good, short, well fed oats are valuable in sickness as well as in health. In the latter periods of convalescence they may be used whole.

Oat Compound.—Take a handful each of oats, bran, rice or pearl barley, malt, hay, chaff, whole linseed, bean meal and celery seed, or any like combination, and mix thoroughly together. A few slices of carrots may be added.

Oat Cake.—The ordinary oat cake is highly relished when given a little at a time by hand, in the lowest state of weakness and complete loss of appetite.

Pea Meal.—This may be used in place of bean meal, or alternately with it, in different mashes.

Barley Water.—Take a pound of pearl barley and boil it in two gallons of water for half an hour; strain through a cloth; let it cool, then give either alone or with ice or lemon juice, or with both. It has the same uses as linseed tea.

Potatoes.—These are a highly useful food for the horse in health, and may be given by way of varying the food during illness. But as they contain a large proportion of starch, they should not be given in liver disorders or its complications.

Potato Mash.—Boil potatoes with their skins on; skin them and beat them up into a mash with milk, whey or skimmed milk. Mix malt with this mash. Useful in later periods of convalescence.

Rice.—This, boiled in a little water till quite expanded, may be given alone as a mash, or may be mixed with malt, bread, carrots, bran, etc., to form most savory food to tempt the remains of appetite.

Rice Water.—Thoroughly wash half a pound of rice with cold water; macerate it for three hours in two gallons or less of water at a tepid heat, and afterward boil slowly for an hour and strain through muslin. A useful drink in dysentery, diarrhoea and irritable states of the alimentary canal. It may be flavored with lemon juice or celery seed.

Skimmed Milk.—This may be used freely as a drink in place of water in most illnesses, and is particularly valuable in diseases of the kidneys and all urinary disorders attended by a want of due amount of secretion from the kidneys.

Whey.—Take fresh warm or warmed milk and curdle it with rennet, then strain off the liquor. This is highly useful as a drink in fevers.

Wine.—Good, sound port wine, a bottle per day, given at frequent intervals, is useful in sinking conditions in tiding the system over a critical period. It may be given alternately with brandy. Other nourishment must be given in fair quantities when wine is given as an article of diet.

FRANKLIN'S MAXIMS.

Temperance.—Eat not to dulness, drink not to elevation.

Silence.—Speak not but what may benefit others or yourself; avoid trifling conversation.

Order.—Let all things have their places; let each part of your business have its time.

Resolution.—Resolve to perform what you ought; perform without fail what you resolve.

Frugality.—Make no expense but to do good to others or yourself; that is, waste nothing.

Industry.—Lose no time; be always employed in something useful; cut off all unnecessary actions.

Sincerity.—Use no hurtful deceit; think innocently and justly, and if you speak, speak accordingly.

Justice.—Wrong none by doing injuries or omitting the benefits that are your duty.

Moderation.—Avoid extremes; forbear resenting injuries as much as you think they deserve.

Cleanliness.—Tolerate no uncleanliness in body, clothes, or habitation.

Tranquillity.—Be not disturbed at trifles or at accidents common or unavoidable.

PROMISSORY NOTES, BILLS OF EXCHANGE, Etc.

A *Promissory Note* is a direct engagement in writing to pay a specified sum named therein, on sight or demand, or at a time therein specified, to a person named, to his order, heirs or assigns, or to the bearer. He who promises the payment is the *maker* or *drawer* of the note. He to whom it is payable is the *payee*. He who indorses it is the *indorser*. He to whom the indorser, by that indorsement, transfers his interest, is the *indorsee*. He in whose possession the note is when due is the *holder*.

The following are essential requisites in law to constitute a promissory note: A promissory note must be in writing. Its promise to pay must be distinctly expressed, and without qualification. It calls for payment in money only. The sum to be paid is definitely stated, both in figures and in words. Should these not agree, the words will rule the figures. If no time of payment is fixed, the note is payable on demand. If the note is not dated, its date is assumed to be the day when its existence was first established. If made payable to a fictitious person, it is payable to the bearer.

An Accommodation Note is one for which the maker receives no consideration for which he promises the payment of the note, but makes it simply to lend his credit to the payee or other party, so that the payee may raise money on the maker's name. He who is so accommodated cannot recover the money promised by the maker. If, however, the note be indorsed over to a third party "for value received," then the maker is holden to the third party, even though the nature of the note was known by the third party when he received the note.

Invalid Notes.—The following notes are invalid: All that lack consideration, which must be some benefit to the party who makes the note, or some act, labor, forbearance, etc., on the part of the payee. Also, all notes founded on fraud or on undue advantage taken of a party, or for illegal considerations, as bribery, wagers, etc. Also, all notes in which material alterations appear. Also, notes dated on Sundays, legal holidays, and on dates yet future when the note is issued.

Negotiable Notes.—The following notes are negotiable: Those payable to a person or order; to a person or bearer; to a person or his assigns;

and to the cashier of any incorporated company or institution, or to his order as cashier.

When the words " or bearer" are introduced, the instrument may pass from hand to hand like a bank bill without indorsement, but when the words " or order" are used, the instrument must be indorsed by the original holder of it.

Three days of grace are usually allowed on all notes and drafts, except those " on demand." These days make no allowance for Sundays or holidays, so that if a note fall due on Thursday, the days of grace are up on Saturday.

As regards the indorsement of notes bear these regulations in mind: A note drawn to a certain person, or bearer, needs no indorsement, though for the sake of tracing it readily indorsement is usually asked. A general indorsement is made by simply writing the payee's name on the back of the note. In this form he remains open to all the consequences if the maker of the note fail to pay it. A special indorsement directs payment to a particular person by writing above the signature the words "Pay to A. B. or order." In this case responsibility falls on this indorser only when those before him on the note fail to pay. If the indorser wishes to avoid all responsibility as such, he must add the words " without recourse" in a general indorsement, and " at his risk," to a special indorsement, or "without recourse upon me." **No indorsement can pass the property included in a note unless the indorser has legal claim to that property. Indorsers become security that the maker of the note shall pay the money due thereon.** If the holder is guilty of neglect or in any way compromises with the holder in respect to the claim the indorsers are discharged from all further responsibility. No compromise can be made with antecedent indorsers to the injury of those subsequently on the paper. Demand for payment when due, and proper diligence in enforcing it, must precede charge upon the indorsers.

Should the holder of a note lose it, he must make a formal demand for its payment when due, but he is responsible to the party paying the note in case trouble should arise. When a note is lost, it is well to give public warning against its negotiation; in some States this is essential.

The demand for payment of a note should be made upon the day that it is due and according to the specifications of the note. A good way to save trouble is to throw the note into a bank for collection, which charges but a small fee.

In case of the non-payment of a note, place it in the hands of a notary public. He formally demands payment, and if not received he at once protests the note and informs the indorsers. **Should any loss occur through the notary's neglect, he is responsible.**

If payment of a note be made to a person because of a forged signature of the payee or other indorser, or if some one fraudulently collects the money who pretends to be the party to whom a note is especially indorsed, the maker is not released from his obligation on account of the fraud played upon him. Should a note be paid before it is due, and should it afterward pass into the hands of a *bona fide* holder for value, the latter can insist upon a full payment at the maturity of the note.

A Bill of Exchange is an order to a person at a distance, which directs him to pay a certain amount to the person in whose favor the bill is drawn, or to his order. Bills of exchange are either foreign or inland. A draft may properly be called an inland bill of exchange.

A Letter of Credit is a letter written by a merchant or correspondent to another, requesting him to advance money or sell goods to the bearer or person named, and undertaking that the debt which may be contracted in pursuance of the request shall be duly paid.

A Lease is a contract in writing whereby a person conveys a portion of his interest in lands or tenements to another in consideration of a certain rent or other recompense. Care should be taken to insert in the lease all the terms of the contract between the parties.

FORMS OF NOTES, Etc.

Note on Demand.

$300.　　　　　　　　　　　　　　ST. PAUL, Feb. 15, 1885.

On demand, I promise to pay John Smith, or order, Three Hundred Dollars, value received.　　　　　　　　　　　JAMES BROWN.

Negotiable Note.

$500.　　　　　　　　　　　　　　NEW YORK, April 10, 1885.

Ninety days after date, I promise to pay James Brown, or order, Five Hundred Dollars, value received.　　　　　JOSEPH ROBINSON.

Note Not Negotiable.

$250.　　　　　　　　　　　　　　NEW YORK, Jan. 5, 1885.

Ninety days after date, I promise to pay James Brown, Two Hundred and Fifty Dollars, value received.　　　　JOSEPH ROBINSON.

Joint Note.

$400.　　　　　　　　　　　　　　CHICAGO, July 12, 1885.

Four months after date, we promise to pay John Smith, or order, Four Hundred Dollars, value received.　　　　JAMES BROWN,
　　　　　　　　　　　　　　　　　　　　　　　　　　　THOMAS JONES.

Joint and Several Note.

$200.　　　　　　　　　　　　　　CHICAGO, July 5, 1885.

Six months after date, we jointly and severally promise to pay George Robinson, or order, Two Hundred Dollars, value received.

　　　　　　　　　　　　　　　　　　　　　　　　GEORGE JONES,
　　　　　　　　　　　　　　　　　　　　　　　　THOMAS LEWIS.

MISCELLANEOUS DEPARTMENT.

Note Payable by Installments.

$400.   CHICAGO, June 6, 1885.

For value received, I promise to pay John Smith, or order, Four Hundred Dollars, in manner following: One Hundred Dollars, in two weeks from date, and Three Hundred Dollars in eight weeks, with interest on the several sums as they fall due.   GEORGE BROWN.

A Due Bill.

$50.   NEW YORK, Feb. 5, 1885.

Due James Robinson, Fifty Dollars, on demand, value received.
                                                                GEORGE JONES.

Order for Money.

MR. JAMES BROWN:

Please pay John Smith, or bearer, Twenty-five Dollars, on my account.   ROBERT SLOAN.

Order for Merchandise.

MR. JOHN HILL:

Please deliver to bearer, John Smith, such goods as he may desire at your store, to the amount of Twelve Dollars, and charge the same to my account.   THOMAS BROWN.

Sight Draft.

$200.   BOSTON, July 7, 1885.

At sight, pay to the order of Jones & Co., Two Hundred Dollars, value received, and charge the same to our account.

To JOHN BROWN, Baltimore, Md.   ROBINSON, BLACK & CO.

Time Draft.

$75.   CHICAGO, June 5, 1885.

Thirty days after date, pay to the order of Smith & Co., Seventy-five Dollars, value received, and charge to our account.

To GIBBS, JONES & CO., Memphis, Tenn.   J. S. SLOAN & CO.

The acceptance of a draft is effected by the drawer, if he consents to the payment, writing "Accepted," the date, and his name across the face of the draft.

Letter of Credit.

                                                        PHILADELPHIA, April 10, 1885.

GENTLEMEN: Let me introduce to your firm the bearer, Mr. John Smith. You will confer a favor by selling him such goods as he may select, to the amount of Six Hundred Dollars, and I will hold myself accountable for that sum in case of non-payment.   Truly Yours,

  To ROBINSON & CO., New York.   JAMES BROWN.

MISCELLANEOUS DEPARTMENT.   163

Receipt in Full.

CHICAGO, June 10, 1885.

Received of John Smith, Sixty Dollars, in full of all demands to date.

$60.   JAMES BROWN.

Receipt on Account.

BOSTON, March 6, 1885.

Received of John Smith, Fifteen Dollars, on account.

$15.   THOMAS MAY.

Receipt for a Note.

$200.   CINCINNATI, Oct. 6, 1885.

Received of John Smith, his note for Four Hundred Dollars, at six months, in full of account.   JAMES STEVENSON.

There are various other business and legal forms which might be given, but as they are printed, and may be purchased almost anywhere for a few cents, it is far more economical, especially as regards time, to buy them already printed than to copy them; all that is necessary is to fill up the blanks.

Business Laws in Daily Use.

A note dated ahead of its issue is void. It may be dated back at pleasure.

A note made on Sunday is void.

Contracts made on Sunday cannot be enforced.

A contract made with a lunatic is void.

A note obtained by fraud or from a person in a state of intoxication cannot be collected.

It is a fraud to conceal a fraud.

If a note is lost or stolen it does not release the maker; he must pay it if the consideration for which it was given and the amount can be proven.

Notes bear interest only when so stated, but by usage of trade they always bear interest from maturity.

The maker of an "accommodation" bill or note (one for which he had received no consideration), having lent his name or credit for the benefit of the holder, is not bound to the person accommodated, but is bound to all other parties precisely as if there was a good consideration.

A note or contract made by a minor is void in some States, and in others is voidable.

One may make a note payable to his own order, and indorse it in blank. He must write his name across the face or back of the note the same as any other indorser. This is transferable by delivery as if made payable to bearer.

After the death of a holder of a bill or note his executor or administrator may transfer it by his indorsement.

The husband who acquires a right to a bill or note which was given to the wife, either before or after marriage, may indorse it.

"Value received" is usually written in a note, but is not necessary. If not written it is presumed by the law or may be supplied by proof.

If the time of payment of a note is not inserted, it is held payable on demand.

The time of payment of a note must not depend upon a contingency. The promise must be absolute.

The payee should be distinctly named in the note, unless it is payable to bearer.

If two or more persons as partners are jointly liable on a note or bill, due notice to one of them is sufficient.

If a note or bill is transferred as security, or even as payment of a pre-existing debt, the debt revives if the note is dishonored.

If the letter containing a protest of non-payment be put into the post-office, any miscarriage does not affect the party giving notice.

Notes of protest may be sent either to the residence or to the place of business of the party notified.

The holder of a note may give notice of protest either to all the previous indorsers, which is the safer method, or only to one of them; in case of the latter, he must select the last indorser, and the last must give notice to the last before him, and so on. Each indorser must send notice the same day or day following. Neither Sunday nor legal holiday is to be reckoned in computing the time in which notice is to be given.

Joint indorsers of a note must both be notified unless they are partners, when notice to one is sufficient. But this does not hold where a notice is served on a partner living elsewhere while none is served on a partner residing in the town where the demand is made.

"Acceptance" applies to bills, and not to notes. It is an engagement on the part of the person on whom the bill is drawn to pay it according to its tenor. The usual way is to write across the face of the bill the word "Accepted," giving date of acceptance.

A bill may be written upon any paper or substitute for it, either with ink or pencil.

An indorsee has a right of action against all whose names were on the bill when he received it.

No consideration is sufficient in law if it be illegal in its nature.

Checks or drafts should be presented during business hours; but in this country, except in the case of banks, the time extends through the day and evening. They should be presented for payment without unreasonable delay.

MISCELLANEOUS DEPARTMENT

Principals are responsible for the acts of their agents.

Each individual in a partnership is responsible for the whole amount of the debts of the firm, except in cases of special partnership. The word "Limited" in connection with a firm name indicates that a limitation of responsibility for each member is fixed.

Ignorance of the law excuses no one.

The law compels no one to do impossibilities.

An agreement without consideration is void.

Signatures made with a lead pencil are good in law.

A receipt for money is not always conclusive.

The acts of one partner bind all the rest.

All claims which do not rest upon a seal or judgment must be sued within six years from the time when they arise.

Part payment of a debt which has passed the time of statutory limitation revives the whole debt, and the claim holds good for another period of six years from the date of such partial payment.

If when a debt is due the debtor is out of the State, the "six years" do not begin to run until he returns. If he afterward leave the State, the time forward counts the same as if he remained in the State.

An oral agreement must be proved by evidence. A written agreement proves itself. The law prefers written to oral evidence because of its precision.

INTEREST RULES AND TABLES.

INTEREST RULES.—For finding the interest on any principal for any number of days: The answer in each case being in cents, separate the two right-hand figures of answer to express in dollars and cents.

Four per cent.: Multiply the principal by the number of days to run; separate right-hand figure from the product, and divide by 9.

Five per cent.: Multiply by number of days and divide by 72.

Six per cent.: Multiply by number of days, separate right-hand figure, and divide by six.

Eight per cent.: Multiply by number of days and divide by 45.

Nine per cent.: Multiply by number of days, separate right-hand figure, and divide by 4.

Ten per cent.: Multiply by number of days and divide by 36.

Twelve per cent.: Multiply by number of days, separate right-hand figure, and divide by 3.

Fifteen per cent.: Multiply by number of days and divide by 24.

Eighteen per cent.: Multiply by number of days, separate right-hand figure, and divide by 2.

Twenty per cent.: Multiply by number of days and divide by 18.

Twenty-four per cent.: Multiply by number of days and divide by 15.

MISCELLANEOUS DEPARTMENT.

SOME SAFE PRESCRIPTIONS.

The few prescriptions that are here subjoined are either for the treatment of such light complaints as may be treated without medical advice, or else they are such as may be safely applied to relieve suffering while waiting for the doctor to come. But few are given, because there are few ailments which should be treated at home without the direct advice of a physician. To attempt much "home doctoring" without proper medical advice is always dangerous, and sometimes leads to the most disastrous results; at the last moment perhaps, a doctor is summoned, but only to find the patient dying from want of proper treatment. Unless a person is a skilled practitioner, it is very easy to mistake the symptoms of a disease, and to give wrong remedies under the delusion that the patient is suffering from some other complaint than the one which really afflicts him. Therefore books which pretend to entirely supplant doctors should never be relied upon. The prescriptions that follow are entirely safe, and may be relied upon. It must be remembered, however, that should any ailment show signs of becoming worse, it may be but a symptom of something more serious to follow, and a physician should be called in. The doses that are given are adult doses.

A good general rule for the determination of the dose for younger persons is this: To the age of the patient add 12, and divide the same by the age for the denominator of the fraction whose numerator is 1. Thus, for an infant two years old the formula will be $\frac{2 \times 12}{2} = \frac{1}{7}$, one-seventh of the adult dose.

Cramps.—A couple of teaspoonfuls of paregoric is a good remedy for any form of cramps. Cramps in the legs and arms may be relieved by cold applications.

Cholera Morbus.—Thirty drops of laudanum or two or three teaspoonfuls of paregoric. Apply a mustard plaster to the stomach or cloth wrung out of hot water and turpentine.

Colic.—Paregoric, one teaspoonful; tincture of cardamon seeds, two teaspoonfuls; tincture of ginger, one-fourth to one-half teaspoonful. Mix in a quarter of a tumblerful of hot water and take at one dose. Apply a mustard plaster to the stomach.

Convulsions.—Twenty-five or thirty grains of bromide of potassium to half a tumblerful of water. The patient should be placed upon his back. The room in which he is kept must be perfectly still, and it is better to have it darkened.

Delirium.—In any case of sudden delirium bromide of potassium in the above quantity is a good remedy.

MISCELLANEOUS DEPARTMENT.   167

Diarrhœa.—One teaspoonful of tincture of kino; one to two table-spoonfuls of blackberry brandy. Mix and repeat three or four times a day. Should this fail to check the attack within a couple of days, a physician should be sent for.

Hemorrhage.—Place the patient in a recumbent position; keep him free from all excitement; endeavor to reassure him; do not allow him to drink either hot or cold drinks nor any stimulants. Give from twenty to thirty drops of laudanum. Lay strips of hot flannel along each side of the spinal column. Keep the patient as quiet as possible until the arrival of the physician.

Hysterics.—Give a teaspoonful of ammoniated tincture of valerian in a little water. Place the patient in a recumbent position.

Mania.—Maniacal Outbreak.—Dissolve half a drachm of bromide of potassium in half a tumblerful of water; administer in one dose. Place a mustard plaster behind the neck.

Nosebleed.—Hold the breath as long as possible. Apply ice to the nape of the neck. Snuff up powdered tannic acid.

Pleuritic Pains—Apply dry heat, as a hot plate, to the painful side, and give a dose of laudanum (thirty drops). Should this fail to abate the pains, send for a physician.

Pain.—For general pains the safest remedy is a teaspoonful of paregoric.

Seat or Pin-Worms.—Wash out the bowels with a pint of cold water by means of a syringe, and inject so an tea of quassia, two ounces of quassia to a pint of water.

Ordinary Sore Throat.—Tincture of chlorate of iron, two-thirds of an ounce; chlorate of potash, half an ounce; water, one pint. Gargle the throat with some of this mixture every two hours. Take ten grains bromide of potassium every three or four hours. Should these means fail to improve the throat, send for a physician.

Spongy and Bleeding Gums.—Wash the gums with weak alum water, about a quarter of a teaspoonful of alum to a tumblerful of water, or with about twenty drops of tincture of myrrh to a half tumblerful of water.

Toothache.—Rub in a mortar ten grains each of chloral and camphor until liquefied; soak a cotton pledget in the liquid and apply it to the tooth; or a drop or two of pure carbolic acid upon the cotton pledget and insert in cavity of tooth.

Vomiting.—If not immediately after meals twenty grains of subnitrate of bismuth. If the vomiting occurs immediately after meals, the attack had better take its course, aided by draughts of warm water.

Sunstroke.—The following is summarized from the last annual circular of the New York Board of Health; under "Prevention" it gives excellent advice for the mode of taking care of one's self during hot spells of weather.

PREVENTION.—Don't lose your sleep; sleep in a cool place; don't worry; don't get excited; don't drink too much alcohol; avoid working in the sun if you can; if indoors, work in a well-ventilated room; wear thin clothes; wear a light hat, not black; put a large green leaf or wet cloth in it; drink water freely and sweat freely; if fatigued or dizzy, knock off work, lie down in a cool place, and apply cold water and cold cloths to your head and neck.

CURE.—Put the patient in the shade; loosen his clothes about the neck; send for the nearest doctor; give the patient cool drinks of water or black tea or black coffee if he can swallow. If his skin is hot and dry prop him up, sitting, against a tree or wall; pour cold water over the body and limbs and put on his head pounded ice wrapped in a cloth or towel. If you can't get ice, use a wet cloth and keep freshening it. But if the patient if pale and faint and his pulse is feeble, lay him on his back, make him smell hartshorn for a few seconds, or give him a teaspoonful of aromatic spirits of ammonia or tincture of ginger in two tablespoonfuls of water. In this case use no cold water, but rub the hands and feet and warm them by hot applications until the circulation is restored.

INVALID DISHES.

These dishes will be relished by sick people, and are often ordered for them.

Chicken Broth. Cut up a small chicken into joints and place it on the fire with a quart of cold water, a teaspoonful of salt, and a sprig or two of parsley. Let the water come to a boil, and then allow it to simmer for fully an hour; strain it through a sieve and it is ready.

The broth may be thickened, if desired, with a little flour. Take out a spoonful or two of the liquid to heat up with the flour, then add it to the broth. As a rule, dishes for invalids should not be highly seasoned; the pure juice of the meat is the great thing to secure.

Mutton Broth. Boil slowly a couple of pounds of lean mutton for two hours; skim it very carefully as it simmers, and add very little salt. If the doctor permits, some vegetable as seasoning may be added, and for some broths a little rice or fine barley is added.

Arrowroot Jelly.—Half a pint of water, to which add one glass of sherry or ginger wine, a little grated nutmeg and fine sugar; put this into a stew-pan, but only let it come to the boil; then mix into it two or three teaspoonfuls of arrowroot, previously broken into pulp in a little cold water, after which boil the whole for a moment or two.

Tapioca Jelly.—Wash the tapioca carefully in two or three waters, then soak it for five or six hours; simmer it then in a stew-pan until it becomes quite clear; add a little lemon juice or wine if required.

Gruel.—If the gruel is preferred to be thick, make it with two tablespoonfuls of oatmeal—if thin, with one spoonful; mix the meal in a basin with a little cold water. Have ready in a stew-pan a pint of boiling water or milk; pour this by degrees into the mixed oatmeal; return it into the stew-pan; set it on the fire; let it boil for five minutes, stirring it all the time; skim and strain it through a hair sieve. It may be seasoned to taste, and wine or brandy added if desired.

Toast Water.—Toast carefully a few crusts of bread (see that they do not burn), and pour over them a pint and a half of boiling water. Let the jug be covered up and stand till the water has become cold; then strain the liquor off, and squeeze into it a few drops of lemon juice.

Barley Water.—Wash a teacupful of pear barley, put it on the fire with two quarts of boiling water, and let it boil down to half the quantity.

Lemonade for Invalids.—Pare the lemons thinly, any number may be used, say a dozen for six pints; and then rub them over with pieces of lump sugar to extract the remaining yellow portions. Lay the sugar after it is used and a pound or so more in a basin with the parings of six of the lemons, and squeeze the juice of the whole dozen into the basin. Add the water—say six pints—pretty nearly boiling, and mix the lot pretty well together; strain carefully, and then pass through a jelly-bag. When cold put it into bottles for use.

Orangeade is made in the same way as above, substituting oranges for lemons.

USEFUL HOUSEHOLD HINTS.

To Dust Carpets and Floors.—Sprinkle tea-leaves on them, then sweep carefully. The former should not be swept frequently with a whisk-brush, as it wears them fast; only once a week, and at other times with the leaves and a hair-brush. Fine carpets should be gently done with a hair hand-brush, such as is used for clothes, on the knees.

To Clean Carpets.—Take up the carpet, let it be well beaten, then laid down, and brush on both sides with a hand-brush; turn it the right side upward, and scour it with oxgall and soap and water very clean, and dry it with linen cloths. Then lay it on grass or hang it up to dry.

Ink spilled on a carpet or woollen article should be attended to at once while still wet, if possible, and then is very easily removed. Take clean blotting paper or cotton batting and gently sop up all the ink that has not soaked in. Then pour a little sweet milk on the spot, and soak it up from the carpet with fresh cotton batting. It will need to be renewed two or three times, fresh milk and cotton being used each time, and the spot will disappear. Then wash the spot with clean soapsuds and rub dry with a clean cloth. If the ink has been allowed to dry in the milk must remain longer and be repeated many times.

To Clean Paper Hangings.—Take small pieces of stale bread, about two days old; commence at the top of the room, and with the crust wipe lightly downward about half a yard at each stroke, till the upper part of the hangings is completely cleaned all around, and so continue until the whole is gone over. This operation, if carefully performed, will frequently make old paper look about equal to new. Great caution must be used not to rub the paper hard nor to attempt cleaning it the cross or horizontal way. The dirty part of the bread must each time be cut away, and the pieces renewed as often as at all necessary.

To Extract Grease from Papered Walls.—Dip a piece of flannel in spirits of wine, rub the greasy spots gently once or twice, and the grease will disappear.

To Clean Mirrors, Looking glasses, etc.—Take a soft sponge, wash it well in clean water, and squeeze it as dry as possible; dip it into some spirits of wine and rub over the glass; then have some powder blue tied up in a rag, dust it over your glass, and rub it lightly and quickly with a soft cloth; afterward finish with a silk handkerchief.

To Take Stains Out of Marble.—Mix unslaked lime in finest powder with the strongest soaplye, pretty thick, and instantly with a painter's brush lay it on the whole of the marble. In two months' time wash it off perfectly clean, then have ready a fine thick lather of soft soap, boiled in soft water; dip a brush in it and scour the marble. This will, with very good rubbing, give a beautiful polish.

To Take Ironstains Out of Marble.—An equal quantity of fresh spirit of vitrol and lemon juice being mixed in a bottle, shake it well; wet the spots and in a few minutes rub with soft linen till they disappear.

Grease on a carpet, if not of long standing, can be readily disposed of by washing the spot with hot soapsuds and borax—half an ounce of borax to a gallon of water. Use a clean cloth to wash it with, rinse in warm water, and wipe dry.

To Clean and Brighten Brussels Carpets.—Take a fresh beef-gall, break it into a clean pan; pour one half into a very clean bucket, and nearly fill it with lukewarm water; take a clean, coarse cloth, and having, brushed the carpet well, rub it hard with the cloth thoroughly wet with gall-water; do a small piece at a time; have ready a dry coarse cloth, and rub the carpet dry; so proceed until the whole carpet is clean. A few drops of carbonate of ammonia, in a small quantity of warm rain water, will change, if carefully applied, discolored spots upon carpets, and indeed all spots, whether produced by acids or alkalies. If one has the misfortune to have a carpet injured by whitewash, this will immediately restore.

Marble can be nicely cleaned in the following manner: Pulverize a little bluestone and mix with four ounces of whiting; add to these four ounces of soft soap and one ounce of soda, dissolved in a very little water. Boil this preparation over a slow fire fifteen minutes, stirring all the time. Lay it on the marble while hot with a clean brush. Let it remain half an hour; then wash off in clean suds, wipe dry, and polish by quick rubbing. If marble is smoked or soiled, either by bituminous coal or too free use of kindling wood, Spanish whiting with a piece of washing soda, rubbed together and wet with only enough water to moisten and make them into a paste, will remove the grease and smoke. Dip a piece of flannel in this preparation and rub the spots while the paste is quite moist. Leave the paste on for hours, and, if need be, remove it and renew with fresh paste. When the spots disappear wash the place with clean hot soapsuds, wipe dry, and polish with chamois-skin.

To Clean Silver.—Silver door and bell plates are most expeditiously cleaned with a weak solution of ammonia and water, say one teaspoonful of ammonia to one teacup of water, applied with a wet rag; it is equally useful in cleaning other silver plate and gold jewelry.

Oil Marks on wall paper, or the marks where inconsiderate people rest their heads, are a sore grief to good housekeepers, but they can be removed without much trouble. Take pipe clay or fuller's earth and make it into a paste about as thick as rich cream with cold water; lay it on the stain gently, without rubbing it in; leave it on all night. It will be dry by morning, when it can be brushed off, and unless an old stain the grease spots will have disappeared. If old, renew the application.

To Remove Mould from Fabrics.—Rub them over with butter, and then apply potash moistened in a little water, and rub the spot until all traces of it disappear; then wash in plenty of water to take out the potash; or the mouldy spot may be wetted with yellow sulphide of ammonia, by which it will be immediately blackened. After a couple of minutes wash it off, and remove the black stain with cold weak chlorohydric acid; then wash well with warmish water.

To Clean Silverware.—Cut some lemons into thick slices, and rub the articles briskly with them; then put the silverware in a pan with the slices of lemons, allowing them to stand for two or three hours. After that rinse them in clear water, and then stir them about in a pan of very hot soapsuds. Then rinse them in hot water, dry them, and rub with chamois-skin.

Or, take an ounce each of cream of tartar, muriate of soda, and alum, and boil in a gallon of water for ten minutes. Then put in the pieces of plate and boil them for ten minutes. Wipe them slightly with a soft linen towel, and rub them dry with chamois-skin. Powdered magnesia is also a good polish for silver.

To Remove Rust from Knives, Forks, Razors, Etc.—Cover with sweet oil, well rubbed on, and let it remain for forty-eight hours; then rub with unslaked lime, powdered very fine, until the rust disappears.

To Prevent Rust on Iron or Steel.—Take one pint of fat-oil varnish, mixed with five pints of highly rectified spirits of turpentine, and rub with a sponge. This varnish may be applied to bright stoves, and even to mathematical instruments, without hurting their delicate polish, and they will never contract any spots of rust.

Stains.—Medicine stains may be removed from silver spoons by rubbing them with a rag dipped in sulphuric acid and washing it off with soapsuds. Stains may be removed from the hands by washing them in a small quantity of oil of vitriol and cold water without soap.

To Clean Paint.—Smear it over with whiting mixed to the consistency of common paste in warm water. Rub the surface to be cleaned briskly, and wash off with pure cold water. Grease spots will in this way be almost instantly removed, as well as other filth, and the paint will retain its brilliancy and beauty unimpaired.

To Scare Woollen Furs, Etc., from Moths.—Carefully shake and brush woollens early in the spring, so as to be certain that no moth eggs are in them; then sew them up in cotton or linen wrappers through which the moths cannot eat, putting a piece of gum camphor, tied up in a bit of muslin, into each bundle or into the chests and closets where the articles are to be. Furs should not be hung out in the sun in the spring before putting away for the season. The moth-miller will be likely to visit them when thus exposed. They should be put in a close box with a piece of camphor, and the box tied up in a pillow-case or bag. Persian insect powder will also keep the moth flies away.

To Take Out Mildew.—Mix soft soap with starch powdered, half as much salt and the juice of a lemon; lay it on the part on both sides with a painter's brush. Let it lie on the grass day and night till the stain comes out.

To Take Grease Out of Silks or Stuffs.—Take a lump of magnesia and rub it wet over the spot; let it dry; then brush the powder off, and the spot will disappear. Take a visiting or other card; separate it, and rub the spot with the soft internal part, and it will disappear without taking the gloss off the silk.

To Take Stains Out of Linens.

Stains Caused by Acids.—Wet the part and lay on it some salt of wormwood; then rub it, without diluting it with more water; or, let the cloth imbibe a little water without dipping, and hold the part over a lighted match at a due distance; the spots will be removed by the sulphurous gas; or tie up in the stained part some pearlash; then scrape some soap into cold soft water to make a lather, and boil the linen till stain disappears.

Stains of Wine, Fruits, etc., After They Have Been Long in the Linen.—Rub the part on each side with yellow soap; then lay on a mixture of starch in cold water very thick; rub it well in and expose the linen to the sun and air till the stain comes out. If not removed in three or four days, rub that off and renew the process. When dry it may be sprinkled with a little water.

Many other stains may be taken out by dipping the linen in sour buttermilk and drying it in a hot sun. Then wash it in cold water and dry it two or three times a day.

To Remove Grease from Clothing.—Take and mix equal parts of ether, ammonia and alcohol, and rub into the grease spot, and allow it to evaporate, the garment having been well shaken and brushed before the liquid is applied with a sponge.

How to Take Ink Out of Boards.—Strong muriatic acid or spirits of salts, applied with a piece of cloth; afterward well washed with water.

Painting and Papering are best done in cold weather, especially the former, for the wood absorbs the oil of paint much more in warm weather, while in cold weather the oil hardens on the outside, making a coat which will protect the wood instead of soaking into it.

Mucilage.—An excellent mucilage may be made by taking one ounce of gum tragacanth, as much corrosive sublimate as will lay on a silver five-cent piece; put in a jar and pour over it one quart of cold soft water; let it stand twenty-four hours, then stir and it is ready for use, and will keep a long time.

To Clean and Tighten Cane-seat Chairs.—Turn up the chair bottom and with hot water and a sponge wash the cane work so that it may be thoroughly soaked. Should it be dirty use a little soap. Let it dry in the air, and it will be as tight and firm as when new, provided the cane be not broken.

Wall Paper.—Paper can be made to stick on whitewashed walls by dissolving glue in good strong vinegar and washing them with the solution. Heat till the glue is dissolved and then apply with a brush.

Cleansing Picture Frames.—Black walnut frames will become dull and rusty looking. They may be renewed by first brushing thoroughly with a stiff brush to remove dust, and then applying pure linseed oil with a proper brush; in the absence of a brush a piece of new bleached muslin will answer the purpose.

To Prevent a Lamp from Smoking, soak the wick in vinegar and dry it well before you use it.

Lamp Chimneys can be prevented from cracking, when exposed to the burning flame, by first placing them in a vessel of cold water and bringing this to a boil over the fire, then removing the vessel and allowing it to cool before taking out the cylinder.

To Remove Glass Stoppers.—When the stopper of a glass decanter is too tight, a cloth wet with hot water and applied to the neck will cause the glass to expand and the stopper may be removed. In a phial the warmth of the finger may be sufficient.

To Get Rid of Ants.—Wash your shelves down clean, and while damp rub fine salt on them quite thick, and let it remain on them for a time, and red ants will disappear.

To Clean Straw Matting.—Wash as seldom as possible, but when it is necessary to do so use salt and water. Salt prevents the matting from turning yellow. Dry as fast as you wash, and wash but a little at a time.

To Clean Stair Rods.—Mix finely powdered rottenstone and sweet oil to a paste, then rub it on each rod with a piece of flannel or woollen. Polish with the dry powder of the rottenstone and a nice leather.

To Clean the Insides of Pots, Pans and Kettles.—Boil in the pot or kettle a little sal-ammoniac for the space of one hour. Be sure to wash out a dirty sauce-pan with boiling water just after using.

COOKERY.

French Bread and French Rolls.—Mix the yolks of twelve eggs and the whites of eight, beaten and strained, a peck of fine flour and a quart of good yeast (but not bitter), with as much warm milk as will make the whole into a thin, light dough; stir it well, but do not knead it. Put the dough into dishes and set it to rise; then turn it into a quick oven; when done rasp the loaves.

French rolls are made by rubbing into every pound of flour an ounce of butter, one egg beaten, a little yeast, and sufficient milk to make a dough moderately stiff; beat it up, but do not knead it. Let it rise, and bake in rolls on tins; when baked, rasp them.

Fine Rolls. - Warm a bit of butter in half a pint of milk; add to it two spoonfuls of small beer yeast and some salt; with these ingredients mix two pounds of flour; let it rise an hour and knead it well; form the rolls and bake them in a quick oven for twenty minutes.

Tea Cakes.---These are prepared the same as bread, substituting for the water warm milk, with a little butter melted in it and sugar; let it rise; knead it into thin cakes, which bake on an iron plate over the fire.

Muffins.---Mix in rather more than a pint of milk a little less than a gill of yeast, into which stir flour to make a thickish batter. Let this stand for some time before the fire, after which add a sufficiency of flour, into which a good sized piece of butter has been rubbed, to make the dough, adding more milk if necessary. Then set the dough before the fire for, say, half an hour, covering it with a napkin. Roll out the dough and cut out the muffins with a shape---the lid of a small pan will do, and cook gently.

Cakes and Cookies.

Pound Cake.---Take of flour, butter and powdered sugar, each one pound, eight yolks and four whites of eggs, and a few caraway seeds; first beat up the butter to a cream, keep beating it one way, then gradually beat in the eggs, sugar and flour. Bake it in a warm oven for an hour and a quarter. Cover the sides and bottom of the tin with buttered paper.

Frosting.---A very little cream of tartar in the frosting for a cake will hasten the hardening process. If the knife is often dipped into water while spreading the frosting, it will give a gloss or polish greatly to be desired.

Cream Cake. --Beat three ounces of butter to a cream, and mix with it very smoothly a half pound of potato flour, a teaspoonful of baking powder, two tablespoonfuls of sugar, pinch of salt, the rind of a lemon, (which has been well rolled to soften), sliced very thinly, and a teacupful of clotted cream. If a little sour, it improves rather than injures the flavor. This should make a light batter. Place it into a well-oiled dish and bake until brown.

Queen Cake.---Queen cake is made of eight eggs, a quarter of a pound of almonds, a pound of butter, a pound of sugar, half a pound of currants, and a pound of flour. Beat the whites of the eggs in a cool place for half an hour. Work the butter to a cream, add slowly and gradually the sugar, and mix all. Beat three yolks with a few drops of saffron-water and put them into the butter; beat all together and then add the currants, flour, spice, etc. Sprinkle all with sugar and place in a shallow tin and bake.

Cocoanut Cake.—Four cupfuls of flour, two cups of sugar, one cupful of milk, five eggs, one cupful of butter, one teaspoonful of soda, two of cream-tartar, one half of the cocoanut put in the cake, the other half put with the whites of three eggs and one half cupful of sugar, and put between the layers of cake. Bake in jelly-pans.

Orange-Ice Cake.—Ten eggs, one pound of sugar, a half pound of flour, one large orange. Beat whites and yolks separately; add to all the yolks and the whites of seven eggs the sugar, the grated rind of the orange, and the juice. Bake as for jelly cake. To the whites of three eggs allow a pound and a quarter of powdered sugar, beaten stiff as for icing; take out enough to cover the top and set aside; add to the rest half the grated rind of a large orange. When the cake is nearly cold spread this between the layers. Beat into the icing reserved for the top a little lemon-juice, and, if needed, more sugar. It should be stiffer than that spread between the cakes.

Marble Cake.—For white part: One cup of butter, three cups of sugar, five cups of flour, a half cup of milk, a half teaspoonful of soda, whites of eight eggs; flavor with lemon. Dark part: A half cup of butter, two cups of brown sugar, one cup of molasses, one cup of sour milk, four cups of flour, one teaspoonful of soda, yolks of eight eggs, one whole egg, spices of all kinds. Put in a pan, first a layer of dark, then a layer of light, and finish with a dark layer.

Snow Cake.—Three-fourths of a cup of butter, two cups of sugar, one cup of milk, one cup of corn starch, two cups flour, one and a half teaspoonfuls of baking-powder; mix corn starch, flour, and baking-powder together; add the butter and sugar alternately with the milk; lastly add the whites of seven eggs; flavor to taste.

Strawberry Shortcake.—One quart of flour sifted dry, with two large teaspoonfuls of baking-powder, one tablespoonful of sugar, and a little salt. Add three tablespoonfuls of butter, and sweet milk enough to form a soft dough. Bake in a quick oven, and when partially cooled split open, spread with butter, and cover with a layer of strawberries well sprinkled with sugar; lay the other half on top and spread in the same manner.

Pocket Cakes.—"Children's pocket cakes" may be made of one pint of flour mixed with the yolk of one egg; sweeten with a cup of soft brown sugar flavor with any favorite seasoning—mace, nutmeg, or cinnamon. Roll out quite thin and cut in fancy shapes. Bake quickly.

Cookies.—One cupful New Orleans molasses, half a cupful of water, half a cupful of shortening (this may be of butter or lard or of nice beef dripping), one teaspoonful each of ginger, cinnamon, and soda. Do not use enough flour to make a hard dough, but have it as soft as you can and yet have the cookies smooth.

Cream Cookies are made of one cupful of sour cream, one cupful of butter, two cupfuls of sugar, two eggs, one teaspoonful of soda, flour enough to make a dough of medium body, neither as soft as possible to roll nor as hard. These may be rolled thin, and will be light and rich. Bake in a quick oven.

Oatmeal Cookies combine many good qualities, and will be relished by children. Make them just like an ordinary sugar cooky, using two-thirds oatmeal and one-third wheat flour.

No-Egg Cookies.—One cup of butter, one of milk, two of sugar, half a teaspoonful of bicarbonate of soda, half a teaspoonful of cinnamon or nutmeg, with flour enough to roll.

Cocoanut Jumbles.—Very nice little cakes are made of two cups of sugar, one cup of butter, two eggs, and a large cup of grated cocoanut, mixed with enough flour to make a dough that can be rolled. Use fancy cutters of various shapes, and bake in a very hot oven.

Soft Gingerbread.—Excellent soft gingerbread is made of one cup of sugar, one cup of butter, one cup of sour cream, one cup of New Orleans molasses, four cups of sifted flour one tablespoonful of ginger three well-beaten eggs, the rind grated of one lemon. Raisins may be added if you please.

A Good Cheap Cake.—A pound and a half of flour, a quarter of a pound of butter, three-quarters of a pound of raisins, a quarter of a pound of of sugar, one eggs, a teaspoonful of carbonate of soda, and half a pint of milk—The milk to be made warm and the soda dissolved in it. Mix all well together, and bake in a slow oven.

Seed Cakes.—Take one pound of eggs (8 generally makes a pound), one pound of crushed lump-sugar, and one pound of flour; mix well together for half an hour or more, and add caraway seeds. Have a dish well greased—any shape that may be required; put the mixture in and bake in a moderate oven.

Family Cake.—Take two pounds of flour, half a pound of currants, half a pound of butter or lard, a quarter of a pound of sugar, four scruples of tartaric acid (half an ounce will be sufficient for three cakes), a quarter of an ounce of carbonate of soda, three eggs, a little lemon peel (or 20 drops of essence of lemon, ginger and nutmeg. Mix with half a pint of milk.

To Ice Cake.—Take about a pound and a half of double-refined sugar, beat it in a morter and sift it through a lawn sieve; when the whole is sifted through mix with it, in a very clean pan, the whites of four large or five small eggs, and stir well for half an hour with a wooden spoon adding by a little at a time, the juice of a lemon. When done, smooth it over the top and the sides of the cakes, and dry them before the fire or at the mouth of an oven.

Ginger Cakes.—Break three eggs into a basin; beat them well, and add half a pint of cream, which must also be well beaten with them, and the whole put into a sauce-pan over the fire, to be stirred till it gets warm. Then add a pound of butter, with half a pound of loaf-sugar and two ounces and a half of ginger, both powdered, carefully stirring the different ingredients together over a very moderate fire, sufficient to melt all the butter. This being done, pour it into two pounds of wheatened flour (fine), and make it into a good paste. Roll it out, without any flour beneath on the dresser, of whatever thickness may be thought proper.

Common Sponge Cake.—Take half a dozen eggs and as much powdered and sifted loaf-sugar as the eggs will weigh, and twice their weight of best flour. Beat up the yolks and whites of the eggs seperately; then add the sugar to the yolks (mixing of course), then stir in the flour, and quickly add the whites, well whisked. Beat the whole up thoroughly and smartly, and bake briskly in one or several tins lined with well-buttered paper. See that your eggs are fresh. The sponge dough may of course be enriched with a little cream, and more sugar may be used, and eggs in proportion. Brush the top of the cake with white of egg and dust with sugar.

Tea Cake.—Take, say, two pounds of flour or as much as you need, which rub lightly into half a pound of butter; add caraway seed, a little allspice, and half a pound of sifted sugar. Mix with the flour, and make the whole into a light dough with a pint of milk to which has been added an eggcupful of yeast. Place the whole in a tin, buttered or papered and then let it stand before the fire for twenty minutes to rise. Bake for about two hours.

Plum Cake.—Taking the above as a basis, make it as large and rich as you like, adding currants, raisins, and a little syrup and preserved lemon-peel and a pinch of powdered ginger. All kinds of fancy cakes can be made from the above as a foundation.

PASTRY AND PIES.

The quality of pie-crust depends much on the baking. If the oven be too hot, the paste, besides being burned, will fall; if too slack, it will be soddened, and consequently heavy.

Paste should be made on a cold, smooth substance, such as marble or slate, with a light, cool hand. It should be made quickly; much handling makes it heavy. Great nicety is required in wetting the paste, too little moisture rendering it dry and crumbly, while too much makes it tough and heavy; and in either case the paste cannot be easily worked. Practice alone can produce perfection in this art.

Before commencing to make paste for pies or puddings it is necessary to place near at hand everything likely to be wanted, to inspect all the utensils, to prepare all the ingredients, and, though last, not least, to wash the hands and nails perfectly clean, for the hands are the best tools to make paste with.

Always use good sweet butter or lard for pie or pudding crust. Some persons entertain the mistaken notion that butter which cannot be eaten on bread will do very well for paste; on the contrary, the baking or boiling of rancid fat increases the bad flavor. It is a good plan to wash the butter in clean spring water before using it. Make two or three holes with a fork in the cover of your pies, that the steam may escape.

Puff Paste.—Rub a quarter of a pound of butter into half a quarter of flour very fine; make it up into a light paste, using as little cold water as you can work it up with; then roll it out about a quarter of an inch thick, put a layer of butter all over, sprinkle on a little flour, double it up and roll it out again; double and roll it out thus four or five times, using another half pound of butter; then it will be fit for any pies or tarts that require puff paste.

A very good and more economical crust for pies may be made in the following fashion: Take two cups of flour, one of lard, one of water, two teaspoonfuls of salt. Have your flour in your pastry-bowl; chop in the lard, drip in the water, using the end of your knife deftly, so as to combine the flour and water into flakes, not dough. Turn the mixture out upon a pie-board; press it gently with your rolling-pin, turning it over and over until it forms a roll; cut this across as you wish to use it. Should you prefer, you can use part butter, part lard.

Apple Pie.—Make a puff-paste crust or one such as is given in the receipt just above; lay some round the sides of the dish; pare and quarter the apples and take out the core; lay a row of apples thick at the bottom of the dish, with half the sugar you intend for the pie, a little minced lemon-peel, a little of the juice, and two or three cloves or a little cinnamon; then the rest of the apples and sugar; squeeze in a little more lemon-juice, and have ready the peels and cores of the apples boiled in some sugar in very little water and strained; pour the liquor into the pie and put on the upper crust. It should be baked very pale. Put no cap in the dish when you make apple pie. The flavor of a quince will greatly improve it.

Apple Pie (excellent).—Use Rhode Island Greenings; peel, core and quarter them. Fill the pie-dish with alternate layers of apple, sugar, a few very small bits of butter, and grated nutmeg. Round the edge of the dish lay an edge of pastry, and over the whole put a cover of good, flaky pie paste. Some cooks put in water but this spoils it. Press the edges, so that no juice will escape, and bake a light brown; eat the same day it is baked. Peach pies are something to dream of when peaches are fresh and can be put in whole, thickly covered with sugar and baked quickly, with an upper crust only. No spice is needed. The stones, in which the pits are enshrined, flavor them sufficiently, provided the peaches are the rich yellow-fleshed variety as they should be.

Open Tarts.—Line your dishes with thin, light paste, fill in with preserved fruits or jam, and lay strips of paste across in squares or diamonds. A short time will bake them.

Mince Pies.—Take equal weights of tender roast beef, suet, currants, raisins, and apples which have been previously pared and cored, with half their weight of soft sugar, one ounce of powdered cinnamon, an equal quantity of candied orange and lemon peel and citron, a little salt, and twelve bitter almonds blanched and grated. Chop the meat and the suet separately; wash and pick the currants; stone the raisins, and chop them with the peel; and having minced all the ingredients very fine mix them together, adding nutmeg grated and the juice of a lemon. A glass or two of wine or spirit greatly improves it. Line your dish or pattypans with puff paste; fill with the mince, cover, and pinch the edges together. Bake for half an hour. Many persons makes the mince without the meat.

Lemon Pie.—Moisten a heaping tablespoonful of corn starch with a little cold water, and add a cupful of boiling water; stir the mixture and allow it to boil. Add a cupful of sugar and a teaspoonful of butter; remove from the fire, and when slightly cooled add a well beaten egg and the juice and grated rind of one lemon.

Pumpkin Pie.—Pare a small pumpkin and take out the seeds. Stew it rather dry and strain through a colander; add three eggs, two quarts of milk, and three tablespoonfuls of molasses; sweeten with sugar to taste; season with two tablespoonfuls of ground cinnamon, one of ginger and two of salt.

PART III.

Consisting of History and Description of Washington, Hackettstown, Belvidere, Phillipsburg and each of the Townships in Warren County, together with names of the residents, occupation and post-office.

Hon. JOHNSTON CORNISH,

MAYOR OF WASHINGTON AND JUN. MEMBER OF THE

CORNISH ORGAN & PIANO COMPANY.

"It is a charming city of which he is the chief executive officer. But everybody is acquainted with Washington, so no more need be said. Mayor Cornish was born in Hunterdon County, in the year 1858, where his father and grandfather were engaged extensively in mercantile business. He was sent to the Easton Business College, where he graduated with high honors. He has been a resident in Washington for 15 years, and for 6 years has been the partner with his father ex-Senator Cornish in the Organ and Piano manufacturing business in that city. As a business man he is active, energetic and prompt, always being found at his office from early morn until late at night. In the Spring of 1884, when not 26 years of age, he was elected Mayor of the city by 22 majority after a most exciting contest, and so popular and satisfactory was his administration of the office that at the next election he was re-chosen without opposition — the first time that such an honor has been conferred on one of its citizens since the city was incorporated. He is a conspicuous also, a member of the De Molay Commandery, Knights Templar; a believer in and advocate of Odd Fellowship; a Past Dictator of the Knights and Ladies of the Golden Star; a member of the American Legion of Honor, and of the Red Men Order." Editorial from the New York World.

WASHINGTON.

THE History of Washington might begin with a period long before the Palefaces came thither, could we place implicit reliance upon Indian traditions. These give us an account of fierce struggles that took place for supremacy, as three tribes, one after the other held the territory hereabouts. These traditions of warfare are attested by the many arrow-heads and spear-points found in our soil; yet we will content ourselves with a more recent date for a beginning. Passing over the time when this spot of earth was under the sway of the proprietors of one of the Jerseys — past the time when the two Jerseys were merged in one colony, ruled over by the Governor of New York, we begin at 1694 when a colony with a Governor of its own appointed by the Mother Country an act was passed by the English Parliament confirming the boundaries of the eight counties into whic.. New Jersey was then divided. This then was a part of Burlington County, but in 1714 the new County of Hunterdon was carved out of Burlington for the convenience of the early settlers who found the County Seat too far off to be readily accessible. From Hunterdon county, in 1738, Morris county was set apart, and again in 1753 Sussex county, and finally in 1824 Warren county was made from a portion of Sussex. This was a part of Mansfield township until 1849, when the town of Washington was set aside, and that again divided in 1868, when a mile square was made into the Borough of Washington.

Port Colden was chosen as the site for a city, but the fates ruled otherwise, and it is now content to be a pretty suburb of its lucky sister. It will be from gross neglect of its opportunities if Washington does not grow into a city of many thousands. The beauty of its location, the healthful climate, the rich surrounding country, the facilities for transportation, all make it likely that it has a future. But the historian must not stop his work to prophesy.

The first we hear of white folks at this place was a cry for preaching, and to this day it is a church-going people that live here. 1740 an application was made to Presbytery "for supplies of preaching in Mr. Barber's neighborhood, Muscanockunk," in response to which appeal the Presbytery erected a log building on the hill, by what is now known as the old cemetery; this being at first called "the Barber Neighborhood Church," the first pastor being an Irishman named McCrea. He had no parsonage here, his home being on the saddle, whence he could overlook the various charges committed to him in the wilderness we now know as the garden section of New Jersey. His sister was murdered by Indians at the Fort Edward massacre, New York State, during the Revolutionary war. His successor was an Irishman, as also was the third pastor, Rev. John Rosburgh, who left his charge to join the Revolutionary army as chaplain, to meet his death at the battle Assunpink, a few days after the battle of Trenton.

At a date unknown the church was re-christened, being known thereafter as the "Mansfield wood-house church"; a name it retained even after the erection of a stone edifice upon the same site. Upon the church records, 1799, is entered a rule that each pew-holder should furnish a bushel of wheat per annum to the man who cared for the building and built fires in the winter. The gradual growth of Washington may best be shown by continuing its Church history. 1822 the church was again re-named and henceforth called the Mansfield Presbyterian Church. 1837 a new building being found necessary, a struggle ensued as to whether it should be upon the old site or down the hill where the town was growing. Those who were disappointed in the removal of the church withdrew from the society and organized a new church at Hampton, now known as the Valley Church. It was finally decided to move, and a brick church erected that was destroyed 1862, upon the ruins of which the present handsome edifice was built. Not until 1877 was the present name given of "First Presbyterian Church of Washington."

The M. E. Church had its beginning in the barn of Abraham Woolston, Port Colden, 1810. After many removals (once to Karrsville) it was strong enough, in 1825, to build a house of worship, and shrewdly it was decided to build at Washington. Col. McCullough and his son-in-law, Maj. Hankinson who were largely instrumental in building up the village, were recent converts when the church was built and through them the building was made possible. 1856 the church was rebuilt in brick. In 1864 it was greatly enlarged, and further improvements have since been made.

The Episcopalians having made several attempts to locate, sometimes at Port Colden, sometimes in Washington, at last effected a permanent lodgment, and many years of struggle with alternate success and failure were finally crowned by the erection of a chapel on Broad street, 1886.

St. Joseph's R. C. Church was erected 1872; the congregation having previously met at private houses for several years.

The Baptists do not appear to have made any effort in this portion of the vineyard until about 1881. Discouragements that would have daunted less persevering souls met their first efforts, but they succeeded in erecting a handsome "little church around the corner", 1886.

The colored people were 20 years getting together material for a congregation, but 1882 their church on the bank of the canal was dedicated, to their great delight.

The first school-house of which we can learn was a log building erected prior to the Revolutionary war, in which the birch was swung until the beginning of the present century. Various private and public schools flourished until the present fine brick structure was built, 1873, at a cost of $24,000; enlarged 1886, at a cost of $4,500.

The earliest tavern stood upon the hill close by the log church. Afterward one was built at the corner where now stands the Windsor House, or at what was then called Washington Crossroads. Why so called is doubtful, for despite the legend that Washington once drank at the well opposite the St. Cloud Hotel, it is almost certain that Washington never enjoyed the privilege of visiting this region. Other inns at an early date were located, one where Elisha Burd's block now is; another the stone house now occupied by Prof. J. M. Rosenberry on Broad street; another where John T. Langstaff resides — that building being, with one exception, the oldest building in the borough. Prior to 1811 there were no buildings within the present borough limits of a better nature than log-huts, but that year Col. McCullough built the brick house now occupied by Dr. J. S. Cook.

The first postoffice was opened 1814, under the name of Mansfield, with John L. Robbins as postmaster. He had so little to do, with the few letters and fewer newspapers that came into his hands, that he combined with his postoffice a harness and shoe store. From that date to 1886 there have been 25 postmasters. Just before 1883 the business of the office had so greatly increased that but two postoffices in the State — Newark and Jersey City — turned in as much revenue to the Postoffice Department.

A stranger in Washington will notice as a peculiar feature that it looks as if recently built. Out West that seems a matter of course, but in Jersey one expects to see new and old side by side. The fact is that Washington has only recently begun to grow. Our townsman, J. V. Creveling, Esq., still in his prime, when a boy ploughed ground that had never before been cultivated, in the limits of what is now known as Washington borough. Another of our justices of peace, A. B. Stewart, Esq., to call whom an old man would be a dangerous experiment, is almost a founder of the present village. 1857 he purchased a farm, cut it up into lots, on which are now built a large part of the borough dwellings. It is a hazardous task to try to give the names and exploits of the early citizens of Washington, as one is sure to omit names that ought to be given prominence. But a very brief roll of honor may be presented without claiming to have it complete. The McCulloughs, Hankinsons, Laceys, Van Horns, VanNattas, Crevelings, Ruslings, Shropes, Robbins, Johnstons, Drakes, Henrys, Beavers, Davis, Hughs, Van Dorens, and many others whose acts deserve to be chronicled.

It is pleasant to know that in the Revolutionary war this section of Jersey had few Tories and furnished many good soldiers, and to remember that in the late Civil war Washington sent its full share of Boys in Blue to fight for the flag.

Long before Washington had factories it had a distillery that has disappeared, and it is worthy of notice that there is not as much drinking now as when Washington was a little cross-road hamlet.

Its industries have been the tannery, the carriage shops the boat yard and the organ factories, by which the town has been made known throughout the world, and finally the shoe factory started 1884. In the manufacture of organs, Robert Hornbaker was the pioneer, though John A. Smith, and after him, H. K. White, made melodeons here before. Among the organ makers who have made Washington famous have been Hornbaker, McMurtrie, Plotts, Dawes, Wyckoff, Alleger, Bowlby, Kennedy, Beatty, Cornish, Cole, Creveling, VanDoren, Herrick and others whose names we cannot just now recall. Of all these Beatty has undoubtedly made the most noise in the world. His career reads like a tale of Munchausen. In ten years, starting a penniless boy, he built up a business of large proportions, turning out 1800 organs per month, spending $400,000 per annum in advertising, but his rapid onward progress was in a moment checked by disaster. The bubble burst and his wonderful prosperity gave way to sudden ruin, and the wonder changed from "how could he achieve success so great in so short a time," to "how could he become so involved in embarrasments." It was a modern "rise and fall of the Roman Empire," in one short chapter, and fiction has no parallel for so unique a career as his. Everybody hopes he may yet succeed in retrieving his fortune. He is young and plucky and having made a start again may once more astonish the world.

Cornish, Alleger and Bowlby, though moving on more slowly, have surely advanced and are giving employment to many men, and are yearly increasing their business.

HISTORY OF WASHINGTON. 187

The shoe factory seems in a fair way to be a decided success.

Of corporations, the First National Bank, organized 1864, and the Washington Water Company, organized 1881, are both in a flourishing condition, their stock much above par, and stockholders happy with regular dividends. The Washington Building Loan Association, started 1870, was not the success its promoters anticipated, yet it has made money for such as held on to their stock with the grip of grim despair.

Washington has had excellent musical organizations. The old brass band won laurels upon many a field and prizes when it competed for them. The orchestra was an unusually fine one until, as with the band, its members were scattered, and could no longer meet together. 1860, two militia companies sprang suddenly into existence, rivalry was intense between them. Real war came soon after, and men from both companies enlisted, forming a company that went to the front; as a result, both of the original companies were disbanded. About 20 years later the same thing again happened. Two rival companies were almost simultaneously raised, between whom much feeling existed. They were speedily equipped and uniformed, but both quickly disbanded, why, "no fellow could ever find out."

Washington has always been a great place to start new societies and the graveyard is full of such, over the graves of some of which the epitaph should be written:

"If I was so soon to be done for,
Why was I ever begun for."

Some have died and been resurrected, but of those who have died to live no more have been— Knights of Pythias, Good Templars, "Young Men's Christian Association," "Emerson Glee Club," Washington Lecture Association, "Sons of Temperance," "Washington Reform Club."

The earliest society of all has been the most prosperous, though even it had a period of several years' slumber that seemed like death. 1814, Mansfield Lodge 31, F. & A. M., was instituted; after ten years it became inoperative and forfeited its charter. It was resuscitated 1855 as Mansfield Lodge 36, F. & A. M. Temple Chapter 12, R. A. M., was instituted at Phillipsburg, 1860, and removed to Washington, 1865. Washington Council 7, R. & S. M., was instituted 1866. DeMolay Commandery 6, K. T., was instituted 1867. It is said that no place of its size in New Jersey has as good opportunities for those who wish to go through the various degrees of masonry. Mansfield Lodge 42, I. O. O. F., was instituted 1846. Hero Encampment 42, I. O. O. F. Liberty Council, O. U. A. M., 15, was instituted 1866. Warren Council 16, Jr. O. U. A. M., was instituted 1868, but after a time lapsed, and was re-instituted as Warren Council 16, Jr. O. U. A. M., 1883. Post Henry 30, G. A. R., was organized 1870, but after nearly ten years of life surrendered its charter. John F. Reynolds Post 66, G. A. R., was organized 1882, and is now in a flourishing condition. In point of finances the Masonic order is the most prosperous, next to which the Odd Fellows, and then the Order United American Mechanics.

The Woman's Christian Temperance Union was started 1876, and waxes stronger from year to year.

The Red Men organized in force some years ago, but faded before the Pale Faces, but 1886, the Ute Tribe 80, I. O. R. M., camped here as if they had come to stay.

Washington Lodge 5, K. & L. of the G. S., and Musconetcong Council 1036, American Legion of Honor, have both flourished since 1884.

The youngest order in our Borough is that of the Knights of Labor. The Band of Hope has for several years drilled the children for the ranks of Temperance. While tender youths of the masculine gender are banded in a secret society of their own getting up and go about wearing the mysterious badge E. The Sons of Temperance may be expected back in force, as they come every once in a while, like a comet, having been organized 1862, 1869 and 1886, the last time existing only a few months.

One thing above all else is remarkable in Washington: The absence of family, neighborhood and church quarrels. But why should people quarrel whose surroundings are so delightful. May the Borough long flourish, and its citizens be ever happy.

Washington has a population of about 3,000, and the present officers of the village are: Mayor, Johnston Cornish; Clerk, John Cushing; Assessor, Wm. P. Milroy; Collector, John C. Weller; Overseer of Poor, Abram Bescherer; Town Attorney, John M. VanDyke; Police and Constable, J. C. Thompson; Councilmen, Mansfield Beatty, Charle Baker, H. H. Crocker, N. Dilts, Jr., J. T. Johnson, J. H. Trimmer; Street Commissioner, Daniel Vanderbilt.

Washington Business Directory.

H. W. Alleger, organs
E. W. Alleger & Son, lumber and building material
Joseph Adams, Brass Castle, general store
F. A. Bowlby, clothing, &c
Wm. M. Baird, physician and surgeon
Bescherer Sisters, millinery and fancy goods

FELIX & LEININGER, Nos. 102 & 104 South 3d St., **Easton, Pa.** **FURNITURE.**

C. C. Bowers, groceries and provisions
L. H. Bowlby, boot and shoemaker
J. T. Bowers, dealer in boots and shoes
Cornish & Co., pianos and organs
J. K. Cooke, dealer in dry goods, groceries, &c
Creveling & Co., dealers in dry goods, groceries, &c
Henry Cummins, dealer in dry goods, groceries, &c
Mark Cyphers, merchant tailor
F. M. Cook, physician and surgeon
J. Fitts & Son, furniture and undertaking
John Fagan, private boarding house
Charles Force, marble yard
Dr. J. R. Gibbs, dentist
Groff & Co., dry goods, groceries, & gen'l merchandise
Thomas V. Gordon, original manufacturer of the
    Gordon Rockers
John M. Huff, barber, &c
Hampton & Oberly, millinery and fancy goods
S. W. Herrick, manufacturer of Herrick's adjustable
    American organ

ANDREWS & NOLF, SELL THE BEST $1.00 AND $1.25 KID GLOVES IN EASTON, PA. 205 NORTHAMPTON STREET.

House furnishing Goods generally. The Best Goods for the Least Money at **H. M. NORTON'S, Easton, Pa.**

Hampton & McKinney, dealers in groceries and provisions
Oscar Jeffery, attorney-at law
Edward Jennings, paint and ornamental slate roofer
Johnston's Sons, hardware, plumbing, &c
Kinneman Brothers, Brass Castle, flour and feed
J. H. Mattison, private boarding house
J. E. Myers, meat market
Mike Meahre, livery and sale stable
Charles Miller, dealer in jewelry, &c
F. P. McMinstry, M. D., physician and surgeon
E. P. McCann, boot and shoemaker
James Nolan, prop'r Washington House
Phila. Shoe Manuf. Co., manufactures boots and shoes
Wm. B. Pool, meat market
Daniel Pittinger, furniture, &c
Prof. J. L. Rosenbery, music teacher
Washington Review, one dollar per year in advance
J. K. Risler, dining rooms and restaurant

FELIX & LEININGER, Nos. 102 & 104 South 3d St., Easton, Pa. **FURNITURE.**

Miss K. M. Shields, bakery and confectionery
Wm. Stites, M. D., physician and surgeon
Wm. A. Stryker, attorney-at-law
Washington Star, one dollar and a half a year in ad
L. G. Smith, harness and collar maker
C. F. Staates, prop'r of St. Cloud Hotel
Wm. M. Stires, clock and watchmaker, box 210
S. S. Teel, photographer

S. S. TEEL,
PHOTOGRAPHER,
WASHINGTON AVE.   WASHINGTON, N. J.

Good work at reasonable prices and satisfaction guaranteed.

Thatcher & Wandling, groceries and provisions
F. M. Uehlein, bakery and confectioner
Warren County Drug Store, drugs, books, etc
John Williamson, restaurant
D. V. Wyckoff, grain merchant

PAINTS and OILS at WADE BROS'., Hackettstown, N. J.

Lodges in Washington.

MANSFIELD LODGE, No. 36, A. F. & A. M.—Stated communications, 1st and 3rd Thursdays in each month. Masonic Hall, Washington. Secretary, J. E. Fulper, Washington, N. J.

TEMPLE CHAPTER, No. 12, R. A. M. Stated convocations, 2nd Tuesday in each month. Masonic Hall, Washington. Secretary, J. E. Fulper, Washington, N. J.

WASHINGTON COUNCIL, No. 7, Royal and Select Masters.—Stated assemblies, 3rd Friday in each month. Masonic Hall, Washington. Recorder, J. E. Fulper, Washington, New Jersey.

DeMOLAY COMMANDERY, No. 6, K. T.—Stated conclaves, 2nd and 4th Wednesdays in each month. Masonic Hall, Washington. Recorder, S. Groff, Washington, N. J.

WARREN COUNCIL, No. 16, Jr. O. U. A. M.—Meetings, every Monday evening. Shields' Hall, Washington. Secretary, Lucien Shrope, Washington, N. J.

WASHINGTON LODGE, No. 5, K. & L. of the G. S.—Stated meetings, 1st and 3rd Friday in each month. Mechanics Hall, Washington. Secretary, W. E. Jennings, Washington, N. J.

LIBERTY COUNCIL, No. 15, O. U. A. M.—Meeting every Tuesday evening in Mechanics Hall, Washington. Secretary, W. E. Jennings Washington, N. J.

HERO ENCAMPMENT, No. 42, I. O. O. F.—Meets 2d and 4th Thursday evenings of each month, in Odd Fellows' Hall, Washington, Scribe, Thomas Tayburn, Washington, N. J.

MANSFIELD LODGE, No. 42, I. O. O. F.—Meets every Saturday evening in Odd Fellows' Hall, Washington, Secretary, T. H. Gulick, Washington, N. J.

MUSCONETCONG COUNCIL, No. 1036, American Legion of Honor.—Meets every 2nd and 4th Monday evenings in each month, at 8 o'clock. Secretary, Miner F. Baty, Washington, N. J.

JOHN F. REYNOLDS POST, No. 66, G. A. R.—Meets 1st and 3rd Monday evenings of each month. (From July 1st to October 1st only on 1st Monday in each month.) Mechanics Hall. Adjutant, J. T. Langstaff, Washington, N. J.

UTE TRIBE, No. 80, I. O. R. M.—Meetings every Friday evening. Shields' Hall. Keeper of Records, Jos. B. Hampton, Washington, N. J.

JULY, 1878,

E. B. Webb came from New York City, and with Geo. H. Hastings bought from W. H. Goodale his stock and fixtures in the Drug Store formerly owned by Dr. Jennings.

At once renovating the store inside and out, and putting in double the stock it had when he took it, he set patiently to work building up a trade. By persistent advertising in various ways he soon made the name he had given to his business—"The Warren County Drug Store"—well known in every corner of the county. March, 1884, he bought out the interest of Mr. Hastings, and has since had sole control. It is no exaggeration to say that his stock is complete in the line of Drugs, Paints, Oils, Books, Stationery, Fishing Tackle, Pictures and Frames. Everybody is invited, all are welcome to the Warren County Drug Store.

WARREN COUNTY DRUG STORE.

Washington Borough.

Alleger E. W., builder and contractor, residence cor School and Church, factory Broad
Alleger A. W., wood carver, Church
Alleger Wm. F., mechanic, Church
Alleger Willard, builder and contractor, Broad
Allen Wm., laborer, Cemetery Hill
Allen Andrew, laborer, Maple
Ammerman Chas. S., clerk, Belvidere ave
Alleger H. W., organ manufacturer, res Church, factory Broad
Andrews George, laborer, Cornish alley
Andrews Benjamin, laborer, New
Andrews Wm., laborer, New
Andrews Abraham, laborer, Cornish alley

FELIX & LEININGER, Nos. 102 & 104 South 3d St., **Easton, Pa.** FURNITURE.

Andrews Geo H., gardener, Broad
Andrews Wm., wood finisher, Belvidere ave
Anderson Wm. E., RR. brakeman, Washington ave
Anderson J. M., mechanic, Washington ave
Anderson Wm. H., laborer, New
Anderson James M., laborer, New
Angard Paul, organ builder, Belvidere ave
Albert Wm., RR. brakeman, Hornbaker
Adams John, mechanic, Broad
Adams Archibald, laborer, New
Adams Geo., laborer, New
Addis, Sam'l A., laborer, New
Beatty Lewis C., poultry fancier, Vannatta
Beatty Mansfield, salesman, Washington ave
Beatty Hibbard, mechanic, Washington ave
Beatty Wellington, shoemaker, Windsor House
Baker Chas. L., RR. engineer, Jane
Bowers S. P., manufacturer, Belvidere ave
Bowers J. T., merchant, residence Broad, store Washington ave

ANDREWS & NOLF, 205 Northampton St., Easton, Pa. The Largest line of DRESS TRIMMINGS etc.

H. M. NORTON, Wholesale and retail dealer in Hardware, Stoves Heaters and Ranges.

Bowers, C. C., merchant, residence Washington ave, store Washington ave
Bowlby Bartley, mechanic, Church
Bowlby Levi H. boot and shoemaker, residence Church, store Broad
Bowlby Chas. P., organ manufacturer, residence Stewart, factory Belvidere ave
Bowlby J. Fletcher, merchant, residence Church store Washington ave
Bowlby Geo. M., organ action maker, Church
Bowlby F. A., merchant, res Church, store Washington ave
Bowlby Alfred, organ salesman, Church
Burd William, book-keeper, Broad
Brown Joseph, stone mason, Church
Bowne Geo. W., janitor pub school, Washington ave
Baty Miner, RR. clerk, Port Washington
Bryant John, laborer, New
Barber B. G., retired, School
Baylor Jesse F., boatman, Pt Washington

FELIX & LEININGER, Nos. 102 & 104 South 3d St., **Easton, Pa.** FURNITURE.

Baylor Wm. A., boatman, Pt Washington
Boyd James L., farmer, Washington ave
Boyd Henry, farmer, Washington ave
Barber Chas., clerk, Washington ave
Barber Miss Jennie, dressmaker, School
Babcock Alphens, RR section supt, Belvidere ave
Babcock Byron, tuner, Belvidere ave
Bescherer Abram, retired, Washington ave
Bescherer Jacob, carpenter, Washington ave
Bescherer Mrs. Jacob, dressmaker, Washington ave
Bescherer Misses, millinery and fancy goods, Washington ave
Beidleman John, mechanic, Belvidere ave
Bird Peter E., salesman, Belvidere ave
Boyer Sam'l, confectioner, carpenter, Washington ave
Boyer Serenus, carpenter, School
Boyer Sylvester, clerk, Washington ave
Barrett B. M., miller, Carlton ave
Bigler A. J., organ action builder, Broad
Burness Samuel, bricklayer, Johnston

SHIELDS' Compound Syrup of Wild Cherry with Hypophosites of Lime and Soda. Sure cure for coughs, croup, etc.

Housefurnishing Goods generally. the Best Goods for the Least Money at **H. M. NORTON'S, Easton, Pa.**

Beers Gilbert, nurseryman, Washington ave
Byrne Thomas, shoemaker, Warren
Byrne Justin, turner, Warren
Baird Wm. M., physician, M. A., Washington ave
Bates James, music teacher, near Lorentz ave
Bryant Jacob, clerk, Washington ave
Bryant Stewart, carpenter, Warren
Bryant Wm. R., carpenter, Washington ave
Bryant Jacob L., carpenter, Washington ave
Bryant Christopher, RR brakeman, Carlton ave
Burd Elisha, mason, Washington ave
Burd Jacob C., mason, Washington ave
Burd Joseph, mason, Washington ave
Barron Frank, hostler, Hornbaker
Barron Wm., saloon keeper, St. Cloud Hotel
Berry Samuel, laborer, New
Beavers Saml. T., action builder, Church
Beavers Jos. A., merchant, Washington ave res Broad
Barnes Wm., carter and laborer, Maple
Beers Geo., clerk, Jane

FELIX & LEININGER, Nos. 102 & 104 South 3d St., **Easton, Pa.** **FURNITURE.**

Bruck Thos., laborer, Cherry alley
Beers Aaron, laborer, Jane
Brown James, mechanic
Brown George, mechanic, Church
Burd John W., wood finisher, Belvidere ave
Blazer Peter W., assoc. ed. *Star*, Broad
Blazer Ira E., telegraph operator, Melodeon
Blazer Charles, farmer, Melodeon
Beam John, farmer, Washington ave
Bowne William, expressman, Washington ave
Bell J. T., blacksmith, res Church, shop Broad
Bennett Calvin, farmer, Washington ave
Beagan Phil, shoemaker, Washington ave
Bryant John, laborer, Broad
Bailey John, fish and oyster dealer, res Church, market Belvidere ave
Creveling A. W., merchant, res Belvidere ave, store Washington ave
Creveling J. V., justice of peace, res Belvidere ave, office Broad

ANDREWS & NOLF, 205 Northampton St. The Largest line of Thompson's Glove Fitting Corsets in Easton.

H. M. NORTON, Wholesale and retail dealer in Hardware, Stoves, Heaters and Ranges.

196 WASHINGTON BOROUGH DIRECTORY.

Creveling Chas., merchant, res Washington ave, store Belvidere ave
Creveling Wm. G., merchant, res Belvidere ave cor Johnston, store Belvidere ave
Creveling James A., mechanic, Belvidere ave
Creveling John R., salesman, Carlton ave
Creveling S. J., carter, Church
Creveling Lewis C., mechanic, Church
Creveling Jacob, foreman organ factory, Railroad ave
Coen Samuel, laborer, Creveling
Cummins Henry, merchant, res Belvidere ave, store Washington ave
Cummins Rodman, salesman, Belvidere ave
Campbell Geo. C., tuner-organ, Broad
Carpenter Jacob, local preacher, Washington ave
Carpenter Henry, baker, Washington ave
Carpenter Enoch, lawyer, Washington ave
Connor John, laborer, Cemetery Hill
Campbell Benj., laborer, New
Campbell John, laborer, New

FELIX & LEININGER, Nos. 102 & 104 South 3d St., Easton, Pa. FURNITURE.

Clinger Lewis, laborer
Collins Rev. R. B., pastor M. E. Church, Jackson ave
Chase Fred, shoemaker, Cherry alley
Case Frederick, laborer
Cushion John, RR clerk, Washington ave
Creveling Elmer, fly finishing, Carlton ave
Case Isaac, blacksmith, Church
Case Wm., laborer, Church
Cushion David, RR workman, Washington ave
Cushion Albert F., clerk and book keeper, Washington ave
Cressman Joseph, mechanic, Belvidere ave
Crocker Henry, mechanic, Washington ave
Craft Samuel C., florist, Washington ave
Craft Alex. J., mechanic, Washington ave
Crotsley J. W., mechanic, Belvidere ave
Crotsley Wm., carpenter, Vannatta
Crotsley Jacob, butcher, Belvidere ave
Cressman Geo., laborer, Belvidere ave
Carr Lewis, laborer, New

ALL KINDS OF HARDWARE at Wade Bros., Hackettstown, N. J.

Housefurnishing Goods generally. The Best Goods for the Least Money at **H. M. NORTON'S, Easton, Pa.**

WASHINGTON BOROUGH DIRECTORY.

Cornish J. B., manufacturer, res Belvidere ave, factory Washington ave
Carling Daniel, RR night watchman, Washington ave
Cornish Johnston, Mayor and organ manufacturer, res Belvidere ave, office Washington ave
Cole A. E., book-keeper, Washington ave
Cook Jas. S., physician, Washington ave
Curby John, shoemaker, St. Cloud Hotel
Cook Frank, physician, Washington ave
Christine Chas. W., switchman, Creveling
Christine Chas. W., Jr., brakeman, Creveling
Christine Wm. W., conductor, RR crossing, Maple
Cyphers Mark, merchant tailor, res Belvidere ave, store Washington ave
Cline Geo. H., finisher, Hornbaker
Cline Wm. H., RR brakeman, Delaware
Cline James, boatman, Delaware
Cline Chas., boatman, Delaware
Cooke John K., merchant, res Belvidere ave, store Washington ave

FELIX & LEININGER, Nos. 102 & 104 South 3d St., **Easton, Pa.** FURNITURE.

Crotsley Isaac, RR fireman, Belvidere ave, cor Johnston
Cyphers Daniel, RR conductor, New, cor Johnston
Cyphers James H., carriage manufacturer, res Church cor School, factory Broad
Cyphers James H., Jr., case maker, Belvidere ave
Christine John S., boatman, Mechanic
Curl Wm., laborer, New
Crane John, carriage finisher, Maple
Crane Wm. L., hard wood finisher, Church
Castner Jacob, farmer, Broad
Conine M. B., canal foreman, Church
Cyphers Jacob H., brakeman, Dumb Corner
Casey Con, puddler, New
Cowel Daniel, farmer, Carlton ave
Cramer N. S., shoemaker, Washington ave
Caufman Nathan, turner, Washington ave
Cougle Jacob, RR brakeman, School
Campbell Wm., mechanic, New
Cravat James, laborer, Washington ave

Andrews & Nolf, 205 Northampton St. The only place to buy the "CONFORMATER" Corset.

H. M. NORTON, Wholesale and retail dealer in Hardware, Stoves, Heaters and Ranges

WASHINGTON BOROUGH DIRECTORY.

Casey Matthews, laborer, Dublin
Carter Jos. S., druggist, res Washington ave
Carter Jos. C., mechanic, Washington ave
Carter John Calvin, merchant, res Stewart, store Washington ave
Cyphers Chas., carpenter, Church cor Stewart
Cyphers Edward O., clerk, Belvidere ave
Cowel Wm. S., engineer, New
Cowel Dan, milk dealer, Carlton ave
Carter John, livery stables, Washington ave
Carter Wm., mechanic, New
Drake J. D., farmer, Broad
Donnelly James, laborer, Carlton ave
Decaker Saml., painter, Carlton ave
Donahoe Dan'l, laborer, Dublin
Davidson Peter, carpenter, Hornbaker
Dildine Wm. M., garment cutter, School
Dufford Miss S. Alice, school teacher, Washington ave
Dufford Wm. G., farmer, Washington ave
Donovan Rev. Wm. J., minister Catholic Church,

FELIX & LEININGER, Nos. 102 & 104 South 3d St., Easton, Pa. **FURNITURE.**

   Belvidere avenue
Dilts Nathan, merchant, res Washington ave, store Washington ave
Dilts Nathan, Jr., merchant, res Washington ave, store Washington ave
Dilts Daniel, painter, Jackson ave
Dilts David, tuner, Washington ave
Dilts Geo. W., tuner, Church
Dilts Capt. Wm., retired blacksmith, Washington ave
Davis Nathan, retired, Washington ave
Davis Job J., mechanic, Warren
Davis Jacob, mechanic, Washington ave
Dowers Frank, porter, St. Cloud Hotel
Doremus Geo., shoemaker, St. Cloud Hotel
Davis Edward, mechanic, Warren
Deremer Smith, farmer, New, cor Johnston
Deremer Isaac, boatman, Jane
Deremer Ralph, carter, New
Douglas A., book-keeper, St. Cloud Hotel
Dolan Edward, laborer

For Coughs, Colds, Croup and Consumption use SHIELDS' **COMPOUND SYRUP** of Wild Cherry with hypo-phosphates of lime and soda

Housefurnishing Goods generally. The Best Goods for the Least Money at **H. M. NORTON'S, Easton, Pa**

WASHINGTON BOROUGH DIRECTORY.

Davison A. K., asst. ed. *Review*, Jane
Defoe Stephen, retired physician, Grand ave
Dawes Geo., postmaster, St. Cloud Hotel
Doughe Joe, merchant, Cornish
Dunham Asa, tin salesman, Washington
Donahoe Edward, RR conductor, Warren
Dazian Saml., shoemaker, Broad
Davis Geo., shoemaker, St. Cloud Hotel
Exton Hugh, veterinary surgeon, Warren
Eilinberger R. M., merchant (A. W. Creveling & Co.), Belvidere ave
Eggins Martin, wood finisher, Hornbaker
Edgerton Chas., cigar merchant, Washington ave
Edgerton Justin P., organ builder, Washington ave
Everett A. H., casemaker, Weller
Emmons I. W., reporter, Washington ave
Ervin Thomas, laborer, Dublin
Ervin Isaac, RR brakeman, Johnston
Fitts Jacob, merchant furniture manufacturer, res and factory Broad, warerooms Washington ave

FELIX & LEININGER, Nos. 102 & 104 South 3d St., **Easton, Pa.** FURNITURE.

Fitts Warren, clerk, Belvidere ave
Fitts Henry, upholsterer, Stewart
Fitts James M., merchant, Broad
Fitts J. W., merchant, res Church, store Washington ave
Fitts Enoch, clerk and book keeper, Washington ave
Fulper J. E., retired, Washington ave
Fox Geo., carter, Vannatta
Fox James, laborer, Vannatta
Fredenberg Ed, RR fireman, Washington ave
Force Wm. W., laborer, Church
Fehr Edward, hostler, Melodeon
Fehr Howard, car inspector, Melodeon
Early Wm. A., mason and carpenter, Creveling
Fagan John, turner, Washington ave
Florey A. F., foreman Cornish organ factory, Church
Frost Frank B., engineer, School
Frost Rev. D. S., retired Baptist minister, School
Flint D. E., plumber, Stewart
Frome Wm., retired, Broad

ANDREWS & NOLF, 26 Northampton Street, Easton, Pa. The reliable store for Black Goods.

H. M. NORTON, Wholesale and retail dealer in Hardware, Stoves, Ranges and Ranges

WASHINGTON BOROUGH DIRECTORY.

Furman Jas., merchant, Belvidere ave
Furman McClellen, tanner, Belvidere ave
Flynn Patrick, night watchman, Dublin
Fox John, organ rubber, Vanuatta
Force John D., marble cutter, Broad
Fitts Miss Maggie, school teacher, Broad
Force Chas., marble cutter and dealer, Broad
Force Peter, retired, Broad
Fisher Christine, retired, Washington ave
Foddle Frank, gardener, etc., Belvidere ave
Foddle Charles, engineer and ice cream freezer, Washington ave
Fleming Geo., laborer, New
Flynn Martin, coal dumper, Dublin
Frome Samuel, saloon keeper, Belvidere ave
Groff Henry S., RR agent, Jackson ave
Groff A. B., merchant, res Washington ave, store Washington ave
Groff J. D., RR freight agent, Washington ave
Gardiner J. W., express and baggage agent, Rail-

FELIX & LEININGER, Nos. 102 & 104 South 3d St., **Easton, Pa.** **FURNITURE.**

road ave
Groff Sylvester, merchant, res Broad, store Washington ave
Gardiner James H., RR engineer, Railroad ave
Gaston John S., billiard and pool room, res Warren, rooms Washington ave
Gordon Morris, clerk, Washington ave
Gibson Chas., farmer, Jackson ave
Gerard G. O., tanner, res Broad, tannery Broad
Gulick F. H., carpenter, Jane
Gunsaulus Geo., mechanic, Washington ave
Godfrey R. W., case maker, Church
Griffith Miss Clara, schoolteacher, Washington ave
Godfrey A. C., RR freight handler, Church
Gibbs J. R., dentist office and res Washington ave
Gunderman Jacob, tanner, Hornbaker
Gaston Elmer, wood carver, Warren
Gunderman Geo., laborer, Hornbaker
Gross Robt., farmer, Washington ave
Gleason John, RR workman, Dublin

PAINTS and OILS at WADE BROS., Hackettstown, N. J.

Housefurnishing Goods generally. The Best Goods for the Least Money at **H. M. NORTON'S, Easton, Pa.**

Glenzbeck Amos, shoemaker, Broad
Gunderman Emery, laborer, Port Washington
Gordon T. V., chair maker, Washington ave
Hornbaker F. K., undertaker, Hornbaker
Hornbaker Robt., sportsman, Hornbaker
Hornbaker John, merchant, res Hornbaker, store Belvidere ave
Hornbaker Daniel, laborer, Hornbaker
Hornbaker A. J., carpenter, Washington ave
Heed Grant, action builder, Belvidere ave
Hann P. H., vice pres 1st Nat Bank, Belvidere ave
Herrick Seth W., organ manfr, Broad
Hann A. P., cashier bank, Belvidere ave
Hann Lewis J., bank clerk, New
Hansler Jos., lather, Brown
Hazard Geo., clerk, Windsor House
Herrick Miss Addie C., school teacher, Broad
Haynes George, shoemaker, Washington ave
Hedden Wm. A., tuner, Hornbaker
Hampton Joseph, merchant, res Washington ave

FELIX & LEININGER, Nos. 102 & 104 South 3d St., **Easton, Pa.** **FURNITURE.**

store Belvidere ave
Hance Jno. H. Jr., butcher, Belvidere ave
Hutchings B. B., shoemaker, Washington ave
Hutchings Wm., painter, Washington ave
Hutchings E. J., mechanic, Warren
Hutchings Peter, laborer, Washington ave
Hutchings Edward, laborer, Washington ave
Hankinson Ira, laborer, Jane
Howel Harvy, painter, Jackson ave
Hampton & Oberly, fancy goods, Washington ave
Hartman Andrew, laborer, New
Hartman Joseph, porter St. Cloud Hotel
Hastings Patrick, laborer
Hayward George, canvasser, Grand ave
Haldren Benj, laborer, Melodeon
Huff John M., barber, Washington ave
Hooker H. C., travelling salesman, Windsor House
Howard Jerome, retired blacksmith, Warren
Hornbaker A. J. Jr., laborer, Washington ave
Hayes Patrick, retired, Belvidere ave

ANDREWS & NOLF, 205 Northampton St., Easton, Pa. You can find it by the fine large awning in front of store.

H. M. NORTON, Wholesale and retail dealers in Hardware, Stoves, Heaters and Ranges.

Hiemer Jas. R., retired, Washington ave
Hoff Wm. L., telegraph operator, School
Honness Aaron, mason, Church
Hoagland U. V. C., retired, New cor Stewart
Hall Wm., RR engineer, Dumb Corner
Hall Chas. B., engineer, Jane and Melodeon
Hartpence Wm. F., physician, Washington ave
Hopple Frank, mechanic, Washington ave
Hahn George, painter, Creveling
Hoff John C., compositor, Jane
Higgins Elisha, laborer, Carlton ave
Higgins Jno. L., foreman car repairers, Railroad ave
Horn Frank, shoemaker, St. Cloud Hotel
Higgins Wm., railroad employe, Railroad ave
Hulsizer Frank, hardware merchant, res Johnston, store Broad
Hamilton Wm., mechanic, Washington ave
Herrick Miss Victoria A., school teacher, Broad
Hamilton Miss Laura S., school teacher, Wash'n ave
Hall L. C., mechanic, Jackson ave

FELIX & LEININGER, Nos. 102 & 104 South 3d St., Easton, Pa. **FURNITURE.**

Hayes Patrick J., conductor, Belvidere ave
Inscho Wm. C., laborer, Washington ave
Inscho George, RR conductor, Church
Irvin Thomas, laborer, Dublin
Johnston Philip, retired, Belvidere ave cor Johnston
Johnston Walter, tinsmith, Broad
Johnston Henry W., merchant, store Belvidere ave, res Belvidere ave
Johnston Henry, hardware merchant, store Washington ave, res School
Johnston Jacob T., agent, Washington ave
Johnston Chas. E., book-keeper, Washington ave
Johnston James H., hardware merchant, store Washington ave, res Stewart
Johnston Joseph W., surveyor, Washington ave
Johnston Wm. E., switchman, Dublin
Johnston Wm. W., clerk, Belvidere ave
Jennings Wm. E., slater, Weller
James John, foreman shoe factory, St. Cloud Hotel
James Wm., cutter and night watchman, Wash'n ave

SHIELDS' INFALLIBLE **Dyspeptic Remedy.** A sure cure for Dyspepsia, Sick or Nervous Headache. Guaranteed.

Jeffery Oscar, lawyer, office Washington ave, res Belvidere ave
Kinneman Joseph, farmer, Karville
Kinneman Whitfield, farmer, Karville
Kelley Thos., section boss, Cemetery Hill
Kelley Patrick, laborer, Dublin
Keifer Jeremiah, horticulturist, Prospect ave
Kator Patrick, laborer, Fisher road
Kelsey Edward, laborer, Jane
Kelsey George, hostler, Washington ave
Kenneday Wm., F., tuner, Stewart
Kenney Wm. laborer, Brass Castle
Kase Frank, book-keeper, Washington ave
King H. L., car repairer, Warren
Losey Jos., merchant, Church
Lynn J. E., marble dealer, Broad
Lynch Daniel, brakeman, Dublin
Lynch Jno., car repairer, Dublin
Libby Frank, mechanic, Belvidere ave
Lunger Morris, engineer, Railroad ave

FELIX & LEININGER, Nos. 102 & 104 South 3d St., **Easton, Pa.** FURNITURE.

Lunger S. J., shoe maker, res Church, shop Bel. ave
Lunger C. R., agent, Windsor House
Leidy Geo., laborer, Hornbaker
Larkin Michael, shoemaker, Warren
Lacy Jno. C., laborer, Washington ave
Langstaff Jno. T., salesman, Washington ave
Lems John S., farmer
Lynch James, car repairer, Dublin
Loehen David, Boatman, Pt. Washington
Lance George H., laborer, Washington ave
Lance Archibald, laborer, Washington ave
LaRoe Wilbur, asso. editor *Star*, Windsor House
Lance Jno., carpenter, Jane
Lance Isaac, car repairer, Belvidere ave
Milroy Geo., rubber, New
Menton Wm. F., carpenter, Washington ave
Miller Henry C., jeweler, res Johnston, store Washington ave
Miller Chas. A., jeweler, res Warren, store Washington ave

Silver-Plated Knives, Forks and Spoons, at WADE BROS.

Miller Wm., tanner, Vannatta
Miller Warne A., fireman, Church
Mount Wm., wheelwright, Broad
Mount Calvin, wheelwright, Broad
Mershon Joab, mechanic, Washington ave
Murphy Patrick, RR yard dispatcher, Railroad ave
Morgan Jeremiah, laborer, Belvidere ave
Morris Jacob H., janitor, Washington ave
McKinstry F. P., physician, Washington ave
Milham James Jr., engineer, New
Milham James, shoemaker, Jane
McKinney Wm., merchant, res Stewart, store Belvidere ave
Milroy W. R., carpenter, Warren
Meagher Michael, livery stables, res Belvidere ave, stables Belvidere ave
Munch Chas., shoemaker, St. Cloud Hotel
Mahoney John, brakeman, New
Middlesworth Isaac, laborer, Mechanic
McMurtrie Jno. H., carpenter, Washington ave

FELIX & LEININGER, Nos. 102 & 104 South 3d St., **Easton, Pa.** FURNITURE.

McMurtrie Jno. S., carpenter, Jackson ave
McMurtrie Thos., carpenter, Church
McClay Alex., boatman, Pt Washington
McClay Jos., boatman, Pt Washington
McClary John, laborer, Pt Washington
McCracken Chas., carriage manfr, res Broad, factory Belvidere ave
McCracken Ira, carriage manfr, res Belvidere ave
McCracken Edward, blacksmith, Broad
McCann Edward, shoemaker, Washington ave

E. P. MCCANN
BOOT AND SHOE MAKER.

Work done with neatness and dispatch and as cheap as can be done anywhere. Thankful for past patronage, I solicit a continuance.

Washington ave.   Washington N. J.

McCann Vincent, shoemaker, Washington ave
Milroy Wm. P., carpenter, New

Andrews & Hoff, 205 Northampton street, Easton, Pa. Sales-room enlarged. Come and see

Myers Jacob, butcher, Creveling
McClary Andrew, boatman, Pt. Washington
McClary Henry, boatman, Jane
McClary Jack, laborer, Jane
McClary Albert, cook, Jane
McClary Edward, laborer, Jane
Miers John H., engineer, Hornbaker
Miers George, laborer, Hornbaker
Miller Henry, boatman, Pt Washington
Mahon Wm. J., music teacher, Warren
Marshall Lewis, shoemaker, Washington ave
Mattison John H., boarding house, Wash'n ave
Mattison J. L. T., mechanic, Jackson ave
Mattison Wm. F., book-keeper, Belvidere ave
Miller L. W., barber, Cherry alley
Morrison Jno., mechanic, Cornish st.
Miller Jno., laborer, Melodeon
Miller J. W., barber, Cherry alley
Morgan Robt., brakeman, School
McClary Jos., boatman, Pt. Washington

FELIX & LEININGER, Nos. 102 & 104 South 3d St., **Easton, Pa.** FURNITURE.

Morgan Chas. H., laborer, Pt. Washington
Miller C. W., laborer,
Moore Isaac, laborer, New
Millham James N., laborer, Pt. Washington
Mahoney Jno. A., wood cutter RR. Dublin
McNaney James, stable boss, Belvidere ave
Mahone Ed., conductor RR. Dublin
Millham Edgar, shoemaker, Johnston

At the MISSES BESCHERER'S
Washington Avenue. WASHINGTON, N. J.
Will always be found the very latest in
MILLINERY AND FANCY GOODS.
STAMPING AND EMBROIDERY MATERIALS A SPECIALTY.
No pains spared to please one and all.

Norris W. N., manager shoe fac., St. Cloud Hotel
Nier John, cabinet maker, Cemetery Hill
Nolan Jas., Washington House landlord, RR ave
Nier Jacob, cigar maker, Cemetery Hill
Nier Henry, mechanic, Cemetery Hill
Nutze J. W., merchant, Washington ave

SHIELDS' Compound Syrup of Wild Cherry with Hypophosites of Lime and Soda. Sure cure for coughs, croup, etc.

H. M. NORTON, WHOLESALE AND RETAIL DEALER IN HARDWARE, STOVES, HEATERS AND RANGES.

26   WASHINGTON BOROUGH DIRECTORY.

Nott Dr. Chas. D., pastor Presbyterian church, Washington ave
Nixon Geo., mechanic, Hornbaker
Osmun William, clerk, Washington ave
Osborne Chas. E., wood finisher, Jane
O'Shea Dennis, woodman RR, Washington ave
Olander Alfred, undertaker and cabinet maker, Washington ave
Paullin George, shoemaker, Washington ave
Pittinger Daniel, furniture manufacturer, Washington ave
Prouty Mrs. W. H., school teacher, Church
Pittinger Jasper, furniture manfr, Wash'n ave
Petty Thompson, merchant, store Bel. ave, res Broad
Petty Jos. K., stone mason, Washington ave
Petty Wm., retired, Washington ave
Petty Samuel V., hostler, Belvidere ave
Perry Wm., engineer, Broad
Person Chris., fish peddler, Washington ave
Poole Ira, shoemaker, Washington ave

FELIX & LEININGER, Nos. 102 & 104 South 3d St., **Easton, Pa.** FURNITURE.

Piche George, shoemaker, New
Peters Jno., farmer, Carlton ave
Pickel Jno., butcher, Washington ave
Pickel Chas., butcher, shop Belvidere ave, res Washington ave
Pickel H. T., butcher, Washington ave
Prouty Wm. H., teacher, Church
Pence George M., engineer RR, Church
Pool Wm. B., butcher, shop Belvidere ave, res Washington ave
Pool Frank, shoemaker, Washington ave
Plotts Jno., farmer, Hornbaker
Plotts Wm., wood finisher, Vannatta
Plotts Edward, organ manuf'r, warerooms Belvidere ave, res Broad
Philhower Jno. E., mechanic, Washington ave
Pidcock Jonathan, farmer, Washington ave
Pidcock Stewart, farmer, Washington ave
Pidcock Theodore, farmer, Washington ave
Robbins J., clerk, Washington ave

Andrews & Nolf, 205 Northampton St. The only place to buy the "CONFORMATER" Corset.

HOUSEFURNISHING GOODS G. NERSLY
The BEST GOODS for the LEAST MONEY at H. M. NORTON'S, Easton, Pa.

Rosenbery James, music teacher, broad
Raub M. K., mechanic, Belvidere ave
Raub Harry, druggist, Belvidere ave
Raub George, clerk, Belvidere ave
Rube John, tinsmith, Washington ave
Richey Jno., boatman, New
Riddle G. R., bartender, Stewart
Ruegg Ed., shoemaker, St. Cloud Hotel
Ryan Patrick, hostler, Dublin
Ryan John, laborer, Dublin
Rocker Wm., tailor, W. shington ave
Roomsaveli Jno., shoemaker, Washington ave
Reynolds J. D., principal pub school, Church
Robberts C. S., engineer RR, Washington ave
Risler John, prop'r restaurant, res Vacoatta, restaurant Washington ave
Russell Jno., organ builder, Washington ave
Russell H. R., organ builder, Washington ave
Rutan R. S., foreman stock dept shoe factory, Belvidere ave

FELIX & LEININGER, Nos. 102 & 104 South 3d St., **Easton, Pa.** **FURNITURE.**

Rockafellow Wm. J., merchant, res School, store Washington ave
Reil Theo., wood finisher, Warren
Radline Nathan, rubber, Washington ave
Rodgers D. J., organ tuner, Carlton ave
Ricker Wm. E., agent, New cor Stewart
Ribble Wellington, druggist, Church
Spangenburg Daniel, merchant, res Wash'n ave, store Washington ave
Smith Jno. K., conductor RR, Carlton ave
Shrope Howard, telephone ex operator, Wash'n ave

F. P. McKINSTRY, M. D.,
Homeopathic Physician and Surgeon.

OFFICE HOURS: { 7 to 9 A. M.
1 to 3 P. M.
6 to 7.30 P. M. } WASHINGTON, N. J.

Smith Adam R., carter, Bel ave cor Carlton ave
Smith Peter, brakeman, Melodeon
Smith L. G., harness maker, Johnston

Garden Seeds a specialty, Wades', Hackettstown.

H. M. NORTON, WHOLESALE AND RETAIL DEALER IN HARDWARE, STOVES, HEATERS AND RANGES.

208   WASHINGTON BOROUGH DIRECTORY.

Smith Reider, mechanic, Warren
Shaw Job J., merchant, res Jackson ave, store Washington ave
Sweeny William, correspondent, Washington ave
Swenson A. J., tinsmith, Warren
Staates C. F., prop'r St. Cloud Hotel, Wash'n ave
Stewart A. B., Justice of Peace, Belvidere ave
Stewart Chas., laborer, Washington ave
Strader Chas. S., mechanic, Belvidere ave
Strader Augustus R., carpenter, Belvidere ave
Strader Charles W., engineer, Belvidere ave
Strader Robt. S., organ case maker, Washington ave
Slack Frank M., laborer, Washington ave
Slack Fred M., stone mason, Cornish
Shrope Jos. A., Surveyor, Washington ave
Shrope Wm. A., laborer, Church
Shrope Jacob W., carpenter, Washington ave
Shrope Lucien, printer, Washington ave
Smith Sim, laborer, New
Smith A. W., book-keeper, Washington ave

FELIX & LEININGER, Nos. 102 & 104 South 3d St., **Easton, Pa.** **FURNITURE.**

Sexton Thos., section boss RR, Dublin
Sexton Martin, brakeman, Dublin
Solomon Abram, blacksmith, Johnston
Solomon Abram Jr., laborer, Johnston
Slater Peter, carpenter, Washington ave

Pleasant Valley Mills,

KINNAMAN & CO.,

MANUFACTURERS AND DEALERS IN

FEED & MEAL, ROLLER FLOUR, GRAIN, &c.

ONE MILE BELOW WASHINGTON, N. J.

Slater Henry, carpenter, Washington ave
Sine D. M., night watchman, Jane
Shields Wm., agent D. L. & W. RR, Wash'n ave

ANDREWS & NOLF, 205 Northampton Street, Easton, Pa.
The reliable store for Black Goods.

Shields Jas L., clerk and coal agt, St. Cloud Hotel
Shields Silas, clerk, Washington ave
Scott Lambert, farmer, Washington ave
Scott Hugh, farmer, Washington ave
Scott George, boatman, Pt. Washington
Stites Wm., physician, Washington ave
Sheats Lewis W., boatman, Church Alley
Smith Wm., clerk, Washington ave
Smith Isaac, engineer, Belvidere ave
Smith Ogden, laborer, New
Stryker Wm. A., lawyer, office Washington ave, res Belvidere ave
Searfoss Barnett, painter, Church
Skinner Smith, farmer, Pt Washington
Snyder Jacob, fireman, Melodeon
Snyder George W., brakeman, Melodeon
Skinner James P., butcher, Belvidere ave
Snyder Willard, action maker, St. Cloud Hotel
Senior Joseph, action maker, Melodeon
Sheats John H., freight handler, Washington ave

FELIX & LEININGER, Nos. 102 & 104 South 3d St., **Easton, Pa.** FURNITURE.

Staples George, brakeman, Church
Seguine Wm. F., brakeman, Broad
Seguine James, shoemaker, Broad
Shrope Theo. B. carpenter, Maple
Stewart Saml. S., night dispatcher RR, Wash'n ave
Stewart Imla, milk dealer, Jane
Smith Arch, laborer, New
Stevenson Austin, butcher, Broad
Shampanore A. J., editor *Review*, Wash'n ave
Shampanore G. W., printer, New cor Stewart
Stewart Harry, shoemaker, Washington ave
Sparry George, clerk, Windsor House
Shields K. M., bakery, Washington ave
Thatcher Saml. S., retired, Broad
Thatcher Jos. R., merchant, Washington ave
Thatcher Wm., retired, Broad
Thatcher Saml., wood-carver, Broad
Thatcher Peter W., carpenter, Washington ave
Teel Samuel, photographer, Broad
Trimmer George, engineer, Carlton ave

H. M. NORTON, WHOLESALE AND RETAIL DEALER IN HARDWARE, STOVES, HEATERS AND RANGES

216   WASHINGTON BOROUGH DIRECTORY.

Trimmer Jacob, conductor, Jackson ave., cor Church
Taylor James, shoemaker, Jane
Taylor J. D., Ins. agent, res Jane, office Broad
Taylor Peter, night watchman, Melodeon
Treat W. L., tinsmith, Washington ave
Thornton Samuel, organ tuner, Washington ave
Teats John, repair shop, Washington ave
Thompson John, tinsmith, Johnston
Tunison A. G., conductor, Church
Tygar P. W., carpenter, Carlton ave
Tygar H. R., carpenter, School
Tayborn Thos., shoemaker, Johnston
Thorp Joseph, laborer, Jackson ave
Townsend Edward, waiter, Windsor House
Thompson Wm. C., boatman, Johnston
Thompson Jos. C., police, Church
Thompson Albert A., organ packer, Johnston
Thompson Saml. C., retired agent, Washington ave
Thompson Chas., brakeman, Belvidere
Thompson Theodore, laborer, Hornbaker

FELIX & LEININGER, Nos. 102 & 104 South 3d St., **Easton, Pa.** FURNITURE

Thompson Charles, laborer, Hornbaker
Thompson Elmer, clerk, St. Cloud Hotel
Thompson Jacob, brakeman, Washington ave
Teeter Obadiah, fireman, Belvidere ave
Tunison Albert W., clerk
Thatcher Jos. H., merchant, res and store Wash'n ave
Uehlein Frank, baker, Washington ave
Uehlein F. M., baker & confectioner, Wash'n ave
Uehlein John, clerk, Washington ave
Uehlein George, baker, Washington ave
Vleit Daniel, lawyer, office Broad, res Wash'n ave
Vough Jacob S., book-keeper, Washington ave
Vough Aaron H., canal supt, Stewart
Vanhorne Richard, laborer, Jane
Vann Joseph, retired, School
Vanderbelt Dan'l, street commissioner, Wash'n ave
Vanderbelt Bart, action maker, Washington ave
Vanderbilt Wm., lawyer, Washington ave
Vanover Jacob, action maker, Warren
Vanover Wm., action maker, Warren

ANDREWS & NOLF, 205 Northampton St., Easton, Pa. You can find it by the fine large awning in front of store.

Vandyke J. M., lawyer, office Belvidere ave resides Windsor House
Vannatta Edward, U. S. mail agt, Washington ave
Vannatta Wm., case maker, Washington ave
Vough Miss Celia H., school teacher, Wash'n ave
Vannatta Samuel, harness maker, res Belvidere ave harness shop Belvidere ave
VanDoren Ten, clerk, Washington ave
Valentine Chas. J., fireman, Washington ave
Vanhorne John L., agent, Washington ave
VanCampen Elwood, shoemaker, Broad
Winter Henry, lumber merchant, Belvidere ave
Winter J. C., Justice of Peace, Belvidere ave
Wandling Peter, farmer, Washington ave
Wright Saml., retired, Church
Wright Wm., brakeman, Church
Wright Wm. R., rubber, Pt Washington
Whippert Daniel, barber, Washington ave
Widener Wm., hostler, Mechanic
Williams G. B., blacksmith, Cornish

FELIX & LEININGER, Nos. 102 & 104 South 3d St., Easton, Pa. **FURNITURE.**

Williams Ermin, blacksmith, Cornish
Warman D. B., laborer, Jane
Warman Andrew, gardener, Jane
Witte Jno. C., harness maker, res Grand ave, shop Washington ave
White George C., action maker, Church
Webber Alfred, laborer, Belvidere ave
Widener Miller, hostler, Belvidere ave
Witte Mrs. John, school teacher, Grand ave
Wyckoff Daniel V., grain merchant, Carlton ave
Whitenight W. H., hostler, Delaware
Washburne John V., mechanic, Melodeon
Washburne E. L., laborer, Melodeon
Washburne McClellen, shoemaker, Church
White Marshal, laborer, Cornish
Woolverton Benj., farmer, Washington ave
Willever Wm., stone mason RR, Pt Washington
Webb Walter M., retired physician, Washington ave
Webb E. B., druggist, Washington ave
Weller Low P., clerk, Belvidere ave

H. M. NORTON, WHOLESALE AND RETAIL DEALERS IN HARDWARE, STOVES HEATERS AND RANGES.

212   WASHINGTON BOROUGH DIRECTORY.

Weller J. C., tobacconist, res Belvidere ave, store Washington ave
Weller Jacob, merchant, Stewart
Weller Capt. Wm., woodfinisher, Washington ave
Weller Peter R., clerk, Stewart
Weller Philip, laborer, Delaware
Weller Samuel, school teacher, Washington ave
Waters Wm. C., fly finisher, Church
Warne J. S., tree agent, School
Wright Chas., wood finisher, Pt Washington
Willamson John, caterer, Washington ave
Weller Miss Lizzie, school teacher, Stewart
Weaver Clinton, laborer, New
Weller Wm., laborer, Delaware
Waters Wm, case maker, Church
Weaver, Wm. R., student, Belvidere ave
Warne J. B., peanut agent, School
Wandling Levi, jig sawyer, St. Cloud Hotel
Wandling Robt., merchant, resides St. Cloud Hotel store Washington ave

FELIX & LEININGER, Nos. 102 & 104 South 3d St., Easton, Pa. FURNITURE

White Fred, barber, Washington ave
Wack Alvin, painter, Carlton ave
Wright John B., brakeman, Church
Weaver Saml., carpenter, Johnston
Weaver Wm. G., nursery agent, Belvidere ave
Yeomans Davison, farmer, Broad
Yeomans Sam'l, teamster, Mechanic cor Cornish
Young Wm. A., brakeman, Brown
Young Geo., blacksmith, Carlton ave

DR. WM. M. BAIRD,
PHYSICIAN AND SURGEON,
Washington,   -   -   New Jersey.
SURGERY AND CHRONIC DISEASES A SPECIALTY

Young Daniel, laborer, Washington ave
Young John, huckster, Carlton ave
Yard Andrew, fireman, Belvidere ave
Yard Frank, organ tuner, Belvidere ave

ANDREWS & NOLF, 205 Northampton St., Easton, Pa. The Largest line of DRESS TRIMMINGS etc.

HACKETTSTOWN.

HACKETTSTOWN was incorporated as a borough in 1853 and has now (1880) about 2,800 inhabitants.

It has an area of about 2½ miles, or 1754 acres. It is bounded on the north and east by Morris county; on the south by Mansfield township, and on the west by Independence. It received its present name from a gentleman by the name of Samuel Hackett, at the time of the raising of the frame of the first hotel on the site of the Warren House. This was most probably in the year 1764. Few places in the county of Warren have such a beautiful natural location as this thriving town. From the summit of Bucks Hill, a rocky height half a mile from town, the town and adjacent country can be seen to the best advantage. Towards the south the fertile valley of the Musconetcong stretches as far as the eye can reach. The hills coming together on the north, and bounding the view in that direction; the Schooley Mountain range on the east; the Musconetcong river meandering through the midst of the valley, and on whose banks the borough stands; the Morris canal at the foot of the hills and the D. L. & W. R. R. track a little below that, presents to the eye a panorama that is indeed most picturesque.

It is said that Samuel Hackett was the first settler of this town, and that he settled there about the year 1720. His father-in-law had received large grants of land from the King of England, and he in turn gave 10,000 acres to Mr. Hackett.

He once lived in a log house that stood on the eastern bank of Bowers' foundry pond. Thomas Shields, Jr., a few years ago removed the Lozear house, which it is said was his last residence. He was one of the judges of Morris county before Sussex and Warren were taken from it. He lived to a ripe old age and died without any heirs.

Hackettstown has three hotels, none of which have license at the present time. There has been a hotel where the Warren House now stands for the last ninety years. The house was rebuilt in 1849, and has been known as the "Warren House" since. The "American House" was kept as a hotel as early as 1823. It has been added to a number of times until it now has a frontage of 160 feet. The Clarendon House, owned by Thomas Shields, Jr., is the one most recently built and is a very neat and attractive hostelry.

Hackettstown is burdened with a considerable debt, most of which was incurred in building the present fine large public school building, which is a credit and ornament to the town. The debt, however, is being gradually wiped out and taxes are easier.

The town is well supplied with churches. The "First Presbyterian Church of Independence" is a strong organization. The first building was a frame one erected about the year 1766. About the year 1849, this old Church was sold and removed to Beattystown and a new one erected. The present church was erected in 1864, when the Rev. G. C. Bush was pastor; is valued at $36,000, with a membership of about 500.

THE ST. JAMES EPISCOPAL CHURCH

was erected in 1859. It is a Mission belonging to the Convocation of Newark.

TRINITY METHODIST EPISCOPAL CHURCH

was organized in 1832. There was no regular Methodist appointment prior to that time. The first church was erected in 1834. There was a new edifice built in front and nearer the street in 1858. The old one is used now as a Sabbath school room.

ST. MARY'S CATHOLIC CHURCH

was erected in 1864. Before its erection the few Catholics in Hackettstown and vicinity worshipped in a house near the Morris and Essex railroad.

The school facilities of Hackettstown are unsurpassed. The fine three-story public school building was erected in 1874, at a cost of $39,000. The school district is number 48, and there are, according to the report of State Superintendent in 1875, 648 scholars in the district. The total amount received from all sources for public school purposes was $5,212.62.

The corner stone of the

CENTENARY COLLEGIATE INSTITUTE

was laid September 9, 1869. It is a Methodist institution under the care of the Newark M. E. Conference. Hackettstown was selected as the site of this institution because of the grandeur of its scenery, the purity of its water and the healthfulness of its climate. The building cost over $200,000 and is free of debt. It has under the Presidency of Rev. George H. Whitney, D. D., enjoyed uninterrupted patronage and prosperity. Each succeeding year has seen this institution increasing in popularity and usefulness. Many students seeking admission are turned away for want of room to accommodate them. It is designated to afford the amplest facilities for both sexes to receive a superior education, and to prepare young men for the higher classes in college or theological seminary.

Hackettstown is favorably situated for the introduction of water, and the reservoir built at Schooley's Mountain amply supplies the town. The income from the water works is a source of profit to the town.

The "First National Bank of Hackettstown" is considered one of the staunchest moneyed institutions in the county. The present officers of the borough are: Mayor, Charles J. Reese; Clerk, Anson G. Protzman; Constables, F. J. Smith, Charles Carpenter, John F. McClellan; Justices of Peace, John R. Carr, S. C. Larison, Jas. K. Rice, L. J. Youngblood; Council, J. L. Winters, J. O. Park, W. K. Hoffman, Amos Read, M. B. Bowers, W. L. Heist, G. W. Smith.

CENTENARY COLLEGIATE INSTITUTE, HACKETTSTOWN, NEW JERSEY.
NEWARK CONFERENCE SEMINARY. REV. G. H. WHITNEY, D. D., PRESIDENT.

New fireproof laboratory for classes in practical Chemistry. The building, which will accommodate nearly 400 students, is pronounced to be one of the finest in the land; heated by steam; lighted with gas; with mountain spring water in every room. Has been crowded during the past six years, and many have been refused from lack of room. Catalogue free.

College Preparatory for Young Men. Ladies College grants degrees. Courses in Science, Art, Music, Elocution, Commercial branches. Gymnasium for young men. New Gymnasium for Ladies.

Hackettstown Business Directory.

F. H. Bryan & Co., real estate, fire and life insurance
Charles Hairhouse, watchmaker and jeweler
L. H. Salmon, lumber, lime, agricultural tools, etc
Centenary Collegiate Institute, Rev. Geo. H. Whitney, D. D., Pres
John Toepfer, bakery, grocery, etc
F. W. Kluppelberg's Son, books, stationery, etc
A. C. Howell, Vienna restaurant, European plan
T. C. Plate, watchmaker and jeweler
R. Q. Bowers & Son, Hackettstown foundry and machine shops
Wade Brothers, hardware, etc
Wm. F. Shields, Ph. G., pharmacies
Aug. Dickerson, fine light carriages and sleighs
W. G. Sutphin, drugs and medicines
J. H. Vesselius, dry and fancy goods
Thomas Shields, Jr., custom tailor, hats, etc
A. B. Buell, photographer

PHOTOGRAPHS

A. B. BUELL,

SUCCESSOR TO C. C. KENNEY,

HACKETTSTOWN, N. J,

Fine Photographs of all kinds. Call and see his pictures.

SHIELDS' COMPOUND SYRUP OF WILD CHERRY.

WITH HYPOPHOSPHITES OF LIME AND SODA.

A POSITIVE CURE FOR

Coughs, Colds, Croup, Pneumonia, Hoarseness. Sore Throat, Bronchitis, Whooping Cough, and all diseases leading to Pulmonary Consumption and Bleeding at the Lungs.

This combination is made by request, to meet the professional demand. It is approved and extensively prescribed by the medical fraternity.

The Hypophosphites contained in this preparation are free from impurities, and neutral, conditions insisted on by Dr. Churchill as necessary to efficiency.

Price 25 cents, 50 cents and $1.00 per bottle.

☞ **CAUTION.**—The Public is strictly cautioned against using so-called Cough Syrups or Cough Mixtures, which are offered for sale with sealed corks, to prevent evaporation. All these contain chloroform, chloric-ether, ether, and other volatile and injurious drugs (may be known by their color) which only give temporary or a false relief, and cause drowsiness, bad after-effects, or leave a burning, sweet taste. By the use of these preparations the system acquires the dreaded opium or morphine habit, and but a small portion of the general public have any adequate idea of the strength of this habit, or of the great difficulty and impossibility, in most cases, of unaided cure. The chief responsibility, indeed, with the habit lies in the initiation rather than in the continuance of the habit; you cannot, like the user of alcohol and tobacco, by a strong effort of the will, shake off its chains.

SHIELDS' INFALLIBLE DYSPEPTIC REMEDY.

COMPRESSED POWDER FORM.

Prepared after a valuable prescription written by the late Dr. Willard Parker, of New York City. Guaranteed a sure cure for

Dyspepsia, Sick or Nervous Headache.

Price 75 cents. Sent by mail, to any address on receipt of price. The above Prescriptions are prepared only by

WM. F. SHIELDS, Ph. G. Pharmacist
Hackettstown, New Jersey.

SOLD BY ALL DRUGGISTS.

WARREN COUNTY DRUG STORE.

Hackettstown Directory.

Albert Ann. E., freeholder, North Hackettstown
Albertson E. H., merchant, North of RR
Albertson Samuel, gentleman, Eastside Plain
Apgar Geo. W., butcher, Plain
Ackley Wm. A., butcher, Main
Allen Samuel H., carpenter, Mechanic
Allen Jacob C., lawyer, Moore
Allen George, laborer, Main
Ayers Amanda, freeholder, Hope
Apgar Mrs. Phoebe, freeholder, Plain
Apgar Archibald, farmer, Willow Grove St
Ayers James, teamster, Moore

FELIX & LEININGER, Nos. 102 & 104 South 3d St., **Easton, Pa.** **FURNITURE.**

Albert Edgar, Plain
Baggot Richard, brakeman, Centre
Baggot Heistand, painter, Centre
Baggot Jesse, laborer, Centre
Bird James F., carriage maker, Willow Grove
Bird James D., Water
Bird Thomas, carpenter, Water
Bird Wm. E., Mechanic
Bird John S., laborer, Mechanic
Bell John J., farmer, Bell's Lane
Bell Milton, presses clothing, Bell's Lane
Bell Wm. H., railroader, Washington
Bell John, huckster, Mechanic
Bell John H., huckster, Mechanic
Bell Rachel H., huckster, Mechanic
Bell Mrs. Elizabeth, householder, cor Mill and Willow Grove
Bell Jacob C., landlord, cor Mill and Willow Grove
Bell Obadiah, farmer, Bell's lane
Bell Wm. P., laborer, Bell's lane

SHIELDS INFALLIBLE Dyspeptic Remedy A sure cure for Dyspepsia, Sick or Nervous Headache. Guaranteed.

H. M. NORTON, WHOLESALE AND RETAIL DEALER IN HARDWARE, STOVES, HEATERS AND RANGES.

Bowlby Frank, furniture, etc, li p
Brown Alfred, manuf of clothing, Church and Main
Brown Mrs. Sarah, householder, Church and Main
Brown Henry, carriage bus, Main
Bowers R. Q., foundry, etc, Willow Grove
Bowers Robert G., foundry, etc, Willow Grove
Bowers Michael B., foundry, etc, Willow Grove
Bowers Elizabeth P., householder, Willow Grove
Brant Thomas H., carriage bus, Hope
Brant Frank H., taxidermist, Hope
Brant James S., carriage trimmer, Main
Baldwin Wm., mason, North Hackettstown
Baldwin Mrs. Margaret, householder, N. Hackettst'n
Burress Robert, laborer, North Hackettstown
Burress Theodore, laborer, N Hackettstown
Bilby Jessie S., grocer, Main
Bilby Johathan, farmer, Willow Grove
Bilby Aaron, laborer, Mechanic
Bilby Eugene, carriage bus, Mechanic
Blackwell, Frank, butcher, Main

FELIX & LEININGER, Nos. 102 & 104 South 3d St., **Easton, Pa.** **FURNITURE.**

Blackwell Isaac N., carpenter, Mechanic
Burrell James, Blacksmith, Main
Branigan Patrick, trackwalker, Railroad
Brotran James, laborer, Dublin
Burt Frank, laborer, Dublin
Beatty Jacob H., mason, Rockport
Beatty Geo. A., merchant, Rockport and Hope
Beatty Robt, J., carriage trimmer, Mechanic
Beatty James, mason, Mechanic
Beatty Wm. T., mason, Mechanic
Beatty John C., grocer, Hope
Buell A. B., photographer, Hight
Beatty John H., miller, Croton Mills
Brands David F., retired, cor Moore and Madison
Bertron John, railroader, Hackettstown
Bryan F. H. & Co., real estate and fire and life insurance agents, Main
Bertron Edwin, railroader, Hackettstown
Bryan Fred H., real estate and insurance agt, Main
Bryan Margaret M., householder, Willow Grove

ANDREWS & NOLF, 205 Northampton Street, Easton, Pa. The reliable store for Black Goods.

HOUSEFURNISHING GOODS GENERALLY
The BEST GOODS for the LEAST MONEY at **H. M. NORTON'S, Easton, Pa.**

HACKETTSTOWN DIRECTORY.

Barker Charles, retired, Sharp
Bird Fred, carriage trimmer, Willow Grove
Bird J. Ferdinand, carriage trimmer, Willow Grove
Crane Dr. Theodore, physician, Washington
Crane Theodore Jr., drug clerk, Main
Crane Isaac W., water superintendent, Crane's Mill
Crane Sophia B., householder, Crane's Mill
Crane John T., laborer, Mechanic
Curtis Joshua, milk bus. Main
Curtis Jos. W., dentist, Main
Curtis Geo. P., printer, Main
Cramer Mrs. Mary B., householder, Washington
Cramer Ephraim D., retired, Washington
Cramer, Wm. B., carriage manfr, Main
Cramer Aaron Jr., carriage manfr, Washington
Crawford David B., carriage manfr, Washington
Clawson Mrs. Catharine, householder, Washington
Clawson Lewis, carpenter, Rockport
Clawson Alpheus, carpenter, Valentine
Cook Dr. John S., physician, Mill

FELIX & LEININGER, Nos. 102 & 104 South 3d St., **Easton, Pa.** **FURNITURE.**

Cook Jos. M., furnaceman, Mill
Cook David M., bank clerk, Moore
Cook S. Pierson, lawyer and publisher, Main
Cook Silas C., printer, Mill
Cook Richard P., physician, Mill
Clawson Talmage, laborer, High
Clawson Jacob S., laborer, Mechanic
Clawson Stephen, laborer, Mechanic

T. G. PLATE
Watchmaker & Jeweler,
HACKETTSTOWN, N. J.
ESTABLISHED 1857.

Clawson Wm. D., laborer, Water
Clawson Alfred, huckster, Washington
Clawson Wm. R., laborer, Washington
Clawson Mrs. Alfred, householder, Washington
Cook Benj. B., painter, Rockport

Clothes Wringers, Washing Machines, etc., at WADE BROS.'

H. M. NORTON, WHOLESALE AND RETAIL DEALER IN HARDWARE, STOVES, HEATERS AND RANGES

Cook Frederick, clerk, Moore
Cook William, clerk, Moore
Cook Charles, printer, Mill
Cook Anna, householder, Main
Cook Kate, householder, Main
Cummins Eliza M., householder, Main
Cummins Thomas, laborer, Dublin
Cummins Patsy J., nightwatchman at depot, Dublin
Cummins John, Dublin
Cummins Charles, Dublin
Coats James, gardener, Moore
Churchfield Thomas, janitor pub school, Washington
Crannon Michael, laborer, Centre
Crannon Patrick, laborer, Dublin
Crate Mary A., householder, Hope
Clark Richard, moulder, Mechanic
Clark Benson S., moulder, cor. Main and Moore
Colclough Susan, milliner, Main
Colclough Phoebe, milliner, Main
Carpenter Chas., chief police, Liberty

FELIX & LEININGER, Nos. 102 & 104 South 3d St., Easton, Pa. **FURNITURE.**

Carpenter Theodore, laborer, Liberty
Chamberlain A. P., householder, Willow Grove
Correll Joseph, laborer, High
Cole Robt. A., cashier bank, Main
Cole Benj. P., retired, Main
Colback John, laborer, Railroad avenue
Carr John R., collector, High
Crone Dennis, railroader, Dublin
Conway Wm., railroader, Dublin
Carter John L., dentist, Hope
Curl David, mason, Rockport
Courtright Edgar, miller, Washington
Cutler A. W., farmer, Rockport
Cornelius Bartley, laborer, Mechanic
Campfield Margaret M., householder, Mechanic
Cole Nelson, Mechanic
Cortright Peter, laborer, Washington
Cregar Chas. W., laborer, Washington
Corwin Harmon, laborer, Mill
Cruykendall Prof., teacher, Institute

BUSE FURNISHING GOODS GENERALLY
The BEST GOODS for the LEAST MONEY at **H. M. NORTON'S, Easton, Pa.**

HACKETTSTOWN DIRECTORY. 223

Cummins Nelson, laborer, Dublin
Davis Jacob W., lawyer, Willow Grove
DeForrest James W., carriage bus., Mechanic
Deremer Isaac, blacksmith, Main
Deremer Abram, machinist, W. Grove
Deremer Watson, moulder, Main
Deremer Wm. P., laborer, Main
Deremer Jacob, grocer, Main
Deremer John, carpenter, Hope
Deremer John, bender, Hope
Deremer Gideon, carpenter, Monroe
Denee David L., butcher, W. Grove
Dilley James B., travelling salesman, W. Grove
Downs Chas. S., huckster, Washington
Downs Edgar P., grocer, Main
Downs Sylvian, retired, Willow Grove
Dow William, blacksmith, Main
Dow Frank, teacher, Main
Dickson John B., painter, Sharp
Dolan Michael, railroader, Dublin

FELIX & LEININGER, Nos. 102 & 104 South 3d St., **Easton, Pa.** **FURNITURE.**

Dolan Wm., railroader, Dublin
Dolan Jas. railroader, Liberty
Dolan Jacob, railroader, Liberty
Dickerman John, laborer, Rockport
Dill Isaac S., retired, Rockport
Douglass Wm. L., tailor, Main
Dalrymple J. W., physician, Hope
Dilts Jonas, teamster, Willow Grove

Hackettstown Foundry & Machine Shops.

R. Q. BOWERS & SON,

Manufacturers of

Agricultural Implements, Plow Castings to fit all plows in general use, Wrought and Cast Iron for building bridges, etc.

Dickerson Pierson, carriage bus., Hope
Drake William, retired, Moore
Drake Rachael, householder, Moore
Dugan John L., laborer, Moore
Dedrick Thomas, librarian, Main

H. M. NORTON, WHOLESALE AND RETAIL DEALER IN HARDWARE, STOVES, HEATERS AND RANGES

Dellicker, A. H., lawyer and surveyor, Rockport
Deman Wm., cutter, Washington
Domblayer Isaac, laborer, Washington
Dubbon John N., laborer, Washington
Dubbon Fred J., laborer, Washington
Drake Chas. M., teacher, Rockport
Emons Joseph, railroader, Mechanic
Everitt J. Milton, harnessmaker, Main
Everitt James, ticket agent, Depot
Everitt, Wm. M., freight agent, Depot
Everitt Geo. T., express agent, Washington
Everitt Frank, Washington
Foster Wallace, laborer, Mechanic
Foster Samuel, laborer, Mechanic
Flock, J. D., merchant, Main
Ferris E. M., mail agent, Washington
Frazer G. W., huckster, Washington
Frazer Peter, laborer, Washington
Freeman A. G., dentist, Main
Fisher Simon, retired, Church

FELIX & LEININGER, Nos. 102 & 104 South 3d St., **Easton, Pa. FURNITURE.**

Fitzgerald Wm., laborer, Church
Fagan Anson, contractor, Moore and Monroe
Goodman John, laborer, Mill
Gibbs Levi B., retired, Main
Gulick Abram, clerk, Washington
Gulick John E., laborer, Washington
Gulick Cornelius, laborer, Washington
Gerard James E., carpenter
Grimes John, carriage trimmer, Washington
Grogan James, railroader, Dublin
Grogan David, railroader, Dublin
Giles Wm. S., retired, Main
Giles Henry, drives hack, Moore
Giles George, carriage bus, Mechanic
Gray Richard B., laborer, Mechanic
Grant Robert, blacksmith, Mechanic
Grovendyke David, farmer
Garrison William, laborer, Rockport
Gaddis John, mason, Water
Glover O. G., agent, Main

ANDREWS & NOLF, 204 Northampton St., Easton, Pa. You can find it by the fine large awning in front of store.

Horn Harrison, railroader, Centre
Horn Anna, householder, Centre
Hoffman Elias, laborer, Centre
Hoffman Wm. K., miller.
Hoffman J. D., merchant, Hope
Hoffman Gilbert, carpenter, Church
Hoffman William, retired, Sharp
Hoffman Alfred, teamster, Lumber
Hoffman Paul D., agent, Wades Row
Hance Alfred, butcher, Main
Hance Stewart, cabinet maker, W Grove
Howell Charles, furniture maker, Plane
Howell Henrietta, householder, Washington
Howell Isaac B., furniture maker, Washington
Howell Thomas B., bakery, Hope
Howell Frank, furniture, Main
Howell Alexander C., Warren
Haywood Edwin, carriage maker, Little
Haines John M., laborer
Haggerty Warren, millwright, Water

FELIX & LEININGER, Nos. 102 & 104 South 3d St., **Easton, Pa.** FURNITURE.

Haggerty Matilda, householder, Mill
Hummer James A., janitor institute, Mechanic
Hummer A. O., sexton M. E. church, Monroe
Hummer B. C., laborer, Madison
Hummer Jos. D., sexton Presby church, Mechanic
Hankison John, tinsmith, Main
Heist Wm. L., boarding house, High
Hairhouse Charles, jeweler, etc., Main

JOHN TOEPFER,
BAKERY, GROCERY and CONFECTIONERY,
MAIN STREET, HACKETTSTOWN, N. J.

Choice Bread, Cakes, Confections, Flour and Groceries of all kinds are always on hand.

Hairhouse William, jeweler, etc., Main
Hildebrant J. T., stock dealer, Main
Hildebrant Cornelius, carpenter, Washington
Hazen John M., sash and blind maker, High
Heed L. H., carriage maker, Mechanic

Guns, Ammunition, &c., at Wades' Hardware Store.

H. M. NORTON, WHOLESALE AND RETAIL DEALER IN HARDWARE, STOVES, HEATERS AND RANGES.

226   HACKETTSTOWN DIRECTORY.

Heed Edward, laborer, Hope
Heed John, musician, Hope
Harry Mrs. Frances, householder, Rockport
Hall Mrs. Anna, householder, Hope
Hall Wm. F., laborer, Hope
Hall James, laborer, Hope
Heyd D. B., trackman,
Hoff G. W., engineer, Main
Herre Chas. G., tailor, Washington
Henehan Thomas, track boss, Railroad ave
Hendershot Fred, mason, Mechanic
Hartman Wm., laborer, Mechanic
Hann Aaron H., laborer, Hope
Heath Emanuel, laborer,
Heath Alexander, laborer,
Hammond A. O., teacher, Institute
Hart Mrs. Abba, householder, Main
Hart Wm. K., carriage maker, Main
Hayes George, laborer, at Furnace
Henry Patrick, laborer,

FELIX & LEININGER, Nos. 102 & 104 South 3d St., Easton, Pa. **FURNITURE.**

Hopkins George, laborer,
Hoover Henry, laborer,
Hawk Walter, laborer,
Harmon Fred, laborer, Seminary
Harden Philander, baker, Seminary
Henber Geo., butcher, Main
Ivory John, watchman RR., Railroad ave
Ivory Thomas, watchman RR., Railroad ave
Ike Jacob, laborer, W. Grove
Johnson Clifford, clerk, Main
Johnson George, merchant, N. Main
Johnson Morris, merchant, N. Main
Johnson Jabe J., wheelwright, Centre
Johnson Wm. L., invalid, Main
Johnson Geo. W. Jr., merchant, Main
Johnson Geo. W. Sr., agent, Washington
Johnson Maria J., householder, Washington
Johnson E. C., boot and shoe store, Main
Johnson Levi, boot and shoe store, Main
Johnson Caleb, hack driver, American House

ANDREWS & NOLF, 205 Northampton Street, Easton, Pa.
The reliable store for Black Goods.

HOUSEFURNISHING GOODS GENERALLY
The BEST GOODS for the LEAST MONEY at **H. M. NORTON'S, Easton, Pa.**

HACKETTSTOWN DIRECTORY. 227

Johnson Marllati, householder, Washington
Jones Casper, retired, Moore
Kelly Charles, laborer, Centre
Kelly Richard, hack driver, Main
Kluppelberg F. W., musician, Rockport
Kluppelberg Enitha, householder, Rockport
Kluppelberg William, merchant, Hope
Keggan M., laborer,
Keggan John S., merchant stoves, etc., Hope
Katz Manness, clothing and dry goods, Main
Klotz Nathan, butcher, Main
Klotz Jos. D., drover, Main
Klotz Abram, drover, Moore
Klotz & Ackley, butchers, Main
Klotz Mrs. Mary E., householder, Moore
Krause Joseph, stone cutter, etc., Main
Kempf Carle. F., boots and shoes, Main
Karr John R., merchant, Rockport
Karr Mrs. Jennie, householder, Rockport
Kinsey Robert, painter, Rockport

FELIX & LEININGER, Nos. 102 & 104 South 3d St., **Easton, Pa.** FURNITURE.

Kemple John E., harness maker,
Kern Charles, retired, Water
Kenney C. C., photographer, High
King Geo. W. Jr. furniture and undertaker, Hope
King Geo. W. Sr., farmer, Hope
King & Bowlby, furniture, etc., Main
King Wm. D., farmer, High
Lozier S. Morgan, blacksmith, Mechanic
Lowery Rev. John, clergyman, pastor pres. ch., Mill

L. H. SALMON,
Hacketts'own, New Jersey.
DEALER IN ALL GRADES OF
Pine and Hemlock Lumber, also Sash, Blinds
Doors, Lime, Cement, Fertilizers, Syracuse Plows and Fixtures.

Lowery Sanford S., retired, Mechanic
Little John S., water rent collector, Mechanic
Loder Gersham, teamster, Main
Loder Robert, carriage maker, Main
Loder Thomas, carriage maker, Main

SHIELDS INFALLIBLE **Dyspeptic Remedy.** A sure cure for Dyspepsia, Sick or Nervous Headache. Guaranteed.

H. M. NORTON, WHOLESALE AND RETAIL DEALER IN HARDWARE, STOVES, HEATERS AND RANGES.

228 HACKETTSTOWN DIRECTORY.

Latsch Leroy, engineer, Main
Lavalier Wm. T., carriages, Main
Lavalier Wm. C., painter, Main
Ledwith Thomas, grocer, Hope
Larrison S. C., coal dealer, Hope
Lake Jefferson, laborer, Mechanic
Lake Mrs. Sarah, householder, Water
Lake Thomas, retired, Water
Langer Jacob, railroader,
Lee Jos. W. A., telegraph office, Rockport
Luff Nutt, cigarmaker, Main
Lord J. H., blacksmith, Main
Lyons Tobias, laborer, Liberty
Lampson J. S., mail agent, Washington
Little Frank, manufacture of clothing, Main
Mosely Patrick, laborer, Cutler's Lane
McCracken Mrs. Sarah, householder, Main
McCracken William, prop. of warren house, Main
McCracken Peter, laborer, Mechanic
McCracken Frank, clerk, Main

FELIX & LEININGER, Nos. 102 & 104 South 3d St., **Easton, Pa.** FURNITURE

Mack S. R., carriages, Main
Mack J. Farley, carriages, Main
Marlatt John, carpenter, Washington
Marlatt Aaron, teamster, Lumber
Marlatt Jacob P., retired, Lumber
Marlatt Wm. H., carpenter, Washington
Marlatt Wm., baggage agent, Washington
Milham Wm., soldier,
Mealer Wm. D., harness maker, Main
Munn Joshua, cutter, Rockport
Miller Dayton B., laborer, Mechanic
Miller Henry, turning bus, Hope
Miller Wm. Sr., blacksmith, Willow Grove
Miller Jerry, mason, Willow Grove
Miller Samuel W., carpenter, Mechanic
Miller William Jr., blacksmith, Willow Grove
Miller Holloway, mason, Willow Grove
Miller Elmer, laborer, Willow Grove
Miller David, retired, Rockport
Miller Jesse S., clerk, Moore

ANDREWS & NOLF, SELL THE BEST $1.00 AND $1.25 KID GLOVES IN EASTON, PA. 295 NORTHAMPTON STREET

Macklow John B., hatter, Main
Martin Amanda, householder, Mill
Martin James C., contractor, Liberty
Martin Alden E., physician, High
Martin Emma E., householder, Main
Martin Charles, retired, Mill
McLean Amos, carriages, Moore and Main
McLean A. W., creamery
McDonald Daniel, railroader
McClellan J. F., detective, American House
McClellan George M., clerk, American House
McClellan David, hardware store, Main
McClellan Emily A., householder, Main
McClellan Silas M., harness dealer, Main
McDead Patrick, laborer, Liberty
Mackmahon Thos. Jr., laborer, Liberty
McCann Wm., laborer, Liberty
Martenis A. Judson, clerk, Hope
Martenis Henry S., laborer, Monroe
Maberry A. & K., milliners, Main

FELIX & LEININGER, Nos. 102 & 104 South 3d St., **Easton, Pa.** FURNITURE.

Menth Edward, blacksmith, Mechanic
Manderville Edward, printer, Main
Murphy James, laborer
Merel Wm. C., clerk, Hope
Merell David, farmer, Washington
Mattison Wm., carriage maker, Valentine
Mattison Amos, millwright, Church
Mattison Oram, clerk, Church
Mucheler J. H., canal boss, North Hackettstown
McConnel Wm. A., laborer, Dublin
McCarty Mrs., householder, Liberty
Mead Peter F., student, Institute
Monroe Rev. John H., pastor M. E. church, Main
McWhei John, laborer
Nipher J. N., blacksmith, Water
Neal A. N., printer, Washington
Nunn Miller R., lumber and undertaker, Hope
Neighbor Theo., sexton cemetery, Washington
Neighbor Lawrence, painter, Washington
Neighbor Morris, carriage trimmer, Washington

Mechanics Tools of all kinds at Wade Brothers.

H. M. NORTON, WHOLESALE AND RETAIL DEALER IN HARDWARE, STOVES, HEATERS AND RANGES

230   HACKETTSTOWN DIRECTORY.

Nolan Thomas, insp of ties on RR, Monroe
Newsome Wm. S., student, Seminary
Osman Sarah A., householder, Willow Grove
Osman Charles, cutter, Main
Osman Elisha, railroader, Main
Osman Anna M., householder, W. Grove
Osman Joseph E., Washington
Osman Joseph, huckster, Main
Osman Ziba, invalid, W. Grove
Osman Jonah H., detective, Liberty
Osman Samuel B., blacksmith, Valentine
Osman E. Milton, engineer, Rockport
Osman Joseph, works on canal, Mill
Osman Ephraim, blacksmith
Osman Wilson, farmer
Ohay Michael, laborer, Dublin
Osmun Mrs. Sarah M., householder, Willow Grove
Odell Frank, machinist, Willow Grove
Palmer Wm. E., Seminary
Price R. S., Co. supt. pub. schools, Church

FELIX & LEININGER, Nos. 102 & 104 South 3d St., **Easton, Pa.** **FURNITURE.**

Price Archibald, retired, Mechanic
Parks John O., grocer, Main
Parks David Jr., shoemaker, Main
Parks Luther, North Hackettstown
Pyles F. C., carpenter, Main

WATCHMAKER, JEWELER & OPTICIAN.

The subscriber has on hand and for sale the best assorted stock of

Clocks, Watches, Jewelry, Silver, Silver Plated Ware and Optical Goods

in town. He confines himself to this business exclusively, and his long experience in the trade entitles him to give the very best satisfaction to all his customers.

CHAS. HAIRHOUSE,
Near Depot, HACKETTSTOWN, N. J.

SEPTEMBER, 1886.   ESTABLISHED 1873.

Pool John, painter
Pool Peter, blacksmith, Mill
Pool Edward, mason, Main
Pool Alvin, laborer, Water

HOUSEFURNISHING GOODS GENERALLY.
The BEST GOODS for the LEAST MONEY at **H. M. NORTON'S**, Easton, Pa.

HACKETTSTOWN DIRECTORY.

Plate F. G., jeweler, Main
Peer Alfred Jr., student, Main
Protzman A. G., printer, Willow Grove
Petty Robt., laborer, Main
Pickle Edward, laborer
Perry Samuel, farmer, Mill
Porter Ruth P. C., householder, Main
Polisse George, peanut stand, Main
Reese Chas. J., mayor of town, Rockport
Read Mrs. Hannah B., householder, High
Read Andrew J., laborer, Mechanic
Read Noah, carpenter, Washington
Read Andrew, laborer, RR ave
Read Amos S., huckster, High
Richardson E. K., teacher, Hope
Rittenhouse Wm. S., teller in bank, Church
Rittenhouse Charles, postmaster, Main
Rittenhouse Brothers, pub. *Gazette*, Main
Rittenhouse Caroline, householder, Main
Rice Jos. K., justice of peace, Washington

FELIX & LEININGER, Nos. 102 & 104 South 3d St., **Easton, Pa.** FURNITURE.

Rice Peter, grocer, High
Rice & Deremer, grocerymen, Main
Rodda Wm. S., butcher, Main
Rusling Robert Jr., lumber business, Hope
Rusling Jos. M., painter, Willow Grove
Rusling & Nunn, lumber and undertaking, Hope
Rusling George M., civil engineer and surv'r, Wash'n
Rusling James J., turning and bending, Hope
Rusling Mrs. Mary, householder, Main
Redinger Jacob, shoemaker, Rockport
Redinger Frederick, barber, Rockport
Redinger Charles, painter, Rockport
Redinger Lewis, laborer, Rockport
Redinger Jacob Jr., barber, Rockport
Ricker David, carpenter, Sharp
Rea Mrs. Mary, householder, Main
Rea Samuel, drugs and medicines, Hope
Rea Geo. M., cutter, Main
Robbins Thomas S., Clarendon Hotel, Rockport
Rolph Aaron, grocer, Main

SHIELDS' Compound Syrup of Wild Cherry with Hypophosphites of Lime and Soda. Sure cure for coughs, croup, etc.

H. M. NORTON, WHOLESALE AND RETAIL DEALER IN HARDWARE, STOVES, HEATERS AND RANGES

Reading Robt. M., retired, Hope
Rusling Geo. M., surveyor, Washington
Richter Edward, barber
Rolph & Skinner, grocers, Main
Smith Mrs. Tamson, householder, Mechanic
Smith Marilda, householder, Main
Smith Mary, householder, Main
Smith Rosilla, householder, Main
Smith Jesse, painter, Mechanic
Smith Isaac R., laborer, Mechanic
Smith Frederick, carpenter, Moore
Smith Geo. W., carpenter, Moore
Smith James L., grocer, Main
Smith Jas. B., retired, Mechanic
Smith Robert, clerk, Mechanic
Smith Edgar A., laborer, Wade's Row
Smith Edward, laborer, Wade's Row
Salmon L. H., lumber, etc., Hope
Saunders Geo. C., carpenter, Warren

FELIX & LEININGER, Nos. 102 & 104 South 3d St., **Easton, Pa.** **FURNITURE.**

Saunders J. E., carpenter, Centre
Sharp Amanda, householder, Washington
Stoddart Walter, livery, Lumber
Stoddart Wm., livery, Lumber
Stoddart Henry, gardener, Mechanic
Stoddart Thomas, gardener, Mechanic
Stoddart Henry Jr., painter, Mechanic
Swayze I. B., blacksmith, High
Swartz Peter, laborer, Water
Shields W. F., drugs and medicines, Main
Shields Jacob A., coal dealer, Hope
Shields John, retired, Mechanic
Shields Imlay, blacksmith, Hope
Shields Thomas Jr., clothing store, Main
Stephens Saml. E., retired, Mechanic
Stephens R. Preston, retired, Washington
Stryker Isaac R., builder and contractor, Washingt'n
Stryker Henry, builder and contractor, Washington
Sutphin W. G., drugs and medicines, Main
Slater A. H., Centre

FINE TABLE CUTLERY at **WADES' HARDWARE STORE.**

Slater Elias R., mason, Moore
Slater Irving, laborer, Moore
Sliker John B., livery, Main
Sliker Thomas, laborer, Warren
Sliker David, laborer, Warren
Sidenor Wm., cooper, Willow Grove
Sidenor Anderson, carriage workman, Centre
Stilwell Radford, painter, Main
Sutton Wm. C., blacksmith, Plane
Sutton Andrew J., engineer, Liberty
Sullivan Dennis, laborer, Railroad ave
Schenck Wm. A., telegraph op, Hope
Stewart Wm. R., farmer, Rockport
Shotwell, Arch., laborer, Washington
Slack Jno. K., conductor, High
Seguine Jos., mason, Washington
Shockinsey Jos., laborer, Liberty
Saatz Ferdinand, upholster
Standish John, laborer, Liberty
Stiff Chas. E., tinsmith, Main

FELIX & LEININGER, Nos. 102 & 104 South 3d St., Easton, Pa. FURNITURE.

Saulesbury L. C., horseman, Willow
Search Geo., brakeman, Hope
Stivers Prof. E. L., teacher, O. C. Institute
Skinner B. F., grocer, Main
Schmeal Walter, boatman, N. Hackettstown
Sharp Jno. D., retired, church
Taylor Eli, carpenter, Main

F. H. BRYAN & CO.,
Hackettstown, N. J.,
REAL ESTATE AND LIFE INSURANCE AGENTS.

Money to loan on Bond and Mortgage. Loans negotiated, Titles Examined. Auctioneering a Specialty.

F. H. BRYAN.   J. W. DAVIS.

Taylor Wallace, carpenter, Main
Teeter John E., telegraph op, Washington
Trimmer Eli, farmer, Willow
Trimmer, Asa, farmer, Willow

H. M. NORTON, WHOLESALE AND RETAIL DEALER IN HARDWARE, STOVES, HEATERS AND RANGES.

HACKETTSTOWN DIRECTORY.

Trimmer A. W., creamery, Main
Trimmer Andrew, retired, Main
Trimmer I. B., market, Hope
Tamblin James, blacksmith, Church
Toepfer John, baker, etc., Main
Tronson Wm., painter, Wade's Row
Titus C. M., tanner, Hope
Titus Rolph, retired, Moore
Titus James J., janitor, Sharp
Tholpe Henry, laborer, Main
Tretheway Wm. R., mining engineer, Washington
Tillman Geo. W., carpenter, Rockport
Tremblan Gustavus, retired, Hope
Thomas David, laborer, Water
Thomas Martin R., laborer, Liberty
Thomas Geo. W., retired, Hope
Thomas James, laborer, Water
Thomas Rev. Richard, M. E. preacher, Rockport
Timmons Michael, brakeman, Railroad ave
Tharp Ira B., laborer, Front Brook

FELIX & LEININGER, Nos. 102 & 104 South 3d St., **Easton, Pa.** FURNITURE.

Tunison Geo. J.
Tunison Henry R., carpenter, Washington
Talmage Wm. R., retired, Main
Terry Robert, laborer, Main
Thompson Geo. W., teamster, Main
Thompson C. F., professor, Institute
Terriberry Jacob, farmer, Mechanic
Vescelius Henry, dry and fancy goods, Main
VanDyke Jacob, bartender, Warren
Vanscyover Mary, retired, Main
Vail James H., trimmer, Plane
Vansyckle, Wm. H., millwright, Washington
Vansyckle John G., grocer, Main
Vansyckle John L., laborer, N. Hackettstown
Vansyckle, Jacob, mason, Washington
Vansyckle A. C., physician, Main
Voorhees Theophilus, photographer, Mechanic
Voorhees Abram, laborer, Mechanic
VanHorn T. S., general store, Hope
Wendt Fred., merchant tailor, Main
Woolever Abm., laborer, Liberty

Woolever George, laborer, Liberty
Woolever Chas., laborer, Liberty
Woolever Stewart, laborer, Liberty
Wire Henry, laborer, Willow
Wire Alonzo, laborer, Warren
Whitney Dr. Geo. H., Pres. Inst., Institute
Whitney E. A., professor, Institute
Weeder Wm., painter, Liberty
Weeder Frank, laborer, Liberty
Widenor Amzi, trackman, Liberty
Weber Herman, barber, High
Weber Charles, jeweler, Main
Winters Jas. L., farmer, Hope
Winters A. J., blacksmith, Hope
Welsh Eliza J., householder, Main
Waters Nancy, householder, Mechanic
Wade Frank E., hardware, Main
White Thomas S., saloon, Hope
White John G., retired, Rockport
Wink Jacob, barber, Hope

FELIX & LEININGER, Nos. 102 & 104 South 3d St., Easton, Pa. FURNITURE.

Waters Wm. L., painter, Centre
Wyley Jacob, carriage maker, Main
Wyley Nelson, blacksmith, High
Ward Marshal, telephone op., Mechanic
Wade Chas. M., hardware, Washington
Williamson Dan'l, carpenter, Mechanic
Wallace Robert, tinsmith, Washington
Wert Jno. C., bakery, Main
Wintermute Archibald, retired, Main
Wintermute Geo., farmer, Washington
Williams Wm. D., clerk, Moore
Waterman N. B., drummer, Warren House
Woodruff Wm. H., clerk, Rockport
Wolf Jno. W., retired, Lumber
Weaver H. J., teacher, Mechanic
Youngblood L. J., justice of peace, Mill
Youngblood W. H. H., miller, Mill
Youngblood Martin J., lawyer, Mill
Young Thomas, retired, Mill
Young Lewis, clerk, Water
Yoder Geo. K., shoemaker, Willow
Young Jacob, tobacconist, Hope

a good assortment of our own manufacture.

PARTIES BUYING CARRIAGES of us may rest assured of getting a stylish, well made and durable vehicle. No efforts will be spared to keep up the reputation of our work, so favorably known.

Aug. Dickerson,
Hackettstown, N. J.

Catalogues and prices furnished on application

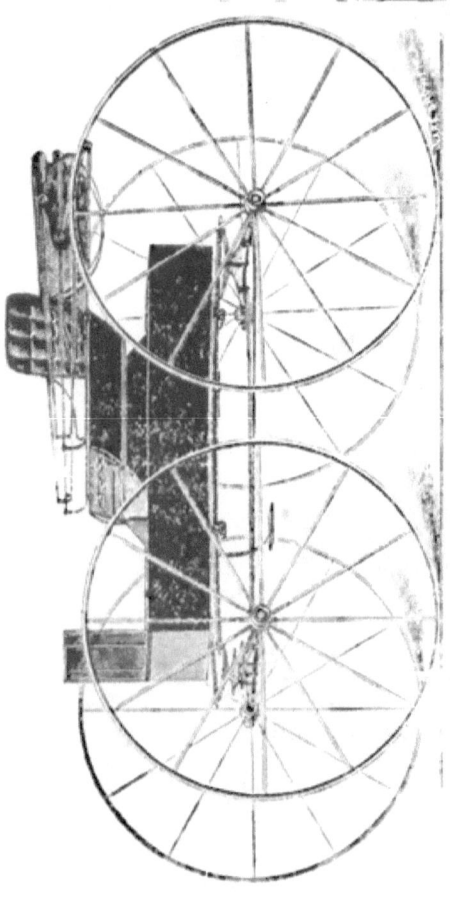

DICKERSON CARRIAGES

have been in use for a half century by

Livery Stables

and other

Hard Drivers.

They never fail to give satisfaction.

BELVIDERE.

THIS is the county seat of Warren county, and is beautifully located on either side of Pequest creek at its confluence with the Delaware river. The south side of the creek was the portion first settled. It is regularly laid out in squares, and about 30 or 40 feet above the level of the river. Here is the public square, the Court House, and the most beautiful part of the town. Around the public park are located, with one exception, the churches of the town, viz: Protestant Episcopal, Methodist Episcopal, Presbyterian and Baptist Churches, facing the east, south and west sides of the park. The Second Presbyterian Church is located on the north side of the river.

Belvidere is situated about 75 miles from New York, 65 miles from Philadelphia and 13 miles above Easton, Pa., and contains about 1,800 inhabitants.

It is supposed that the portion of the town upon the south side of the Pequest was at one time an Indian village. Robert Patterson was the first pioneer of Belvidere, and probably built the first house, which was torn down in 1838 by Major Depue. It was a block house, or double log house, as they were called in those days. The next land owner was Robert Morris, who in 1793 "gave a deed of the entire tract to his son-in-law and daughter, Charles and Mary Coxall." By deed dated Sept. 30, 1825, the entire 614 acres embraced in this tract were transferred to Garret D. Wall by Charles Coxall—Mary Coxall having previously died. Subsequently Mr. Wall generously donated to Warren county the grounds upon which the county buildings stand, and the public square. To his generosity, also, all the churches which face the park, with the exception of the Baptist, owe the lands upon which the churches and parsonages stand. The Baptists purchased their church lot of Hon. Geo. M. Robeson, in 1866. Major Robert Hoops came to Belvidere about the year 1770. He gave Belvidere its present name, and was an extensive land proprietor in and about the place. He acquired by purchase some 500 acres of land on either side of the Pequest, including the mill and water power. He afterwards erected a large slaughter house on the lot where now stand the buildings of D. C. Blair. In this building "large numbers of cattle and hogs were slaughtered and packed, which together with the flour manufactured at the mill were transported to middle Jersey for the use of the Revolutionary army, and not unfrequently at that period, all the farmers wagons and sleds were put into requisition to convey these articles to the half-starving thousands under the command of Gen. Washington, in the vicinity of Morristown."

During Major Hoop's ownership of the land to the north of the Pequest, he had it surveyed and divided into town lots, and called the town "Mercer," which remained its name for many years. This was, at that time, the only business part of the town, except the double-log or block-house, of Patterson's, which was occupied as a store, and subsequently as a tavern, and the Coxall mansion, which was in all probability built by Robert Morris about the year 1780. Belvidere is at the western terminus of the Lehigh & Hudson railroad, and also on the Belvidere & Delaware Division of the Pennsylvania railroad, and is well supplied with good hotels. The Warren House, the American House, the Pequest House are all kept in a first-class manner, and receive a liberal patronage.

The "Belvidere House," which was built in 1831 by Chapman Warner, and originally intended for a store, and a dwelling, was torn down this Summer, (1886), and will be replaced by a large and commodious structure, with all the conveniences of a first-class hotel. The

BELVIDERE BANK

was chartered Feb. 13th, 1830, principally through the efforts of Hon. John I. Blair. The first President of the institution was John Kinney Jr. who held the position till his death, 1850, when John I. Blair, Esq., was elected to fill the vacancy, and has held the position ever since. The first cashier was John Stuart, who was succeeded in 1854 by the present incumbent, Israel Harris. It was organized as a National Bank in 1865 with a capital of $500,000, but, in 1876, by a vote of its stockholders, the capital was reduced to $300,000.

Belvidere is very favorably situated for manufacturing purposes. Its water power is reckoned as second to none in the State, and with all the other natural advantages taken into consideration it probably has no superior as a site for manufacturing purposes. The principal manufacturing establishments are the flouring mills, of which there are several first-class ones.

Belvidere is well supplied with churches, and has a good public school. The first school house was a small frame structure of 14 by 26 feet. The present building is a common frame one, and was erected in 1861. In 1885 the total amount received for school purposes was $3,

765.00; value of school property, $5,500; total number of children in district between the ages of five and eighteen, 495. The school house will seat comfortably 360.

The present officers of the town are: Mayor, John W. King; Clerk, Geo. B. Given; Freeholder, Levi Ott; Assessor, Wm. R. Brokaw; Collector, J. Bittenbender; Constables, Augustus Laubach, Nelson Teeter; Council, Alonzo D. Cornell, Mahlon C. Cass, Samuel Rees, Janson K. Wildrick, John V. Deshong, Asa Kinney.

FAUST BROS.,

Water Street, BELVIDERE, NEW JERSEY,

DEALERS IN

Pure Drugs and Medicines, Paints, Oils, Glass, Varnishes, etc., of the Best Grades.

Perfumes, Trusses, and Surgical

Appliances. Also a full line of TOILET SOAPS.

REMEMBER THE PLACE.

FAUST BROS., Druggists,

BELVIDERE, N. J.

PEQUEST HOUSE,

Belvidere, N. J.,

H. K. Ramsey, Prop'r.

ADAPTED TO THE WANTS OF THE PUBLIC.

First-Class Accommodations for Transient Guests.

GOOD STABLING. TERMS MODERATE.

Belvidere Business Directory.

King's West End Pharmacy
Depue Son & Co., fertilizing material
C. H. Beasley, attorney at-law
G. A. Angle, attorney-at-law
P. F. Brakely, physician
Warren Journal, two dollars a year in advance
John B. Brookfield, deputy bank cashier
John D. Deisel & Son, clothing store and tailors
Faust Brothers, drugs, medicines and paints
Edward Hutchinson, constable and detective
Henry S. Harris, attorney-at-law
Charles Hoagland, grocery store
Theodore Hopler, county clerk of Warren County
Belvidere Apollo, two dollars a year in advance
Charles A. Lott, attorney-at-law
Frank Lefferts, homepathist physician
William H. Morrow, ex judge and lawyer
William O'Neill, Surrogate of Warren county
Irvin Quick, deputy county clerk
Solomon Parsons, pastor M. E. church
Samuel J. Kaub, dry goods and groceries
Joseph Roseberry, J. attorney-at-law
H. K. Ramsey, proprietor Pequest House
Martin C. Swartzweller, ex-surrogate
J. G. Shipman & Son, attorney-at-law
William Silverthorn, speculator
L. Dewitt Taylor, attorney-at-law
George H. Vancampen, sheriff of Warren county
William S. White, dentist

J. Diesel & Sons,
ONE-PRICE CLOTHIERS and MERCHANT TAILORS,
BELVIDERE, NEW JERSEY.
Fine Merchant Tailoring a Specialty.

◁KING'S▷
West ✦ End ✦ Pharmacy,

Cor. Front and Mansfield Streets.

BELVIDERE, N. J.

Drugs, Paints, Oils, and Medicines

LOWEST PRICES.

Sole Agent for JNO. W. MASURY & SON'S Pure Liquid Paint.

REMEMBER when you have a COLD to take DR. BEESLEY'S TONIC

EXPECTORANT.

◁KING'S ✦ WEST ✦ END▷ PHARMACY,

BELVIDERE, N. J.

WARREN COUNTY DRUG STORE.

Belvidere Directory

Armstrong George, laborer, Market
Angle John H., fish market, Water
Ackerman Abram, carriage shop, Water
Alliger Saml. R., painter, Depue
Allen Jos. E. railroader, Depue
Armstrong Mrs. Lizzie, householder, Fourth
Angle Geo. A., lawyer, office First
Allen Aaron H., agent, Water
Aiken James, laborer, Water
Barret Nathaniel, carpenter, Fourth
Barren John, hostler, Mansfield
Barron Howard, hostler, Mansfield

FELIX & LEININGER, Nos. 102 & 104 South 3d St., **Easton, Pa.** **FURNITURE.**

Barron Oscar, hostler, Mansfield
Beesley C. H., lawyer, Third
Beesley E. M., dentist, First
Bowers George B., miller, Mansfield
Brokaw Wm. R., assessor, Mansfield
Brophy John, laborer, Paul
Blackwell James, laborer, Depue
Bruen J. Dehart, Presbyterian pastor, Mansfield
Boyer George, gentleman, Hardwick
Blair D. C., capitalist, Hardwick and Second
Britton Nathaniel, laborer, Mill
Bair Henry B, Delaware ave
Bair James Sen., carpenter, Delaware ave
Bair James B. Jr., blacksmith, Delaware
Bair & Reher, store etc, cor Water and Market
Barlow, A. M., weaver, Market
Butler John C., Water
Brands James H., carriage maker, Water
Bebler Peter, expressman, Paul
Burd & Hoagland, grocery, Market

Mechanics Tools of all kinds at Wade Brothers.

HOUSEFURNISHING GOODS GENERALLY The BEST GOODS for the LEAST MONEY at **H. M. NORTON'S, Easton, Pa.**

Burd Elisha, merchant
Brackley P. F., physician, Third
Best Michael, carpenter, First
Bittenbender James, marble yard, First
Bittenbender Emanuel, Depue
Brink Morris, restaurant, Mansfield
Bittenbender Ira E., stone cutter, First
Burdett Jacob, fireman, Water
Bellis Jacob, tinsmith, Depue
Bellis Peter, laborer, Spring
Bellis Samuel, railroader, Fourth
Bellis Adam., editor *Warren Journal*, Front
Brittin Jas. A., telegraph repairer, Greenwich
Barry Wm. Sr., laborer, Fourth
Bee Manufacturing Co., pail factory, Front
Belford Mrs. James, Hardwick
Belford James, gentleman, Hardwick
Belford Edward, gentleman, Third
Barry Wm. Jr., laborer, Fourth
Baker Chas. laborer, Depue

FELIX & LEININGER, Nos. 102 & 104 South 3d St., **Easton, Pa.** FURNITURE.

Brookfield John B., deputy bank cashier, Front
Barrett John E., railroader, Hardwick
Bradley I. M., gentleman, First
Case Howard, laborer, Second
Cramer Wm. J., cabinet maker, Water
Cramer Amos, speculator, Market
Cramer Benjamin, hostler etc, Second
Crats Marshal, laborer, Water
Crats Jacob, laborer
Courtright John, fireman, Depue
Craig John, gentleman, Warren House
Coleman John, carpenter, Water
Cole John C., sexton at 1st Pres. church, Second
Cole Henry, clerk, Second
Cole Allie, school teacher, Second
Cowell Gideon, carpenter, Mansfield
Clymer John, sawyer, Mansfield
Cyphers George L., shoemaker, Water
Collins Edward, laborer, Oxford
Crane Jenny, school teacher, Third

H. M. NOR... WHOLESALE AND RETAIL DEALER IN HARDWARE, STOVES, HEATERS AND RANGES.

Cooper Mrs. B. B., householder, Third
Carter Jacob, gentleman, Water
Clark Mrs. Jane, householder, Second
Case Mahlon, miller, Mill
Cornell A. D., miller, Fourth
Calahan Timothy, railroader, Mansfield
Carhart Theodore, speculator, Mansfield
Clark Benjamin, teacher, etc., Seminary
Dereamer John, laborer, Paul
Donohue John, blacksmith, Water
Donohue Joseph, Belvidere House
Decker Isaac, gentleman, Paul
Decker John L., miller, Mill
Dildine Wm. M., tailor, Water
Davis D., carpenter, Market
Daily Peter, carpenter, Water
DeWitt Moses A., dealer in peaches, First
Dickey John P., railroad boss, First
Dickey John P. Jr., First
Ditz Joseph B., undertaker, &c., Water

FELIX & LEININGER, Nos. 102 & 104 South 3d St., Easton, Pa., FURNITURE.

Deisel John & Son tailors and clothing, First
Deisel Harry, tailor, First
Deisel John, tailor, Adams
Davis George, railroad watchman, Fourth
Davis & Hartung, proprietors of the American House
Davis George, hotel keeper, Mansfield
Dalke John, lawyer, Mansfield
Depue James & Son, fertilizing factory, near Depue
Depue James A., residence Third
Deshong John V., carriage factory, Water
Deshong William, proprietor rink, etc., Water
Dagget A. S., speculator, First
Dowd M. E., carpenter, First
Dickey E. P., printer, First
Davis Charles, pail factory, Oxford
Drake Richard, ins. agent, Mansfield
Douglas Rev. Charles, pastor episcopal church, Second
Discol John, railroad laborer,
Evans James P., carpenter, Paul

READ CAREFULLY Page 218

GENTS FURNISHING GOODS GENERALLY
The BEST GOODS for the LEAST MONEY at A. M. NORTON'S, Easton, Pa.

BELVIDERE DIRECTORY. 245

Everett Zenith, truckster, S. Water
Eylenberger Alfred, laborer
Eylenberger Hiram, blacksmith, Maiden Lane
Everett Wilson, expressman, Water
Emery Reeder F., carpenter, Fourth
Emery Albert, tinsmith, Second
Emery James, laborer.
Frome Wm. E., carpenter, Water
Fox Valentine, mason, Paul
Fox William, laborer, Paul
Fairclo Paul F., speculator, Water
Fritts John F., painter, Water
Fromer Mrs. Jacob, jeweler, Water
Folkner Cummins H., grocer, Water
Freeman Brothers, clothiers, cor. Water and Market
Freeman Sam, tobacco store, Water
Freeman Nathan, clerk, Water
Faust Brothers, drug store, Water
Faust M. S., drug store, Water
Faust H. W., drug store, Water

FELIX & LEININGER, Nos. 102 & 104 South 3d St., Easton, Pa. **FURNITURE.**

Forman William, huckster, Water
Fisher William, soldier, Mansfiled
Fisher Joseph, hotel keeper, First
Fisher John
Fisher Daniel, Hardwick
Fleming Elisha, deputy p. m., Mansfield
Foster Michael, laborer, Mansfield
Forge Quinn, blacksmith, Water
Flumerfelt P. C. B., wheelwright, Hardwick
Gardner David, saloon, Mansfield
Gardner Mathias, mason, Third
Gardner John, ex-sheriff, Third
Gardner George L., lumber dealer, S. Water
Gleatille Freemont, laborer.
Gross John G., bakery, First
Guis Sam, laborer, Hardwick
Guis Lewis, laborer, Hardwick
Givins George Jr., printer, Water
Givins George, hotel prop. cor. Hardwick and Front
Gibbs Silas, Water

Andrews & Nolf, 205 Northampton St. The only place to buy the "CONFORMATER" Corset.

H. M. NORTON WHOLESALE AND RETAIL DEALER IN HARDWARE, STOVES HEATERS AND RANGES.

Garry Philip, clerk at Pequest House, Water
Hutchinson Zack, bridge-tender, Water
Hutchinson Edward, con. and detective, Water
Hollander Wm., laborer, Water
Hollander Joseph, laborer, Greenwich
Hollander John, laborer, Water
Hays A. J., policeman, Water
Hunt Oliver, painter, Water
Hays B. D., wheel maker, Water
Hays Wm., laborer, Water
Hamburg August, tailor, First
Hansler J. S., shoemaker, Depue
Hyman John, carpenter, First
Heem Joseph, laborer, Hardwick
Hoff Mrs. Louisa, Mansfield
Helderbrant Dan, grocer, First
Hanes George, laborer, Spring
Huntsberger Mrs., dressmaker, Third
Harris Mag E., retired, Water
Harris Israel, bank cashier, First

FELIX & LEININGER, Nos. 102 & 104 South 3d St., **Easton, Pa.** FURNITURE.

Harris Henry S., lawyer, Water
Harris Chas., lawyer, First
Haughawort Isaac farmer Race
Haughawort Philip, speculator, Second
Hazlet Joseph, work in wheel factory, Front
Hoagland Geo., in county clerks office, Mill
Hoagland Chas., merchant, Water
Hoagland Wm., retired, Water
Hoagland & Randolph, carpenters, Water
Hilton Thomas, clerk, First
Hoagan James, laborer, Mansfield
Howard Mathew, farmer, Market
Holstein George, speculator, Market
Holstein L. H., speculator,
Holstein Mrs. Anna, retired
Harris Nicholas, lawyer, First
Hopler Theodore, county clerk, Second
Hefner Dan, telegrapher, Mansfield
Heed Henry, carpenter, Depue
Hopler Marcus, clerk, Second

Carriage Trimmings at Wade Bros., HACKETTSTOWN, NEW JERSEY.

Hendrickson Samuel, printer, Water
Harris Amelia, householder, Water
Innis George, general store, Water
Johnson Mrs. Margaret, householder, Hardwick
Johnson Carrie, householder, Hardwick
Jecohe Francis, carpenter, Wall
Jones John, laborer, Water
Jennings Joseph H., laborer, Water
Jennings Wm. H., cooper, &c., Depue
Jones Henry, barber, Mill
Jackson James & Co., dry goods millinery, etc., First
Jackson James A., merchant, First
Johnson Levi, farmer, Hardwick
Joiner Frank fireman, Greenwich
Keighen Cornelius, laborer, Paul
Kist John G., harness and saddler, Water
King Halsey, farmer, Water
Kethiege Peter, photographer, Mill
Kizzelbaugh Aaron, oysters, fish, fruit etc., Greenwich
Knice Peter, wood chopper, Greenwich

FELIX & LEININGER, Nos. 1, 2 & 101 south 3d St., Easton, Pa. **FURNITURE.**

Kohlman Edward, farmer, Spring
Kohlman Edward, Jr., miller, Spring
Kinney Asa, farmer, etc., Spring
Kitchen S. B., millwright, Oxford
Karr Jacob, carpenter, Water
Kleerchanie Dan, retired, Third
Kline John J., retired, Hardwick
Knights of Pythias, office over Wade's store, Water
Kimenour Andrew, lumber dealer, Depue
Kimenour Joseph, Depue
Kimenour John, painter, etc., Paul
Ketcham Josiah, editor of Apollo, First
Keener Ira B., miller, Mill
Kennedy Robert, farmer
Kelsey A. B., postmaster, Mansfield
King John H., architect and builder, Mansfield
King George H., druggist, cor. front and Mansfield
Kern Mrs. J. T., householder, Mansfield
Looman Andrew, laborer, Paul
Looman John, Jr., laborer, Paul

ANDREWS & NOLF, 205 Northampton St., Easton, Pa. You can find it by the fine large awning in front of store.

H. M. NORTON — WHOLESALE AND RETAIL DEALER IN HARDWARE, STOVES, HEATERS AND RANGES.

Lime Augustus, team driver, Water
Lee John, Market
Lomason Thomas, gardener, Depue
Lomason George, Depue
Lauterman George, laborer, Water
Lauterman George, Jr., team driver, Water
Litzenberger Benj., blacksmith, Water
Litzenberger A. G., barber, First
Lee Henry D., blacksmith, Water
Linn Levi, laborer, Water
Lake Chrales, cabinet ware-room, Water
Large Augustus, inspt. of cars, Greenwich
Lomerson Elizabeth, householder, Greenwich
Lott Charles A., lawyer, Hardwick
Lippincott Charles, railroader, Depue
Lockard Sam, boarding house, Greenwich
Lockard Jerry, tailor, First
Lockard George, tobacco store, Mill
Laire Wm. R., railroad ticket agt., American House
Laubach Augustus, constable, First

FELIX & LEININGER, Nos. 102 & 104 South 3d St., **Easton, Pa.** **FURNITURE.**

Land Charles, shoemaker, Paul
Lefferts Frank, physician, Mansfield
Lomping Wm., bartender, American House
Laurence Mrs. C., householder, Greenwich
Lerch Chris., laborer, Market
McQuinn Michael, laborer, Water
Mucklin Andrew, laborer, Water
Mucklin Henry, laborer, Market
McLane James, laborer, Water
McIntise Thomas, laborer, Adam
McGinnis, Williams laborer, Water
Metler Peter, laborer, Water
Metler Lewis, laborer, Water
Mace James, blacksmith, Second
Montgomery Edward, railroad fireman, Hardwick
McCammon Aaron, hardware dealer, Water
McCammon & Perry, hardware, &c., Water
Metler Amanda, dressmaker, First
Miller Caroline, tailorist, First
Myers Mary, teacher, Hardwick

For Coughs, Colds, Croup and Consumption use SHIELDS' **COMPOUND SYRUP** of Wild Cherry with hypophosphates of lime and soda.

HOUSEFURNISHING GOODS GENERALLY.
The BEST GOODS for the LEAST MONEY at **H. M. NORTON'S, Easton, Pa.**

Meadagh Wm., laborer, Depue
Mann Mahlon M., carpenter, First
Mann Joel, carpenter, Fourth
Mezses Jane, householder, Water
Mezses Sam, clerk, Water
McIlhany Wm., truck, etc., Hardwick
Mezses Jacob, wheel factory, Hardwick
Melela Augustus, gardener, Oxford
Martenis Morris, farmer
McCord D., Greenwich
Mildrick Morris, laborer, Race
Mildrick John, laborer, Race
Morgan Sabre, Race
Miller Wm., farmer, Oxford
Maberry & Milton, crockery and lamp store, First
Melick Sharp, stationery store, Second
Maier Frank, jeweler, Greenwich
Miller Abram, clerk at Warren House
Menshauzen Wm. K., miller
Mackey Miss Mary, householder, Water

Felix & Leininger, Nos. 102 & 104 South 3d Street, **Easton, Pa.** **Furniture.**

Mertz Mrs. Roza, householder, Water
Moser Josiah, railroader, Depue
Mackey Wm. M., Paul
McMurtrie & Co., lumbermen, First
Miller Philip, householder, Greenwich
Morrow Wm. H., ex-judge and lawyer, Greenwich
McMurtrie George, retired, Hardwick
McGee William, physician, Mansfield
Melroy Hiram, team driver, Depue
Mertz James, painter, etc., Water
McCalister John, soldier
Naylor Chas., Market
Norton Thos., carpenter, Third
Norton Mrs. Catherine, householder, Oxford
Nicholas Anna, school teacher
Norton Marshal, blacksmith, Water
O'Neill Michael, laborer, Race
O'Neill William, Surrogate of Warren county, Third
Ott Sern, freeholder, Water

E. M. NORTON, WHOLESALE AND RETAIL DEALER IN HARDWARE, STOVES, HEATERS AND RANGES.

256 BELVIDERE DIRECTORY.

Ott William, clerk, Water
O'Brine John, railroader, Greenwich
Quick Irvin, deputy county clerk, Water
Person Jeremiah, drover, Water
Person Fannie, school teacher, Water
Payne Thos. C., railroader, Paul
Person Miss Kate, school teacher, Water
Perry Daniel, S. Water
Parson Solomon, Pastor M. E. Church
Paul J. M., Jr., physician, Front
Paul T. S., Water
Prall George, general store, Water
Paul Sedgwick, Water
Prall & Witte, general store, Water
Rush John, laborer, Market
Rittenhouse Miss Tillie, teacher, Water
Robison John H., painter, Paul
Reemer Robert, speculator, Oxford
Reemer Frank, laborer, Oxford
Reemer P. H., tobacconist, Market

Felix & Leininger, Nos. 102 & 104 South 3d Street, **Easton, Pa.** **Furniture.**

Reemer Jonathan, segar store, Market
Randolph A. B., Market
Randolph Irwin, groceryman, First
Rynolds Stephen, agent, Market
Raseley Reubin, wheelwright, Water
Raseley Mathias, shoemaker, Race
Raub S. J., general store, First
Reese Sam, carriage maker, Paul
Reher Levi, Market
Roseberry Joseph Sr., Greenwich
Roseberry Joseph, Jr., lawyer, Mansfield
Ribble Miss Susie, milliner store, Mill
Ribble Mrs. Elizabeth, First
Richard H. R., butcher, Mill
Ribble Philip, retired
Rusling John, retired, Fourth
Rosencrans S. B., clerk
Ramsey H. K., hotel keeper, Pequest House
Robeson A. B., householder, Water
Shields John, carpenter, Water

FISHING TACKLE AT WADE BROS.', HACKETTSTOWN.

HOUSEFURNISHING GOODS GENERALLY.
The BEST GOODS for the LEAST MONEY at **H. M. NORTON'S, Easton, Pa.**

BELVIDERE DIRECTORY.

Slack Julia, householder, Paul
Slack Chas., laborer, Paul
Seeple Henry, mason, Water
Smozer R. B., shoemaker, Market
Stephens Mary A., householder, Mill
Scadden Thos., farmer, Market
Swartz Frederick, butcher, Market
Swartz Mrs. Mary, householder, Greenwich
Snyder Wm. A., watchman, Market
Snyder James, undertaker, Water
Snyder Mary A., householder, Water
Snyder George, sawyer, Depue
Snyder Perry, tailor, Depue
Snyder Zander, printer, Depue
Shannon Mark T., carpenter, Oxford
Stocker Geo., laborer, Mansfield
Silvers John, railroader, Depue
Scoch Lorenzo, mason, Market
Scoch Henry, painter, Market
Snyder Zachariah, musician, Depue

FELIX & LEININGER, Nos. 102 & 104 South 3d St., **Easton, Pa.** **FURNITURE.**

Snyder Palmer A., farmer, Mill
Smith John, painter, Water
Smith Jas. C., painter, Water
Smith Joseph, painter, Water
Smith Thos. L., farmer, Water
Smith Geo. W., retired, Water
Smith Daniel C., laborer, S. Water
Smith Wm. T., lawyer, S. Water
Smith Geo. W., well-digger, Market
Smith Benton T., laborer, Mill
Smith Marshal R., lawyer, Mansfield
Smith Vincent, retired, Greenwich
Smith Chas., telegraph operator, Greenwich
Slem Jefferson, peddler, First
Smith George, laborer, Paul
Sutton Wm., laborer, Hardwick
Sutton H., laborer, Hardwick
Swartzweller H. C., ex surrogate, Oxford
Swartzweller John, truckman, Oxford
Snover Joseph, laborer, Third

Snover Eugene, printer, Third
Sharp Caroline, householder, Third
Sharp George, clerk, Third
Simerson, assistant editor of the *Journal*, Second
Simerson A., printer, Hardwick
Simerson Martin, printer, Hardwick
Somers Frank, butcher, Mill
Sampsell Alexander, barber, Mill
Snyder Jas. S., laborer, First
Shipman J. G., lawyer, Third
Shipman & Son, lawyer, Third
Stone Jacob, railroader, Depue
Searles A. B., miller, Water
Searles Hugh, carpenter, Water
Searles George, carpenter, Third
Searles John C., laborer, Wall
Searles Joseph, miller, Wall
Searles Horace, telegraph operator, Water
Searles Jas., carpenter, Depue
Searles Frederick, retired, Third

Searles Wm. H., carpenter, Water
Shull A. B., carpenter, Prospect
Shull Peter, carpenter, Prospect
Shaffer R. B., book keeper, Third
Shaffer Geo., hotel keeper, Market
Shaffer Zebulon, vandue crierer, etc., S. Water
Serbert Chas., tannery, Water
Serbert Chas. Jr., butcher, Water
Serbert Edward, butcher, Water
Serbert & Bro., tobacconist
Stock Christian, laborer
Shetter Eugene F., team driver, Depue
Sampsell Hattie, school teacher, Mill
Simmers Lizzie, dress maker, Third
Singer Mrs., dress maker, Market
Stultz Josiah, carpenter, Depue
Suydam Geo., trimmer, First
Strouse Reubin, janitor, Prospect
Stephen James E., fireman, Depue
Stilwell Margaret, householder, Water

Solmon Wm. P., lawyer
Shartz Jacob F., retired, Water
Silverthorn Wm., speculator, Water
Tunis Sarah, gardner, Paul
Teters Nelson, constable, Water
Tresler Jacob, shoe store, Water
Tinsman Wm. H., First
Taylor Mrs. Nancy, householder, Third
Taylor Dewitt, lawyer, Third
Taylor Theodore, carpenter, Third
Uhler & Lake, cabinet makers, Market
Uhler Thomas, Hall
Valentine Caleb, machinist, Oxford
Valentine Jas., laborer, First
Vannatta Sam, Third
Vannatta Elisha, Third
Vandixon Edward, wagon factory, Oxford
Vancampen Geo., sheriff
Vancampen Walter, deputy sheriff
Wilson Philip, trimmer, Market

FELIX & LEININGER, Nos. 102 & 104 South 3d St. **Easton, Pa.** FURNITURE.

Wilson Joseph, lawyer, Paul
Wilson Richard, speculator, Paul
Wilson Jesse S., book keeper, Paul
Wilson Chas., clerk, Paul
Wilson M. S., railroader, First
Williams Geo., laborer, Market
Williams Edward, laborer, Market
Williams Theodore, laborer, Water
Williams Jerry, teamster, Adams
Wilcox Isaac, teamster, etc., Oxford
Weidner Geo. T., shoe store, Water
Weidner Wilson, laborer, Mansfield
Weidner Fred S., hardware store, Water
Weir Elbridge, musician, Mansfield
Weaver Geo. H., coal dealer, Depue
Weaver Geo. H. & Co., hay, straw etc., First
White Wm. S., dentist, Third
White Mrs. Mary G., householder, Greenwich
White Wm. S., farmer
White Mrs. Roze, householder, Second

Carriage Trimmings at Wade Bros., HACKETTSTOWN, NEW JERSEY.

H. M. NORTON WHOLESALE AND RETAIL DEALER IN HARDWARE, STOVES, HEATERS AND RANGES.

BELVIDERE DIRECTORY.

Witte Wm. C., miller, Greenwich
Witte Sam, merchant, Greenwich
Wildrick Jason, general store, Market
Woodruff Elisha, blacksmith, Mansfield
Wyckoff Mrs. L. C., householder, Mansfield
Wyckoff John W., retired, Third
Woolever Jacob, harness maker, Mansfield
Woolever Geo., laborer, Hardwick
Wade Simon, First
Wagner Geo., agent, First
Wintermute Wm., printer, Greenwich
Wintermute O. B., cabinet maker, Mill
Warner Alonzo, wheel factory, First
Walton Joseph, tailor, Mill
Weaver E. G., hotel keeper, First
Willever E., harness maker, Mansfield
Young Able, farmer, Market
Young Anna E., householder, Wall
Young Mrs. Ellen, householder, First
Young Peter, railroader, Mansfield

FELIX & LEININGER, Nos. 102 & 104 South 3d St., **Easton, Pa.** **FURNITURE.**

Young Talmage, railroader, Third
Young John, railroader, Wall
Yetter Peter S., Depue
Yard Edward, pail factory, First

S. J. RAUB,
—DEALER IN—
DRY GOODS, GROCERIES, BOOTS and SHOES.
GENERAL EXCHANGE STORE.
BELVIDERE, N. J.

Zink Geo., engineer, res. near Stand Pipe
Zink John, fireman, Depue
Zanita Lewis, candy store, etc., Water

ANDREWS & NOLF, SELL THE BEST $1.00 AND $1.25 KID GLOVES IN EASTON, PA. 225 NORTHAMPTON STREET.

PHILLIPSBURG.

THE present site of Phillipsburg was in 1654 an Indian village, and according to a map published at that time by a Dutch engineer named Vander Donk was called chintewink. It is said to have been the favorite fishing ground of the Indians. The "history of the Lehigh Valley," published in 1860, gives the following interesting facts:

"The origin of the name of Phillipsburg is not well-known, the impression being that it was named after a large landholder by the name of Phillips, who resided here at an early day; but the more plausible supposition is that it was derived from the Indian chief Philip, who took up his abode in this place. This Indian chief was an intimate friend of the great chief Teedyuscung. The name of Phillipsburg was found on the map of the inhabited parts of Pennsylvania and New Jersey, published in 1749 by Evans, which was before the time of Mr. Phillips' residence here."

"Phillipsburg was evidently settled by the white people before Easton, inasmuch as Easton was not laid out until some time after the different maps were published giving the name of Phillipsburg. About the time Easton was laid out the land upon which Phillipsburg was built was owned by the heirs of David Martin, a ferryman, and a Mr. Coxe, a merchant of Philadelphia, Mr. Coxe owning the principle part—about four hundred and eleven acres, among which were the 'Old Fields'— on which, on account of their beautiful location and the advantages they appeared to have possessed for the purposes of a town over the land on the opposite side of the Delaware river he contemplated in 1752 to lay out a town. The intention of Mr. Coxe appeared to greatly alarm the proprietors of Pennsylvania, who were afraid that it would injure the infant town of Easton. In a letter from Thomas Penn, dated March 9,

1752, to Richard Peters, he said, 'I think we should secure all the lands we can on the Jersey side of the water;' the intention being evidently to get this land in their possession, and thus prevent any settlement there."

Phillipsburg was not incorporated as a town until March 8, 1861. Its growth had been slow, and in 1850 it was but a straggling village.

The presence of the flourishing town of Easton on the opposite bank of the Delaware seemed to operate against its growth. In 1832 the Morris Canal was completed, and Phillipsburg made one of the termini of that water-way. That was a step upward. A bigger one was made in 1848, when the Trenton Iron Company established a furnace here; and again in 1852, when the New Jersey Central Railway was completed to that place. In 1854 the Belvidere Delaware Railroad was completed, manufacturing began to enlarge, and it was fairly upon that road to prosperity which it enjoys to-day. The railways touching at Phillipsburg are the New Jersey Central, Belvidere Delaware, Lehigh Valley, Morris & Essex, and Easton & Amboy. It is an iron manufacturing centre, and its industries in that line give employment to about eleven hundred men. Communication is had with Easton by means of a toll-bridge, and a double railway bridge. The business portion of Phillipsburg is confined chiefly to Main street, which runs northwest and southeast for about a mile and a half. "Back from the river the land rises into an abrupt elevation, and along its summit, whence a magnificent view of the landscape may be obtained, lies a pretty thickly populated portion of the town."

Phillipsburg is divided into four wards, the aggregate population being about eight thousand. In 1860 the population was but 1300, while in 1870 it numbered 5,950. That shows a rapid growth.

SCHOOLS.

Phillipsburg is famed for its excellent schools and handsome architectural accommodations for them. There are 2,568 children of school age in the town. The total amount received from all sources for school purposes in 1885 was $18,839.71; value of school property, $72,440; average number who attended school during time it was kept open, 1,600; number of children that can be comfortably seated, 1,794; number of teachers employed, male, 3; female, 31; total, 34; average salary per month paid to male teachers $80, and the female teachers $33.63. Edwin C. Beers is the present Superintendent.

RELIGIOUS HISTORY.

The religious history of Phillipsburg dates back to 1737 and to the time when David Brainerd the "Apostles of Indians," labored in this region. Missionaries were sent in 1737 by the Presbytery of New Brunswick to the " Forks of the Delaware to preach to the Indians." It was during Brainerd's missionary work here—1740—to 1744, that a log church was erected in Phillipsburg, and the word preached from the pulpit to both whites and Indians alike. "There was a Lutheran church here prior to 1762, but whether it occupied the log church above referred to is not known."

THE PRESENT PRESBYTERIAN CHURCH

was dedicated September 12, 1858. Its erection was begun in 1854, but financial embarrassments delayed its completion. Rev. S. S. Sturges, was the first pastor of the new church, and remained till September, 1856. At that time the membership of the church numbered 63. Sturges was succeeded by Rev. W. C. Cottrell, who acted as supply till May 11th, 1857, when J. Y. Mitchell was called and installed July 26th of the same year. The time of experiment was now over and the church was thoroughly established. The present pastor, Rev. H. B. Townsend was called in March, 1867. The church now is the leading one of the town, possessing a pipe-organ, and a paid choir.

THE FIRST METHODIST EPISCOPAL CHURCH

was organized in 1855. The present church edifice was dedicated complete Oct. 3, 1858, although the basement had been dedicated January 27, 1856. The church property including church and parsonage is valued at $35,000.

WESLEYAN METHODIST EPISCOPAL CHAPEL.

In November, 1871, members of the Main St. Methodist Episcopal church living in the Third Ward began to have class-meetings in the Fitch school-house. These were continued for about a year, when, in the fall of 1872, a church was organized. In the month of October 1872 Wesleyan chapel was occupied and dedicated and has been a flourishing chapel ever since. The old structure is now being remodeled into a more handsome edifice and the congregation under the guidance of J. R. Wright bids fair to become in a short time a very large one in numbers.

THE FREE METHODIST CHURCH

was built during Rev. Markham's pastorate in 1875. Rev. J. J. Haviland is the present pastor.

SAINTS PHILIP AND JAMES' CHURCH.

Prior to 1860 the Catholics of Phillipsburg worshipped at Easton. Services were first held in Phillipsburg during that year by Rev. John Smith of Paterson. He organized a congregation and immediately began to solicit subscriptions for the building of a church. He was not, however, permitted to finish the enterprise, death putting an end to his labors October, 1860. Rev. C. O'Reilly was sent to fill his place and under his vigorous leadership the construction of the new church was pushed so rapidly that it was completed in the Spring of 1861. The parsonage was built in 1864. In 1873 to accommodate the increased membership a new and larger church edifice was erected. The church is now (Oct. 1, '86) being remodeled at a great expense. Rev. R. E. Burke is the present pastor.

The other churches of Phillipsburg are the Grace (Evangelical Lutheran) church, organized in the Winter of 1869-70, by Rev. M. H. Richards; the St Luke's (Protestant Episcopal) church, organized December 1856, and the building consecrated June 9, 1861 by Bishop W. H. Odenheimer — the present congregation worship in a new church built during the past year and a half; the St. John's (German Evangelical Lutheran) church, organized February 5th, 1875, by Rev. R. F. Widener; and the First Baptist Church, organized early in 1880, by Rev. A. E. Francis and continued by H. A. Chapman, which ceased 2 years later.

PHILLIPSBURG NATIONAL BANK

was organized under the State laws March 19, 1856, with a capital of $200,000 divided into 4000 shares. In 1865 the institution was chartered as a national bank, with the capital still fixed at $200,000. Charles Sitgreaves was the first president and continued to act as such till his death in 1878, when Samuel Boileau was chosen to succeed him. Mr. Lewis C. Reese was the first cashier and acted in that capacity until December 1877. Since then the post of cashier has been occupied by John A. Bachman. The directors, October 1886, were Joseph C. Kent, Wm. F. Boileau, Wm. M. Davis, James Lomerson, Benjamin Riegel, Samuel Boileau, Wm. B. Shimer, Levi Hiles and Daniel Runkle.

The bank has an average loan and discount account of $400,000, a deposit account of $300,000, a surplus of $40,000, an undivided profit and loss account of $97,846.85, and a circulation of $180,000.

The following are the present officers of the borough: Mayor, Peter H. Hagerty; Town Clerk, P. F. Brakeley; Superintendent of Public Instruction, Edwin C. Beers; Prosecuting Attorney for Warren county, Sylvester C. Smith; Justices of the Peace, James E. Smith, J. M. R. Shimer, William Smith, Peter H. Haggerty; Guardians of the Public Peace, 1st Ward, Charles Nixon; 2nd Ward, James Callannann; 3rd Ward, Michael Hughes; 4th Ward, Charles Coleman; Constables, John Norton, George Creveling.

WHERE TO WORSHIP.

First Presbyterian Church, corner Main and Market streets, Rev. H. B. Townsend, pastor; services every Sunday morning throughout the year at 10.30; every Sunday evening, at 7 p. m. during the winter, and 7.30 p. m. during the summer season; pastor's residence, 317 Washington street (on the hill).

HISTORY OF PHILLIPSBURG.

Sts. Philip and James' Church, corner Main and Stockton streets, Rev. R. E. Burke pastor, Rev. P. Hanley asst.; first mass at 7.30 a. m.; children's mass at 9 a. m., and high mass at 10.30 a. m.; Sunday-school at 2 p. m., and vespers and benediction at 7.30 p. m.; pastor's and asst.'s residence adjoining.

Wesley Methodist Episcopal Church, Lewis street, near Hudson (on the hill); services at the usual hour; Sunday-school at 2 p. m.; pastor's residence adjoining; pastors elected by Conference every three years.

Free Methodist Chapel, Fillman street, between Hudson and Bullman (on the hill). Rev. J. J. Haviland, presiding; services every Sunday morning and evening at the usual hour; pastor's residence on Lewis street; Sunday-school at 9 a. m.

Grace Lutheran Church, Main street, below Stockton, Rev. G. D. Bernheim, D. D. pastor; services every Sunday morning and evening at the usual hour; Sunday-school at 9 a. m.; pastor's residence 231 Brainard.

Second Presbyterian Church (Westminster—third ward), no regular pastor, preaching by W. H. Waygood.

First Methodist Episcopal Church, Main street, Rev. J. K. Bryan pastor; services every Sunday morning and evening at the usual hour; pastor's residence adjoining; Sunday-school at 2 p. m.; pastor elected every three years by Conference.

St. Luke's Episcopal Church, Rev. P. S. Robottom in charge; pastor's residence adjoining.

SECRET, LITERARY SOCIETIES, ETC.

Chatauqua Literary Circle meets on anniversary nights of some distinguished poet, author, etc.; Mrs. A. L. B. Griswald, Secretary.

"Senate" Club—membership limited, no ladies admitted—the advancement of education is its primary object, meets semi-monthly; Augustus I. Wood, Secretary.

Warren Social Club, meets in Hagerty's Building, corner Main and River streets; John W. Flynn, Secretary.

Home Rule Club, meets every Sunday afternoon in Parochial Building; Patrick Walsh, Secretary.

Delaware Lodge and Eagle Chapter, No. 30, F. & A. M., meet over Lee building, corner Main and Market streets; J. Irvin Lake, Secretary.

HISTORY OF PHILLIPSBURG.

Warren Assembly, Knights of Labor, meets weekly regularly, twice on Sunday and twice on Monday evenings monthly,—session rooms on the third floor of Parochial Building; George W. Kellogg, Secretary.

Montana Lodge No. 23, Knights of Pythias, meets every Friday evening over Bel. Del. depot; Robert B. Carhart, K. of R. & S.

Phillipsburg Division, No. 28, Sons of Temperance, meets over Bel. Del. depot, membership about 85; E. T. Barnet, secretary.

Victory Council No. 12, Jr. O. U. A. M., meets every Thursday evening over Bel. Del. depot; J. V. Metz, Sec'y.

Knights of Honor, meet in Council room on Market street on Wednesday evenings of each month; Allen J. Clifton, Sec'y.

Accho Lodge No. 124, I. O. O. F., meets every Monday evening over Bel. Del. depot; Thomas Castles, Sec'y.

Twilight Social Club, meets over P. F. Brakeley's drug store; John Johnson, Secretary.

Brotherhood of Locomotive Engineers No. 30, meet on Sunday afternoon over Phillipsburg National Bank; Jacob Rustay, Secretary.

Brotherhood of Locomotive Firemen, Excelsior Lodge No. 11, meets at Parochial Hall; John St. Clair, Secretary.

Brotherhood of Railroad Brakemen; Elmer Carhart, Sec'y.

Teedyuscong Tribe of Red Men, No. 17, meets every Thursday evening over Bel. Del. depot; James Hess, Sec'y.

Phillipsburg Reform Club, meets every Sunday afternoon in Hagerty's Hall, corner So. Main and River streets, Charles Stakes, Secretary.

Haymaker Tribe of Red Men, No. 17½, meets every Wednesday evening over the Bel. Del. depot; Wm. F. Keepers, Sec'y.

United Order of American Workmen, meets every first and third Wednesday evenings over Bel. Del depot; Robert H. Leich, secretary.

Emerald Beneficial Society, meets in Parochial Building; Michael Conlan, of Mercer street, secretary.

United Ancient Order of Druids meets Wednesday evening at Gwinner's Hall; George R. Wilking, secretary.

HISTORY OF PHILLIPSBURG. 261

John S. Little Section No. 1, Cadets of Temperance, meets every Wednesday evening at Hagerty's Hall, membership about 60; Samuel Quear, worthy patron.

Malaska Council of the O. U. A. M.

Ancient Order of Hibernians, meets once a month in Parochial Hall; Patrick Stanley, secretary.

Musconetcong Tribe of Red men, meets every Thursday evening at Hagerty's Hall; John P. Hermes, secretary.

Phillipsburg Pleasure Party, meets over A. S. Deichman's Insurance Office, near the Delaware Bridge; Elmer Carhart, secretary.

John G. Tolmie Post No. 50, G. A. R., meets every Monday evening at Hagerty's Hall; James Gilien, adjutant. The Ladies Loyal League, an aid to the Post, also meet on Monday evening in the same building.

INDUSTRIES.

American Sheet Iron Works.
Andover Furnace.
American Brick and Tile Co.
Central Round House and Machine Shop.
Morris & Essex Round House and Machine Shop
Delaware Rolling Mill.
Borough Water Works.
Phillipsburg Stove Works.
Phillipsburg Silk Mill.
Phillipsburg Gas Works.
Shimer's Smoke House.
Tippet & Wood's Boiler Works.
Vulcan Iron Works.
Warren Foundry and Machine Co.

Phillipsburg Business Directory.

J. M. Butler, cigars and tobacco
R. J. Ritter, cigars and tobacco
John H. Haggerty & Sons, hardware and lumber
W. H. Walters, attorney-at-law
John Lee, photographer
A. Moenig, fine furniture
John Eilenberg, wholesale liquor dealer
Robert H. Lerch, bookseller and stationery
O. Kidney, oyster and ice cream saloon
O. D. McConnell, groceries and provisions
Thomas Carroll, cigars and tobacco
C. C. Conklin, watches, clocks and jewelry
Samuel A. Metz, drugs and medicines
Chas. J. Able, confectionary
R. B. Carhart & Co., wall paper
Long & Boileau, lumber and hardware
Huges & Cyphers, groceries
Samuel Teets, merchant tailor
Abram Miller, grocer
Thomas Heiberger, butcher
Walter Freeman, druggist
J. H. Sweeny, fish and oysters
George Meyers, groceries
John Yob, tombstones, 198 S. Main
William T. Randall, groceries
J. C. Butler, agent Equitable Life Assurance Society
J. M. R. Shimer, general dealer
Clemens Kupke, merchant tailor

ROBERT H. LERCH,
BOOKSELLER AND STATIONER.

Miscellaneous, School and Blank Books,

Legal and Justice Blanks,

MUSIC AND MUSICAL INSTRUMENTS.

122 MAIN STREET,

PHILLIPSBURG N. J.

WARREN COUNTY DRUG STORE.

Phillipsburg Directory

Atwood Wm., engineer, 234 Bullman
American Sheet Iron Co., office 353 Broad
Almond Wm. H., laborer, cor. Broad and Second
Almond John L. laborer, cor. Broad and Second
Andrews Thomas C., engineer, cor. Sec. and N. Main
Arndt Frank, clerk. 283 N. Main
Arnold George, laborer, 388 Lewis
Arnold Geo. Jr., hostler, bds., 388 Lewis
Apgar Alfred B., brakeman, 310 Chambers
Alpaugh Wesley, railroader, 356 Washington
Achenbach Joseph, brakeman, 550 Washington
Ayers Theo., fireman, 466 Washington

FELIX & LEININGER, Nos. 102 & 104 South 3d St., **Easton, Pa.** FURNITURE.

Arner James P., fireman, 457 Lewis
Apgar Carter, carpenter, bds., 98 Detweiler's Row
Alley R. C., insurance agent, Henderson
Able C. J., confectionery, near Delaware Bridge
Able Percival, clerk, Main near Delaware Bridge
Aten Milton lawyer and stenographer, Union Square
Alsover George, foreman, bds. Lee House
Anderson Oliver, hostler, bds. Lee House
Alpaugh John, foreman, bds. 118 S. Main
Apgar Matthias, carpenter, Reese Alley
Alpaugh John, master mechanic, 148 S. Main
Altemus Mrs. R. J., boarding, 224 S. Main
Altemus Alexander, retired, 224 S. Main
Altemus Charles, clerk, 224 S. Main
Amey William, brakeman, near Lehigh Junction
Arnold Wm., expressman, 207 Hanover
Alpaugh Benj. J., fireman, bds. Phillipsburg Hotel
Apgar Adam, brakeman, 20 Haggerty's Row
Ames Anna D., boarding, 228 Sitgreaves
Applegate Jacob, Sr., retired, 530 Sitgreaves

SHIELDS' Compound Syrup of Wild Cherry with Hypophosites of Lime and Soda. Sure cure for coughs, croup, etc.

Applegate Jacob, Jr., wiper, bds. 530 Sitgreaves
Applegate Edward, machinist, 530 Sitgreaves
Ammerman Wm. D., painter, Howard
Arndt Mrs. Anna, widow, 603 S. Main
Arndt Frank, wiper, 603 S. Main
Able Theodore, railroader, bds 1028 S. Main
Abrams Mrs. Caroline, fancy notions, 714 S. Main
Abrams Charles, auctioneer, 714 S. Main
Armbruster John, boatman, cor. McKean and Chesnut
Apgar Sloan, railroader, 948 Mercer
American House, Jos. H. Hulsizer prop, cor. Jefferson and Main
Apgar Jacob, carpenter, Jefferson
Albert Mrs. Annie M., 748 Mercer
Armbruster John J., laborer, Spruce alley
Andrews Isaac, foundryman, 613 Sitgreaves
Andover Hotel, Ed Gartland, prop., 1032 S. Main
Albus Albert, shoemaker, 850 S. Main
Ashmore Wm. A., clerk C. R. R. of N. J., res. 180 S. Main

FELIX & LEININGER, Nos. 102 & 104 South 3d St., Easton, Pa. **FURNITURE.**

Butler J. C., agent for the Equitable Insurance Co., of New York, office 22 Union Square, res. 327 Washington
Brakeley Philip F., drugs and medicines, 104 S. Main, bds. Lee House
Bird Col. E. H., watchman, bds. Lee House
Ballantyne James, candy maker, 124 S. Main
Andover Furnace and Iron Works, Jos. C. Kent, Supt. office S. Main, on P. R. R.
Butler A. M., cigars and tobacco, finest 5c. cigar in the world "Principes" leads all others, 220 Union Square, next door to the Lee House, bds. 327 Washington
Beers Henry W., railroader, 216 Brainard
Beers Ida, teacher, bds. 216 Brainard
Beers Lewis Osman, student, 216 Brainard
Beers Stephen, railroader, 166 Brainard
Bereaw Samuel, watchman, 203 Brainard
Bernhim Rev. C. D., pastor Grace Luthern Church, 234 Brainard

ANDREWS & NULF, 255 Northampton St., Easton, Pa. The Largest line of DRESS TRIMMINGS etc.

Beers Thomas, retired, 228 Brainard
Bowman Elmer, freight office, bds. Columbia House
Bah John, barber shop, 205 S. Main, h. 213 Hanover
Bowers John S., dispatcher, 211 S. Main
Bogardus S. W., dentist, 185 S. Main
Bennett J. C., farmer, 197 Market
Bennett Sadie, teacher, 197 Market
Baumaunn Jacob, laborer, 124 Detweiler's Row
Brown Mrs. Louisa, widow, 98 Detweiler's Row
Bowlby Robt., miner, 628 Chambers
Bunn Wm., core turner, 626 Chambers
Brannan Mrs. Maria, widow, Chambers near Heckman
Brailer Barney, laborer, 522 Chambers
Brailer John, laborer, bds. 522 Chambers
Butler Charles, watchman, 524 Lewis
Bird John W., brakeman, 511 Lewis
Brady Charles, foundryman, 502 Wilson
Barnet Sarah, widow, 321 Heckman
Barnet James, foundryman, bds. 321 Heckman
Barnet Edward, invalid, bds. 321 Heckman

FELIX & LEININGER, Nos. 102 & 104 South 3d St., **Easton, Pa.** **FURNITURE.**

Beers Henry, carpenter, 636 Railroad ave
Baker John, laborer, 576 Railroad ave
Bercaw Henry, bookkeeper, 752 Howard
Burke James, railroader, 839 Howard
Barber Whitfield, railroader, 707 Fayette
Ball Bernard, number taker, 741 Fayette
Boyle Connel, laborer, Fayette near McKean
Boyle Hugh, laborer, Fayette near McKean
Bercaw Joshua, car checker, 933 Mercer
Boehn Augustus, barber, 931 Mercer
Brunner Matthias, laborer, foot of Mercer
Beckworth Thomas, foundryman, 845 S. Main
Bigelow Daniel, retired, 333 Washington
Benjamin Thomas, fireman, 385 Washington
Brant Lewis, engineer, bds. 393 Washington
Brant Edward, tinsmith, bds. 393 Washington
Beers Mrs. Mary A., teacher, bds. 330 Washington
Beiter Matthias, cabinet maker, Hudson
Brown James, machinist, 501 Washington
Bradshaw Wm., conductor, Hudson

The **BISSLE PLOWS** are the best of all. For sale at Wades' Hardware Store.

Bowers Wm. K., machinist, 434 Lewis
Banner Ephraim, mason, 416 Fulton
Bryan Wm., boarding, 447 Lewis
Benn Urah, silk mill, bds. 447 Lewis
Beers Elle, clerk, 435 Lewis
Brown Charles, shoemaker shop, 417 Chambers res. 411 Lewis
Bellis Lemuel, clerk, 409 Lewis
Baylor Lewis, railroader, 438 Chambers
Butler Theodore, laborer, 454 Chambers
Beers Samuel, carpenter, 407 Chambers
Beers Peter, fireman, bds. 407 Chambers
Bowers Chris., machinist, bds. 434 Lewis
Bates O. E. & Co., groceries and prov., 479 Chambers
Bruns Fred., railroader, 529 Chambers
Bilger B., laborer, cor. Delaware and First
Bachman Wm., ironworker, Delaware
Burke John, laborer, Morris turnpike
Bishop Henry, laborer, Morris turnpike
Butler Wm. C., laborer, 429 Fillmore

Felix & Leininger, Nos. 102 & 104 South 3d Street, **Easton, Pa. Furniture.**

Barnet John, railroader, 431 Fillmore
Banner Wm., mason, 466 Fillmore
Beam Mrs. Kate, widow, 472 Davis
Beam Frank, moulder, bds. 472 Davis
Beam Wilson, moulder, bds. 472 Davis
Beam John, plumber, 472 Davis
Benjamin Dan'l, hod carrier, 120 N. Main
Burwell Sam'l, insurance agent, 356 Lewis
Burwell Miss Linnie, teacher, bds. 356 Lewis
Burwell Benjamin, laborer, bds. 356 Lewis
Burwell George, clerk, bds. 356 Lewis
Branner Joseph, foundryman, 366 Lewis
Brink Wm., brakeman, 377 Lewis
Bock Reeves, railroader, 381 Lewis
Bush Moses, grocery store, 384 Chambers
Burs John K., carpenter, 347 Chambers
Bosch Christian, beer saloon, 470 Chambers
Bosch Christian, meat market, 472 Chambers
Brown John, railroader, Front
Barnitz Sam'l, expressman, bds. 118 Bullman

Andrews & Nolf, 205 Northampton St. The only place to buy the "CONFORMATER" Corset.

Britain Mrs. R. S., widow, 128 Bullman
Beers Wm., Railroad detective, Front
Beers Wm. Jr., railroader, bds. Front
Beers E. C., Sup't of Public Instruction, bds. Front
Baker Sam'l, huckster, 222 Washington
Boofman Wm., chief engineer, Broad
Brinzer Andrew, ironworker, 356 Broad
Bayard John M., horse jockey, Third
Butler Henry, clerk, Rose
Brady Patrick, laborer, Rose
Bachman Sam'l, ironworker, Rose
Beaman Silas, melter, Rose
Bachman John, ironworker, N. Main
Bush, E. M., shoemaker, 319 N. Main
Bonder Levi, sup't street cars, 303 N. Main
Beaman Mrs. Jane, widow, First
Beaman Wm., laborer, bds. First
Butz Jacob, ironworker, 360 Broad
Black John, laborer, Spruce Alley
Brunner Wm., foreman, 823 S. Main
Bilgert Isaac, furnaceman, 815 S. Main

FELIX & LEININGER, Nos. 102 & 104 South 3d St., **Easton, Pa.** **FURNITURE.**

Bird Joseph, retired, 713 Mercer
Bell Watson, painter, Cherry Alley
Burr Charles, laborer, Cedar Alley
Rose John, butcher, 765 S. Main, h 767
Burke R. E., pastor St. Philips and St. James church, h 761 S. Main
Beck Frank, engineer, 747 S. Main
Bachman John A., cashier P. N. B., h 225 Washington
Brannon Patrick, section boss, 755 S. Main
Barnett Ezra T., machinist, 316 McKean
Brady James, foundryman, 856 Sitgreaves
Burke Elizabeth, widow, 956 Sitgreaves
Brackan Patrick, laborer, 971 Sitgreaves
Bahr Frank, furnaceman, 917 Sitgreaves
Brennan Thomas, furnaceman, 815 Sitgreaves
Brodell Charles, barber, 664 S. Main h 637 Sitgreaves
Berry Walter, railroader, bds. 643 Sitgreaves
Bowden Tillie, widow, Spruce Alley
Brooks Jane C., candy, etc., 709 Sitgreaves
Bird Peter, laborer, 747 Sitgreaves

For Coughs, Colds, Croup and **COMPOUND SYRUP** of Wild Cherry with hypo-Consumption use SHIELDS' phosphates of lime and soda

Bennett Annie, teacher, 197 Market
Brant Halsey, conductor, 191 Market
Bryan Rev. J. R., pastor Main Street Methodist Episcopal Church, res. 430 S. Main
Brink Morris, car inspector, bds. 528 Sitgreaves
Berry Alexander, brakeman, 532 Sitgreaves
Bowlsby Thomas, laborer, Union
Bereaw Henry, laborer, River
Bowers Joseph, laborer, Cedar Alley
Blake John F., wiper, 525 Mercer
Barber Joanna, widow, 531 Mercer
Bachman John, watchman, 627 Mercer
Baker Adam, carpenter, 621 Fayette
Boat yard (Morris Canal Co.,) opp. Howard
Barton James, section boss, Fox
Barber Eldridge, railroader, 135 Fox
Barnett M. A., druggist, 621 S. Main
Brunner Elizabeth, widow, 615 S. Main
Barber Hiram, boiler maker, 613 S. Main
Barber Isaac, physician, 531 S. Main bds. 224

Felix & Leininger, Nos. 102 & 104 South 3d Street, **Easton, Pa.** **Furniture.**

Bouden C. B., engineer, 652 Howard
Britain S. J., railroad clerk, 668 Howard
Burger Samuel, carpenter, 744 Howard
Bowers Daniel, railroader, 742 Howard
Brody John, laborer, 824 S. Main
Bowers Joseph, railroader, 638 S. Main
Brewer Joseph, saloon, 634 S. Main
Bieber L. D., physician, 624 S. Main
Bardux Henry, book binder, h Warren
Butt Samuel A., editor, 134 River
Bauman Joseph, engineer, Dempster's Hill
Botz James, laborer, Dempster's Hill
Crutz Wm., railroader, Bennett
Carkuff Amos, carpenter, 232 Bullman
Carpenter shop, I. B. Wolf, prop., Front
Cyphers H. M., grocer, 136 Washington
Cyphers Mrs. Amanda, widow, 216 Washington
Carfrey George, freight agent, 224 Washington
Cullen James, watchman, cor. Third and Broad
Connolly James, puddler, bds. on Broad

ANDREWS & NOLF, 205 Northampton Street, Easton, Pa.
The reliable store for Black Goods.

PHILLIPSBURG DIRECTORY. 269

Connolly Michael, watchman, Broad
Case Frank, laborer, 349 N. Main
Clifton John L., laborer, 301 N. Main
Co-operative store No. 3, 237 N. Main
Clymer Charles, laborer, Morris Turnpike
Cargo Matthias, laborer, 459 Fillmore
Chamberlain Chris., washing, 120 N. Main
Carhart Edward, foreman, 224 Harris
Crowle Edward, machinist, 337 Lewis
Coleman Mrs. Mary, widow 370 Lewis
Cosgroff John, laborer, 383 Lewis
Castles Thomas, clerk, 374 Chambers
Carhart Wm. M., foreman, 357 Chambers
Carling Wm., engineer, 345 Chambers
Campbell John, engineer, 335 Chambers
Charles Milton, foundryman, 349 Washington
Cole Samuel, railroader, 357 Washington
Cook Charles, railroader, 375 Washington
Carhart Mrs. Lydia, widow, 366 Washington
Cattel Caleb, foreman, 378 Washington

FELIX & LEININGER, Nos. 102 & 104 South 3d St., **Easton, Pa.** **FURNITURE.**

Carpenter Isaac, railroader, 326 Washington
Cook Lewis, cigarmaker, Hudson
Co-operative grocery, No. 4, cor. Hudson, Reese alley
Clark James, bridge builder, 614 Hudson
Carhart, H. O., doctor, cor. Washington and Hudson
Carpenter Frank, clerk, bds. 403 Washington
Crause Mrs. W., widow, 522 Washington
Colbath Orem, laborer, 530 Washington
Cook Wm., railroader, 450 Washington
Cook John, wire-worker, 450 Washington
Crater Philip, railroader, 442 Washington
Crater Annie, dressmaker, 442 Washington
Cease Wm., machinisit, 438 Washington
Cease Daniel, brakeman, 438 Washington
Champlin Edward, engineer, 406 Lewis
Carr Andrew S., pipe inspector, 410 Lewis
Carr Mrs. Sophia, widow, 410 Lewis
Carey Mrs. Annie, dressmaker, 440 Lewis
Campbell Samuel, fireman, 451 Lewis
Cowell Henry, laborer, 441 Lewis

The **BISSLE PLOWS** are the best of all. For sale at Wades' Hardware Store.

Cowell Frank, laborer, 442 Chambers
Cowell Wm. F., laborer, 442 Chambers
Coleman Edward C., carpenter, 457 Chambers
Corcoran Thomas, foundryman, 557 Railroad ave
Canavan John, blacksmith, 573 Wilson
Conover Horace J., laborer, 652 Railroad ave
Curlis Mrs. Rebecca, widow, Heckman
Cullen Kate, teacher, cor. Third and Broad
Carhart R. B. & Co., wall paper, 100 S. Main
Carhart Jesse F., wall paper, res. 609 S. Main
Cooley Morris D., tailor, bds. 118 S. Main
Case Oliver P., boilermaker, 151 Randall
Case George, fireman, bds. 151 Randall
Cheeseman Geo. W., plasterer, 154 Randall
Cronce H. S., agent, Shimer
Cole George, laborer, Shimer
Cole John, car inspector, Shimer
Cole Abraham, engine wiper, Hudson
Cook Rev. Isaac, missionary, Reese Alley
Case Frank, butcher, 182 Brainard

Felix & Leininger, Nos. 102 & 104 South 3d Street, **Easton, Pa.** **Furniture.**

Creveling John, engineer, 196 Brainard
Coleman Kate, dressmaker, 204 Brainard
Clifton George, switch tender, 181 Brainard
Carling Wm. K., railroader, 173 Brainard
Carling Wilbur A., manager Becker's Easton tea store, bds. 173 Brainard
Comstock S. A., retired, bds. 174 S. Main
Carling John, geologist, 180 S. Main
Case Whit., brakeman, 194 S. Main
Crater Angelina, confectionery, 206 S. Main
Calvin Mrs. Charles, widow, 218 S. Main
Carpenter John O., timekeeper, 240 Brainard
Columbia Hotel, John O'Grady, prop. 314 S. Main
Capwell John N., brakeman, bds. Columbia Hotel
Carroll Jacob, merchant tailor, res. 201 Hanover
Carroll Clara, teacher, 201 Hanover
Carroll Gertie, teacher, 201 Hanover
Clifton Allen J., ass't dispatcher, 220 Hanover
Central Railroad Depot, Market
Central Railroad freight house, 316 S. Main

Andrews & Nolf, 205 Northampton St. The only place to buy the "CONFORMATER" Corset.

HOUSEFURNISHING GOODS GENERALLY
The BEST GOODS for the LEAST MONEY at **H. M. NORTON'S, Easton, Pa.**

Coogan Michael, Jr., clerk, Golden
Coogan Ellie, teacher, Golden
Creveling Wm., railroader, 413 S. Main
Caldwell Hugh, peddler, 7 Haggerty's Row
Caldwell William, laborer, 7 Haggerty's Row
Creveling George, constable, 511 S. Main
Clymer Wesley, railroader, bds. foot of Hanover
Crispen R. B., candy store, Union
Creveling Howard, shoemaker, Union
Christern John, number taker, 138 River
Christern Hannah, dressmaker, 138 River
Carhart Wm., invalid, Cedar Alley
Cope A. S., engineer, 615 Mercer
Cope Chas., fireman, bds. 615 Mercer
Caffey Joseph, brakeman, 621 Mercer
Clark John J., number taker, 545 Fayette
Clark Charles S., foundryman, bds. 545 Fayette
Cody Thomas, engineer, 550 Howard
Cooper Wm., railroader, 620 Howard
Calanman James, 2d ward policeman, 630 Howard

FELIX & LEININGER, Nos. 102 & 104 South 3d St., **Easton, Pa.** **FURNITURE.**

Cornish Wm., rag dealer, Fox
Case Jacob, fish and oysters, 541 S. Main, h Chestnut Alley
Cocklin C. C., jewelry, 539 S. Main, bds. Phillipsburg Hotel
Cocklin R. T., jeweler, bds. Phillipsburg Hotel
Coyne Frank, laborer, 862 Howard
Cahill John, laborer, Dempster's Hill

C. C. COCKLIN,

Dealer in FINE

WATCHES CLOCKS AND JEWELRY.

Repairing of Fine Watches a Specialty.

539 SOUTH MAIN STREET,

PHILLIPSBURG, - - - NEW JERSEY.

The **BISSLE PLOWS** are the best of all. For sale at **Wages' Hardware Store.**

M. M. NORTON, WHOLESALE AND RETAIL DEALER IN HARDWARE, STOVES, HEATERS AND RANGES.

Coyne Elizabeth, 862 Howard
Coyne Patrick, laborer, 862 Howard
Coyne Benjamin, laborer, 862 Howard
Condon James, foundryman, 841 Mercer
Carpenter Edward, foundryman, 824 Mercer
Call Anthony, laborer, 806 Mercer
Carling John, watchman, 933 S. Main
Coleman Charles, 4th ward policeman, Cedar alley near McKean
Coleman John, laborer, Cedar alley near McKean
Caffrey Mary, teacher, res. 843 S. Main
Clifford Cornelius, boatman, Cherry alley
Case Calvin, railroader, 743 Mercer
Cord John, car painter, 721 Mercer
Crosley Thomas, foundryman, 649 Mercer
Campbell Archibald, machinist, Dempster's Hill
Carpenter Edward, laborer, Dempster's Hill
Crosley James, foundryman, 704 Mercer
Crosley Lawrence, foundryman, 700 Mercer
Connlain Michael, machinist, 734 Mercer

Felix & Leininger, Nos. 102 & 104 South 3d Street, **Easton, Pa.** **Furniture.**

Cooney William, boiler-maker, 738 Mercer
Conners Daniel, laborer, Cedar alley
Carlin David, laborer, Cedar alley
Carty William, grocer, 751 S. Main, h do
Consolly Lewis, chinaware, 747 S. Main
Creveling Jacob, flour and feed, 733 S. Main, h do
Creveling Charles, clerk, 733 S. Main
Co-operative grocery No. 1, 717 S. Main
Catholic Church, cor. Main and Stockton
Clark Mrs. Mary, Dempster's Hill
Coudlet Patrick, laborer, Dempster's Hill
Case George, teamster, 640 Sitgreaves
Caffey George, fireman, bds. 755 S. Main
Caffey Frank, fireman, bds. 755 S. Main
Carhart Samuel, flagman, 656 Sitgreaves
Case John R., brakeman, Foundry alley
Carey Thomas, brakeman, Foundry alley
Carling George S., clerk, Jefferson
Cope George, farmer, 307 McKean
Coyle John, laborer, 938 Sitgreaves

H. M. NORTON, WHOLESALE AND RETAIL DEALER IN HARDWARE, STOVES, HEATERS AND RANGES

PHILLIPSBURG DIRECTORY. 273

Carpenter Henry, railroader, 949 Sitgreaves
Correll Charles, laborer, 976 Sitgreaves
Conover Charles W., laborer, 986 Sitgreaves
Carpenter Philip, laborer, 988 Sitgreaves
Cripps James, machinist, 975 Sitgreaves
Casey Patrick, laborer, 973 Sitgreaves
Carpenter George, laborer, 957 Sitgreaves
Comiskey Mary, widow, 951 Sitgreaves
Cruts Peter, quarryman, 829 Sitgreaves
Caton Daniel, laborer, 813 Sitgreaves
Cochran Stephen, railroader, bds. Spruce alley
Cummings Patrick, street commissioner, 635 Sitgreaves
Coxe Bridget, widow, 661 Sitgreaves
Cope Thomas, baker, bds. Mercer
Christian Annie, 743 Sitgreaves
Creveling George L., boat builder, 1063 S. Main
Call Patrick, brakeman, 910 S. Main
Cummings Thomas, machinist, 856 S. Main
Connell Matthew, laborer, 854 S. Main
Conover John, shoemaker, 852 S. Main

FELIX & LEININGER, Nos. 102 & 104 South 3d St., Easton, Pa. **FURNITURE.**

Cavanaugh James, physician, 662 S. Main, h 535 do
Cramer Caroline, restaurant, 666 S. Main
Cahill James, laborer, Dempster's Hill
Case Theodore, fireman, 664 Howard
Clark Philip, machinist, 762 Howard
Cox John, foundryman, 764 Howard
Croseley Daniel, foundryman, 820 Howard
Call Joseph S., brakeman, 825 Howard
Central Hotel, C. O. Lantz, prop., 211 and 213 Market, h do
Centennial engine house, 207 and 209 Market
Couch G. M., engineer, 201 Market
Clickner Augustus, baggage master, 193 Market
Clickner Minnie, teacher, 193 Market
Campfield Morris P., Sup't American Brick & Tile Co., bds. 163 S. Main
Carlesey Thomas, foundryman, Phillipsburg Hotel
Carling John M., engineer, bds. Phillipsburg Hotel
Coogan Michael, Roadmaster Amboy Div L. V. R. R., Golden street, opp. S. Main

ALL KINDS OF HARDWARE at Wade Bros., Hackettstown, N. J.

Carrol Thomas, cigars and tobacco, 644 S. Main h do
Cannon M. T., grocer, 640 S. Main h do
Dingler Joseph, brakeman, 531 Lewis
Davis Wm., laborer, 250 Heckman
Damford David, watchman, Heckman
Dalrymple Franklin, boatman, 9 Haggerty's Row
Dugan John, ferryman, 19 Haggerty's Row
Denny George, engineer, 516 Sitgreaves
Drake James, groceries, 517 S. Main h 515 do
Drake Wm. C., clerk, bds. 515 S. Main
Doll Michael, cigar manufacturer, 447 S. Main, house rear Sitgreaves
Dereamer Charles, railroader, 299 S. Main
Davis Wm., railroader, 134 River

THOMAS CARROL,
DEALER IN
FINE CIGARS AND TOBACCO,
644 SOUTH MAIN STREET.
Phillipsburg, N. J.
A Choice Line of Havana Cigars, Smoking and Chewing Tobacco always on Stock, at Bottom Prices.

FELIX & LEININGER, Nos. 102 & 104 South 3d St., **Easton, Pa.** FURNITURE

Dennis John, railroader, 537 Mercer
Divett Martin, laborer, 619 Mercer
Divett Frank, boiler maker, bds. 619 Mercer
Dawson Philip, railroader, 531 Fayette
Durkam Michael, laborer, 526 Howard
Dunworth John Sr., laborer, 608 Howard
Dunworth John Jr., laborer, 608 Howard
Dinan Thomas, brakeman, Fox
Duffy John, moulder, 142 Fox
Davitt John, flagman, 662 Howard
Demass Lewis, switchman, 746 Howard
Dereamer Peter, laborer, 837 Howard
Davidge Charles, laborer, Howard
Dewitt Silas W., law judge of Warren county, office over Bel. Del. depot, Union Square, bds. 174 S. Main
Davis Wm. M., lawyer, 16 Union Square, res. above Howell School House
Deichman A. S., insurance agent, 18 Union Square, res. Centre Square, Easton

ANDREWS & NOLF, 205 Northampton St., Easton, Pa. The Largest line of DRESS TRIMMINGS etc.

H. M. NORTON, WHOLESALE AND RETAIL DEALER IN HARDWARE, STOVES, HEATERS AND RANGES.

Davis Sam'l V., prop. Lee House, 24 Union Square
Dumont Jane, widow, 184 Brainard
Dilts Edward W., conductor, 192 Brainard
Daub Anna, widow, 604 Mercer
Dickerson Irene, near Central Railroad Round House
Dixon John, station agent, bds 224 S. Main
Daubert A. A., tombstones, 309 S. Main h 604 Sitgreave
Dereamer Jesse L., carpenter, Elizabeth's Court
Dale Eldridge, railroad supervisor, Dale's ave
Dale Mrs. Irene, widow, 175 S. Main
Dumont J. F., lawyer, 149 S. Main h 147 do
Dumont Jennie, teacher, 147 S. Main
Dumont Fred, student, 147 S. Main
Dilts Calvin, conductor, bds. Phillipsburg Hotel
Dougherty James, laborer, South Market
Durling Jerome B., Asst. Supt. Morris Canal, res. 411 South Main
Dickey Peter, driver, 444 S. Main
Danley S. B., retired, S. Haggerty's Row
Dewitt Levi, wire-drawer, 239 Burnett

FELIX & LEININGER, Nos. 102 & 104 South 3d St., Easton, Pa. **FURNITURE.**

Dewitt Washington, retired, 144 Chambers
Dalton Stewart T., retired, 230 Bullman
Dinsmore Mrs. Phoebe, teacher, cor. Bullman and Front
Dick L. A., laborer, Rose near Second
Davis William, laborer, 305 N. Main
Dickey Peter, ironworker, Broad
Delaware Rolling Mill office, cor. Delaware and First
Divine Edward, fireman, Delaware
Dalrymple George, laborer, Delaware
Drinkhouse F. Y., machine shop, Delaware
Duncan Mrs. Kate, widow, 120 N. Main
Dawes Col. W. H., retired, 339 Chamber
DeWitt Peter, wiredrawer, 332 Chambers
Davis Ephraim, carpet weaver, 420 Washington
Dunlap George C., engineer, 450 Lewis
Dennis John, brakeman, 461 Lewis
Dull C. J., butcher, 416 Chambers
Dodd Vincent R., railroader, 437 Chambers
Dailey J. V., shoemaker, 455 Chambers

ALL KINDS OF HARDWARE at Wade Bros., Hackettstown, N. J.

Bailey Mrs. Mary, dressmaker, 453 Chambers
Dereamer James, brakeman, 543 Chambers
Deats John, laborer, 120 Detweiler's Row
Dingler Wm., saloon, 528 Chambers
Dwyer John, furnaceman, 725 Fayette
Doren Casper, quarryman, bds. 930 Mercer
Dennis Joseph, boiler maker, 826 Mercer
Dean M., boiler maker, 817 Mercer
Duffy John, laborer, bds. 806 Mercer
Dilts Levi, brakeman, 941 S. Main
Devinney James, laborer, 651 Mercer
Doyle Thomas, foundryman, 708 Mercer
Duffy John, furnaceman, 704 Mercer
Dibble Edgar A., engine inspector, bds. 751 S. Main
Dowd James, grocer, 737 S. Main, bds. 735 do
Ditton Charles, butcher, 721 S. Main h 719 do
Ditton Charles, Jr., butcher, 719 S. Main
Ditton John, clerk, 719 S. Main
Ditton Annie, teacher, 719 S. Main
Dempster Wm., horseman, Dempster's Hill

FELIX & LEININGER, Nos. 102 & 104 South 3d St., Easton, Pa. FURNITURE

Dempster Robert, boss, Dempster's Hill
Dempster Robert, Jr., horseman, Dempster's Hill
Dempster M. M., blacksmith, Dempster's Hill
Dempster Joseph, blacksmith, Dempster's Hill
Dempster Mrs. Susan, Dempster's Hill
Duffy James, laborer, bds. 755 S. Main
Dorsey Thomas, flagman, bds. 755 S. Main
Dilts William, foundryman, Jefferson
D. L. & W. Freight House, rear Columbia Hotel
Duckworth Samuel, railroader, McKean Hotel near Main
Dick Charles, mason 924 Sitgreave
Doloney Thomas, teamster, 975 Sitgreave
Desley Lewis, laborer, 735 Sitgreaves
Davis Patrick, laborer, 763 Sitgreaves
Dean Kate, widow, 767 Sitgreaves
Davis Daniel, carpenter, 1059 S. Main
Dalrymple Charles, brakeman, 928 S. Main
Dalrymple David, foundryman, 926 S. Main
Duckworth John, railroader, 832 S. Main

ANDREWS & NOLF, 205 Northampton St., Easton, Pa. The Largest line of DRESS TRIMMINGS etc.

Daneger Jacob, saloon, 816 S. Main
Diehl Fred, crockery, &c., 706 S. Main
Dodd Alfred, engineer, 610 S. Main
Ewing Joseph, car inspector, 214 Brainard
Ewing James, monkey wrencher, bds 214 Brainard
Ewing Lizzie, dressmaker, 214 Brainard
Edline Daniel, foreman, 212 So. Main
Everback Sarah, widow, 211 Hanover
Engle Henry, engineer, 524 Sitgreaves
Everitt Alexander, fireman, 529 Fayette
Eilenberg John, wholesale liquor dealer, residence and store 525 So. Main
Eilenberg George, student, 535 So. Main
Erbacker John, plumber, 828 Mercer
Ehly Frank, brakeman, 636 Mercer
Ehly Edward, foundryman, bds 636 Mercer
Egan Michael, mason, 656 Mercer
Eppler William H., blacksmith, h 636 Sitgreaves
Eckhart Margaret, widow, Foundry alley
Eckhart Henry, foundryman, Foundry alley

FELIX & LEININGER, Nos. 102 & 104 South 3d St., **Easton, Pa.** **FURNITURE.**

Elridge Taylor, laborer, 926 Sitgreaves
Eldridge Ziebie, foundryman, 960 Sitgreaves
Edgerton Alvin, carpenter, 1060 So. Main
Eppler Robert H., wall paper, 704 So. Main

JOHN EILENBERG,

WHOLESALE LIQUOR DEALER

553 So. Main St., PHILLIPSBURG, N. J.

Pure Wines and Liquors for Medicinal Use a Specialty.

Eilenberger H. A. cigar manufacturer, store 648 So. Main, house 646 So. Main
Elyea F. H., laborer, Bennett

ANDREWS & NULF, 205 Northampton St., Easton, Pa. The Largest line of DRESS TRIMMINGS etc.

H. M. NORTON, WHOLESALE AND RETAIL DEALER IN HARDWARE, STOVES, HEATERS AND RANGES.

PHILLIPSBURG DIRECTORY.

Ensley David, mason, 247 Bennett
Egbert E. B., painter, 118 Bullman
Ecoff Wilson, iron worker, Rose
Eckert William, brakeman, North Main
Exton Wm. H., driver, bds 160 N. Main
Exton Mansfield, driver, bds 160 N. Main
Eilenberg John, retired, 383 Washington
Eckert John, carpenter, Hudson
Eckert Frank, laborer, Hudson
Eckert Gustavus, laborer, Hudson
Eckert John C., baker, 554 Washington
Eckert William, laborer, bds 554 Washington
Eckert Adam, mason, bds 554 Washington
Eversole John C., fireman, 426 Washington
Ealer Harvey, laborer, 465 Chambers
Eckert Mrs. William, baker shop, Detweilers row
Engle William, trackman, Dempters Hill
Eldridge Samuel, laborer, Mounts Hill
Force Edward, railroader, 132 Chambers
Fisk M. M., principal, 213 Bullman

Felix & Leininger, Nos. 102 & 104 South 3d Street, **Easton, Pa.** **Furniture.**

Flynn Jeremiah, laborer, Front
Frey Jesse, iron worker, corner Third and Broad
Ford Michael, puddler, North Broad
Ford Joseph, clerk, bds North Broad
Frantz Norman, carpenter, 432 Broad
Foster Isaac, grocer, 237 N. Main, h 285 N. Main
Foster D. L., clerk, 285 N. Main
Force Kate, widow, 233 North Main
Fraunfelter James, engineer, North Main
Fisher John, laborer, Davis
Fishbaugh Wm., car inspector, 479 Davis
Frost Isaiah, laborer, 245 Jane Louisa
Freck Anthony, laborer, 124 Detweilers Row
Folk Charles, laborer 108 Detweilers Row
Folk John, mason, 100 Detweilers Row
Folk Charles, mason, 102 Detweilers Row
Fehrer Charles, boiler maker, 544 Lewis
First Jacob, laborer, 549 Lewis
Fry Albert, retired, Marshall
Firth Mrs. Mary, retired, near Cemetery

Andrews & Nolf, 205 Northampton St. The only place to buy the "CONFORMATER" Corset.

HOUSEFURNISHING GOODS GENERALLY — The BEST GOODS for the LEAST MONEY at **H. M. NORTON'S**, Easton, Pa.

PHILLIPSBURG DIRECTORY.

Flory Cyrus, brakeman, 702 Howard
Fisher Mrs. Mary T., widow, 731 Howard
Fehr Newberry, railroader, 856 Howard
Fehr William, shoemaker, 856 Howard
Fehr Warren, boatman, 856 Howard
Frankenfield Hugh, brakeman, 721 Fayette
Fishbaugh Peter, railroader, 814 Mercer
Fisher John, laborer, 810 Mercer
Fitzgerald Richard, laborer, 805 Mercer
Flummerfelt Jesse, book keeper, 969 S. Main
Frame William, foundryman, 945 S. Main
Frame James, furnaceman, 927 S. Main
Frame Miss Christina, teacher, 927 S. Main
Fitzpatrick Michael, laborer, Cherry alley
Fox John, laborer, cor Fox and Mercer
Flynn Michael, RR detective, 658 Mercer
Flynn John, railroader, 730 Mercer
Flynn Wm. F., brakeman, Foundry alley
Frye John R., painter, 602 Sitgreaves
Flynn Bernard, engineer, 602 Sitgreaves

FELIX & LEININGER, Nos. 102 & 104 South 3d St., Easton, Pa. **FURNITURE.**

Franks Mary, 972, Sitgreaves
Fisher Lewis, laborer, 929 Sitgreaves
Flynn William, laborer, 933 Sitgreaves
Fisher Annie, widow, Spruce alley
Fister George, foundryman, 649 Sitgreaves
Folk Charles, carpenter, 711 Sitgreaves
Ferry Joseph, laborer, 735 Sitgreaves
Fisher Lewis, foundryman, 769 Sitgreaves
Finnegan John, laborer, 1067 S. Main
Frame Samuel, machinist, near Andover Furnace
Fitzcharles Lawrence, laborer, 953 S. Main
Flemming Robert, foreman, 964 S. Main
Flemming George, ass't foreman, 940 S. Main
Fitzsimons Thomas, laborer, 936 S. Main
Fenton George H., painter, 732 S. Main
Fiske William H., books, stationery and music, 702 S. Main, h do
Flummerfelt John, gent, bds 969 S. Main
Fulper Abraham, railroader, 152 S. Main
Flummerfelt Charlotte, widow, 164 Randall

The **BISSLE PLOWS** are the best of all. For sale at **Wades' Hardware Store.**

Frasher Wm. W., conductor, 237 Brainard
Fitch Charles F., editor *Warren Democrat*, and attorney-at-law, office 102 South Main
Franks John, freight agent, also member of the firm of Meeker & Franks, dealers in coal and wood, bds Lee House, rooms cor Market and S. Main
Freeman Walter, drug store, cor Main and Market
Fulper Robert, brakeman, 205 Market
Fuller Mrs. Elizabeth, widow, 338 S. Main
Fuller Edward, brakeman, 338 S. Main
Fulper Rebecca, widow, Cedar Alley
Foulker William, laborer, Dempster Alley
Fiske Rufus, railroader, 716 S. Main
Frizell James, farmer, Roseberry
Fisher David, blacksmith, Dempters Hill
Focklin John, laborer, 626 Mercer
Fahley Martin, laborer, 608 Mercer
Flynn Bernard, railroader, 592 Mercer
Fishler Thomas, railroader, 617 Fayette
Funk John N., engineer, 525 Fayette

Felix & Leininger, Nos. 102 & 104 South 3d Street, **Easton, Pa.** **Furniture.**

Fitzgerald Matthew, track walker, 628 Howard
Fitzpatrick Patrick, laborer, Chestnut Alley
Fogle Benjamin, carpenter, Fox
Furnace School Building (foot of Sitgreaves)
Ferguson John S., carpenter, 323 Lewis
Folk John, mason, 367 Lewis
Folk John Jr., laborer, 367 Lewis
Fauerbach Philip, brakeman, 375 Lewis
Freeman Mrs. Samuel, boarding, 325 Chambers
Freeman Annie, private school, 325 Chambers
Fahely James, laborer, Taylors alley
Frost B. C., lawyer, Union Square, h 304 Chambers
Frace Simon, carpenter, 408 Washington
Fuller Geo. E., grocery, 405 Chambers, store 400 Lewis
Frith Joseph, foundryman, 446 Lewis
Fishbaugh Calvin, railroader, 448 Lewis
Fry Jacob, laborer, 460 Lewis
Fisher Fred, engineer, 525 Chambers
Gallagher Charles, laborer, 602 Mercer
Gordon Charles, brakeman, 523 Mercer

ALL KINDS OF HARDWARE at Wade Bros., Hackettstown, N. J.

H. M. NORTON, WHOLESALE AND RETAIL DEALER IN HARDWARE, STOVES, HEATERS AND RANGES.

PHILLIPSBURG DIRECTORY.

Gordon Granville, wiper, 552 Howard
Grube Harvey, laborer, bds. 552 Howard
Gordon Emanuel, wrencher, 624 Howard
Gordon Reading, brakeman, 626 Howard
Grace G. H., Supt. Tel. C. R. R. of N. J., Dept.
    h Ferry street, Easton
Gipp Christian, laborer Dempster's Hill
Gischel Charles, engineer, 670 Howard
Gischel Charles, Jr., job printer, 670 Howard
Gruber Gottlieb, railroader, 728 Howard
Gibney Christopher, laborer, Chesnut Alley
Grenninger Martin, moulder, 719 Fayette
Gordon Elwood, railroader, Chesnut near McKean
Gallagher, Helen, teacher, bds. Lee House
Gamble James E., saloon, 110 and 112 S. Main
Godley Mrs. Mary, widow, 134 S. Main
Gillaspy Charles, fireman, bds. Columbia Hotel
Gooley Patrick, brakeman, bds. Columbia Hotel
Griswoold Alice E., music teacher, bds. 224 S. Main
Gove Frank, telegraph operator, bds. on Hanover

FELIX & LEININGER, Nos. 102 & 104 South 3d St., **Easton, Pa.** **FURNITURE.**

Gulick Aaron, car inspector, 301 S. Main
Gulick Amanda, dressmaker, 301 S. Main
Goehler Philip, laborer, 15 Haggerty's Row
Gibney Matthew, fireman, 22 Haggerty's Row
Gibney Edward, retired, 502 South Main
Gorgas Jacob, railroader, Union
Garrison Wm., RR carpenter, Cedar Alley
Gorgas David, engineer, 618 Mercer
Gallagher Hugh, railroader, 944 Mercer
Gallagher Daniel, laborer, foot of Mercer
Gorman Patrick, contractor, 822 S. Main
Gardiner James, teamster, 653 Mercer
Gray Henry, brakeman, 635 Mercer
Godder Banks, conductor, 761 S. Main
Grace Lutheran Church, 727 S. Main, below Stockton,
    Rev. G. D. Bernhim, pastor
Gaffney John, laborer, 958 Sitgreaves
Glenville Albert, laborer, 309 McKean
Gipp Francis, furnaceman, 614 Sitgreaves
Gipp Joseph, foundryman, bds. 614 Sitgreaves

Andrews & Nolf, 205 Northampton St. The only place to buy the "CONFORMATER" Corset.

HOUSE FURNISHING GOODS GENERALLY. **E. M. NORTON'S** Easton Pa.
The BEST GOODS for the LEAST MONEY at

PHILLIPSBURG DIRECTORY.

Gilinger Jeremiah, engineer, 429 Lewis
Griffith T. H., physician, office 412 Chambers
Griffith Wm. A., baggage-master, bds. 410 Chambers
Griffith Mrs. S. P., widow, 449 Chambers
Guygar G. A., carpenter, Fulton
Griffith Percival, clerk, 449 Chambers
Groondyke Andrew, brakeman, 569 Chambers
Greenwood Wm., foundryman, Wilson
Glackin Moses, moulder, 603 Railroad ave
Gilluly Mrs. Anna, widow, Heckman
Gelphart Chas., laborer, bds. Heckman
Gamill Patrick, laborer, Dempster's Hill
Gallagher Frank, laborer, 922 S. Main
Gilluly Benjamin, prop., 2d Ward Hotel, 760 S. Main, h 758 do
Gavin Richard, grocer, 740 S. Main, h do
Grouney Philip, laborer, 626 S. Main
Grouney Rosa, dressmaker, 626 S. Main
Gabert John, laborer, 346 N. Main
Gallagher John, laborer, N. Main

FELIX & LEININGER, Nos. 102 & 104 South 3d St., Easton, Pa., FURNITURE

Griffith Thomas, puddler, 346 Broad
Gabert Lewis, ironworker, 346 N. Main
Goolupsky Henry, agent, N. Main
Gallagher Mrs. Sarah, widow, 154 N. Main
Gross John, sash factory, 335 Morris Turnpike
Gipp John, laborer, 337 Fillmore
Gleason Martin, laborer, 523 Fillmore
Gross Adam, hostler, 120 N. Main
Gorgas Edward, driver, 353 Washington
Gorgas Samuel, railroader, 393 Washington
Gilroy Henry, shoemaker, h 334 Washington
Goodwin Jeremiah, engineer, bds. on Hudson
Gardner J. H., machinist, 416 Hudson
Gardner Forrest, laborer, bds. 416 Hudson
Gertson Fred., laborer, Hudson
Green Wm., agent, 411 Washington
Googas Joseph, engineer, 462 Washington
Gray Andrew, foundryman, 455 Lewis
Gorgas Charles, butcher, 231 Washington
Grinning Chris., laborer, Rose
Gaston Joseph, laborer, 351 N. Main

H. M. NORTON, WHOLESALE AND RETAIL DEALER IN HARDWARE, STOVES, HEATERS AND RANGES.

Gallagher James, laborer, 958 Sitgreaves
Gallagher Neil, confectionery, 990 Sitgreaves
Garis Aaron, foundryman, 955 Sitgreaves
Garis Wm. E., laborer, 955 Sitgreaves
Glenville Chauncey, laborer, 853 Sitgreaves
Gelpke Charles, compositor, 633 Sitgreaves
Galligan Edward B., peddler, 653 Sitgreaves
Garrecht George, shoemaker, 810 S. Main
Hartland Edward, prop. Andover Hotel 1032 S. Main
Gallagher John, laborer, rear Andover Hotel
Gray Mrs. Annie, dressmaker, 948 S. Main
Gillen James, photograph agent, Bennet
Gelpke Mrs. Charlotte, widow, Bennet
Gillen George, driver, Bunnel Alley
Grooby Mrs. Elizabeth, widow, 239 Bullman
Grooley Edward, telegraph operator, 239 Bullman
Greigs George, car cleaner, 228 Washington
Hagenbuch Wm., bookkeeper, cor. Morris and Chambers
Hildebrand Lewis, carpenter, 224 Bennett

FELIX & LEININGER, Nos. 102 & 104 South 3d St., **Easton, Pa.** **FURNITURE.**

Harrison Wm., shoemaker, Bennett
Hawk Isaac, railroader, Bennett
Herbert Wm. F., railroader, 134 Chambers
Huff Simeon, engineer, 244 Bullman
Huff Wm. H., car inspector, 302 Bullman
Huff Samuel, railroader, 227 Bullman
Harris J. M., crockery and prop. Delaware Pottery, residence on Bullman
Harris Benj. F. Genr'l Agt. C. R. R., Bullman
Hulsizer Silas, conductor, 229 Washington
Howell Joseph, carpenter, Third
Howell Mrs. Ellen, widow, Third
Harrison Daniel, railroader, Third
Harris Robert, ironworker, Rose
Hauck F. F., moulder, 403 N. Main
Hummel Peter, puddler, N. Main
Hess John, carpenter, 329 N. Main
Hively Jacob, laborer, bds. 317 N. Main
Harrison Mrs. Euphemia, dressmaker, 312 N. Main
Hickson Charles, laborer, 378 Broad
Horn John, boat builder, Mercer

ALL KINDS OF HARDWARE at Wade Bros., Hackettstown, N. J.

Hughes James, horse jockey, bds. 142 N. Main
Housman John, car driver, 213 Morris Turnpike
Higgins Samuel, Jr., Baggage Master, bds. Morris Turnpike
Higgins Samuel, P., station agent, P. R. R., depot h 321 Morris Turnpike
Higgins Kate, artist studio, 321 Morris
Hoffman Aug., laborer, Morris Turnpike
Hawk Edward, laborer, Morris Turnpike
Hamilton Jacob, laborer, 449 Fillmore
Hines Andrew, laborer, Davis
Honch Rinehard, laborer, Filmore
Haggerty Elizabeth, widow, Fillmore
Harrison R. G., engine wiper, 428 Broad
Hawk Cornelius, wire drawer, 220 Harris
Harwig Mrs. Wm., widow, 372 Chambers
Harwig Josephine, brace maker, 372 Chambers
Harvey Wm., railroader, 353 Chambers
Hicks Bartley, conductor, 341 Chambers
Hunt W. W., expressman, 339 Chambers

FELIX & LEININGER, Nos. 102 & 104 South 3d St., **Easton, Pa.** FURNITURE

Harle Wm., carpenter, 308 Chambers
Heckman Charles, retired, 321 Washington
Hofford Mahlon, mason, 367 Washington
Hofford Elmer, mason, 367 Washington
Harris Mrs. Mary, dressmaker, 379 Washington
Hofford Emma, fore lady, bds. 379 Washington
Henshaw Peter, laborer, 633 Hudson
Hogen Daniel, laborer, 646 Hudson
Hughes Michael, 3d ward policeman, 428 Washington
Harle John, fireman, 452 Lewis
Harle Herbert, brakeman, 452 Lewis
Houston James, machinist, 420 Fulton
Hedmrig Wm., carpenter, 467 Lewis
Hagerman Jacob, fireman, 433 Lewis
Hoff Joseph, conductor, 427 Lewis
Hartzell Herbert, grocer, res. 436 Chambers
Haggerty Francis, railroader, bds. 452 Chambers
Hauck Charles, machinist, 537 Chambers
Henry David, brakeman, 128 Detweiler's
Hannan Samuel, railroader, 116 Detweiler's

The **BISSLE PLOWS** are the best of all. For sale at **Wades' Hardware Store**

HOUSEFURNISHING GOODS GENERALLY
The BEST GOODS for the LEAST MONEY at **H. M. NORTON'S, Easton, Pa.**

PHILLIPSBURG DIRECTORY. 285

Hulon Albert, laborer, 112 Detweiler's
Heater Wm., brakeman, 104 Detweiler's
Height Mrs. Elizabeth, widow, Chamb's near Heckman
Hann J. W., fireman, 527 Lewis
Heery Mrs. Anna, widow, 539 Lewis
Heery Luke, laborer, bds. 539 Lewis
Hann Alfred, spring maker, bds. 526 Lewis
Hendershot Chauncey, brakeman, 546 Lewis
Holmes Frank, G. D., machinist, Fillmore
Haley Alfred, foundryman, 576 Wilson
Hamler Isaac, boots and shoes, 631 S. Main res. 627 Wilson
Heath Albert, brakeman, 608 Railroad ave
Hazzard Wm. S., brakeman, 271 Heckman
Hoff Wm. H., pipe maker, Heckman
Hoff James, pipe maker, Heckman
Huff Peter, foundryman, Heckman
Hermes Peter, shoemaker, cor Heck and Fill
Hammel Joseph, gardener, Henderson
Hughes and Cyphers, grocers, 16 and 18 Union Sq

FELIX & LEININGER, Nos. 102 & 104 South 3d St., Easton, Pa. **FURNITURE.**

Higgins Peter, RR clerk, bds Lee House
Heiberger Thomas, butcher, 128 S. Main, h 156 do
Heiberger Lorenzo, butcher, res 156 S. Main
Houser Wm., conductor, bds 152 S. Main
Hess James, carpenter, 159 Randall
Hoffman Wm. F., foreman, 157 Randall
Hance Charles M., express messenger, 219 Hudson
Horn Richard, engineer, Hudson
Heller Samuel, fireman, 200 Brainard
Hummer Andrew, laborer, 205 Brainard
Hess Edward, conductor, 197 Brainard
Hummer Wm. A., foreman, 191 Brainard
Heitzman Stewart, farmer, 180½ S. Main
Heitzman Frank B., retired, bds 180½ S. Main
Hartzell & Kracher, grocers, 196 S. Main
Hefferman John, conductor, 246 Brainard
Hunter James, railroader, 238 Brainard
Hurley Daniel, RR carpenter, bds Columbia Hotel
Heller William, brakeman, 312 S. Main
Hulsizer Hugh, express messenger, bds 224 S. Main

SHIELDS' Compound Syrup of Wild Cherry with Hypophosites of Lime and Soda. Sure cure for coughs, croup, etc.

M. M. NORTON, WHOLESALE AND RETAIL DEALER IN HARDWARE, STOVES, HEATERS AND RANGES.

PHILLIPSBURG DIRECTORY.

Hoffman Joseph, clerk, bds 224 S. Main
Hendricks Christopher, brakeman, Elizabeth
Hoffman George E., railroader, 131 S. Main
Hadler A. A., insurance agt, bds Phillipsburg Hotel
Hendricks Joseph, fireman, Phillipsburg Hotel
Home School, (private) 339 S. Main
Harzell Reuben, painter, South Market
Hagerman P. R. & Son, grocers, 403 South Main, house 409 do
Hagerman Charles, grocer, 409 S. Main
Harrison George, laborer, 25 Hagerty's Row
Harrison Jonah, laborer, 25 Hagerty's Row
Hoagland James, fireman, 534 Sitgreaves
Hagerman Caroline, milliner, 514 S. Main
Hagerty Peter H., Mayor of the town, and undertaker, 449 S. Main
Hagerty Frank, boots & shoes, 447 S. Main
Hagerty F. P., stoves, tinware, and ice, 443 S. Main,
Hagerty Martin, clerk, 525 Union
Harrison Firman, teamster, 175 Union

Felix & Leininger, Nos. 102 & 104 South 3d Street, **Easton, Pa.** **Furniture.**

Howell Roger, machinist, Union
Hixon Martin, railroader, 611 S. Main
Hixon Andrew, railroader, 611 S. Main
Housel John, brakeman, Cedar Alley
Heitzman George, engine wiper, Cedar Alley
House William, engineer, 605 S. Main
Howell H. Budd, principal High School, bds 537 South Main
Hagerty John H., lumber, hardware, etc., 517 S. Main, h 527 do

John H. Hagerty & Sons,
WHOLESALE AND RETAIL DEALERS IN
HARDWARE AND LUMBER,
Paint, Oils, Varnish, Glass, Putty, etc.,
AND MANUFACTURERS OF
MOULDING, SASH, BLINDS, DOORS, SHUTTERS, ETC.,
NO. 519 SOUTH MAIN ST.   PHILLIPSBURG, N. J.

Hagerty's Hall, occupied every Sunday afternoon at 3.30 o'clock by Phillipsburg Reform Club
Hendrickson Wm., railroader, 826 Howard

For Coughs, Colds, Croup and Consumption use SHIELDS' **COMPOUND SYRUP** of Wild Cherry with hypophosphates of lime and soda

HOUSEFURNISHING GOODS GENERALLY. **H. M. NORTON'S, Easton, Pa.**
The BEST GOODS for the LEAST MONEY at

PHILLIPSBURG DIRECTORY. 287

Hanly Rev. P., ass't in St. Philip and James' church h 661 S. Main
Heinly Abraham, conductor, 701 Fayette
Hager John, butcher, 635 Fayette
Hoagland Terrence, laborer, Fayette near McKean
Herbert John, foreman, 930 Mercer
Hawk Ervin, hostler, 831 Mercer
Hawk Frank, brakeman, bds 831 Mercer
Headley Jacob, fireman, 827 Mercer
Hyre George, boiler maker, 807 Mercer
Holleran Bartholomew, laborer, 851 S. Main
Holden Jacob, traveling salesman, 853 S. Main
Hurley Thomas, foundryman, 845 S. Main
Harris John, laborer, 813 S. Main
Harrison Abbey, widow, 813 S. Main
Hulsizer Joseph H., prop'r American House, 801 S. Main
Hoag Richard, laborer, Jefferson
Hoag Robert, boatman, Cherry alley
Hoag James, laborer, Cherry alley

FELIX & LEININGER, Nos. 102 & 104 South 3d St., **Easton, Pa.** **FURNITURE.**

Hayes John, clerk, 655 Mercer
Herbert Charles, fireman, 710 Mercer
Haley Friend, foundryman, bds 712 Mercer
Haley Earle, foundryman, bds 712 Mercer
Hans Peter, shoemaker, 718 Mercer
Heitzman Wm., railroader, 736 Mercer
Howell School Building, North Main
Hamlen John, farmer, Dempster's Hill
Hamlen Cyrus, wheelwright, 752 Mercer
Heater George M., laborer, Cedar alley
Hammerman Emil, carpets, etc., 745 S. Main
Hawk Daniel, grocer, 900 S. Main, h 707 do
Hunt James, fireman, bds 755 S. Main
Hawk Gustavus, laborer, 608 Sitgreaves
Hawk Joseph, monkey wrencher, 610 Sitgreaves
Hawk Horton, railroader, bds 608 Sitgreaves
Hann Jacob, machinist, 630 Sitgreaves
Hess James, railroader, 652 Sitgreaves
Haily Jeremiah, laborer, 944 Sitgreaves
Hally Lawrence, laborer, 946 Sitgreaves

ANDREWS & NOLF, 205 Northampton St., Easton, Pa. The Largest line of DRESS **TRIMMINGS** etc.

Hager Peter, wire drawer, 608 S. Main
Hogan James, driver, 952 Sitgreaves
Heist Charles, laborer, 954 Sitgreaves
Harrison George, sawyer, 970 Sitgreaves
Harrison Lemuel, teamster, Spruce alley
Halley Jeremiah, Jr., laborer, 849 Sitgreaves
Hansen Thorwald, boiler maker, 825 Sitgreaves
Hub Peter, saloon, 645 Sitgreaves, h 643 do
Hub Peter A., slater, bds 643 Sitgreaves
Hughes Mrs. P., prop's Union Hotel, cor Sitgreaves and Stockton
Hendricks Fred, foundryman, 705 Sitgreaves
Huff Isaac, laborer, 725 Sitgreaves
Hance Albert, laborer, 747 Sitgreaves
Haley Dennis, laborer, 749 Sitgreaves
Hagerty D. W., lumber, etc., 1067 S. Main
Hughes George, laborer, 1063 S. Main
Hawk Geo. H., coal yard, 1003 S. Main, h do
Hager Nicholas, butcher, 710 S. Main, h 708 do
Hurbert John, engineer, 908 S. Main

Felix & Leininger, Nos. 102 & 104 South 3d Street, **Easton, Pa.** **Furniture.**

Hulsizer Stewart, railroader, 846 S. Main
Heaton Thomas, machinist and present assessor, 830 South Main
Harms G. H., tinsmith, 656 S. Main
Harms H. H., tinsmith, 656 S. Main
Harms Wm., tinsmith, 650 S. Main
Hager & Co., butchers, 710 S. Main
Hess William, blacksmith, Dempster's Hill
Hoadley Demons, railroader, foundry alley
Hummel John, laborer, Dempster's Hill
Huff Holley, laborer, Dempster's Hill
Imlay John C., ironworker and inventor, 352 Broad
Ieely Frank, engine wiper, 465 Fillmore
Ingham Charles, Asst. Supt. Warren Foundry, 566 Lewis
Ingham Walter, foreman, Warren Foundry, 571 Lewis
Ingham John, Sup't Warren Foundry, 236 Heckman
Job William, car cleaner, Shimer
Imlay Charles, brakeman, 943 S. Main
Ihrie Irwin, foundryman, 740 Sitgreaves

Andrews & Nolf, 205 Northampton St. The only place to buy the "CONFORMATER" Corset.

H. M. NORTON, WHOLESALE AND RETAIL DEALER IN HARDWARE, STOVES, HEATERS AND RANGES.

PHILLIPSBURG DIRECTORY.

Icely Frank, laborer, Foundry Alley
Ihrie Elmer, foundryman, 752 Sitgreaves
Ihrie Robert, fireman, 754 Sitgreaves
Inscho Philip, railroader, 29 Haggerty's Row
Inscho David, car inspector, 24 Haggerty's Row
Inscho Jacob, clerk, 502 S. Main
Johnson W. Scott, laborer, bds. 758 S. Main
Johnson Alex., laborer, Rose street
Johnson John, laborer, Rose
Johnson Chris., brakeman, 373 Lewis
Johnson Mrs. Ella, dressmaker, 412 Washington
Johnson Wm., canal man, Chambers near Heckman
Johnson Lewis, carpenter, 456 Chambers
Johnson Harry, laborer, bds. 412 Washington
Jones Henry T., roller, 354 Broad
Jones Thomas R. L., clerk, 354 Broad
Jones John Washington, representative the *Easton Daily Express*, and gen'l adv. agt
Jones William, laborer, bds. Broad
Justice Mrs. Mary, widow, bds. 341 Chambers

FELIX & LEININGER, Nos. 102 & 104 South 3d St., **Easton, Pa.** FURNITURE.

Johnson Wm., machinist, 120 Chambers
Johnson Wm. H., railroader, bds. 118 Bullman
Johnson Elisha, barber, 30 Union Square, h 108 Del
Johnson Alexander, railroader, 160 Randall
Johnson Thomas, conductor, bds. 311 S. Main
Judge Mrs. Rosanna, widow, 137 S. Main
Johnson Wesley, blacksmith, Cedar
James Joseph, machinist, 609 Mercer
Johnson Charles, laborer, Fayette near McKean
Johnson George, engineer, 724 Mercer
Johnson Frank, laborer, Cedar alley
Johnson Charlie, hooker up, Rose
Johnson Philip, laborer, 928 Sitgreaves
Johnson Alexander, carpet weaver, Spruce alley
Kelly Patrick, miner, Third
Kerkendall Reuben, laborer, N. Main
Kotee Adam, laborer, 358 N. Main
Kotee Henry, clerk, Broad
Keller Frank, laborer, 322 Broad
Krouse Casper, tailor, Broad

READ CAREFULLY, Page 218

Krinket Charles, laborer, Morris Turnpike
Kimmer George, carpenter, N. Hudson
Keller John, silk mill, bds. 447 Lewis
Kidney Michael, blacksmith, Fillmore
Keating Bartholomew, moulder, 333 Fillmore
Kromer Martin, 461 Davis
Koch Peter, peddler, 359 Lewis
King A. W., engineer, 381 Chambers
Kern Theodore, conductor, 364 Chambers
Kinney Stewart, pattern maker, 319 Chambers
Kupka Clemens, tailor, 163 S. Main, h 315 Chamb's
Keese Wm., stone-cutter, 605 Hudson
Keese Wm., Jr., boilermaker, 603 Hudson
Keas John, laborer, 513 Hudson
Kitchart A. F., druggist, cor. Hudson and Lewis, h do
Karcher Jacob, foundryman, 460 Chambers
Karcher Edward, (Hartzell & Karcher,) grocers, res. 460 Chambers
Kent Fred., clerk, bds. 470 Chambers
Karcher Mrs. Elizabeth, widow, bds. 464 Chambers

FELIX & LEININGER, Nos. 102 & 104 South 3d St., **Easton, Pa.** FURNITURE.

Keating James, shoemaker, 429 Chambers
Kenna James, brakeman, 433 Chambers
Kichline Samuel, brakeman, 459 Chambers
Kenney Michael, confectionery, cor. Chambers and Hudson
Kaler Lewis, locksmith, 630 Chambers
Kichline Reuben, laborer, 548 Chambers

CLEMENS KUPKA,
FASHIONABLE MERCHANT TAILOR,

Fine Suitings made to order at reasonable rates.
Give me a call at
165 SOUTH MAIN STREET,
PHILLIPSBURG, - - - NEW JERSEY

Kramer Henry, bakery, 540 Chambers
Kline Edwin, engineer, Fillmore
Kinney John, carpenter, 269 Heckman
Keiter Mrs. Eliza, candy store, Chamb's near Heckman

SHIELDS' Compound Syrup of Wild Cherry with Hypophosites of Lime and Soda Sure cure for coughs, croup, etc

H. M. NORTON, WHOLESALE AND RETAIL DEALER IN HARDWARE, STOVES, HEATERS AND RANGES

Kaiser Anthony, saddler, 12 Union Square
Kenny C., clerk, bds. Lee House
Kinsley Wm., laborer, Shimer
Kinsley Charles, huckster, Shimer
Kelogg George, engineer, Hudson
Kocher John, railroader, 198 Brainard
Kemerer Edward, carpenter, 208 Brainard
Kinney Thomas, railroader, 169 Brainard
Kelty John, fireman, bds. Columbia Hotel
Kane Patrick, trackman, bds. Columbia Hotel
Kellcher Patrick, laborer, Dempster's Hill
Keenan Thomas, engineer, bds. Columbia Hotel
Keepers W. F., tin and sheet iron works, 199 Market
Kelog Wm. H., Sup't Morris Canal, L. V. R. R., depot, res. 185 S. Main
Knedler Frank, postmaster, bds. 157 S. Main
Kitchen Smith, railroader, Fifth
Kerkendall Jacob, foundryman, Fifth
Kearney Maria, widow, S. Market
Kressly George, laborer, 17 Haggerty's Row

FELIX & LEININGER, Nos. 102 & 104 South 3d St., **Easton, Pa.** **FURNITURE.**

Kelly William, railroader, 508 Sitgreaves
Kirkuff Elmer, driver, Union
Kinney George, laborer, River
Kinney Freeman, clerk, 139 River
Kinney John, railroader, Henderson
Kroesen Samuel, carpenter, Cedar alley
King John, railroader, 539 Mercer
Kidney Oliver, cigars and tobacco, confectionery, ice cream, etc., 606 S. Main
Kugler William, driver, 607 Mercer
Kugler Edward, brakeman, 543 Fayette
Koabel Andrew, blacksmith, Chestnut alley
Kemery Willam, brakeman, Fox
Kupbelsberger, Harry, baker, 607 S. Main
Kocher Israel, engineer, 601 S. Main
Knecht James M., carriage painter, 757 S. Main
Kessler Harry, printer, bds. Brainard
Kauffman Christian, carpenter, 824 Howard
Kugler Frank, laborer, Jefferson
Kipp Frank, foreman, 747 Fayette

Andrews & Nolf, 205 Northampton St. The only place to buy the "CONFORMATER" Corset.

Kelly Daniel, laborer, 805 Fayette
Knauss John D., car inspector, 808 Mercer
Kerkendall Rinaldo, railroader, bds. 808 Mercer
Kellogg John, railroader, 923 S. Main
Kane George, watchman, Cedar alley near McKean
Kane John, teamster, Cedar alley near McKean
Kane George, Jr., teamster, Cedar alley near McKean
Kane Thomas, teamster, Cedar alley near McKean
Kelly Francis, saloon, also grocery, 805 and 807 S Main h do
Knobloch John, moulder, bds. 646 Sitgreaves
Kugler Irvin, railroader, 702 Sitgreaves
Kisselbach John C., cripple, 305 McKean
Keaghan Thomas, laborer, 949 Sitgreaves
Kutzler David, blacksmith, 626 Sitgreaves
Kenealy Mrs. Mary, widow, Foundry alley
Kurley Mrs. Mary, widow, 956 Sitgreaves
Korp Edward, teamster, 969 Sitgreaves
Kinney Terrence, foundryman, 929 Sitgreaves
Kerkendall Peter, laborer, 801 Sitgreaves

FELIX & LEININGER, Nos. 102 & 104 South 3d St., Easton, Pa. FURNITURE

Kinney Patrick, retired, Spruce alley
Kerkendall Frank, laborer, 739 Sitgreaves
Kelly John, laborer, near Andover Furnace
Kent Joseph C., Supt. Andover Furnace, h near same
Krutendall Christopher, laborer, 991 S. Main
Kichline William, laborer, 946 S. Main
Kase Arthur, clerk, 808 S. Main
Klusmeyer Jacob, laborer, 740 S. Main
King Ida, candies, 718 S. Main
Lake Alva D., telegraph operator, Bullman
Laubach Issac, huckster, 216 Washington
Lee House, S. V. Davis, prop'r, 24 and 26 Union Sq
Long and Boileau, lumber and hardware, 20 Union Sq
Lerch Robert H., stationery and books, 122 South Main
Loveridge Mrs. G., 134 South Main
Lee A. H., retired, 160 South Main
Ludrig William, laborer, Tindall ave
Lommasson Abram, carpenter, 153 Randall
Lomasson Miss Emily, principal, 153 Randall

ANDREWS & NOLF, 205 Northampton St., Easton, Pa. The Largest line of DRESS TRIMMINGS etc.

HOUSEFURNISHING GOODS GENERALLY.
The BEST GOODS for the LEAST MONEY at **H. M. NORTON'S, Easton, Pa.**

Lewis Elezeaor, blacksmith, 152 Randall
Lamb Mrs. Rosetta, widow, 156 Randall
Lary Lafayette, engineer, 167 Reese alley
Londenbery Isaac, fish, oysters, and milk, 198 South Main, h 195 Brainard
Lowt Mrs. Jermina, invalid, 222 Washington
Lumber yard, (Long & Boileau), N. Main
Lamb George, painter, cor. Fillmore and Fulton
Lewis David, machinist, bds 354 Broad
Lyle John, laborer, 120 N. Main
Lee Walter, waiter, 120 N. Main
Lerch Mrs. Jane, widow, 230 Harris
Lerch Susan A., vest maker, 230 Harris
Lerch Peter, sexton, 232 Harris
Lerch Anthony, railroader, 236 Harris
Leminger Joseph, fireman, 365 Chambers
Lafey James, laborer, 330 Chambers
Leiberman Anthony, lumber, 324 Chambers
Lewis George H., blacksmith, 312 Chambers
Lewis George, Jr., puddler, bds. 312 Chambers

FELIX & LEININGER, Nos. 102 & 104 South 3d St., **Easton, Pa.** **FURNITURE.**

Loville Jacob R., clerk, 204 South Main
Leslie, W. J., telegraph operator, bds Columbia Hotel
Laird Charles, conductor, bds Columbia Hotel
Lee John, photographer, 441 South Main

For Good and First Class Pictures
GO TO
LEE THE PHOTOGRAPHER.

We guarantee a finer picture, and one for less money than any other Gallery in the County.
Cabinet Pictures, $2.00 per dozen.
Tin Types, 4 for 35 cents.

JOHN LEE,
441 So. Main Street.   PHILLIPSBURG, N. J.
Near the Methodist Church.

Lyman James, engineer, bds Phillipsburg Hotel
Linden Moses, watchman, South Market
Lampfield Nancy, widow, 27 Hagerty's Row

ANDREWS & NOLF, 205 Northampton St., Easton, Pa. The Largest line of DRESS TRIMMINGS etc.

H. M. NORTON, WHOLESALE AND RETAIL DEALER IN HARDWARE, STOVES, HEATERS AND RANGES.

Lee Edward, telegraph operator, Hanover
Lehigh Valley RR. depot, Market near Hanover
Lee Joseph (colored), driver, Randall
Laird Frank W., engineer, 130 River
Lovell Asbury, laborer, 600 Mercer
Lehigh Valley freight house, Golden, near Union
Lanigan Wm., laborer, Dempster's Hill
Lewis Nelson, moulder, bds. 312 Chambers
Lurken Mrs. M., widow Taylor's alley
Lewis Thomas, apprentice, bds. 446 Lewis
Lyons John, brakeman, bds. 452 Lewis
Lamb Robert, confectionery, etc., N. Fulton
Lehr George, fireman, 450 Lewis
Lloyd Alfred, foreman, 447 Lewis
Liedy Howard, laborer, 406 Chambers
Lutz Charles, laborer, 122 Detweiler's row
Leidy John T., pattern maker, 106 Detweiler's row
Lambert Wilson, laborer, 526 Lewis
Lake Irvin, machinist, 247 Heckman
Lynch Barnet, laborer, 306 Heckman

Felix & Leininger, Nos. 102 & 104 South 3d Street, **Easton, Pa.** **Furniture.**

Leibelsperger Samuel, insurance agent, 605 RR. ave
Lukens Thomas, conductor, 202 Heckman
Lawton Philip, laborer, Dempster's Hill
Leary James, laborer, Mounts Hill
Leary James Jr., laborer, Mount's Hill
Leary John, laborer, Mounts Hill
Leidy John H., moulder, 915 S. Main
Leidy George, moulder, bds 915 S. Main
Lambach Casper, builder, 724 Mercer
Lambach Gothart, carpenter, 724 Mercer
Lilly Charles, section boss, 858 Howard
Lowers Rudolph, railroader, 745 Fayette
Laughlin James, blacksmith, Fayette near McKean
Lauer Joseph, retired, 939 South Main
List Abraham, boatman, Cedar Alley, near McKean
Lilly Lucius, quarryman, 703 Mercer
Loare Samuel, manager No. 1 co-operative grocery, res. 609 Sitgreaves
Lewis William, huckster, Spruce alley
Lomasney Timothy, laborer, rear Andover Hotel

READ CAREFULLY Page 218

HOUSEFURNISHING GOODS GENERALLY. The BEST GOODS for the LEAST MONEY at **H. M. NORTON'S, Easton, Pa.**

PHILLIPSBURG DIRECTORY.

Loudenberger Osborne, prop. Osborne House, 600 S. Main
Launan Bernard, laborer, Howard
Lutz David, railroader, Howard
Leigh Mary D., drug store, 637 S. Main h 635 do
Lewis Lorenzo, engineer, 731 Mercer
Lutz Hugh, carpenter, 661 Mercer
Lavery Wm., laborer, 637 Mercer
Lang Oscar, retired, 715 South Main
Loare Peter, quarryman, 606 Sitgreaves
Lott Henry, engineer, 644 Sitgreaves
Levers Mrs. Emma, widow, 654 Sitgreaves
Lutz John, brakeman, Foundry Alley
Lawler Thomas, foundryman, 748 Sitgreaves
Lynch Edward, foundryman, Spruce Alley
Lance Edward, laborer, 910 Sitgreaves
Lerch Abraham, railroader, 932 Sitgreaves
Laushe Nicholas, laborer, Spruce Alley
Lutz Godfrey, laborer, 833 Sitgreaves
Lauder John, retired, 171 S. Main

FELIX & LEININGER, Nos. 102 & 104 South 3d St., **Easton, Pa.** **FURNITURE.**

Marsh Ed. H. machinist, Third
Miers Alfred, puddler, 407 N. Main
Malt House, unoccupied, 409 N. Main
Mack George, brakeman, bds. N. Main
Mack Robert, boiler maker, bds. N. Main
Muck Wm., painter, N. Main
McConnel, O. D., grocer, 350 Broad
Merritt Michael, laborer, bds. 338 N. Main
Myers Peter, driver, bds. 317 N. Main
Mutchler Mrs. Nettie, tailoress, 308 N. Main

O. D. McCONNEL, EX'R.,
NO. 350 BROAD ST. - - - - PHILLIPSBURG, N. J.
Choice Groceries and Provisions,
AT BOTTOM PRICES

Highest cash market price paid for butter, eggs and all kinds of
COUNTRY PRODUCE.

Morrow Charles, grocer, 348 Broad
Mixsell Theodore, laborer, N. Main
Major John W., carpenter, 380 Broad
Murray James, puddler, 374 Broad

ANDREWS & NOLF, SELL THE BEST $1.00 AND $1.25 KID GLOVES IN EASTON, PA. 205 NORTHAMPTON STREET.

Moyer Catherine, widow Delaware
Mose Genther, laborer, Delaware
Miller Daniel, car inspector, N. Main
McQuillen James, mining engineer, N. Main
Morris Samuel A., carpenter, Fillmore
McGuire Hugh, boiler maker, 335 Fillmore
Miller John, engineer, Davis
Mildenberger Frank, laborer, 485 Davis
Morris Robert, laborer, 243 Bennett
Merrick Andrew, puddler, 204 Harris
Merrick Elizabeth, widow, 204 Harris
McCorkell Joseph, machinist, 216 Jane Louisa
McCorkell Charles, coppersmith, 216 Jane Lousia
McDaniel David, sexton, 314 Lewis
Metz Henry J., fireman, 313 Lewis
Montgomery Charles, railroader, 376 Lewis
Moyer Amos, miller, 380 Lewis
Moyer Lizzie, teacher, bds. 380 Lewis
Moyer Samuel, grocer clerk, bds. 380 Chambers
Mann Wm. H., clerk, bds. 384 Chambers

Felix & Leininger, *Nos. 102 & 104 South 3d Street,* **Easton, Pa.** **Furniture.**

Mapp Mrs. Elizabeth, widow, bds. 364 Chambers
Mason Wm., engineer, 367 Chambers
McCracken George, brakeman, 363 Chambers
Myers Harry, fireman, bds. 357 Chambers
Miller Wm., engineer, 108 Chambers
Miller A. G., presiding elder, Bennett
Mason H. P., retired, 224 Bennett
Miller Isaac, engineer, 224 Bullman
Myers John S., carpenter, 146 Front
Mutchler Sarah, widow, 225 Front
Moore Alexander, foundryman, 146 Washington
Mutchler A. J., mason, 226 Washington
McGinley Thomas, foundryman, 346 Chambers
Miller Charles, carpenter, 344 Chambers
Metz James, telegraph operator, 321 Chambers
Miller George H., car inspector, 314 Chambers
Marsh Isaac, book agent, 351 Washington
Metz Catherine, widow, 355 Washington
Miller John, painter, 372 Washington
Miller Jesse, painter, 372 Washington

FISHING TACKLE AT WADE BROS.', HACKETTSTOWN.

McClary Walter, painter, 467 Washington
Miller Joseph, brakeman, 469 Washington
McCorkell Fred., laborer, Taylor's alley
McGloskey John, railroad carpenter, 452 Washington
McGloskey Wm., railroader, bds. 452 Washington
McGloskey Henry, barber, bds. 452 Washington
Meyers Wm., brakeman, 459 Lewis
McNamara Michael, laborer, 265 Heckman
Miller Valentine, painter, 412 Fulton
McBride J. C., silk mill, bds. 747 Lewis
McAuliff Dennis, conductor, 425 Chambers
Moore, J. J., clerk, 451 Chambers
Miller Fred., builder, 463 Chambers
Metz Wm. L., laborer, 541 Chambers
Mahon Martin, laborer, 565 Chambers
McNally Wm., laborer, Chambers and Heckman
Messinger Wm., brakeman, 516 Chambers
Meyers Uriah, railroader, 504 Chambers
Moule James, fireman, bds. 539 Lewis
Metz Laurence, milkman, 540 Lewis

FELIX & LEININGER, Nos. 102 & 104 South 3d St., **Easton, Pa.** FURNITURE.

Murray Robert, teamster, 544 Lewis
Mason Charles E., engineer, 548 Lewis
Maloney Michael, foundryman, Wilson
Marks Daniel, foreman, bds. Lee House
Moon Hon. James E., Senator, 155 Randall
Mixsell Edward, monkey wrencher, Hudson
Meyers J. O., brakeman, Reese alley
McNally James, engineer, 172 Brainard
Martindell Richard, carpenter, 174 Brainard
Martindell Mabel, teacher, 174 Brainard
Mellen John, machinist, 202 Brainard
Merritt Cyrus, fireman, 204 Brainard
Meyer Isaac, oysters, 106 and 108 S. M., h 209 Hanover
Matz Benjamin, book-keeper, 201 Brainard
Mixsell Lewis, local expressman, 193 Brainard
Meyers Samuel, brakeman, 191 Brainard
McCann John, shoemaker, 220 S. Main, h 185 Brainard
McCann David, ass't postmaster, bds. 185 Brainard
Mutchler Howell, mason, 179 Brainard
Metz Elizabeth, widow, 167 Brainard

Andrews & Nolf, 205 Northampton St. The only place to buy the "CONFORMATER" Corset.

H. M. NORTON, WHOLESALE AND RETAIL DEALER IN HARDWARE, STOVES, HEATERS AND RANGES.

Mixsell Jacob, retired, bds. 174 S. Main
Mixsell Harry, painter, bds. 174 S. Main
Miller John H., brakeman, bds. Columbia Hotel
Miller Chas. P., engineer, bds. Columbia Hotel
Meeker George, dispatcher, 226 S. Main
Mixsell David, lawyer, 102 S. Main, res. 36 South 4th
Moore John, baggage master, h. C. R. R., depot
Morris canal office, over L. V. R. R., depot
Myers George, groceries, 195 S. Main, h do
Morris & Essex depot, (D. L. & W.,) Market
Moser Isaac, watchman, 129 S. Main
Massey Edward, boiler maker, 406 S. Main
Metz Reuben, engineer, 407 S. Main
Main Street M. E. Church, Rev. J. R. Bryan, pastor, 434 S. Main
Mortz Cortlandt, painter, 23 Haggerty's row
Moenig Augustus, furniture warerooms, 513 S, house 515 do
McDavis George, plane tender, foot of Hanover
McKenney George, brakeman, 112 River

FELIX & LEININGER, Nos. **102 & 104 South 3d St.,** **FURNITURE.** **Easton, Pa.**

Monaghan Ellen, candies, 604 Mercer
Metzgar Charles, railroader, Fayette
Metzgar Andrew, railroader, 140 Fox
McClary Charles D., foreman painter, 139 Fox

A. MOENIG

Dealer in

FINE FURNITURE.

Upholstering done in all its branches
PARLOR AND BED-ROOM SUITES A SPECIALTY.

Leading House in the County.

513 & 515 SOUTH MAIN STREET.

PHILLIPSBURG, - - - NEW JERSEY

McNally Patrick, brakeman, Fox
McHale Edward, boots and shoes, 529 S. Main h do
McHale Mary E., millinery, 529 S. Main,

For Coughs, Colds, Croup and Consumption use SHIELDS' **COMPOUND SYRUP** of Wild Cherry with hypophosphates of lime and soda

Mutchler S. B., contractor, 114 S. Main
Murphy Thomas, laborer, 750 Howard
Murphy John, railroader, bds. 750 Howard
Martin Thomas, foundryman, 860 Howard
Martin William, boilermaker, bds. 860 Howard
Mura John, laborer, Jefferson
Meyers J. M., clerk, 633 Fayette
Maroney James, car cleaner, 651 Fayette
McDavitt Westley, clerk, 715 Fayette
Martin Susanna, widow, 715 Fayette
McLaughlin Thomas, laborer, Fayette near McKean
McDermott Frank, grocer, 755 S. Main, h 834 Mercer
Mellick Jacob, teamster, 816 Mercer
McShafrey Michael, laborer, foot of Mercer
McKue Edward, laborer, foot of Mercer
Moser Thomas, railroader, Cedar Alley
McHale Thomas, contractor, 913 S. Main
Murray Dennis, mason, 903 S. Main
Morgan Charles, blacksmith, 724 S. Main
Mayer George, bakery, 741 S. Main, h 406 do

FELIX & LEININGER, Nos. 102 & 104 South 3d St., **Easton, Pa.** FURNITURE.

Martin Thomas, moulder, 811 Sitgreaves
Metz Samuel A., drugs, medicines, paints, oils, etc., 660 S. Main, h 623 Sitgreaves

SAMUEL A. METZ,
DEALER IN
FINE DRUGS AND MEDICINES.

A choice line of Patent Medicines, Perfumery, Paints, Oils and Varnishes always in Stock.

All Medicines Guaranteed Strictly Pure.

SPECIAL ATTENTION TO PHYSICIANS' PRESCRIPTIONS.

ORDERS BY MAIL PROMPTLY ATTENDED TO

660 SOUTH MAIN STREET,
PHILLIPSBURG N. J.

Maddock Pierson, railroader, bds American Hotel
Metz J. C., laborer, 753 Mercer
Mellick John, laborer, 755 Mercer
Markey Matthew, laborer, 721 Mercer

ANDREWS & NOLF, 205 Northampton St., Easton, Pa. You can find it by the fine large awning in front of store.

H. M. NORTON, WHOLESALE AND RETAIL DEALER IN HARDWARE, STOVES HEATERS AND RANGES.

McClair Henry, mason, 663 Mercer
McClair James, laborer, bds 663 Mercer
Murray John, foundryman, 638 Mercer
Mack Margaret, widow, 640 Mercer
Mitchell Thomas, machinist, bds 712 Mercer
Martin Joseph, watchman, 716 Mercer
Meyers John, fish and oysters, 713 S. Main h do
Martinus Andrew B., carpenter, 749 S. Main
Metz Daniel, fireman, 638 Sitgreaves
Matthes Leopold, foundryman, 646 Sitgreaves
Miller Prof, musician, 658 Sitgreaves
Meyers Charles O., monkey wrencher, Stockton
McDavis Jacob, laborer, Foundry Alley
McCann Patrick, foundryman, Spruce Alley
Martin Margaret, widow, Foundry Alley
Mooney William, foundryman, Spruce Alley
McShane Peter, watchman, Spruce Alley
Murray Bernard, mason, McKean near Main
Maloney Patrick, foundryman, 906 Sitgreaves
Meisenhelder Christian, mason, 916 Sitgreaves

FELIX & LEININGER, Nos. 102 & 104 South 3d St., Easton, Pa. FURNITURE

Morrisey Michael, laborer, 945 Sitgreaves
Morey Sylvester, blacksmith, 941 Sitgreaves
Mooney Patrick, furnaceman, 931 Sitgreaves
McHale Edward, stone cutter, 639 Sitgreaves
McHale Patrick, mason, 641 Sitgreaves
McHale Joseph, mason, 641 Sitgreaves
McHale William, mason, 641 Sitgreaves
McHale James, mason, 641 Sitgreaves
Milroy Lewis, carpenter, Spruce Alley
Mordan Elizabeth, widow, 715 Sitgreaves
Mordan Tunis, laborer, Spruce Alley
Mullen John, laborer, Spruce Alley
Mullen Patrick, railroader, Spruce Alley
Mooney Michael, furnaceman, 925 S. Main
McMullen Daniel, laborer, 924 S. Main
Murray Neil, mason, 906 S. Main
McIlhaney Mrs. Catharine, saloon, 868 S. Main
McIlhaney John, mason, 864 S. Main
Moule E. G., shoemaker, 862 S. Main
Meyers Charles, foundryman, 860 S. Main

FINE TABLE CUTLERY at **WADES' HARDWARE STORE.**

HOUSEFURNISHING GOODS GENERALLY. The BEST GOODS for the LEAST MONEY at **H. M. NORTON'S, Easton, Pa.**

PHILLIPSBURG DIRECTORY.

Monaghan Wm., laborer, 858 S. Main
Mellick Howard, general merchandise, 800 Main, h do
McLaughlin Wm., saloon, 748 S. Main
McDavis George, ferryman, 712 S. Main
Martin Adam, groceries, 700 S. Main
Moyer M. W., engineer, 652 S. Main
Marsh Edward, grocery, 632 S. Main, h do
Muttle Joseph, engineer wiper, Stockton
McCafrey John, laborer, 953 Sitgreaves
McCafrey Charles, laborer, bds 953 Sitgreaves
Macauley Walter, laborer, 945 Sitgreaves
Mooney James, laborer, 847 Sitgreaves
McLaughlin Owen, boatman, 1058 S. Main
McEnroe James, watchman, near Andover Furnace
Maddock Thomas, laborer, Mounts Hill
Masterson John J., agent, Mounts Hill
McAnally Bernard, laborer, Mounts Hill
McCann Owen, contractor, Dempster's Hill
McMennamim Edward, laborer, Dempster's Hill
McRea Thomas, laborer, Dempster's Hill

FELIX & LEININGER, Nos. 102 & 104 South 3d St., **Easton, Pa.** FURNITURE.

Mooney Daniel, laborer, Dempster's Hill
Nixon Frank, heater, 254 Bullman
Nixon Charles, 1st ward policeman, 233 N. Main
Nixon Charles, Jr., puddler, N. Main
Noble Amos, laborer, 142 N. Main
Nixon Wm, laborer, Fillmore
Nixon Wm., laborer, N. Main
Nixon James, laborer, Fillmore
Nixon Thomas, moulder, 318 Lewis
Nagle Henry, invalid, 352 Chambers
Nagle August, brakeman, Heckman
Newhart Hattie, forelady, bds. 366 Washington
Nixon John, brakeman, 460 Washington
Noonan Mrs. P., widow, 552 Chambers
Newman Patrick, blacksmith, 536 Chambers
Nixon George, engineer, 238 Harris
Nalon John, brakeman, bds. Heckman
Newman Thomas, coal, hay and straw, livery stables, Union Square, coal yard River
Nixon Robert, railroader, 127 S. Main

ANDREWS & NOLF, 205 Northampton Street, Easton, Pa. The reliable store for Black Goods.

H. M. NORTON, WHOLESALE AND RETAIL DEALER IN HARDWARE, STOVES, HEATERS AND RANGES.

Newman Wesley, car insp. bds. Phillipsburg Hotel
Niece John S., engineer, Mercer
Niece John E., Jr., carpenter, bds Mercer
Newman Christopher, hostler and gardner, Andover Iron Works
Nixon James D., conductor, 642 Howard
Nixon Catherine, widow, 629 Fayette
Nixon Milton, boatman, Cedar alley, near McKean
Neice Asa, fireman, 647 Mercer
Nicholas George, laborer, 729 Sitgreaves
Norton John, brakeman, 644 S. Main
Newman Ellis, ice cream parlor, 720 S. Main
Newman John W., clerk, 720 S. Main
Nolan Dennis, laborer, Mounts Hill
Newman W. H., laborer, Dempsters Hill
Newman Robert, laborer, Dempsters Hill
Ochs Wm., cabinet maker, Hudson near Lewis
O'Brien James, brakeman, 454 Washington
O'Hara Arthur, laborer, bds. on Heckman
Oehler Wm., machinist, 640 Railroad ave

Felix & Leininger, Nos. 102 & 104 South 3d Street, **Easton, Pa. Furniture.**

Osmun Wm., section boss, 507 Washington
Otterbach Charles, machinist, 530 Lewis
Opitz Henry, huckster, Morris Turnpike
Omick Jesse, laborer, 143 Fillmore
Opitz Carl, shoemaker, 224 N. Main
Oliver Oscar, car driver, N. Main
Opdyke Geo. W., laborer, Delaware
Ozenbaugh James, blacksmith, 313 N. Main
O'Brien Mrs. Jane, widow, Chestnut alley
O'Neill Michael, engine wiper, 828 Howard
Osmun Daniel, boat caulker, Fayette near McKean
Ommert Michael, oyster saloon, 749 S. Main
O'Brien James, foundryman, 630 Sitgreaves
O'Brien George, foundryman, bds. 630 Sitgreaves
Osterstock Alfred, carpenter, 817 Sitgreaves
O'Brien Bartholomew, laborer, Spruce alley
Osborne House, Osborne Loudenberger, prop. 600 S. Main
Osmun L. C., (Ramsey & Osmun), physicians, 210 S. Main, res. do

SHIELDS' Compound Syrup of Wild Cherry with Hypophosites of Lime and Soda. Sure cure for coughs, croup, etc.

HOUSEFURNISHING GOODS GENERALLY. **H. M. NORTON'S**, Easton, Pa.
The BEST GOODS for the LEAST MONEY at

PHILLIPSBURG DIRECTORY. 303

O'Neill O., stone mason, bds. Columbia Hotel
O'Grady John, prop. Columbia Hotel, 314 S. Main
O'Hara Robert, engineer, 620 Mercer
O'Hara Anna, widow, 622 Mercer
O'Connor John, stone cutter, 138 Fox
Osterstock Peter, laborer, Dempsters Hill
Osmun Milton, drug clerk, bds. 224 S. Main
Odenwelder John, telegraph operator, C. R. R. of N.
 J., res. Easton
O'Hern Jeremiah, laborer, Dempsters Hill
Phillips Charles, machinist, 220 Bullman
Price Mrs. Anna, widow, Bennett
Perdae John, conductor, 331 Bullman
Patterson Lewis F., conductor, Harris and Bullman
Phillips Samuel, D., moulder, Rose
Paul Lodorus, laborer, 349 North Main
Powers Martin, laborer, 338 North Main
Pendergraf James, shoemaker, 319 North Main
Parker E. C., clerk, 309 North Main
Pierson Wm. K., huckster, First

FELIX & LEININGER, Nos. 102 & 104 South 3d St., **Easton, Pa.** **FURNITURE.**

Price John H., blacksmith, 312 Broad
Phillipsburg Stove Foundry, office First
Phillipsburg High School Building, cor Hudson and
 Fillmore
Phillipsburg Cemetery, intersection Fillmore and
 Fulton
Page Wm., laborer, 385 Lewis
Person John, yard master, 378 Chambers
Person Edw., brakeman, bds 378 Chambers
Phipps Samuel, conductor, 384 Washington
Pierson Frank R., railroader, 330 Washington
Paff John, laborer, Hudson
Peters Joseph, laborer, bds Hudson
Peters Lafayette, monkey wrencher, 404 Washington
Peacher E. P., watchman, 404 Lewis
Parker William, foundryman, 411 Fulton
Plummer Wm. M., carpenter, 404 Chambers
Parks John R., brakeman, 437 Chambers
Powelson J. C., fireman, bds 451 Chambers
Prall Wm. E., brakeman, 529 Chambers

ANDREWS & NOLF, SELL THE BEST $1.00 AND $1.25 KID GLOVES IN EASTON, PA. 205 NORTH-AMPTON STREET.

S. M. NORTON, WHOLESALE AND RETAIL DEALER IN HARDWARE, STOVES, HEATERS AND RANGES.

Post Mrs. Kate, widow, 549 Chambers
Post Mrs. Eva, widow, 549 Chambers
Pendergrast Mrs. Thomas, widow, 556 Chambers
Prendergast Kate, teacher, 556 Chambers
Prendergast Edw., laborer, 556 Chambers
Person Hugh, conductor, 504 Lewis
Person Johnson, number taker, bds 507 Lewis
Paustian John F., baggage master, 532 Lewis
Pymer Chris., laborer, 543 Lewis
Pfeiffer Henry, brakeman, Heckman
Phillipsburg National Bank, John Bachman cashier, Union Square
Pocachard Capt. Richard, supt. of "The Standard Silk Mill Co.," bds Lee House
Pensyl Thomas, bricklayer, bds Lee House
Phillipsburg PostOffice, Frank Knedler, postmaster, 116 South Main
Purcel John, pattern maker, bds Union Square Hotel
Peeney Ralph, machinist, 199 Brainard
Prall George, brakeman, 243 Brainard

Felix & Leininger, Nos. 102 & 104 South 3d Street, **Easton, Pa.** **Furniture.**

Perdoe Charles, engineer, 242 Brainard
Perdoe Lizzie, teacher, 242 Brainard
Perry John, fireman, bds Columbia Hotel
Pierson George, clerk, bds Columbia Hotel
Purcel Peter C., book-keeper, bds 224 S. Main
Purcel Mrs. P. C., teacher, bds 224 S. Main
Philips George, railroader, 205 Hanover
Partner Matilda, saloon, 215 Market
Presbyterian Church, Rev. H. B. Townsend pastor, cor Main and Market
Petrie James A., retired, 169 Main
Patterson Susan, widow, 159 S. Main
Person Charles, railroader, 157 S. Main
Philips Isaac, machinist, 145 S. Main
Philips Jos. C., agent, bds 145 S. Main
Pursell Andrew, clerk, 141 S. Main
Phillipsburg Hotel, cor Hanover and Main, W. H. Carey, prop'r
Pollock Robert M., blacksmith, bds Phil'b'g Hotel
Pyatt Miner, railroader, 285 Hagerty's Row

Mechanics Tools of all kinds at Wade Brothers.

Phillipsburg Gas Works, Union
Potter Brazil, engineer, Union
Peacher John, laborer, Union
Promoly Charles, agent, River
Pendergast John, foundryman, 537 Mercer
Pyatt Wm., boatman, 601 Fayette
Pyatt Henry, brakeman, bds 552 Howard
Peevey Ralph, laborer, Dempster's Hill
Philips James, engineer, 816 Howard
Price Andrew, 835 Howard
Page Annie, McKean
Peterman John, laborer, Chestnut Alley
Pursell Wm., carpenter, 643 Fayette
Post Eva S., teacher, 715 Fayette
Price James, blacksmith, 925 Mercer
Pyatt Howard, switch tender, 829 Mercer
Piatt I. W., shoemaker, 812 Mercer
Pettit Samuel, foundryman, 937 S. Main
Piatt Anna, dressmaker, 803 Mercer
Pettit Robert Jr., switch tender, bds 935 S. Main

Pettit Robert, moulder, 935 S. Main
Pyatt Edward, fireman, 929 S. Main
Pettit W. H., laborer, Dempster's Hill
Price W. S., blacksmith, McKean, h 963 Sitgreaves
Pattenburg Mary, confectionery, 813 S. Main
Pursel John, butcher, 809 S. Main, h 811 do
Paustian Henry, coal yard, also tax collector, 727 Mercer
Parker John, carpenter, 757 S. Main
Parochial Hall, cor Main and Stockton
Powe Moses, blacksmith, 634 Sitgreaves
Pfeiffer Joseph, cigar maker, bds 646 Sitgreaves
Patterson Aaron, railroader, 650 Sitgreaves
Pefrnmanshleg Frank, foundryman 904 Sitgreaves
Pefrnmanshleg John, foundryman, 908 Sitgreaves
Prall Angeline, widow, 615 Sitgreaves
Philips Aaron, laborer, 619 Sitgreaves
Patterson Edward, laborer, 731 Sitgreaves
Pursel S. C., general merchandise, 1070 S. Main
Pursel Ephraim D., clerk, 1070 S. Main

H. M. NORTON, WHOLESALE AND RETAIL DEALER IN HARDWARE, STOVES, HEATERS AND RANGES.

PHILLIPSBURG DIRECTORY.

Pointon John, saloon, 1057 S. Main
Peters Alexander, furnaceman, bds 1026 S. Main
Pierson Joseph, flour and feed, 762 S. Main, h 764 do
Pefrmanshleg Joseph, laborer, 730 S. Main
Quear Samuel, carpenter, 946 S. Main
Quigley John, fireman, 660 Howard
Reynolds Wm., night boss, 223 Bennett
Rubert Vincent, moulder, 235 Bullman
Rooker Wm., potter, 251 Front
Robbins Mrs. Jane, widow, 222 Washington
Reese W. E., clerk, 203 Market
Redmond Samuel B., book keeper, 411 N. Main
Rodenbough Irvin, ironworker, 352 N. Main
Reaser Charles, carpenter, 348 N. Main
Raub Levi, ironworker, 313 N. Main
Rinker Edward B., tailor, First
Rinker Geo. W., laborer, bds. First
Rinker Edward, printer, bds. First
Richard Mrs. C., grocer, Broad
Rhodes Mrs. Emma, widow, Broad

FELIX & LEININGER, Nos. 102 & 104 South 3d St., Easton, Pa. **FURNITURE.**

Robinson Rebecca, widow, 156 N. Main
Ruche Andrew, laborer, Morris turnpike
Reed John D., blacksmith, 205 Morris turnpike
Reuss Joseph, laborer, 352 Fillmore
Roth John, Jr., cabinet maker, 451 Fillmore
Roth John, carpenter, 453 Fillmore
Ricker Theodore, telegraph operator, 208 Harris
Ricker Mrs. Mary, widow, 208 Harris
Ricker Frank, telegraph operator, bds. 208 Harris
Ricker Geo. E., painter, 208 Harris
Rooks Sylvester, retired, 247 Jane Louisa
Rooks Asher, quarryman, bds. 247 Jane Louisa
Roadarmel Wm., retired, 311 Lewis
Rodgers Jos. R., laborer, 333 Lewis
Reynolds Thomas, engineer, 313 Chambers
Rogers Charles, engineer, 306 Chambers
Richards Wm., grocer clerk, bds. Broad
Richard Edward, grocer clerk, bds. Broad
Reese Adam R., car checker, 325 Washington
Ricker Charles, carpenter, 383 Washington

SHIELDS' INFALLIBLE **Dyspeptic Remedy.** A sure cure for Dyspepsia, Sick or Nervous Headache. Guaranteed.

HOUSEFURNISHING GOODS GENERALLY.
The BEST GOODS for the LEAST MONEY at **H. M. NORTON'S Easton Pa.**

PHILLIPSBURG DIRECTORY.

Roseberry Jacob, retired, 336 Washington
Raub Wm. H., brickmaker, Henderson
Roseberry Shipman, painter, 324 Washington
Raub Flemming, laborer, Henderson
Roth John, carpenter, Hudson
Roberts Wm., engineer, 417 Hudson
Reichenbach John, laborer, Hudson
Richline Fred., railroader, 506 Washington
Roseberry Peter, machinist, 448 Washington
Robinson Wm., carriage maker, factory 753 S. Main h 440 Lewis
Robinson Millard, carriage maker, bds. 440 Lewis
Robinson Lafayette, switchman, cor. Fulton & Lewis
Reed Jacob, carpenter, 463 Lewis
Rahrig Samuel, carpenter, 408 Chambers
Ryan Edward, laborer, 567 Chambers
Rehfuss Otto, sign painter, 126 Detweilers row
Rehfuss Gustavus, printer, 126 Detweilers row
Rinehart Wm., laborer, 118 Detweilers row
Riegeleine Charles, laborer, Chambers near Heckman

FELIX & LEININGER, Nos. 102 & 104 South 3d St., **Easton, Pa.**, **FURNITURE.**

Riegeleine Andrew, laborer, Chambers near Heckman
Reilley John, moulder, 530 Chambers
Reed Jennie, shirt maker, bds. 546 Lewis
Roseberry Anderson, foundryman, Wilson

O. KIDNEY'S
OYSTER AND ICE CREAM SALOON.

Confectionery, Fruit, Etc.
Choice Line of Cigars and Tobacco.

OYSTERS

Raw. Stewed and Fried. and Families Supplied in Large and Small Quantities at
433 So. Main Street.   PHILLIPSBURG, N. J.

Ripple Howard, foreman, Heckman and Wilson
Roseberry A. C., laborer and carmaker, 646 RR. ave
Roseberry Charles, car maker, 630 Railroad ave

Andrews & Uolf, 205 Northampton street, Easton, Pa. Store-room enlarged. Come and see

H. M. NORTON, WHOLESALE AND RETAIL DEALER IN HARDWARE, STOVES, HEATERS AND RANGES.

Randolph Phineas, engineer, Dale's ave
Roth Penrose, Ass't Supt. "Prudential Life Insurance Company," Dale's ave
Reese Mrs. L. C., widow, 181 S. Main
Reiley John I. Blair, lawyer, 165 S. Main
Reiley Mrs. A. C., widow, 5th ave., bds. 204 do
Reese Mrs. Mariah, widow, 333 S. Main
Reese Charles, retired, 341 S. Main
Reiley A. L., clerk, bds. 5th ave
Robbins John, waiter, S. Market
Rustay Julia, washing, etc., River
Raub Andrew J., ticket agent, Cedar alley
Reynolds Michael, baggage master, 623 Mercer
Rustay Samuel, railroader, Cherry alley
Roger Matthias, laborer, Cherry alley
Reynolds John, night caller, 551 Fayette
Rupert William, moulder, 533 Fayette
Robottom P. J., pastor St. Luke's Episcopal church, res. adjoining
Rockafellow George, laborer, 829 Howard

FELIX & LEININGER, Nos. 102 & 104 South 3d St., **Easton, Pa.** FURNITURE.

Rose Martha C., 841 Howard
Ryan John, blacksmith, Chestnut alley
Rosenbery Charles, foreman, 645 Fayette
Riddle J. C., railroad carpenter, 647 Fayette
Reaser John, conductor, 709 Fayette
Raul Benjamin, conductor, 731 Fayette
Russel Philip, mason, 804 Mercer
Rush George, carpenter, 800 Mercer
Richard Silas, foundryman, 931 S. Main
Rhodes H. M., wall paper and organs, 651 S Main h do
Reily James, laborer, Dempster's Hill
Rinker Edward, foundryman, 704 Sitgreaves
Raub Leopold, foundryman, 742 Sitgreaves
Reiley Edward, stone cutter, 948 Sitgreaves
Roarity Collom, laborer, 962 Sitgreaves
Rourke Bernard, laborer, 980 Sitgreaves
Reese Killian, machinist, 655 Sitgreaves
Ripley Joseph, boatman, 743 Sitgreaves
Ray Jacob, laborer, Spruce alley
Rooks Charity, widow, 1080 S. Main

PAINTS and OILS at WADE BROS.', Hackettstown, N. J.

HOUSEFURNISHING GOODS GENERALLY. **H. M. NORTON'S, Easton, Pa.**
The BEST GOODS for the LEAST MONEY at

PHILLIPSBURG DIRECTORY.

Riley Thomas, foundryman, Heckman
Randolph Wm. M., clerk, Lee House
Ritter J. C., cigars and tobacco, 38 Union Square h do
Rapp R. F., millwright, 118 S. Main
Reamer Wm., railroad carpenter, 124 S. Main
Reamer Lillie, teacher, 124 S. Main
Reese Catherine, 162 S. Main
Randall Wm. T., grocery, 216 S. Main, h 162 Randall
Reese John, invalid, Hudson
Rutan Charles L., railroader, 206 Brainard
Reese J. M., physician, 180 S. Main
Ramsey James, physician, 210 S. Main
Reese A. R., inventor, 108 S. Main
Rogers Constance, moulder, Elizabeth
Ramsey James, physician, 210 S. Main
Rich Harry, engineer, 1077 S. Main
Rich Wm., ass't engineer, 1077 S. Main
Rippley Constance, carpenter, 904 S. Main
Reuff John E., foreman, 814 S. Main
Rustay Jacob, engineer, 616 S. Main

FELIX & LEININGER, Nos. 102 & 104 South 3d St., **Easton, Pa.** **FURNITURE.**

Rinehart A. R., milkman, 606 S. Main
Swartz James, brakeman, 120 Chambers
Smith Wm., Justice of the Peace, 189½ S. Main, h 222 Bennett
Smith Wm. Jr., railroader 222 Bennett
Smith Stephen, printer, 222 Bennett
Smith Andrew, railroader, 220 Bennett
Sitgreaves Irwin, machinist, 289 Bennett
Schicka Albert, hod carrier, Bunnell
Savacool Elias W., laborer, 358 Bullman
Smith Charles A., laborer, 333 Bullman
Scott Edward, engineer, 221 Bullman
Scott Bella, teacher, 221 Bullman
Spinner Henry T., clerk, 207 Bullman
Stone Peter W., insurance agent, 201 Chambers
Savacool Aaron, RR carpenter, 253 Front
Shimer Joseph, smoked meats, N. Main, h 148 Front
Savacool George, supt. car cleaners, Front
Sheppard Mrs. Emily, widow, 138 Washington
Souders John, driver, 212 Washington

ANDREWS & NOLF, 205 Northampton Street, Easton, Pa.
The Best Selected Line of Hosiery and Gloves.

M. M. NORTON, WHOLESALE AND RETAIL DEALER IN HARDWARE, STOVES, HEATERS AND RANGES.

PHILLIPSBURG DIRECTORY.

Stabp Robert, iron worker, 358 Broad
Slaven John, laborer, cor 3d and Broad
Stabp Valentine, iron worker, 384 Broad
Schrope Geo. W., butcher, Broad
Stocker Azariah, cor Rose and Second
Slaven Wm., laborer, Rose
Snyder Wm. D., laborer, Rose
Snyder Archibald, laborer, Rose
Snyder David, laborer, Rose
Snyder Thomas, ass't engineer, bds 317 N. Main
Stausburg David, iron bundler, 376 Broad
Snyder Alonzo, iron worker, 382 Broad
Skillman Henry P., engineer, Delaware
Snyder Wm., puddler, Delaware
Stratton Ed. L., laborer, Delaware
Stone John, butcher, 221 N. Main
Smith James P., heater, 146 N. Main
Schnoor H., carpet weaver, Morris turnpike
Schnoor John, laborer, Morris turnpike
Schull Charles, musician, bds 317 Morris turnpike

Wonderful Bargains in OVERCOATS at CREVELING & CO.'S

Schull Peter, stone mason, 317 Morris turnpike
Smith John, stone mason, 315 Morris turnpike
Schmelse John, gardener, 337 Morris turnpike
Schaffer John, fireman, Morris turnpike
Shaffer Thos., farmer, Morris turnpike
Sheppard Wm. O., clerk, Fillmore
Snyder Edward, laborer, 489 Fillmore
Strong George, brakeman, 507 Fillmore
Smith James D., book-keeper, 471 Davis
Stamets Wm. T., carpenter, 458 Davis
Street Car Stables, near Union Square
Souders Daniel, grocery, 325 Lewis, h 327 Lewis
Sterner John, railroader, 365 Lewis
Sterner Monroe, railroader, 365 Lewis
Sterner Andrew, clerk, 365 Lewis
Snyder Christian, machinist, 372 Lewis
Smith John J., shoemaker, 194 S. Main, h 374 Lewis
Smith Aaron, hod carrier, 382 Lewis
Seibler Mrs. Julia, widow, 386 Lewis
Seibler Fred, painter, bds 386 Lewis

SHIELDS' Compound Syrup of Wild Cherry with Hypophosites of Lime and Soda. Sure cure for coughs, croup, etc.

Seibler John, laborer, bds 386 Lewis
Snyder Fred, coppersmith, 384 Chambers
Snyder Benj., watchman, 359 Chambers
Shafer Mrs. Eliza, widow, 352 Chambers
Setner Thomas, wire drawer, 346 Chambers
Slight Mrs. Anna, nurse, North Main
Skinner P. W., flour and feed, 189 South Main, res 331 Washington
Sitgreaves Henry, conductor, 347 Washington
Shiner John, engineer, bds 355 Washington
Scott C. T., agent, 373 Washington
Stokes C. S., railroader, 387 Washington
Schrantz Benj., carpenter, 389 Washington
Stites Wm. conductor, 395 Washington
Stites Sanford, operator, bds 395 Washington
Stites Charles, brakeman, 395 Washington
Stephens John K., retired, Washington and Hudson
Stevenson Wm. J., foreman, 360 Washington
Stevenson Charles, fireman, bds 360 Washington
Souders John W., engineer, 368 Washington

Sheldon Agnes, forelady, 366 Washington
Smith Alonzo, laborer, 354 Washington
Stott Mrs. Annie, 336 Washington
Salzman V. E., barber, Hudson, h do
Sinclair Mrs. Jane, widow, Hudson
Schultz Alexander, florist, Hudson
Schultz Elwood, tutor, Hudson
Schultz Irwin W., lawyer and insurance, Lee Building cor Main and Market, bds 174 S. Main
Sharps C. B., telegraph operator, 409 Washington
Sutphen John R., telegraph operator, 413 Wash'ton
Schooley Mary E., dressmaker, 415 Washington
Schooley Frank, laborer, bds 415 Washington
Schooley John, carpenter, 415 Washington
Snyder Theodore, laborer, 463 Washington
Sheets Samuel, blind, Taylors alley
Snyder Simpson, blind, Taylors alley
Swayze Lizzie, widow, 436 Washington
Scofield James, railroader, 430 Washington
Sterner & Treloar, grocers, 418 Washington

H. M. NORTON, WHOLESALE AND RETAIL DEALER IN HARDWARE, STOVES, HEATERS AND RANGES.

Sterner Milton, grocer, res 418 Washington
Smith Elwood, railroader, 458 Lewis
Sepfel John, foundryman, 463 Lewis
Sharp Wm., engineer, 437 Lewis
Sheppard Clara, dressmaker, 429 Lewis
Stiles Ira, brakeman, 423 Lewis
Steiner Reding, iron worker, 428 Chambers
Stamets Daniel, boat builder, 440 Chambers
Stein Mrs. Christiana, widow, 452 Chambers
Schlabach Wm., milkman, 357 Chambers
St. John German Lutheran Church, Rev. Jacob Zentner, pastor, cor Chambers and Fulton
Shergan George, mason, 505 Chambers
Schaeffer Charles, laborer, 535 Chambers
Shafer Theophilus, blacksmith, 118 Detweilers
Smith Frank, laborer, 625 Chambers
Schwank Fred, laborer, 627 Chambers
Shultz August, carpet weaver, 629 Chambers
Schweikhardt Charles, clerk, 538 Chambers
Saltzman Mrs. Mary, widow, 538 Lewis

If You Want To See a Fine Line of MILLINERY Go To **CREVELING & CO'S**

Saltzman John, laborer, 538 Lewis
Seyer John, foreman, 542 Lewis
Sherry Jacob, fireman, 551 Lewis
Strouse Dennis, laborer, Wilson
Sheffel Christian, cabinet maker, 263 Heckman
Strouse Nathan, engineer, Heckman
Sutton Alfred, laborer, bds on Heckman
Smith Adam, laborer, Heckman
Strader Lewis, foundryman, Heckman
Searfoss Peter, hostler, Heckman
Sweeney Daniel, clerk, h over collector's office, Port Delaware, Morris Canal
Smith S. C., prosecuting attorney, office over Phillipsburg Bank, h 164 S. Main
Smith David W., pool room, 32 Union Square
Sitgreaves Edward, laborer, 134 S. Main
Smith Forrest, bds 152 South Main
Shrope Theodore, conductor, 463 Randall
Sanderson James, contractor, Dempsters Hill
Stiles Chas., boiler maker, 856 Howard

Mechanics Tools of all kinds at Wade Brothers.

HOUSEFURNISHING GOODS GENERALLY
The BEST GOODS for the LEAST MONEY at **H. M. NORTON'S** Easton Pa.

PHILLIPSBURG DIRECTORY. 313

Slant William, fireman, Shimer
Sweeney Mrs. C. H., widow, 217 Hudson
Schrantz Isaac, carpenter, Hudson
Smith Isaac, clerk, 170 Brainard
Seip B. F., miller, 178 Brainard
Spruel James H. & Co., card and job printers, 184 Brainard
Sprowl Mary, tailoress, 189 Brainard
Shields T. J., ticket ag't, C. RR. of N. J., 198 Brain'd
Stull Robert, machinist, 183 Brainard
Stull Emma, dressmaker, 183 Brainard
Seigel Jacob, retired, 176 S. Main
Stewart R. A., physician, 170 S. Main
Snyder Peter, railroader, 208 S. Main
Saeger Henry, pattern maker, 222 S. Main
Saeger Edw. L., clerk, 222 South Main
Stewart James, express messenger, 233 Brainard
Smith John H., engineer, bds Columbia Hotel
Street Isaac, engineer, bds Columbia Hotel
Sellers Amos J., baggage master, 207 South Main

CREVELING & CO. have the Largest Stock of Men's, Youths, Boys and Childrens Clothing in Northern N. J.

Snyder H. M. & Co., hats and caps, 187 S. Main
Shrope Sylvester, conductor, Roseberry

J. M. R SHIMER,
Dealer in Everything.

1086 So. Main Street. **PHILLIPSBURG, N. J,**

*Justice of the Peace, Counselor of Deeds,
General Insurance Agent for
Fire, Life, Accident
and Live Stock.*

General Business Office, Room No. 6.
(over Bel. Del. Depot.)

Insurance affected in any Locality.

Shimer J. M. R., general store, 1086 South Main, insurance office over Bel. Del. depot
Sanderson Wm., teacher, Dempster's Hill
Smith Edward, railroader, 164 Randall
Slant Landis, hostler, Shimer

ANDREWS & NOLF, 205 Northampton St. Keep the Largest line of Silks and Dress Goods on E. Northampton

H. M. NORTON, WHOLESALE AND RETAIL DEALER IN HARDWARE, STOVES, HEATERS AND RANGES.

Smith Barnet, carpenter, 195 Market
Slawter Charles, telegraph operator, 189 Market
Smith Mrs Green, widow, 183 S. Main
Sullivan Isaac, painter, 615 Fayette
Smith James E., foreman, 603 Fayette
Steiner Wm., railroader, 549 Fayette
Smith Paul, monkey wrencher, 547 Fayette
Smith Christopher, boiler maker, bds 629 Fayette
Salter Matthias, brakeman, 535 Fayette
Sitgreaves Samuel, carpenter and builder, 539 Fay't
Sharps Lambert, engineer, Howard
Smith Jacob A., railroader, 632 Howard
Steinmetz Rachel, widow, Chestnut Alley
Seifert D. I., jeweler, 619 S. Main, h 617 do
Sheppard J. F., physician, 173 S. Main
Stewart Jacob S., lawyer, 167 S. Main
Sheppard R. H., dentist, 161 S. Main
Stryker T. G., commercial traveler, 157 S. Main
Schlabach Jennie, forelady, bds Phillipsburg Hotel
Sheridan N. I., engineer, Phillipsburg Hotel

The Latest Novelties in GENT'S HATS AND CAPS at **CREVELING & CO.'S**

Snyder Jacob, mineralogist, bds Phillipsburg Hotel
Schooley V. Y., clerk, Phillipsburg Hotel
Shillinger Clarence, brakeman, bds Phillipsb'g Hotel
Snyder Mary A., widow, 333 S. Main
Smith John Wesley, brakeman, 5th ave
Skinner Wilson, miller, 5th ave
Sheod A. F., engineer, 5th ave
Sliker Rufus, agricultural implements, 340 S. Main
Sliker Miss Kate, teacher 340 S. Main
Simms Robert, car inspector, S. Market
Smith James R., railroader, 11 Hagerty's Row
Steiner John A., foundryman, 13 Hagerty's Row
Smith Peter, blacksmith, bds 502 S. Main
Smith Edward, conductor, 520 Sitgreaves
Stiles Eliza, boarding, 522 Sitgreaves
Smith Jacob, watchman, bds 536 Sitgreaves
Schrantz George, brakeman, 538 Sitgreaves
Stone D. F., coal yard, 542 Sitgreaves, h 540 do
Snyder Joseph, cigars and shaving, 532 S. main, res 639 Mercer

SHIELDS' INFALLIBLE **Dyspeptic Remedy.** A sure cure for Dyspepsia, Sick or Nervous Headache. Guaranteed.

Stamets Walter, railroader, 136 Union
Sigafuss Oscar, laborer, Union
Smith John, clerk, 177 Union
Scarborough Charles, mechanic, Union
Souders James, teamster, Union
Slack George, brakeman, 108 River
Smith Wm. H., brakeman, 110 River
Scott William, laborer, 132 River
Sigafoos Michael, boiler maker, 618 Mercer
Smith John, blacksmith, bds 606 Mercer
Smith Anna, widow, 606 Mercer
Snyder Albert, laborer, Cherry Alley
Snook Wm., telegraph operator, 942 S. Main
Stadelhafer Matthew, machinist, 842 S. Main
Shipman J. C., clerk, 804 S. Main
Stamets Ed. L., conductor, 726 S. Main
Shulte August, cigar maker, 724 S. Main, h 722 do
Stamets H. H., groceries, 630 S. Main, h do
Sloan C. S., groceries, 622 S. Main
Shewell Edward, boiler maker, 719 Fayette

CREVELING & CO.'S Boot and Shoe Department Unequaled in Washington, N. J.

Sts. Philip and James' Church, Rev. Robt. E. Burke, pastor, cor Main and Stockton
Smith James, foundryman, 935 Sitgreaves
Sine Israel, laborer, 823 Sitgreaves
Skinner John, railroader, 629 Sitgreaves
Smith Julia, widow, Spruce alley
Scofield Wm., laborer, 723 Sitgreaves
Seitz Andrew, laborer, 727 Sitgreaves
Smith Thomas, laborer, 749 Sitgreaves
Smith James, boatman, 1085 S. Main
Skinner Howard C., miller, 1082 S. Main
Sullivan Jeremiah, laborer, Purcel
Shimer S. L., retired, 1079 S. Main
Smith John, laborer, 1062 S. Main
Stocker Wm., laborer, near Andover Furnace
Sherrer Daniel, laborer, 1026 S. Main
Smith James, laborer, near Furnace School
Smith Annie, widow, near Furnace School
Smith John, teamster, 970 S. Main
Stafford George, moulder, 952 S. Main

ANDREWS & NOLF, Proprietors of the "DOWN TOWN" Dry Goods House, 205 Northampton Street, Easton, Pa.

Sex Matthias, teamster, Sheet Mill yard
Santee Herman, boiler maker, 730 Howard
Sender John, laborer, Dempsters Hill
Stanley Patrick, boiler maker, Chestnut alley
Seabold Charles, engineer, 631 Fayette
Smith John E., foundryman, cor. Stockton & Fayette
Stevenson Edward, railroader, 703 Fayette
Smith Adam H., millwright, 705 Fayette
Sigafoss Jehile, carpenter, 723 Fayette
Sigafoos David, boiler maker, 727 Fayette
Scofield John, brakeman, Fayette near McKean
Sigafoos Asher, brakeman, 800 Fayette
Smith James M., car inspector, 904 Mercer
Smith John W., retired, 845 Mercer
Smith Wm. E., telegraph operator, 845 Mercer
Smith David, furnaceman, Cedar alley
Sheridan Bridget, candies, etc., 911 S. Main
Schooley G. W., butcher, 901 S. Main, h cor. McKean and S. Main
Schooley Sharps, clerk, cor. McKean and Main

GO TO **CREVELING & CO'S** FOR SILKS AND VELVETS.

Smith James, laborer, Cedar alley near McKean
Shively Harry W., hostler, bds. American House
Storm Anthony, boatman, Cherry alley
Smith Holdren, brakeman, 653 Mercer
Sigafoos James, laborer, 740 Mercer
Skillman John, brakeman, Cedar alley
Stocker Daniel, railroader, bds. 755 S. Main
Stocker Wm. C., railroader, bds. 755 S. Main
Stocker Stewart, blacksmith, bds. 755 S. Main
Stocker Wm., blacksmith, Cedar alley
Shafer George, railroader, 763 S. Main
Slacker David, railroader, 759 S. Main
Shafer Joseph, saloon, 711 S. Main
Smith Jacob, foreman, 645 S. Main
Smith Ellsworth, moulder, 645 S. Main
Smith Floyd, mail carrier, 645 S. Main
Smith William, foreman, 645 S. Main
Smith E. L., Secretary Phillipsburg Stove Foundry, 639 S. Main
Stamets Lewis, brakeman, 612 Sitgreaves

PAINTS and OILS at WADE BROS., Hackettstown, N. J.

HOUSEFURNISHING GOODS GENERALLY. The BEST GOODS for the LEAST MONEY at **H. M. NORTON'S, Easton, Pa.**

PHILLIPSBURG DIRECTORY. 317

St. John Mrs. Catherine, widow, 660 Sitgreaves
Saegar Wm., brakeman, Stockton
Stretcher George, laborer, Foundry alley
Snyder George, foundryman, 708 Sitgreaves
Shafer John, foundryman, 746 Sitgreaves
Smith Isaac, foundryman, Jefferson
Styres Rebecca, widow, Jefferson
Styres John, laborer, bds. Jefferson
Styres Cyrus, laborer, bds. Jefferson
Shine Mrs. Barbara, widow, Spruce alley
Sugan Mrs. Sarah, widow, 902 Sitgreaves
Strahle Anthony, laborer, 966 Sitgreaves
Silliman John, blacksmith, 965 Sitgreaves
Smith Theresa, widow, 941 Sitgreaves
The Standard Silk Co., Richard Pocachard, Sup't Standard st., 3d ward
Tarleton Wm., laborer, Chambers near Heckman
Tobin Christopher, foundryman, Wilson
Tighe Patrick, section boss, 654 Railroad ave
Teel John K., grocer, res. 307 N. Main

What Good Tea and Coffee I Got At CREVELING & CO.'S.

Teel Edward, brakeman, 287 N. Main
Thomas E. W., book-keeper, 211 N. Main
Tilton Charles, laborer, Fillmore
Tilton Forrest, railroader, 229 Chambers
Thomas Henry, mason, 379 Lewis
Thomas John, machinist, bds. 374 Chambers
Townsend Rev. H. B., pastor of the Main Street Presbyterian Church, h 317 Washington
Trimmer Josiah, railroader, 349 Washington
Tinsman Mrs. Joseph, widow, Taylor alley
Thatcher Mrs. Catherine, widow, Taylor alley
Taylor S. L., tinsmith, 414 Fulton
Tuloar Jas., blacksmith, 459 Lewis
Treloar James, Jr , (Sterner & Treloar, groceries,) bds. 459 Lewis
Tinsman Matthias, brakeman, 431 Lewis
Third ward shaving parlors, 416 Chambers
Tracey John, brakeman, 461 Chambers
Tieff Frank, foundryman, 509 Chambers
Tate John, number taker, Bennett

ANDREWS & NOLF, The CORRECT Place to Buy SILKS and MOURNING GOODS. 205 NORTHAMPTON ST, EASTON, PA.

H. M. NORTON, WHOLESALE AND RETAIL DEALER IN HARDWARE, STOVES, HEATERS AND RANGES.

318   PHILLIPSBURG DIRECTORY.

Thompson Joseph, car inspector, 704 Howard
Thatcher Anna, widow, 706 Howard
Tippit and Wood, boiler worker, cor. Jefferson and Hanover
Tindall Reuben, fireman, 801 Howard
TenEyck George, shoemaker, 827 S. Main
Tighe Catherine, ice cream garden, 825 S. Main
Tax Collector's office, 725 Mercer
Taylor Rosa, widow, 719 Mercer
Thorne Charles H., engineer, 717 Mercer
Taylor Wm., car inspector, 634 Mercer
Tippet Ebenezer, machinist, 712 Mercer
Thatcher David, railroader, 750 Mercer
Taylor Philip, cart driver, Randall
Taylor Wm., railroader, 632 Sitgreaves
Thatcher George, railroader, 706 Sitgreaves
Tomer Andrew, railroader, 746 Sitgreaves
Toye James, machinist, 657 Sitgreaves
Tanner J. H., cake bakery, 663 Sitgreaves
Thatcher Jacob, foundryman, 721 Sitgreaves

Woolen Blankets How Nice They Feel at **CREVELING & CO.'S**

Troxell J. J., engineer, 950 S. Main
Thomas Mahlon, driver, 864 S. Main
Thatcher J. M., laborer, 834 S. Main
Trudewind Charles, carpets, etc., 734 S. Main, h do
Thompson James, boatman, 514 Sitgreaves
Trumbore Samuel, Sup't Gas Works, 518 Sitgreaves
Tully Thomas, horseman, Dempsters Hill
Tolmie T. G., foreman, Union
Thomas James, railroader, Bennett
Tiffany James, machinist, 142 Washington
Tindall George, brakeman, 230 Washington
Thomas James, watchman, Dempsters Hill
Toadwin Allison P., gent, bds. Union Square Hotel
Teets Samuel, tailor, 120 S. Main, h 118 do
Teets D. Hoyt, tailor, 118 S. Main
Teel Edwin E., engineer, 152 S. Main
Tolles Edwin, clerk, 142 S. Main
Tolles Mrs. F. C., widow, 142 S. Main
Tolles Frederick, teacher, 142 S. Main
Tanner Thomas, editor and reporter, 180 Brainard

LUBRICATING   OILS of all kinds at **WADE BROS.'**

Teel Wm., boarding, 174 S. Main
Teel Edmund, grocer, bds. 174 S. Main
Tinsman J. F., groceries, 182 S. Main h do
Titus Thomas L., member of N. J. Legislature, 188 S. Main
Teel L. M., lumber, etc., 440 S. Main, h 200 do
Treadway Elizabeth, teacher, bds. 224 S. Main
Troxell Daniel, tinware and stoves, 203 S. Main. h 201 do
Titus Richard J., brakeman, 207 Market
Teel S. H., groceries, 165 S. Main
Thomas Samuel, grain, 153 S. Main
Tinpett Jacob, (Tippett & Wood,) 329 S. Main
Tippett George, clerk, 329 S. Main
Thatcher Charles, railroader, 415 S. Main
Thornbury Thomas, grocer, 623 S. Main. res. 594 Mercer
Taylor Daniel, car inspector, Mercer
Taylor Theodore, car inspector, 611 Mercer
Tenecliff John, engineer, Fayette

Call and be charmed with CREVELING & CO.'S Ranges.

Taylor Jacob, railroader, Fox
Taylor John, invalid, Fox
Thornbury Charles, clerk, 594 Mercer
Unangst Maria, widow, bds. 224 Harris
Unangst Irvin, clerk D. L. & W., freight office, lives on Ferry street, Easton
Ulmer Martin, boiler maker, 406 Washington
Updegraff J. W., clerk, 110 Bullman
Union Square Hotel. W. C. Smith, prop. 28 Union
Unangst Christopher, car inspector, 599 S. Main
Union Hotel, Mrs. M. P., Hughes, propritoress, cor. Sitgreaves and Stockton
Vanatta Lewis, monkey wrencher, 304 Bullman
Vanscoten Ellen, widow, First
VanNorman Oscar, ironworker, cor. First and Del
Van Norman Jacob, laborer, Delaware
Vaughn Matthew, laborer, 162 N. Main
Vought Henry C., brakeman, 215 N. Main
Vogle Samuel, laborer, Fillmore
Vanatta Wesley, engineer, 228 Harris

H. M. NORTON, WHOLESALE AND RETAIL DEALER IN HARDWARE, STOVES, HEATERS AND RANGES.

320　　　PHILLIPSBURG DIRECTORY.

Vogle Theodore, tinsmith, 329 Lewis
VanAmburgh Henry, laborer, 377 Chambers
Vought Henry, Jr., hostler, 500 Washington
Vought Henry, furnaceman, 518 Washington
Vought Lewis, railroader, 518 Washington
Vanatta James, fireman, bds. 436 Washington
Vanatta Frank, brakeman, bds. 436 Washington
VanScoten George, insurance agt., RR. ave near Davis
VanScoten Thaddeus, mason, 165 Randall
VanScoten Jeremiah, railroader, 165 Randall
Vanatta Jacob, engineer, 218 Brainard
Vandegrift Augustus, fireman, 190 Brainard
Vandegrift James, engineer, 194 Brainard
Vandegrift Hudson, switchman, bds. 194 Brainard
Voorhees George, engineer, 236 Brainard
Voorhees John M., clerk, 446 S. Main
Vail Henry, marble and stone yard, 404 S. Main h do
Vorhees Mrs., dressmaker, 446 S. Main
VanSyckle Joseph, laborer, bds. 536 Sitgreaves
Vogle Valentine, laborer, 624 Mercer

HANDSOME DECORATED TOILET SETS AT CREVELING & CO.'S

Van Camp Garret, plasterer, 603 Mercer
Vansyckle John, railroader, 625 Fayette
Vandirken Albert, car cleaner, Fox
Vanatta Isaac, passenger agent, 644 Howard
Vulcan Iron Works, N. Main, F. F. Drinkhouse, prop. res. Easton
Vanatta Abraham, fireman, 660 Howard
Volkert Frank, saloon, 905 S. Main
Vandorn Mrs. E. C., boarding, 755 and 757 S. Main
Ventline Wm., foundryman, 839 Sitgreaves
Vandegrift William, railroader, bds. 619 Sitgreaves
Vernaltrik Sarah, widow, 707 Sitgreaves
Vetter Casper, (C. V. & Son), 838 S. Main
Vetter Casper, Jr., iron and steel, 838 S. Main
Vetter & Son, iron and steel, Spruce alley
Vetter Wm., foundryman, 836 S. Main
Vocht John, engineer, 728 S. Main
Van Ambury Wm., truck farm, Belvidere roads
Williams Wm. J., watchman, Second and Broad
Williams Isaac, puddler, N. Main

For Coughs, Colds, Croup and Consumption use SHIELDS' **COMPOUND SYRUP** of Wild Cherry with hypophosphates of lime and soda

HOUSEFURNISHING GOODS GENERALLY.
The BEST GOODS for the LEAST MONEY at **H. M. NORTON'S** Easton Pa.

PHILLIPSBURG DIRECTORY.

Warne M. T., coal yard, N. Main
Wisley David, butcher, Morris turnpike
Wrinkle Alfred, laborer, Fillmore
Wagner Stephen, grocer, Fillmore and Davis
Winkler Peter, laborer, 454 Davis
Wildrick Fred. H., grocer, 237 Harris h do
Wolverton Aaron, railroader, bds. 245 Jane Louisa
Willever Mrs. Mary, dressmaker, bds. 374 Lewis
Wilson Robert, machinist, bds. 374 Chambers
Weller Samuel, carpenter, 362 Chambers
Walmsley Joseph, retired, 327 Chambers
Wilson Frank, brakesman, 323 Chambers
Wilking James, engine wiper, 322 Chambers
Warren Thomas, railroad clerk, 317 Chambers
Wolf Isaac, carpenter, 339 Washington
Warne Edward J., book keeper, 139 N. Main, bds in Easton
Wilson Wm. R., Secretary " Warren Foundry and Machine Co., h 220 Bushkill, Easton
Wilhelm Wm., laborer, Bennett

Go To CREVELING & CO.'S For Hosiery and Gloves.

Whiteman Jacob, machinist, 252 Bullman
Warner Thomas, laborer, 256 Bullman
Wright W. L., veterinary dentist, Front
Walton John, foreman, 148 Washington
Walton Ella, dry goods clerk, 148 Washington
Walters Stewart, blacksmith, 355 Washington
Willever Stewart, conductor, 371 Washington
Wolfram John, blacksmith, Hudson
Wolfram Harry, barber, Hudson h do
Wolfram Wm., laborer, Hudson
Winters Peter A., laborer, bds. Taylor's alley
Wilson Thomas, conductor, 446 Washington
Wesley M. E. Church, Rev. J. R. Wright, pastor, res. Lewis Church, do
Weil Harry S., railroader, 460 Lewis
Warwick Wm., clerk, bds. 447 Lewis
Wright J. R., pastor of the new Wesley M. E. Church, 428 Lewis
Wendland August, furnaceman, 443 Lewis
Weygood W. H., student, bds., 414 Chambers

ANDREWS & NOLF, 205 Northampton St., Easton, Pa. The reliable Dry Goods Store for Silks and Dress Goods.

H. M. NORTON, WHOLESALE AND RETAIL DEALER IN HARDWARE, STOVES, HEATERS AND RANGES.

Ward Edward, hostler, 413 Chambers
Ward Wm., student, bds. 413 Chambers
Ward Fred., confectionery, 415 Chambers
Warner Mrs. Sarah, widow, 456 Chambers
Warner Amos, clerk, bds. 456 Chambers
Weidman Wm., laborer, 464 Chambers
Wenner George, brakeman, 475 Chambers
Ward Michael, laborer, 110 Detweiler's
Wieghorst Fred., brakeman, 525 Lewis
Wagner Mrs. Matthias, 517 Lewis
Weikly James, fireman, Marshall
Wagner Adam, boiler maker, Wilson
White Patrick, laborer, Wilson
Winters Daniel, laborer, 600 Railroad ave
Welsh John, laborer, Heckman
Walters Wm. Henry, lawyer, Union Square, (over Bel. Del. depot, h 229 Brainard)
West H. R., physician, 142 S. Main, bds. Lee House
Willever P. B., section boss, 158 S. Main
Willever Chauncey, clerk, 158 S. Main

Just Look at CREVELING & CO.'S
Velvet and Brussels Carpets.

Wohlback Thomas, car cleaner, Shimer
Willever Elizabeth, 202 Brainard
Wamsley Rebecca, 205 Brainard
Wamsley Harry, painter, 202 Brainard

Wm. H. Walters,
ATTORNEY-AT-LAW.
OFFICE over Bel. Del. Depot in Union Square. Residence on Brainard Street.

Walmsley Sallie, teacher, 202 Brainard
Wilson Irvin, conductor, 175 Brainard
Wilson Matthias, conductor, 194 S. Main
Walters Silas C., teamster, Reese alley near Hudson
Walters Henry, retired, 229 Brainard
Wildoner Jacob, engineer, 244 Brainard
Warren Democrat, Charles F. Fitch, editor, office 125 S. Main

EMPIRE SOLID CAST STEEL SCISSORS AND SHEARS For Sale at **Wades' Hardware Store.**

HOUSEFURNISHING GOODS GENERALLY. The BEST GOODS for the LEAST MONEY at **H. M. NORTON'S** Easton Pa.

PHILLIPSBURG DIRECTORY.

Wilson Garrett, telegraph operator, bds. Hanover
Wilhelm George, dispatcher, 218 Hanover
Waite John, engineer, bds. 301 S. Main
Winters Maria, dressmaker, 331 S. Main
Weil Daniel, freight agent, Golden
Wolfe Winfield, foundryman, 536 Sitgreaves
Wolf Winfield, foundryman, 536 Sitgreaves
Wolf Catherine, boarding, 536 Sitgreaves
Wilson Charles, fireman, Union
Wolverton Philip, brakeman, Cedar alley
Welsh Patrick, laborer, 610 Mercer
Way Samuel, laborer, 625 Mercer
Wismer Joseph, brakeman, 607 Fayette
Walsh Mary, widow, 553 Fayette
Walsh Bridget, teacher, 553 Fayette
Wheeler Wm., conductor, 527 Fayette
Wilson John, driver, Howard
Warford Norman, laborer, 612 Howard
Warford Amos, railroader, 612 Howard
Wagner Mrs. A., dressmaker, Chestnut alley

A Splendid Line of CLOAKS and WRAPS at **CREVELING & CO'S**

Willever John P., carpenter, 150 Fox
Wilkins John, laborer, bds 136 Fox
Warne Mark, switchman, Dempster's Hill
Weaver John, boatman, Henderson
Weaver Joseph, boatman, Henderson
Weaver Henry, laborer, Henderson
Wright George, laborer, Warren
Wright William, laborer, Warren
Wismer George, railroader, 700 Howard
Wagner John, boilermaker, 732 Howard
Warner Hoagland, railroader, 748 Howard
Ward Abraham, retired, 818 Howard
Wettlaufer Jacob, shoemaker, 814 South Main, res Fayette
Ward James, laborer, Fayette near McKean
Warner Joseph, engineer, 938 Mercer
Warner Sheridan, railroader, 938 Mercer
Warner Frank, boiler maker, 938 Mercer
Weaver Benjamin, foundryman, 940 Mercer
Warner John, moulder, 853 Mercer

Andrews & Nolf, 205 Northampton St., Easton, Pa. The reliable HOUSE for Mourning Goods.

H. M. NORTON, WHOLESALE AND RETAIL DEALER IN HARDWARE, STOVES, HEATERS AND RANGES.

PHILLIPSBURG DIRECTORY.

Warner George, moulder, 853 Mercer
Welsh Patrick, furnaceman, bds 802 Mercer
Welsh Richard, furnaceman, 802 Mercer
Wright Orville, laborer, 701 Mercer
Warner Reuben, carpenter, 747 Mercer
Warner Sheridan, carpenter, 747 Mercer
Wilson John, blacksmith, 722 Mercer
Walmsley Walter, switch tender, 729 Fayette
Wilson Sarah, widow, Cherry alley
Woodruff Wm. B., brakeman, 702 Mercer
Wisley John, huckster, Cedar alley
Wallace Peter, mason, Cedar alley
Wright John, fireman, 729 S. Main
Warner August, retired, 731 S. Main
Warren Assembly, K. of L., Parochial Hall
Walters Irvin, boiler maker, 959 Sitgreaves
Winters Robert, furnaceman, 835 Sitgreaves
West George T., huckster, 651 Sitgreaves
West George Jr., job printer, 651 Sitgreaves
Walton Richard, engineer, 746 S. Main

Flower Pots at CREVELING & CO.

Weikly James, fireman, Wilson
Warner Christian, railroader, Marshall
Wallace W. K., mason, Grant
Whitcoff Robert, blacksmith, 628 Sitgreaves
Wilking George, switch tender, 648 Sitgreaves
Wilson Thomas, foundryman, Jefferson
Warren Foundry & Machine Co., John Ingraham, supt., office cor Jefferson and Sitgreaves
Woepple Charles, laborer, Spruce alley
West Elmer, laborer, 713 Sitgreaves
Wells Susan, widow, Spruce alley
Widener Milton, furnaceman, bds 1026 S. Main
Wagner James, furnaceman, bds 1026 S. Main
Ward Allison, groceries, 999 S. Main
Walker James, engine wiper, 822 S. Main
Werkheiser Monroe, harness maker, 802 S. Main
Wambold Latinus, cigar maker, 766 S. Main
Wood A. I., clerk, bds Randall
Young T. K., brakeman, 222 Bullman
Yocum Abraham, carpenter 237 Bullman

RAED CAREFULLY Page 218

HOUSEFURNISHING GOODS GENERALLY. The BEST GOODS for the LEAST MONEY at **H. M. NORTON'S, Easton, Pa.**

PHILLIPSBURG DIRECTORY.

Young Wilson J., engineer, 311 North Main
Youngkin Peter, installment merchant, 452 Broad
Young Jacob, laborer, 405 North Main
Young William, car painter, bds 311 N. Main
Young Martin, brakeman, 235 N. Main
Young Daniel, brakeman, 351 Chambers
Young Jacob, moulder, 504 Washington
Yoder John, bricklayer, bds Lee House
Yong William, stove maker, 207 Brainard
Yob John, marble and granite works, 197 S. Main, res 54 N. 7th, Easton
Young Joseph, carpenter, bds 536 Sitgreaves
Young John, boiler maker, 138 Union
Young George, laborer, 107 River
Young Philip A., invalid, Cherry alley
Young Joseph, flagman, 743 Fayette
Yntz Herbert, baker, 668 S. Main
Zellers John R., dramatic agent, 1080 S. Main
Zentner Jacob, pastor of St. John's Lutheran Church, res Fulton

---

Fringes and Dress Trimmings at CREVELING & CO'S

Zink Kaiser, peddler, Spruce alley
Ziegler Lewis, railroader, 545 Lewis
Zwald Charles, watchman, 612 Hudson

BUY THE RIEGEL & LUCH
ORGAN
IF YOU WANT A GOOD ORGAN.
THE UPRIGHT PIANO ORGANS, SIX OCTAVES,

Are becoming the leading Organ of the country. See them before you buy any other.

Factory Pine St., EASTON, PA.

Zwald Charles Jr., messenger, 612 Hudson
Zulauf Mrs. Annie, 732 Mercer
Zulauf John H., engineer, Broad

ANDREWS & NOLF, Proprietors of the "DOWN TOWN" Dry Goods House, 205 Northampton Street, Easton, Pa.

The Washington Star,

A Weekly Newspaper published at Washington, N. J.

SUBSCRIPTION $1.50 PER YEAR.

Six Months 75 cts.   Sample Copy Free.

The most enterprising newspaper published in Warren county. Contains all the State and County News, with a full local page.

A LIVE LOCAL PAPER.

The Daily Star, published whenever occasion requires and the people demand it.

A WELL-STOCKED JOB OFFICE,

Equipped with the latest styles of type and an abundance of material.

Work done Tastefully, Neatly, and Satisfaction Guaranteed.

LA ROE & BLAZER,
Publishers.

ALLAMUCHY TOWNSHIP.

ALLAMUCHY is situated in the eastern corner of Warren county. It is bounded on the north by Frelinghuysen township and Sussex county; on the east by Sussex and Morris counties; on the south by Morris county, the borough of Hackettstown and Independence township; and on the west by Independence township. The township has an area of 20.72 square miles or 13,260 acres of land, of which about 2,500 acres belong to the "Great Meadows" and is untillable, though a portion of this has been reclaimed by drainage. It was formed from Independence township in the year 1873; population of the township about 900.

The surface of Allamuchy is rough and uneven, covered more or less with hills. The township has an abundant supply of water, furnished by the many small streams flowing from its hill sides. The principal stream is the Pequest river, which enters from Frelinghuysen on the north and flows southwest through the township. The farming land is mostly rolling—some, however, being comparatively level, and is perhaps as susceptible of cultivation as any in the county. The soil is principally limestone, though in the valleys may be found a dark rich loam. The farms of Allamuchy are well cultivated and are held at a high figure, which speaks well for the thrift of the township.

A portion of the "Great Meadows" is found in this township. This is a vast tract of swamp or bog land, covering an area of about 6,000 acres, and embracing portions of four townships along the course of the Pequest—Hope, Independence and Allamuchy in Warren, and Green in Sussex. In the year 1872 commissioners were appointed by the Supreme Court, and constituted a Board of Managers for the purpose of draining the "Great Meadows." The work has now been going on several years, and good results are being realized in the reclaiming of the land, and in the improved sanitary condition of this district. Previously it was a famous malarial district, which has been considerably relieved by this system of drainage. Allamuchy Pond, the only lake in the township, is a small and rather pretty sheet of water, and is the source of a somewhat rapid little stream, running from its momentum rather than its magnitude, two or three grist mills.

The exact date of the first settlement in Allamuchy cannot be given. The most prominent and enterprising *business* man among the early settlers was one Joseph Demund, who settled here about the year 1800. He purchased 640 acres of land, where Allamuchy village now stands, planted orchards, built a grist mill and distillery attached, and did business on what was then considered a large scale. He was fond of speculating, won the confidence of his neighbors, borrowed large amounts of money, failed finally, and ruined a number of his securities. However, through his enterprise, Allamuchy in the early part of this century was more prominent as a business place than Hackettstown. The Quakers were also among the early settlers of the township. In 1764 they built the first Quaker church in this portion of New Jersey, upon a site the deed for which was given by William Penn, for the purpose of "a Friends meeting-house forever," which is the site of the present school house of Quaker settlement, used also for church services. This building contains a stove taken from the old one, and bearing the date "1764." About 200 yards east of the school house is the old Quaker graveyard, surrounded by a well built stone wall five feet high, and still used for burial purposes.

There are but few villages in the township. Allamuchy, the chief village, and the only business village, is located a little northeast of the centre of the township, and was probably the site of an old Indian village. It has two stores, blacksmith shop, wheelwright shop, postoffice, hotel, creamery and two grist mills in close proximity.

Warrenville is a hamlet, midway between Allamuchy and Hackettstown. It was once quite a prosperous business place, but at present is unimportant in that particular. Allamuchy has no regular church organization. The Lehigh and Hudson River Railroad crosses the township. Schools 4; scholars, 212.

Vienna Restaurant
—AND—
Ladies' Dining Saloon.
European Plan.   Meals at all Hours.
ICE CREAM and OYSTERS a Specialty.

Confectionery, Fruits, Nuts, etc. Finest brands Cigars

Main Street near the Bank, HACKETTSTOWN, N. J.

A. C. HOWELL, Proprietor.

WARREN COUNTY DRUG STORE.

TOWNSHIP DIRECTORY.

Postoffice addresses Allamuchy, N. J.

Allen Samuel, farmer; Arnold Stephen, farmer; Arnold Philip, farmer; Appleby Wm., laborer; Axford Jacob, laborer; Ayers James, farmer; Ayers Emma E., retired; Allen David, laborer; Axford Wm., farmer; Applegate Moses, farmer; Ayers Geo. H., farmer; Ayers John D., laborer; Ayers W. S., civil engineer; Adams Jesse, farmer; Adams John, laborer; Applegate Peter M., laborer.

Buckley Alfred, farmer; Barber Abner, retired; Bell Philip, farmer; Batley Huldah, widow; Batley Wm., laborer; Barret Christopher, farmer; Baylor Chas. W., blacksmith; Baylor John W., blacksmith; Bartron Elsa, widow; Blackwell Mary, widow; Barber Malon, farmer; Bartron Wm., laborer; Barton Jacob, laborer; Bartron Chas., merchant; Bird Morris, lock tender.

WHERE DO YOU GET THOSE DELICIOUS **HAMS. Why at CREVELING & CO.'S**

Cook Hiram, farmer; Cummins N. N., farmer; Crammer John M., farmer; Cooper Robt. M., laborer; Cunningham James, farmer; Cooper B. R., farmer; Chamberlin Jas. M., farmer; Cooper Zackariah, laborer; Crate Mary; Cummins W. M., farmer; Cummins Amanda, widow; Campfield Margaret; Conley Hannah, widow; Conley Peter, boatman; Cook M. L., lives on a lot; Crammer George, laborer; Crammer Wm., laborer; Crammer Sarah, dressmaker; Chamberlin D. P., express and freight agent; Chamberlin John C., drummer; Cron Joseph, farmer; Cooper W. S., laborer; Clawson Harvey, laborer; Cummins Andrew, laborer.

Deremer Eli, laborer; Depue Chas., farmer; Depue Henry, carpenter; Dickerson Wm., farmer; Dickerson Caleb R., farmer; Dawson Thomas, laborer; Drake George, laborer; Decker Joseph, laborer; Downs Patrick, gardner; Dunn Joseph, laborer; Dunn Al-

ANDREWS & NOLF, 205 Northampton St. Keep the Largest line of Silks and Dress Goods on E. Northampton

H. M. NORTON, WHOLESALE AND RETAIL DEALER IN HARDWARE, STOVES, HEATERS AND RANGES.

ALLAMUCHY TOWNSHIP.

mond, laborer; Dunn Samuel, laborer; Dunn Alexander, farmer; Phillips Dolan, miner; Drake Samuel, farmer; Drake R. H., sawyer; Drake J. W., sawyer; Dilly John F., retired; Deurmer Wm., farmer; Deurmer John H., laborer; Davis Thomas, laborer; Dennis A. J., farmer; Deremer John F., cooper; Decker Joel, farmer.

Foster Thomas, laborer; Feasler Huldah, widow.

Gibbs George G., teacher; Gibbs Clinton, farmer; Gibbs James N., farmer; Guess George, laborer; Gray John, farmer; Guess S. Y., laborer; Gillson John Sr., carpenter; Gillson John, Jr., carpenter; Gillson Albert, carpenter; Grube Maxmilian, shoemaker.

Hannas Isaac, laborer; Harrington P. L., laborer; Hendershot Benj., laborer; Harden E. J., farmer; Hubert John, laborer; Hibler S. L., farmer; Hering George, laborer; Huff Joseph, laborer; Huff Samuel, laborer; Huff Aquilla, laborer; Harden Lemuel, book agent; Hawk Philip G., laborer; Hawk Edward, laborer; Hinch Richard, coachman; Hibler Lutitia,

What Beautiful Prints at CREVELING & CO.'S

widow; Hibler Matthias, farmer; Harris W. A., farmer; Haggerty Thomas, merchant; Haggerty Stephen, merchant; Haggerty Geo., miller; Haggerty Morris, miller.

Jones George, farmer; Johnson G. F., farmer; Johnson Orace, laborer; Hibler Cristopher, retired farmer.

Kelly James, laborer; Kinney Michael, farmer; Kettle Judson, farmer.

Lundy Eli, farmer; Lundy Eli Jr., farmer; Lambert Jacob, laborer; Lyons Martin, laborer; Lewis Josiah, farmer; Lineberry W. L., physician.

Meeker Aaron, laborer; McDonough Michael, laborer; Mott Maria, widow; Martin Richard, merchant; Mooney Eliza, widow; Mooney Wm., laborer; Martin John, blacksmith.

Niper Azubah, widow; Neigh James, miller.

Polhemus Wm., farmer; Parks S. G., farmer; Parks Samuel, farmer; Pool John, laborer; Pool Geo., laborer; Pettit John, laborer; Philips Martha, widow;

ALL KINDS OF HARDWARE at Wade Bros., Hackettstown, N. J.

ALLAMUCHY TOWNSHIP.

Parks Gersham, farmer; Pyles Wm., farmer; Pyles John, laborer; Pyles Elbridge, laborer.

Runion J. C. farmer; Runion L. M., farmer; Reader S. R., farmer; Riker Lewis; Rutherford Stuyvesent, retired; Rutherford L. M., retired; Reynolds Richard, laborer; Runion Winfield, laborer.

Staley Alexander, farmer; Staley Mary, widow; Staples James M., laborer; Snyder C. G., laborer; Shotwell Emelissa, no occupation; Shackelton S. R., laborer; Smith Milton, laborer; Staples Hiram, retired; Sergant Charles, laborer; Shafer James N., laborer; Shafer Effa, widow; Sutton George, laborer; Sutton Wm., laborer; Sherer George, laborer; Sutton W. O., farmer; Sipley Sarah, widow; Sipley Johnson J., farmer; Swisher Garret, farmer; Swartsweller Michael, farmer; Stevens Theron, miner; Schooley Stephen, farmer; Stiff Adam, farmer; Stiff Marshal, laborer; Schooley Aaron, laborer; Savacool Charles, laborer; Seals Wm., hotel keeper; Sidnar Edward, laborer; Staples Wm., laborer.

Tims Jas. W., farmer; Tims Wm., farmer; Tims Wesley, farmer; Telfer John, farmer; Townsend George, blacksmith; Townsend Chas., wheelwright; Till John, farmer; Till Joel, farmer.

Vanduser H. H., farmer; Van Horn Wm. farmer; Vanhouter T. G., laborer.

Willson Amos, retired farmer; Willson John, farmer; Willson David, retired; Wheeler Isaac, laborer; Willson Frank, laborer; Wheeler John, laborer; Wheeler Peter, laborer; Willson Abner, farmer; Willson Ezra, farmer; Whitesell Emma; Williams John, laborer; Waldron William, laborer; White Wm., boatman; White Catharine, widow; Willson George, farmer; Wheeler James, laborer.

Young Mary D., widow; Young D. A., farmer; Young W. H., laborer; Young John M., laborer; Young Dewitt, farmer.

BLAIRSTOWN TOWNSHIP.

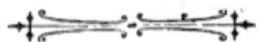

BLAIRSTOWN is one of the most northern townships of Warren County, and is so named in honor of one of her most distinguished sons, John I. Blair, a railroad king and millionaire of the present day. It was set off from Knowlton township by an act of the State Legislature in February, 1845, and embraced 27.30 sq. miles, or 17,472 acres of land. It has a population of about 1500. It is bounded as follows: North, Pahaquarry township; east, Hardwick and Frelinghuysen; south, Hope; and west, Knowlton.

The Blue Mountains on the north form the boundary between the townships of Pahaquarry and Blairstown. From the summit of this range is a series of hills and valleys, like a giant staircase, leading down to the valley of the Paulinskill, near the centre of the township. On the south side of the Paulinskill is a gradual rise extending nearly to the southern boundary of the township, where a ridge is reached, running in a northeasterly and southwesterly direction across it and forming a local watershed; the streams on the north running into the Paulinskill, and those on the south into Hope township. The soil is composed chiefly of a gravelly loam, susceptible of a high state of cultivation, and is very productive when placed under proper treatment.

The principal stream in this township is the Paulinskill, which runs through the central portion in a southwesterly direction and empties into the Delaware. There are numerous other small and unimportant streams. Cedar Lake, sometimes called Buttermilk pond from the milky appearance of its waters, is a pretty sheet of water situated about one and a half miles from the village of Blairstown, and has become quite popular as a local picnic ground and as a general summer resort. One of the natural curiosities of this township, and perhaps the only specimen of the kind to be found in the United States, is Elephant Rock. It is situated along the road leading from Jacksonburg to Walnut Valley, about midway between the two places, and resembles very exactly a big elephant asleep.

It is probable that the earliest settlements were made in the vicinity of Walnut Valley and along the Paulinskill. The red men were here ahead of the white settlers. There are still to be found the remains of an Indian village along the Paulinskill, on the farm of David F. Brands, not far from the western border of the township. On the high knoll above what is now known in this vicinity as the "big spring" was the old Indian burying-ground, where lie the remains of many a red man whose spirit has long since gone to the "happy hunting ground." Mounds and rude headstones, marking the resting-places of the dead, are still visible though overgrown by trees and underbrush.

The first town-meeting in Blairstown was held April 14, 1845.

The villages of the township are as follows: Blairstown, the "gem of the Paulinskill", is beautifully and romatically situated on the right bank of that stream, nine miles from its confluence with the Delaware river, and about half-way between the capitals of Warren and Sussex counties, being thirteen miles southwest of Newton and fifteen miles northeast of Belvidere. Blairstown is the natural centre of an extensive scope of territory embracing all the northern part of the county, and even parts of western Sussex county, bounded on the north by the Delaware, extending to the eastward of Stillwater in Sussex, south to the Jenny Jump mountains, and west also to the Deleware. Its merchants and business men have always been noted for their enterprise and have always commanded a large share of the patronage, not only of the district just described, but also a very liberal patronage from Monroe and Pike counties, Pa. The exact date of its settlement is not known, but there are evidences that it is one of the oldest towns in the county. It was originally called "Smith's Mills", in honor of the Smith who settled there at a very early date and built a large grist-mill and saw-mill along the Paulinskill and near where King's blacksmith shop now stands. It was next called "Butts' Bridge"; then "Gravel Hill", and finally, Jan. 24, 1839, by a vote of the citizens it was called Blairstown, in honor of Hon. John I. Blair, before referred to. At this place was located one of the old-time whipping-posts. The *Blairstown Press* was established in 1877; the building of that name was erected in 1880. Blair Academy, a Presbyterian college preparatory school is located here. There are in Blairstown: two churches, Presbyterian and Methodist; academy; public school; public hall; hotel; postoffice; general and grocery stores; *Blairstown Press*; carriage manufactory, and numerous smaller business places. Jacksonburg, a small hamlet located about one mile to the northwest of Blairstown. It was at one time quite a business place. At the present time it has a school-house, blacksmith and wheelwright shop, distillery, store and gristmill. Walnut Valley, about four miles from Blairstown, was so called because of the large number of blackwalnut trees growing in that section. The postoffice at this place was established in 1827, and was conducted by the original postmaster for about 50 years. It has a hotel building, blacksmith shop, and school building, used also for church services.

No. schools in township, 9; scholars 447.

THE BLAIRSTOWN PRESS.

(Only Paper in Northern Warren County.)

ESTABLISHED IN 1877.

Published every Wednesday Morning at the office on Main Street, *BLAIRSTOWN, N. J.*

Circulation over 1000 Copies Weekly.

D. C. CARTER, - Editor and Proprietor.

THE PRESS is a well printed, thirty-two column paper, devoted to the local news of Warren county. It is independent in politics, circulating as it does among the best classes of people in the county, and especially the farming community. It is unexcelled as an advertising medium. Advertising rates moderate and furnished upon application.

SUBSCRIPTION - - - $1.50 PER YEAR.

Our system of correspondence is the most complete in the county. Special reporters at every town in the northern end of the county, and a special correspondent at the county seat.

It's columns are filled with the latest and most reliable news. Try it and be convinced. Send postal for sample copy.

OUR JOBBING DEPARTMENT

has gradually acquired a reputation second to none in the county. New type is being added from time to time, good workmen are employed and with the steam power lately added, we are prepared to turn out first-class work at low rates. Persons in need of printed envelopes, bill boards, note heads, circulars, posters, vendue bills or anything in our line will do well to write us for estimates before giving out the work.

Subscribe for THE PRESS. You will like it.

All the news for $1.50 per year.

WARREN COUNTY DRUG STORE.

Township Directory.

All whose vocation is not mentioned are farmers.

Angle Frederick, Blairstown; Angle David, laborer, Blairstown; Ayers George, butcher, Blairstown; Ayres Laura, tailoress, Blairstown; Auble Robert, carter, Blairstown; Auble Geo. D., miller, Blairstown; Auble Geo. W., miller, Blairstown; Andress Roderick B., carpenter, Blairstown; Andress Isaiah P., laborer, Blairstown; Alpaugh Nathan, blacksmith, Blairstown; Allen John M., Blairstown; Allen & Titman, lumbermen, Blairstown; Armstrong Milton N., M. D., Blairstown; Albertson Rachel, weaving, Paulina; Albertson Philip, mail carrier, Blairstown.

Blair John I., railroad king, Blairstown; Bellis John, Blairstown; Bellis John R., Blairstown; Butler Henry S., minister of gospel, Blairstown; Bowers John A., Blairstown; Bowers Jacob S., Blairstown; Branigan George, druggist, Blairstown; Ball Joseph G.,

Polite and Handsome Clerks at CREVELING & CO.'S

Blairstown; Ball Jacob, mason, Blairstown; Ball Marcus, mason, Blairstown; Ball George, blacksmith aprentice, Blairstown; Bird Thomas S., mason, Paulina; Bird John, laborer, Blairstown; Bird Isaiah, miller, Paulina; Barker Harvey G., mason, Blairstown; Brown Nicholas E., laborer, Blairstown; Brown Alvin, railroad conductor, Blairstown; Brown Benjamin, railroad conductor, Walnut Valley; Brown Issac L., Blairstown; Blazier Charles, creamery hand, Blairstown; Babbitt Hampton, carriage painter and trimmer, Blairstown; Beegle Elias E., cooper, Blairstown; Beegle William E., cooper, Blairstown; Beck Ervin, lumberman, Walnut Valley; Bunnell J. Fletcher, Blairstown; Bunnell Isaac, Blairstown; Bunnell Henry, Blairstown; **Bunnell Frank P.**, confectioner, dealer in gent's furnishing goods, hats caps, segars, notions etc., Bunnell Leslie C., assistant postmaster, Blairstown; Bunnell Lizzie, milliner, Blairstown; Bunnell Jennie, secretary for Jno. Bunnell, Blairstown; Bartow Isaiah, Hainesburg; Bartow John H., railroad engineer,

ANDREWS & NOLF, 205 Northampton St. Keep the Largest line of Silks and Dress Goods on E. Northampton

E. M. NORTON, WHOLESALE AND RETAIL DEALER IN HARDWARE, STOVES, HEATERS AND RANGES.

BLAIRSTOWN DIRECTORY.

Blairstown; Brands William C., Blairstown; Brands Nelson, Hainesburg; Bunnell James K., Blairstown; **Bunnell John**, fire and life insurance agent, Blairstown; Brugler Charles S., printer, Blairstown; Brugler James O., laborer, Mt. Herman; Bentz Jacob, marble dealer, Blairstown.

Carter John A., horseshoer and general blacksmith, N. Jersey; Craig Robert Jr., merchant, N. Jersey; Cowell A. R., blacksmith, Walnut Valley; Conklin Edward H. Jr., lime dealer, Blairstown; Conklin E. H., minister of the gospel, Blairstown; Cyphers Williams, Blairstown; Castner Jacob T., sawyer, Blairstown; Carter George, sawyer, Blairstown; **Carter D. C.**, editor *Blairstown Press*, Blairstown; Cornell Theodore P., Paulina; Cook John, Blairstown; Cook Elisha, Blairstown; Cook Marshall, Blairstown; Cook Simeon, laborer, Blairstown; Christian Myron, Blairstown; Crisman Edgar, retired, Blairstown; Crisman Morris, retired, Blairstown; Crisman Cassius, retired, Blairstown; Crisman Calvin, retired, Blairstown;

LAUBACH'S, Easton, Pa. SPECIAL ATTENTION TO SILKS AND DRESS GOODS. NEW GOODS DAILY.

Crisman Lemuel, retired, Blairstown; Crisman Morris R., laborer, Blairstown; Crisman Marshall, laborer, Blairstown; Crisman John L. B., Blairstown; Chase D. L., shoemaker, Blairstown; Clifford B. R., Hainesburg.

Decker Alex., Blairstown; Decker Geo., Blairstown; Divers Fannie, dressmaker, Blairstown; Divers John, Blairstown; Divers Lizzie, dressmaker, Blairstown; **Drake L. C.**, wheelwright, wagon and carriage manufacturer, Blairstown; Davidson John, Hainesburg;

JOHN BUNNELL,
LIFE AND FIRE INSURANCE AGENT,
OFFICE ON MAIN STREET.
Blairstown, New Jersey.

Dorland G. H., miller, Blairstown.
Elder Fred. W., landlord, Blairstown; Ervine William, cooper, Walnut Valley; Ervine Joseph D., freighter, Blairstown; Edmonds A. F., U. S. mail

For Coughs, Colds, Croup and Consumption use SHIELDS' COMPOUND SYRUP of Wild Cherry with hypophosphates of lime and soda

BLAIRSTOWN TOWNSHIP. 337

agent, Paulina; Edgerton James, town clerk, Blairstown; Edgerton Byron C., liveryman, Blairstown.

Firth Eli, cabinet maker, Paulina; Flummerfelt J. R., Mt. Hermon; Flummerfelt John W., Mt. Hermon; France James C., laborer, Walnut Valley; France Abram, laborer, Walnut Valley; France Ira, mason, Blairstown; France Jacob, carpenter, Blairstown; Freeman E. H., jeweler, Blairstown; Freeman Aaron, laborer, Walnut Valley.

Gulnup Alfred, Walnut Valley; Gougher Gershom, Walnut Valley; Gougher Marshal, laborer, Walnut Valley; Gougher John H., laborer, Walnut Valley; Gougher James, Walnut Valley; Gougher Johnson, Walnut Valley; Glass Reuben, cabinet maker, Walnut Valley; Garrison Philip, laborer, Mt. Hermon; Garrison Seth D., laborer, Blairstown; Green Charles, Blairstown; Gibbs Isaac, Blairstown; Gibbs Abram, freighter, Blairstown; Groover Martin, Blairstown.

Hiles Lymon, Mount Hermon; Huff Silas, laborer, Mount Hermon; Hall John, laborer, Blairstown;

Hartman Andrew, laborer, Blairstown; Hartman Ira, Blairstown; Hull David, laborer, Blairstown; Howell William C., ticket and freight agent, Blairstown; Howell Margarette A., milliner, Blairstown; Harris Elias, clerk drug store, Blairstown; Heater James, laborer, Blairstown; Heater James R., Blairstown; Heater Samuel S., Blairstown; Heater Elias L., Knowlton; Heldemore Charles, sash and blind maker, Paulina; Hoagland Edward, Knowlton; Hill Isaac, Blairstown; Hill Alonzo, justice of the peace, Blairs-

JOSEPH M. MANN,
Barber and Hairdresser,
BLAIRSTOWN. - - - NEW JERSEY.

A full line of Gents' Furnishing Goods always in stock. Fine Shirts, Laundried and Unlaundried, Underwear, Neckties, Collars, Cuffs, Silk Handkerchiefs, and in fact everything in Gents Furnishings. Gloves for Winter and Summer wear always in stock. Tobacco and Cigars a specialty.

town; Hill James D., justice of the peace, Walnut Val'y; Hill And'w, B'rst'n; Hill Jos. D., Wal. Val'y; Hill J. Fletcher, painter, Blairstown; Hill Abram,

H. M. NORTON, WHOLESALE AND RETAIL DEALER IN HARDWARE, STOVES, HEATERS AND RANGES.

BLAIRSTOWN TOWNSHIP.

Walnut Valley; Hill Alva B., Walnut Valley; Hartman David W., Blairstown; Hartman Myron C., butcher, Blairstown; Hartman Theodore, clerk, Blairstown; Hibler Silas, Blairstown; Hankinson Belden H., mechanic, Paulina.

Jones Joshua, Blairstown; Jones Charles F., Walnut Valley; Jones William M., Blairstown; Johnson John C., M. D., Blairstown; Johnston Samuel, carpenter, Blairstown; Johnston William L., blacksmith, Blairstown; Johnson Alfred K., carpenter, Blairstown; Johnston Charles P., Paulina.

Keyser Jacob, Blairstown; Kirkhoff Cornelius, Walnut Valley; Kirkhoff George B., Walnut Valley; Kinney James C., laborer, Blairstown; Kinney Jesse, laborer, Blairstown; Kinney Bartley L., Blairstown; Kishpaugh Nelson, Mount Hermon; Kishpaugh Elmer W., Blairstown; Kishpaugh John, Blairstown; Kishpaugh Isaac, laborer, Blairstown; Kishpaugh William R., ex-teacher, Blairstown; Koukle John, Blairstown; Koukle Milton S., fancy stock dealers, Blairstown;

LAUBACH'S EASTON, PA. Largest Store, Largest Assortments, and One Price to All

Koukle Lewis A., teacher, Blairstown; Koukle Anna M., fancy goods dealer, Blairstown; Kise Jacob, laborer, Blairstown; Kise Emanuel, carpenter, Blairstown; Kentz Aaron, laborer, Walnut Valley; Keepers Charles, merchant, Blairstown.

Lanterman Isaac D., Blairstown; Lanterman Edward L., surveyor, Blairstown; Lanterman Aaron J., Blairstown; Lanterman Peter A., proprietor of Cedar Lake House, Blairstown; Lanterman John P., Blairstown; Lanterman J. Clark, Blairstown; Lanterman Clinton, laborer, Blairstown; Kehnroth Charles H., teacher at Blair Hall, Blairstown; Larue Bartley, Blairstown; Luse Jacob L., retired farmer, Blairstown; Lewis T. L., Blairstown; Lanning Andrew, Mount Hermon; Lanning Elmer E., Mount Hermon; **Logan John R.**, carpenter and builder, contracts taken for erection of all kinds of buildings, Blairstown; Lundy George, laborer, Blairstown; Lance John, Walnut Valley; Lance George M., Walnut Valley; Lance Anthony, wheelwright, Walnut Valley; Lance Isaiah, carpenter,

EMPIRE SOLID CAST STEEL SCISSORS AND SHEARS For Sale at **Wades' Hardware Store.**

BLAIRSTOWN TOWNSHIP.

Walnut Valley; Lance J. B., teacher, Walnut Valley; Linabery Philip, Blairstown; Linabery Gershom C., Blairstown; Linabery Josiah D., Walnut Valley; Linabery Samuel B., Walnut Valley; Linabery Calvin C., Walnut Valley; Linabery Hiram C., Blairstown; Linabery Silas A., constable, Blairstown; Linabery Jabez J., Blairstown; Linabary James H., Walnut Valley; Linabery William L., blacksmith, Blairstown.

Mann Marshall, laborer, Blairstown; Mann Horace, laborer, Blairstown; **Mann Joseph M.**, barber, etc., Blairstown; Mann Charles, clerk, Blairstown; Mackey Elias J., Blairstown; Mackey Charles, Blairstown; Mackey Marshall, cooper, Walnut Valley; Messler Simeon, Blairstown; Miller Conrad, President of Bangor Railroad Company, Blairstown; Maines Ralph, laborer, Blairstown; Maines Jacob, carpenter, Blairstown; Metzgar John N., Blairstown; McGuiness George, tailor, Blairstown; McCarly James, laborer, Blairstown; McConachy Samuel, miller, Blairstown;

LAUBACH'S EASTON, PA. CLOAKS and WRAPS of every description. **Our Own Manufacture.**

McConachy Clinton, Blairstown; McConachy William M., Blairstown; McConachy John C., Blairstown; Mitchel Robert, Blairstown; Mingle Jacob, Paulina; McCain Jeremiah, Mount Herman; McCain Lewis, Mount Herman; McCain Melvin C., blacksmith, Blairstown; McCracken William, laborer, Blairstown; McCracken John, painter, Blairstown; Merrick Peter, Walnut Valley; Merrick Jacob B., Walnut Valley; McCleary Robert, laborer, Knowlton; Mullen James, baker, Blairstown.

Opdyke John W., gentleman, Blairstown.

Perry George W., lawyer, Blairstown; Perry William S., carriage trimmer, Knowlton; Perry George Jr., colporteur, Knowlton; Potter Samuel, laborer, Walnut Valley; Place J. M., millright, Blairstown; Pope Charles E., carpenter, Blairstown; Parr Gershom, laborer, Walnut Valley; Perry Mrs. S. D., summer boarding house, Knowlton; Pullis George, Walnut Valley; Pullis Read, undertaker and cabinet maker, Blairstown; Pullis William M., laborer, Wal-

H. M. NORTON, WHOLESALE AND RETAIL DEALER IN HARDWARE, STOVES, HEATERS AND RANGES.

BLAIRSTOWN TOWNSHIP.

nut Valley; Painter John, miller, Blairstown; Pierson John, tinsmith, Blairstown.

Quick Benjamin, Blairstown.

Raub William C., butcher, Blairstown; Raub Calvin E., farmer and butcher, Blairstown; Raub Albert, Blairstown; Raub Erastus V., Blairstown; Rusling R. H., tinsmith, Blairstown; Reader David H., laborer, Blairstown; Reader Geo. F., Blairstown; Reader Alfred, Blairstown; Robins George, shoemaker, Blairstown; Rice Robt. G., Blairstown; Rhodes Peter, Hainesburg; **Rice Geo. C.,** clerk, Blairstown; Rice Lizzie, mantua maker, Blairstown; Read Isaac F., distiller and farmer, Blairstown; Read John A., laborer, Blairstown.

Snover Andrew N., Blairstown; Snover Emanuel, Blairstown; Sipley Melissa, milliner, Blairstown; Sipley John, carpenter, Blairstown; Sly C. W., prop. Blairstown creamery, Blairstown; Strickland Chas., shoemaker, Blairstown; Swisher Abram, Blairstown; Seigler Wm. R., printer, Blairstown; Seigler Isaac,

LAUBACH'S, Easton, Pa. Largest stock of CARPETS, lowest prices. Best attention always.

laborer, Blairstown; Shotwell George M., laborer, Blairstown; Shotwell John, laborer, Blairstown; Shotwell James, laborer, Blairstown; **Smith Ervin W.,**

BLAIR PRESBYTERIAL ACADEMY.
JOHN I. BLAIR, Foundation.

Both Sexes. Experienced Teachers. English, Latin, Greek, French, German, Music, Drawing and Painting. Building Refurnished; Warmed by Steam; Hot and Cold Water on Each Floor; Latest Scientific Sanitary Arrangements; New Gymnasium; Large Play Grounds.

Boarding, Tuition, Furnished Room, Light, Fuel and Washing $225 a year,

J. H. SHOEMAKER, Ph. D., Prin.

agent for Champion plows and Hench's walking and riding cultivators, Walnut Valley; Shuster Isaac, Blairstown; Shuster Timothy, hostler, Blairstown;

SHIELDS' Compound Syrup of Wild Cherry with Hypophosphites of Lime and Soda. Sure cure for coughs, croup, etc.

Savercool Robt., Walnut Valley; Silverthorn John, painter, Blairstown; Shipman George, painter, Blairstown; Snyder Jeremiah, painter, Knowlton; Snyder Paul G., retired, Knowlton; Snyder Aaron, Knowlton; Snyder William, laborer, Knowlton; Snyder Robert M., Blairstown; Snyder John F., Knowlton; Snyder Andrew W., sash and blind maker, Paulina; Snyder Jas., laborer, Mt. Hermon; Stiff J. N., harness maker, Blairst'n; Smith Nathan S., Blairsto'n; Smith Joshua, Walnut Valley; Smith Charles C., Walnut Valley; **Shumaker J. H.**, principal of Blair Hall, Blairstown; Smith Wm. J., Blairstown; Smith Henry K., Knowlton; Smith Conrad, Blairstown; Smith Wm. C., Knowlton; Smith Abram H., merchant, Blairstown; Smith Geo. W., laborer, Blairstown; Smith Franklin M., justice of peace, Blairstown; Smith Jacob A., Blairstown; Smith Irvin W., prop'r of Willow Farm boarding house, Blairstown; Smith Critendon, wheelwright, Blairstown; Smith Theo. H., laborer, Blairstown; Smith Abram L., Walnut Val'y;

LAUBACH'S EASTON, PA. CLOAKS and WRAPS of every description. **Our Own Manufacture.**

Smith Lodor, laborer, Blairstown; Smith Read, Blairstown; Smith Jacob T., RR. fireman, Blairstown; Shubert A. A., dentist, Blairstown; Stout Gideon L., sawyer, Walnut Valley; Swartz John W., laborer, Blairstown; Shanon Jas. H., prop. Evergreen Lake Farm, Knowlton; Stoll Robt. S., merchant and collector, Blairstown; Sliker Caleb W., laborer, Blairstown; Sliker David S., RR. engineer, Blairstown; Snover Geo. F., Blairstown; Snover Lemuel, Blairstown; Snover Elias J., Blairstown; Snover Wm. S., butcher, Blairstown; Snover Marshall, RR fireman, Blairstown.

Titus Andrew, laborer, Walnut Valley; Titus Jos. F., laborer, Blairstown; Tinsman Wm., Knowlton; Teel Albert, Blairstown; Teel Isaiah, laborer, Blairstown; Teel John D., Walnut Valley; Teel Andrew, Blairstown; Teel Jordan, Blairstown; Teets Adam, Blairstown; Teeter Philip, Walnut Valley; Teeter Jehill, Walnut Valley; Teeter Isaac, Walnut Valley; Titman Geo. W., carpenter, Blairstown; Titman Al-

ANDREWS & NOLF, Proprietors of the "**DOWN TOWN**" Dry Goods House, 205 Northampton Street, Easton, Pa.

H. M. NORTON, WHOLESALE AND RETAIL DEALER IN HARDWARE, STOVES, HEATERS AND RANGES.

exander, Blairstown; Titman Isaac R., Blairstown; Titman Simeon F., painter, Blairstown; Titman Geo., farmer and dealer in lumber, Walnut Valley.

Vangorden Henry, laborer, Blairstown; Vass Mathias, retired, Blairstown; Vanauken Reuben, Blairstown; Vanauken David, laborer, Blairstown; Vanauken Reuben H., Blairstown; Vail C. E., secretary of John I. Blair, Blairstown; Vail John D., postmaster, Blairstown; Vanscoten P. K., carpenter, Blairstown; Vanscoten Chas. W., stone mason, Walnut Valley; Vanscoten Thaddeus, Blairstown; Vanscoten John A., mail carrier, Walnut Valley; Vanscoten Owen D., laborer, Walnut Valley; Vankirk Wm., Walnut Valley; Vankirk Louis, Walnut Valley; Vankirk James, Walnut Valley; Vankirk John Astor, Walnut Valley; Vankirk Burns, laborer, Walnut Valley.

Warner James, Blairstown; Walters Andrew J., Blairstown; Wilson John S., Blairstown; Willson Walter, retired, Blairstown; **Willson Milton L.**,

LAUBACH'S, Easton, Pa. THE LARGEST DRY GOODS AND CARPET HOUSE. BARGAINS ALWAYS.

clothing, boots, shoes, hats, and gents' furnishing goods, Blairstown; Willson Lemuel F. L., Blairstown; Woodruff James, laborer, Blairstown; Wintermute Isaac, carpenter, Blairstown; West John, Blairstown; West Mathias, Blairstown; West Thomas D., Mt. Herman; West Jacob E., Blairstown; Wildrick Geo. A., blacksmith, Blairstown; Wildrick W. Preston, creamery employee, Blairstown; Wildrick Aaron K., assessor, Blairstown; Wildrick Chas. C., laborer, Blairstown; Wildrick John A., Blairstown; Wildrick Henry, creamery employe, Blairstown; Wildrick Ferdinand, Blairstown; Wildrick Westfield J., Blairstown; Wildrick Isaac, auctioneer, Blairstown; Wildrick Warren H., laborer, Blairstown; Wildrick Jacob B., laborer, Blairstown; Wildrick Kelsie, laborer, Paulina; Wildrick Mellie, fancy goods and dressmaker, Blairstown.

Yetter Andrew, merchant and lumber dealer, Blairstown; Yetter George, Blairstown; Youmans William M., miller, Paulina; **Yetter & Craig**, dry goods, groceries, boots, shoes, etc., Blairstown.

LUBRICATING OILS of all kinds at **WADE BROS.'**

FRELINGHUYSEN TOWNSHIP.

THIS township was formed from Hardwick township in 1848, and is one of the N. E. border townships. It was named in honor of Hon. Theodore Frelinghuysen. The township is about five and a half miles long and four and half wide, and covers an area of 22.69 square miles or 14,522 acres, with a population of about 1100. It is bounded on the N. and N.E. by Hardwick township and Sussex county on the E. and SE. by Sussex county, and the townships of Allamuchy and Independence; on the SW. by Hope and Blairstown, and on the NW. by Blairstown and Hardwick. Paulin's Kill creek forms the boundary line between Hardwick and Frelinghuysen.

The surface of this township is very uneven, being covered with hills, hollows, and rocky knobs. The Jenny Jump mountains run along the South Eastern border, "Mount Rascal," is a lofty limestone knob, near the village of Johnsonsburg, covered with evergreens and scrub oaks ; it is said to be a resort for Sunday card players, hence the name. The Northwestern portion of the township is drained by the several small tributaries of the Paulin's Kill, Bear creek and its tributaries drain the Southeastern corner, and Trout Brook the Southwestern. There are several small and beautiful lakes or "ponds," as they are called, sprinkled throughout the township, generally bearing the name of the individual who owns or has at some time owned the land upon which they are found.

This township was first settled by German pioneers, at a very early date—long before Warren county was thought of—whose love for freedom and religious liberty led them into this section of country, when it was but a howling wilderness, in search of a home where they might enjoy freedom of thought, and act according to the dictates of their own conscience without fear of molestation from any one. Among these early pioneers was Dr. Samuel Kennedy, who located at Johnsonsburg, and was the first practicing physician of a fixed location in all this section of country. His practice extended so far over the country that professional visits of twenty-five or thirty miles were no uncommon event in his career. He was an able practitioner, and prepared a number of students for the medical profession. Drs. Linn and Everitt, who practiced among later generations, were among the number who received their first medical instruction from Dr. Kennedy.

The first voting place for this township, of which we have knowledge was at Trenton, then a village of Hunterdon county, though of course, as in our day the voting place could be appointed elsewhere by vote of the people.

Among the ancient land marks of this township are the "old log jail," and the "Dark Moon tavern." On the 21st of March 1754, a meeting of the Board of Justices and freeholders of the county, (then embracing both Sussex and Warren,) met at the house of Samuel Green, near the present site of Johnsonsburg, (the first body of the kind ever convened in the county,) and appointed a meeting of all the qualified persons of the county to be held at said Green's house on the 16th, 17th and 18th days of April, 1754, " to elect a place to build a jail and court-house." The meeting was accordingly held and the jail ordered to be built near Jonathan Pettit's tavern and the county to bear the expense. Jonathan Pettits tavern was located near what is now Johnsonsburg. The jail was cheaply and poorly built, and very unsatisfactorily served the purpose of a jail. During the nine years of its existence as a jail the county became responsible, on account of the flight of imprisoned debtors to the amount of nearly £600 or about $3,000, which was equal to about fourteen times the expense of building the jail.

The courts were held at the house of Jonathan Pettit, near the log jail, from Nov. 1753 to Feb. 1756, when Newton was made the seat of holding the courts.

The "Dark Moon tavern" was located about 1½ miles from the log jail, on the road to Greenville, and was kept prior to and long after the Revolutionary war. Its large, old fashioned swinging sign had a black moon painted on a white background, which gave to it and the surrounding country the name of "Dark Moon tavern." Many stories and thrilling adventures are told of this tavern, which in its palmy days was the rendezvous of the most desperate characters for miles around. The three principal villages of Frelinghuysen are Johnsonsburg with a population of about 200; Marksboro, 150, and Paulina 75. Johnsonsburg has a christian and M. E church, and Presbyterian chapel, a school house, grist mill, hotel, three stores, a cabinet shop, wheelwrights, coopers, tinsmiths, blacksmith, shoemakers, etc.

Marksboro and Paulina have each a school-house and grist mill; Marksboro a Presbyterian church, and Paulina a Presbyterian chapel, and a sash and blind factory, with such other business places as are common to country villages. There are in the township five schools with a total of 259 children of school age.

WARREN COUNTY DRUG STORE.

Township Directory.

All whose vocation is not mentioned are farmers.

Allen J. V., Paulina; Allen Andrew, school teacher, Paulina; Allen Jacob, school teacher, Paulina; Armstrong George B., justice of the peace, Marksboro; Ayers Robert C., Johnsonsburg; Albertson Jay, Hope; Albertson Isaac R., Hope; Albertson Edgar, Hope; Ackerson Walter, Johnsonsburg; Anthony Jesse, gentleman, Johnsonsburg.

Barton E. S., tailor, Marksboro; Burt Rev. Robt. J., minister of gospel, Marksboro; Ball Wm. H., telegraph operator, Marksboro; Brown James H., blacksmith, Marksboro; Brown Ervin, blacksmith, Marksboro; Bescherer John, Johnsonsburg; Boice Mrs. Mary, Hope; Bartow Aaron, Hope; Blair Robert, gentleman, Johnsonsburg; Beegle Gershom, constable, Johnsonsburg; Ball Mrs. Mary, householder, Marksboro; Bartow William, tinsmith, Marksboro.

Clouse Alonzo, Johnsonsburg; Clouse Jacob, laborer, Marksboro; Cook Alfred W., Marksboro; Cook Adrain L., tinsmith, Marksboro; Cool Edward, Creveling J. B. C., resident, Asbury; Cruts Reuben

LAUBACH'S, Easton, Pa., Largest stock of CARPETS, lowest prices. Best attention always.

Marksboro; Cook George Edward, Marksboro; Cook Winfield, Marksboro; Coursen J. H., Marksboro; Coursen Miss Emma, Marksboro; Cooke Jacob, Paulina; Cook J. W., Marksboro; Cook J. M., Marksboro; Cook Marvin, Hope; Cook Aaron R., Johnsonsburg; Cook Elmer, Hope; Cook Albert L., Marksboro; boro; Cook Richard P., Hope; Cooke Zackery, Hope; Cooke Thomson T., Johnsonsburg; Cool Geo., Hope; Cook Mrs. Mary Y., householder, Marksboro; Cook Frederick, gentleman, Johnsonsburg; Cassidy Wm., Johnsonsburg; Dyer Joseph E., Johnsonsburg; Durling William, Sen., Johnsonsburg; Durling John, Johnsonsburg; Durling Joseph, hotel keeper, Johnsonsburg; Dildine Lydia Mrs., householder, Johnsonsburg; Durling William Jr., school teacher, Johnsonsburg; Dennis Lewis, gentleman, Johnsonsburg.

ANDREWS & NOLF, 205 Northampton St. Keep the Largest line of Silks and Dress Goods on E. Northampton

FRELINGHUYSEN TOWNSHIP.

Everitt Mathias, Marksboro; Fisher Joseph, laborer, Johnsonsburg; Forsman Rev. R. B., minister of gospel, Johnsonsburg.

Gibbs George, hotel keeper, Marksboro; Gibbs William, clerk, Marksboro; Gibbs Jeremiah, laborer, Johnsonsburg; Gray George A., carpenter, Johnsonsburg; Gunnip Geo., wheelwright, Marksboro; Gunnip John, cabinetmaker, Marksboro.

Hazen Nathan K., gentleman, Marksboro; Howell George, laborer, Marksboro; Howell Harrison, laborer, Marksboro; Harris George, Marksboro; Huff Ralph, Marksboro; Heater George, laborer, Marksboro; Howell Vancleve, Marksboro; Hauke Geo. W., Johnsonsburg; Hauke William, justice of peace, Johnsonsburg; Henry Watson V., Johnsonsburg; Howell Levi J., miller, Hope; Hoit Henry, miller, Hope; Howell Jonah, Hope; Hixson Levi, Hope; Hendershot Jeremiah, laborer, Hope; Hart John W., Johnsonsburg; Hart Jos. W., Johnsonsburg; Harris C. O., Johnsonsburg; Hibbler Albert, Johnsonsburg; Hall John, Johnsonsburg; Hibler George, Johnsonsburg; Howell Isaac, Johnsonsburg; Howell Levi, Johnsonsburg; Huff Charles, Marksboro; Harden Samuel, miller, Johnsonsburg; Harden Elbridge, merchant, Johnsonsburg; Hazen Nathan, gentleman, Johnsonsburg; Haggerty Wm., fruit grower, Paulina; Hendershot Ira, Marksboro; Howell Frank, clerk, Marksboro.

Jennings Soloman, Marksboro; Jennings Rufus, Marksboro; Jennings Fred F., constable, Marksboro; Johnson Mrs. Maria, householder, Marksboro.

Kinney Aaron, Marksboro; Kishpaugh Lewis, Johnsonsburg; Kishpaugh James, Johnsonsburg; Kishpaugh Seron, Johnsonsburg; Kerr Ira, Marksboro; Kerr William, Marksboro; Kerr Nathan, Marksboro; Kerr George P., Marksboro; Kerr Isaac R., Marksboro; Kerr Clinton, Marksboro; Kishpaugh Miss Alueda, Paulina; Kettle Levi, Johnsonsburg; Kerr John, Johnsonsburg; Kise Charles, Johnsonsburg; Kerr Samuel, Marksboro; Kise Jonas, Marksboro.

FRELINGHUYSEN DIRECTORY.

Lanning Isaiah, Marksboro; Lewis John P., gentleman, Marksboro; Lanning Milton R., tax collector, Marksboro; Lanning Cyrus, barber, Marksboro; LaHommidieu Job S., harnessmaker, Marksboro; Lanterman Wm. L. Jr., clerk, Marksboro; Luce Aaron, Marksboro; Luce Joseph, Johnsonsburg; Luce Henry, Paulina; Lundy George, Johnsonsburg; Longcore Theodore, Johnsonsburg; Longcore Alonzo, Johnsonsburg; Lemmons Jacob, gentleman, Johnsonsburg; Lewis Charles, Johnsonsburg; Lanning Levi, Johnsonsburg; Luce Joseph B., gentleman, Johnsonsburg; Losey Nathan, laborer, Johnsonsburg; Lundy Jacob, Johnsonsburg.

Mott Austin P., laborer, Marksboro; Mingle John, gentleman, Marksboro; Mayberry John C., postmaster and merchant, Marksboro; Mott George W., Marksboro; Mains Thomas, Johnsonsburg; Minion Isaac, carpenter, Johnsonsburg; Mitchell T., cheesemaker, Marksboro; Mushback Miss Saville, householder, Johnsonsburg; Mushback Miss Mary, householder, Johnsonburg; Miller David, blacksmith, Johnsonsburg; Miller John, laborer, Johnsonsburg; Miller William, laborer, Johnsonsburg; McClane William, gentleman, Johnsonsburg.

O'Brien Edward, blacksmith, Johnsonsburg.

Potter Allanson. K., cheesemaker, Marksboro; Potter Wesley, cheesemaker, Marksboro; Potter & Co., proprietors creamery, Marksboro.

Ryman David, assessor and shoemaker, Johnsonsburg; Ryman John, blacksmith, Marksboro; Rice Edward, strawberry grower, Marksboro; Ribble Charles, miller, Hope; Ramsey Edward, farmer, Johnsonsburg; Ramsey Stewart, farmer, Johnsonsburg; Rorback Frederick, physician, Johnsonsburg; Rose George, blacksmith, Johnsonsburg.

Strayley Freeman, Johnsonsburg; Savercool John, laborer, Marksboro; Savercool William, Marksboro; Savercool Lewis, Marksboro; Savercool Frederick, Marksboro; Savercool Fred., Johnsonsburg; Swisher J. W., cheesemaker, Marksboro; Shuster Charles, carpenter, Marksboro; Shuster Jacob, Paulina; Sullivan Lester, laborer, Marksboro; Stout Joseph, Marksboro; Stout Frank, Marksboro; Shaver John, Johnsonsburg; Shaver William, Johnsonsburg; Smith George, Paulina; Smith John, Paulina; Smith Jacob, laborer, Paulina; Smith Marshall R., Marksboro; Sharp Ozias, Hope; Stickles Price, Johnsonsburg; Stickles John, Johnsonsburg; Strickles Isaac, Johnsonsburg; Strayley Peter C., carpenter, Johnsonsburg; Sharp Joseph, Marksboro; Stillville John, Marksboro; Sidner Walter, laborer, Johnsonsburg; Stockbower Abram, gentleman, Johnsonsburg; Stillwell Isaac, gentleman, Johnssnsburg; Saveroool Elmer, Marksboro; Saverool Theodore, Johnsonsburg.

Titus Robert B., laborer, Hope; Tillman John, blacksmith, Johnsonsburg.

Vanhorn Jacob C., Marksboro; Vanhorn Wm. S. Jr., merchant, Marksboro; Vanhorn Wm. S. Sen., gentleman, Johnsonsburg; Vanhorn George, merchant, Johnsonsburg; Vought Wm., Marksboro; Vought Levi L., Marksboro; Vought Miss Harriet.

LAUBACH'S, Easton, Pa. SPECIAL ATTENTION TO SILKS AND DRESS GOODS. NEW GOODS DAILY.

householder, Marksboro; Vought Miss Kate, householder, Marksboro; Vought Miss Margaret, householder, Marksboro; Vliet Daniel, Hope; Vanauken Cole, Johnsonsburg; Vanhorn Edward M., Johnsonsburg; VanCamp James V., Paulina; VanCamp John, Paulina; VanCamp Aaron, Paulina; VanCamp Harvey Paulina; Vasbinder John, Johnsonsburg; Vasbinder Elwood, Johnsonsburg; Vasbinder N. Davison, Johnsonsburg; Vanvoy Joseph, wheelwright, Johnsonsburg; Voss Miss Electa, householder, Johnsonsburg; Vannes Peter, gentleman, Johnsonsburg.

Wildrick Edward, railroader, Marksboro; Wildrick Albert, Marksboro; Wildrick Ira, laborer, Hope; Wildrick Mark, laborer; Hope; Ward Nathan, carpenter, Johnsonsburg; Ward Andrew, housepainter, Johnsonsburg; Waterfield Thomas John, Johnsonsburg; Wilson George, Johnsonsburg; Westbrook Kelly, Johnsonsburg; Westbrook Isaac, Johnsonsburg; Westbrook Charles, Johnsonsburg; Westbrook John, Johnsonsburg; Wintermute Miss Mercy, householder, Johnsonsburg; Willet Isaac, gentleman, Johnsonsburg; Willet Thompson, gentleman, Johnsonsburg, Johnsonsburg.

Youmans Esick, Johnsonsburg.

FRANKLIN TOWNSHIP.

THIS township, though not among the latest settled in the county, can make but little claim to antiquity, being one of the townships that was organized in 1839.

The act which erected Franklin an independant township was passed Feb. 15, 1839, and is as follows :

"*Be it enacted* by the Council and General Assembly of this State and it is hereby enacted by the authority of the same, That all that part of the townships of Greenwich, Oxford and Mansfield, lying within the descriptions and boundaries following—to wit: Beginning at a point in the centre of the Musconetcong creek, half a mile above the Bloomsbury bridge; thence to a white oak tree on the north bank of Merrel's brook, one mile and a quarter above its junction with the Morris turnpike; thence to a point where the Brass Castle stream crosses the Oxford and Mansfield township line; thence to the point where the bridge crosses the Musconetcong creek, near the house of William Runkle; thence down the middle of said stream to the place of beginning—shall be and hereby is set off from the township of Greenwich, Oxford and Mansfield, in the county of Warren, and made a separate township, to be called and known by the name of the 'township of Franklin."

"*And be it enacted*, That the inhabitants of the township of Franklin shall hold their first annual township meeting at the inn now occupied by Benjamin C. McCullough, in the village of Broadway, in the said township of Franklin, on the day appointed by law for holding the annual township meetings in other townships in the county of Warren."

Franklin is bounded on the northeast by Washington township; on the southeast by the township of Bethlehem in Hunterdon county ; on the northwest by Harmony, and on the southwest by Greenwhich.

The Musconetcong river runs along its entire eastern border, separating it from Hunterdon county, and the Pohatcong mountains traverse its entire extent from the northeast to southwest.

It embraces an area of 4½ miles square, or 12,621 acres, most of which is tillable land. It has a population of about sixteen hundred

The Morris and Essex division of the Delaware, Lackawanna and Western railroad passes through the township. There is a station at Broadway. The Central Railroad of New Jersey has a station at Asbury, in the eastern part of the township, near the Hunterdon county line. The Morris Canal traverses the northern portion of the township.

The soil of the township is principally clay, with a mixture of gravel. Scarcely any sand is found within its borders. In the southern portion there is a ridge of slate about one and a half miles in extent. The soil is fertile and well adapted to the raising of most grains.

The grain in Franklin township is usually good, large and prolific crops being annually gathered. The surface of the township is undulating, exhibiting to the traveler alternate elevations and depressions.

Franklin township has three villages within its limits, viz: Asbury, Broadway and New Village. Asbury derived its name from Bishop Asbury, who in 1800 laid the corner stone of the Methodist Episcopal Church. It was known previously as Hall's Mill. The church that was erected in 1800 was simple in construction, and but 28x30 feet in dimensions. A new building was erected in 1842, and dedicated during December of that year. The Bloomsbury church was connected with the Asbury charge until 1858, when it became a separate organization.

The First Presbyterian Church of Asbury was erected and dedicated to God Sept. 23, 1869. It is a neat brick structure, capable of seating 400 persons. It was built at a cost of about $18,000 and is free from debt. Broadway is a quiet little hamlet containing two stores, a hotel, a school house, and a Methodist Episcopal Church. The church edifice was erected in 1842. New Village, located upon the Morris Canal, is a small collection of houses, with but little pretensions to business enterprise. There are six school districts in the township, and 391 scholars.

—GO TO—
J. T. BOWERS,
FOR YOUR
Fine Boots and Shoes
Washington Ave.,   WASHINGTON, N. J.

The Washington Review,
The Largest, Cheapest and Best Paper in Warren county. $1.00 a Year.

WARREN COUNTY DRUG STORE.

Township Directory.

All whose vocation is not mentioned are farmers.

Allshouse Wm., New Village; Apgar James G., Bloomsbury; Apgar Charles, Bloomsbury; Andros Wm., laborer, New Village; Albright Geo. P., school teacher, Bloomsbury; Axford John C., Broadway.

Bowman John L., Broadway; Bowers M. B., merchant, Broadway; Baylor John S., Broadway; Bowman N. L., Broadway; Brink John C., Broadway; Bodine Henry, Broadway; Beers John, New Village; Beers Elijah, New Village; Berry William, retired, Asbury; Berry Harvey, laborer, Asbury; Bodine Robert, New Village; Butler David, Broadway; Burd David, Montana; Burd Philip, Montana; Beers David, Asbury; Baylor Wm. A., Broadway; Britton John V., Asbury; Baylor James B., laborer, Asbury; Boaz William, gardener, Asbury; Bowers James S., Asbury; Bennett Isaac, retired, Asbury; Biglow Henry M.

LAUBACH'S EASTON, PA. CLOAKS and WRAPS of every description. **Our Own Manufacture.**

merchant, Asbury; Burd Christopher, Broadway; Bryan C. H., Broadway; Baylor Samuel, Broadway; Baylor Geo. F., Broadway; Bowman David, railroad ticket agent, Broadway; Baylor Geo. W., laborer, Broadway; Butler Henry E., merchant, Broadway; Brittan Wm., laborer, Broadway; Brittan Stewart, Broadway; Bowers J. C. Broadway.

Carling Wm., hotel-keeper, New Village; Crisman Levi, miller, Stewartsville; Conkling William H.,

PROF. JAMES L. ROSENBERY,
WASHINGTON, N. J.

Gives instructions in music on Piano or Organ. Pupils attended at their own residence, or at his home. Long and successful experience. Terms moderate.

Broadway; Cruts John, laborer, Broadway; Cruts William, laborer, Broadway; Cline John W., New Village; Cline Holloway H., New Village; Cook Geo. B., boatman, New Village; Cook Sylvanus, broom maker, New Village; Creveling E. N. L., Asbury;

ANDREWS & NOLF, The CORRECT Place to Buy SILKS and MOURNING GOODS, 205 NORTHAMPTON ST., EASTON, PA

H. M. NORTON, WHOLESALE AND RETAIL DEALER IN HARDWARE, STOVES, HEATERS AND RANGES.

352 FRANKLIN DIRECTORY.

Creveling, J. R. C., resident, Asbury; Cruts, Reuben H., laborer, Broadway; Curlis, Ziba H., bartender, Asbury; Cummins, John W., Asbury; Carling, Jos., wheelwright, Asbury; Chamberlain, Walter, clergyman, Asbury; Compton, Johnston, Asbury; Compton, Mahlon, Asbury; Cougle, Lewis C., teacher, Broadway; Creveling, George, laborer, Asbury; Carpenter, Chas. R., retired gentleman, Asbury; Cook, Philip, laborer, Broadway; Cushman, Samuel S., New Village; Creveling, P. G., physician, Broadway; Cruts, John D., laborer, Montana; Conover, Jacob, New Village; Conover, John B. New Village; Conover, James M., New Village; Creveling, Isaac C., Asbury; Cowell, Benjamin, laborer, Asbury; Cowell, Wm., Broadway; Carhart, Samuel, Stewartsville; Carhart, Elmer E., Stewartsville.

Ditmer, Christopher, New Village; Drake, Elmer E. Broadway; Dalrymple, John M., New Village; Dalrymple, Peter, New Village; Dugan, James, boatman, Broadway; Ditmer, Frederick, shoemaker, New

LAUBACH'S, Easton, Pa. THE LAREST DRY GOODS AND CARPET HOUSE. BARGAINS ALWAYS.

Village; Ditmer, James, New Village; Deremer, Jas. P., carpenter, New Village; Daly, James, boatman, New Village; Duckworth, Gordon E., laborer, Asbury; Deremer, Abram, laborer, New Village; Dehart, Isaac H., drover, Asbury; Dehart, Isaac, drover, Asbury; Dalrymple, Thos. J., blacksmith, Asbury; Deremer, Philip, laborer, Broadway; Dagan, W., boatman, Broadway; Davis, Wm. Stewartsville; Davis, Geo. A. Stewartsville.

THATCHER & WANDLING,
Wholesale and Retail Dealers in
FINE GROCERIES AND PROVISIONS,
Arcade building, opposite P. O.   **WASHINGTON, N. J.**
We make a specialty of fine Teas and Coffees, and if you can be pleased anywhere in Washington on these articles, we can do it. All kinds of fruit in season. Produce sent anywhere else, as we will not be undersold. Call on us.

Every John, Broadway; Emery William, drover, Asbury; Emory John, laborer, Asbury; Egbert Richmond, New Village.

Fitts Andrew, Asbury; Frey Geo., New Village; Fox Mahlon, Valley; Fox Peter, Valley; Fox Lewis,

LUBRICATING OILS of all kinds at **WADE BROS.'**

Mammoth Bazaar.

Creveling & Co., dealers in dry goods, groceries, hardware, boots and shoes, hats and caps, oils and paints, stoves and ranges, carpets, oil cloths, rugs, tinware, gents underwear and neckwear,

Clothing and Lumber,

And all kinds of building material, crockery, glassware, wall paper, wood and willowware, trunks, silverware, clocks and watches, jewelry, cloaks, stationery, carriages, sole leather, eye glasses, lamps, chimneys, medicines, perfumes, and in fact everything needful for man or beast.

Special attention is called to their **TAILORING, MILLINERY, DRESS MAKING, AND TIN DEPARTMENTS.**

Building nearly 200 feet deep; four floors. Come and see what we have for sale.

Creveling & Co.,
Washington, N. J.

H. M. NORTON WHOLESALE AND RETAIL DEALER IN HARDWARE, STOVES HEATERS AND RANGES.

FRANKLIN TOWNSHIP

drover, Asbury; Francis Alex., laborer, New Village; Fitts Daniel, Broadway.

Gardner George, locktender, Stewartsville; Graner John, mail carrier, New Village; Gale Alfred, physician, Asbury; Groff Sylvester, laborer, Broadway.

Hunt John, laborer, New Village; Hunt John W., laborer, New Village; Hazard Edward, Asbury; Hulshizer Wm. S., Bloomsbury; Hulshizer Eugene, Bloomsbury; Hummer Andrew, laborer, New Village; Hulshizer Wm. K., Asbury; Harley Wm. C., laborer, Asbury; Hiner George, Asbury; Hevener Henry K., saloon keeper, Asbury; Hulshizer Wm. K., Asbury; Hoagland John, hotel keeper, Asbury; Hazard Chas., farmer and drover, Asbury; Hoffman Geo W., Asbury; Hulshizer Thomas L., Asbury; Hoffman J. M., miller, Asbury; Hummer John C., harnessmaker, Broadway; Housel Jacob S., laborer, Broadway; Hummer Mahlon Oscar, laborer, Broadway; Hull Isaac P., blacksmith, Broadway; Hummer Mahlon, Broadway; Hoffman Wm., Asbury; Hevener Wm.,

LAUBACH'S, Easton, Pa. Largest stock of CARPETS, lowest prices. Best attention always.

butcher, Asbury; Hixon Andrew C., Broadway; Hiner Wm., Asbury; Hiner Philip, Asbury; Hixon Andrew, Broadway; Housel John Y., laborer, Broadway; Hoff Aaron, laborer, Stewartsville; Hoff Geo., laborer, Stewartsville; Hawk Joseph H., laborer, Stewartsville; Hazlett George M., clergyman, Asbury; Hull Joseph S., New Village.

Inscho, Wm. F. laborer, Asbury; Inscho, James, shoemaker, Broadway; Inscho, John, laborer, Broadway; Inscho, Wm., laborer, Broadway.

TO BUYERS OF FURNITURE.
The proprietor of the long-established Pittenger Stand on Washington Ave., below the St. Cloud Hotel, begs leave to call your attention to his New Stock of Furniture and Material. Buys at lowest cash prices, runs business at small expense, thus giving every advantage to the purchaser. Sole agent for the best woven wire bed in the market. Looking Glasses, Upholstered Patent Carpet Rockers, etc., etc. Repairing, Upholstering, and caning chairs, neatly done. Goods delivered at reasonable distances. DANIEL PITTENGER.
Washington, New Jersey.

Johnson, Jacob A. carpenter, Asbury; Johnston, Mahlon, wheelwright, Asbury.

Kries, Samuel, Montana; Kinney, Wm., New Village; Kirkwood, Thomas J., boatman, Broadway;

SHIELDS' Compound Syrup of Wild Cherry with Hypophosites of Lime and Soda. Sure cure for coughs, croup, etc.

HOUSEFURNISHING GOODS GENERALLY. **H. M. NORTON'S, Easton, Pa.**
The BEST GOODS for the LEAST MONEY at

FRANKLIN TOWNSHIP.

Kinney, Jacob, New Village; Kinney, Albert, New Village; Kinney, Daniel, New Village; Kinney, Jacob Jr., New Village; Kinney, Jesse, Asbury; Kishling, Henry, Asbury; Krinle, Peter, Asbury; Keefe, Frank, shoemaker, Asbury; Kinney Tunis, boatman, Broadway; Kinney, James C., laborer, New Village; Kinney, Stewart A., laborer, New Village.

Low, John, boatman, New Village; Locklin, John O., New Village; Lewis, Jos. B., laborer, Broadway; Lomerson, James, Broadway; Lightcap, L. C. undertaker, Asbury; Lewis, Peter, boatman, Broadway; Lockwood, R. B., clergyman, Broadway; Lewis C., laborer, Broadway; Lewis, Josiah, boatman, Broadway; Lomerson, Wm. M. Broadway; Lomerson, Jas., Asbury.

Metler, L. L., New Village; McIllroy, James, laborer, New Village; Myers, Wm. B., New Village; Maguire, Peter, laborer, Broadway; Maguire, Frank, laborer, Broadway; Mullen, Wm. boatman, Broadway; McIllroy, John P., churn maker, New Village;

LAUBACH'S, Easton, Pa. THE LAREST DRY GOODS AND CARPET HOUSE. BARGAINS ALWAYS.

Mason, Wm. A., laborer, Broadway; Myers, William, New Village; Muchler, John, canal overseer, Broadway; Magee, Geo. F., boatman, Broadway; Muchmore, David B., merchant, Broadway; Myers, Dan'l, laborer, Broadway; Moore, John, Asbury; Moore, Casper, Asbury; Moore, Geo., Asbury; Muchler, W. R. Asbury; Mulligan, Alex., laborer, Asbury; McKinney, John, Broadway.

WM. A. STRYKER,
Civil and Criminal Law Practitioner.
Notary Public. Master in Chancery.
Washington Ave. **WASHINGTON, N. J.**

NewKirk, Henry C., merchant, Broadway; Nelson, John, laborer, Broadway; Nelson, Simon, laborer, Broadway.

Osmun, Samuel, New Village; Osmun, John D., Asbury; Osmun, Frank H., retired, Asbury; Osborn, Archibald, drover, Asbury; Osmun, Peter, Asbury;

ANDREWS & NOLF, 205 Northampton St., Easton, Pa. Sell the best Black and Colored Silks. Guaranteed.

H. M. NORTON, WHOLESALE AND RETAIL DEALER IN HARDWARE, STOVES HEATERS AND RANGES.

356 FRANKLIN TOWNSHIP.

Osmun, Geo. C., Asbury; Osmun, John, Asbury; Oberly, John F., Asbury; Osmun, Daniel, Asbury.

Pursell, Wm., New Village; Pinkner, Andrew, laborer, Broadway; Prower, G., laborer, New Village; Prower, Elmer, laborer, New Village; Proctor, Chas., laborer, Asbury; Parker, Stewart, Bloomsbury; Petyt, Jeremiah, New Village; Petty, James, New Village; Petty, John, New Village; Purcell, David, New Village; Parker, Jos. A., Broadway.

Rush Abram, New Village; Rush James D., New Village; Rush Asa K., Montana; Rinehart John R., Montana; Reed Jeremiah, laborer, New Village; Richey Samuel S., Asbury; Richey Robert K., retired merchant, Asbury; Rodenbaugh John, retired farmer, Asbury; Richey Chas. W., citizen, Asbury; Riddle David C., carpenter, Broadway; Rush Jacob, laborer, Rymond A. J., harnessmaker, Broadway; Rodenbaugh Lee, Asbury; Rodenbaugh Geo., Asbury; Ranch William, laborer, Asbury; Riddle Johnston F., Asbury.

LAUBACH'S EASTON, PA. Largest Store, Largest Assortments, and One Price to All

Schooley Albert, Stewartsville; Smith James B., drover, Asbury; Smith Reuben, laborer, New Village; Sickle Samuel, wheelwright, New Village; Snyder Philip, laborer, Broadway; Sebold Gilbert B., laborer, Asbury; Snyder Wm. L., dealer, Broadway; Slack Chas. A., Bloomsbury; Spencer John, laborer, Asbury; Stoff Joseph, Bloomsbury; Smith Mathias, resident, New Village; Snyder Andrew, hack driver

F. A. BOWLBY & BRO,
CLOTHIERS AND GENT'S FURNISHERS,
Washington, New Jersey.
Bargains in Boy's and Children's, as well as Men's and Youths' Clothing. The latest styles of Hats, etc., always in stock. The latest novelties in Neckwear. Sell as cheap as you can buy anywhere. We won't be undersold.

and mail carrier, Asbury; Slater W. E., dealer in agricultural implements, Asbury; Smith Wm. C., driver, Asbury; Smith Theodore J., drover, Asbury; Smith James, blacksmith, New Village; Smith Lewis B., drover, Asbury; Shipman James, Asbury; Shrope Christopher, retired farmer, Asbury; Simeton W.

ALL KINDS OF HARDWARE at Wade Bros., Hackettstown, N. J.

HOUSEFURNISHING GOODS GENERALLY
The BEST GOODS for the LEAST MONEY at **H. M. NORTON'S, Easton, Pa.**

FRANKLIN TOWNSHIP.

M., Asbury; Snyder Jasper, Broadway; Scadden Andrew, laborer, Asbury; Sigler Peter H., Asbury; Stout Samuel S., drummer, Asbury; Stout James, gentleman, Broadway; Snyder William, laborer, Broadway; Snyder William, peddler, Broadway; Snyder Edward, laborer, Broadway; Strunk Frank, laborer, Broadway; Stocker Geo., miller, Broadway, Snyder Samuel, laborer, Broadway; Snyder Chas., Broadway; Snyder Geo., Broadway; Sickle Peter, Washington; Smith Franklin P., Broadway; Stutes Aaron H., clerk, Broadway; Snyder John H., Broadway; Shurts Wm., Asbury; Shurts John, Asbury; Shipman Wm. W., Broadway; Shipman James, Asbury; Shipman Abraham, Broadway; Shipman Wm., Jr., Broadway; Silmon John, blacksmith, New Village; Smith Leonard, New Village; Schooley James, Stewartsville; Smith Isaac C., Asbury; Smith John C., Asbury; Shaw Job J., resident, Asbury; Shaw Frank W., clerk, Asbury.

LAUBACH'S EASTON, PA. Largest Store, Largest Assortments, and One Price to All

Thatcher Stephen, laborer, New Village; Thatcher Thomas T., merchant, New Village; Thompson Wm. H., drummer, Asbury; Tichelor Thomas, Asbury; Thatcher Geo., Stewartsville; Terriberry A. M., merchant, Asbury.

Vliet James, surveyor, New Village; Vliet Garret L., Valley Postoffice; Vanderbilt Franklin B., laborer, Asbury; Vliet D. L., drover, Asbury; Vannatta, Geo., New Village; Vanderbilt, J. B., laborer,

HOFF'S POSITIVE CURE

For **Drunkeness**. Destroys all desire for Strong Drink, saves thousands of Dollars, is tasteless in Tea or Coffee. Try it and be convinced. Forwarded free by mail to all parts of the United States. Enclose One Dollar. Address

DR. J. P. HOFF,
131 Northampton Street,   EASTON, PA.
Pure Drugs and Medicines, Chemicals, Paints, etc., always in Stock.

Asbury; Vanderbilt, W. S., teamster, Asbury; Vanderbilt, Peter, laborer, Asbury; Vliet, Wm. assessor, Asbury; Vliet, Jacob M., Asbury; Voorhees, C. E., Asbury; Vliet, David V., Stewartsville; Vliet, Wm. M., laborer, Stewartsville; Vliet, Marshall, New Village.

ANDREWS & NOLF, 205 Northampton St., Easton, Pa. Sell the best Black and Colored Silks. Guaranteed.

H. M. NORTON, WHOLESALE AND RETAIL DEALER IN Hardware, Stoves and Housefurnishing

358 FRANKLIN TOWNSHIP.

Woodruff, Wm., laborer, New Village; Wolverton, Moses, Broadway; Weller, Peter, B., Broadway; Winters, Daniel L., laborer, New Village; Willever, John P., laborer, New Village; Willever, Joseph A., Asbury; Willever, Peter, New Village; Willever, Irwin, Broadway; Willever, John J., Asbury; Willever, John S., laborer, Asbury; Willever, Theodore, Asbury; Willever, John A., retired, Asbury; Willever, Daniel, mason, Broadway; Willever, Joseph, hotel keeper, Broadway; Warne, Elijah, Asbury; Warman, Thomas, Broadway; Warman, Samuel, laborer, Broadway; Warne, Adam G., Broadway; Weller, Garner, New Village; Warman, Simon, Stewartsville; Warman, John C., Stewartsville; Warman Geo., Stewartsville; Warman, Peter, Stewartsville; Warman, Chas. F., Stewartsville; Warman, Samuel S., Stewartsville; Welsh, S. A., physician, Asbury; Warne, Nichodemus, Broadway; Wise, Wm., laborer, Stewartsville; Williamson, C. M., Valley; Williamson, Daniel, Valley; Wolverton, Isaac, Asbury;

LAUBACH'S, Easton, Pa. SPECIAL ATTENTION TO SILKS AND DRESS GOODS. NEW GOODS DAILY.

Wolverton, John C., Broadway; Wolverton, W., speculator, Broadway; Wyckoff, Martin, lawyer, Asbury; Watson, Wm. H., merchant, Asbury; Weller, Jos.,

J. M. BUTLER,
Manufacturer and Wholesale and Retail Dealer in
Fine Havana and Domestic Cigars,
CHEWING AND SMOKING TOBACCO,
JOBBER IN FINE CUT,
A Fine Line of Meerschaum and Briar Pipes and Smokers' Articles.
No. 22 Union Square.   Under Lee House.
PHILLIPSBURG, N. J.

Broadway; Woodruff, Jos. J., laborer, Broadway; Weller, Benjamin, Broadway; Wydner, Milton, New Village.

SHIELDS' INFALLIBLE **Dyspeptic Remedy**, A sure cure for Dyspepsia, Sick or Nervous Headache. Guaranteed.

GREENWICH TOWNSHIP.

GREENWICH township was originally one of the four civil divisions of Sussex county, and was until very recently the most southerly of the township of Warren. When first formed it comprised a vast extent of territory, but has been reduced from time to time until at present it is comparatively small, having a population of less than 1,200.

Greenwich is bounded on the north by Lopatcong, east by Franklin, south by Hunterdon county and Pohatcong, west by Pohatcong.

The township is crossed by the Morris & Essex Railroad, and the Morris Canal. The Lehigh Valley Railroad also traverses the western portion. The surface of Greenwich is undulating, presenting a great variety of scenery, portions of which are very beautiful. The soil is generally fertile, much of it being a combination of limestone clay, and sand. Clay is mostly found in the central portion, with but little sand interspersed. This is the most productive section of the township. The principal occupation is farming, though mining interests have begun to spring up in this portion of the county. The several lime-kilns, located here and there, add another item to the industries of the township. The fine water-power facilities have given rise to manufacturing and milling interests in various portions of Greenwich. One of the largest flour and feed mills of the county is located at Cooksville, about one mile from Stewartsville.

Perhaps the most interesting evidence of the antiquity of this township is the ancient burial place connected with the Greenwich Presbyterian Church, in which lie the remains of many settlers who came hither prior to the war of the Revolution. Indeed it is a relic of Revolutionary times. The visitor who gazes upon the plain, ancient slabs that mark the final resting place of so many of our country's early settlers, cannot refrain from calling up in his imagination the dark days of old, and in his vision there appeared many a manly and heroic form whose sturdy, daring and faithful adherence to the principals of duty, have rendered Greenwich the happy dwelling place of hundreds, and whose ashes now render sacred Greenwich cemetery. There are in the township some other burial places of less than ancient date.

Stewartsville is the chief town of Greenwich. It has a population of nearly (600) six hundred or about one-half the population of the entire township. There are in Stewartsville at present three stores, two hotels, of which one is a temperance house, one tin shop, one wheelwright and blacksmith shop, two carpenter shops, two undertakers, one tailor shop, two justices of the peace, two physicians and two ministers. A number of retired farmers have made this their place of residence. Stewartsville has a public school of two departments, with a total enrollment of over 150 pupils, two churches in good condition, Presbyterian and Lutheran, and a depot of the Morris & Essex Railroad, at which a good grain and coal trade is carried on. Besides the churches already mentioned, is the M. E. Church of Pleasant Valley.

Kennedysville and Still Valley have each a public school, making the total number of schools in the township 3, with a total of 286 pupils.

G. C. Young, M. D.

Physician and Surgeon.

OFFICE AT RESIDENCE.

Stewartsville, N. J.

WARREN COUNTY DRUG STORE.

TOWNSHIP DIRECTORY.

All whose vocation is not mentioned are farmers.

Able John, laborer, Bloomsbury; Apgar D. M., Bloomsbury; Anderson Aaron, laborer, Stewartsville.

Beers Geo. P., Stewartsville; Berger Reuben, laborer, Stewartsville; Berger Hiram, lime burner, Stewartsville; Benwood Henry, laborer, Stewartsville; Bowers Chris., carpenter, Stewartsville; Barber J. K., gentleman, Stewartsville; Benward G. W., miller, Stewartsville; Boyer Sarah H., Stewartsville; Bigley Wm., laborer, Bloomsburg; Brotzman Reuben, Bloomsbury; Banker Elizabeth, widow, Stewartsville.

Cline Elizabeth D., householder, Stewartsville; Cline E. F., school teacher, Stewartsville; Cline Caleb, Stewartsville; Cline Michael, Stewartsville; Cline E. A., Stewartsville; Conover Leonard, laborer, Stewartsville; Carling Wm., laborer, Stewartsville; Cook P. C., Stewartsville; Cook James, laborer, Stewartsville;

LAUBACH'S EASTON, PA. CLOAKS and WRAPS of every description. **Our Own Manufacture.**

Cook Wm., agent, Stewartsville; Carling John B., laborer, Cooksville; Carling Peter, carpenter, Cooksville; Carling Thomas, shoemaker, Stewartsville; Cole George B., Cooksville; Cooper Henry, gentlemen, Stewartsville; Cyphers John H., huckster, Stewartsville; Carter C. S., Stewartsville; Carter J. W., Stewartsville; Creveling Wm. N., Bloomsbury; Creveling John W., lawyer, Bloomsbury; Creveling David, Bloomsbury.

Durling Wm., school teacher, Stewartsville; Dilts Jas. E., laborer, Stewartsville; Deremer Moses, laborer, Stewartsville; Dalrymple Thompson, laborer, Stewartsville; Dolan Thomas, laborer, Stewartsville; Depue Shrader, laborer, Stewartsville; Dehart Wm., laborer, Bloomsbury; Deemer Fred., laborer, Bloomsbury; Davis Daniel, Bloomsbury; Drake Clayton, Bloomsbury.

Eichline Levi, laborer, Bloomsbury; Ervin Peter, boatman, Stewartsville.

Fritts John, gentleman, Stewartsville; Frey Harry.

ANDREWS & NOLF, The CORRECT Place to Buy SILKS and MOURNING GOODS. 205 NORTHAMPTON ST. EASTON, PA

H. M. NORTON, *WHOLESALE AND RETAIL DEALER IN* **Hardware, Stoves and Housefurnishing.**

GREENWICH TOWNSHIP.

stone cutter, Stewartsville; **Frey Henry L. Tomb and Monumental Works,** Stewartsville; Furman Abe., laborer, Stewartsville; **Fulmer A. Jackson, Gen. Mdse.,** Stewartsville; Fritts, Wm. D., Bloomsbury.

Gaston Jacob, laborer, Cooksville; Garmer Wm., boatman, Cooksville; Godfry Harry A. Cooksville; Godfry Charles H., Stewartsville.

Hulshizer William F., plane tender, Stewartsville; Hulshizer Oscar, brakeman, Stewartsville; Hulshizer P. F., clerk, Stewartsville; Hulshizer Peter F., physician, Stewartsville; Hulshizer H. Furman, Stewartsville; Hulshizer Theodore, Stewartsville; Hulshizer A. carpenter, Stewartsville; Hulshizer John H., Stewartsville; Hulshizer James, Stewartsville; Hartung Philip C., Stewartsville; Hartung John, carpenter, Stewartsville; Hommadeine Jason, laborer, Stewartsville; Heller Lewis, laborer, Stewartsville; Heller John, laborer, Stewartsville; Heller Abe, laborer, Stewartsville; Heller Palmer, laborer, Stew-

LAUBACH'S, Easton, Pa. THE LARGEST DRY GOODS AND CARPET HOUSE. BARGAINS ALWAYS.

artsville; Heller John Jr., laborer, Stewartsville; Holden James M., miller, Stewartsville; Hartzell Simon, laborer, Stewartsville; Hance John, Stewartsville; Hance Abraham, Stewartsville; Hance Robert, music teacher, Stewartsville; Hance Philip, Bloomsbury; Hyndshaw John, Stewartsville; Hyndshaw Thomas, Stewartsville; Hyndshaw James, Stewartsville; Housel Henry, horse dealer, Bloomsbury; Heang Howard, Bloomsbury; Hess John, laborer, Stewartsville; Heil Levi, Stewartsville; Hamlen John H., Stewartsville; Hamlen George E., Stewartsville; Heigley Frank, laborer, Bloomsbury; Hyndshaw Elizabeth, widow, Stewartsville.

Insley George, Stewartsville; Inscho Theo. K., Bloomsbury; Inscho Charlotte, widow, Stewartsville. Johnson David, boatman, Cooksville.

Kinney Andrew P., carpenter, Stewartsville; Kinney John W., Stewartsville; Kase George W., Stewartsville; Kase A. R., agent, Stewartsville; Kase Theodore, laborer, Stewartsville; Kase Philip S., com-

RAED CAREFULLY Page 218

THE BEST GOODS FOR THE LEAST MONEY AT **NORTON'S Easton, Pa.**

GREENWICH TOWNSHIP. 363

mission merchant, Stewartsville; Kremer Charles, tinsmith, Stewartsville; Kinkle Henry, tanner, Stewartsville; Kinkle Henry, laborer, Stewartsville; Kennedy John F., Bloomsbury; Kennedy Theodore F., Bloomsbury; Kennedy R. H., Bloomsbury; Kennedy E. L. Mrs., widow, Bloomsbury; Kitchen Solomon W., Bloomsbury; Kinney Jacob Jr., carpenter, Stewartsville.

Loder William A., Stewartsville; Lambert Dewitt, laborer, Cooksville; Lantz Jessie, Stewartsville; Lantz John, Stewartsville; Lantz George, Stewartsville; Lantz Peter, Stewartsville; Lark Valentine, laborer, Stewartsville; Loudenberry Henry, laborer, Bloomsbury; Loudenberry David, Bloomsbury; Lamping John, carpenter, Stewartsville; Love James, carpenter, Stewartsville; Lanning John A., Bloomsbury; Lott A. H., laborer, Bloomsbury; Lake Jesse J., Bloomsbury; Long Thomas S. Rev., pastor of Greenwich Presbyterian Church, Bloomsbury; Low Mary, housekeeper, Stewartsville.

LAUBACH'S EASTON, PA. CLOAKS and WRAPS of every description. **Our Own Manufacture.**

Metz Arch C., Shimers; Metler Samuel B., inn keeper, Shimers; Metler Hadoran, Shimers; Metler Wilson, Shimers; Maxwell Amos S., Bloomsbury; Myers David, harness maker, Cooksville; Melick Charles, laborer, Stewartsville; Melick James, laborer, Stewartsville; Melick Abraham, laborer, Stewartsville; Melick John H. inn keeper, Stewartsville; Mullen J. R., laborer, Stewartsville; Miers Sebastin, laborer, Springtown; Mitchell Wm., laborer, Stewartsville; McFern B. M., stone mason, Stewartsville; Mills John, laborer, Bloomsbury; Mitchell Elmer, laborer, Stewartsville; Martin Rachael, temperance house, Stewartsville; Mongel Enos, carpenter, Stewartsville; **Martin Mrs. Joseph, Temperance Hotel and Boarding House**, Stewartsville.

Opdyke William, Cooksville; Oliver George, laborer, Stewartsville; Oberly Charles, Stewartsville; Oberly, Wm., Stewartsville; Oberly Owen, Stewartsville; Oberly Mrs. Anna, widow, Stewartsville

Price John S. carpenter, Stewartsville; Price Geo.

Andrews & Nolf, 205 Northampton St., Easton, Pa. The reliable HOUSE for Mourning Goods.

T., school teacher, Stewartsville; Paulus Chas., Stewartsville.

Ruple Jos. F., wheelwright, Shimers; Raub Barnet, Stewartsville; Rugg Charles H., laborer, Springtown; Rugg Arthur B., laborer, Springtown; Rush Wm. C., Springtown; Raisner Joshua, laborer, Stewartsville; Rush Wm. J., Stewartsville; Rush Caleb, Stewartsville; Rush Mary Ann, widow, Stewartsville; Rush Rachael, Stewartsville.

Stiff Andrew B., miller, Bloomsbury; Shipman Isaac, Bloomsbury; Shipman Wm., physician, Shimers; Shipman Sharps, Stewartsville; Shipman Peter, Stewartsville; Shipman Wm., Stewartsville; Sloyer Peter A., Stewartsvill ; Stone Robt. H., and John S., carpenters and undertakers, Stewartsville; Stone Charles, carpenter, Stewartsville; Stone Jacob J., blacksmith, Shimers; Stone Wm., carpenter, Stewartsville; Stone Benton, laborer, Stewartsville; Stone Henry H., merchant, Stewartsville; Shillinger George, merchant, Cooksville; Shillinger Jacob, mil

LAUBACH'S, Easton, Pa., Largest stock of CARPETS, lowest prices. Best attention always.

ler, Cooksville; Shillinger Samuel, Stewartsville; Shillinger Stewart, miller, Cooksville; Snyder Geo. S., laborer, Cooksville; Stewart Jesse, gentleman, Stewartsville; Stewart Thomas K., Justice of Peace, Stewartsville; Stock Fred., merchant, Stewartsville; Strader B. F., postmaster and clerk, Stewartsville; Stewart Isaac, physician, Bloomsbury; Stone Matilda, widow, Stewartsville; Sidders Henry, laborer, Springtown; Schooly Henry, laborer, Bloomsbury; Stocker G. R., blacksmith, Stewartsville; Severs A., Stewartsville; Smith John, Stewartsville; Smith W. J., Bloomsbury; Smith Robt. J, Bloomsbury; Smith Water G., Bloomsbury; Smith S. E. G., widow, Bloomsbury; Smith Chester, Bloomsbury; Scott Samuel, Esquire, Stewartsville; Shively J. P., Stewartsville; Shewser Wm., Bloomsbury; Strader Mary, widow, Stewartsville; Steck A. R., pastor Lutheran Church, Stewartsville; Thatcher John K., wheelwright, Shimers; Thatcher John, gentleman, Stewartsville; Thatcher Jesse, laborer, Stewartsville;

EMPIRE SOLID CAST STEEL SCISSORS AND SHEARS For Sale at **Wades' Hardware Store.**

HOUSEFURNISHING GOODS GENERALLY. The BEST GOODS for the LEAST MONEY at **H. M. NORTON'S, Easton, Pa.**

GREENWICH TOWNSHIP

Thompson Charles R., station agent, Stewartsville; Thompson John H., laborer, Stewartsville; Thompson Willard, station clerk, Stewartsville; Thompson Rev.

C. W. GARIS
Has the Largest and Finest Line of
PARLOR FURNITURE,
In the Lehigh Valley,
228 Northampton Street.   Below the Circle.

Easton, Pa.

Wm., pastor Presbyterian church Stewartsville; Thompson Annie, widow, Stewartsville.

Weider David, Shimers; Woodruff Peter C., brakeman, Stewartsville; Wallace Charles, laborer, Stewartsville; Warman James C., laborer, Cooksville;

LAUBACH'S EASTON, PA. Largest Store, Largest Assortments, and One Price to All

Warman David, laborer, Stewartsville; Whitesell Henry, Cooksville; Wolf Lemuel, lime burner, Cooksville; Wolf John, laborer, Cooksville; Wolf George, laborer, Cooksville; Weller Jane E., widow, Stewartsville; Weller Margaret, Stewartsville; Weller Daniel, butcher, Stewartsville; Weller Wm., laborer,

The Washington Review,
The Largest, Cheapest and Best Paper in Warren county. $1.00 a Year.

Stewartsville; Weller Wm., Stewartsville; Weller Charles, laborer, Stewartsville; Williamson Ingham, carpenter, Bloomsbury; Wilson John, Stewartsville.

Young G. C., physician and surgeon, Stewartsville; Young Andrew, carpenter, Cooksville.

ANDREWS & NOLF, 205 Northampton St., Easton, Pa. Sell the best Black and Colored Silks. Guaranteed.

HOPE TOWNSHIP.

HOPE is the central interior township of the county. Its name is derived from the pioneer Moravians, who settled here in 1769, and gave that name to the locality in which they settled which finally became the present village of Hope. This township was cut off from Oxford in 1839. Hope township is bounded on the north by Blairstown and Frelinghuysen on the northeast and east by Frelinghuysen and Independence; on the southeast and south by Mansfield and Oxford, and southwest and west by Oxford and Knowlton. The township contains 3,017 square miles or 19,309 acres of land; present population about 1,600.

The surface of Hope township is hilly and mountainous. The Jenny Jump mountain range crosses the township from northeast to southwest. Limestone knolls abound throughout the township. A great variety of scenery is presented in the township, portions of it being picturesque and beautiful. The soil along the valleys of the Pequest River and other streams is very fertile, while that upon the mountain sides is not commendable for its fertility. Green's Pond, a picnic and excursion resort of local fame, is a beautiful sheet of water located in the southwestern part of the township. It is one mile long, and from one half to three-quarters of a mile wide, and is said to be named from the first settler in the township.

Silver Lake, so called because of the clear silvery appearance of its surface, covers about 500 acres in the northeast corner of the township. There are a number of small streams in the township, among which are Beaver Brook, Honey Run and Muddy Brook. Upon these streams are numerous good mill sites, some of which are occupied.

North of the village of Hope, and along the Beaver Brook, are 557 acres of land called "Wet Meadow."

About one mile southwest of Hope is a deposit of marl, where it is said to be four feet thick, under from two to four feet of muck.

The first settler within the present limits of Hope township is supposed to be Samuel Green, who came from Long Island about the commencement of the French and Indian war. The exact place of his location is not positively known, though supposed to be either in the vicinity of Green's Pond or near what is now the village of Hope. Mr. Green was a deputy surveyor for the West Jersey proprietors, and was the owner of a large tract of land, embracing about the whole of the present township. Other settlers followed, among whom were Samson Howell, who settled at the foot of the Jenny Jump mountains built a saw mill, and supplied the Moravians with what lumber they required for their buildings at Hope. The Moravian brethren came here in 1769 from Bethlehem, Pa., and purchased of Samuel Green 1500 acres of land, for which they paid about $1 per acre. They founded the village of Hope; lived there for about 35 years, suffered pecuniary loss, and returned to Bethlehem in 1805 or 1806. The Moravian were a thoroughly honest class of people, but by relying too much on the honesty of those whom they dealt with, they suffered loss and were compelled to abandon their Hope enterprise.

The towns of Hope township are: Hope, the principal town of the township, was founded by the Moravians, or United Brethren, in 1769, and was for a short time the seat of justice for Warren county. It is located in the north central part of the township, being beautifully situated near the head waters of Beaver Brook, upon the banks of which it is built. It is an inland town, lying among the picturesque hills and surrounded by smiling valleys, and is a terminus of the old Hope and Elizabeth turnpike. It is 12 miles from the famous Water Gap, 16 from Newton, 9 from Belvidere, and about 6 each from Blairstown, Delaware Station, and Bridgeville, which are its nearest railroad stations. A stage, carrying the mail, runs daily to the last named place; also one from Hope to Warrington.

One of the peculiarities of the history of Hope, is the conversion of the old stone church of the Moravians into a hotel at present, and for several years passed occupied by H. W. Rundle, while on the site of the old Moravian tavern, stands the Christian church of to-day.

In the building which is now the Union Hotel, in the year 1824, were held the first courts for Warren county, and thus Hope became a rival of Belvidere when the question of a county seat was to be determined. Hope has the advantages of a very pleasant summer resort, and has a fair prospect of being thus patronized. The Union House is already accommodating a number of summer boarders.

Hope has at present two hotels, four general stores, one drug store, one hardware store, merchant tailor, harnessmaker, foundry and machine shop, wheelwright shop, blacksmith shop, shoe shop, furniture and undertaking establishment, meat market, saw mill, four churches, physicians, lawyer, a public and private school, and a grist mill; population, 250.

Mt. Herman, a neat little hamlet in the northwest corner of the township, has a church, school-house, store and postoffice.

Townsbury is situated in the southern part of the township, in the Pequest Valley and on the Lehigh and Hudson railroad and is the only point in the township having a railway station. It has a store, blacksmith shops, grist-mill, saw-mill and postoffice. Schools in township, 6 scholars. 863.

WARREN COUNTY DRUG STORE.

Township Directory.

All whose vocation is not mentioned are farmers.

Acher Mrs. Geo., freeholder, Hope; Acher Wm., Hope; Adams John L., peddler, Hope; Adams C., laborer, Danville; Albert Monas. Hope; Albert Amos, Danville; Albert John, Danville; Albert Jas., Danville; Albert Jacob, Hope; Albertson Gideon L., Hope; Albight J. J., laborer Danville; Allen Wm. P., miller, Hope; Almer Chas., Townsbury; Amadas Joseph, laborer, Townsbury; Ambusher Geo., lumberman, Townsbury; Anderson David, Buttzville; Angle Wilson, laborer, Hope; Angle John W., Townsbury; Appleman Grover, Buttzville; Aten Henry, foundryman, Hope; Ayers Simon A., Hope.

Babcock Jacob, Hope; Bailey Jacob, carpenter, Hope; Bailey Fletcher, carpenter, Hope; Bailey George, miner, Hope; Bartow Chas R., Hope; Bartow Johnson, Mt. Hermon; Bartow Jason, miller,

YOU CAN ALWAYS FIND WHAT YOU WANT AT LAUBACH'S, Easton, Pa.

Hope; Bartow Wesley, Mt. Hermon; Bartow Milton, Hope; Beatty Hon. Geo. H., Judge, Hope; Beatty Lewis C., State Prison official, Hope; Bennett John C., laborer, Hope; Bennett Fletcher, laborer, Hope; Bennett George, laborer, Hope; Bennett Elisha, laborer, Hope; Bergen Dr. E. J., physician, Hope; Bice Rev. Henry, minister, Hope; Bird Andrew, laborer, Danville; Bird Frederick, laborer, Danville; Bird George, laborer, Danville; Black John H., wheelwright, Hope; Blain Silas, laborer, Hope; Blain Jehile, laborer, Hope; Blain John, hostler, Danville; Bowers Wm. H., Hope; Brader Samuel, laborer, Hope; Brinkerhoff Isaac, Danville; Brown Albanus, Hope; Brown Peter, Hope; Burdge John, laborer Hope; **Bryan Charles**, Dealer in Blankets, Whips, Harness and Robes, Hope; Burdge Wm. S., laborer, Hope; Burdge Herman laborer Hope; Burdge U., laborer, Hope; Burdge Joseph, laborer, Hope; Burdge Amos S., laborer, Hope; Bushlock Martin,

LUBRICATING OILS 'of all kinds at WADE BROS.'

THE BEST GOODS FOR THE LEAST MONEY AT **NORTON'S Easton, Pa.**

HOPE TOWNSHIP.

laborer, Danville; Boyer Oscar, Bridgeville; Burdge Wm. W., laborer, Hope.

Christian A. L. Bro., Dealer in Stoves, Copper, Tin and Hardware, Hope; Case Jacob, laborer, Danville; Christian F. H., bl'ksmith Hope; Christian J. S., trucker, Hope; Christian George F., Hope; Christian Archibald, tinsmith, Hope; Christian Ambrose, tinsmith, Hope; Christian Geo. B., laborer, Hope; Clifford Franklin, miner, Danville; Colburn Wm., miner, Danville; Conner Geo., laborer, Townsbury; Cook John H., Hope; Cook Charles H., Hope; Cook Wm. S., Hope; Cook James J., Hope; Cook Geo. A., mechanic, Hope; Cook Leslie, Hope; Cook Chas. C., Hope; Cortwright Chas., laborer, Danville; Corwin Joseph, laborer, Townsbury; Congle Alfred, laborer, Danville; Cox Charles, laborer, Danville; Crisman Clark, Hope; Crisman James, laborer, Townsbury; Crusen Wm. A., undertaker, Hope; Crusen Jacob, laborer, Hope; Cummings John, Hope; Cummins Joseph, Danville; Cunningham Charles, blacksmith,

LAUBACH'S, Easton, Pa. SPECIAL ATTENTION TO SILKS AND DRESS GOODS, NEW GOODS DAILY.

Hope; Cunningham Jerome, blacksmith, Hope; Curlis John, Danville; Curlis James, Hope; Cyphers J. C., Hope; Cyphers Rodman, Hope; Cyphers Clark, Hope.

Damon Rev. Austin, minister, Hope; Dean Marshal, laborer, Townsbury; **Dean Wm.**, Confectioner, etc., Hope; Deats George, Hope; Deats David, laborer, Hope; Dell George, Hope; Dennis Jacob, laborer,

WILLIAM DEAN,

Confectioner and Dealer in Candies, Nuts and Fruits in their season. Ice Cream in Summer, Oysters in Winter.

HOPE. New Jersey.

Hope; Depue Geo., Mt. Hermon; Dill John, Hope; Dill George G., Hope; Dilley J. F., blacksmith, Danville; Drake James P., Hope; Drake Hezekiah, Hope; Drake Barnet S., Townsbury; Drake George, Townsbury.

ANDREWS & NOLF, Proprietors of the "DOWN TOWN" Dry Goods House, 205 Northampton Street, Easton, Pa.

H. M. NORTON, *WHOLESALE AND RETAIL DEALER IN* Hardware, Stoves and Housefurnishing.

HOPE TOWNSHIP.

Everett Epenetus, Hope; Everett Theodore, stage driver, Hope; Everett Irving, stage driver, Hope; Everett David, Hope.

Faulkner W. C., drover, Townsbury; Faulkner B. C., Hope; Fisher Samuel, Mt. Hermon; Fleming C., Danville; Fleming J. W. C., Danville; Fleming Albert, Danville; Fleming James F., Danville; Fleming Lewis, Danville; Fleming Wm. E., Danville; Flumerfelt John S., gentleman, Danville; Flumerfelt J. B., laborer, Danville; Flumerfelt Michael C., trucker, Danville; Flumerfelt Zachariah, Danville; Flumerfelt Charles, mechanic, Mt. Hermon; Flumerfelt J. C., Mt. Hermon; Flumerfelt John, carpenter, Mt. Hermon; Flumerfelt David B., Hope; France David C., laborer, Hope; Freese John, merchant, Hope; Freeman Clinton, laborer, Hope; Frome T. P., Justice of Peace, Townsbury; Fitch Miss Rosa, music teacher, Hope.

Gallager Terrence, laborer, Danville; Gallager Daniel, laborer, Hope; Garretson Asher, carpenter, Hope;

LAUBACH'S, Easton, Pa. THE LARGEST DRY GOODS AND CARPET HOUSE. BARGAINS ALWAYS.

Garretson Peter, laborer, Hope; Garretson Peter Jr., laborer, Townsbury; **Gibbs I. R.**, Veterinary Surgeon, Townsbury; **Gibbs Dr. A. L.**, Dealer in Drugs, Paints and Oils, Hope; Gibbs Silas, agent, Hope; Gibbs James M., Hope; Gibbs Edward P., trucker, Hope; Gibbs Isaac, laborer, Hope; Gibbs John, Hope; Gibbs Martin, Hope; Gibbs David V., teamster, Hope; Gibbs Prof. Charles, carpenter, Mt. Hermon; Gibbs Wm., stage driver, Townsbury; Goble David, laborer, Hope;

Israel R. Gibbs,
VETERINARY SURGEON.
All Diseases of Domestic Animals Scientifically treated.
HOPE, NEW JERSEY.

Green John Sr., freeholder, Townsbury; Green Dan., Gentleman, Townsbury; Green Wesley, laborer, Danville; Green Samuel, Danville; Green James A., laborer, Danville; Green Jeremiah, Danville; Green

THE BEST GOODS FOR THE LEAST MONEY AT **NORTON'S Easton, Pa.**

HOPE TOWNSHIP.

Richard, laborer, Danville; Green George, carpenter, Mt. Hermon; Green John Jr., laborer, Hope; Gorkey Henry, laborer, Danville; Grover Albert, butcher, Hope; Gouger John, Hope; Gould Edward, Townsbury; Gould Simon, laborer, Hope.

Hagarman Wm. P., Cooper, Hope; Hann Ira L., carpenter, Hope; Hann D. M., Hope; Hann Jacob, Danville; Harris John, Danville; Hartman Cornel, Hope; Hartung John R., Delaware; Hartung Alpheus, Delaware; Hendershot Jas. H., gentleman, Hope; Hendershot James P., Hope; Hendershot Abram V., Hope; Hildebrant Stewart B., Hope; Hildebrant A. D., Hope; Hildebrant Daniel J., Hope; Hildebrant Winfield, Hope; Hildebrant Isaiah B., Hope; Hildebrant George F., Hope; Hildebrant Smith J., Hope; **Hildebrant Jas. F.**, Auctioneer, Hope; Hibbler Andrew H., Hope; Hill Albert, Danville; Hill Thos., Danville; Hill Robert, Hope; Hiles Wm. J., Mt. Hermon; Hoit John B., Hope; Hoit Stewart B., Hope; Hoit Lewis, Hope; Hopkins Jacob, laborer,

LAUBACH'S EASTON, PA. CLOAKS and WRAPS of every description. **Our Own Manufacture.**

Hope; Hopkins Philip, laborer, Hope; Howell John H., gentleman, Hope; Howell Isaac L., Hope; Howell, Gideon G., landlord, Hope; Howell Edger C., Hope; Howel Millard F., Hope; Howell Edward A., clerk, Hope; Howell Garret C., Hope; Howell Chas. W., Hope; Howell Frank B., Hope; Howell Geo. B., Mt. Hermon; Howland Rev. E. O., clergyman, Mt. Hermon; Holland Michael, laborer, Danville; Holbach Andrew J., laborer, Danville; Huff Silas, laborer, Hope.

Ingersoll John B., Townsbury.

Jayne Philip, laborer, Hope; Jane Isaac, laborer, Hope.

Keg Lewis, laborer, Danville; Kelsey Abram W., Danville; Ketcham Thomas, laborer, Townsbury; Kerr W. A., teacher, Hope; Kishpaugh Abram F., Danville.

Lance Freman, Danville; Lanning Edward, Mt. Hermon; Lanning Amos E., Mt. Hermon; LaRue James, gentleman, Mt. Hermon; LaRue George, gen-

Andrews & Nolf, 205 Northampton St., Easton, Pa. The reliable HOUSE for Mourning Goods.

H. M. NORTON, *WHOLESALE AND RETAIL DEALER IN* **Hardware, Stoves and Housefurnishing**

tleman, Mt. Hermon; LaRue Jerry, gentleman, Hope; J. LaRue, laborer, Hope; Letson Jacob, mason, Mt. Hermon; Letson James F., Mt. Hermon; Locey Moses, laborer, Hope; Lozier Marshal, laborer, Townsbury; Loller Jefferson B., merchant, Mt. Hermon; Lusk Wm. laborer, Hope; Lusk Daniel, laborer, Hope; Lusk Wm. Jr., laborer Hope; Lusk Marcus, laborer, Hope.

Mains Theodore, laborer, Hope; Matlock Daniel P., Hope; Matlock George, Hope; Martenis Wm., Townsbury; McDavit Henry, painter, Hope; McCain James, Mt. Hermon; McElroy Anson, laborer, Hope; Miller Wm, C., butcher, Hope; Miller Dennis, Townsbury; Miller Isaac, Hope; Miller Dell, Hope; Merrill Lewis L., Hope; Merral Amos H., laborer, Hope; Merrill Dennis K., laborer, Townsbury; Mericle W., Hope; Moore Stephen, Townsbury; Moore Wm. A., Townsbury; Moore Wm. B., miller, Townsbury; Moore Daniel G., Townsbury; Moore Jesse, Townsbury; Morrison Benjamin, tailor, Hope; Morris George, Hope.

LAUBACH'S, Easton, Pa., Largest stock of CARPETS, lowest prices. Best attention always.

Naragarard Lewis, miner, Danville; Newman S. B., Hope; Newman Alvin, Mt. Hermon.

Osmun Joseph, Delaware; Osmun Otto, laborer, Hope; Ort Jesse, laborer, Danville.

JAMES F. HILDEBRANT,
Experienced Auctioneer

Is prepared to do all kinds of Vendue Crying. People wishing my services should see me before having bills printed.

HOPE, NEW JERSEY.

Parks John N., Hope; Parks Wm., Hope; Parks Samuel G., Townsbury; Parks Jos., Townsbury; Parks John, Townsbury; Parr Peter, laborer, Hope; Parr Isaac, laborer, Hope; Parr Wm., laborer, Hope; Parr John, laborer, Hope; Parsell Lewis, blacksmith, Townsbury; Parsell Herman L., miller, Townsbury; Peterson Hance, Danville; Petty Jacob M., general mdse., Townsbury; Pierson Joseph, Mt. Hermon; Poyer James K., laborer, Danville; Poyer Abraham,

EMPIRE SOLID CAST STEEL SCISSORS AND SHEARS For Sale at **Wades' Hardware Store.**

THE BEST GOODS FOR THE LEAST MONEY AT **NORTON'S, Easton, Pa**

HOPE TOWNSHIP.

laborer, Hope; Poyer Irving, laborer, Hope; Poyer Joseph, laborer, Hope; Poyer Caleb, laborer, Hope; Price Richard, laborer, Hope; Price Abram, laborer, Hope; Price Ziba, laborer, Hope; Price George, laborer, Danville.

Quick John, Townsbury; Quick George, Townsbury; Quick Jacob, Mt. Hermon.

Rader Aaron, laborer, Hope; Read John C., laborer, Mt. Hermon; Read Aaron, gentleman, Mt. Hermon; Read Samuel, Mt. Hermon; Read Isaac S., Hope; Read Saron W., Hope; Read Ira C., Hope; Read Jos. M., miller, Hope; Read Wm., Hope; Read Elias, Hope; Rice Benton, Hope; Robinson B. C., Hope; Roe James V., Hope; **Rundle H. W.,** Proprietor Union House, Hope; Runyan Nelson, Hope; Runyan John W., Hope.

Seals Lawrence, Hope; Seals Simon, clerk, Hope; Shultz Daniel, Danville; Shultz Peter, Delaware; Siney Joseph, Hope; Ships Lewis, laborer, Hope; Smith Philip, laborer, Hope; Smith Wm. V., laborer,

LAUBACH'S EASTON, PA. Largest Store, Largest Assortments, and One Price to All

Hope; Smith John G., laborer, Hope; Smith Joseph, laborer, Hope; Smith Francis, Buttzville; Smith Geo. R., Buttzville; Smith Ravington G., Buttzville; Snover John, laborer, Hope; Snyder Frederick, Mt. Hermon; Stackhouse Cornelius, laborer, Hope; Stephens John, laborer, Hope; Still David B., Hope; Stout Wm., laborer, Hope; Stout John, laborer, Hope; Swayze Caleb, merchant, Hope; Irving Swayze, clerk, Hope; Swayze Alpheus, Hope; Swayze Asa Sr., gentleman, Hope; Swayze Asa Jr., teamster, Hope; Swayze Alpheus J., Hope; Swayze Isaac S., Hope; Swayze Henry J., laborer, Hope; Swayze A. J., banker, Hope; Swayze A. B., gentleman, Hope; Swayze G. B., clerk, Hope; Swayze Edward, Hope; Swayze Winfield, carpenter, Hope; Swayze Witfield, carpenter, Hope; Swayze John B., Hope; Strunk Wm., Hope; **Swayze Miss Camilla,** Dealer in Fine Millinery Goods and Lace, Hope.

Taylor James H., laborer, Delaware; Tims Ellis, laborer, Townsbury; Tims Calvin, laborer, Townsbury;

ANDREWS & NOLF, Proprietors of the "DOWN TOWN" Dry Goods House, 205 Northampton Street, Easton, Pa.

H. M. NORTON, *WHOLESALE AND RETAIL DEALER IN* Hardware, Stoves and Housefurnishing.

HOPE TOWNSHIP.

Tinsman Daniel M. gentleman, Mt. Hermon; Tinsman John T., Mt. Hermon; Treat S. J., gentleman, Hope; Tims John, Bridgeville; **Turner Bros.**, Dealers in General Merchandise, Hope.

Updegrove David, laborer, Danville.

Van Camp David, mason, Mt. Hermon; Van Camp Daniel, foundryman, Mt. Hermon; Van Gorden Daniel, laborer, Hope; Van Horn A. S., gentleman, Hope; **Van Horn Alvin A.**, Dealer in General Merchandise, Hope; **Van Horn R. M.**, Attorney at Law and Solicitor and Master in Chancery, Hope; Van Horn Garret A., Hope; Van Sickle Daniel, laborer, Hope; Van Sickle John, laborer, Hope; Van Scoten Johnson, laborer, Hope; Van Vorst Charles, Hope; Voorhees John, Townsbury; Vliet Nelson, Justice of Peace, Townsbury; Vliet Harry, miller, Townsbury; Vliet Benjamin, blacksmith, Townsbury; Vus'er Jas., farmer, Mt. Hermon; Vusler Edward, farmer, Hope.

Walters Peter, laborer, Hope; West Jacob, speculator, Hope; West John C., farmer, Hope; Wel'er

LAUBACH'S, Easton, Pa. THE LARGEST DRY GOODS AND CARPET HOUSE BARGAINS ALWAYS.

Cornelius, laborer, Townsbury; Welch Patrick, laborer, Danville; White Wm., laborer, Danville; Whitesell Wm. M., Townsbury; Wire Amos, Townsbury; Wilson Lewi, laborer, Townsbury; Williams J. J., Mt. Hermon; Wintermute Geo. A., laborer, Hope; Wintermute Wm., laborer, Buttzville; Wintermute Geo. M., Buttzville; Winters Ogden, Hope; Wildrick Marshal, Hope; Wildrick Jerome, laborer, Hope; Wildrick James M., laborer, Hope; Wildrick Isaac, Hope; Wildrick Stephen, Hope; Wildrick George W., Danville; Wildrick Samuel, Danville; Winters Mrs. M., dressmaker, Hope; Wolfe John B., carpenter, Hope; Wolfe George, Hope; Woolverton Henry, foundryman, Hope.

Yancer Albert, farm hand, Hope; Youmans Wesley, laborer, Hope; Youmans Luther, Hope.

RAED CAREFULLY Page 218

HARDWICK TOWNSHIP.

HARDWICK is one of the northern northeast border townships of the county, and is bounded on the northeast by Sussex county, on the south and southwest by Paulinskill, which forms the boundary between this and Frelinghuysen townships, on the southwest by Blairstown township, and on the northwest by the township of Pahaquarry. It contains 15.91 square miles, or 10,182 acres of land. Population at present about 650.

The surface of Hardwick is very uneven. All the streams of this township flow in a southerly or southwesterly direction, which indicates the general slope of land. The Blue Mountains on the north form the boundary between this and Pahaquary townships. This is the most elevated portion of the township, and from this part southward to the Valley of the Paulinskill is a succession of hills, valleys and ridges. The principal stream passing through this township is Blair Creek, which rises in the northeastern part, flows in a slightly southwestern direction, crossing the township almost diagonally, and emptying into the Paulinskill at the village of Blairstown. This stream provides several good mill sites, some of which are already occupied. Jacksonburg Creek rises also in the northeastern part, among the Blair Mountains, flows southwest through Hardwick and Blairstown townships into the Paulinskill. White Pond is a beautiful sheet of water, situated about half a mile north of Paulinskill, and about halfway between the northeast and southwest borders of the township. This name is given to the pond on account of the deposits of white shells, which are plainly visible at its bottom. Shuster Pond, named from an early settler of that name, and Mud Pond, so-called because of its muddy appearance, are small bodies of water found in the township.

There are no settlements of importance in this township, which is doubtless due to the fact that the surroundings necessary to suggest and invite the building of a town are wanting. There is good farming land in the township, and considerable timber resources, with probable mineral wealth, and many of the people are in comfortable circumstances. The first settlers came here about the year 1735. Among the first were a number of Quakers, who, after a time, constrained to migrate into Hunterdon county, that they might carry on their business as millers, there being no mills in Hardwick at this early date. The first mill in this township was built about the year 1783, near the present village of Paulina. The mill at Marksboro was soon afterward built. The first general election in this township, which at that time embraced also Frelinghuysen, was held in 1791. The division of the township was made in 1848. The original Hardwick was formed by royal patent in 1713. The first town meeting of which we have any record met at the house of one Deborah Hettit, on the 8th of March, 1774. At this time the "Town Committee" was known as a "committee to settle with the Overseers of the Poor and to assist them." The words "and for other purposes" became a part of the title in 1775. In 1779 they were termed "Commissioners of Appeals and a committee to settle with the Overseers of the Poor;" in 1781 "a committee to settle all the public business of the town," in 1799 "committee of the town;" in 1801, "committee of five;" in 1843, "township committee;" and in 1844 "town committee," which title is still retained. The first school committee seems to have been organized in 1834. In 1847 the committee was composed of one person. The last township school superintendent was Lemuel F. L. Wilson, who held office in 1866.

Among the business interests of Hardwick may be mentioned the following: The saw-mill of A. J. Hill, which stands on the site of the old pioneer grist-mill, built by Peter B. Shafer about the close of the war of the Revolution. A sash and blind factory at Paulina; the old Wintermute saw-mill; a sorghum factory on Paulinskill near Wintermutes saw-mill; a saw-mill and tannery at Slabtown; a saw-mill on Blair Creek, and one on Jacksonburg Creek, and a grist-mill on Blair Creek. Hardwick once had a cotton factory on the banks of the Paulinskill, and about midway between Paulina and Marksboro, the walls of which may still be seen. It has not been in active operation since about the year 1855. There is no regular church organization in the township at the present time, and but one cemetery, situated in the southern part of School District No. 78, on the road leading from Slabtown to Marksboro, in which a number of the pioneer settlers are sleeping.

A temperance society was formed in this township as early as 1830, and was known as the "Hardwick Temperance Society." It has long since dwindled into insignificance, and is now only a thing of the past, and the fathers who formed it have been long in possession of their reward. There are but two schools in the township with 99 scholars,

WARREN COUNTY DRUG STORE.

TOWNSHIP DIRECTORY.

All whose vocation is not mentioned are farmers.

Bird James C., Blairstown; Blackford Andrew, laborer, Blairstown; Bale Peter, Blairstown; Bale Jas. Biairstown; Bale Henry, Blairstown; Bale David, Blairstown; Bunnell Henry, Blairstown; Budd Geo., freighter, Marksboro.

Conklin John, sawyer, Blairstown; Cook Aaron, Stillwater; Cole Samuel, Hardwick; Cole Samuel Jr. Hardwick; Cole Jacob, Blairstown; Croup Jonas, Blairstown; Croup Amos, laborer, Blairstown; Castner, Wm., lumberman, Hardwick; Castner George, miller, Hardwick; Castner Samuel, teamster, Hardwick; Crouse Baltis, Marksboro; Crisman John C., Blairstown; Crissman Marshall, Blairstown; Castner Fordham, laborer, Hardwick.

Dickerson John, laborer, Marksboro; Dickerson Alfred, Marksboro.

LAUBACH'S EASTON, PA. CLOAKS and WRAPS of every description. **Our Own Manufacture.**

Ervey Walter, Hardwick; Engersoll Caleb Marksboro.

France Hiram, pension agent, Blairstown; Fisher Wm., Hardwick; Fisher Levi H., laborer, Hardwick; Fritze David, Stillwater.

Gouger Wesley, Blairstown; Gouger Baltis, laborer, Blairstown; Grover John, laborer, Blairstown. Hill Andrew J., mason and contractor, Paulina; Hill Abram, Blairstown; Hill I. L., laborer, Blairstown; Hill Samuel, tanner, Blairstown; Hill Andrew R., carpenter, Blairstown; Hill James, Blairstown; Hill Wm., Blairstown; Hill John M., Blairstown; Hill Clark, Blairstown; Hill Marcus C., laborer, Blairstown; Hill Wm. R., retired, Blairstown; Hunt Robert, laborer, Blairstown; Harris Charles, Blairstown; Harris Jacob, Blairstown; Harris Isaac, Blairstown; Honey Christopher, Blairstown; Honey Samuel, Blairstown; Horton George, Blairstown; Huff Jacob S., Blairstown; Huff Jacob E., Stillwater; Huff Alonzo, Stillwater; Harden Alex., Blairstown; Hull John.

Andrews & Nolf, 205 Northampton St., Easton, Pa. The reliable HOUSE for Mourning Goods.

H. M. NORTON, *WHOLESALE AND RETAIL DEALER IN* Hardware, Stoves and Housefurnishing

378   HARDWICK TOWNSHIP.

mason, Stillwater; Hull Charles, mason, Stillwater; Hull George, laborer, Stillwater; Hendershot Josiah, laborer, Stillwater; Hyther Wm., laborer, Stillwater; Harris Wm., tree agent, Blairstown; Harris Elias, druggist, Blairstown; Huston Abram, laborer, Marksboro; Huff Eugene, laborer, Marksboro; Huff Schooley, laborer, Marksboro; Hisom Wm., laborer, Hardwick.

Johnson Philip, miller, Marksboro; Johnson Lewis, agent and operator, Marksboro.

Konkle Isaac R., Marksboro; Konkle D. R., Blairstown; Kice Wm., shoemaker, Hardwick; Kice Henry, Hardwick; Kise Jacob, Hardwick; Keer Hampton, Stillwater.

Lanterman James D., Paulina; Lanterman Frank, Paulina; Lanterman Jason, laborer, Paulina; Lanterman George, laborer, Paulina; Lanterman Wm., Marksboro; Luse Aaron, Marksboro; Lanterman Wm. Jr., clerk, Marksboro; Laurenson J. H., carpenter, Marksboro; Laurenson M. E., laborer, Marks-

YOU CAN ALWAYS FIND WHAT YOU WANT AT **LAUBACH'S, Easton, Pa.**

boro; Linabery Benj., Blairstown; Laton John, Blairstown; Losey Wm. D., Stillwater; Lambert Jacob, laborer, Blairstown.

Mann Enola D., carpenter, Blairstown; Mann John, laborer, Blairstown; Maring Mrs. Sarah J., postmistress, Hardwick; Mott Wm., Marksboro; Mott Austin, laborer, Marksboro; Mott Jacob, retired, Marksboro; Mann Enos O., Marksboro; Mesler John, Marksboro; Mesler Kinney, laborer, Marksboro; Mesler Daniel, lumberman, Blairstown; Morrison W., laborer, Stillwater; Morrison Guy, laborer, Stillwater; Mowery Emanuel, Blairstown.

McCracken John, Blairstown; McGrath John, Blairstown; McGrath Eugene, sawyer, Blairstown.

Newman Levi, Blairstown; Newman David R., Blairstown; Nulton Mrs. Sarah, dressmaker, Blairstown.

Primrose George, Marksboro; Primrose George Jr., Marksboro; Pooster Jonas, Blairstown; Primrose Jos., Marksboro; Primrose Samuel, Marksboro.

SHULDS' INFALLIBLE **Dyspeptic Remedy.** A sure cure for Dyspepsia, Sick or Nervous Headache. Guaranteed.

HARDWICK TOWNSHIP.

Quick Embla D., tree agent, Blairstown.

Rice Lewis R., laborer, Blairstown; Roof Jacob S., laborer, Stillwater; Rutanr C. S. laborer, Blairstown; Roof Lemnel, laborer, Stillwater.

Shuster Wm Plairstown; Shuster Israel, Blairstown; Shuster Ira, Blairstown; Shewster Andrew, Blairstown; Shuster Elijah, Marksboro; Shuster Abram B., Stillwater; Simmons George, Stillwater; Specht Henry C. M., lumberman, Blairstown; Specht Frank, laborer, Blairstown; Savercool J. B., Blairstown; Savercool Mathias, Blairstown; Savercool Seldon, laborer, Blairstown; Savercool Martin, laborer, Paulina; Savercool George, laborer, Hardwick; Savercool Phillip, S. Marksboro; Sipley J. D., laborer, Paulina; Sipley Philip, Paulina; Sipley Rachael, Blairstown; Squire Philip, Marksboro; Simonson Frank, laborer, Hardwick; Simonson Nicholas, laborer, Hardwick; Simanton George, laborer, Hardwick; Schoonover Catharine, grocer, Hardwick.

Teel John L. Blairstown; Teel James C., Blairstown; Teel Lewis B., Blairstown; Titman Zadock, laborer, Blairstown; Toten Henry, laborer, Blairstown; Toten Edward, laborer, Blairstown; Tew George, laborer, Marksboro.

Vass John W., Blairstown; Vass Philip, Blairstown; Vass Isaac S., Marksboro; Vass Charles, Marksboro; Vass Frank, Marksboro; Voss Martin, Marksboro; Vough Isaac, Marksboro; Vough Jas. F., laborer, Marksboro; Vough John, laborer, Marksboro; Vanauken Chris, laborer, Blairstown.

Walters Wm., Blairstown; Walters J. B., Blairstown; Wilson L. F. L., Blairstown; Wilson Frank, Blairstown; Wilson Theodore, Marksboro; Warner John W., Marksboro; Warner Frank, Marksboro; Warner George, laborer, Marksboro; Wildrick Clinton, Marksboro; Wintermute A. K., Marksboro; Wintermute James, laborer, Marksboro; Wintermute Mrs. Diantha, Hardwick; Warner Marcus B., laborer, Marksboro; Wildrick George G., laborer, Marksboro.

HARMONY TOWNSHIP.

HARMONY is one of the southwestern border townships of Warren county, being situated in the southern part of the tier of townships along the Delaware, and was formed in 1839, having up to that time embraced portions of Greenwich and Oxford. Its dimensions are six miles long by five miles in breadth, and it contains 13,881 acres of land.

The Belvidere division of the Pennsylvania Railroad crosses the western part of the township, along and nearly parallel with the Delaware river, and has a station at Martin's Creek, and flag stations at Hutchinsons and Roxburg. Harmony is bounded on the north by Oxford and the Delaware, on the east by Franklin, on the south by Lopatcong, and on the west by the Delaware.

The surface of this township is considerably varied, being covered with mountains, hills and valley. Scott's Mountain extends into the township of Oxford, running northeast and southwest near the eastern boundary. Marble Mountain, and its extension Ragged Ridge cross the township in the center, running also northeast and southwest.

The soil of the township, like its surface, is varied. Along the Delaware is a flat composed mostly of sand and limestone. Marble Mountain has a soil made up also of limestone and other coarse material of a character not to be highly commended for its fertility. There is also a small portion of wet land, but the greater part of the township is fertile and productive. Harmony township is well watered. Its western border is washed by the Delaware; Lopatcong Creek, a tributary of the Delaware, rises in Scotts Mountain and flows in a southwestern direction through the township; Merrets Brook has its source in the same mountains, and flows south into Greenwich township. Harmony is one of the most picturesque townships in the county.

The first settlements were made prior to the Revolutionary War, but the exact date cannot be given. The early settlers were probably mixed, coming from different fatherlands. Among the most important were those of English extraction.

The villages of Harmony are as follows: Montana, situated in the

HARMONY TOWNSHIP.

northeastern corner of the township on Scott's Mountain, has a Presbyterian church, a Baptist church, school-house, blacksmith shop, store and post office.

Roxburg, in the northern part of the township, has a grist mill, blacksmith shop, store and and post office, a foundry, and the best public school building in the township, used also for union church services. It is about one mile from the Delaware and four from Belvidere.

Upper Harmony, located near the center of the township, has a store, post office, blacksmith shop, undertaker's establishment, public school, and a fine Presbyterian church, recently erected on the site of the old one, adjoining which is "Fairview Cemetery," the finest burial place in the township.

Brainards, situated in the central western part of the township, along the Delaware, and at the junction of the Martin's Creek division of the Bangor R.R. with the Bel. Del. R.R., is simply a post hamlet.

Lower Harmony, located about a mile southwest of Upper Harmony, has two grist mills, a blacksmith shop, store, public school, and a Methodist church. It has no post office. Lower Harmony has a burial ground supposed to have been used over one hundred years.

Population of the township about 1,300. Schools, 7; Scholars, 444.

DEPUE, SON, & CO.,

Manufacturers of
Ground Bone, Bone Phosphate, and Neats
FOOT OIL.

Dealers in new and second-hand grain and phosphate drills and other agricultural machinery. We also keep constantly a general line of

FERTILIZING MATERIAL,

consisting of Sulphate of Potash, uriate Potash, Sulphate of Soda, Kanite, Sulphate Ammonia, ground and dissolved bone, dissolved

North Carolina Rock Phosphate,

Cayuga and Nova Scotia plaster, etc., at very reasonable prices for cash. Farmers given instructions in preparing fertilizers for their own use.

BELVIDERE, NEW JERSEY.

James Depue.   A. Brands.   Wm. H. K. Depue.

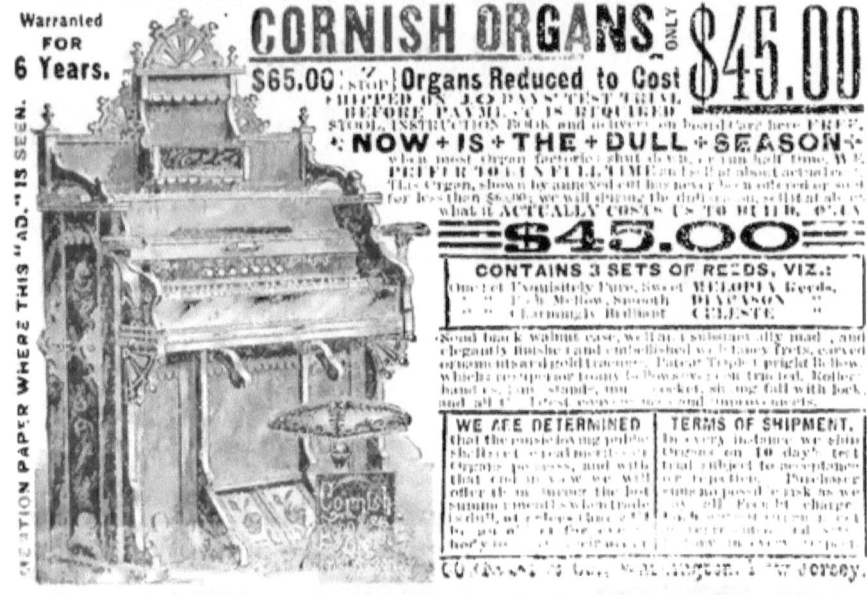

MESSRS. CORNISH & COMPANY

Would call the attention of the residents of Warren county to their latest style Parlor Organ "The Favorite," style 12, shown above, the regular price of which is $65, but which is reduced to about cost $45.00.

A GREAT OFFER.

Any resident of Warren Co., can purchase above organ and pay $5 down after ten days test trial, and $5 per month thereafter until all is paid. Besides this we will pay the expenses of any resident of Warren Co., who chooses to visit our Factory and select an organ in person. Address or call on

CORNISH & CO.
WASHINGTON,

WARREN CO.   NEW JERSEY

WARREN COUNTY DRUG STORE.

Township Directory.

All whose vocation is not mentioned are farmers.

Alshouse Emanuel, Montana; Alshouse Henry, Montana; Alshouse Marcus, Harmony; Amey Margaret, seamstress, Harmony; Amey Catharine, seamstress, Harmony; Amey John C., Harmony; Amey J. H., Phillipsburg; Amey Wm., Harmony; Amey H. H., retired, Harmony; Allen Elijah, Sr., grist mill, Harmony; Allen Elijah, Jr., Harmony; Angle Richard, Roxburg; Amey James M., Harmony; Amey David, Harmony; Alshouse John, laborer, Harmony; Alshouse Mary, retired, Harmony; Alshouse Ellen, retired, Harmony; Apgar G. H., minister, Harmony.

Beers Elisha, mason, Harmony; Burr Andrew, laborer, Stewartsville; Burr Alva, laborer, Stewartsville; Bird Henry E., Montana; Beers Maria, Montana; Bird Adam, Montana; Butler Nathan, Montana; Beers David, laborer, Montana; Beers Benja-

LAUBACH'S, Easton, Pa. THE LARGEST DRY GOODS AND CARPET HOUSE. BARGAINS ALWAYS

min, Montana; Beers Wm., Montana; Bard John L., Montana; Beers Luke V., Montana; Beers Garner, Montana; Beers Aaron, Montana; Benward James, laborer, Harmony; Bellis Philip, Harmony; Beers George L., Montana; Bitner Wm., laborer, Harmony; Beers John C., Montana; Peers Charles, laborer, Montana; Butler Holloway, Roxburg; Butler Thomas, laborer, Roxburg; Buchman Hiram, Harmony; Buchman Oscar, laborer, Harmony.

Carling Elizabeth, Stewartsville; Culver Wilson R., Montana; Cook Joseph, Montana; Cole Asa K., Justice of the Peace, Montana; Cole George, laborer, Montana; Cole Peter E., Montana; Carhart Jacob, undertaker, Harmony; Culver Silas, laborer, Montana; Clymer John, Brainard; Cline Jacob W., Harmony; Carhart Charles, Harmony; Cline Garner, Harmony; Crutz Ezekiel, laborer, Harmony; Crutz Peter, Montana; Campbell Matilda, Roxburg; Crutz John H., laborer, Montana; Cline John L., Roxburg; Cline Price L., teacher, Roxburg; Cobb

ANDREWS & NOLF, Proprietors of the "DOWN TOWN" Dry Goods House, 205 Northampton Street, Easton, Pa.

H. M. NORTON, WHOLESALE AND RETAIL DEALER IN Hardware, Stoves and Housefurnishing.

HARMONY TOWNSHIP.

R. P., minister, Harmony; Carling T. F., Harmony; Cline Lewis, retired, Harmony; Cline G. H., physician, Harmony; Cline David, Retired, Harmony; Cyphers George, laborer, Harmony.

Dida John, Harmony; Dilts John, laborer, Stewartsville; DeWitt Isaac, Montana; DeWitt J. D., physician, Harmony; DeWitt Paul P., Montana; Dalrymple George, Montana; Dunn Samuel, laborer, Harmony; DeWitt Thomas, Harmony; Depue Calvin, Phillipsburg; Depue Abram, Harmony; Depue James, Harmony; DeWitt James W., Harmony; DeWitt Geo. M., laborer, Phillipsburg; DeWitt Jas., Phillipsburg; Dempsey Michael, railroader, Phillipsburg; Duckworth Angeline, laborer, Roxburg; Duckworth James, laborer, Roxburg; Dereamer Isaac, laborer, Montana; Davison Eliza, Roxburg; Dalrymple Wm., laborer, Montana; Depue Samuel A. Harmony.

Evans James, Montana; Eberly George, Montana; Eberly Henry, Montana; Edinger David, Montana;

LAUBACH'S EASTON, PA. CLOAKS and WRAPS of every description. Our Own Manufacture.

Eckert Otto, Harmony; Eckert Jacob Sr., laborer, Harmony; Eckert Jacob Jr., laborer, Harmony; Engler Christopher, Harmony; Engler Marshall, Phillipsburg; Eckert Garner, laborer, Harmony; Eckert John, laborer, Harmony; Easterday Darius, laborer, Phillipsburg.

Fine Barnet D., Roxburg; Fine Irvin, Roxburg; Fine Howard, Roxburg; Fine George, carpenter, Roxburg; Fox John, Harmony; Fry Jesse, Brainards; Fitts Mary, Montana; Fangboner Abram, Montana; Flynn Patrick, Montana; Fuller Wm, C., grest mill, Harmony; Fry John, Brainards; Fulse Jacob, laborer, Brainards; Fritz Wm., Harmony; Fry Isaac, Harmony; Fulker Peter, billiard hall, Roxburg.

Gross Edmund, laborer, Montana; Gross Daniel, Montana; Gross George W., laborer, Montana; Garren, Daniel blacksmith, Harmony; Gorman J. D., laborer, Montana; Green Hosea, Montana; Garr's Jacob, Harmony; Grotz Jacob, retired, Roxburg; Gross Wm., laborer, Roxburg; Gardner George B., Brain-

ROPE, TWINE, etc. at **WADE BROS.** Hackettstown.

HARMONY TOWNSHIP.

ards; Garris Reuben, laborer, Brianards; Gray Geo. W., laborer, Stewartsville; Gardner Mathias, carpenter, Harmony.

Housman Michael, laborer, Stewartsville; Hager George, Montana; Hixon Wm., Montana; Holden John, gristmill, Harmony; Hineline M. B., carpet weaver, Harmony; Handlong John, mail carrier, Harmony; Horner Sarah E., retired, Montana; Hineline Samuel V., huckster, Harmony; Hildenbrand Jacob, laborer, Harmony; Howell John, Harmony; Hulshizer Milton, laborer, Roxburg; Hulshizer David, stone mason, Roxburg; Hofacker Peter, laborer, Roxburg; Hiles Samuel Sr., retired, Roxburg; Hiles Samuel Jr., Roxburg; Harper George, laborer, Harmony; Hawk Wm., Harmony; Hess Bernaldo, Brainards; Hoff Benjamin, Brainards; Hoff Moses, stone mason, Brainards; Hoff Henry, Bernards; Hoff Abel H., Brainards; Hoff Wm. P., Brainards; Hoff Wm. S., railroader, Brainards; Hoff Jacob, laborer, Brainards; Hess Benjamin, Harmony; Hamlin Frank, huckster, Harmony; Howey Charles, laborer, Harmony; Hill Edward, Roxburg.

Jumper Catharine, laborer, Roxburg; Jumper Amos, laborer, Brainards.

Kinney Robert C., carpenter, Harmony; Kinney Wesley, Harmony; Kinney John, Harmony; Kuhns Mary A., laborer, Harmony; Kneiper William, Harmony; Kline Peter, S., retired, Harmony; Kline Peter Jr., retired Harmony; Koch Charles C., Brainard; Kent James P., Roxburg.

Lamb Edward, minister, Montana; Love Anna T., retired, Harmony; Loughran Edward, Montana; Lommason William, laborer, Roxburg; Luty Samuel, laborer, Harmony; Lightcap Levi, Roxburg; Lightcap Irvin, laborer, Roxburg; Lommasson George H., laborer, Brainard; Lightcap Peter, laborer, Harmony.

McElroy Frank, blacksmith, Harmony; Meyers Daniel, Montana; Metz Benjamin, Harmony; Messinger Benjamin, Phillipsburg; Melroy Elijah, carpenter, Roxburg; Metz William K., Roxburg; Mc-

H. M. NORTON, *WHOLESALE AND RETAIL DEALER IN* Hardware, Stoves and Housefurnishing

386　　　　　HARMONY TOWNSHIP.

Cracken James, constable, Roxburg; Martenis Ralph, Harmony; Metz Henry, Harmony; Merritt William, retired, Brainard; Mackey Joseph, Harmony; Mellick Henry, retired, Phillipsburg; Mellick Moses D., retired, Phillipsburg; **Miller J. W.**, Surveyor, Harmony; Miller Anzie, Harmony; Miller Henry Y., Harmony; Miller James, retired, Harmony; Miller John, retired, Harmony; Miller John H., retired, Harmony; Miller John M., laborer, Harmony; Miller Irvin, Harmony; Miller Martha, Harmony; Miller Samuel B., laborer, Harmony; Miller Frederic, laborer, Brainards; Mutchler Garner H., retired, Harmony; Mutchler W. Newton, Harmony; McCracken Levi, laborer, Roxburg.

Osmun Jonas, carpenter, Montana; Ott Leonard, Harmony; Oberly Anthony, retired, Brainard.

Pearson William, Montana; Piggott John, Montana; Piggott Edward, Harmony; Post Robert, laborer, Roxburg; Petty Robert, laborer, Roxburg; Probasco Daniel, laborer, Roxburg; Probasco Charles,

LAUBACH'S, Easton, Pa. SPECIAL ATTENTION TO SILKS AND DRESS GOODS. NEW GOODS DAILY.

shoemaker, Harmony; Price Harvey, laborer, Roxburg; Price Abner, laborer, Roxburg; Petty Samuel, Roxburg; Petty Alfred, Harmony.

Read Isaac, laborer, Brainards; Rush Jacob F.,

J. C. BUTLER,
No. 22 Union Square, or 327 Washington St.
PHILLIPSBURG, N. J.
AGENT FOR
The Equitable Life Assurance Society of the United States.
120 Broadway, New York.
THE STRONGEST AND MOST RELIABLE COMPANY IN THE WORLD

ASSETS　　　　　　　　　　　　　$70,000,000
SURPLUS OVER,　　　　　　　　　$18,000,000
NEW BUSINESS IN 1885,　　　　　$96,011,378
NEW BUSINESS FROM JANUARY TO JULY 1886, OVER　$50,000,000

It is the originator of the popular Semi-Tontine *and other improved forms of non-forfeiting Policies, and has never contested a policy.*

Send for Estimates for yourself.

Montana; Raub Abram, Harmony; Rice Noah, railroader, Brainards; Rush Lewis S., Montana; Ramsey William, Stewartsville; Rush Jacob, laborer, Mon-

SHIELDS' INFALLIBLE **Dyspeptic Remedy.** A sure cure for Dyspepsia, Sick or Nervous Headache. Guaranteed.

HARMONY TOWNSHIP.

tana; Radle Ludwig, Montana; Radle Christopher, laborer, Montana; Rush Abram F., Montana; Raesly Daniel, blacksmith, Montana; Rush Emanuel, Montana; Rush Ralph, merchant, Montana; Rush Geo. W., Montana; Rush David B., Montana; Rush Levi F., Montana; Ross John, laborer, Harmony; Rush John D., Montana; Rush John J., Montana; Rush John M., laborer, Montana; Ramsey Charles, merchant, Harmony; Rush Daniel F., Montana; Rush Peter P., laborer, Roxburg; Rush William C., Harmony; Rice Silas, laborer, Phillipsburg; Ross William, stone mason, Harmony; Reilly William, Harmony; Rice Anthony, laborer, Phillipsburg; Raub Levi, Brainards; Raub Jesse, Brainards; Rice Chas., Phillipsburg; Robins Peter, laborer, Roxburg; Rush Peter R., carpenter, Harmony; Rasner Simon, Roxburg; Rinehart Samuel, Montana; Roseberry John, Harmony; Reilly Henry, Brainards; Rush Amzie, Montana; Burd Ann, Montana; Rush James D., Montana; Rush Alfred, carpenter, Harmony; Reilly

Warner, laborer, Brainards; Rush Geo. W., Roxburg.

Smith James R., laborer, Harmony; Schreiber August, laborer, Stewartsville; Simons Robert, Stewartsville; Sapp Charles, Montana; Simons Henry, merchant, Harmony; Sheridan Margaret, retired, Harmony; Stiles Hannah, retired, Harmony; Smith David B., laborer, Montana; Smith Peter, stone mason, Harmony; Smith Adam R., stone mason, Montana; Smith Tunis, carpenter, Montana; Stabp John, Harmony; Snyder Philip, laborer, Harmony; Stires Eber, laborer, Harmony; Snyder James, Harmony; Stout David B., carpenter, Harmony; Stout John, Phillipsburg; Stout Jacob, railroader, Phillipsburg; Smith Eleanor, retired, Roxburg; Scadding Augustus, Roxburg; Smith Isaac J., Montana; Shular William, Roxburg; Steel Vendel, Roxburg; Stires Alexander, laborer, Roxburg; Stull Mary, retired, Roxburg; Stull George, merchant, Roxburg; Shultz James, laborer, Brainards; Shimer Jacob, retired, Brainards;

H. M. NORTON, *WHOLESALE AND RETAIL DEALER IN* **Hardware, Stoves and Housefurnishing**

Smith Aaron B., carpenter, Harmony; Smith Nancey, retired, Brainards; Seguine James, painter, Montana.

Teel Henry, retired, Harmony; Thatcher Joseph, laborer, Montana.

Unangst Catharine, retired, Stewartsville; Unangst David, laborer, Harmony.

Vannatta Wm., retired, Harmony; Vannatta Alexander, laborer, Roxburg; Vannatta Samuel, Roxburg; Vannatta Roderic, Roxburg; Vannatta James D., Roxburg; Vannatta Silas B., Justice of Peace, Brainards; Vannatta George, agent, Brainards; **Vannatta John R.,** Harmony.

Wolf Henry, Stewartsville; Wolf John, Stewartsville; Wolf Lida, laborer, Stewartsville; Wilkins H. A. laborer, Stewartsville; Woolever Barnabas, Montana; Williamson Jacob, laborer, Harmony; Williamson John, laborer, Harmony; Woolever Levi, laborer, Brainards; Warman Lev., Montana; Warner Benj, Montana; Werkheiser Jerry, laborer, Phillipsburg;

LAUBACH'S, Easton, Pa. SPECIAL ATTENTION TO SILKS AND DRESS GOODS. NEW GOODS DAILY.

Williams John, painter, Harmony; Woolever Philip, laborer, Harmony; Woodruff Isaac, blacksmith, Roxburg; Werkeiser John, Brainards.

THE MANAGEMENT OF EASTON COLLEGE OF BUSINESS.

Guarantees a thorough course of practical training to every patron. Our school is without doubt one of the oldest and best in the United States. Formerly known as T. H. Stevens' Institute of Business and Finance, and Knorrs' Institute of Business. We claim to advance a pupil more rapidly than any other school in this section, from the simple fact that our methods are *actual business* and thus a pupil will realize at once. Our rates of tuition and board are reasonable and within the reach of all. Our catalogue, handsomely illustrated, is second to none of any school in the U. S. Send for it.

Address
CHARLES L. FREE, Pres.
EASTON, PA.

Young Isaac, Roxburg; Young Peter, Roxburg; Young Wm., Harmony; Young Peter, Harmony; Young Semple, Harmony; Young George, clerk, Roxburg.

ANDREWS & NOLF, 205 Northampton St., Easton, Pa. Sell the best Black and Colored Silks. Guaranteed.

INDEPENDENCE TOWNSHIP.

INDEPENDENCE, located in the eastern part of the county, is bounded on the northwest by Frelinghuysen; on the northeast by Allamuchy; on the southeast by Hackettstown and Mansfield; and on the west and north by Mansfield and Hope. It contains 16.88 square miles, or 10,836 acres, and has a population of about 1100. The Morris canal is the dividing line between Independence and Hackettstown, and the Jenny Jump mountains between Independence and Frelinghuysen. The Pequest River crosses the township from northeast to southwest, and with its many tributaries supplies it well with water, and fits it for agricultural products. The Lehigh & Hudson R. R. crosses the township just a little north of the centre.

The land in Independence is very uneven, being composed in the southeastern part of ranges of high hills and deep gullies.

"On the road leading from Hackettstown, northwest to Vienna—a steep hill, nearly a mile long has to be surmounted. When the top is reached the land is found to be rolling, but laid out in good farms. As Vienna is approached, a long hill is descended fully a mile in length. Then the beautiful valley of the Pequest is reached, where may be seen some of the finest farms in the country. Rough as the uplands are they afford abundant crops. The soil is largely composed of limestone on the hills and hillsides; in the valleys is a dark loam and needs but little cultivation to be made to produce most beautifully. The "Jenny Jump" mountains is a high range of hills bordering the township on the northwest. The origin of its name is a matter of tradition. Probably the most reliable account is that as an old settler was driving down the steep side of the mountain his team became unmanageable, and being in great danger of being capsized, he called to his wife whose name was Jenny, to jump—which she did, thereby saving her life. Be this as it may, the mountains have born this name far back of the memory of any living man."

There is an abundance of limestone throughout the township, large quantities of which are quarried for fertilizing purposes. The soil of nearly all the farming land is composed of this disintegrated limestone. The rock extends from the Pequest Valley well up the slope of the hillsides, where a dark slate crops out. There is an abundance of iron ore in various parts of the township, although not worked to any great extent.

Vienna, Danville and Petersburg are the three villages located in the township. Vienna is situated one mile southeast of Danville, and is a pleasant village of about 300 inhabitants. It was settled at a very early date. Danville is located in the western part of the township near the Hope township line. It has fewer inhabitants than its more beautiful neighbor, Vienna. Petersburg is a small hamlet of half a dozen houses.

There are three churches in the township, viz.: The Pequest Methodist Episcopal Church; the Danville Presbyterian Church, and the Christian Church, at Vienna. The Methodist Church was projected in 1810, but was not finished till 1824. The site for the church was purchased of John Cummins for the sum of thirty dollars. Prior to 1810, the Methodists held meetings in the old stone house of Mr. Philip Cummins. Here Bishop Asbury occasionally stayed and preached. It is said that this was the first Methodist Church in what was then Sussex county. A new church in which the congregation now worship, was built in 1855. The Danville Presbyterian Church was formerly an outpost or mission connected with the Hackettstown Church. In 1824 a stone church was built, and in 1863 it was remodelled to its present condition—one of the most beautiful and comfortable in the Presbytery. The Christian Church was first organized at Caddington, now called Petersburg, in 1839, and the present church at Vienna built in 1858.

The drainage of the Great Meadows was a great thing for Independence, and some of the finest and most profitable land in the State is now cultivated where formerly was simply marsh and bog. There are three schools in Independence township, viz.: Vienna, Danville and Petersburg with a total of 200 scholars.

The Washington Review,
The Largest, Cheapest and Best Paper in Warren county. $1.00 a Year.

WARREN COUNTY DRUG STORE.

Township Directory.

All whose vocation is not mentioned are farmers.

Ayers Nelson E., Hackettstown; Ayers Isaac, Hackettstown; Ayers Theodore, Vienna; Ayers William, Hackettstown; Ayers James, Hackettstown; Ayers Robert, Jr., Vienna; Albertson C. H., general business, Vienna; Ayers David, Hackettstown; Aber George, mason, Vienna; Ayers Wm. A., Hackettstown; Ayers Robert, Sr., Hackettstown; Almer Edward, cabinet maker and undertaker, Danville; Aber Caleb, laborer, Vienna; Aber Isaac, stone-mason, Vienna; Aber Andrew, mason, Vienna; Allen Mary A., householder, Vienna; Allen Robert, laborer, Vienna; Ackley Archibald, Hackettstown; Ayers Andrew, Hackettstown; Allen Jacob C., Hackettstown; Ackley James, Hackettstown.

Ball Theo., Danville; Barry Lemuel, laborer, Danville; Burdge P., laborer, Danville; Bird Ed., F., Danville;

LAUBACH'S EASTON, PA. Largest Store, Largest Assortments, and One Price to All

Bird Steward, Vienna; Boyd James, Vienna; Boofman John, moulder, Vienna; Bulgin Edwin G., Vienna; Bartron Elisha, shoemaker, Vienna; Bartron Rhuel, shoemaker, Vienna; Baylor Samuel, blacksmith, Hackettstown; Burk Alexander, laborer, Hackettstown; Barker Wm. J., miller, Vienna; Bartoe Andrew, house painter, Vienna; Banghart Nelson, laborer, Danville; Betson Stephen, laborer, Danville; Bayley John, Hackettstown; Bayley Geo. Hackettstown; Barker Charles, Hackettstown; Bryant Robert Rev., minister, Danville; Bartoe Charles, laborer, Hackettstown; Banghart Nelson, laborer, Hackettstown; Bush Charles R., house painter, Vienna; Burdge Joseph, laborer, Danville; Bennett Charles, bartender, Danville; Bescherer John, laborer, Vienna.

Cook Joseph, railroad laborer, Hackettstown; Cummins Johnson J., Vienna; Cummins Geo. O., Vienna; Cummins R. Ayers, Vienna; Clancey Wm. O., machinist, Vienna; Cummins John F., Vienna; Cummins Andrew J., Vienna; Cummins Theodore, Vienna; Cummins Jacob P., storekeeper, Vienna; Cummins Isaac, Vienna; Cummins Nelson, Vienna; Cummins Edward, Vienna; Cummins Philetus, Vienna; Cummins Christian, Vienna; Cummins Silas, Vienna; Cummins Polemus, Vienna; Criger David, team driver, Danville; Conover Wm. O., Hackettstown; Clark B., Hackettstown; Cooper Peter, laborer, Johnsonsburg; Crammer John; Coursen Isetions.

Deremer George, undertaker, Vienna; Deremer Charles, carpenter, Vienna; Deremer Steward, laborer, Vienna; Durmer Wm., Vienna; Dolan Mark, laborer, Vienna; Deremer Daniel, Vienna; Decker George; Dunn John, Vienna; Delicker Wm., Hackettstown; Dill Isaac R., Hackettstown; Dan Jacob R., Hackettstown; Decker Edmond, Hackettstown; Dilly George, laborer, Hackettstown; Doland William, laborer, Vienna; Dickerson R. E., laborer, Hackettstown; Drake Nathaniel, Vienna; Dye Frank, laborer, Hackettstown; Dalrymple Edward.

LAUBACH'S EASTON, PA. CLOAKS and WRAPS of every description. **Our Own Manufacture.**

Frasher George, railroad laborer, Hackettstown; Fleming Misses A. and E., retired, Vienna; Fine Isaac, laborer, Vienna; Fleming Nelson, Danville; Fleming Erving, Vienna; Frace John, Hackettstown; Frace Isaac, Hackettstown; Frace George, Hackettstown; Fisher Jacob, Vienna.

Grace Michael, laborer, Hackettstown; Grey Chas., laborer, Hackettstown; Green John, hotel prop., Danville; Gulick Walter, groceryman, Vienna; Gulick Ezra P., general business, Vienna; Goodrich Amedis, merchant, Danville; Graudin William, laborer, Danville; Globe Philip, blacksmith, Danville.

Hoffman David, blacksmith, Vienna; Howell D. H. painter, Vienna; Howell George, Vienna; Howell John, merchant, Vienna; Howell Aaron, Vienna; Howell Benjamin, Vienna; Hance James, Vienna; Hall Benjamin, bending business, Vienna; Homadue Edward, Hackettstown; Huntsman A. J., carpenter, Vienna; Hart Joseph, laborer, Vienna; Hann Jeremiah, Danville; Hance W. B., Vienna; Howell Nel-

Extra quality Carving knives and forks at Wade Bros., Hackettstown.

INDEPENDENCE TOWNSHIP.

son, Vienna; Howell Wm., Vienna; Hoffman John, blacksmith, Vienna; Hill Theodore, Vienna; Heath Emanuel, Vienna; Hart Wm. Vienna; Henry John, laborer, Hackettstown; Henry Alfred, Danville; Henry George, Danville; Henry Philip, Danville.

Inscho Levi, laborer, Vienna; Inscho David B., laborer, Vienna.

Johnson Samuel Hackettstown; Johnson Oakly, teacher, Hackettstown; Johnson James, teacher, Hackettstown; Johnson Rev. W. M., Vienna.

Kipp John, laborer, Hackettstown; Ketcham Morris, Hackettstown; Keegan Jacob, Hackettstown; Kennady Daniel, merchant, Danville; Ketcham John F., Vienna; Kinney George, Vienna; Linnaberry J. A., Hackettstown; Linnaberry J. N., Hackettstown; Langdon Jacob Y., Danville; Letson Jonah, mason, Vienna; Leigh Isaac, Danville; Leigh Aaron B., general business, Danville; Larkins Patrick, Vienna; Lafaucherie John C., assessor, Hackettstown; Leigh Daniel, Vienna; Leigh Isaiah, Vienna; Leigh Milton,

YOU CAN ALWAYS FIND WHAT YOU WANT AT LAUBACH'S, Easton, Pa.

Vienna; Milton Henry, Danville; Martin Christopher, tanner, Hackettstown; Martin James H. tanner, Hackettstown; McLaughlin John, school teacher, Vienna; Merrell Lewis E., Vienna; Merrell Lewis E. laborer, Vienna; Martin Robert, laborer, Vienna; Mitchell Wm., Vienna; Mitchell Samuel, Vienna; Merrell John, carpenter, Danville; Mitchell Henry, Vienna; Mahoney Patrick, laborer, Hackettstown; Merrell George B., laborer, Vienna; Martin R. L. laborer, Vienna; Martenis George, Vienna; Martenis Wm., Vienna; Marlatt John, Vienna; Merrell Frank, Vienna; Morris George, Vienna.

Osmun James, laborer, Vienna; Osmun Wm. trucker, Vienna; Orr Joseph, laborer, Danville.

Park James H., laborer, Hackettstown; Park Geo., laborer, Hackettstown; Park John, Vienna; Park Wm., Vienna; Park Charles, Vienna; Park David, Vienna; Pierce John, Hackettstown; Pierce Charles, Vienna; Park Elisha, Vienna; Pendy Michael, laborer, Hackettstown; Park Samuel, Vienna; Park Edward, Vienna; Park Buckley, Vienna; Park Theo,

ANDREWS & NOLF, Proprietors of the "DOWN TOWN" Dry Goods House, 205 Northampton Street, Easton, Pa.

H. M. NORTON, *WHOLESALE AND RETAIL DEALER IN* Hardware, Stoves and Housefurnishing.

INDEPENDENCE TOWNSHIP.

Vienna.

Quinn Hugh, laborer, Hackettstown; Quick Caleb, carpenter, Vienna; Quick George, laborer, Vienna.

Roberts Wm., Hackettstown; Repp Phillip, Danville; Roe Dr. Jacob J., Vienna; Roe Dr. Wm J., Danville; Reed John, Danville; Raub Jacob, laborer, Vienna; Reeves E. W., Vienna; Rodgers Frank, laborer, Danville; Pierce Patrick, laborer, Hackettstown; Pyles Joseph, Vienna; Slyker Jacob S., Vienna; Shields Jacob, Vienna; Swianton Rev E., Hackettstown; Swianton John, miller, Hackettstown; Smith James, Hackettstown; Sigler Stilson, merchant, Vienna; Shackelton L. R., laborer, Vienna; Smith Peter, Vienna; Smith Nelson, laborer, Vienna; Smith Charles, Vienna; Schenk Lewis, Vienna; Schrumpf John G., Vienna; Sutton Erving, Vienna; Sutton Martin, laborer, Vienna; Sullivan John, laborer, Vienna; Sullivan John, laborer, Vienna; Simanton Andrew, Vienna; Schenk John J., Vienna; Sutton John, Vienna; Sheets Stewart, Vienna;

LAUBACH'S, Easton, Pa. THE LARGEST DRY GOODS AND CARPET HOUSE. BARGAINS ALWAYS

Shackelton J., laborer, Vienna; Staples David, engineer, Vienna; Sigler John, Danville; Titus John, Danville; Shields John, laborer, Vienna.

Tinsman William, Vienna; Tinsman Samuel J., Vienna.

Vreeland William, dealer in stock, Danville; Vreeland Garrett, trucking, Danville; Vreeland Henry, Danville; Vansyckle Abram, Vienna; Vannatta Jos., Hackettstown; Vansyckle John F., Justice of the Peace, Danville; Van Buskirk Sarah, retired, Danville; Van Buskirk Aaron, Vienna.

Wise Morris H., Hackettstown; Winchell Timothy, school teacher, Hackettstown; Whitesell Albert, laborer, Vienna; Whitesell Ogden, constable, Vienna; Whitesell Jacob, Vienna; Wheeler Peter, Allamuchy; Wilson Eli, laborer, Vienna; Wilson Richard, stone mason, Vienna; Wilson Geo., Hackettstown; Wolf Daniel, Vienna.

Young Thomas, Vienna.

ANDREWS & NOLF, 205 Northampton St., Easton, Pa. Sell the best Black and Colored Silks Guaranteed.

KNOWLTON TOWNSHIP.

KNOWLTON is one of the three northern townships of the county, and whose northern boundary is formed by the Kittatinny Mountains. It was formed from Oxford in 1764, at which time it embraced parts of Hope and Blairstown townships. The name of the township is said to be derived from the appearance of its surface. It is bounded on the north by Pahaquarry, on the east by Blairstown, on the south by Hope and Oxford, and on the west by the Delaware River. It has an area of 25.13 square miles or 16,083 acres of land. This township presents a considerable variety of surface. Along the Delaware, and in the valley of the Paulinskill, the soil is rich and of alluvial formation, while along the mountains in the north it is mostly a gravelly loam and less fertile. The soil in the southern part of the township varies with the location. The surface of the township is uneven, having upon it a large number of small knolls or hills, some of which are limestone knobs. From this fact the township was written for a number of years as *Knoll-town*. The principal streams of Knowlton are, the Paulinskill which crosses the central portion of the township in a southwestern direction and empties into the Delaware; Yard's Creek, a tributary of the Paulinskill; and Shawpocussing and Centreville Creeks, both tributaries of the Delaware. The New Jersey side of the famous Delaware Water Gap, is in the northwestern part of this township.

The first settlers were Germans who came here to enjoy religious liberty. Among these pioneers was one Robeson, whose son was shot by the Indians while endeavoring to cross the river at the point now known as "Robeson's Rift." In honor of this son the rift was named.

The chief business of this township is farming, though the slate factories, bending works, etc., carry on an amount of trade worthy of mention.

Present population about 2,000.

Among the towns are the following: Ramsaysburg, located along the Delaware in the southwestern part of the township, and was named in honor of James and Adam Ramsay who were the pioneer settlers of the town, locating here in 1795. A pioneer Episcopal, and a pioneer Baptist church, were built here. The chief business of the place at present is carried on in the steam saw-mill.

Delaware Station, also located in the southwestern part of the township, on the D. L. & W. R.R. and at the southern terminus of the Blairstown division of the N. Y. & S. railroad, a town of recent date. It is beautifully and favorably located, and is an enterprising town. The land upon which the village stands was purchased by Hon. John I. Blair, and in 1856 surveyed into squares and building lots. It has at present stores, churches, bending works, a post office, public school, blacksmith shop, hotel, R.R. station and restaurant.

Hainesburg, an "old time" village located on the Paulinskill, four miles from its confluence with the Delaware, and about the same distance from Columbia. It was named in honor of John Haines, one of the pioneer settlers of the place. It has a church, store, blacksmith shops, post office, school, hotel, grist mill, and depot of the N. Y. & S. R.R. Also some other small business places.

Centreville, in the southwestern part of the township, about three miles from Hainesburg. It was once quite a public center for the surrounding country, from which it probably derived its name. It has at present a blacksmith shop, store and post office, known as Knowlton P. O.

Polkville, situated about a mile and a half from Centreville. The place is named in honor of James K. Polk, during whose administration the post office was established. It has a store, post office and school.

Warrington, on the Paulinskill, and about half way between Hainesburg and the Delaware River, also on the N. Y. & S. R.R. There are here a grist mill, blacksmith shop, hotel building, post office and R.R. depot.

Columbia, in the central western part of the township on the Delaware, is situated on a plane about 40 ft. above the river level. It has one of the finest locations imaginable, and was once quite enterprising, but at present it is very much wanting in that particular. Glassblowing was once carried on here. At the present time it has a church, two stores, post office, hotel, saw mill, depot of the New York and Susquehanna R.R., and school.

No. of schools in the township, 7. Scholars, 412.

WARREN COUNTY DRUG STORE.

TOWNSHIP DIRECTORY.

All whose vocation is not mentioned are farmers.

Aten John J., laborer, Warrington; Angle Mrs. Jacob, mill owner, Warrington; Angle Eliza, domestic, Delaware; Atchley Susan, house holder, Warrington; Albert S. R., Columbia; Anderson James, saloon keeper, Delaware; Adams George, Delaware; Adams D. C., Delaware; Adams Sarah, Delaware; Addis Wm. C., Delaware; Albertson Mrs. H., house holder, Delaware; Albertson Philip, Delaware; Albertson Levi, wheelwright, Delaware; Albertson John H., Delaware; Albertson John G., Delaware; Albertson Henry, Delaware; Albertson Samuel, Polkville; Allen Jacob, mail carrier, Hainesburg; **Andress Jacob**, merchant, Hainesburg; Andress Joseph, gentleman, Hainesburg; Andress Wm. laborer, Hainesburg; Adams Wm. S., railroad section master, Hainesburg; Angle Emma, teacher, Delaware; An

LAUBACH'S EASTON, Pa. Largest Store, Largest Assortments, and One price to All

gerson Calvin, Marble cutter, Delaware; **Anderson Marshall**, marble cutter, Delaware; Anthony Jerre, settler, Delaware; Ammerman Ward, blacksmith, Delaware; Ammerman Albert, blacksmith, Delaware; Allen M. C., Delaware; Abers Edward, Delaware; Angle J. Wesley Sr., gentleman, Polkville; **Angle J. W. Jr.**, agent and operator N. Y. S. & W. R. R., Columbia; Angle Sarah, householder, Delaware; Angle E., domestic, Delaware; Angle J. G., Delaware; Angle David C., Delaware; Ayers Daniel, hotelkeeper, Delaware; Albert Samuel, laborer Knowlton; Aten Philip, laborer, Warrington; **Angle A. L.** telegraph operator, Delaware; Angle Catharine, domestic, Delaware; Albertson Elbert C., Polkville; Allen Sarah, carpet weaver, Hainesburg; Allen Helen, carpet weaver, Hainesburg; Abers Wm., laborer, Knowlton.

Bebis Snyder, Columbia; Brugler Trumbower, Columbia; Brugler Frank, Columbia; Brugler Peter, Columbia; Brugler Peter M., Columbia; Brugler J.

Andrews & Nolf, 205 Northampton St., Easton, Pa. The reliable HOUSE for Mourning Goods.

H. M. NORTON, *WHOLESALE AND RETAIL DEALER IN* Hardware, Stoves and Housefurnishing.

KNOWLTON TOWNSHIP.

M., Columbia; Brugler Irven, Columbia; Brugler W. H., laborer, Columbia; **Brugler Woodley**, Undertaker and P. M., Columbia; Brugler Henry G., Columbia; Brugler Andrew R., Columbia; Brugler George, laborer, Columbia; Brugler Henry, Columbia; Brugler Edward, Justice of Peace, Hainesburg; **Bellis A. J.,** blacksmith, Hainesburg; Bellis Wm. C. carpenter, Hainesburg; Bellis John M., wheelwright; Bellis Nelson L., Polkville; Bellis Mrs. A., householder, Delaware; Bellis Wm., telegraph operator, Delaware; **Bellis Annie,** Dressmaker, Delaware; Brands DeWitt, laborer, Warrington; Brands Jabez G., Warrington; Brands Wm., Warrington; Brands James, Delaware; Brands Isaac, Delaware; Brands A. H., Delaware; Brands Abram, Delaware; Brands David B., Polkville; Brands Nelson L., Hainsburg; Brands Lewis C., laborer, Polkville; Brands J. F., Delaware; Brands David A., Delaware; Brands W. D. machine agent, Columbia; Brands Peter, Delaware; Brands Mary Ellen, teacher, Delaware; Beck

LAUBACH'S EASTON, PA. CLOAKS and WRAPS of every description. **Our Own Manufacture.**

J. J., Hainesburg; Beck Mashall, Hainesburg; Beck Elizabeth, householder, Hainesburg; Beck Jehiel, Hainesburg; Beck John Sr., Hainesburg; Beck John L. Jr., Hainesburg; Beck Abram, Hainesburg; Beck Philip, Hainesburg; Beck Henry, Hainesburg; Beck Matthias, Hainesburg; Beck Theodore, Hainesburg; Beck Jacob B., blacksmith, Hainesburg; Billings Lewis, Hainesburg; Baird Geo. N., gentleman, Delaware; Bird John, gentleman, Delaware; Broderick J. R., laborer, Columbia; Berry Patrick, laborer, Delaware; Brown Carlisle, Delaware; Brown John L., Delaware; Brown Jacob, laborer, Delaware; Brown Jabez, Columbia; Bogart Samuel, Delaware; Bogart George, Delaware; Bogart John, miller, Warrington; Powers Wm., Delaware; Bowers Albert, Delaware; Butler Mary J., domestic, Delaware; **Bond Robert,** Physician, Knowlton; Brown J. R., laborer, Hainesburg; Brown Joseph Sr., laborer, Hainesburg; Banghart J. A., laborer, Polkville; Blair Harrison, Knowlton; Broderick Wm. F., laborer,

ANDREWS & NOLF, 205 Northampton St. Keep the Largest line of Silks and Dress Goods on E. Northampton

THE BEST GOODS FOR THE LEAST MONEY AT **NORTON'S, Easton, Pa**

KNOWLTON TOWNSHIP.

Columbia; Brich Harvey B., laborer, Polkville; Brich Richard, laborer, Polkville; Brinkerhoff Edward, Delaware; Bodine E. E., milliner, Delaware; Brands George, Delaware; Brugler Augustus, telegraph opertor, Delaware; Boyer R., laborer, Delaware; Beck George, clerk, Delaware; Brich Mary, domestic, Knowlton; Brich Euphemie, domestic, Polkville; Brown Joshua, laborer, Hainesburg; Brown Wm., laborer, Columbia; Bellis Abi, householder, Columbia; Brands Edith, dress maker, Delaware; Brands Amelia, dress maker, Delaware.

Cool Charles, Delaware; Cool Clark, Delaware; Cool Wm., Delaware; **Cool Marshall**, assessor, Columbia; Cool Sarah, householder, Columbia; Cool John F., gentleman, Columbia; Cooper George, laborer, Dunfield; Chambers Frank, carpenter, Delaware; Chamberlain Jacob, Hainesburg; Cramer Edward, Delaware; Cramer Catherine, householder, Delaware; Cramer Lewis, Columbia; Cramer Robert, laborer, Columbia; Cramer Jeremiah, Dunfield;

YOU CAN ALWAYS FIND WHAT YOU WANT AT **LAUBACH'S, Easton, Pa.**

Cramer George, laborer, Dunfield; Cummins Martha, Delaware; Craig Wm., Delaware; Collins Ephraim, laborer, Dunfield; Cowell Letitia, domestic, Hainesburg.

Dewitt Marshall, teacher, Warrington; Gewitt Josiah, farmer, Justice of the Peace, Warrington; Dewitt Anson, Warrington; Gewitt Milton, clerk, Columbia; Dietrick Sylvanus, laborer, Columbia; Dietrick Valentine, blacksmith, Columbia; Dietrich Wm., gentleman, Columbia; Deitrich Ephraim, teacher, Columbia; Dean George, Delaware; Dean David, Knowlton; Dean Albert, laborer, Knowlton; Dean Phœbe, householder, Delaware; Denee Alfred M., carpenter, Delaware; Davidson John C., Hainesburg; Dunfield Jacob, Knowlton; Dunfield John, Polkville; Dunfield Malvin, Knowlton; Davenport C. L., railroad section master, Columbia; Davis R. Hamil, Pastor Presbyterian Church, Delaware; Dugan Milton, laborer, Delaware; Decker John, laborer, Dunfield; Dietrick John, laborer, Columbia; Dunn

All kinds of PAINTS and OILS at WADE BROS.

H. M. NORTON, WHOLESALE AND RETAIL DEALER IN Hardware, Stoves and Housefurnishing

400   KNOWLTON TOWNSHIP.

Clara, domestic, Delaware; Davidson Alvin, teacher, Hainesburg; Dickinson Alfred, laborer, Knowlton; Dickinson Sarah, domestic, Knowlton.

East Frank, laborer, Columbia; East Daniel, laborer, Dunfield; East Ella, Dunfield; Englet Joseph, Polkville; Englet Henry P., shoemaker, Hainesburg; Edinger John F., laborer, Delaware; Edinger Elmer, laborer, Delaware; Eilenberger James, tailor, Delaware; Eilenberger, George L., laborer, Delaware; Elliot Charlotte, householder, Delaware; Easy Charles, mason, Delaware; Easy George, laborer, Delaware; Evans Wm., laborer, Dunfield; Evans Robert M., teacher, Dunfield; Egbert George, laborer, Columbia.

Fell Steven, Hainesburg; **Flummerfelt Amos,** merchant, Polkville; Flummerfelt Alfred L., carpenter, Polkville; Flummerfelt Sarah, householder, Polkville; Flummerfelt Macrina, householder, Polkville; Faunce John D., gentleman, Knowlton; Foster Wm. G., mason, Polkville; **Fitzer William,** hotelkeeper, Hainesburg; Freeman Alexander, laborer, Haines-

LAUBACH'S Easton, Pa. THE LARGEST DRY GOODS AND CARPET HOUSE   BARGAINS ALWAYS

burg; Frutchey Peter, teacher, Columbia.

Geise Henry, Columbia; Geise Herman, Columbia; Gardener Joseph Sr., Columbia; Gardener Joseph, Hainesburg; Gardener Hampton, Columbia; Gardener John K., laborer, Columbia; Gardener Phillip M., Columbia; Gilbert Ephriam, gentleman, Columbia; Grismiller Henry, laborer, Delaware; Green Milton, Knowlton; Green Ephriam, laborer, Knowlton; Garrison Andrew, laborer, Knowlton; Garrison, Martin, Delaware; Gelogey John, laborer, Knowlton; Griffith John F., laborer, Polkville; Gariss Floyd, laborer, Knowlton; Gibbs Wm., teacher, Hainesburg.

Hildebrant Freeman, Delaware; Hildebrant Elmer, Delaware; Hagerman Sarah, householder, Polkville; Hagerman Ellen, tailoress, Polkville; Hagerman Sallie, domestic, Polkville; Hopler George, laborer, Polkville; Hopler Alfred, laborer, Polkville; Hopler Abram, Knowlton; Hopler Frank, machinist, Knowlton; Hopler Wm., laborer, Knowlton; Heitsman Emeline, householder, Delaware; Hay Theodore, Dela-

ANDREWS & NOLF, Proprietors of the "DOWN TOWN" Dry Goods House, 205 Northampton Street, Easton, Pa.

THE BEST GOODS FOR THE LEAST MONEY AT **NORTON'S Easton, Pa.**

KNOWLTON TOWNSHIP. 401

...are; Hiles Jeremiah, Knowlton; Hiles Hulelah, householder, Knowlton; Hutchinson A. J., lawyer and farmer, Delaware; Hutchinson Bartley, lawyer and farmer, Delaware; Huff James, laborer, Knowlton; Hutchinson James, miller, Delaware; Hutchinson Wm., gentleman, Delaware; Hutchinson Charles, miller, Delaware; Hornbeck Samuel, mason, Warrington; Heater Solomon, laborer, Delaware; Henningway Wm. A., agent N. Y. S. & W. R. R., Delaware Henningway Wm. H., agent N. Y. S. & W. R. R., Delaware; Hunt Wellington, constable, Hainesburg; Hunt George, laborer, Hainesburg; Hall James, Dunfield; Haines Jeniel, Knowlton; Harris Adam S., laborer, Polkville; Howell John, laborer, Polkville; Hallet Joseph, Polkville; Hallet John, Polkville; Hallet Ulysses, Polkville; Hartung Chas., paper manufacturer, Delaware; Hartung Alfred, paper manufacturer, Delaware; Hartung Wm. H., paper manufacturer, Delaware; Hartung Robert H., Delaware; Harding J. L. laborer, Delaware; Henry E., Dela-

LAUHACH Leads in prices and quality of goods. EASTON Pa.

ware; Henry Wm., Delaware; Honeywell Margaret, householder, Hainesburg; Heller Edmund, Columbia; Hicks Priscilla, householder, Knowlton; Histon Harry, gentleman, Knowlton; Howey B. F., school slate manufacturer, Dunfield; Hulsizer Aaron, laborer, Delaware; Hartung Albert, laborer, Delaware; Holden Mary, Delaware; Hall Caroline, householder, Dunfield; Hill Chas., laborer, Columbia; Howell Janson, clerk, Polkville; Howell Elwell, laborer, Polkville.

Jones Robert W., Columbia; Jones Jas. P., merchant, Delaware; Jones Hugh P., laborer, Columbia; Jones John G., laborer, Columbia; Jones Thomas R., slater, Columbia; Jones Robert R., Columbia; Jones Evan R., slater, Columbia; James C. T., bending works, Delaware; James Wm. H., bending works, Delaware; Johnson Wm., tailor, Delaware; **Johnson Samuel,** physician.

Kinney John, Columbia; Kinney Geo. S., laborer, Columbia; Kinney Lemuel, Columbia; Kinney Wm.

Extra quality Carving knives and forks at Wade Bros., Hackettstown.

G., Columbia; Kinney Charles, laborer, Hainesburg; Kinney Judson, laborer, Hainesburg; Kinney Mahlon, laborer, Delaware; Kitchen Joseph, laborer, Columbia; Kitchen Reuben, gentleman, Columbia; Kitchen John C., Columbia; Kitchen Peter, laborer, Hainesburg; Kitchen Wm., Hainesburg; Kitchen R., laborer, Hainesburg; Kitchen Isaac, laborer, Hainesburg; Kirkhuff R. A., gentleman, Delaware; Keyser Joseph, Hainesburg; Keyser Irven, Hainesburg; Kays Amos, gentleman, Polkville; Lewis Frederick, laborer, Delaware; Larue Irven, laborer, Delaware; Larue Anna, householder, Polkville; Leida Alfred, huckster, Delaware; Leida Charles, merchant, Knowlton; Leida Isaac, Knowlton; Leida Isaac Jr., laborer, Knowlton; Leida Goodwin, laborer, Knowlton; **Lisk Chas.** Hotelkeeper, Columbia; Lisk James, laborer, Columbia; Loller J., laborer, Polkville; Linnabery Andrew, laborer, Hainesburg; Linnabery Calvin, laborer, Hainesburg; Linnabery Wesley, Delaware; Linnabery John, miller, Hainesburg; Linnabery

LAUBACH'S Easton, Pa. THE LARGEST DRY GOODS AND CARPET HOUSE. BARGAINS ALWAYS

Charles, miller, Hainesburg; Leida Wm., laborer, Knowlton; Lanning George, Knowlton; Labarre Wilson, laborer, Columbia; Low Hannah, householder, Polkville; Low David, Polkville; Love Mary E., householder, Columbia; Lundy Wm., laborer, Warrington; Love Harvey, Columbia; Labarre Robert, laborer, Columbia; Linnabery Parmer, laborer, Knowlton; Michaels Alfred, laborer, Warrington; Michaels Deliah, householder, Warrington; Michaels George, laborer, Dunfield; Michaels James, laborer, Dunfield; Moore Wm. B., Columbia; Moore John B., gentleman, Columbia; Moore Chester, laborer, Columbia.

Milles George, Hainesburg; Miller George C., laborer, Hainesburg; Meshac Wm., Columbia; **McCollum Theodore**, Merchant, Delaware; Mc Murtry Oscar, creamery, Delaware; Mericle Nathan, Hainesburg; McCain Daniel, Polkville; McCain Malvin, blacksmith, Polkville; McCracken Wm., Polkville; McCracken Levin, Polkville; McCracken Geo. Milton, Polkville; Messinger Zachariah, laborer,

Andrews & Nolf, 205 Northampton St., Easton, Pa. The reliable HOUSE for Mourning Goods.

Champions of the World.

I have exhibited at all the largest **Poultry Shows** in the United States, and have never been beaten. I own and breed the highest scoring birds in the World:

Brown Leghorns, White Leghorns, White face Black Spanish, Plymouth Rocks and Light Brahmas.

My stock is from the best known strains in existence, and have been carefully bred by me for the last ten years, and I guarantee them to be second to none

Fowls, Chicks and Eggs for sale.

Send two cent stamp for beautifully illustrated circular showing greatest record ever known.

H. M. COX, M. D.
Port Murray, Warren Co., N. J.

H. M. NORTON
WHOLESALE AND RETAIL DEALER HARDWARE, STOVES AND HOUSE FURNISHING GOODS.

KNOWLTON TOWNSHIP.

Warrington; McElroy Charles, Polkville; Meyer Wm., Delaware; Michaels Peter, laborer, Warrington; Mann Catharine, householder, Delaware; Meler George, laborer, Delaware; Morgan George, laborer, Dunfield; Moyer John, blacksmith, Knowlton; Mains Peter, Delaware; Mann Edward, gentleman, Delaware; Mann Mary, domestic, Hainesburg; Moor Paul, laborer, Columbia; Freeman Moore, laborer, Columbia; McCain Wm. A., Polkville.

Nyce Henry B., Knowlton; Nyce Adrian, Knowlton; Nyce Warren, Knowlton; Newbaker Jacob, carpenter, Columbia; Nicholas Wm., laborer, Knowlton; Osmun Alvah, Delaware; Osmun Jeryme, Delaware.

Ozenbaugh Jacob, laborer, Hainesburg.

Prall George, Merchant, Delaware; Prall Jane, Delaware; Pitson Peter, laborer, Columbia; P ler Mary, domestic, Knowlton; Philips Samuel, laborer, Knowlton; Philips Owen, laborer, Knowlton; Philips John, laborer, Knowlton; Pierce David, wool carder, Pitney James, laborer, Hainesburg; Paul Wm., labor

LAUBACH'S, Easton, Pa. SPECIAL ATTENTION SILKS AND DRESS GOODS. NEW GOODS DAILY

er, Columbia; Pollis Wm., laborer, Delaware; Pattison Edward, laborer, Delaware; **Peters Harry**, gen'l D. L. & W. RR Delaware; Payer Isaiah, laborer, Delaware; Paul Henry, laborer, Delaware; Price Mary, dressmaker Hainesburg; Quick Wm., laborer, Columbia; **Quig Charles**, merchant, Delaware; Randolph James, shoemaker, Columbia; Rice Wm., laborer, Warrington; Rice Ann, householder, Warrington; Rice Abraham, Confectioner Hainesburg; Ribble Winfield, laborer, Delaware; Ridgeway John, laborer, Dunfield; Robbins David, cooper, Hainesburg; Rorbach John, blacksmith, Hainesburg; Roberts G. E., laborer, Polkville; Ryman Elmer, laborer, Columbia; Rusling Margaret, boarding house, Polkville; Rusling Mary, milliner, Polkville; Read Minnie, teacher, Knowlton; Rundle Mr., teacher, Hainesburg.

Simpson J. T., gentleman, Columbus; Sexton John, railroad section master, Delaware; Silverthorn David B., Delaware; Silverthorn Albert, Delaware; Smith

KNOWLTON TOWNSHIP.

Jabez B., farmer and drover, Delaware; Smith George L., farmer and drover, Delaware; Smith Lemuel C., farmer and drove, Delaware; Smith Wm. L., laborer, Columbia; Smith Clark, Knowlton; Smith Chas., Hainesburg; Smith Alfred, Knowlton; Smith Isaac N., Hainesburg; Smith Alvin, Knowlton; Smith Marshall G., Polkville; Smith Josiah L., sawyer, Delaware; Seitz John J., carpenter, Delaware; Sisco H. M., mason, Washington; Snyder Robert, laborer, Hainesburg; Snyder Clark, teacher, Columbia; Snyder James W., laborer, Warrington; Snyder Zadoc, laborer, Warrington; Snyder Alex., laborer, Warrington; Snyder Isabella, householder, Columbia; Snyder Richard, laborer, Columbia; Snyder Chas., laborer, Warrington; Snyder J., laborer, Columbia; Shoemaker Wm., laborer, Columbia; Shafer Hiram, laborer, Delaware; Swayze Joseph, Delaware; Swayze Jebiel, Polkville; Swayze Wm., laborer, Polkville; Sterling G. J., telegraph operator, Delaware; Snover Carmel, Hainesburg; Snover Charlotte, householder, Hainesburg; Snover George, miller, Hainesburg; Swisher W. H., Knowlton; Shafer George, laborer, Delaware; Slack Moses, Delaware; Shannon Elmer, laborer, Delaware; Snover Ella, domestic, Columbia; Seals F., Polkville; Snyder Olivia, tailoress, Warrington; Shafer Almeda, domestic, Delaware; Snyder Irvan, laborer, Delaware; Swisher Bina, domestic, Hainesburg; Swisher Frank, Knowlton; Snyder Frederick, laborer, Warrington; **Smith Oscar**, merchant, Delaware; Space Wm., laborer, Knowlton.

Timmar Milton, merchant, Columbia; Timmar John A., Columbia; Timmerman Chas., laborer, Columbia; Thomas Joseph P., Columbia; Trimmer Augustus, Columbia; Teel Andrew R., laborer, Columbia; Thomson Thomas, gentleman, Delaware; Thomson Geo. D., Hainesburg; Troxel Lorenzo, gentleman, Delaware; Transue Sufferine, Delaware; Titman Brakley, Hainesburg; Turner Edna, domestic, Knowlton; Trimmer Elias, Columbia.

VanKirk John J. Sr., gentleman, Columbia; Van Kirk John J. Jr., teacher, Delaware; Van Vorst Cor-

H. M. NORTON — WHOLESALE AND RETAIL DEALER IN HARDWARE, STOVES AND HOUSEFURNISHING GOODS.

KNOWLTON TOWNSHIP.

nelius, lawyer, Columbia; Van Kirk Sarah, householder, Columbia; Van Kirk Edward, laborer, Columbia; Van Kirk James, laborer, Columbia; Van Kirk James, laborer, Hainesburg; Vanhorn George, Columbia; Vanhorn Andrew, Hainesburg; Vanhorn Johnson, Delaware; Voss Lizzie, householder, Delaware; Vroom Jacob, Columbia; Van Duzen Albert, Pastor M. E. Church, Columbia; Van Vorst Wm., lawyer, Columbia; Van Vorst E. J., lawyer, Columbia; Vough Elmer, painter, Hainesburg; Vough Edward, laborer, Hainesburg; Vanscoten J. K., clerk, Hainesburg.

Weidman Samuel C., clerk, Columbia; Weidman Webster W., merchant, Columbia; Weidman Wm. F., gentleman, Columbia; Weller Michael, slate factory, Columbia; Weller Lewis C., laborer, Columbia; Weller Samuel, laborer, Columbia; Weller Isaiah, mason, Columbia; Weller John Sr., laborer, Columbia; Weller John Jr., teacher, Columbia; Winters Stewart, laborer, Columbia; Wallace Horace F., laborer,

LAUBACH Leads in prices and quality of goods. EASTON Pa.

Columbia; Walters Depue, Hainesburg; Wolfe Abram, laborer, Hainesburg; Wolfe Benjamin, Delaware; Wolfe Thomas B., Delaware; Wolfe Joseph, Knowlton; Ward Wm. O., Hainesburg; Ward Frank, teacher, Hainesburg; Ward John A., shoemaker, Delaware; Ward Wm. A., laborer, Delaware; Widner A. C., wheelwright, Delaware; Wildrick

GEORGE C. RICE,
Breeder of Thoroughbred Wyandotes, Rose and Single Comb, Brown Leghorns.

Eggs and Fowls for sale at moderate prices. I also keep a supply of Poultry Powders, German Roup Pills, Imperial Egg Food. Eggies and almost everything needed in the Poultry Yard. Write for what you want; satisfaction guaranteed. Send for circulars and price list.

Abram, Knowlton; Walters John A., clerk, Knowlton; West Samuel, Delaware; Wiley Samuel, laborer, Delaware; Wolfe Wm., laborer, Delaware; Winters James, Warrington; Wilgus Brit., laborer, Warrington; Wallace Eva, teacher, Columbia.

Yeomans B. D., Columbia; Yeomans A. C., reporter, Columbia; Young George, Columbia; Young Judson, Columbia; Young Peter Y., Hainesburg.

Zanser Albert, Delaware.

LOPATCONG TOWNSHIP.

LOPATCONG is one of the smallest townships of Warren County and is situated in the southwestern part, along the Delaware.

It is odd in outline, having the shape of a wedge, as if to split Harmony from Greenwich. Its extreme length and breadth are about equal, each being about four miles. It is bounded on the north by Harmony, on the east and south by Greenwich, and on the west by the borough of Phillipsburg and the Delaware, which separates it from Pennsylvania.

The surface is uneven, and in parts somewhat mountainous. The agriculture of the township is in a flourishing condition, which fact is attested by the existence of many well-to-do farmers within its limits. There is considerable mineral wealth in Lopatcong, but no important developments in this line have yet been made.

This township has no village within its limits, a fact possibly due to the proximity of Phillipsburg and Easton. It is traversed by the railway lines of the New Jersey Central, the Morris & Essex, the Belvidere-Delaware, and the Easton and Amboy. The Morris Canal passes near the southern and eastern borders.

The date of the first settlement cannot be definitely ascertained, but there are evidences that the history of the township began as early as 1740, and perhaps even earlier. Among the very earliest settlers was one John Feit, who emigrated to America from the Rhine country, between Germany and France, and settled in the vicinity of the present town of Phillipsburg about the year above mentioned. It is known that he married there in 1741. The only circumstance, of which we have knowledge, influencing his emigration, is that he came hither to escape military proscription, which was at that time driving so many Germans to the New World. He came to this country when about eighteen years of age, and must have been the son of wealthy parents, as at that age he could hardly have acquired a fortune for himself, his extensive land purchases showing that he was well supplied with money. The old homestead of the pioneer Feit has remained in the family line while three generations have passed away, and has been for some time the home of the fourth.

Other German pioneers are supposed to have been among the early settlers, but no important records of them have been preserved.

The Shipmans, who for more than a century have figured in the history of Warren County, are also identified with the early history of Lopatcong. It is rather a peculiar and remarkable fact that a number of the pioneer properties are still in their respective family lines.

The township was formed in 1851 from Greenwich and Harmony, and was first called the township of Phillipsburg, after the town of that name. In 1868, some time after the incorporation of Phillipsburg, the name of the township was changed to Lopatcong, after the creek of the same name.

The business interests of the township are almost identical with those of Phillipsburg, all the business places of importance being in close proximity to the borough limits.

Population about 1,700. Schools, 5. Scholars, 570.

E. W. ALLEGER.   WILLARD ALLEGER.

E. W. ALLEGER & SON,

Lumber Yards and Planing Mills.

MANUFACTURERS, WHOLESALE AND RETAIL DEALERS IN

All kinds of Floorings, Ceilings, Sidings, Lath, Shingles, Rough and Dressed Lumber, Slate, Brick, Lime, Cement, Sand and Plaster.

We have constantly on hand a large stock of

Sash, Doors, Blinds, Shutters, Mouldings and General House Trim, and can make to order at short notice.

We have also Hand-Rails, Balusters, Newels and Turned Work at prices to which we def. competition. Planing, Scroll and Circular Sawing, Wood Turning, &c. Our prices are as low as the lowest for good work.

BROAD STREET,   **WASHINGTON, N. J.**

WARREN COUNTY DRUG STORE.

Township Directory.

*All whose vocation is not mentioned are farmers.
The Post Office addresses not given in this township are Phillipsburg.*

Allshouse Jacob; Allshouse James; Amey John; Ashton William, laborer; Aten James, car inspector.

Bauman Joseph, foundryman; Bauman William, foundryman; Beers Charles M., railroader; Burke John, laborer, Shimer's; Bishop Geo. W., laborer, Shimer's; Baker Amsey, laborer, Shimer's; Brady Patrick, furnaceman, Shimer's; Bullman James, brakeman; Bullman Thomas, laborer; Bullman Jeremiah, laborer; Browne Robert D., physician; Brakely John H., laborer; Beeman Jasper, laborer; Beers Levi R., teamster, Shimer's; Burdock Henry, trackman; Barber Robert K., Stewartsville; Bozzo Lewis, engineer; Baylor Michael, laborer, Stewartsville; Baylor Jesse, laborer, Stewartsville; Boyer John C., re-

YOU CAN ALWAYS FIND WHAT YOU WANT AT LAUBACH'S, Easton, Pa.

tired, Stewartsville; Baker Philip, laborer; Bennett Theodore K.; Brotzman Daniel; Brakely Matthias; Brakely George, retired; Bittner Phaon; Brotzman Daniel Jr., agent; Bittner Amandus, laborer; Beatty Thomas, boatman, Shimer's; Beatty Elmer, boatman, Shimer's; Beatty Alvin, boatman, Shimer's; Beatty Wm., boatman, Shimer's; Black Morris, boatman, Shimer's; Bercaw Chester, boatman, Shimer's.

Clark Philip, laborer; Clark Hugh, trackman; Culver Jacob, boatman, Stewartsville; Cool Aaron, F., Stewartsville; Cline Clarence E; Cressman Benjamin; Conn James, railroader; Cusick John, railroader; Crampton Michael, furnaceman, Shimer's; Conway Andrew, furnaceman, Shimer's; Caton John, foundryman, Shimer's; Caton Michael, foundryman, Shimer's; Conner Daniel, laborer, Shimer's; Clark Edward, laborer, Shimer's; Conklin John A., gardener; Caseby Jesse, Sheet-mill-man; Cahill James, furnaceman; Conlogue Patrick, laborer; Connor John laborer, Shimer's; Cooper David, laborer; Cava-

ANDREWS & NOLF, 205 Northampton St. Keep the Largest line of Silks and Dress Goods on E. Northampton

H. M. NORTON, WHOLESALE AND RETAIL DEALER IN Hardware, Stoves and Housefurnishing.

410 LOPATCONG TOWNSHIP.

naugh Michael, boatman, Shimer's; Cox Michael, foundryman; Cowell Geo. W., carpenter; Clymer Jacob, milkman; Clymer Lemuel; Cole John Sr., retired; Cole John Jr., car inspector; Cole Charles W., blacksmith; Cole Clark, machinisit; Creveling William, engine-wiper; Crotsby Jacob, foundryman; Cooley Mahlon, brakeman; Cline Garner H.; Chalmers James, patternmaker.

Drake Lorenzo; Drake Howard, milkman; Dutt Geo.; Daily Philips, laborer; Deremer Isaac; Deremer Jas. S.; DeWitt Moses; DeWitt Barnet, retired; DeWitt George; DeWitt Oliver, laborer; Deats Jonathan, laborer; Donnelly John, laborer, Shimer's; Davis David, laborer, Shimer's; Davis Wilson, laborer, Shimer's; Draney William; Dalton Ed., brakeman, Shimer's; Dundass Thomas, foundryman; Dundass Arthur, foundryman; Davis William M., lawyer.

Eckert Garner, laborer, Harmony; Eckert Frank, sheet mill man; Eckert George, huckster.

Fritts David H.; Fritts Joseph; Fritts John; Fry

LAUBACH'S, Easton, Pa. SPECIAL ATTENTION SILKS AND DRESS GOODS. NEW GOODS DAILY.

Samuel, milkman; Fulmer Samuel, laborer; Firth David, stone-cutter; Firth David J., stone-cutter; Fulmer William, huckster; Fine Philip G., mail carrier, Shimer's; Felker David, foundryman; Fox Thomas, furnaceman, Shimer's; Feit Paul; Feit Daniel, retired; Feit John Sr., retired; Feit John Jr.; Feit Jacob; Feit George W.; Freck George, foundryman; Fell John C., foundryman.

Gephart Joseph, engineer; Garner Levi, miller; Gaghan Martin, foundryman; Garrecht George, laborer; Gaughran Thomas, furnaceman, Shimer's; Gaughran Owen, furnaceman, Shimer's; Gaughran Matthew, printer, Shimer's; Greagor H. Harman, furnaceman, Shimer's; Gaven John, furnaceman, Shimer's; Gruver Irvin, carpenter; Gruver John; Gruver Jeremiah; Geary Nelson, carpenter; Gross William F., laborer, Shimer's; Gammell Patrick, furnaceman; Gibb Christopher, Sr., laborer; Gibb Christopher, Jr., laborer; Gaten William, furnaceman, Shimer's.

SHIELDS' Compound Syrup of Wild Cherry with Hypophosites of Lime and Soda. Sure cure for coughs, croup, etc.

Haml n Wil iam Sr.; Hamlen William Jr.; Hamlen William H., retired; Hamlen Wm. F., milkman; Hamlen Wm. A., laborer; Hamlen Robert, milkman; Hamlen John; Hamlen Mahlon; Huff James, laborer; Helm William, blacksmith, Stewartsville; Halpin Daniel R.; Hildeorand Peter, shoemaker, Stewartsville; Heid John, laborer, Stewartsville; Hawk William D.; Hawk John; Huff John R., laborer, Shimer's; Huff John, laborer, Shimer's; Heffendreger Milton, laborer, Shimer; Hetzler Enoch, laborer, Shimer's; House Edward, watchman, Shimer's; Howell Joseph, retired; Howell Charles, laborer; Henry John S., laborer; Hess William H., blacksmith; Hess Peter, shoemaker; Hoff Holloway, foundryman; Hummell John, foundryman; Hofschild August, furnaceman, Shimer's; Hofschild William, furnace foreman, Shimer's; Hartzell John, switchman.

Insley Jacob, Stewartsville; Insley Isaac, Stewartsville; Insley Godfrey, retired, Stewartsville; Iliff Joseph A.; Iliff Mrs. Margaret.

LAUBACH'S EASTON, PA. Largest Store, Largest Assortments, and One rice to All

Johnson Alvin, laborer, Shimer's; Johnson James, laborer, Shimer's; Johnson Charles, retired; Johnson Theodore, wheelwright; Jacoby Alpheus, millwright, Shimer's.

Kitchen Daniel; Kitchen Thomas W., blacksmith; Kinney Charles E., laborer; Kitchen Mrs. Eliza, householder; Kinney Mrs. Sarah, householder, Stewartsville; Kline William, collector and constable; Kananhan William N., laborer; Kelso James, laborer, Shimer's; Kelegher Patrick, foundryman, Knowles Arthur, foundryman; Keck Benjamin, boatman; Kearney Thomas, foundryman; Koose William, mason; Kisselbach Edward, car inspector; Kisselbach Eugene, car inspector; Kichline Aaron, painter; Kinneybrook Charles, switchman; Kelly Peter, foundryman; Kinney Alfred G., carpenter.

Larue George; Lehr Anson, machinist; Lesher William H., carpenter; Lance Jesse R., boatman, Stewartsville; Lambert Jackson, boatman, Stewartsville; Lambert John, boatman, Stewartsville; Lambert Al-

ANDREWS & NOLF, Proprietors of the "DOWN TOWN" Dry Goods House, 205 Northampton Street, Easton, Pa.

NEW PIANOS

FROM

Steinway & Sons, Kranich & Bach, Hallet & Davis, J. & C. Fischer, &c.

Lowest Prices, Cash, Installments or Rent, and one year's rent allowed if purchased from

WM. H. KELLER.

NEW ORGANS

From Estey & Co., Mason & Hamlin, Smith American, Taylor & Farley, Worcester Co. Sterling Co., Etc., Etc.

Lowest Prices, Cash, Installments or Rent, and one year's rent allowed if purchased only at

WM. H. KELLER'S 223 & 225 Northampton St., Easton, Pa.

LOPATCONG TOWNSHIP.

phonso, boatman, Stewartsville; Lerch Lycurgus, boatman; Lanagan William, furnaceman; Lennon Edward, foundryman; Lee George, foundryman; Lyons Thomas, laborer; Lesher Andrew M., R. R. brakeman; Lesher John P., carpenter; Lesher Millard, R. R. conductor, Loughland John, foundry foreman.

McClary James; McNeill Garner, laborer, Stewartsville; McNeill Martin, laborer, Stewartsville; Merritt Abel H. farmer and drover; Merritt George E.; Metz Theodore, laborer, Stewartsville; Melroy John, carpenter; Melroy Robert D., gardener, Melroy Jesse, huckster; Myers Whitfield; Melick Miss Rebecca, householder; Metz A. W. L., gardener; Mitchell Joseph, sheetmillman; McElroy Frederick laborer, Shimer's; Murphy Thomas, furnaceman, Shimer's; Murphy James, furnaceman, Shimer's; Murphy Bartholomew, furnaceman, Shimer's; McDermott Thomas Sr., laborer, Shimer's; McDermott James, laborer, Shimer's; McDermott Thomas, Jr., clerk; Shimer's;

McCan John, laborer, Shimer's; Mettler William A., R R brakeman; Metz Lawrence, Shimer's; Melick William S.; McClure John J., stonecutter; McClure Margaret Mrs;, householder; Myers Robert, laborer; McCrary Thomas, Jr., quarryman; McCrary Thomas, Sr., gardener; McMannen Edward, foundryman; McCan Owen, quarryman; Mooney Daniel, laborer; Muldenhauer August, laborer, Shimer's; McNamee Thomas, furnaceman, Shimer's; Mernell Walter, furnaceman, Shimer's; Miller Alfred, laborer, Shimer's; Maddock Thomas, laborer, Shimer's; Murren Charles, plane brakeman; McCormick Thomas, R. R. contractor; Mearion William, foundryman; Mearion Richard, foundryman; Merrick John, engineer; Manning John, foundryman; Miller William H., foundryman; Miller John F., foundryman; Middleton William, foundryman; McInerney Dennis, foundryman.

Norris Eugene, laborer; Nunnemaker Jacob, laborer; Neno Reinhard, laborer, Shimer's; Neencteil Maurice, laborer; Norton Mrs. Mary, householder.

H. M. NORTON *WHOLESALE AND RETAIL DEALER IN HARDWARE, STOVES AND HOUSEFURNISHING GOODS.*

LOPATCONG TOWNSHIP.

Oswald John, laborer; Osterstock Daniel, brickmaker; O'Brian James, laborer, Shimer's; O'Herren John, furnaceman, Shimer's; Owens Nicholas, furnaceman, Shimer's; O'Hagan Michael, mason.

Probasco George, laborer; Pierson Robert, gardener; Person Richard, gardener; Potraz Harman, laborer; Parker George, laborer, Shimer's; Price Thomas, laborer, Shimer's; Price George W., plane tender; Pratt Albert, grocer, Shimer's; Pierson Edward, grocer, Shimer's; Pursell Lefferd H., lock tender, Shimer's; Pursell Thomas, miller; Pursell Stewart C., merchant; Poole U. S., poultryman; Petit William H., laborer; Piatt Orton, laborer, Shimer's; Paulus Abraham, grocer; Paulus Edwin H.; Paulus Daniel; Potts James E., machinist foreman; Person John M., laborer.

Roseberry John, agent; Roseberry Isabella, householder; Rush William C., laborer, Stewartsville; Rinedart Samuel; Riddle Samuel P.; Stewartsville; Richline John, laborer, Stewartsville; Richline Andrew, laborer, Stewartsville; Richline George, laborer, Stewartsville; Reimer Owen; Reinert Cosmos B., laborer; Resh Irvin, engineer; Rooney Jeremiah, nightwatchman, Shimer's; Rooney Timothy, laborer, Shimer's; Rooney Barney, laborer, Shimer's; Reimel Edward; Rice Charles, laborer; Rodenbaugh James, laborer; Ready Frank, laborer; Rudden Peter, furnaceman, Shimer's; Reis James, saloon keeper; Reis William, foundryman; Renner Urban, foundryman; Raub John J., foundryman; Richard Philip, railroad brakeman.

LAUBACH LEADS IN PRICES AND QUALITY OF GOODS, EASTON, PA.

Shipman Philip, retired; Shipman John, retired; Sleight Frederick, Stewartsville; Smith Charles C., laborer, Stewartsville; Smith Allison, laborer, Stewartsville; Smith John B., laborer, Stewartsville; Smith Daniel, laborer, Stewartsville; Smith Lawrence, furnaceman; Smith James, furnaceman; Smith Jeremiah, engine hostler; Smith Patrick, boatman, Shimer's; Stewart William S., Stewartsville; Styers Edward, carpenter, Stewartsville; Searles Alonzo, la-

Extra quality Carving knives and forks at Wade Bros., Hackettstown.

borer; Searles Charles, laborer; Searles William, laborer; Searles Albro, laborer; Searles Alfred, laborer; Searles Theodore, railroad flagman; Schiffert Uriah, gardener; Schuyler Aaron M.; Stansberry Jacob, sheet mill man; Sass Frederick, retired; Shoener Thomas, laborer; Sanderson James, quarry foreman; Seas George, railroader, Shimer's; Stone Mrs. Elizabeth, householder, Shimer's; Seas James, railroader, Shimer's; Seas John, railroader, Shimer's; Seas Philip, laborer, Shimer's; Snyder Penrose, miller, Shimer's; Snyder Peter K., miller, Shimer's; Strouse Samuel, railroader, Shimer's; Schooley Samuel, miller, Shimer's; Schedler Frederick, junk merchant, Shimer's; Stocker John; Sheard Francis W., stone cutter; Sheard William, stone cutter; Slowey John, furnaceman, Shimer's; Steber Ferdinand, furnaceman, Shimer's; Snyder Henry M., boatman, Shimer,s; Steele Joseph, Shimer's; Sherry Peter Sr., laborer; Sherry Peter Jr., foundryman; Sinclair Jno., railroad engineer; Stamets Samuel, engine wiper;

LAUBACH'S EASTON, PA. Largest Store Largest Assortments, and One Price to All

Stryker Joseph J.; Stryker John W.; Shimer Hubler; Shimer Hervey; Stark Ferdinand, engine wiper; St. John Richard, foundryman; Smith Wm., laborer, Stewartsville.

Tinsman Martin; Tinsman Peter, retired; Tilton William K., gardener; Thatcher Thomas, sheet mill man; Taylor James H., laborer, Shimer's; Tully Christopher, laborer, Shimer's; Thatcher Elisha, truckman; Tute Walter, furnaceman, Shimer's; Travers Peter, laborer; Trump John, foundryman; Trump George, foundryman; Tully Thos., laborer, Shimer's.

Unangst Barnet, laborer, Stewartsville; Unangst William, Stewartsville; Unangst Henry, shute foreman; Unangst Arthur, carpenter; Unangst George, canal foreman.

VanNorman William, rolling mill man; VanSickle Martin, laborer, Shimer's; Vetter Charles, blacksmith Shimer's; Vanatta Elisha; Van Amburg William, gardener.

ANDREWS & NOLF Immense Stock, Low Prices. The "DOWN TOWN" Dry Goods House. EASTON Pa.

H. M. NORTON *WHOLESALE AND RETAIL DEALER IN HARDWARE, STOVES AND HOUSEFURNISHING GOODS.*

LOPATCONG TOWNSHIP.

Wright Nathan; Wright William T., huckster; Walters Allen H.; Walters Henry; Walters George W., laborer; Walters Joseph; Weller John, laborer, Stewartsville; Wolf Calvin, boatman, Stewartsville; Workheiser Jeremiah; Worman John, laborer, Shimer's; Wilson Edmund O., merchant; Willever John A., railroader; White Benjamin, laborer; Wagner Stephen, carpenter; Way Isaac, laborer; Wighorst Henry F., gardener; Wallace Patrick, furnaceman, Shimer's; Wendland August, retired, Shimer's; Waldbeiser Frederick, laborer, Shimer's; Wallace William, mason; Wintergarst Max, laborer; Warner Christopher, laborer; Weidon John B., retired.

Yeisly Jeremiah, teacher; Yeisley George L., clerk; Young John C., mason, Stewartsville; Young Andrew, shoemaker; Young William, laborer; Yearance Peter, laborer.

ST. CLOUD HOTEL,
C. F. STAATES, Prop'r,
WASHINGTON, N. J.

THIS HOTEL has recently been thoroughly renovated throughout, and the liberal patronage of Commercial Agents and Travelers, as well as the large number of permanent boarders, is a sufficient guarantee of its excellent accommodation and good management. It stands among the first Hotels of the State. Owned by the proprietor and every effort possible is put forth for the comfort and accommodation of its guests.

Parlors, Reading-Rooms, Billard Hall and Bar

are well-arranged and conveniently heated. You are welcome.

MANSFIELD TOWNSHIP.

MANSFIELD is one of the two south central border townships of the county. The area of the township is 27.8 square miles or 17,805 acres. It is bounded on the north by Hope township, on the northeast by Independence, on the east by the Musconetcong, on the south by Washington, on the southwest by Washington and Oxford, and on the west and northwest by Oxford and Hope. It has a population of about 1,800. The Morris canal and the Delaware, Lackawanna and Western Railroad pass through the entire township from east to west.

The surface of the township is undulating, two chains of hills running its entire length from east to west. The Musconetcong River forms the entire southern boundary of the township, and the beautiful Musconetcong valley, filled with picturesque and productive farms, comprises the whole southern portion of the township, running parallel with the chain of hills on the north. Just north of the valley and almost parallel with it, run the Morris & Essex Canal and D. L. & W. R. R. Some of the most productive farms of the county are found in this township and in this valley, though much of the land, on account of its location and slaty nature, is not susceptible of a high state of cultivation. The land in the valley bottoms and to a considerable extent the uplands are unusually rich and easily cultivated. Many of the farms in the Musconetcong valley yield from sixty to seventy-five bushels of corn and from one and a half to two tons of hay per acre.

The valley along the Morris Canal is wide, the hills on the south side sloping off gradually, but on the north side in some places the hills rise abruptly from the canal. Beyond this ridge, on the north, is the Pohatcong valley, through which runs the creek of that name. This creek has its source in Independence township, on the stock farm owned by Dr. W. A. Conover. The soil in this valley is very rich, and the farms throughout the entire township give evidence of considerable scientific agricultural knowledge on the part of the farmers.

Two other streams Old Hollow Brook and Trout Brook, run through the township in a southwestern direction, both discharging their waters into the Musconetcong.

There are also indications of considerable mineral wealth in the township, though at the present time these resources are comparatively neglected.

Mansfield was set off from Greenwich in 1754, about twenty years before the first bloodshed in the Revolutionary War. The township was named in honor of Lord Mansfield, who was a prominent royal jurist of England, at the time of the setting off of Mansfield from Greenwich.

The Poor-house of Warren County, is located in the northwestern part of this township. It is a four story building, 80 by 50 feet, having a wing upon the northeast, 50 by 24 feet, and two and a half stories high. The county owns 396 acres of land, surrounding the building. The Poor house was erected here about the year 1839, and the stewards have been as follows: William Richards, William McDonald, Samuel Lowder, T. H. Tunison, L. H. Martenis, J. K. Poel, Samuel Frome, R. H. Tunison, and J. H. Hance, who is the present steward.

Among the recent business interests of the township are the creamery lately established at Port Murray, and the Poultry Yard of Dr. H. M. Cox of the same place. Dr. Cox has in his yard, though so lately established, some of the finest birds to be found anywhere in the country, and his patronage is fast becoming extensive. For some time he was the only resident physician of the township.

The Warren Slate Co., located at Port Murray, does a thriving business and turns out a good quality of slate.

There are several small towns in the township, some of which are very enterprising. The oldest is Beattystown which in 1869 was a thriving hamlet. In 1825 it was said to be more of a business place than Hackettstown, being then the chief market of this vicinity for grain and all kinds of produce. There were also more residences in Beattystown then, than at the present time. It has a store and post office, grist mill, school house, M. E. church, blacksmith shop and wheelwright shop. Present population about 240. Anderson is in the southwestern part of the township and is situated next to the Washington line. It has a store and post office, hotel, school, M. E. church and blacksmith shop. Population, 100. Rockport is a small hamlet located in the eastern part of the township, having a store school and eight or ten dwellings. Mount Bethel in the northeastern part of the township has a M. E. church. Karrsville is located on Pohatcong Creek about 1½ miles from Port Murray. It has a school, and a store kept by H. M. Cregar, doing a good business. Port Murray is the youngest and most flourishing town in Mansfield. It is the only point in the township situated on the railroad and is hence the shipping point for that entire section. The location is a desirable one, being about half way between Washington and Hackettstown, and on the direct line of railroad between the two places. It is an enterprising village of about 300 inhabitants with a good store kept by John W. Forker, a Baptist church, a beautiful Hall in which the M. E. Society worship, a school house, hotel and blacksmith and wheelwright shop, beside the enterprises already mentioned, there are several fine residences. There are in Mansfield 6 schools with a total of 397 scholars.

WARREN COUNTY DRUG STORE.

Township Directory.

All whose vocation is not mentioned are farmers.

Apgar Ebenezer, Stevensburg; Apgar Elizabeth, freeholder, Beattystown; Albert J. M., carpenter, Port Murray; Albert A. G., laborer, Port Murray; Albert Wm., carpenter, Port Murray; Albert D. M., carpenter, Karrsville; Adams Mary, freeholder, Port Murray; Adams George, laborer, Port Murray; Anthony Mary, freeholder, Port Murray; Anthony John, Anderson; Anthony Jacob, Anderson; Anderson Margaret, freeholder, Karrsville; Anderson John, Hackettstown; **Anderson Joseph**, propr. of Port Murray Hotel, Port Murray; Anderson Sarah, Port Murray; Anderson Elizabeth, freeholder, Port Murray; Anderson Lewis, gentleman, Port Murray; Anderson Wm., millwright, Karrsville; Anderson Nelson, millwright, Karrsville; Ackley Zeim, Beattystown; Ackley James, laborer, Beattystown; Ackley Theodore, laborer, Beattystown.

YOU CAN ALWAYS FIND WHAT YOU WANT AT **LAUBACH'S, Easton, Pa**

Beatty, H. T., Hackettstown; Beatty Alexander, Port Murray; Beatty H. L., miller, Port Murray; Beatty Eva, freeholder, Port Murray; Beatty James, Port Murray; Beatty Amos, Port Murray; Beatty Jacob, carpenter, Port Murray; Beatty J. B., carpenter, Hackettstown; Beatty Lewis, Port Murray; Beatty Robt., carpenter, Beattystown; Beatty Theodore, laborer, Port Murray; Beatty Wm., miller, Beattystown; Bryan George, Sr., Port Murray; Bryan Albert, Port Murray; Bryan George, Jr., Port Murray; Bryan Isaac, Beattystown; Beam Joseph, carpenter, Port Murray; Beam Abraham, carpenter, Port Murray; Beam Andrew, carpenter, Port Murray; Bartow John, shoemaker, Anderson; Bartow Wm., laborer, Beattystown; Beri H. J., laborer, Port Murray; Bell William, laborer, Karrsville; Bigler James A., Port Murray; Bigler John, teamster, Port Murray; Bigler Alonzo, laborer, Port Murray; Bigler Larison, Port Murray; Bigler J. H., Port Murray; Bigler

William, railroader, Port Murray; Bertron Anna, freeholder, Port Colden; Bertron William, boatman, Port Colden; Barber C. D., boatman, Beattystown; Burk John, laborer, Beattystown; Bercaugh Isaac, laborer, Port Murray; Bartley Cornelius, Beattystown.

Conine Charles, brakeman, Port Colden; Carhart Matilda, Anderson; Cornish W. T., laborer, Port Murray; Cougle Wm., laborer, Beattystown; Cougle Robert, laborer, Beattystown; Cougle Charles V., carriagemaker, Beattystown; Cougle Peter, laborer, Beattystown; Cougle Wm., laborer, Port Murray; Cougle John, agent, Beattystown; Cougle Smith A., saloonkeeper, Port Murray; Cougle Charles, milk peddler, Port Murray; Smith A. W., laborer, Port Murray; Carpenter David, laborer, Beattystown; Curl John, carpenter, Beattystown; Curl Jacob, merchant, Beattystown; Castner Adam, Karrsville; Castner Jane, freeholder, Karrsville; Castner Charles, laborer, Karrsville; Castner Miller, clerk, Karrsville;

LAUBACH'S, Easton, Pa. 328 NORTHAMPTON ST. LARGEST Dry Goods and Carpet House.

Cougle Dallas, shopkeeper, Beattystown; Cole David, brickmaker, Karrsville; Cole Jacob, Port Colden; Cregar John, Karrsville; **Cregar H. M.**, dry goods, groceries, etc., Karrsville; Cregar Andrew M., Port Murray; Cregar Emanuel, Port Murray; Cregar Adam F., blacksmith, Beattystown; Cregar Marcus, Beattystown; Cregar Wm., painter, Beattystown; Cregar Andrew, Karrsville; **Cox H. M.**, physician and surgeon, Port Murray; Cox John, carpenter, Port Murray; Carling Sarah, freeholder, Anderson; Carling Joseph, laborer, Anderson; Cowell Daniel, wheelwright; Canfield Uzal, Judge, Port Murray; Canfield Caroline, freeholder, Port Murray; Cummins Mathias, mason, Port Murray; Cummins James, mason, Port Murray; Cummins Wm., laborer, Stephensburg.

Davis A. N., Stephensburg; Davis S. W., Stephensburg; Davis J. R., Stephensburg; Davis Frank, laborer, Stephensburg; Davis W. J., Beattystown; Deats Joseph, laborer, Anderson; Deats Emma, free-

Carriage Trimmings at Wade Bros., HACKETTSTOWN, NEW JERSEY.

UNDERTAKING AT PORT MURRAY.

The undersigned have had about ten years experience in the undertaking business, and are prepared to do it in the most approved style and at the lowest rates possible. We have a handsome hearse and

Furnish an extra conveyance for friends free of charge.

We use J. C. Taylor & Son's Patent Improved Ice Casket for preserving the dead with cold air.

We also do embalming. Our embalming keeps the body for any ordinary length of time desired without ice.

The body after three or four days looks better than when first embalmed.

We furnish any style of coffin at short notice. For all distances within 15 miles rates the same. Night attendance same as day. Flowers and stools provided if desired. Connection by telephone with Belvidere, Oxford, Broadway, Washington, Port Colden, Beattystown, Hackettstown and Schooley's Mountains. Orders by telephone received, and telephone charges paid by us.

We do not take advantage of these occasions, but charge very reasonably.

Very respectfully,

THOMPSON & CO.

holder, Anderson; Deats Jacob, boatman, Anderson; Deats Samuel, laborer, Anderson; Dega, Jacob, laborer, Port Colden; Drake J. K., Beattystown; Drake Charles M., school teacher, Beattystown; Dickson James, shoemaker, Beattystown; Danly John C., carpenter, Beattystown.

Everitt George W., Karrsville; Everitt Wm., Karrsville; Eakley John, laborer, Karrsville.

Forester Wm., laborer, Port Murray; Fisher J. B., Esquire, Beattystown; Fisher James, lawyer, Beattystown; Fisher Martin, Beattystown; Fisher Adam, Beattystown; Fenrick George, Karrsville; **Forker John W.**, dry goods, groceries etc., Port Murray; Fritts C. N., Anderson; Frome J. Hill, Karrsville.

Garey Miss Susanah, freeholder, Anderson; Garey Wm., huckster, Anderson; Garey Brackley, laborer, Port Murray; Gardner Alfred, Port Colden; Gardner Hanlon, Port Colden; Gardner Mary, Port Colden; Gardner Wesley, laborer, Port Colden; Gardner Amanda, freeholder, Port Colden; Gibbs Richard,

LAUBACH Leads in prices and quality of goods, EASTON Pa.

Townsbury; Gulick Samuel, brakeman, Port Murray; Gulick Amanda, freeholder, Karrsville; Gulick Sarah, freeholder, Port Murray; Gulick J. Q., boatman, Port Murray; Gulick Rachel, freeholder, Port Murray; Gulick James, laborer, Karrsville; Gulick Sarah, freeholder, Karrsville; Gulick Ervin, laborer, Karrsville; Gruver John W., laborer, Karrsville; Gruver Anna S., freeholder, Port Murray; Gray Aaron, boatman, Karrsville; Gearcke Mary, freeholder, Port Murray; Gaston Wm. C., freeholder, Port Colden; Gibson James, Port Colden; Gould James, Karrsville; Groondyke Thomas, Karrsville.

Hance Wm., Stevensburgh; Hance Philip, laborer, Beattystown; Hance Jos., Beattystown; Hance John, Beattystown; Hance J. H., steward county house, Karrsville; Hann Jeremiah, laborer, Beattystown; Hann Lawrence, Jr., laborer, Port Murray; Hann John, Jr., laborer, Port Murray; Hann Arthur B., Karrsville; Hann John, hotel keeper, Anderson; Hann Alfred, Anderson; Hann Wm., Jr., laborer,

Extra quality Carving knives and forks at Wade Bros., Hackettstown.

THE BEST GOODS FOR THE LEAST MONEY AT **NORTON'S Easton, Pa.**

MANSFIELD TOWNSHIP. 423

Anderson; Hann Stewart, laborer, Port Murray; Hann Lawrence, laborer, Anderson; Hendershot Holaway, laborer, Anderson; Hendershot John, laborer, Anderson; Hendershot Robert S., Anderson; Hull Benjamin, laborer, Beattystown; Hook Augustus, laborer, Beattystown; Huff Charles E., laborer, Beattystown; Husselton H. S., Beattystown; Husselton Jos., laborer, Beattystown; Hoover Theodore, laborer, Port Murray; Hoover Elizabeth, freeholder, Port Murray; Hoppaugh Samuel, laborer, Port Murray; Hoppaugh Teeter, Karrsville; Hoppaugh Vernon, laborer, Karrsville; House George, Anderson; Holden Frank, Laborer, Karrsville; Hoagland Theo., Townsbury; Hoagland Wm. H., Townsbury; Henry Jacob, Townsbury; Hoffman George, laborer, Karrsville; Hoffman Rebecca, freeholder, Karrsville; Hoffman Ephniah, miller, Beattystown; Hoffman Oliver B., Beattystown; Hipp John, Beattystown; Hipp Elizabeth, freeholder, Port Murray; Hipp James, gentleman, Port Murray; Hipp Frances A., freeholder,

LAUBACH'S EASTON, PA. Largest Store, Largest Assortments, and One rice to All

Port Murray; Hipp Mark, laborer, Port Murray; Howell Lemuel, laborer, Port Murray; Hill Wm., Karrsville.

Insho Wm., laborer, Anderson.

Jorden Eden, laborer, Karrsville; Jorden James, Karrsville; Jorden Jonathan, Karrsville; Johnson Henry, merchant, Beattystown; Johnson & White, millers, Beattystown; Johnson Ezra, clerk, Beattystown; Johnson Wm., laborer, Beattystown; Johnson David, laborer, Beattystown; Jones Mary A., freeholder, Port Murray; Jones Robert T., laborer, Port Murray.

Ketcham W. H., Karrsville; Ketcham Lewis, painter, Karrsville; Ketcham John, Karrsville; King Wm. D., Hackettstown; Karr Walter, wheelwright, Karrsville; Karr Jos. K., Karrsville; Karr Mark, Karrsville; Karr Lewis, Anderson.

Lee Ichabod, Port Murray; Larison Wm., miller, Karrsville; Labar M. H., school teacher, Beattystown; Labar Lewis T., Beattystown; Lance Fred-

ANDREWS & NOLF, Proprietors of the "DOWN TOWN" Dry Goods House, 205 Northampton Street, Easton, Pa.

H. M. NORTON WHOLESALE AND RETAIL DEALER IN HARDWARE, STOVES AND HOUSEFURNISHING GOODS.

MANSFIELD TOWNSHIP.

erick, laborer, Anderson; Lance Alonzo, laborer, Townsbury; Longcore George M., painter, Rockport; Lawrence George, laborer, Port Murray.

Marlatt Wm., Townsbury; Marlatt Edward, Karrsville; Marlatt John R., Karrsville; Marlatt Nathan, laborer, Beattystown; Marlatt John F., laborer, Karrsville; Marlatt Lewis, railroader, Port Murray; Marlatt Newton, laborer, Port Murray; Marlatt John, Port Murray; Marlatt Benjamin, laborer, Karrsville; Marlatt Emanuel, laborer, Karrsville; Miller J. H., Anderson; Miller John, blacksmith, Anderson; Miller Jacob Jr., Anderson; Miller Henry, railroader, Port Murray; Miller Hugh, Port Murray; Martin R. C., Beattystown; Miller Wm., laborer, Townsbury; Martenis Nicholas, Karrsville; Martenis James, laborer, Port Murray; Martenis Jacob, Townsbury; Martenis Zorenda, Townsbury; Martenis Jacob Jr., laborer, Townsbury; Martenis Samuel, laborer, Port Murray; Merrell H. W., carpenter, Townsbury; Mare Cyrus, Port Murray; McCatharine Theodore, mason,

LAUBACH'S, Easton, Pa. SPECIAL ATTENTION -SILKS AND DRESS GOODS. NEW GOODS DAILY.

Port Murray; Mayberry Andrew, Port Murray; Mayberry Frederick, laborer, Port Murray; Mayberry Edward, laborer, Port Murray; Mayberry Lawrence, laborer, Port Murray; Mayberry John H., laborer,

MARK CYPHERS,
MERCHANT TAILOR,
Washington Ave. *WASHINGTON, N. J.*

The foremost merchant tailor of Washington and Warren county is Mr. Mark Cyphers, who has for many years been engaged in this special business, he having over thirty years practice. He has in stock, which he is always pleased to show, a well-selected line of foreign and domestic worsted cassimeres, etc., of latest styles, as will be found in this part of the country. He enjoys a large patronage from among the leading citizens of Washington and surrounding towns. In fit and workmanship, he guarantees perfect satisfaction. The latest fashion plates are in prominent positions, so that one is able to make good selections as to style of cut wanted. Mr. Cyphers is the son of Wm. L. Cyphers whom old timers will remember as making their best fitting suit.

Port Murray; Mayberry William, laborer, Port Murray; Mowrey Samuel, laborer, Port Murray; Mitchell Reuben, distiller and farmer, Karrsville; Mitchell Jacob, Karrsville; Mitchell John, carpenter, Karrs-

EMPIRE SOLID CAST STEEL SCISSORS AND SHEARS For Sale at **Wades' Hardware Store.**

MANSFIELD TOWNSHIP.

ville; Mitchell Ira, Port Colden; Monder Daniel, boatman, Port Colden; **Mowder W. H.**, utcher, Anderson; Mowder John, Anderson; Mowder Catherine, freeholder, Anderson; Mowder Ellen, freeholder, Anderson; Mowder Susan, freeholder, Anderson; Murphy Terence, laborer, Karrsville; Myers James, blacksmith, Anderson; Myers Clarissa, freeholder, Anderson; McNee James, boatman, Karrsville; McCrea Samuel, gentleman, Port Murray; McCrea John, merchant, Port Murray; McCracken Cline, laborer, Anderson; McCathern John, laborer, Port Murray; McCatherine Samuel, laborer, Port Murray.

Nunn G. T., Karrsville; Nunn Edward, boatman, Karrsville; Nunn Andrew M., weighmaster, Port Colden; Nunn Alfred, Port Murray; Nunn John, Port Colden; Nunn Thomas, laborer, Stephensburg.

Osmun Joseph E., Beattystown; Osmun John, laborer, Beattystown; Osmun James, Karrsville.

Parks Lewis S., Townsbury; Parks Lewis Jr., Townsbury; Parks Thomas, laborer, Port Murray;

Petty Aaron, Karrsville; Petty Wm., carpenter, Karrsville; Petty John A., laborer, Karrsville; Petty Jacob, carpenter, Karrsville; Petty Steven, laborer, Karrsville; Petty Joseph, laborer, Karrsville; Petty James, la orer, Beattystown; Petty Jacob P., carpenter, Port Murray; Petty George W., carpenter, Karrsville; Pool Isaac, blacksmith, Beattystown; Pool Oscar, blacksmith, Beattystown; Pierce William, laborer, Karrsville; Perry S. R., laborer, Port Murray; Perry Margaret, freeholder, Port Murray; Perry Mary A., freeholder, Port Murray; Perry Lewis, laborer, Port Murray; Perry B. C., Port Murray; Perry Francis, freeholder, Port Murray; Perry Elisha, laborer, Port Murray; Perry Calvin, clerk, Port Murray; Pidcock Mariah, Port Murray; Price David, wheelwright, Port Murray; Price James, gentleman, Port Murray; Prime Theodore, Beattystown; Prime Thomas, Beattystown

Quick John, Townsbury.

Robeson Elizabeth, freeholder, Beattystown;

JOHN W. FORKER,

DEALER IN

GENERAL ✸ MERCHANDISE,

PORT MURRAY, N. J.

THE proprietor of this popular bazaar was born in New York city about 37 years ago, and came to this county about 16 years ago. He was at that time selling the popular organs of Peloubet, Pelton & Co., manufactured at Bloomfield, N. J. By his push and pluck he made a paying busines of it. Fifteen years ago he settled at Port Murray and commenced with a small capital, the business which he is still pursuing. By indomitable courage and perseverance, together with strict attention to his business, he has built up a large and lucrative trade. He has the best village store that there is in the county to-day. He carries from eight to ten thousand dollars worth of stock, and is prepared to furnish you with what you want no matter what you may call for. He deals in everything. Goods are delivered free of charge, and sold at the lowest living profit. Give him a call and be convinced.

THE BEST GOODS FOR THE LEAST MONEY AT **NORTON'S, Easton, Pa**

MANSFIELD TOWNSHIP.

Robeson John R., groceries and provisions, Port Murray; Rea Daniel, laborer, Port Murray; Ruple Peter, mason, Port Murray; Ruple John, railroader, Port Murray; Reed Wm., lime burner, Beattystown; Reed Jeremiah, laborer, Beattystown; Reed Jeremiah Jr., laborer, Beattystown; Robertson Samuel, laborer, Beattystown; Rush Levi, Karrsville; Ross David, laborer, Port Murray; Ross Charles, laborer, Port Murray; Ramsey Samuel, Anderson; Ramsey Wm., gentleman, Port Murray; Ross Silas, laborer, Karrsville.

Smith Jacob, Port Colden; Smith David, laborer, Beattystown; Smith Luke, boatman, Anderson; Smith Alfred G., Port Colden; Smith Samuel, blacksmith, Port Colden; **Smith John**, blacksmith, machinist and scale repairer, Port Colden; Smith George D., boatman, Karrsville; Smith P. V., Karrsville; Smith Wm., laborer, Karrsville; Smith Samuel, Jr., brakeman, Port Colden; Smith Wood, laborer, Port Colden; Smith James, wood dealer, Hackettstown;

YOU CAN ALWAYS FIND WHAT YOU WANT AT **LAUBACH'S, Easton, Pa.**

Shumaker Henry S., blacksmith and wheelwright shop, Port Murray; Sharp Aaron L., Townsbury; Sutton Robert, Port Murray; Sutton L. W., Port Murray; Sutton Lewis, laborer, Port Murray; Sutton Eugene, laborer, Port Murray; Sowers Henry, boatman, Port Colden; Sowers Wm., laborer, Port Murray; Searfoss Frederick, track boss, Port Murray; Stevenson Hannah, freeholder, Port Murray; Stevens Harvey, Port Murray; Stevens Ransom, Port Murray; Somerville James, Ex Judge, Port Murray; Scott Joseph, brakeman, Port Murray; Scott Isaac, Port Colden; Scott Abraham, plane-tender, Port Colden; Slater John, laborer, Beattystown; Stires J. R., miller, Karrsville; Stires Wm. H. H., mill wright, Port Murray; Starker Jacob D., laborer, Port Colden; Starker George, teamster, Anderson; Shafer John, Anderson; Snyder J. P., laborer, Port Murray; Seals Harriet, freeholder, Port Murray; Skinner Archibald, carpenter, Beattystown; Skinner Emma, freeholder, Beattystown; Skinner Jacob, carpenter, Beattystown;

ANDREWS & NOLF, 205 Northampton St., Easton, Pa. Sell the best Black and Colored Silks. Guaranteed.

H. M. NORTON, *WHOLESALE AND RETAIL DEALER IN* **Hardware, Stoves and Housefurnishing**

428   MANSFIELD TOWNSHIP.

Wm. Shields, laborer, Beattystown; Shanon David, Beattystown; Shrope Wm., laborer, Anderson; Sliker David, laborer, Anderson; Sliker John B., Hackettstown; Simanton Robert, Port Murray; Simanton Frank, Port Murray; Stewart J. R., Hackettstown; Stewart George, tailor, Hackettstown; Stewart John O., conductor, Port Murray; Stewart William, Hackettstown; Stewart David, Hackettstown; Sickles Wm., laborer, Hackettstown; Stewart Samuel, Hackettstown.

Trimmer Elias, Beattystown; Trimmer Jacob, Beattystown; Tinsman Charlotte, freeholder, Hackettstown; Tinsman Samuel, laborer, Hackettstown; Thomas Samuel, Beattystown; Thomas Jacob, Karrsville; Thaw B. F., track-boss, Port Colden; Thomson W. H., miller, Beattystown; Thomson Samuel, miller, Beattystown; **Thompson S. F.**, carriagemaker and undertaker, Port Murray; Turner Wm., laborer, Port Murray; Taylor Sarah, Washington; Tunison Cornelius, Karrsville; Tunison John, laborer, Karrsville.

LAUBACH'S EASTON, PA. CLOAKS and WRAPS of every description. **Our Own Manufacture.**

Vansyckle A. G., Anderson; **Vansyckle Mrs. Mary C.**, dry goods, groceries etc., Anderson; Vleit William D., Beattystown; Vleit George, Beattystown; Vangordon Moses, Karrsville; Vandoren Thomas, laborer, Beattystown; Vanatta Samuel, Anderson; Vanatta John H., Anderson; Voss John B., Karrsville; Vusler Joseph, laborer, Anderson; Varus John W., laborer, Townsburry.

**CHARLES A. MILLER,
WATCHMAKER AND JEWELER,
Washington, New Jersey.**
Dealer in Jewelry of all kinds. Musical Instruments, Pens, Pencils, Ink, Mucilage and Novelties of every description. Watches, Clocks and Jewelry repaired and warranted.

White H. D., Beattystown; **White Roswell, Beattystown**; White Wm., Beattystown; Weller A. W., Port Colden; Weller Eugene, Port Colden; Weller S. K., Port Colden; Winters Daniel, boatman, Port Murray; Winters Manning, boatman, Port Murray; Waters E., Stevensburg; Waters J., Stevensburg;

All kinds of PAINTS and OILS at WADE BROS.

THE BEST GOODS FOR THE LEAST MONEY AT **NORTON'S Easton, Pa.**

MANSFIELD TOWNSHIP.

Waters John, Stevensburg; Wolf Wm., Karrsville; Wolf Peter, laborer, Karrsville; Wiley Jackson, laborer, Port Murray; Winter Mute, laborer, Beattystown; Willever Jacob H., agent, Port Murray; Willever Jos., laborer, Karrsville; Woodruff Jacob, Karrsville; Wandling W. C., Stephensburg; Welsh J. C., Hackettstown; Witson Clarissa, freeholder, Hackettstown.

Young Nancy D., Hackettstown; Youngblood L. J., Hackettstown; Yawger John, carpenter, Karrsville; Yawger James, engineer, Port Murray.

Zellers John, Hackettstown; Zellers William, Port Murray; Zellers Robert, Port Murray; Zellers Elisha, laborer, Port Murray; Zellers Morris, laborer, Port Murray; Zellers Obadiah, laborer, Port Murray.

H. M. CREGAR,

◆ Proprietor of the ◆

New Jersey Bargain House,

KARRSVILLE, N. J.

Dealer in all kinds of merchandise. **Boots** and **Shoes** a Specialty. Ready-made **Clothing** in endless variety. Ladies and Gent's Furnishing Goods. Agent for the **New York Sewing Machine**. Also agent for **The Largest Carpet House in New York City**. On these goods I defy competition. **Crockery** in abundance. Parlor, Range and Cook **Stoves** always on hand and at the lowest possible prices. Give me a call and be convinced.

CHARLES FORCE,

Manufacturer of

MARBLE AND GRANITE

MONUMENTS, HEADSTONES,

TABLETS, ETC.

Cemetery plots enclosed with marble or granite posts, and with galvanized railing. Also dealer in all kinds of Cemetery Fixtures, as

Grave Borders, Flower Fixtures, etc.

Designs furnished cheerfully to all persons on application. Prices reasonable and work done in the very best style.

Thankful for past favors, I solicit a continuance of the same. I always try to please.

Shop and Yard, Broad St,
WASHINGTON, N. J.

OXFORD TOWNSHIP.

OXFORD is one of the western border townships of the county. It is bounded on the northeast by Hope, southeast by Mansfield and Washington, on the southwest by Harmony, and on the west and northwest by the Delaware river and Knowlton township.

It was formed from Greenwich township about the year 1753 or 1755, and received its name in honor of Oxford University, England, at which place the father of one of Oxford's chief pioneers was educated. The township contains 32.17 square miles or 20,589 acres of land. The soil of the township is a mixture of clay and gravelly loam, with a layer of limestone and slate underneath. In the valley it is especially fertile and susceptible of cultivation, the hills also, yielding readily to the farmer's plow.

The surface of Oxford is perhaps as uneven as any in the county. It has however, a proportionately extensive front along the Delaware, which, when added to the Pequest valley, gives it considerable flat surface.

There are numerous mountain ranges in the township, among which are Scott's along the southeast border of the township, going westward or northwestward we have next the Ragged Ridge, an extension of Marble mountain running into this township, from Harmony and parallel with Scott's; Manunka Chunk mountain in the northwest and along the Delaware is the next and last westward range, of importance. Scott's mountains lie between Scott's and Ragged Ridge, and Mount Nomore, just west of Oxford Furnace, beside several others that are up to this time, nameless.

The principal streams are Pequest Creek, which flows through the township in a southwesterly direction and empties in the Delaware at Belvidere. Beaver Brook and Furnace Creek both tributary to the Pequest Creek; Oxford Creek, a tributary to the Delaware and Buck Horn Brook flowing into Harmony township. The Delaware river may also be numbered among the the streams of Oxford. It washes the western side of the township and furnishes excellent water power at various points. About half a mile below what is known as Paphandusing Creek, is Foul Rift, where the channel of the river is rapid and navigation is dangerous.

The pioneer settlers of Oxford, were, a Mr. Oxford and a Mr. Green, who were soon followed by a number of other families, most of whom came between 1735 and 1740. The first congregation was formed at Oxford Furnace about the year 1746, a short time after the starting of the Furnace. The second congregation was formed at old Oxford in 1749.

OXFORD TOWNSHIP.

The towns of the township are as follows:

Oxford Furnace, the chief town, is situated on the Delaware, Lackawanna and Western Railroad, in the southeastern part of the township. The first settler was Jonathan Robeson, the son of the Robeson in honor of whose alma mater the township was named. Jonathan Robeson built the old pioneer furnace at this place, and was hence the furnace of the town. Oxford Furnace is really made up of several small towns, Furnace Hill on the east, Jonestown on the south, Dutch Hill on the west, Pittengerville on the northwest and Smithville on the north, all of which are so peculiarly located that the town taken as a whole cannot be distinctly seen from any one of these, and no one passing through the place would suppose the population to be even nearly what it is. The mercantile business of the place is mostly conducted by the company store, which is perhaps the largest of its kind in the county. Jonestown has a general store, Dutch Hill two stores, Smithville a small store and drug store besides some other small business places scattered throughout the Furnace. The principal business enterprises are the rolling mills and nail works in which several hundred hands are employed. There are four churches at this place, Methodist, Presbyterian, Roman Catholic, and Lutheran.

Buttzville, a small town, is situated also on the line of the D. L. & W. RR. in the eastern part of the township and in the Pequest Valley. It has a Methodist Church, school house, grist mill, hotel building, store and post office. The Lehigh and Hudson Railroad also has a depot at this place.

Bridgeville is situated also in the Pequest Valley, a little to the northwest of Buttzville. The Cedar Grove grist mill, a school house, an old hotel building, and depot of the D. L. & W. RR. are located here.

Sarepta, in the northern part of the township, has a grist mill, school house and blacksmith shop. The principal business interests of this section is the Limestone quarry, which employs a number of men, and does considerable business. Oxford now known as "Hazen Post office" in honor of the third assistant Postmaster General of the United States, is situated a little southwest of the center of the township. It has in addition to its post office, a store, school house and blacksmith shop. The old Oxford church is located at this place.

Oxford township has much mineral wealth, which is in course of progressive developement and promises to be a very important industry. The recent developements in this direction have been considerable.

There are seven cemetaries in the township, two at Oxford Furnace, two at Oxford village, Summerfield cemetery, Buttzville cemetery, and an old grave yard on the Young farm in the southwest corner of the township.

The township has excellent water power facilities furnished by the Pequest Creek and the Delaware river. Present population about 4500. Schools in the township, 9, scholars, 1,199.

WARREN COUNTY DRUG STORE.

Township Directory.

All whose vocation is not mentioned are farmers. The Post Office addresses not given in this township are Oxford.

Anderson Fred, laborer; Albra Fred., laborer; Allshouse Charles, miner; **Allen James A.**, druggist; Allen B. O., Buttzville; Albrect John, laborer, Buttzville; Atwood F. F., teacher; Ayroe Sorrein, factory-hand, Buttzville; Ayres Peter, laborer, Buttzville; Appleman Geo. M., laborer; Anderson Wm., miller, Buttzville; Ayers Aaron, watchman, Buttzville; Amendt William, laborer; Angle I. J., operator, Bridgeville; Ayers John B., Buttzville; Allen E. C., storekeeper; Appleman Joab, teacher; Actard Chas., miner; Appleman Peter; Allen Wm., clerk, Buttzville; Anderson Daniel, Buttzville; Axford Eugene, telegraph operator; Anderson Andrew, laborer; Armstrong Wm. B.; Aaroye Peter C., laborer; Arndt Fred., miner; Arndt Augustus, laborer;

LAUBACH'S Easton, Pa. THE LARGEST DRY GOODS AND CARPET HOUSE. BARGAINS ALWAYS

Arndt Chris., laborer; Arndt Herman, laborer; Arndt Julia, householder; Amendt Wm. Jr., miner; Amendt Henry, miner; Anderson Hugh E., miller, Bridgeville; Anderson A., miner; Angle W., Belvidere; Anderson Peter, laborer; Atkins Charles, teacher; Appleman Jacob, laborer; Abb Joseph, miner; Axford M. J. book agent; Axford Wm., station-agent.

Boofman George, laborer; Bush Philip E., laborer; Belka Wm., laborer; Rosenberry John, carpenter; Bullock Samuel, laborer; Burke John, laborer; Burke Patrick, laborer; Briening Nick, puddler; Briening John, puddler; Bushlock Martin, laborer; Bushlock Yerkie, laborer; Bardrow August, laborer; Burge Joseph, laborer; Beck Chas., laborer, Buttzville; Burdine Joseph, Bridgeville; Biger George, laborer; Barry Thomas, puddler; Bartron David, lawyer; Bartron George, shoemaker; Bartron Harvey G., shoemaker; Burd J. C., cooper; Burd George W., laborer; Burd Theo. P., superintendant cooper shop; Burd John; Bush Chas. A., carpenter; Bush John A., laborer; Burns Patrick, puddler; Burns Robert, puddler;

ANDREWS & NOLF, Proprietors of the "DOWN TOWN" Dry Goods House, 205 Northampton Street, Easton, Pa.

H. M. NORTON, *WHOLESALE AND RETAIL DEALER IN* **Hardware, Stoves and Housefurnishing.**

OXFORD TOWNSHIP.

Buckley Edward; Buckley James, blacksmith; Baylor M. B., merchant; Baylor William, mason, Baylor J. C., carpenter; Brown James, laborer; Brown John W., puddler; Bumgardner Fred., laborer; Bumgardner Charles, nailer; Bowman Wm. H., laborer; Bell Thomas, moulder; Biglow Fred., clerk; Belka Fred., miner; Belka Theodore, miner; Brecker John, laborer; Barrett John, laborer; Bennett James, laborer; Bennett J. R., bookkeeper, Buttzville; Burmiller Paul, puddler; Blessing Manx, miner; Burdenback Lewis, laborer; Branahan Martin, laborer; Beam Lyman C., laborer; Beam Erastus, laborer; Beam William, carpenter; Bembler Wm., nailer; Breman Lawrence, machinist; Beam Jacob, laborer, Bridgeville; Bowers Jeremiah, laborer, Belvidere; Balog Michael, laborer, Bridgeville; Banghart Alpheus, Buttzville; Banghart Henry A.; Banghart Geo. W.; Banghart Michael, Bridgeville; Brands W. S., Belvidere; Boardman Wm., laborer, Belvidere; Beam A., laborer; Bird Wm., Hazen; Buttz John R. Sr.,

LAUBACH'S EASTON, PA. Largest Store, Largest Assortments, and One Price to All

Bridgeville; Banghart William M., Bridgeville; Beam Jacob, laborer; Brokaw Samuel, hotel, Buttzville; Bowers Samuel, Roxburg; Buttz Henry, Belvidere; Buttz Edward, Belvidere; Banghart John, Buttzville; Bowlby R. M., Montana; Beers David, Montana; Beers Edward, Roxburg; Butler Daniel H., Belvidere; Butler Gershom C., Belvidere; Bennett Wm. H., Bridgeville; Becher Jacob, laborer, Hazen; Buttz John H., Bridgeville; Boyer Thomas M. Bridgeville; Boyer George, Bridgeville; Bird John W., laborer, Bridgeville; Bird Jacob J., Montana; Bird Jacob M., Hazen; Bird Elijah W., Hazen; Bird Barton B., Hazen; Bird E. P., mechanic; Baylor J. C., engineer; Brost John, miner; Bell John F., moulder; Butler Edward, Montana; Beam Conrad, laborer; Brokaw Cornelius, Hazen; Banghart George, Buttzville; Baylor Moses A., Montana; Brokaw John, Hazen; Burd J. W., Hazen; Baylor Wm., blacksmith, Hazen; Bush J. S., laborer, Hazen; Burd Calvin, cooper; Butler Wm., Belvidere; Brands Henry, Belvidere;

SHIELDS' INFALLIBLE **Dypeptic Remedy,** A sure cure for Dyspepsia, Sick or Nervous Headache. Guaranteed.

OXFORD TOWNSHIP. 435

Burns Patrick, laborer; Burns Peter, watchman; Brown John, puddler; Burd John, Montana; Beam Philip, Bridgeville; Bessus Jack, laborer, Bridgeville; Bishop Robert, shoemaker, Bridgeville; Bropsky Patrick, laborer, Bridgeville; Bowlby Jacob, laborer, Bridgeville; Beam Cornelius, laborer; Beam John P., Bridgeville; Beam Geo. F., Bridgeville; Bonnell Wm. P., milk dealer, Belvidere; Beers Elisha; Burd J.; Boyer George, Bridgeville; Burd Jacob A., Montana; Bishop A. C., Bridgeville; Burns John, puddler.

Cutsler James, boilermaker; Cutsler William, cooper; Custler Morris, laborer; Cooper Aaron; Cooper Britton, laborer; Creager Wm. S., carpenter; Cyphers William, laborer; Christian C., Montana; Clymer John, Bridgeville; Costinalker John, miller, Bridgeville; Cline G. M.; Clymer Isaac, Buttzville; Craig Robert, Buttzville; Craig M J., clerk, Buttzville; Craig S. J., Buttzville; **Craig Thomas,** merchant, Buttzville, N. J.; Craig John J., Buttzville; Curts E., Buttzville; Cline William, Bridgeville; Cole Samuel, brickmaker, Hazen; Cyphers A. B., laborer, Belvidere; Cyphers Philip, Roxburg; Cowell E., wheelwright, Buttzville; Creager James, Buttzville; Cyphers James, Belvidere; Chamberlain Wm., retired farmer, Hazen; Cole J. R., agent, Hazen; Cole Cornelius, laborer; Cole Chris J.; Cole Thomas; Cole James, brickmaker; Hazen; Cole George, brickmaker, Hazen; Cole Jesse, brickmaker, Hazen; Cox William, blacksmith; Compton Samuel; Cronon Mahlon; Cocron John; Cline Wm. B., laborer; Cooper Jacob, engineer; Cooper C. C., Hazen; Cooper Frederick, engineer; Casey David, laborer; Casey James, laborer; Cline Fred, laborer; Cline Peter, miner; Cline Rev. E. C., Presbyterian pastor; Cowell John S., wheelwright, Buttzville; Cooper John W.; Cooley Thomas, miner; Cook William, laborer; Cook Garret A.; Call Wm. R., Jr., nailer; Call Wm. R., Sr., nailer; Collins Daniel, laborer; Collins William, puddler; Camp A. D., laborer; Coy Thomas, puddler; Cross William, laborer; Christianson Jacob, laborer;

H. M. NORTON *WHOLESALE AND RETAIL DEALER IN HARDWARE, STOVES AND HOUSEFURNISHING GOODS.*

436 OXFORD TOWNSHIP.

Calpin Thomas, laborer; Cole William, brickmaker, Montana; Cressman David, cooper, Montana; Creager John B., nailer, Montana; Creager Jacob, nailer, Montana; Closky David, puddler; Cottle Theodore, nailer; Cawley S., milliner; Clawson Sigler, harness shop; Clawson J. S., miner; Cosgrove John, puddler; Coleman John, laborer, Bridgeville; Carroll John, laborer, Bridgeville; Cyphers E. B., Belvidere; Cronon Matt, laborer, Bridgeville; Coughlin John, laborer, Bridgeville; Case Stewart, laborer, Buttzville; Cline Elijah J.; Cressman Christian; Cole Henry G., laborer; Cole Henry C., Montana; Cox Elijah; Christianson James, laborer; Christianson Jacob, laborer; Christianson Peter M., miner; Craft Henry, laborer; Childs James, laborer; Cryan Hugh, laborer; Carley Michael, puddler; Calpin Thomas, laborer; **Coy** Thomas, puddler; Casey Daniel, trackman; Casey James, laborer; Conroy Conrod, laborer; Cole Wilson, laborer, Hazen.

Docker Joseph, nailer; Docker William, nailer;

LAUBACH Leads in prices and quality of goods. EASTON Pa.

Docker Henry, laborer; Docker George, huckster; Docker Walter, nailer; Dougherty Stephen, gatetender; Dougherty James, laborer; Dempsey Martin, puddler; Davis David, puddler; Duff John, puddler; Dee Daniel, teamster; Dell M. R., teamster; Devany Patrick, laborer; Dolbey Lewis, laborer; **Devens** George, laborer; Drake J. W., laborer; Davis A. W., teacher; Dernberger Jacob; Dearborn G. S., physician and surgeon; Daly William, laborer; Dearborn G. H., agent; Dresback G. H.; Dean David, laborer, Bridgeville; Donnelly Hugh, puddler; Davis Lewis, laborer; Derringer George, laborer, Bridgeville; Dopkie Fred, Belvidere; Davison John, Belvidere; Davison Lewis, Hazen; Daly Solomon, laborer, Hazen; Donnelly John C., laborer, Bridgeville; Dean Geo. W., Bridgeville; Dickinson Simon, laborer, Bridgeville; Deumboss Elias, laborer, Belvidere; Dalrymple Wm., Montana; Dalrymple Wm., Sr., Montana; Dalrymple Wm. C., Montana; Dalrymple Daniel, Montana, Montana; Dalrymple Benjamin, Montana; Dal-

Extra quality Carving knives and forks at Wade Bros., Hackettstown.

THE BEST GOODS FOR THE LEAST MONEY AT **NORTON'S Easton, Pa.**

OXFORD TOWNSHIP.

rymple John, Montana; Dalrymple Thomas, puddler; Dalrymple Henry, laborer; Dean Nelson, laborer; Drikit John, laborer; Donovan Cornelius, puddler; Dillworth John, laborer.

Emery Joseph, Bridgeville; Exler Jacob, hostler; Eckmeker John, puddler; Estler Ezra, nailer; Estler Lewis, clerk Euler Alex, Jr., nailer; Euler Alex, Sr., saloon; Edwards James, puddler; Edinger E., Bridgeville; Edgar Josiah, Bridgeville; Earye C. W., Bridgeville; Edinger Amos, Jr., Montana; Edinger Alexandria, Montana; Erickson Peter, laborer; Erambenst A. C., laborer; Echart Rudolph, miner; Fountain George, puddle; Foley Thomas, laborer; Foley Peter, millhand; Foley W. M., millhand; Fowler Frederick, clerk; Fowler Mrs., boarding house; Forrester H. C.; Finnegan John, puddler; Folkner J. D., teamster; Folkner Albert, puddler; Forgus John; Forgus Dan'l; Fox Wilson, nailer; Fox Samuel, laborer; Fox George, nailer; Foss Daniel, carpenter; Fitzgerald Thomas, laborer; Fitchtel Michael,

LAUBACH'S EASTON, PA. CLOAKS and WRAPS of every description. **Our Own Manufacture.**

feeder; Flynn John, laborer; Frome Jacob P., huckster; Frome William, Montana; Frome John, book agent; Frome Jacob, Bridgeville; Frome Peter, laborer, Montana; Freet John, laborer, Bridgeville; Folk-

THOMAS CRAIG,
DEALER IN
DRY GOODS AND GROCERIES, HATS, CAPS, BOOTS, SHOES,
Clothing, Carpets, Oilcloth and General Merchandise.

Agent for

Lehigh and Free Burning Anthracite Coal, and Mapes' Complete Manures and Fertilizers.

Highest Cash Prices paid for grain and all orders for the same promptly filled. All Merchandise delivered free of charge.

BUTTZVILLE, N. J.

ner Dennis R., laborer, Buttzville; Freeman Henry, Bridgeville; Forrester Andrew, Bridgeville; Fritts Benjamin, Bridgeville; Flumerfelt Geo. F., Bridgeville; Flumerfelt Geo. B., Bridgeville; Fitts Joseph,

Andrews & Nolf, 205 Northampton St., Easton, Pa. The reliable HOUSE for Mourning Goods.

H. M. NORTON *WHOLESALE AND RETAIL DEALER IN HARDWARE, STOVES AND HOUSEFURNISHING GOODS.*

438   OXFORD TOWNSHIP.

Montana; Fitts George, Montana; Fitts Samuel, Hazen; Fitts W. L., Hazen; Fitts Jacob, Hazen; Foley Thomas, puddler; Foley Peter, puddler; Foley William, laborer; Foss Andrew, carpenter; Fangbonner Abram, Montana; Franson George, trackman; Frick Fred, laborer; Francis George, machinist; Fulmer Jacob, laborer, Buttzville; Fray Peter, laborer, Belvidere; Fray Joseph, Belvidere; Flatt Charles, laborer; Finns George, laborer, Belvidere.

Gardner Jacob, puddler; Gross John, laborer; Glynn Thomas, teamster; Gartland James, nailer; Griffin John, puddler; Garvey Owen, boarding house; Gano Joseph, miller; Gano Herbert, clerk; Gariss Jason, mail-agent, Buttzville; Gulick John M., Buttzville; German William, laborer, Buttzville; Gray William, merchant; Gray Robert, merchant; Grogerson Hans, laborer; Grogerson Michael, laborer; Grogerson Nelson, laborer; Girke Julius, laborer; Guy Samuel, Montana; Grundahl Jeff, laborer; Gardner Samuel; Gross Jacob, laborer; Gi'l Patrick,

LAUBACH'S EASTON, PA. Largest Store largest Assortments, and One price to All

laborer; Giese William, laborer; Grern Jeremiah G., laborer, Bridgeville; Gingles James M., Bridgeville; Gingles Peter, Bridgeville; Garrison Amos D. Buttzville; Gougher Joseph, laborer, Bridgeville; Gulick Lemuel, laborer, Bridgeville; Gulick Theodore, Bridgeville; German George, laborer, Buttzville; Groff Enoch, laborer; Guile William, carpenter; Guise Samuel, laborer.

Haycock George, nailer; Haycock Lewis, nailer; Hunt Isaac, nailer; Hyler H. A., nailer; Hardaman John, miner; Hornbaker Wm., nailer; Hornbaker John, stable keeper; Heath Samuel B., laborer; Heath Israel, puddler; Hanlan Dominick, laborer; Hilbert Joseph, postmaster; Hilbert Michael, engineer; Hochgsend Chas., nailfeeder; Hays Wm., puddler; Hoagland L. B., physician; Hoagland B., druggist; Hoagland Nathan R.; Hill S. B., bookkeeper; Higgins Michael, laborer; Hixon George, Buttzville; Howell Geo., Hazen; Heater Elias, laborer; Hartman John, laborer; Hartman Geo., la-

RAED CAREFULLY Page 218

THE BEST GOODS FOR THE LEAST MONEY AT **NORTON'S Easton, Pa.**

OXFORD TOWNSHIP.

borer; Hendershot Henry; Hendershot Ellsworth, laborer; Hendershot Michael, Bridgeville; Hysinger Geo.; Harbers Henry, blacksmith; Hoit Theodore, Buttzville; Hoit Nathan, Buttzville; Hoit John G., Buttzville; Hamson Ansel, laborer, Buttzville; Hopler Henry, Hazen; Hoit Thomas, laborer, Buttzville; Hissam Moses, laborer, Bridgeville; Hixon John, Bridgeville; Hixon Wm., laborer; Hartpence E. C., mine prospector, Buttzville; Herman Fred., Hazen; Herman Henry, Belvidere; Herman Henry, laborer; Howard Charles, laborer, Hazen; Haley Michael, watchmaker; Howell Chas., laborer; Howell Thomas, laborer; Harling Thomas laborer; Harling Henry, furnace manager; Harling Wm., laborer; Harling Benjamin, laborer; Hessel John, laborer; Hyler Moses, nailer; Hoffman John, wheelwright; Hoffman Christopher, mason; Hoffman Peter, laborer; Hoffman Samuel, laborer; Hoffman Abram, laborer, Bridgeville; Hoffman Fred., mason, Bridgeville; Henderson Wm., puddler, Bridgeville; Henderson

YOU CAN ALWAYS FIND WHAT YOU WANT AT **LAUBACH'S, Easton, Pa.**

Robert Sr., freeholder, Bridgeville; Henderson Robert Jr., puddler, Bridgeville; Henderson Martin, puddler, Bridgeville; Hendershot Jacob, Bridgeville; Hender-

MARVIN A. PIERSON,
MILK DEALER,
OXFORD, NEW JERSEY.

shot John, Bridgeville; Hardyman Hugh, puddler; Honan Patrick, track boss; Honan John, laborer; Harden Frank, laborer; Hummer Wm. S., engineer; Hill Obediah; Hamilton Patrick, laborer; Heist Jas., laborer; Hayes Isaac L., Bridgeville; Hayes Rev. J. L., clergyman, Buttzville; Henderson Christopher, laborer; Hussin Fred., laborer; Hoffman Jonathan, laborer; Hoffman Chas., laborer, Bridgeville; Honglan Levi; Honglan Enos; Hornbaker Geo., Hazen; Hunt Charles L., painter, Buttzville; Hunt Wm. L., painter, Buttzville; Henry Wm., nailer; Henry Jacob

ANDREWS & NOLF, Proprietors of the "DOWN TOWN" Dry Goods House, 205 Northampton Street, Easton, Pa.

H. M. NORTON *WHOLESALE AND RETAIL DEALER IN HARDWARE, STOVES AND HOUSEFURNISHING GOODS.*

OXFORD TOWNSHIP.

H., Bridgeville; Henry Jerome, laborer; Howell Aram, laborer, Bridgeville; Hutchinson S. M., minister, Hazen; Hixon Richard, Buttzville; Hilderbrant J. H., Belvidere; Henry Joseph, Bridgeville; Hopler Theodore, county clerk, Belvidere; Hoit Lewis B., Buttzville; Hendershot M., Buttzvile; Hoit M., Buttzville; Hyster Henry, laborer, Buttzville; Hornbaker Geo., Montana; Hixon Jasper, Bridgeville; Hixon Samuel S., Bridgeville; Hoagland E. W.; Hoit Caleb, Buttzville; Howard Wm., Hazen; Homadieu Joseph, Hazen; Hansen Peter, laborer; Hansen Chris. D., laborer; Hanson Chris., laborer; Husselton Samuel V., Bridgeville; Husselton Irvin, Bridgeville; Hanson Hans, laborer; Hartzell A. G., Belvidere; Halsted Albert, Belvidere; Holaren Frank, laborer, Bridgeville; Hellman John, Buttzville.

Irvin Nelson, mason; Iusco Dan. D., puddler; Ike Geo., miner, Buttzville; Ike Andrew, miner, Buttzville; Hick Charles, laborer, Belvidere; Irwin Hans,

LAUBACH'S, Easton, Pa. SPECIAL ATTENTION TO SILKS AND DRESS GOODS. NEW GOODS DAILY.

laborer; Jemieger Jacob, laborer; Johnson Carl, laborer; Johnson John, laborer; Johnson Benj., puddler; Johnson Gustave, heater; Johnson Chas. J., laborer; James Jacob, laborer; Jones Newman;

S. J. ODSTED,
OXFORD, - - - - - NEW JERSEY.
DEALER IN

GROCERIES, FLOUR, FEED,
TOBACCO AND CIGARS.

Agent for Steamship Lines.   P. O. Box 227

Jones Alfred, teamster; Jones Samuel; Jones Wm. A.; Jones John; Jones John A., Buttzville; Jones William, puddler; Jones Peter, nailer; Jones Isaac; Jones Jacob; Johnson Andrew, miner; Jones J. P.,

STEP LADDERS at Wades' Hardware Store, Hackettstown.

THE BEST GOODS FOR THE LEAST MONEY AT NORTON'S, Easton, Pa

OXFORD TOWNSHIP.

Hazen; Jones Edward, Buttzville; Jingles William, Buttzville; Johnson John A., Bridgeville; Johnson Richard C., merchant, Hazen; Johnson Nels, laborer; Johnson Jesse, laborer; Johnson Chris, laborer; Johnson Lewis, laborer; Jones William, laborer; Jones Samuel D., farmer, Hazen; Janney Fred, saloon; Janney Chris, laborer; Jepson Otto, miner; Jepson Myers, miner; Jepson Uhler, miner; James David, puddler.

Kemple William, laborer; Kemple Wm. F., laborer; Kemple Antone, boarding house; Kempsey Patrick, miner; Kempsey Bartley, miner; Kern James, nailer; Kean Charles, nailer; Kingman Nathan, nailer; Kempsey Pat., Jr., engineer; Kries Levi, Montana; Kries George, Montana; Kirkpatrick David, laborer; Kistenbader John N., laborer, Bridgeville; Kemple Chris, laborer; Kemple Fred, laborer; Kelagher Mike, laborer; Keyser George, retired farmer, Kelley Mike, laborer; Kelley Cornelius, laborer; Kane Daniel, puddler; Kerwitzkey Fred, miner; Ker-

LAUBACH'S, Easton, Pa., Largest stock of CARPETS, lowest prices. Best attention always.

witzkey Isaac, miner; Krull Herman, miner; Kielson Cornelius, laborer; Kinney Joseph, laborer; Kiefer F., Hazen; Kennedy George, laborer.

Lanning Charles B., porter; Lanning Stephen, blacksmith; Lanning George B., puddler; Lanning Chris, mason; Lanning William; Lanning Daniel; Lanterman Henry, machinist; Lanterman S. H.; Little William, laborer; Little George, nailer; Little George, laborer; Lacy J. C., laborer; Lacy George, laborer; Lukens E. T., gen'l manager; Lu-

DR. G. ORLANDO TUNISON,
PHYSICIAN AND SURGEON,
OXFORD, N. J.

pelt Chas., laborer; Leonard Thos., miner; Lane Thos., laborer; Lantz Joseph, Bridgeville; Little Jesse, Oxford; Lightcap John, Bridgeville; Lanning Cyrus, shoemaker, Bridgeville; Lippincott E., mason,

ANDREWS & NOLF'S DRY GOODS HOUSE, 205 NORTHAMPTON ST., EASTON, PA. THE LARGEST LINE OF HOUSE FURNISHING GOODS

H. M. NORTON, *WHOLESALE AND RETAIL DEALER IN* Hardware, Stoves and Housefurnishing.

OXFORD TOWNSHIP.

Buttzville; Lantz Wm., collector, Bridgeville; Litts Wm., laborer, Bridgeville; Litts John, laborer, Bridgeville; Lantz Jacob, Bridgeville; Lantz A., Bridgeville; Lantz Isaac, Bridgeville; Linaberry Wm., R.R. agent, Buttzville; Linaberry Eugene, act. R.R. agent, Buttzville; Lantz George, Bridgeville; Larrison James L.; Lomerson Geo. L., Belvidere; Lomerson John, Belvidere; Lanning L. M., teacher, Montana; Lanning J. S., Montana; Lanning M., painter, Lanning Stephen, Sr.; Lanterman G. D., Belvidere; Lanterman John, Belvidere; Lynn Levi, laborer, Hazen; Lentz Joseph, laborer, Belvidere; Lewis Benjamin, puddler; Lomerson Henry, Belvidere; Litz John, laborer, Bridgeville; Lippincott Samuel, mason, Buttzville; Loder James, Belvidere; Lynn George, laborer, Hazen; Lippincott W., laborer, Hazen; Lockhoven R., laborer; Lawson Nels, laborer; Linaman George, miner; Lawrence E., laborer, Bridgeville; Lorenson Levi, laborer.

Mountain Thomas, puddler; Mountain Michael,

LAUBACH Leads in prices and quality of goods. EASTON, Pa.

shoemaker; Martin William, nailer; Martin George A.; Martin Michael, laborer; Medangile George; Mackey Levi, Hazen; Mackey William, Hazen; Mackey Marshal, Belvidere; McMutrie A., miller, Belvidere; Major William, Buttzville; Matthews John, carpenter; Mickler C., laborer; Miller Wm. F., blacksmith, Hazen; Major William, laborer; Matthews Daniel, mason, Hazen; McConnell Joseph, Hazen; Martin Philip, watchman; Martin Michael, constable; Mahoney Thomas, blacksmith; Moray James, laborer; Marlatt

JOHN ZULAUF,
Baker & Confectioner,
OXFORD, NEW JERSEY.

Joseph, laborer; Marlatt Jerry, laborer; Marlatt George; Marlatt J.; Mackey M. P., Hazen; Mackey Ed. B., Hazen; Mackey Wm. B., Hazen; Mulchey Ed., laborer, Bridgeville; Miller William, blacksmith;

SHIELDS' INFALLIBLE **Dypeptic Remedy.** A sure cure for Dyspepsia, Sick or Nervous Headache. Guaranteed.

OXFORD TOWNSHIP.

Miller Ashel; Mershon Peter, laborer, Bridgeville; Mershon Miller, laborer, Bridgeville; Matthews David R., mason; Miller William, Hazen; Matthews Charles, Hazen; Matthews John, laborer; Matthews Joseph F., laborer, Hazen; McAfee Nathan, laborer, Hazen; McConvell Patrick, puddler, Hazen; McDevitt Dominick, laborer, Hazen; Mornaugh James, laborer, Hazen; Malley Peter, laborer, Hazen; McLean John, laborer, Hazen; Murray William, laborer, Hazen; Mayhew Charles, mill boss; Mooney Michael, puddler; Moran Michael, laborer; Moran Dominick, laborer; Massandahe Andrew, laborer; Minan Patrick, laborer; Myers Isaac, clerk; Myers Samuel, nailer; Myers George, butcher; Myers Henry, merchant; Myers J. C., nailer; Mooney James, laborer; Mooney Matt, plate carrier; Miller William, laborer; Mellberger Fred, merchant; Morris Andrew, watchman; Manning Pat, laborer; Manning Michael, laborer; Matthews Wm., laborer; Matthews George, puddler; Mickler Jacob, laborer; McCarthy Andrew, laborer;

McKeifer James, laborer; McNear John, engineer; McDermott Thomas, puddler; McGowen Barney, laborer; McHannan John, laborer; McDonough Thos., track boss; McCabe Michael, saloon; McCabe John, laborer; McDonough Walter, clerk; McConnell Castrine, nailer; McNear Theodore, nailer; McGowen Thomas, laborer; McConnell Patrick, puddler; Mackey Edward, Belvidere; Matthews J., laborer; Mulroy Peter, laborer.

Nyhart Wm. H., miller, Buttzville; Nelson August, laborer; Nelson Soreen, laborer; Nelson John, carpenter; Nelson Cornelius, miner; Nelson John N., laborer; Nelson Chris., laborer; Noll Eugene, miner; Nessen Hans, miner; Nee Thos. Sr., miner; Nee Thomas Jr., miner; Nolan James, machinist; Newman Abram, retired farmer; Norgard John, laborer; Norgard Hans, laborer; Nassendshot Andrew, laborer; Nicholls Wm. H.; Nyhart James, Buttzville.

Odsted S. J., merchant; O'Neill Cornelius, laborer; O'Neill Michael, laborer, Belvidere; O'Neill James, laborer, Belvidere; O'Neill John, laborer, Belvidere; O'Brien Richard, miner; O'Heron John, laborer, Bridgeville; O'Heron David, laborer, Bridgeville; Osmun Chas. J., Bridgeville; Osmun Albert, laborer, Bridgeville; Owens Frank, nailer; Ort Winfield, laborer, Montana; Ort Jesse laborer, Bridgeville; Oleson Soren, laborer; Oleson Jane, laborer.

Price Harvey, laborer; Pohle Theodore, miner; **Pierson Marvin A.**, milk dealer; Pursell Benjamin; Pierson David; Perry James, laborer; Pierson Lars, engineer; Paul Thomas, retired; Pott John Sr.; Polhemus W. C., laborer; Pittenger Daniel, Sr., Pittenger James; Pittenger John S., nailer; Pittenger John L., engineer; Pittenger Eugene, nailer; Pittenger Daniel Jr., nailer; Petty Walter, puddler; Pole Albert, puddler; Pierson Clark, cooper; Powers Michael, puddler; Pierson Robert, cooper; Peterson P. M., laborer; Pape Ludwig, painter; Parks Joseph R., teacher; Paul John, nailer; Polley Britton, laborer; Puff Frank, laborer; Pierson Jas L., car-

YOU CAN ALWAYS FIND WHAT YOU WANT AT **LAUBACH'S, Easton, Pa.**

penter; Perry D. M., time-keeper; Pierce Chas., laborer; Pierson Wm., laborer; Peterson Fred., laborer; Perry O N., time-keeper; Pursell James, laborer; Pyles J. H., Hazen; Pyles Roderick, Hazen; Prall J.

JAMES A. ALLEN,
OXFORD, NEW JERSEY.
Wholesale and Retail Dealer in

Drugs, Medicines, Chemicals, Fancy & Toilet Articles,

Sponges, **Brushes, Perfumery, Etc.**

Physicians Prescriptions Carefully Compounded.
ORDERS FILLED WITH CARE AND DISPATCH.

C., Hazen; Prall B. B., drover, Hazen; Potts George, Oxford; Petty Cornelius, laborer, Buttzville; Petty Robert, Buttzville; Prall Thomas, retired farmer, Hazen; Pittenger Marshal, laborer, Buttzville; Petty Daniel, Buttzville.

Extra quality Carving knives and forks at Wade Bros., Hackettstown.

THE BEST GOODS FOR THE LEAST MONEY AT **NORTON'S Easton, Pa.**

OXFORD TOWNSHIP. 445

Quinn James, laborer, Oxford; Quick Peter, laborer, Oxford; Quick Geo. W., laborer, Oxford; Quinn Michael, boss at mines, Oxford; Quick Philip, Bridgeville; Quick Ayers, laborer, Hazen; Quigley James, laborer.

Ryan A. M., bookkeeper,; Ryan John, laborer; Reagan Patrick, laborer; Reagan John Jr., puddler; Reagan Dennis Jr., puddler; Rafter Thomas, puddler; Radle Lewis, blacksmith; Raisley John; Radle George, miner; Robbins John, carpenter; Ryan Hugh, laborer; Rush Milton, laborer; Ryder John, jeweler; Reagan Wm., laborer; Rush Calvin, laborer; Reagan John Sr., laborer; Reagan James, laborer; Reagan Michael, puddler; Reagan Thomas, puddler; Ryan Jerry, mill-hand; Ryan Michael, laborer; Ryan Roger, laborer; Reese Isaac, teamster; Reese Thomas, nailer; Root Charles, laborer; Repp Michael, machinist; Radle Philip, nailer; Repp Wm. S., nailer; **Raisley S. G.**, confectionery, tobacco and segars; Roseberry D. K.; Roseberry A. D.; Rush

LAUBACH'S EASTON, PA. CLOAKS and WRAPS of every description. Our Own Manufacture.

Wm., Montana; Race Henry; Rhinehart Peter O., Asbury; Raub Jacob; Rush Calvin, Montana; Raub John A., laborer; Renyan Dennis Jr., laborer; Ryan Wm., laborer; Reese Henry, laborer; Reese George, laborer; Rasmussen Hans, laborer; Ray Daniel, laborer; Repp Henry, miner; Repp Mathias, laborer; Raisley Philip, laborer; Roberts John, laborer; Rush William, Bridgeville; Ross George, laborer; Rittenhouse Peter, laborer; Rittenhouse Wm., laborer; Rittenhouse Reuben, laborer; Radle Ludwig, Montana; Ramber George, laborer, Belvidere; Rosenberry J., Belvidere; Rosenberry Cline, Belvidere; Rosenberry Jos. M., Belvidere; Rosenberry A. Depue, Belvidere; Raw Charles.

Slack James, engineer; Sarson John, blacksmith; Snyder Thomas, laborer; Shafer George, laborer; Sharps E. W., undertaker; Swick Nicholas, shoemaker; Struble George W., puddler; Shanon George, laborer; Shafer Peter L., heater; Shafer Hiram, huckster; Sheridan Samuel; Sackman Fred, boarding

Andrews & Nolf, 205 Northampton St., Easton, Pa. The reliable HOUSE for Mourning Goods.

H. M. NORTON, WHOLESALE AND RETAIL DEALER IN Hardware, Stoves and Housefurnishing.

OXFORD TOWNSHIP.

house; Stelter Henry, miner; Sullivan Daniel, laborer; Swick Joseph, laborer; Shafer A. E., laborer, Pequest; Snyder John, puddler; Steller Albert, engineer; Scranton S. T., retired; Sweeney John; Slack Enoch, mason; Sweeney Morgan, laborer; Swick Nicholas, shoemaker; Shemps Antoine, miner; Sipple Henry, laborer; Sheridan Michael, laborer; Sorenson Gus, laborer; Searles Henry, laborer, Montana; Searles Edward, laborer, Bridgeville; Stout Theo. P., cooper; Stout Theodore, furnaceman; Stout DeWitt, shoemaker, Buttzville; Stout Henry, laborer; Smith Nicholas, laborer; Smith Irven B.; Smith Edward G., Belvidere; Smith Samuel, Belvidere; Smith John W., Hazen; Smith Andrew J., laborer, Hazen; Smith Frank, laborer, Hazen; Smith Sylvanus, laborer, Bridgeville; Smith Lorenzo, laborer, Buttzville; Smith Abram, laborer, Buttzville; Smith Reuben, laborer, Buttzville; Smith Jesse, laborer, Bridgeville; Smith Jacob R., carpenter; Smith Joseph, laborer; Stout Mark A., blacksmith; Smith Henry, saloon; Stinson

YOU CAN ALWAYS FIND WHAT YOU WANT AT **LAUBACH'S, Easton, Pa.**

L. T., harness dealer; Sohner John, livery; Strackbine John; Searing George R., time-keeper; Sweeney Daniel Sr.; Stepp David, laborer; Sullivan Patrick, laborer; Sweeney Michael, laborer; Silverthorn

ROCKAFELLOW & WELLER,
SIGNISTS.
WASHINGTON - - NEW JERSEY.

Plain, Fancy, Ornamental, Wayside and Sign Painting. Our motto, "Best Work, Lowest Prices and all Work Guaranteed." Write us for prices on any kind of painting you desire. First-class references. Wagon Lettering and Wayside Painting a specialty.

Lewis; Struble Jacob, puddler; Scranton Charles; Smith John, laborer; Smith John T., blacksmith; Sawyer John, cooper; Shafer John, laborer; St. Ledger John, laborer; Stout William; Shanly John, sa-

SHIELDS INFALLIBLE **Dyspeptic Remedy** A sure cure for Dyspepsia, Sick or Nervous Headache. Guaranteed.

THE BEST GOODS FOR THE LEAST MONEY AT **NORTON'S, Easton Pa.**

OXFORD TOWNSHIP.

loon; Swick Lewis, puddler; Smith John, laborer; Smith A. S., laborer; Smith Philip, laborer, Buttzville; Schuyler Simon, laborer, Buttzville; Stone George, laborer, Buttzville; Stocher David, laborer, Bridgeville; Stocher Isaac, laborer, Bridgeville; Shaw Martin, Bridgeville; Sechler Abram, Bridgeville; Schultz Andrew, laborer; Snyder Isaac W., laborer; Snyder Peter, laborer; Snyder James, laborer, Bridgeville; Snyder Adam, nailer; Snyder John, puddler; Snyder Charles, laborer; Sutton A. E., laborer, Bridgeville; Sutton Jos. C., laborer, Bridgeville; Schuler Charles, Buttzville; Schuler William, Belvidere; Searles A., miller, Belvidere; Steele Wendell, laborer, Belvidere; Snyder Thomas, nailer; Shafer Thomas, laborer, Buttzville; Shafer Jacob S., laborer, Buttzville; Shafer Wm. P., laborer; Sawyer Abram, cooper; Stout Theodore, laborer; Scaley John, miner; Smith Peter S.; Seiple Abram, miner; Skinner A. H., teacher; Snyder Jesse, teamster; Stout Edward, nailer; Shultz Hiram; Smith William, laborer; Sullivan

LAUBACH'S, Easton, Pa., Largest stock of CARPETS, lowest prices. Best attention always.

James, laborer; Switzer Philip, nailer; Snyder Adam, nailer; Strong James, nailer; Sherrer John, nailer; Searing John M., nailer; Switzer Samuel, nailer; Searles Frederick, merchant; Shafer Peter H., nailer; Seiple Henry, laborer; Schuyler S. H., laborer, Buttzville; Seiple William, laborer; Snyder James, blacksmith, Bridgeville; Smith A., carpenter, Buttzville; Snyder Isaac, Bridgeville; Schuler Charles, Buttzville; Seiple A., laborer; Smith Frank, Buttzville; Searles Henry, laborer Buttzville; Serell John, Buttzville; Smith Irving, carpenter, Bridgeville; Sarson William, Montana; Smith Jason, laborer, Hazen; Searles George E., Bridgeville; Slack Aaron, laborer; Stout Jacob, laborer; Schuler Freeman, Oxford; Suff C. T., Montana; Shoemaker A. V., Hazen; Sarsin C. T., Montana; Savercool James, Bridgeville; Shoemaker Edward, Hazen; Sarson Geo. W., Hazen; Smith S., laborer; Searles Reuben, carpenter, Bridgeville; Spangenberry D. S., Hazen; Stone John, laborer, Buttzville; Sutton Joseph, furnace boss, Pequest;

ANDREWS & NOLF, 205 Northampton St. Keep the Largest line of Silks and Dress Goods on E. Northampton

H. M. NORTON — *WHOLESALE AND RETAIL DEALER IN HARDWARE, STOVES AND HOUSEFURNISHING GOODS.*

448   OXFORD TOWNSHIP.

Swayze Amos, Bridgeville; Shafer Amasa, laborer; Shafer James, laborer; Shafer Casteni, laborer; Shoemaker Abram; Shoemaker, A. L.; Shoemaker George, Hazen; Shoemaker James M., Bridgeville; Shoemaker Edward, Hazen; Shoemaker John, Hazen; Seibert Samuel; Seibert Wells; Spangenberry D. S., Hazen; Spangenberry Jos. L., Hazen; Spangenberry John F., Hazen; Spangenberry Marshall, carpenter; Slack Aaron, laborer, Bridgeville; Slack Cornelius, mason; Slack Charles, laborer; Slack John J., mason; Spoty Peter, laborer; Sullivan Daniel, laborer; Sullivan Dennis Sr., laborer; Sullivan Michael, iron worker; Stires Alex., Belvidere; Sarson Charles; Stongel Andrew, laborer; Sorosain Nels, laborer; Struckhin Henry, laborer; Sherrer John, laborer; Schueigart John, miner; Sonnson George, laborer; Sonnson Carl, laborer; Sonnson Michael, laborer; Shimrock Frank, laborer; Shultz Edwin T., laborer; Steinberg Ed., laborer; Shannon John, laborer; Swenson Savon, laborer; Shoemaker Jacob, Bridgeville; Shurtz John, laborer, Bridge-

LAUBACH'S, Easton, Pa. — *SPECIAL ATTENTION SILKS AND DRESS GOODS. NEW GOODS DAILY.*

ville, Skillman F., laborer, Bridgeville; Sorenson Nels.

Tunison G. O., physician and surgeon; Tunison W. A. H., insurance agent; Thomas Jabez, puddler;

J. FITTS & SON,
Furniture Manufacturers
WASHINGTON, N. J.

Invite the special attention of housekeepers to their immense stock of every description of Furniture, which they are selling at

About One-half of Former Prices.

Wise and economical people should not fail to give them a call.

J. FITTS & SON,
WASHINGTON AVENUE.   WASHINGTON, N. J.

Thomas John, puddler; Toomey M., miner; Tool J. R., laborer; Teal William, puddler; Trimmer G. H., carpenter; Taylor John P., laborer; Thompson W. F., blacksmith; Thompson F. J., merchant; Titman

PEACH BASKETS at Wades' Hardware Store, Hackettstown.

OXFORD TOWNSHIP.

W. B., Buttzville; Thatcher E., Montana; Titman J. F. G., Buttzville; Titus Robert, laborer, Buttzville; Teel James, teacher, Bridgeville; Thatcher George, laborer; Thatcher James, laborer; Tims George, laborer; Tims John, laborer, Bridgeville; Teel Robert, Hazen; Thatcher Lemuel, Montana; Thatcher Elijah, Montana; Titler James, laborer, Bridgeville; Teetes Elisha, Hazen; Toosen Otto, laborer; Thaw Levi, laborer; Trimmer George, laborer; Trimmer David, laborer; Tauger Fred., laborer; Tiffany James, laborer; Toomey Thomas, laborer; Thawson John, laborer; Thawson Otto, laborer.

Unangst John, Hazen; Uptegraw Daniel, laborer.

Voorhees Joseph, laborer, Montana; Voster Daniel, teamster; Voster Cyrus, puddler; Voorhees Cornelius, brakeman; Vosler Philip, nailer; Vosler John, nailer; Vorhees C. C., laborer; Vasbinder A. C., laborer, Buttzville; Vannatta Robert; Vass A. J., Bridgeville; Vannatta Jacob, laborer; Vannatta Samuel, laborer, Hazen; Vannatta George, laborer, Hazen;

Vannatta William, laborer, Hazen; Voorhees John, Montana; Voorhees C. E., laborer; Vortenburg, Peter, laborer; Vanskey August, laborer.

Willet John, Buttzville; Willet Edward, Buttzville; Willever Samuel, laborer, Buttzville; Willever Brakley, laborer, Montana; Willever James, Hazen; Watts Robert, laborer, Bridgeville; Woite Michael, laborer, Bridgeville; White Thomas, laborer, Bridgeville; White Wm. B., Hazen; Wildrick John B., laborer; Wildrick Andrew, laborer; Winfield John; Wolfe J.

N., laborer, Hazen; Wolfe William, laborer, Hazen; Widenor Joseph, Buttzville; Warne Wm. W., Hazen; Woodruff Geo. W., Montana; Wiggins Charles, puddler; Warner Axel, laborer; Wrestregard Peter,

H. M. NORTON, WHOLESALE AND RETAIL DEALER IN Hardware, Stoves and Housefurnishing

OXFORD TOWNSHIP.

laborer, Bridgeville; Winkely Arthur, nailer; Walbery Peter, laborer; Weaver John, laborer, Pequest; Widenor Peter, laborer, Roxburg; Wagner John; Warren Wm. N., Montana; Warren W. W., Montana; Willever Peter W., Montana; Wideoner Henry; Wildrick George; Wolfe William, miller, Hazen; Wyckoff G., Belvidere; Willever James, laborer, Roxburg; White Thomas, Roxburg; Walters Edward, laborer, Bridgeville; Widenor John, mason, Hazen; Walter Wm. J., laborer, Buttzville; Winkley J. B., nailer; Weitrecht Wm. M., agent; Wilkinson Alden, puddler; White Anson Sr., laborer; Wildrick G. A.; Wisebrown Charles, puddler; White Wm., laborer; Widenor James, puddler; Winkley George, nailer; Wright James, nailer; Wolfinger Henry; Weber George, agent; Weston Edward, nailer; Wyckoff David L.; Weston C. C., nailer; Wildrick J.; Warner H. C., engineer; Weston Charles B., superintendent nail factory; Walton Benjamin, tailor; White James, puddler; Wilson Peter, boss, Hazen;

LAUBACH'S Easton, Pa. THE LARGEST DRY GOODS AND CARPET HOUSE. BARGAINS ALWAYS

Wilson G. H., clerk, Hazen; Wolback Jesse, laborer; Wintermute Chas., Buttzville.

Young Henry R., nailer; Young John, nailer; Young Levi J., Belvidere; Young Benjamin, laborer, Belvidere; Young Robert S., laborer; Belvidere; Young Levi Sr., Belvidere; Young Abel, Belvidere;

OSCAR JEFFERY,
Counsellor-at-Law, Examiner in Chancery,
NOTARY PUBLIC AND SUPREME COURT EXAMINER.
WASHINGTON, N. J.

Yernson Peter, laborer; Yonson Andrew, laborer; Yerkley Judson, laborer; Yanston Peter, laborer; Youmans Ira, Bridgeville.

Zulauf Henry Jr., engineer; **Zulauf John,** baker; Zulauf Henry Sr., miner; Zapp J. J., clerk; Zapp Chris., watchman.

READ CAREFULLY Page 218

PAHAQUARRY TOWNSHIP.

PAHAQUARRY. This township, sometimes spoken of as "the State of Pahaquarry," is the extreme northern township of Warren County, running across the entire county, and was formed from Wallpack township, Sussex County, in 1824. It is bounded on the north by the Delaware River, on the east by Sussex Co., on the south by Hardwick, Blairstown, and Knowlton townships, and on the west by the Delaware River. It is a peculiarly secluded township, having for its northern boundary the Delaware River, and for its southern boundary the Blue Mountain. The length of the township is 12 miles, average width 1½ miles. Its area is 19.04 square miles or 12,186 acres of land. The name of the township is derived from an Indian village, of the Minisink tribe, once located within its limits.

The Blue Mountain, which forms the entire southern boundary of the township, occupies the greater part of its surface. The remaining portion consists of but a small strip along the Delaware, about one fourth of a mile in width, running also the entire length of the township. The rustic beauty, and mountain scenery of Pahaquarry is truly picturesque and sublime in no ordinary degree. Foremost among the natural attractions of the township is the celebrated "Delaware Water Gap," located at the southwestern end. At this point in the township, the rocks rise almost perpendicularly in rugged masses, presenting a bold threatening front forty or fifty feet in hight. This is known as the "Indian Ladder," the Indians having formed here a ladder for themselves from a tree, the upright position of which served their purpose. The whites also for their accommodation constructed a rope ladder, but its use was attended with considerable danger and it was finally abandoned. At the present time a wagon and also a railroad run along the river, making the use of the former contrivance unnecessary.

PAHAQUARRY TOWNSHIP.

On the summit of the Blue Mountain, near the northeastern end of the township, is "Cat Fish Pond," the line of the township running just southeast of the pond. Its outlet flows into Blairstown. About two miles southwest of this is "Sun Fish Pond," also on the summit of the mountain, 1,000 ft. above the Delaware, and having two outlets, one natural and one artificial, both flowing into the Delaware. About three quarters of a mile farther to the southwest is "The Paint Spring," which deposits ferruginous ochre. The summit of the Blue Mountain is the highest ground in the State, being at the Water Gap nearly 1,500 ft. above sea level.

The *first settlement in Warren County*, was made in this township, perhaps by a hundred and fifty years. The pioneer settlers were Hollanders, who came here in search of minerals as early as 1650, and, it is thought, discovered copper, within the present limits of the township. But the natural obstructions of this section (which might be turned into natural advantages), were such as to prevent any important development in this direction. This township used to be visited by Horace Greely when on his rustic excursions.

There is but one village in the township. Mill Brook, in the northeastern part, at the foot of the Blue Mountain, and on Mill Brook Creek, has a grist mill, blacksmith shop, store and post office, M. E. Church, hotel and school house.

The Delaware Slate Company have their works in the southwestern end of the township. At this place is a small collection of houses for the accommodation of the employees. There are two other post offices in the township, known as Calno and Pahaquarry.

Population, 150. Schools, 3. Scholars, 108.

WARREN COUNTY DRUG STORE.

Township Directory.

All whose vocation is not mentioned are farmers.

Burk Wm., Calno; Bunnel Isaac, Calno; Beford Samuel, Dunnfield; Barnes W. E., Dunnfield.

Cortright Oliver, Calno; Depue M. M., Calno.

Depue Daniel, Calno; Dimmock M. H., Calno; Dimmock Chauncey, Calno; Dingman Daniel, miller, Millbrook; Dingman Henry, saloon, Millbrook; Duryee Samuel, laborer, Millbrook; Davey G. H., Dunnfield; Deats M. R., agent, Dunnfield.

Fleet Joseph, laborer, Dunnfield; Fuller Bartley, miller, Millbrook; Fuller Fletcher, Calno; Freer Louis, laborer, Dunnfield.

Garris P. J. S., Freeholder, Millbrook; Garris E. L., collector, Millbrook; Garris Garnet, Millbrook; Garris John, Millbrook; Garris Elmer, laborer, Millbrook; Garris Isaiah, laborer, Millbrook; Garris A. A., Millbrook; Gardner Joseph, engineer, Dunnfield; Garris

LAUBACH'S EASTON, PA. CLOAKS and WRAPS of every description. **Our Own Manufacture.**

Hamilton, carpenter, Millbrook; Garris George, laborer, Millbrook.

Hunterdon Daniel, merchant, Millbrook; Henry George, Calno; Hall George, Calno; Howell John, laborer, Millbrook; Hill Jason, Millbrook; Hall Frank, laborer, Dunnfield; Huff Frank, Millbrook; Hism J. K., laborer, Millbrook; Hunt Peter, laborer, Dunnfield.

Kitchen Simon, slate factory, Dunnfield; Kitchen John, slate factory, Dunnfield; Kitchen Jacob, slate factory, Dunnfield; Kimball Calvin, blacksmith, Millbrook; Kimball James, laborer, Millbrook.

Labar Charles, Millbrook; Loun Stephen, Dunnfield.

Michell John, Calno; Michell P. Z., Calno; Michell William, Calno.

O'Brien Daniel, Dunnfield; O'Conner Martin, laborer, Dunnfield.

Rible Angeline, Calno; Rible W. R., Calno.

Spansunburg Andrew, Millbrook; Spansunburg Wil-

ANDREWS & NOLF, 205 Northampton St., Easton, Pa. The best place to buy Merino **Underwear** for Gents, Ladies and Children.

H. M. NORTON, *WHOLESALE AND RETAIL DEALER IN* **Hardware, Stoves and Housefurnishing.**

PAHAQUARRY TOWNSHIP.

liam, laborer, Millbrook; Smith Jacob, Dunnfield; Smith Daniel, Dunnfield; Smith David, clerk, Dunnfield; Stronk J. M., laborer, Calno; Suttan M. M., Calno; Stires George, laborer, Calno; Snover Hampton, laborer, Calno; Sisco Robert, mason, Millbrook; Stires F. C., Justice of Peace, Millbrook; Shoemaker Daniel, laborer, Calno.

Tillman G. M., Dunnfield; Transue Adam, Dunnfield; Transue Godfrey, Dunnfield; Tillman I. R., Calno.

Vancamp Moses, Calno; Vanuken John, Calno; Vangordon Abraham, mason, Calno; Vangordon Andrew, laborer, Millbrook; Vangordon Abraham, laborer, Millbrook; Vancampen W. O., laborer, Millbrook; Vanetten William, school teacher, Millbrook; Vanetten John, school teacher, Millbrook; Vanetten Susan, Millbrook; Vencampen Frank, laborer, Millbrook.

Welter John, laborer, Millbrook; Warner Obidiah, laborer, Millbrook; Warner Ouston, laborer, Millbrook;

LAUBACH'S, Easton, Pa., Largest stock of CARPETS, lowest prices. Best attention always.

Wilgus Joseph, laborer, Millbrook; Warner Israel, Millbrook; Walker Charles, Dunnfield; Walker Chas., Dunnfield; Walker C. M., Dunnfield; Wyckoff M.

WASHINGTON HOUSE,

WASHINGTON, N. J.   *JAMES NOLAN, Prop.*

NEArly Opposite D. L. & W. Depot,
Permanent and transient guests well entertained. Prices reasonable.

A., Dunnfield; Wyckoff S. D., laborer, Dunnfield; Walter Abram, laborer, Millbrook.

Zimmerman John, Calno; Zimmerman Hiram, Calno.

SHIELDS INVALUABLE **Dyspeptic Remedy.** A sure cure for Dyspepsia, Sick or Nervous Headache. Guaranteed.

POHATCONG TOWNSHIP.

POHATCONG is the southwestern township of Warren County. It was until recently embraced in Greenwich, from which it was formed by an act of the State Legislature, approved March 24, 1881. The township contains 8,315 acres of land, or a little less than 13 square miles. It is bounded north and northwest by the Delaware River, east and northeast by Greenwich, southeast by the Musconetcong, and southwest by the Delaware. The Pohatcong Creek crosses the township from northeast to southwest, a little south of the centre.

In physical characteristics it very much resembles Greenwich. The land is rolling and hilly, and the soil fertile. The chief industry is farming, for which the township has special advantages. The proximity of the cities of Phillipsburg and Easton, makes it a desirable location for the farmer, who thus finds a ready and convenient market for his produce. The water facilities of Pohatcong also, are worthy of special mention, and are such as would invite the manufacturer to locate his business within her limits.

Of the first settlements within the present limits of the township, we have but little definite information. The Seigles, the descendants of whom are quite numerous in the township, are known to be among the first settlers. They came to this country with William Penn, and settled in the township, now known as Pohatcong, which was a part of Penn's grant. It is probable that the first settlers located in the vicinity of the present town of Seigleville, formerly Middleville. The present name of the town will probably perpetuate the historic name of its founders.

The following are the towns of Pohatcong:

Reiglesville, in the southwest part along the Delaware, has a paper mill, grist mill, hotel, store, post office and R. R. station.

Finesville, in the south part along the Musconetcong, has a knife factory, two stores, blacksmith and wheelwright shop, carriage factory, M. E. and Christian churches, and public school.

Seigleville, about a half a mile from Finesville, has an earthenware manufactory, grist mill and grain cradle manufactory.

Hughesville, also along the Musconetcong, is the seat of the Warren paper mill, and has a store and an unoccupied mill seat.

Carpentersville, in the northwest, along the Delaware, has a church, depot and school house.

Springtown, in the east, along the Pohatcong, has two stores, blacksmith shop, grist mill and a Christian church.

Schools, 4. Scholars, 328. Population, about 1,150.

There is one other town in the township which is really a suburb of Phillipsburg, and its business is rather related to that town than to the township.

LIVERY, SALE
AND
EXCHANGE STABLES

MICHAEL MEAGHER, Prop'r.
WASHINGTON, N. J.

Carriages and Light Wagons

Furnished at short notice and

At Reasonable Prices.

Office connected with Telephone.

HOTEL AND CITY OMNIBUS.

WARREN COUNTY DRUG STORE.

Township Directory.

All whose vocation is not mentioned are farmers.

Austin Charles H., grinder, Reiglesville; Apgar Levi, farmer and peach grower, Reiglesville.

Brown Huton, laborer, Warren paper mills; Burns Henry R., laborer, Springtown; Bapp John, laborer, Warren paper mills; Backman Charles, clerk, bookkeeper and postmaster, Warren paper mills; Burkett C. S., laborer, Warren paper mills; Bidleman Abram R., miller, Reiglesville; Buss Daniel, boatman, Shimers; Beers George, shoemaker, Shimer's; Beers Wm. S., laborer, Shimer's; Bird Peter, laborer, Carpenterville; Bennett Solon, laborer, Carpentersville; Boyer Jacob O., Justice of the Peace, Reiglesville; Butler Philip, laborer, Reiglesville; Brotzman Philip, Reiglesville; Bell E. J., teacher, Carpentersville; Butler Robert, blacksmith, wagon maker and carriage builder, Reiglesville; Bloom John D., farmer, drover and

LAUBACH Leads in prices and quality of goods. EASTON Pa.

agent for farming implements, Reiglesville; Bloom John S., proprietor Riverside House and carpenter, Reiglesville; Brotzman Christopher, well borer and carter, Reiglesville; Brotzman Edward, teamster, Reiglesville; Clendening Charles, gentleman, Springtown; Casey James, trucker, Springtown; Carpenter Wm. S., Springtown; Carpenter Robert S., Springtown; Carpenter Nathan, agent for agricultural implements, Springtown; Carpenter J. S., gentleman, Springtown; Crouse R. T., dealer and peach grower, Springtown; Crouse J. M., farmer and peach grower, Reiglesville; Ceran James, blacksmith and machinist, Warren paper mills; Cackender Fred., fireman, Warren paper mills; Cole John, paper maker, Warren Paper Mills; Crouse Briten, laborer, Warren paper mills; Carpenter John, agent for agricultural implements, Shimer's; Couch Samuel, miner, Carpentersville; Crouse Thos. M., farmer and peach grower, Riegelsvile; Carpenter R. K., farmer and peach grower, Carpentersville;

Andrews & Nolf, 205 Northampton St., Easton, Pa. The only place to buy the celebrated "Cold Blast" feathers Guaranteed free from odor and dirt.

H. M. NORTON *WHOLESALE AND RETAIL DEALER IN HARDWARE, STOVES AND HOUSEFURNISHING GOODS.*

POHATCONG TOWNSHIP.

Carpenter S. D., gentleman and peach grower, Carpentersville; Carpenter James A., farmer and peach grower; Chamberlain Wm., laborer, Warren paper mills; Casey James Jr., laborer, Warren paper mills; Case I. F., Warren paper mills; Carpenter J. B., Springtown; Cline Harry, laborer, Springtown; Clark R. H., Rieglesville; Cope Broth. lime burners and miners, Carpentersville; Cooley Henry, laborer, Carpentersville; Cole Daniel, miner, Riegelsville; Cyphers John R., general store, Finesville, Rieglesville; Cooley Simon, laborer, Carpentersville; Cathers James, lime burner and moulding sand, Carpentersville; Cather William, clerk, Carpentersville; Carpenter J. D., general store, postmaster, agent Belvidere Division P. R. R., Carpentersville; Case Nathan, M. D., Rieglesville; Carpenter Joseph, broker, lumberman, Carpentersville.

Dalrymple James F., constable, Sprucetown; Dalrymple Levi, Springtown; Dalrymple James G., laborer, Springtown; Dalrymple Chris. S., laborer, Spring-

LAUBACH'S, Easton, Pa. SPECIAL ATTENTION TO SILKS AND DRESS GOODS. NEW GOODS DAILY.

town, Deemer Frank, teacher, Springtown; Duncan Thomas, colored, trader, Springtown; Draney Robert, laborer, Warren paper mills; Davis Lewis, fireman, Warren paper mills; Druckenmiller Nathan, miller, Springtown; Dalton Wm. F., boatman, Shimer's; Dickson John R., retired, Carpenterville; Donnell Daniel, laborer, Carpentersville; Donnelly Daniel, retired, Rieglesville; Deemer John H., gardener, Rieglesville; Duckworth Wm. H., Rieglesville; DeJoy Cornelius, furnaceman, Rieglesville.

Edinger Abram, trackman, Rieglesville; Easterly Furman, laborer, Carpentersville; Edinger Abram, lime-burner, Carpentersville; Easterly Godfry, laborer, Carpentersville; Eipper Henry F., blacksmith, Rieglesville; Edinger Wm., sand paver and fisherman, Reiglesville; Edinger Jesse, sawyer and peach grower, Rieglesville.

Freeman Mart. Sr., colored, laborer, Warren Paper Mills; Freeman Martin Jr., laborer, Warren Paper Mills; Forgus Samuel, laborer, Warren Paper Mills;

THE BEST GOODS FOR THE LEAST MONEY AT **NORTON'S, Easton Pa.**

POHATCONG TOWNSHIP. 459

Fretts Jacob A., Warren Paper Mills; Frace David, Shimers; Force Wm. A., painter and paper hanger, Springtown; Fair John V., Carpentersville; Fry Wm. H., Carpentersville; Freeman Isaac, colored, laborer, Warren Paper Mills; Farrell Wm. T., colored, laborer, Rieglesville; Fretz Samuel, laborer, Rieglesville; Flenard Edward, machinist, Rieglesville; Fine Millard, butcher, Rieglesville; Fritz Henry, gentleman, Rieglesville; Fair Wm., laborer, Carpentersville; Frankenfield Jacob, teamster, Rieglesville; Fine Spencer, butcher, Rieglesville.

Gano Sansberry, Springtown; Goodyear Francis, Springtown; Garner Casper, miller, Springtown; Godwin Geo., general store, Warren Paper Mills; Gilbert Robert C., paper maker, Warren Paper Mills; Grube Louis, Warren Paper Mills; Grube Samuel, Shimers; Grube Quintus S., laborer, Shimers; Gano Samuel, laborer, Carpentersville; Griffin Charles, book keeper, Rieglesville.

Hawk Henry, laborer, Springtown; Hawk Isaac,

LAUBACH'S Easton, Pa. THE LARGEST DRY GOODS AND CARPET HOUSE. BARGAINS ALWAYS

laborer, Springtown; Hawk Samuel, Springtown; Hawk Isaac H., laborer, Springtown; Hawk R. M., laborer, Springtown; Harrison Alferdy, laborer, Springtown; Hamlin John T., Springtown; Hamlin J. C., Springtown; HoneyBoam Wm., laborer, Springtown; Hawk H. B. Carpentersville; Hawk John W., laborer, Carpentersville; Hawk Joseph, R. R. agent and mail carrier, Warren Paper Mills; Hawk Hiram, railroader, Springtown; Harrison Wm. H., laborer, Warren Paper Mills; Hughes Wm. J., trucker, Warren Paper Mills; Huff J. D., laborer, Warren Paper Mills; Harrison David, carpenter, Warren Paper Mills; Hagerty Wm., laborer, Warren Paper Mills; Harrison Daniel, blacksmith, Warren Paper Mills; Hughes Sam, Warren Paper Mills; Hawk Wm. N., drover, Shimers; Hulshyer J. S., Shimers; Herber Phaon, laborer, Springtown; Hughes H. G., gentleman, Warren Paper Mills; Hager Peter, Carpentersville; Hawk R L.,milkman,Shimers, Heder John,gentleman,Shimers; Hawk Warren,Shimers; Hawk Marshal, music teacher

ANDREWS & NOLF'S Easton, Pa., sell Terry's Scissors and Shears. Every pair warranted.

H. M. NORTON, *WHOLESALE AND RETAIL DEALER IN* Hardware, Stoves and Housefurnishing

POHATCONG TOWNSHIP.

and dealer in instruments, Shimer; Hoadly David S., shoemaker, Shimers; Hummer Johnson, Shimers; Hamlen Edward, Shimers; Hoadley Samuel, laborer, Carpentersville; Hulshryer Frank, teamster, Rieglesville; Henesy John, gentleman, Carpentersville; Howel Jacob, boatman, Carpentersville; Heater William H., laborer, Carpentersville; Heater John, laborer, Carpentersville; Hughes John, Carpentersville; Hulshryer Richard, coal merchant, Rieglesville; Holmen Joel, trip hammer forger, Rieglesville; Hawk Henry, gentleman cigars and tobacco, Carpentersville; Hunt Luther, laborer, Rieglesville; Hunt John, peach grower, Rieglesville; Hawk R. S., laborer, Springtown; Hunt J. S., town treasurer, Rieglesville.

Jones Richard, Shimers; Jones Burge, trip hammer forger, Rieglesville; Jacoby L. M., merchant miller and grain dealer, Rieglesville.

Kinney Wm. P., Springtown; Keller Jesse, retired, Springtown; Kocker Samuel, teamster, Warren Paper Mills; Kressler Moses, millwright and machinist, Rie-

YOU CAN ALWAYS FIND WHAT YOU WANT AT **LAUBACH'S, Easton, Pa.**

glesville; Kelley R. S., gentleman, Rieglesville; Kelley J. R., Rieglesville; Kressler Warren, laborer, Rieglesville; Kinney Theodore, Shimers; Kelt Patrick, watchman, Rieglesville; Kutner Charles, painter and paper hanger, Rieglesville; Knecht Joseph, miller and merchant, Carpentersville; Kelty Conrad, gentleman, Rieglesville; Kressler James, millwright and machinist, Rieglesville; Kelty Wm., watchman, Rieglesville.

Loudenburg John, carpenter and cooper, Springtown; Loudenburg Amos, laborer, Springtown; Lyons Manning, laborer, Springtown; Lauback Wm., laborer, Springtown; Loose Philip, laborer, Warren Paper Mills; Loose Jacob, laborer, Carpentersville; Loose Wm., peach grower, Carpentersville; Lauback Levi, peach grower, Carpentersville; Loose George W., Warren Paper Mills; Loudenberg John, railroader, Shimers; Lippincott Wm. H., sawyer, Carpentersville; Layton C. M., shoemaker, Rieglesville; Lauback J. F., teamster, Rieglesville; Lauback I. S., lime burner and mason, Rieglesville.

ROPE, TWINE, etc. at **WADE BROS.** Hackettstown.

THE BEST GOODS FOR THE LEAST MONEY AT **NORTON'S, Easton Pa.**

POHATCONG TOWNSHIP.

Mutchler J. G., shoemaker, Springtown; Myers Sylvester, boatman, Shimer's; Mousley Louis H., paper maker, Warren paper mills; Mires Peter, broom maker and farmer, Springtown; Moyers Charles J., railroader, Shimer's; Moyers William H., railroader, Shimer's; Moyers John S., railroader, Shimer's; Mires Casper, laborer, Shimer's; Mires Chas. P., railroader, Shimer's; Melick John, Shimer's; Mullen A. W., laborer, Shimer's; McClain Barney, laborer, Shimer's; Mickel Thomas, laborer, Carpentersville; Merritt Winfield, laborer, Rieglesville; Moses Eli, laborer, Carpentersville; Mickel Samuel H., laborer, Carpentersville; Mechner William, laborer, Carpentersville; Mullen James, grinder, Rieglesville; Metler Wm. S., laborer, Reiglesville; Millick Alvin, Springtown; Miller Frank B., laborer, Springtown; Meleck John W., hotel and saloon keeper, Rieglesville.

Neilly John, stone mason, Springtown; Northelfer Edward, carriage and blacksmith, Shimer's.

LAUBACH'S EASTON, PA. CLOAKS and WRAPS of every description. **Our Own Manufacture.**

O'Brine Thomas, watchman, Carpentersville.

Parker Jeremiah, carpenter, Springtown; Painter Jacob, miller, Springtown; Perry C. C., carpenter, Warren paper mills; Pinkerton Cyrus, laborer, Warren paper mills; Painter A., farmer and freeholder, Shimer's; Painter H. S., laborer, Shimer's; Piatt Henry, lock tender, Shimer's; Pursell Wm. H., laborer, Shimer's; Pritchard Rev. T. C., Lutheran, Shimer's; Pursell H. W., milkman and farmer, Shimer's; Piatt Thomas, laborer, Shimer's; Pursell Leford H., gentleman, Shimer's; Piatt J. H., laborer, Shimer's; Piatt Aaron, laborer, Shimer's; Piatt Jos., laborer, Shimer's; Piatt Philip, grocery and stone mason, Shimer's; Pursell Andrew, stone dealer, Shimer's; Pursell Wm. S., milkman, Shimer's; Pursell Spencer C., gentleman, Shimer's; Pursell Howard, Shimer's; Pursell Brice, laborer, Carpentersville; Precour J. G., laborer, Reiglesville; Pursell James, Carpentersville; Pursell Joseph C., laborer, Carpentersville; Person Frank, bartender, Reiglesville.

ANDREWS & NOLF, 205 Northampton St., Easton, Pa. The best place to buy **Merino Underwear** for Gents, Ladies and Children.

Quick Wm. H., trucker, Springtown.

Riddle Samuel, laborer, Warren paper mills; Rinkert Geo., laborer, Springtown; Rinkert Gothial, laborer, Springtown; Rosenbery Geo., sexton Lutheran Church, Shimer's; Roberts H. J., Superintendent, Warren paper mills; Riegle Edward, laborer, Carpentersville; Rapp Andrew, mining, Carpentersville; Rugg C. H., lime-burner, Springtown; Roseberry James M., mason, Reiglesville; Roseberry Wm., grinder, Reiglesville; Roseberry Thomas, laborer, Reiglesville; Reese Philip, Carpentersville; Reese Hiram, gentleman, Carpentersville; Reese John, gentleman, Carpentersville; Raymon H. C., painter, Reiglesville; Robin Cornelius, Springtown; Riegel John L. & Son, coal, Springtown; Reigel Benjamin, store keeper, Reiglesville.

Seagraves Charles, Warren Paper Mills; Stecker Jacob, Warren Paper Mills; Swackhammer, store and ticket agent P. R. R., Springtown; Stocker Wm. M., laborer, Warren Paper Mills; Stamates Aaron, laborer, Springtown; Stamates Edward, laborer Springtown; Smith Charles, railroader, Springtown; Stocker Matison, clerk, Springtown; Spangenburg Joseph R., Springtown; Stocker Sanford, general store and postmaster, Springtown; Stocker Josiah, watchman, Springtown; Striker Paul P., Springtown; Stocker Edmund L., Springtown; Stocker Sylvester, Springtown; Stocker Abram, general blacksmith, wagons, etc., Springtown; Stocker Samuel, railroader, Springtown; Stocker Ervin, blacksmith, Springtown; Stocker Wm., railroader, Springtown; Stocker Charles, railroader, Springtown; Stamates James G., miner, Carpentersville; Sidders Wm., teamster, Reiglesville; Stamates Robert, Springtown; Swink Otto, laborer, Warren Paper Mills; Smith Wm. G., Springtown; Stamates Samuel, laborer, Warren Paper Mills; Seigle Jacob, miller, Reiglesville; Siegle Benj., carpenter and cradle maker, Reiglesville; Seigle Thomas, Reiglesville; Seigle A. C., carpenter, Reiglesville; Seigle J. R., Reiglesville; Seigle Charles, laborer, Reigles-

POHATCONG TOWNSHIP.

ville; Schooley A., boss, Shimer's; Stiner Levi, laborer, Shimer's; Stiner Reading, Shimer's; Schooley Nicholas, boatman, Shimer's; Small John, gentleman, Shimer's; Sherrer Charles, Springtown; Sherren W. W., Springtown; Stocker Peter, huckster, Springtown; Stocker Harry, railroad r, Springtown; Smith Geo. F., laborer, Shimer's; Shoup Samuel, tinsmith, Shimer's; Snyder Charles M., laborer, Shimer's; Snyder Wm., railroad carpenter, Shimer's; Smith Wm. H., mason, Reiglesville; Siegel W. R., carpenter, Reiglesville; Sailer Alonzo, Carpentersville; Sheninger John, gentleman, Carpentersville; Fred. W., laborer, Carpentersville, Sampson Geo., boss miner, Carpentersville; Seigle Judar, laborer, Reiglesville; Seagraves James, trucker. Springtown; Searfass Wm., S., carpenter, Reiglesville; Schug Edwin F., teacher, Springtown; Searfass Wm. H., clerk, Reiglesville; Sinclair Elmer, laborer, Reiglesville; Seyler Henry, carpenter, Reiglesville; Seyler Jacob E., wagon maker, Reiglesville; Sailer Jacob, carpenter, Riegles-ville; Slater John, laborer, Reiglesville; Sullivan Timothy, boss, Carpentersville; Sullivan Daniel, railroader, Carpentersville; Sullivan Dennis, railroader, Carpentersville; Stone H. R., Carpentersville; Smith Peter, laborer, Carpentersville; Smith Laurence M., miner, Carpentersville; Sinclair Henry, watchman, Reiglesville; Searfoss Jacob C., laborer, Reiglesville; Stiles Francis, knife manufacturer, Reiglesville; Snyder J. F., blacksmith, Reiglesville; Snyder Geo. W., carriages and sleighs, Reiglesville; Seigle Abram, commissioner of deeds, Reiglesville; Shimer Wm. S., railroader, Shimer's; Shimer Thomas, teacher, Shimer's; Souder Sanford W., clerk, Rieglesville; Shimes Wm. B., gentleman, Shimer's; Smith John M., gentleman, Reiglesville; Schultz Henry, miller, Reiglesville; Super Henry, gentleman, Reiglesville; Super James, furnaceman, Reiglesville; Shimer Robert A., store, Reiglesville.

Transue Milton, laborer, Warren paper mills, Warren paper mills; Tomer Newton, teacher, Reiglesville;

H. M. NORTON — WHOLESALE AND RETAIL DEALER IN HARDWARE, STOVES AND HOUSEFURNISHING GOODS.

POHATCONG TOWNSHIP.

Tomer Wm. C., miner, Carpentersville; Terney John, railroader, Shimer's; Todd Roland, carpenter, Carpentersville; Tomer Margaret, seamstress and tailor, Rieglesville; Taylor F. S., manufacturer of knives, Reiglesville; Tormer Wm. S., gentleman, Rieglesville.

Ulmer David, shoemaker, Springtown.

Vought William, laborer, Springtown; Vannatta A. H., teacher, Carpentersville; Vanderbilt Furman, peach grower, Reiglesville.

Welch John S., laborer, Warren paper mills; Welch Peter T., Warren paper mills; Warman Isaac, Springtown; Warman John, gentleman, Springtown; Weydemyer Jonas, milk dealer, Springtown; Wallace T. L., laborer, Shimer's; Wallace Christain, Shimer's; Wieder Sam'l S., laborer, Shimer's; Wallace Howard, laborer, Shimer's; Welch George S., railroader, Warren paper mills; Wiegle Charles E., finisher, Warren paper mills; Winter Spencer, laborer, Warren paper mills; Wolverton V. R., gentleman, Warren paper

LAUBACH'S, Easton, Pa. 328 NORTHAMPTON ST. LARGEST Dry Goods and Carpet House.

mills; Weiant Samuel, laborer, Shimer's; Weller Robert, Springtown; Wieder Jacob S., Reiglesville; Watson Harry, paper maker, Warren paper mills; Weller Joseph C., Shimer's; Weller Calvin, trucker, Springtown; Willever Henry, boatman, Shimer's; Winter Peter, railroader, Springtown; Wyatt Richard, gardener, Reiglesville; Wernert Charles A., laborer, Carpentersville; Warner Samuel, groceries, Reiglesville; Walkner James G., miller, Reiglesville; Wolfinger S. M., clerk, Reiglesville; Wardell Henry, paper maker, Reiglesville; Office Warren Manufacturing Company, Reiglesville; Wieder Solomon W., postmaster, Reiglesville; Wieder John S., Reiglesville.

Young Joseph, mason, Springtown; Younkins Jonas, wheelwright, Springtown; Younkins James, railroader, Springtown; Young Alfred H., trucker, Springtown; Young Abram, trucker, Reiglesville; Young Geo. H., plasterer, Reiglesville.

Zigenfoose Henry, miner, Carpentersville; Zigle,

BARGAINS IN HORSE WHIPS at Wades', Hackettstown.

THE BET GOOD FOR THE LEAST MONEY AT NORTON'S Easton, Pa.

POHATCONG TOWNSHIP.

Asher, laborer, Carpentersville; Zigler John, laborer, Carpentersville; Zearfoss Levi, gentleman, Carpentersville; Zeller Peter, carpenter, Reiglesville; Zeller Samuel, Reiglesville; Zeller Jacob, laborer, Reiglesville; Zeller James, gentleman, Springtown; Zeller Isaac, Springtown; Zeller Henry, Springtown; Zeller Wendle, Springtown.

VICTOR CASTNER,

DEALER IN

General Merchandise!

FERTILIZERS, NURSERY STOCK, Etc.,

General Farmer and Peach and Small Fruit Grower.

Producer of large quantities of Peach trees for setting out. Best varieties. Established 30 years.

CHANGEWATER, N. J.

WASHINGTON TOWNSHIP.

WASHINGTON township is situated about midway between the northern and southern ends of Warren county along the Musconetcong. As a township it may be called "The Flower of the Musconetcong." No more beautiful scenery is presented in the county than is to be seen in this township.

From Washington Borough, looking westward, in the direction of Phillipsburg, may be seen a landscape truly picturesque and strikingly beautiful.

In shape, the township is almost square, its eastern and western sides being at right angles with the Musconetcong, and its northern boundary in general direction, almost parallel with it. It is bounded as follows: north, Oxford; east, Mansfield; south, the Musconetcong, and west, Franklin.

The Borough of Washington is located in the centre of the township and is described elsewhere in this work.

Present population of the township, about 2,300.

The physical features of this township are considerably varied. Smiling valleys, hills rising along and above them, and mountains looming up here and there are its characteristics. It is well watered with numerous springs and small streams, the township being drained almost wholly by the Musconetcong and the Pohatcong, the one forming its southern boundary, the other crossing its central portion.

The Pohatcong mountains as the principal range. The loftiest mountain in this section of country is Scott's Mountain, near Oxford Furnace, being about 1,120 feet above the sea level. The elevation of the Pohatcong Mountains in the vicinity of Washington is much less, being but about 500 feet. Most of the mountains in this section have a marked characteristic—to the northeast they slope very gradually until they sink out of sight, while at their southwest ends the decline is broken and sudden, which is possibly the result of the diluvial period.

One of the most romantic places, for a single day's rustication, to be found anywhere, may be visited in this township. "Roaring Rock," of local fame, is a miniature cataract in the course of Brass Castle Creek, situated about a mile and a half from Washington Borough, and is much visited by picnic parties and the lovers of romantic and picturesque

WASHINGTON TOWNSHIP.

scenery. The Rock is about 10 feet wide and 20 feet long. It was originally called the "Indian Stomper" from the fact that it was once used by the Indians for grinding or crushing corn.

There are evidences that the history of the township begins with that of Changewater, in 1787, and that Changewater was more prosperous than Washington prior to 1800. There were settlers in the township, however, as early as 1769.

The principal occupation of the inhabitants of the township, is farming, and stock raising. Several other industries are represented, such as milling, tanning, stone quarrying etc., but are not carried on to any great extent.

Formery other industries received attention in this township, which are now not existing, among which was that of canal-boat building. Two boat yards were in active operation, one at Washington and one at Port Colden, in which many boats were built annually. The Morris Canal and the Morris & Essex RR. furnish employment to a number of men in the township.

The towns are: Port Colden, situated on the Morris & Essex RR. and the Morris Canal, and is said to be named in honor of Cadwalader Colden, who was Governor of the State of New York, under the second period of the English administration, during the year 1760-61. The settlement was first called "Dusenberry's Folly," in contempt for Wm. Dusenberry, one of the founders of the place, for being so foolish as to think that a large town would at some time occupy the present site of the village.

The oldest settler here was Newbold Woolston, grandfather of the present James B. Woolston. It has three stores, a blacksmith shop, post office and schoolhouse. It is about one mile from Washington.

Changewater, so called because of the separation and conducting of the waters from the upper and lower banks of the Musconetcong, into two counties, Warren and Hunterdon, by the mill races of the "Old Forge," is located in the southern part of the township, where the D. L. & W. RR. crosses the Musconetcong. It was the scene of the murder of the Castner family, by Carter and Parks, whose graves are along the road leading to Port Colden, and just north of the village of Changewater. Parks was a brother-in-law of Castner. Date of the murder, 1844. Changewater has an excellent flouring mill, a picture frame factory, store post office, school house and limestone quarries.

Brass Castle, supposed to be so called because one Jacob Brass, in the old pioneer days erected at this place his log castle, is located in the northwestern part of the township upon the north bank of the Morris canal. It has a grist mill, blacksmith shop, saw mill, school house and store of recent date.

Imladale has a store and grist mill.

Fairmount has a school house and foundry.

Washington Borough is described elsewhere. Schools 5, scholars 360.

WARREN COUNTY DRUG STORE.

TOWNSHIP DIRECTORY.

*All whose vocation is not mentioned are farmers.
The Post Office addresses not given in this township
are Washington.*

Anderson J. H., car repairer, Port Colden; Alshouse A. W., teamster, Port Colden; Apgar W. H., level tender, Port Colden; Adams B B., wheelwright; Adams Joseph, merchant; Ackerman Charles, boatman; Allen William, sexton; Apgar Emanuel, retired, Port Colden; Apgar Jennie, householder; Apgar Geo., laborer; Ackmen John, laborer.

Bryan Reuben, New Hampton; Bryan Ezra, New Hampton; Bryan Alonzo, New Hampton; Bryan Chester, New Hampton; Bowlby Joseph, laborer, New Hampton; Blinn Othniel, laborer, New Hampton; Burd Marshal, frame maker, Changewater; Burd George, laborer, Changewater; Burd Caleb, laborer, Changewater; Burd Wm., laborer, Changewater; Bar-

LAUBACH'S Easton, Pa. THE LARGEST DRY GOODS AND CARPET HOUSE BARGAINS ALWAYS

net Wm., teamster, Changewater; Barber Wm. T., organ builder, Port Colden; Barber Charles, railroader, Port Colden; Burd James, boatman, Port Colden; Bamrick John, railroader, Port Colden; Bryan Rachel, freeholder; Bryan Joseph, laborer; Bryan Harry, laborer; Baker Jacob, laborer; Baker Daniel, laborer; Baker John R., blacksmith, Port Colden; Burd Theo., laborer, Changewater; Bodine Enos; Bodine Wm.; Bodine John; Bowlby Richey, New Hampton; Bowlby Chester, New Hampton; Bowlby Wm., New Hampton; Bowlby Miller, New Hampton; Beideman Joseph; Beideman Harry; Benward Wm., painter; Benward Irvin, painter; Benward Ira, painter; Bowman Adam; Bowman Samuel; Bowman Edward; Boyd Edward; Baylor Wm., Broadway; Baylor Ira, laborer, Broadway; Baylor Frank, laborer, Broadway; Baylor Alfred, laborer, Broadway; Bryan Michael, laborer, Broadway; Beatty Wm. H., laborer; Bannahan Patrick, Oxford; Bannahan Michael, laborer, Oxford; Bannahan Pat-

ROPE, TWINE, etc. at **WADE BROS.** Hackettstown.

THE BEST GOODS FOR THE LEAST MONEY AT **NORTON'S, Easton Pa.**

WASHINGTON TOWNSHIP.

rick, laborer, Oxford; Broad Martin, laborer, Oxford; Broad Geo., laborer, Oxford; Broad Fred., laborer, Broad Oliver, laborer, Oxford; Broad Martin, laborer, Oxford; Bannahan John, laborer, Oxford; Bannahan Thomas, laborer, Oxford; Bigelow John, tailor, Oxford; Bickle David, huckster, Oxford; Bickle John, laborer, Oxford; Brinck Daniel, laborer, Oxford; Brinck Lewis, laborer, Oxford; Brinck Wm., laborer, Oxford; Brinck John, laborer, Oxford; Benward John, brickmaker; Bowers & Mitchell, plow makers; Bowlby Gelson, Port Colden; B H William, New Hampton; Burns Patrick, laborer, Oxford; Bloomfield Wilson, freeholder, Changewater; Brow Peter, laborer, Changewater; Britne Christian, laborer, Changewater.

Cramer Peter, flour, feed etc., New Hampton; Cramer Samuel, miller, New Hampton; Cowell Geo., laborer, New Hampton; Cowell Walter, laborer, New Hampton; Cowell David, laborer, New Hampton; Cowell W., New Hampton; Collins Oliver, laborer,

LAUBACH'S EASTON, PA. CLOAKS and WRAPS of every description. **Our Own Manufacture,**

Port Colden; Collins Edward, laborer, Port Colden; Collins John, Railroader, Port Colden; Castner John P., Changewater; **Castner Victor**, dry goods and groceries, Changewater; Cramer Jacob, laborer, Changewater; Cline Lawson, New Hampton; Cline Gardner, New Hampton; Creveling Wm., New Hampton; Creveling John, New Hampton; Creveling George, laborer,

WILLIAM JENNINGS,
Washington, N. J.
PAINT and ORNAMENTAL SLATE ROOFER,
Work done in best of style and at reasonable prices.

New Hampton; Chandler Peter, teamster, New Hampton; Castner Whitfield, carpenter, Port Colden; Carling Peter, carpenter, Changewater; Carling Geo.; Carling Jacob, laborer, Changewater; Canon Thomas, laborer, Oxford; Canon Patrick, laborer, Oxford; Curl Nathan, carpenter, Port Colden; Curl Isaiah L., clerk, Port Colden; Curl Charles, brakeman; Cyphers

ANDREWS & NOLF, 205 Northampton St. Easton, Pa. The best place to buy **Merino Underwear** for Gents, Ladies and Children.

H. M. NORTON, *WHOLESALE AND RETAIL DEALER IN* **Hardware, Stoves and Housefurnishing**

WASHINGTON TOWNSHIP.

Robert, shoemaker, Port Colden; Cyphers Lindlow, carpenter, Port Colden, Cyphers Anna, shoe factory, Port Colden; Cyphers Carrie, shoe factory, Port Colden; Creager Peter, laborer; Creager Wm., laborer; Creager Whitfield, laborer; Creager Thomas, Cole Christopher; Cole John; Cole George, carpenter; Cole Archibald; Cole Christopher; Cole Thomas, laborer; Cole John Sr., laborer; Campbell Wm. Sr., laborer; Campbell Wm. Jr., organ maker; Cole Gardner, boatman; Chamberlin George; Chamberlan Peter; Cougle Jacob, railroader, Port Colden; Castner Robert, New Hampton; Castner Aaron, New Hampton; Canon Thomas, laborer, New Hampton; Creager Patrick, laborer, New Hampton; Cook Joseph, laborer, Oxford; Cook Peter, Oxford; Cook Adam, laborer, Oxford; Cole C. P., drover; Cravat Elijah, Port Colden; **Christine J. W.**, boot and shoemaker, Port Colden; Cowell David, laborer, New Hampton; Crine Thomas, laborer, Oxford; Creveling John, laborer, Changewater; Cowder Jacob, laborer, Oxford; Chamberlain Jacob,

LAUBACH'S, Easton. Pa., Largest stock of CARPETS, lowest prices. Best attention always.

laborer, Oxford.

Dunn Jacob, New Hampton; Dilts E. V., Port Colden; Dilts Henry, Port Colden; Dilts Peter, Port Colden; Dilts W. A., soldier, Changewater; De-

JACOB HILL, JR.,
Changewater, N. J.,
DEALER IN

Dry Goods, Groceries,
BOOTS and SHOES, HATS and CAPS,
CROCKERY, Etc.

Agent for Frank Coe's Fertilizers. Proprietor of Changewater Peach Nursery. A choice lot of trees to select from.

reamer Abraham, laborer, Changewater; Dereamer John W., car repairer, Port Colden ; Dereamer Miller, railroader, Port Colden; Denee Jehile, laborer; Donahue Jerry, laborer; Donahue Jerry, laborer; Dona-

BARGAINS IN HORSE WHIPS at Wades', Hackettstown.

hue Jerry Jr., laborer; Dorine John, laborer; Dresbock George, laborer; Dalrymple John R. Devine John, Denee Jehile, laborer; Dalrumpel John, laborer, Oxford; Dereamer Isaac, boatman; Denee Wm., laborer; Drake Wm., laborer.

Ester Charles, laborer.

Fritts Benjamin, carpenter, Changewater; Fritts Martin, laborer, Changewater; Fritts James, Changewater; Fritts Watson, Changewater; Fritts William, Fitts John; Fitts Henry; Fisher Austin; Felver Clark,; laborer, Port Colden; Felver Samuel, organ carver, Port dolden; Felver Benjamin, shoemaker, Port Colden; Fritts William; Frome Walter; Frome Marvin; Fox George, moulder; Fox Charles, moulder; Foss Frank, laborer; Foss Enoch, laborer; Foss Solomon, Foss Jacob, boss railroad carpenter; Foss Christopher; Foss Author; Foss Harvey, laborer; Foss Edward; Force Jesse, laborer; Force Jacob, laborer; Frick Lewis, moulder, Oxford; Fox Frederick, moulder.

Gaylord Nancy, Freeholder, Port Colden; Gaylord

LAUBACH'S EASTON, PA. Largest Store Largest Assortments, and One Price to All

George, telegrapher, Port Colden; Garey Whitfield, railroader, Port Colden; Garey Philip, shoemaker, Port Colden; Gouger Joseph, retired, Port Colden; Garey Charles, brakeman, Port Colden; Grand Lewis, laborer; Gross Joseph, laborer; Gross John, laborer; Gross Henry, laborer; Gulick Mark, Port Colden; Gulick Howard, Port Colden; Gulick Wesley, Port

WILLIAMSON'S RESTAURANT,
Washington, N. J.

☞ Give me a call. Everything in its season.

JOHN WILLIAMSON, Prop.

Colden; Gass Zenas, laborer; Gass Simon, laborer; Gardner Wm., laborer; Gardner Albert, laborer; Gardner Robert, carpenter, Port Colden; Gerard Lewis, laborer; Grentendoler Christian, laborer, New Hampton; Gass David, organ builder.

Hass Tillman, laborer; Hankinson Irvin, New

ANDREWS & NOLF, EASTON, PA. The place for all kinds of fine goods. **DOWN TOWN STORE,** 205 Northampton street.

ESTABLISHED 1865.

A. B. GROFF & CO.,

152 Washington Avenue, Washington, N. J.

— DEALERS IN —

GENERAL MERCHANDISE

Dry Goods, Wall Paper, Boots and Shoes, Crockery,

BALED HAY, LONG AND CUT.

ALL KINDS OF

COUNTRY PRODUCE

TAKEN.

HEADQUARTERS FOR

SEWING MACHINES,

The ROYAL ST. JOHN our specialty. Runs FORWARD or BACKWARD, without breaking the needle or thread or changing the stitch.

CALL AND EXAMINE THEM!

THE BET GOOD FOR THE LEAST MONEY AT NORTON'S Easton, Pa.

WASHINGTON TOWNSHIP.

Hampton; Hankinson Wm., New Hampton; **Hill Jacob**, dry goods, groceries, etc. Changewater; Hedden Theodore, railroader, Port Colden; Hummer Frank, clerk, Port Colden; Hummer C. C., merchant, Port Colden; Hummer George, ticket agent M. & E. R. R., Newark; Hummer Alonzo, fireman, Port Colden; Hansler Abram, mason, Port Colden; Hansler Isaac, laborer, Port Colden; Hamilton Wm., railroader, Port Colden; Hamilton Edon, railroader, Port Colden; Hughes James; Holdman Howard, laborer; Hendershot Oscar, ice dealer; Henderson George, teamster; Harrison Frank, laborer; Hardy Peter, laborer, Port Colden; Hays Roger, railroad conductor; Hays John, railroader; Hays Wm., railroader; Hardy John G., laborer, New Hampton; Harrison Edgar; Hildebrandt Howard, railroader; Hixson Abrm, blacksmith; Hartpence John, retired; Hartpence Armitage, retired; Hartman Jacob, miner, Oxford; Hartman George, miner, Oxford; Hartman Harvey, miner, Oxford; Hartman Elmer, miner, Oxford; Hartman Adam,

LAUBACH'S, Easton, Pa. 328 NORTHAMPTON ST. LARGEST Dry Goods and Carpet House.

miner, Oxford; Hawk Philip, New Hampton; Hatcher Anthony, laborer, Oxford.

Insco Henry.

Jefferson John, carpenter, Port Colden; Jefferson Mary, dressmaker, Port Colden; Jefferson Martha, dressmaker.

Kline Freeman; Kline James; Kline Oliver; Kinna-

MYERS' MEAT MARKET.
Fresh and Salt Meats
ALWAYS ON HAND AT THE LOWEST PRICES
J. E. MYERS, Washington, N. J.

man Peter; Kinnaman Wm.; Kinnaman John, laborer, Port Colden; Kinnaman Samuel; Kinnaman Hamilton, miller; Kinnaman Peter; Kinnaman Samuel; Kinnaman Joseph, miller; **Kinnaman Bros.**, flour, feed, etc.; Kenney Thomas, laborer; Knapp John, laborer, Oxford; Knapp Wm., laborer, Oxford; Knapp Robert, laborer, Oxford; **Kern, E. G., schoolteacher**, Port

Andrews & Nolf, 205 Northampton St., Easton, Pa. The only place to buy the celebrated "Cold Blast" feathers. Guaranteed free from odor and dirt.

H. M. NORTON *WHOLESALE AND RETAIL DEALER IN HARDWARE, STOVES AND HOUSEFURNISHING GOODS.*

474   WASHINGTON TOWNSHIP.

Colden; Kinney Joseph, laborer; Kinney Jacob, truck raiser; Kinney Castner, laborer; Kinney Tunis, laborer; Kinney Samuel, laborer; Kinney Peter, laborer; Kavitz Charles, laborer, Oxford; Kempsey Charles, butcher, Oxford.

Lewis Frederick; Lewis Henry, agent; Lewis James; Lunger John, railroader, Port Colden; Lee Joseph, carpenter, Port Colden; Lee Jabe, lock-tender, Port Colden; Lee John, laborer, Port Colden; Lee Austin, laborer, Port Colden; Lee Alfred, laborer, Port Colden; Lee Stewart, milk peddler, Port Colden; Lake Thomas B.; Lake Frank; Lukins Jos., laborer; Lanning Edward, Oxford; Lanning Frank, Oxford; Lanning Stephen, Sr. Oxford; Lanning Stephen, Jr., milk peddler; Lanning James, Oxford; Lanning Alfred, Oxford.

Minnick Samuel, laborer, Oxford; Minnick Clayton, laborer, Oxford; Marlatt John R.; Marlatt Alfred; Marlatt Paul; Marlatt Howard; Mills Baron, laborer; Mills James, laborer; Martin Mary, freeholder; Mar-

---

LAUBACH'S Easton, Pa. THE LARGEST DRY GOODS AND CARPET HOUSE. BARGAINS ALWAYS

---

tin Thomas; Miller Catharine, freeholder; Moore Geo., railroader, Port Colden; Moore Grant, laborer, Changewater; Moore Charles, laborer, Changewater; Miller Leonard, carpet weaver, Port Colden; Milligan

C. C. BOWERS,
NEW GROCERY AND PROVISION STORE,
IN BEATTY BUILDING, ON WASHINGTON AVENUE,
WASHINGTON, N. J.

I respectfully call the attention of housekeepers and others to my select stock of

CHOICE FAMILY GROCERIES.

Including all kinds of Meat, domestic and foreign Fruits, French and other mixed Candies, canned goods, bacon, lard, chip beef, all the different brands of Flour, Meal, Vegetables, etc., etc.

Cigars and Tobacco a Specialty. Full Stock of Lamps and Crockery Ware.

Alexandra, laborer, Port Colden; Mowder William; Mowder Samuel, Port Colden; Mowder Jacob, Port Colden; Mackey George, New Hampton; Metler Albert, New Hampton; Mitchell F. B., foundryman;

ROPE, TWINE, etc. at **WADE BROS.** Hackettstown.

WASHINGTON TOWNSHIP.

Melroy Wm. R., carpenter.

Nixson Frank, laborer; Nixson Peter, laborer; Nixson Morris, laborer; Nixon Wm., laborer; Nunn David P. S., merchant, Port Colden; Nunn Simon W., merchant, Port Colden; Nixson Abraham, laborer; Naplas Wm., laborer.

Opdyke S. R., canalman, Port Colden; Opdyke Oliver, canalman, Port Colden; Opdyke Wm., section boss, Port Colden; Opdyke John, mason, Port Colden; Opdyke Jacob P., carpenter, Port Colden; Opdyke Benjamin, conductor RR., Port Colden; Opdyke Lizzie, music teacher, Port Colden; Opdyke Samuel, miller; Opdyke Mary, shoe factory, Port Colden; Omick James, laborer; Omick Charles, laborer; Omick Phillip; Omick George, laborer; Osman Daniel; Osman Irvin; Osman Robert C.; Osman Zibe; Osman John, laborer; Opdyke Archibald, huckster; Otts Michael, laborer, Oxford; Otts Henry, laborer, Oxford; Otts George, laborer, Oxford; Otts Wm., laborer, Oxford; Oakes Wm., laborer; Oakes George, laborer;

Oakes Ernest, laborer; Opdyke Elmer, laborer; Opdyke Wm., laborer; Opdyke Eugene, laborer, Opdyke Charles, laborer.

Petty Morris, Changewater; Petty Wm., laborer, Changewater; Petty Charles, laborer, Changewater; Petty Morgan; Petty Theodore; Petty William; Probasco Isaiah, laborer; Paxon Wm., laborer, Port Colden; Perry Ira, railroader, Port Colden; Perry Elisha; Perry Oron; Pickle Thomas, laborer; Plotts Sarah, Freeholder; Plotts John; Pierson John, laborer, Oxford; Perry Elisha; Pool Wm.; Powers Frank; Parker Wm., laborer; Pursel Lafayette, railroader, Port Colden.

Quigley Sylvester, boatman, Port Colden.

H. M. NORTON, *WHOLESALE AND RETAIL DEALER IN* Hardware, Stoves and Housefurnishing

Rupie Charles, laborer, New Hampton; Reed Frederick, laborer, New Hampton; Riddle James, New Hampton; Riddle Harry, New Hampton; Rinehart George; Roseberry Simon; Roseberry Michael, Port Colden; Roseberry Abraham, Port Colden; Riegle John, Riegle Urban; Rounceville Oakey, laborer; Rounceville Wm., laborer; Richey Frank, laborer; Rush Wm. P., painter; Rush Ralph D.; Rush C. L., laborer; Rush George, laborer; Riddle Lewis, laborer, New Hampton; Riddle Frank, laborer, New Hampton; Riddle Joseph, laborer, New Hampton; Riddle John, laborer, New Hampton; Rityer Anthony, laborer; Rityer Frederick, laborer; Rody Wm., laborer; Rody John, laborer; Rody George, laborer; Roddaty Chas., Roddaty August, laborer; Roddaty Frederick, laborer; Renard Edward, laborer, Oxford; Renard Frederick, laborer, Oxford; Renard Howard, laborer, Oxford; Rea Samuel, farmer, Port Colden.

Sill John, New Hampton; Silker James, New Hampton; Silker James Sr., retired, New Hampton; Sheats

LAUBACH Leads in prices and quality of goods. EASTON Pa.

Adam, canalman; Stires Wm. M., merchant; Stewart Joseph C., miller, Changewater; Snyder Jacob, Changewater; Snyder Frank, Changewater; Snyder Ziba, wheelwright; Snyder James, boatman; Snyder Samuel, mason; Snyder Emanuel, laborer; Snyder Luther, laborer; Snyder Elmer, laborer; Stevenson James, laborer; Stevenson Whitfield, laborer; Stevenson

BRASS CASTLE STORE,
JOSEPH ADAMS, Proprietor.

This store was built in a new by the present proprietor, and has come that far for general trade, dry goods, boots and shoes, hats, caps, tinware, etc., according to be a first class general store. If you want a good article at a cheap price go to the Brass Castle Store.

Nicholas; Scomp Wm., railroader, Port Colden; Scomp Fletcher, railroader, Port Colden; Smith Jacob, laborer; Skinner James, Port Colden; Skinner Nelson Jr., organ builder, Port Colden; Skinner Wm., Port Colden; Scott John B., clerk, Port Colden; Scott Charles, laborer; Scott Morris; Scott Edward; Smith Wm., laborer; Smith Peter, laborer; Smith

SHIELDS INFALLIBLE **Dyspeptic Remedy** A safe cure for Dyspepsia, Sick or Nervous Headache. Guaranteed.

WASHINGTON TOWNSHIP.

Lewis, laborer; Smith Jasper; Snyder Ira, laborer; Snyder Jonas, laborer; Snyder Christopher, laborer; Scaden Lewis, laborer; Scaden Thomas, laberer; Stull James, freeholder; Stull Jane, freeholder; Snyder Staufel, mason; Sunday Frederick, laborer; Sunday George, laborer; Sunday Jacob, laborer; Sunday Henry, laborer; Sunday Irvin, laborer; Slater Samuel laborer; Starker Henry, laborer, Port Colden; Snyder John, laborer; Snyder Harry, laborer; Snyder Harvey, laborer; Snyder Miller, laborer; Snyder McCallan, laborer; Snyder Jasper, overseer of poor; Snyder Little, laborer; Snyder Alonzo, laborer; Stevenson Jacob, laborer; Stevenson George, laborer; Stevenson Wm., laborer; Sexton Martin, railroader; Sutton Jacob, laborer; Shurts Wm., New Hampton; Sine John, laborer.

Teitsworth Wm., lumberman. Port Colden; Teitsworth, J. S., organ builder, Port Colden; Teitsworth Lydia, boarding house, Port Colden; Teitsworth Alonzo, factory hand, Port Colden; Teitsworth J. T.,

LAUBACH'S EASTON, PA. CLOAKS and WRAPS of every description. **Our Own Manufacture.**

factory hand; Thaw Samuel, railroader, Port Colden; Tice Levi, laborer; Tice Howard, laborer; Thomas Peter, laborer, Port Colden; Thomas Martin, laborer, Port Colden; Thompson Robert, railroader, Port Colden; Thompson Lola, shoe factory, Port Colden; Thorp Daniel, laborer; Thorp John, laborer; Thorp Moses, laborer; Thorp Grant, laborer; Thorp Andrew, laborer; Thorp Wm., laborer; Thomas Whitfield, Tinsman J. F.

Vusler Edward, Port Colden; Vusler Jacob, Port Colden; Vusler Uriah, Port Colden; Vusler Joseph, laborer; Veilt Catharine; Vleit Alonzo; Vanatta Jos.; Vanatta John; Vanatta H. T. B.; Vanatta Joseph; Vanatta Ervin; VanSyckle David, Port Colden; VanSyckle John, laborer.

Weller William; Weller Peter, Sr.; Weller Wm., laborer; Weller Peter; Weller Daniel; Weller John; Willever Adam G.; Willever Wm.; Winters Retta, shoe factory, Port Colden; Winters Benjamin, railroader, Port Colden; Winters Henry; Wall Thomas,

ANDREWS & NOLF, 205 Northampton St., Easton, Pa. The best place to buy **Merino Underwear** for Gents, Ladies and Children.

WASHINGTON TOWNSHIP.

laborer; Winters Prescilla, shoe factory, Port Colden; Woolston J., Port Colden; Wamsley Milton; Wamsley John; Walker Joseph, laborer; Walker Charles, laborer; Walker Gardner, laborer; Warren John; Wire Samuel, railroader, Port Colden; Weaver Wm. R., teacher, Port Colden; Warner John; Warner Lewis, laborer, Port Colden; Weiss David; Weber John, freeholder, Oxford; Weber Henry, laborer, Oxford; Wyckoff Jacob, Port Colden; Wyckoff Geo. P., retired, Port Colden; Wyckoff John Jr.; Wyckoff Daniel, laborer; Wyckoff William, laborer; Wyckoff Elmer, laborer; Wyckoff J. H., teamster; Wandling Frank B., lime burner; Wandling John; Wandling Enoch, organ builder; Wandling Adam; Wandling Henry, carpenter; Wette Mary, freeholder; Woolf Susan, freeholder; Woodruff Jacob.

Youmans Simon; Youmans Hugh; Youmans Hannah.

Zenbrick Clark, laborer; Zenbrick Frederick, laborer; Zellers George.

SIMON W. NUNN,

DEALER IN

GENERAL MERCHANDISE,

PORT COLDEN, N. J.

Dry Goods, Groceries,

Hats, Caps, Crockery, STOVES, BOOTS AND SHOES,

and everything usually kept in a general store. The highest price paid for Country Produce.

GOODS DELIVERED FREE.

Give him a call and be convinced.

T. SHIELDS, JR.,

MANUFACTURER OF

FINE CLOTHING.

All Orders Promptly Executed and Satisfaction Guaranteed.

DEALER IN

READY-MADE CLOTHING,

Gents' Furnishing Goods,

HATS, CAPS, &c., &c.

HACKETTSTOWN, N. J.

www.ingramcontent.com/pod-product-compliance
Lightning Source LLC
Chambersburg PA
CBHW020835020526
44114CB00040B/785